Fodor's

D0611641

NEW MEXICO

7th Edition

Where to Eat and Stay
for All Budgets

Must-See Sights
and Local Secrets

Ratings You Can Trust

Fodor's Travel Publications   New York, Toronto, London, Sydney, Auckland
www.fodors.com

FODOR'S NEW MEXICO
Editor: Eric B. Wechter

Editorial Contributors: Lynne Arany, Andrew Collins, Francesca Drago, Barbara Floria, Georgia de Katona

Production Editor: Jennifer DePrima
Maps & Illustrations: David Lindroth, *cartographer*; Bob Blake, Rebecca Baer, *map editors;* William Wu, *information graphics*
Design: Fabrizio La Rocca, *creative director*; Guido Caroti, Siobhan O'Hare, *art directors*; Tina Malaney, Chie Ushio, Ann McBride, Jessica Walsh, *designers*; Melanie Marin, *senior picture editor*
Cover Photo: (Sand painting, Farmington): Ted Spiegel/Corbis
Production Manager: Angela McLean

7th Edition

ISBN 978-1-4000-0811-7

ISSN 1526-4734

SPECIAL SALES
This book is available at special discounts for bulk purchases for sales promotions or premiums. Special editions, including personalized covers, excerpts of existing books, and corporate imprints, can be created in large quantities for special needs. For more information, write to Special Markets/Premium Sales, 1745 Broadway, MD 6-2, New York, New York 10019, or e-mail specialmarkets@randomhouse.com.

AN IMPORTANT TIP & AN INVITATION
Although all prices, opening times, and other details in this book are based on information supplied to us at press time, changes occur all the time in the travel world, and Fodor's cannot accept responsibility for facts that become outdated or for inadvertent errors or omissions. So **always confirm information when it matters**, especially if you're making a detour to visit a specific place. Your experiences—positive and negative—matter to us. If we have missed or misstated something, **please write to us.** We follow up on all suggestions. Contact the New Mexico editor at editors@fodors.com or c/o Fodor's at 1745 Broadway, New York, NY 10019.

PRINTED IN THE UNITED STATES OF AMERICA

10 9 8 7 6 5 4 3 2 1

Be a Fodor's Correspondent

Your opinion matters. It matters to us. It matters to your fellow Fodor's travelers, too. And we'd like to hear it. In fact, we need to hear it.

When you share your experiences and opinions, you become an active member of the Fodor's community. That means we'll not only use your feedback to make our books better, but we'll publish your names and comments whenever possible. Throughout our guides, look for "Word of Mouth," excerpts of your unvarnished feedback.

Here's how you can help improve Fodor's for all of us.

Tell us when we're right. We rely on local writers to give you an insider's perspective. But our writers and staff editors—who are the best in the business—depend on you. Your positive feedback is a vote to renew our recommendations for the next edition.

Tell us when we're wrong. We're proud that we update most of our guides every year. But we're not perfect. Things change. Hotels cut services. Museums change hours. Charming cafés lose charm. If our writer didn't quite capture the essence of a place, tell us how you'd do it differently. If any of our descriptions are inaccurate or inadequate, we'll incorporate your changes in the next edition and will correct factual errors at fodors.com immediately.

Tell us what to include. You probably have had fantastic travel experiences that aren't yet in Fodor's. Why not share them with a community of like-minded travelers? Maybe you chanced upon a beach or bistro or B&B that you don't want to keep to yourself. Tell us why we should include it. And share your discoveries and experiences with everyone directly at fodors.com. Your input may lead us to add a new listing or highlight a place we cover with a "Highly Recommended" star or with our highest rating, "Fodor's Choice."

Give us your opinion instantly at our feedback center at www.fodors.com/feedback. You may also e-mail editors@fodors.com with the subject line "New Mexico Editor." Or send your nominations, comments, and complaints by mail to New Mexico Editor, Fodor's, 1745 Broadway, New York, NY 10019.

You and travelers like you are the heart of the Fodor's community. Make our community richer by sharing your experiences. Be a Fodor's correspondent.

Happy Traveling!

Tim Jarrell, Publisher

CONTENTS

MAPS

Fodor's Features

ABOUT THIS BOOK

Our Ratings

Sometimes you find terrific travel experiences, and sometimes they just find you. But usually the burden is on you to select the right combination of experiences. That's where our ratings come in.

As travelers we've all discovered a place so wonderful that its worthiness is obvious, a place is so unique that superlatives don't do it justice. These sights, properties, and experiences get our highest rating, **Fodor's Choice**, indicated by orange stars.

Black stars highlight sights and properties we deem **Highly Recommended,** places that our writers, editors, and readers praise for consistency and excellence.

By default, there's another category: any place we include in this book is by definition worth your time, unless we say otherwise. And we will.

Disagree with any of our choices? Care to nominate a place or suggest that we rate one more highly? Visit our feedback center at www.fodors.com/feedback.

Budget Well

Hotel and restaurant price categories from ¢ to $$$$ are defined in the opening pages of each chapter. For attractions, we always give standard adult admission fees; reductions are usually available for children, students, and senior citizens. Want to pay with plastic? **AE, D, DC, MC, V** following restaurant and hotel listings indicate whether American Express, Discover, Diners Club, MasterCard, and Visa are accepted.

Restaurants

Unless we state otherwise, restaurants are open for lunch and dinner daily. We mention dress only when there's a specific requirement and reservations only when they're essential or not accepted—it's always best to book ahead.

Hotels

Hotels have private bath, phone, TV, and air-conditioning and operate on the European Plan (aka EP, meaning without meals), unless we specify that they use the Continental Plan (CP, with a Continental breakfast), Breakfast Plan (BP, with a full breakfast), or Modified American Plan (MAP, with breakfast and dinner) or are all-inclusive (including all meals and most activities).

We always list facilities but not whether you'll be charged an extra fee to use them.

Many Listings	
★	Fodor's Choice
★	Highly recommended
⊠	Physical address
✛	Directions
⌂	Mailing address
☎	Telephone
🖷	Fax
⊕	On the Web
✉	E-mail
💷	Admission fee
☉	Open/closed times
Ⓜ	Metro stations
▭	Credit cards

Hotels & Restaurants	
🏨	Hotel
⇱	Number of rooms
♨	Facilities
⦿	Meal plans
✕	Restaurant
⇱	Reservations
⬀	Smoking
🔃	BYOB
✕🏨	Hotel with restaurant that warrants a visit

Outdoors	
🏌	Golf
⛺	Camping

Other	
ℭ	Family-friendly
⇨	See also
⊠	Branch address
☞	Take note

Experience New Mexico

WORD OF MOUTH

"[September]...in New Mexico is so beautiful. The trees are turning a golden yellow, the pinon burning, green chiles roasting, the people are just, I don't know, it's like they "know" something that everyone else doesn't. "

—BeachGirl247

WHAT'S WHERE

The following numbers refer to chapters.

2 Albuquerque. Albuquerque is the gateway to New Mexico, by far the state's largest city, and its business and education capital. Its residents—like its architecture, food, and art—reflect a confluence of Native American, Hispanic, and Anglo culture.

3 Santa Fe. On a 7,000-foot-high plateau at the base of the Sangre de Cristo Mountains, Santa Fe is one of the most visited small cities in the United States, with an abundance of museums, one-of-a-kind cultural events, art galleries, and distinctive restaurants and shops.

4 Taos. World-famous museums and galleries, stunning views of the desert and Sangre de Cristo Mountains, and charming, cottonwood-shaded streets lined with adobe buildings are a few of this small town's attractions. Nearby Taos Pueblo and Taos Ski Valley are major draws.

5 Side Trips from the Cities. Encompassing the stunning mountains and the remnants of a 2,000-year-old Pueblo civilization, this region includes the many artsy and historic villages surrounding Albuquerque, Santa Fe, and Taos. Scenic drives abound.

6 Northwestern New Mexico. Red-rock canyons shelter ancient hamlets and high, fortresslike plateaus crowned by Native American villages. Can't-miss places: El Morro National Monument, Chaco Canyon, Zuni Pueblo, Aztec Ruins, and Acoma Pueblo.

7 Northeastern New Mexico. The brilliantly clear light of northeastern New Mexico—the area east of the Sangre de Cristo range that includes parts of Carson National Forest and a large portion of the Santa Fe Trail—illuminates seemingly endless high-desert plains.

8 Southeastern New Mexico. This region contains Carlsbad Caverns National Park, one of the largest cave systems in the world; Roswell, which draws UFO enthusiasts from far and wide; the lush, high-elevation Lincoln National Forest; and the surreal gypsum wonderland of White Sands National Monument.

9 Southwestern New Mexico. Shimmering mirages born of desert heat hover here above mesquite-covered sand dunes. Near Silver City, the ore-rich mountains are dotted with old mining ghost towns. Fish, swim, or boat along the miles of lake water at Elephant Butte Reservoir, near Truth or Consequences.

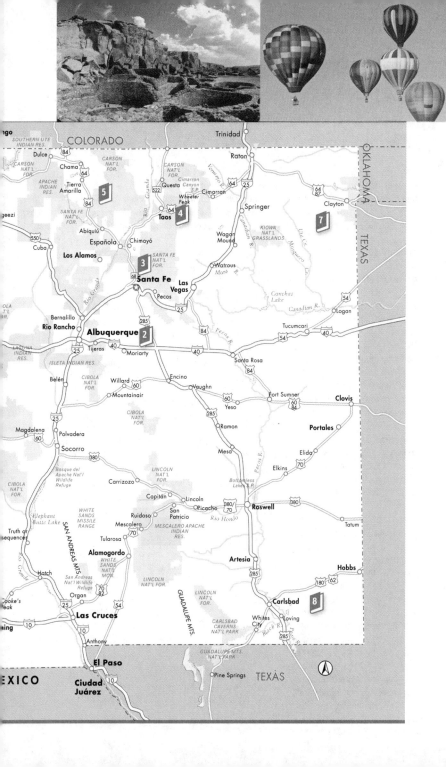

NEW MEXICO PLANNER

When to Go

The cool, dry climates of Santa Fe and Taos are as much a lure in summer as the skiing in Taos and Santa Fe is in winter. Christmas is a wonderful time to be in New Mexico because of Native American ceremonies as well as the Hispanic religious folk plays, special foods, and musical events. Santa Fe is at its most festive at this time, with incense and piñon smoke sweetening the air and the darkness of winter illuminated by thousands of *farolitos* (glowing paper-bag lanterns), which line walkways, doorways, and rooftops. Most ceremonial dances at the pueblos occur in summer, early fall, and at Christmas and Easter. Other major events—including the Santa Fe Opera, Chamber Music Festival, and Native American and Spanish markets—are geared to the heavy tourist season of July and August. The Santa Fe Fiesta and New Mexico State Fair in Albuquerque are held in September, and the Albuquerque International Balloon Fiesta in October. Hotel rates are generally highest during the peak summer season but fluctuate less than those in most major resort areas. If you plan to come in summer, **be sure to make reservations in advance.** Avoid the heaviest crowds by coming in spring or fall.

Flying in and Getting Around

New Mexico is easy to reach by plane but a full day's drive from major metro areas in the neighboring states of Arizona, Utah, Colorado, Oklahoma, and Texas. Unless you're a big fan of long road trips (the scenery getting here is spectacular, especially coming from Arizona, Utah, and Colorado), it generally makes the most sense to fly here.

Northern and central New Mexico's main air gateway is Albuquerque International Sunport (ABQ), which is served by virtually all of the nation's major domestic airlines as well as some smaller regional ones; there are direct flights from all major West Coast and Midwest cities and a number of big East Coast cities. From here it's an easy 60-minute drive to Santa Fe, or a 2½-hour drive to Taos (shuttle services are available). To reach southern New Mexico, it's more convenient to fly into El Paso International Airport (ELP), 50 mi southeast of Las Cruces, 160 mi southeast of Silver City, 135 mi southwest of Ruidoso, and 160 mi southwest of Carlsbad. El Paso's airport is smaller but still has direct flights from many major carriers. There are also flights between El Paso and Albuquerque, and a handful of cities around the state (Ruidoso, Carlsbad, Alamogordo) have regional air service.

A car is your best way to get around the region, whether traveling among New Mexico's main cities, or even exploring them in depth. You can see much of downtown Santa Fe, Taos, Ruidoso, and Silver City on foot or using buses, but in Albuquerque and Las Cruces a car is really a necessity for any serious touring and exploring.

For more flight information and ground transportation options, see the Travel Smart section at the back of this book.

WHAT'S NEW IN NEW MEXICO

Happy Anniversary

What's old is new in the Land of Enchantment: Santa Fe will roll out dozens of special events and programs through 2010 as this second-oldest city in America celebrates the 400th anniversary of its founding. Festivities kick off on March 30, 2009, with a commemoration of the date on which the Spanish viceroy officially decreed the establishment of Santa Fe as a permanent city. During the months that follow, until the end of 2010, the City Different will pay homage to its heritage with celebrations, performances, and museum exhibits. The annual Fiestas de Santa Fe, held in mid-September to commemorate the resettlement of the city in 1692 following the Pueblo Revolt, will be an especially prominent affair both in 2009 and 2010.

History in a New Light

Santa Fe's venerable **Palace of the Governors**, the oldest public building in America, is the site of the state's newest attraction, the **New Mexico History Museum**, which is planning a Memorial Day weekend opening in 2009. The new, sleek new facility has been constructed behind the palace and will tell the rich and complex story of the state's founding through an incredible collection of artifacts that, up to this point, only made brief appearances in temporary exhibits at the Palace of the Governors. The 20,000-square-foot facility will use interactive, state-of-the-art audio and visual technology to bring New Mexico's heritage to life—a refreshing contrast to the sometimes static methods many of the state's museums employ in their exhibits (in fairness, some of the museums occupy extremely old, historic buildings).

In Albuquerque, another venerable dedication to the state's earliest inhabitants, the **Indian Pueblo Cultural Center**, completed a dramatic expansion in August 2008. Built with local flagstone and timber, the new 15,000-square-foot building and adjoining 4,000-square-foot covered patio includes considerably more space for art and history exhibits as well as a display of 19 exterior columns with the official seal of each New Mexico Pueblo embossed on the top of each. The center's **Pueblo Harvest Cafe**, which serves such indigenous-inspired fare as buffalo tenderloin and grilled salmon, has been dramatically expanded and will now serve three meals a day and feature live entertainment.

Training for Success

At the tail end of 2008, **New Mexico Railrunner Express** rail service began connecting Albuquerque to Santa Fe, thus extending the existing rail service from Albuquerque north to Bernalillo and south to the airport, Los Lunas, and Belén. A new station was also added for Isleta Casino and Resort, just south of Albuquerque, in fall 2008. This is big news in a part of the country where a car has been a necessity and was the most convenient way to get from Santa Fe to Albuquerque. The service in Santa Fe terminates in the city's new **Santa Fe Railyard District**, a revitalized section of the hip Guadalupe neighborhood, within easy walking distance of the Plaza. Features of this 13-acre plot include a park (where a huge empty lot once stood), a new space for the city's farmers' market, shops and galleries, restaurants, a new movie theater, and loft residences.

QUINTESSENTIAL NEW MEXICO

Ancient Peoples

Nowhere in the United States will you find communities that have been continuously inhabited for a longer period than the oldest pueblos of New Mexico, Acoma, and Taos. Acoma has been a living, working community for more than 1,000 years—the cliff-top city here is perhaps the most dramatically situated pueblo in the state, and a must-see attraction, especially since the tribe opened a stunning cultural center and museum in 2006. Taos Pueblo, which contains the largest collection of multistory pueblo dwellings in the country, also dates back more than a millennium.

But these are just two of the state's 19 pueblos, not to mention the Indian Pueblo Cultural Center (which was dramatically expanded in 2008) in Albuquerque, and outstanding museums on Native American arts and culture in Santa Fe. Ancient, now-deserted sites, such as Chaco and Aztec, offer further opportunities to explore and learn about New Mexico's thriving indigenous culture.

The Cradle of Creativity

New Mexico draws all kinds of vibrant spirits, both to visit and relocate, but the state is particularly a magnet for artists. Santa Fe, with its dozens of prestigious galleries and art museums, claims the third-largest art market in the nation, after New York City and Los Angeles. The much smaller town of Taos claims a similarly exciting gallery scene, and the state's largest city, Albuquerque, is no slouch when it comes to the arts—galleries have popped up all over the city in recent years.

Although New Mexico's prestigious gallery scene is concentrated in its cities, many of the state's most talented artists live in small, scenic villages and work out

1

If you want to get a sense of New Mexico culture, and indulge in some of its pleasures, start by familiarizing yourself with the rituals of daily life. These are a few highlights that you can take part in with relative ease.

of their home studios. Some of these studios are open year-round, but the best way to visit them—and also discover some of the most charming and distinctive communities in the state—is to participate in a Studio Tour Weekend. More than 40 of these events are held year-round, most of them from early fall through December, with others taking place in the spring. During tour weekends, the private studios in a given town open their doors to visitors—it's a great time to converse with artists, shop for their creations, and get off the beaten path. Some particularly noteworthy studio tours include those in Galisteo (late October), a funky little village near Santa Fe; Silver City (late May), which combines its studio tour with a rollicking blues festival; Ruidoso (mid-June), whose cool-climate Art in the Pines event features 25 artists; and Abiquiu (mid-October), where Georgia O'Keeffe lived and some 70 artists participate.

Peak Experiences

With nearly 50 peaks towering higher than 12,000 feet, New Mexico is a wonderland for people who love the mountains—it's partly this vertiginous topographical feature that gives the state its unparalleled beauty. The southern spine of the Rocky Mountain range, known as the Sangre de Cristos, runs right through the center of the state, looming over Taos and Santa Fe. The stunning Sandia Mountains face the city of Albuquerque, and similarly beautiful peaks dot the landscape as far south as Cloudcroft. Much of the Land of Enchantment's high-country is accessible. Hiking trails lead to some of the highest points in the state, and several first-rate ski areas have been carved out of New Mexico's mountains, including Taos Ski Valley, Angel Fire, and Ski Santa Fe to the north, and Ski Apache in Ruidoso.

IF YOU LIKE

Historic Sites

There's no state in the Union with a richer historical heritage than New Mexico, which contains not only buildings constructed by Europeans well before the Pilgrims set foot in Massachusetts but also still-inhabited pueblos that date back more than a millennium.

The entire state can feel like one massive archaeological dig, with its mystical Native American ruins and weathered adobe buildings. Stately plazas laid out as fortifications by the Spanish in the 17th century still anchor many communities, including Albuquerque, Las Cruces, Las Vegas, Santa Fe, and Taos. And side trips from these cities lead to ghost towns and deserted pueblos that have been carefully preserved by historians. Here are some of the top draws for history buffs.

One of the most well-preserved and fascinating ruin sites on the continent, the ancient **Chaco Culture National Historical Park** in Chaco Canyon was home to the forerunners of today's Pueblo Indians more than 1,000 years ago.

Santa Fe's **San Miguel Mission** is a simple, earth-hue adobe structure built in about 1625—it's the oldest church still in use in the continental United States.

A United Nations World Heritage Site, the 1,000-year-old **Taos Pueblo** has the largest collection of multistory pueblo dwellings in the United States.

The oldest public building in the United States, the Pueblo-style **Palace of the Governors** anchors Santa Fe's historic Plaza and has served as the residence for 100 Spanish, Native American, Mexican, and American governors; it's now the state history museum.

Hiking Adventures

At just about every turn in the Land of Enchantment, whether you're high in the mountains or low in a dramatic river canyon, hiking opportunities abound. Six national forests cover many thousands of acres around New Mexico, as do 34 state parks and a number of other national and state monuments and recreation areas. The ski areas make for great mountaineering during the warmer months, and the state's many Native American ruins are also laced with trails.

Hiking is a year-round activity in New Mexico, as you can virtually always find temperate weather somewhere in the state. Consider the following areas for an engaging ramble.

About midway between Santa Fe and Albuquerque, **Kasha-Katuwe Tent Rocks National Monument** is so named because its bizarre rock formations look like tepees rising over a narrow box canyon. The hike here is relatively short and only moderately challenging, offering plenty of bang for the buck.

One of the more strenuous hiking challenges in the state is **Wheeler Peak**. The 8-mi trek to New Mexico's highest point (elevation 13,161 feet) rewards visitors with stunning views of the Taos Ski Valley.

From the northeastern fringes of Albuquerque, **La Luz Trail** winds 9 mi (with an elevation gain of more than 3,000 feet) to Sandia Crest.

Gila National Forest's short **Catwalk Trail**, in the southwestern corner of the state, is a metal walkway that clings to the sides of the soaring cliffs in White Water Canyon.

Burger Joints

In a state with plenty of open ranching land and an appreciation for no-nonsense, homestyle eating, it's no surprise that locals debate intensely about where to find the best burger in town.

In New Mexico, the preferred meal is a green-chile cheeseburger—a culinary delight that's available just about anyplace that serves hamburgers. Burgers served in tortillas or sopaipillas also earn kudos, and increasingly, you'll find establishments serving terrific buffalo, lamb, turkey, and even tuna and veggie burgers.

With about 75 locations throughout the state, the New Mexico chain **Blake's Lotaburger** has become a cult favorite for its juicy Angus beef burgers. Just order at the counter, take a number, and wait for your meal (which is best accompanied by a bag of seasoned fries).

A friendly and funky little roadhouse about a 15-minute drive south of Santa Fe, **Bobcat Bite** is a much-loved source of outstanding green-chile burgers. Loyalists order them rare.

Feasting on a burger at the **Mineshaft Tavern** is a big reason to stop in the tiny village of Madrid, as you drive up the fabled Turquoise Trail from Albuquerque to Santa Fe. This rollicking bar serves hefty patties.

Although it's most famous for its delicious homemade pies, the **Pie-O-Neer Cafe**, in Pie Town along a lonely but beautiful stretch of U.S. 60, serves exceptionally good green-chile cheeseburgers.

Dramatic Photo Ops

New Mexico's spectacular landscapes and crystal-clear atmosphere can help just about any amateur with a decent camera produce professional-quality photos. Many of the common scenes around the state seem tailor-made for photography sessions: terra-cotta-hued adobe buildings against azure-blue skies, souped-up low-rider automobiles cruising along wide-open highways, and rustic fruit and chili stands by the side of the road. In summer, dramatic rain clouds contrast with vermilion sunsets to create memorable images. Come fall, shoot the foliage of cottonwood and aspen trees, and in winter, snap the state's snow-capped mountains.

The **High Road to Taos**, a stunning drive from Santa Fe with a rugged alpine backdrop, encompasses rolling hillsides studded with orchards and tiny villages.

More than 1,000 balloons lift off from the **Albuquerque International Balloon Fiesta,** affording shutterbugs countless opportunities for great photos—whether from the ground or the air. And there are year-round opportunities to soar above the city.

The dizzyingly high **Rio Grande Gorge Bridge,** near Taos, stands 650 feet above the Rio Grande—the reddish rocks dotted with green scrub contrast brilliantly against the blue sky.

White Sands National Monument, near Alamogordo, is a huge and dramatic expanse of 60-foot-high shifting sand dunes—it's the largest deposit of gypsum sand in the world, and one of the few landforms recognizable from space.

GREAT ITINERARIES

ALBUQUERQUE TO TAOS: NEW MEXICO MOUNTAIN HIGH

Day 1: Albuquerque

Start out by strolling through the shops of Old Town Plaza, then visit the New Mexico Museum of Natural History and Science. Also be sure to check out the Albuquerque Museum of Art and History, and try to make your way over to the Albuquerque Biological Park, which contains the aquarium, zoo, and botanic park. For lunch, try the atmospheric Monica's El Portal or the sophisticated St. Clair Winery and Bistro, both near the Old Town center.

Later in the afternoon, you'll need a car to head east a couple of miles along Central to reach the University of New Mexico's main campus and the nearby Nob Hill District. Start with a stroll around the UNM campus with its many historic adobe buildings; if you have time, pop inside either the Maxwell Museum of Anthropology or the University Art Museum. When you're finished here, walk east along Central into Nob Hill and check out the dozens of offbeat shops. If it's summer, meaning that you still have some time before the sun sets, it's worth detouring from Old Town to Far Northeast Heights (a 15-minute drive), where you can take the Sandia Peak Aerial Tramway 2.7 mi up to Sandia Peak for spectacular sunset views of the city. Either way, plan to have dinner back in Nob Hill, perhaps at Zinc or Flying Star. If you're still up for more fun, check out one of the neighborhood's lively lounges; head back downtown for a bit of late-night barhopping.

Days 2 & 3: Santa Fe

On Day 2, head to Santa Fe early in the morning by driving up the scenic Turquoise Trail; once you arrive in town, explore the adobe charms of the downtown central Plaza. Visit the Palace of the Governors and browse the wares of the Native American vendors there. Also check out the adjacent New Mexico History Museum (slated to open in May 2009). At the nearby Museum of Fine Arts you can see works by Southwestern artists, and a short drive away at the Museum of International Folk Art you can see how different cultures in New Mexico and elsewhere in the world have expressed themselves artistically. Give yourself time to stroll the narrow, adobe-lined streets of this charming downtown, and treat yourself to some authentic New Mexican cuisine in the evening, perhaps with a meal at La Choza or Maria's.

On your second day in town, plan to walk a bit. Head east from the Plaza up to Canyon Road's foot, perusing the galleries. Have lunch at one of the restaurants midway uphill, such as Geronimo or El Farol. From here, you can either continue walking 2 mi up Canyon, and then Upper Canyon, roads to the Randall Davey Audubon Center, or you can take a cab there. If you're up for some exercise, hike the foothills—there are trails within the center's property and also from the free parking area (off Cerro Gordo Road) leading into the Dale Ball Trail Network. You might want to try one of Santa Fe's truly stellar, upscale restaurants your final night in town, either La Boca on Marcy Street, or the restaurant at the Inn of the Anasazi, a couple of blocks from the Plaza. Later in the evening, enjoy cocktails at famed Dragon Room Lounge at the historic Pink Adobe restaurant.

Day 4: Abiquiu

From Santa Fe, drive north up U.S. 285/84 through Española, and then take

U.S. 84 from Española up to Abiquiu, the fabled community where Georgia O'Keeffe lived and painted for much of the final five decades of her life. On your way up, before you reach Española, make the detour toward Los Alamos and spend the morning visiting Bandelier National Monument. In Abiquiu, plan to tour Georgia O'Keeffe's home.

Days 5 & 6: Taos
Begin by strolling around Taos Plaza, taking in the galleries and crafts shops. Head south two blocks to visit the Harwood Museum. Then walk north on Paseo del Pueblo to the Taos Art Museum at the Fechin House. In the afternoon, drive out to the Rio Grande Gorge Bridge. Return the way you came to see the Millicent Rogers Museum on your way back to town. In the evening, stop in at the Adobe Bar at the Taos Inn and plan for dinner at Joseph's Table. On the second day, drive out to the Taos Pueblo in the morning and tour the ancient village while the day is fresh. Return to town and go to the Blumenschein Home and Museum, lunching afterward at the Dragonfly Café. After lunch drive out to La Hacienda de los Martinez for a look at early life in Taos

and then to Ranchos de Taos to see the San Francisco de Asís Church.

Day 7: The High Road
On your final day, drive back down toward Albuquerque and Santa Fe via the famed High Road, which twists through a series of tiny, historic villages—including Peñasco, Truchas, and Chimayó. In the latter village, be sure to stop by El Santuario de Chimayó. Have lunch at Léona's Restaurante or Rancho de Chimayó, and do a little shopping at Ortega's Weaving Shop. From here, it's a 30-minute drive to Santa Fe, where you can spend a final night, or a 90-minute drive to Albuquerque.

Alternatives
On Day 4, as you drive up through Abiquiu, if you're more a fan of historic railroads than Georgia O'Keeffe, continue up U.S. 84 to Chama, and ride the famed Cumbres & Toltec Scenic Railroad in the morning, and then cut east on U.S. 64 to reach Taos. After visiting Taos Pueblo on Day 6, consider doing the Enchanted Circle tour rather than returning to town. This 84-mi loop runs through the scenic villages of Questa, Red River, Eagle Nest, and Angel Fire.

TOP NEW MEXICO EXPERIENCES

Ski the Southern Rockies

It may sound like a mere novelty—skiing less than 100 mi from the Mexican border, which, indeed, you can do at the relatively small and casual downhill facility in **Cloudcroft**. But the Land of Enchantment offers some of the most difficult and breathtaking ski terrain in the country, and is home to several outstanding facilities. The southern spine of the Rockies, with elevations topping out at 13,000 feet and well over 250 inches of annual snowfall in some places, runs right down the center of New Mexico. Often recognized by major ski magazines for its first-rate ski school and demanding trails, **Taos Ski Valley** is the state's most famous winter-sports destination—it comprises a friendly, handsomely developed village of condos and restaurants. Other nearby northern New Mexico venues with great alpine and cross-country skiing, snowboarding, snowshoeing, and snowmobiling include **Red River, Angel Fire, Pajarito** (an underrated gem in Los Alamos), **Santa Fe,** and **Sandia** (just east of Albuquerque). And down in the state's southern reaches, in addition to Cloudcroft, you can tackle some 750 well-groomed acres at **Ski Apache**, just outside the resort town of Ruidoso.

Browse the Art Markets of Santa Fe

New Mexico's most popular destination, Santa Fe is also one of the great cultural treasures of the Southwest, packed as it is with first-rate museums. The best season for appreciating the arts is summer, when the **Santa Fe Opera** comes into full swing, as does the **Santa Fe Chamber Music Festival**. But the biggest weekends of summer are when the legendary Indian and Spanish markets come to town, and there's no more exciting time to take in Santa Fe.

The **Spanish Market** dominates the city's historic Plaza the last weekend of July and draws more than 250 local artisans versed in the traditional regional practices of straw appliqué, hide painting, metalwork, *retablo* and santo carving, weaving, and furniture making. During the third weekend in August, more than 1,200 artists representing some 100 tribes throughout North America display their jewelry, textiles, paintings, and other fine works during the **Santa Fe Indian Market**. Additional antiques-related markets take place in mid-August, and the city hosts a smaller but still excellent **Spanish Winter Market** in December.

Sample New Mexico's Wines

You might think beer would be the state's most celebrated drink, given the laid-back nature of New Mexicans and the fiery nature of the local cuisine. In fact, the region has developed into an increasingly fruitful (pardon the pun) and critically acclaimed wine producer, its soil and climate perfect for growing a number of varietals, from pinot noir in the cooler upper elevations to chardonnay and cabernet sauvignon in warmer areas. There are about two dozen vineyards in the state, and half have tasting rooms. Albuquerque's **Gruet Winery** now ranks among the nation's most esteemed producers of champagne-style sparkling wines, and others around the state—**Black Mesa, La Chiripada, Casa Rondena, St. Clair**—have garnered prominent awards. But you can also try local vintages during several popular festivals. The **Southern New Mexico Wine Festival** in Las Cruces and the **Albuquerque Wine Festival** both take place in late May. Las Cruces then hosts the **Harvest Wine Festival** over Labor Day Weekend, which is when Bernalillo holds

its **New Mexico Wine Festival**. Other communities with wine events include Ruidoso (mid-June), Santa Fe (early July), and Alamogordo (late September).

Usher in the Holidays, New Mexico Style

The piñon-scented air, cozy adobe architecture, and traditional Native American and Spanish festivals have long made New Mexico a great place to visit during the December holiday season. In Carlsbad, boats cruise by lighted holiday displays during the town's Christmas on the Pecos celebration. Christmas in Santa Fe is perhaps the city's most festive time of year. During the 10 days of **Las Posadas at San Miguel Mission,** the story of Mary and Joseph's journey to Bethlehem is reenacted. **The Feast Day of Our Lady of Guadalupe,** December 12, is grandly celebrated at the Santuario de Guadalupe, and **Christmas at the Palace** resounds with hours of festive music emanating from the Palace of the Governors in mid-December. The traditional Christmas Eve stroll down Canyon Road, complete with snacks and costumed carolers, is the way to celebrate the night before Christmas when in Santa Fe. Christmas Native American Dances take place at most pueblos. The Spanish-inspired dance-drama Los Matachines is performed at Picurís Pueblo. There are also pine-torch processions and kachina dances at Taos Pueblo and Basket, Buffalo, Deer, Harvest, Rainbow, and Turtle dances at Acoma, Cochiti, San Ildefonso, Santa Clara, and Taos pueblos.

Take the Tramway to Albuquerque's Sandia Peak

Take the aerial tramway to the top of the Sandia Mountains for an incomparable view over Albuquerque. You can ride the world's longest aerial tram (it climbs over 5,000 feet in elevation, and covers nearly 3 mi in distance) to the top, take in the soaring panoramas of the entire Rio Grande Valley from Santa Fe down toward Socorro, and enjoy drinks plus lunch or dinner at the lofty **High Finance Restaurant & Tavern,** which clings precipitously to the sheer edge of Sandia Peak. But if you have time, use the tram as a means to an exhilarating outdoor adventure—at the top you can access the **Sandia Peak Ski Area** in winter for fun in the snow, or for challenging mountain biking down these very slopes in summer. You can hike on short and easy trails or choose far more challenging ones, including the famed **La Luz trail,** which descends down the face of the Sandias back into Albuquerque's Northeast Heights neighborhood. You can also drive to the ski area and ranger station (and then hike or take the chairlift to the tram station)—this beautiful drive takes about 45 minutes.

FAQs

Just how spicy is New Mexican food? Compared with food served in most parts of the country, traditional New Mexico fare—green- and red-chile sauces, the salsa that comes with chips—ranks pretty high on the fire meter. If you've spent a bit of time in Louisiana, Texas, or elsewhere in the Southwest, you've likely encountered plenty of kick in the local cuisine. In New Mexico, on average, the heat factor is even a tad higher. If you're averse to spicy fare, it's easy enough to request milder salsa with your meal, or to ask the staff at restaurants for recommendations about which foods pack the least heat. In less touristy areas, however, or in restaurants that cater primarily to locals, expect food that's considerably spicier than what you may be used to.

Should I visit New Mexico in the winter for a warm getaway, and avoid it in summer because of excessive heat? Actually, New Mexico doesn't conform to the stereotypes of hot desert destinations. Much of the state (including its largest city, Albuquerque) sits a mile above sea level, and popular destinations like Ruidoso, Santa Fe, and Taos all have elevations of around 7,000 feet. Although New Mexico is sunny and quite beautiful all winter, it's nevertheless extremely cold in many parts of the state—the average January low temperature in Santa Fe is 15°F, which is actually lower than you'll find in Chicago or Boston during this time of year. It does often warm up considerably during the day, but you still shouldn't come to New Mexico in winter expecting a toasty break from Old Man Winter: remember, this is a prime skiing destination. In summer, these same high-elevation communities remain consistently cool and dry—in Ruidoso, which is at the same latitude as Phoenix and Dallas, the average high in July is just 83°F, which is comparable to the temperature in Minneapolis.

What's the best strategy for including New Mexico as part of a larger Southwestern road trip? If you have at least 10 days, and ideally a bit more, road-tripping through New Mexico and into the adjoining states that make up the famed Four Corners region (Arizona, Utah, and Colorado) is a fantastic way to experience the Southwest. Just keep in mind that distances are vast, and you'll spend a lot of time driving, albeit through some of the country's most amazing scenery. An excellent strategy is to fly into Albuquerque and drive in a counterclockwise loop into north-central Arizona (Flagstaff, Sedona, Grand Canyon), southern Utah (Bryce and Zion national parks, Moab), southwestern Colorado (Mesa Verde, Durango), and return through New Mexico to visit Farmington, Taos, and Santa Fe. A drive like this can easily run close to 2,000 mi, but the incredible scenery will leave you wanting more.

FLAVORS OF NEW MEXICO

CHILE TIME

Chile peppers, which have been locally grown since ancient times, are a defining ingredient of New Mexican cuisine. Combined with corn tortillas, beans, tomatoes, and potatoes, chiles bind together the New Mexico that for centuries sustained indigenous people, the Spanish, and subsequent arrivals. A fan will travel any distance—down any highway—in pursuit of a great chile sauce (which is referred to in these parts as simply "chile"). From Chope's south of Las Cruces to M&J's Sanitary Tortilla Factory in Albuquerque and JoAnn's Ranch-o-Casados in Española (to name a few classic hot spots), the pursuit of the most flavorful—but not necessarily the hottest—chile remains a personal quest akin to proving one's honor.

How chiles first arrived in New Mexico is the subject of debate. Some believe the Spanish introduced them to the Pueblo Indians on their travels north from Mexico. Others say they were grown in New Mexico centuries prior to the arrival of the Spanish, having been introduced through trade with the peoples of Mexico and South America.

The source of the chile's heat is the chemical capsaicin, found in the pepper's heart and membrane. In addition to providing a culinary delight to chile lovers, capsaicin has been used medicinally since prehistoric times; it's thought to prevent blood clots and heart attacks, and has been found to hinder cholesterol absorption. Low in fat and high in vitamins A and C and beta-carotene, it also speeds up metabolism and helps digestion. When you eat chile, or even touch it, endorphins (the "hormones of pleasure") are released in the brain.

The same chemical reaction that produces "chile addiction" also blunts pain.

The green variety of chile, generically called "Hatch" (for the New Mexico town that produces the bulk of the state's crop), is the commercially developed type known as New Mexico 6–10 and the Big Jim. The best red chiles are said to be grown from the old stock cultivated in Chimayó and other high mountain villages of the north—Española, Dixon, Velarde, and Peñasco.

By far the state's most important vegetable crop, New Mexico chiles are grown on 30,000 acres, mostly in Luna and Doña Ana counties. Sixty percent of the nation's chile crop comes from the Land of Enchantment.

From mid-August through the fall, the New Mexican air is scented with the warm, enticing fragrance of chiles roasting outdoors in large, wire, propane-fired cages. Around State Fair time in September, people head for their favorite roadside stand to buy a sack of fresh-roasted green chiles. Once stored in the freezer, they're used all winter long, in stews, enchiladas, salsas, and burritos.

As the season progresses into October, it's time to buy a red chile *ristra*, a string of chiles, to hang full, heavy, and sweet, near the front door, a sign of warmth and welcome. It's said the ristra brings good luck—and it certainly is convenient to have the makings of soul-warming red-chile salsa right at hand.

—Sharon Niederman

FLAVORS OF NEW MEXICO

MENU GUIDE

Aguacate: Spanish for avocado, the key ingredient of guacamole.

Albóndigas: Meatballs, usually cooked with rice in a meat broth.

Bizcochitos: Buttery cookies flavored with cinnamon and anise seeds and served typically at Christmas but available throughout the year.

Burrito: A warm flour tortilla wrapped around meat, beans, and vegetables and smothered in chiles and cheese; many New Mexicans also love breakfast burritos (filled with any combination of the above, along with eggs and, typically, bacon or sausage and potatoes).

Calabacitas: Summer squash, usually served with corn, chiles, and other vegetables.

Carne adovada: Red-chile-marinated pork (or, occasionally, chicken).

Chalupa: A corn tortilla deep-fried in the shape of a bowl, filled with pinto beans (sometimes meat), and topped with cheese, guacamole, sour cream, lettuce, tomatoes, and salsa.

Chicharrones: Fried pork rinds.

Chilaquiles: Often served at breakfast, this casserolelike dish consists of small pieces of fried tortillas baked with red or green chiles, bits of chicken or cheese, and sometimes eggs.

Chile relleno: A poblano pepper peeled, stuffed with cheese or a special mixture of spicy ingredients, dipped in batter, and fried.

Chiles: New Mexico's infamous hot peppers, which come in an endless variety of sizes and in various degrees of hot-

ness, from the thumb-size jalapeño to the smaller and often hotter serrano. They can be canned or fresh, dried or cut up into salsa. Most traditional New Mexican dishes are served either with green, red, or both types of chiles (ask for "Christmas" when indicating to your server that you'd like both red and green). Famous regional uses for green chile include green-chile stew (usually made with shredded pork), green-chile cheeseburgers, and green-chile-and-cheese tamales.

Chili: A stewlike dish with Texas origins that typically contains beans, beef, and red chile.

Chimichanga: The same as a burrito, only deep-fried and topped with a dab of sour cream or salsa. (The chimichanga was allegedly invented in Tucson, Arizona.)

Chipotle: A dried smoked jalapeño with a smoky, almost sweet, chocolaty flavor.

Chorizo: Well-spiced Spanish sausage, made with pork and red chiles.

Enchilada: A rolled or flat corn tortilla filled with meat, chicken, seafood, or cheese, an enchilada is covered with chili and baked. The ultimate enchilada is made with blue Native American corn tortillas. New Mexicans order them flat, sometimes topped with a fried egg.

Fajitas: A Tex-Mex dish of grilled beef, chicken, fish, or roasted vegetables and served with peppers, onions, and pico de gallo, served with tortillas; traditionally known as *arracheras*.

Flauta: A tortilla filled with cheese or meat and rolled into a flutelike shape ("flauta" means flute) and lightly fried.

Frijoles refritos: Refried beans, often seasoned with lard or cheese.

Frito Pie: Originally from Texas but extremely popular in New Mexican diners and short-order restaurants, this savory, humble casserole consists of Fritos snack chips layered with chili, cheese, green onions, and pinto beans.

Guacamole: Mashed avocado, mixed with tomatoes, garlic, onions, lemon juice, and chiles, used as a dip, a side dish, or a topping.

Hatch: A small southern New Mexico town in the Mesilla Valley, known for its outstanding production and quality of both green and red chiles. The "Hatch" name often is found on canned chile food products.

Huevos rancheros: New Mexico's answer to eggs Benedict—eggs doused with chili and sometimes melted cheese, served on top of a corn tortilla (they're best with a side order of chorizo).

Nopalitos: The pads of the prickly pear cactus, typically cut up and served uncooked in salads or baked or stir-fried as a vegetable side dish. (The tangy-sweet, purplish-red fruit of the prickly pear is often used to make juice drinks and margaritas.)

Posole: Resembling popcorn soup, this is a sublime marriage of lime, hominy, pork, chiles, garlic, and spices.

Quesadilla: A folded flour tortilla filled with cheese and meat or vegetables and warmed or lightly fried so the cheese melts.

Queso: Cheese; an ingredient in many Mexican and Southwestern recipes (cheddar or Jack is used most commonly in New Mexican dishes).

Ristra: String of dried red-chile peppers, often used as decoration.

Salsa: Finely chopped concoction of green- and red-chile peppers, mixed with onion, garlic, and other spices.

Sopaipilla: Puffy deep-fried bread that's similar to Navajo fry bread (found in Arizona and western New Mexico); it's served either as a dessert with honey drizzled over it or savory as a meal stuffed with pinto beans or meat.

Taco: A corn or flour tortilla served either soft, or baked or fried and served in a hard shell; it's then stuffed with vegetables or spicy meat and garnished with shredded lettuce, chopped tomatoes, onions, and grated cheese.

Tacos al carbón: Shredded pork cooked in a mole sauce and folded into corn tortillas.

Tamale: Ground corn made into a dough, often filled with finely ground pork and red chiles; it's steamed in a corn husk.

Tortilla: A thin pancake made of corn or wheat flour, a tortilla is used as bread, as an edible "spoon," and as a container for other foods. Locals place butter in the center of a hot tortilla, roll it up, and eat it as a scroll.

Trucha en terra-cotta: Fresh trout wrapped in corn husks and baked in clay.

Verde: Spanish for "green," as in chile verde (a green chile sauce).

A LAND APART

Almost every New Mexican has a tale or two to tell about being perceived as a "foreigner" by the rest of the country. There's the well-documented case of the Santa Fe man who tried to purchase tickets to the 1996 Olympic Games in Atlanta, only to be shuffled over to the department handling international requests. Even the U.S. Postal Service occasionally returns New Mexico–bound mail to its senders for insufficient "international" postage.

Though annoying to residents, such cases of mistaken identity are oddly apt (keep an ear open to how often New Mexicans themselves refer to their state, one of the nation's poorest, as a Third World country). New Mexico is, in many ways, an anomaly: it has its own cuisine, architecture, fashion, and culture, all of these an amalgam of the designs and accidents of a long and intriguing history. In prehistoric times indigenous peoples hunted game in New Mexico's mountains and farmed along its riverbanks. Two thousand years ago Pueblo Indians began expressing their reverence for the land through flat-roofed earthen architecture, drawings carved onto rocks, and rhythmic chants and dances. The late 16th and early 17th centuries brought the Spanish explorers who, along with the Franciscan monks, founded Santa Fe as a northern capital of the empire of New Spain, a settlement that was contemporaneous with the Jamestown colony of Virginia.

Although the Spanish brutally enslaved and mistreated the Native Americans, during the course of several hundred years tolerance has grown and traditions have commingled. Pueblo Indians passed on the use of chiles, beans, and corn, and the Spanish shared their skill at metalwork, influencing the Native American jewelry that has become symbolic of the region. The Spanish also shared their architecture, which itself had been influenced by 700 years of Arab domination of Spain, and the acequia method of irrigation still in use in the villages of northern New Mexico.

The last of the three main cultures to make its mark was that of the Anglo (any nonindigenous, non-Hispanic person in New Mexico is considered an Anglo—even groups who don't normally identify with the Anglo-Saxon tradition). Arriving throughout the 19th century, Anglos mined the mountains for gold, other precious metals, and gemstones and uncovered vast deposits of coal, oil, and natural gas. Their contributions to New Mexican life include the railroad, the highway system, and—for better or worse—the atomic bomb.

The resulting mélange of cultures has produced a character that's uniquely New Mexican: Spanish words are sprinkled liberally through everyday English parlance; Spanish itself, still widely spoken in the smaller villages, contains numerous words from the Pueblo Indian dialects. Architectural references and culinary terms in particular tend to hew to the original Spanish: you can admire the vigas and bancos that adorn the restaurant where you can partake of posole or sopaipilla.

But beyond the linguistic quirks, gastronomic surprises, and cultural anomalies that make New Mexico unique, there remains the most distinctive feature of all—the landscape. At once subtle and dramatic, the mountains and mesas seem almost surreal as they glow gold, terracotta, and pink in the clear, still air of

the high desert. The shifting clouds overhead cast rippling shadows across the land, illuminating the delicate palette of greens, grays, and browns that contrast with a sky that can go purple or dead black or eye-searingly blue in a matter of seconds. It's a landscape that has inspired writers (such as D. H. Lawrence and Willa Cather), painters (such as Georgia O'Keeffe and Peter Hurd), and countless poets, dreamers, filmmakers, and assorted creative spirits for centuries.

Indeed, watching the ever-changing sky is something of a spectator sport here, especially during the usual "monsoons" of summer. So regular that you could almost set your watch by them, the thunderheads start to gather in late afternoon, giving visual warning before the inevitable downpour. In the meantime, the sky dazzles with its interplay of creamy-white clouds edged by charcoal, sizzling flashes of lightning, and dramatic shafts of light shooting earthward from some ethereal perch.

The mountains absorb and radiate this special illumination, transforming themselves daily according to the whims of light and shadow. The very names of the major ranges attest to the profound effect their light show had on the original Spanish settlers. The Franciscan monks named the mountains to the east of Santa Fe *Sangre de Cristo,* or "blood of Christ," because of their tendency to glow deep red at sunset. To the south, east of Albuquerque, the Sandia Mountains ("watermelon" in Spanish) also live up to their colorful name when the sun sets. Georgia O'Keeffe once joked about the Pedernal mesa in the Jemez range, "It's my private mountain, it belongs to me. God told me if I painted it enough, I could have it."

The awe-inspiring beauty of the landscape renders New Mexico's tag lines more than just marketing clichés. The state is truly a "Land of Enchantment," and Santa Fe is indeed "the City Different." Surrounded by mind-expanding mountain views and filled with sinuous streets that promote foot over car traffic, Santa Fe welcomes with characteristic adobe warmth. Rapid growth and development have prompted many local residents to worry about becoming too much like everywhere else, but the surfeit of trendy restaurants, galleries, and boutiques that tout regional fare and wares, both authentic and commercial, are still distinctly Santa Fean. Commercialism notwithstanding, Santa Fe's deeply spiritual aura affects even nonreligious types in surprising ways, inspiring a reverence probably not unlike that which inspired the Spanish monks to name it the City of Holy Faith. (Its full name is La Villa Real de la Santa Fe de San Francisco de Asís, or the Royal City of the Holy Faith of St. Francis of Assisi.) A kind of mystical Catholicism blended with ancient Native American lore and beliefs flourishes throughout northern New Mexico in tiny mountain villages that have seen little change through the centuries. Tales of miracles, spontaneous healings, and spiritual visitations thrive in the old adobe churches that line the High Road that leads north of Santa Fe to Taos.

If Santa Fe is spiritual, sophisticated, and occasionally snobby, Taos, 65 mi away, is very much an outpost despite its relative proximity to the capital. Compared with Santa Fe, Taos is smaller, feistier, quirkier, tougher, and very independent. Taoseños are a study in diverse convictions, and most anyone will share his or

A LAND APART

hers with you if you lend an ear. Rustic and comfortably unpretentious, the town contains a handful of upscale restaurants with cuisines and wine lists as innovative as what you might find in New York. It's a haven for aging hippies, creative geniuses, cranky misanthropes, and anyone else who wants a good quality of life in a place that accepts new arrivals without a lot of questions—as long as they don't offend longtime residents with their city attitudes.

Sixty miles south of Santa Fe, Albuquerque adds another distinctive perspective to the mix. New Mexico's only big city, it shares many traits with cities its size elsewhere: traffic, noise, crime, and sprawl. But what sets it apart is its dogged determination to remain a friendly small town, a place where pedestrians still greet one another as they pass and where downtown's main street is lined with angle parking (a modern-day version of the hitching post). Old Town, a congenial district whose authentic historical appeal is tempered by the unabashed pursuit of the tourist buck, is a typical example of how traditional small-town New Mexico flourishes amid a larger, more demanding economy without sacrificing the heart and soul of the lifestyle. San Felipe de Neri Catholic Church, built in 1793, is still attended by local worshippers.

The unifying factor among these and other towns and the terrain around them is the appeal of the land and the people. From the stunning natural formations of Carlsbad Caverns to the oceanic sweep of the "badlands" north of Santa Fe, it's the character of the residents and respect for the land that imbue New Mexico with its enchanted spirit. First-time visitors discover the unexpected pleasures of a place where time is measured not only by linear calculations of hours, days, weeks, and years but also by the circular sweep of crop cycles, gestation periods, the rotation of generations, and the changing of seasons.

Summer is traditionally the high season, when the arts scene explodes with gallery openings, performances at Santa Fe's open-air opera house, and a variety of festivals and celebrations. In autumn the towering cottonwoods that hug the riverbanks turn gold, days are warm and sunny, and the nights are crisp. Those beehive-shaped kiva fireplaces get a workout in winter, a time when life slows down to accommodate occasional snowstorms, and the scent of aromatic firewood like piñon and cedar fill the air like an earthy incense.

Even after you leave, New Mexico will sneak into your consciousness in unexpected ways. As much a state of mind as it is a geographic entity, a place where nature can be glimpsed simultaneously at its most fragile and most powerful, New Mexico truly is a land of enchantment.

—Nancy Zimmerman

Albuquerque

Updated by
Lynne Arany

AT FIRST GLANCE, ALBUQUERQUE APPEARS to be a typical Sun Belt city, stretching more than 100 square mi with no grand design, architectural or otherwise, to hold it together. The city's growth seems as free-spirited as the hot-air balloons that take part in the Albuquerque International Balloon Fiesta every October. In reality, this spread-out city has been inhabited for more than 300 years (2006 ushered in a jubilant year of tricentennial celebrations). With a bit of exploration, your initial impression of an asphalt maze softens. The distinctive blend of Spanish, Mexican, Native American, Anglo, and Asian influences spreads throughout its neighborhoods, making Albuquerque a vibrant multicultural metropolis.

Albuquerque was established in 1706 as a farming settlement near a bend in the Rio Grande. Named for Spain's duke of Alburquerque (the first "r" was later dropped), it prospered, thanks to its strategic location on a trade route. Its proximity to several Native American pueblos, which were another source of commerce, provided protection from raiding nomadic tribes. Farming thrived right from the start in the fertile Rio Grande Valley. Settlers built a chapel and then a larger structure, San Felipe de Neri Catholic Church, named after a 16th-century Florentine saint. For protection, the first homes were built around a central plaza like those in other Spanish settlements. The fortress-like community could be entered from the four corners only, making it easier to defend. This four-block area, Old Town, is now the city's tourist hub, filled with shops, galleries, and restaurants.

In 1880 the railroad came to central New Mexico, its tracks bypassing Old Town by a good 2 mi to the east, and causing a population shift. Old Town wasn't exactly abandoned, but New Town sprouted near the depot and grew in all directions; the separation of New and Old was blurred. The city experienced huge growth around the turn of the 20th century, as railroad workers flooded the city. Then came Route 66. Opened in 1926 and nicknamed "The Mother Road" by John Steinbeck, it sparked much of Albuquerque's modern economic development. Surging through town during the 1930s and '40s, the route had as much impact as the railroad and the river combined. The burgeoning city swelled around the asphalt—motels, gas stations, diners, and truck stops formed a sea of neon that celebrated American mobility. During World War II Albuquerque flourished with the growth of a major air base, Kirtland. It and other military-related facilities such as Sandia National Laboratory remain economic linchpins.

Today Albuquerque is the center of New Mexico's educational institutions and financial, manufacturing, and medical industries. It's an unpretentious, practical city with a metro population of nearly 850,000 easygoing inhabitants. Albuquerque's economy continues to diversify. Intel, the world's largest computer-chip maker, has one of its biggest manufacturing centers here, in the fast-growing northern suburb of Rio Rancho. To the south, the immense Mesa del Sol project has taken root. In addition to a progressive, planned community, it brings with it key international solar-power developers and two very heavy anchors

TOP REASONS TO GO

■ For a drive up the **Camino Real** (N. 4th St.) or south into Barelas where you'll glimpse vintage shops and taquerias with hand-painted signage in idiosyncratic script and blazing-hot colors. Be sure to pause for a bite at **Red Ball, Barelas Coffehouse**, or **Mary & Tito's**.

■ To visit the spectacularly embellished Pueblo Deco **KiMo Theatre**, in the center of downtown right on old Route 66.

■ To walk or bike the **Paseo del Bosque** along the Rio Grande. The scenery along the 16-mi trail is a menagerie of cottonwoods, migrating birds, and the ever-present river rippling quietly at your side.

■ To experience **The National Hispanic Cultural Center**, a one-of-a-kind music and arts venue.

■ To witness the sunset over the volcanoes in the Western desert—a brilliant pink flood that creeps over the valley making its way east to illuminate the Sandias before disappearing. Even better when the scent of roasting green chiles fills the late August air.

for the state's burgeoning film industry: Albuquerque "Q" Studios and Sony Pictures Imageworks.

The city's substantial arts scene, proudly distinct from those of Santa Fe and Taos, is apparent the moment you step off a plane at Albuquerque International Sunport and see the works of New Mexican artists throughout the terminal. Significant museums and galleries draw much local support, and feed off the creative energy of the many artists, writers, poets, filmmakers, and musicians who call this area home.

Outdoors enthusiasts and seekers of places off the beaten path will also find plenty of options both in town and a very short drive away. Engaging mountainside frontier towns, unique wilderness areas, and the Indian pueblos of the high desert and the Rio Grande Valley all lie just beyond Albuquerque's city limits.

ORIENTATION & PLANNING

GETTING ORIENTED

Colorful Historic Route 66 unifies the diverse areas of the city—Old Town cradled at the bend of the Rio Grande; the downtown business, government, arts, and entertainment center to the east; the University of New Mexico farther east (and EDo, or East Downtown, in between); and the Nob Hill strip of restaurants and shops past the university. Uptown and the Heights are north and east of Nob Hill. The North Valley area is west, above Old Town. The South Valley and Barelas are just below Old Town and Downtown. The railroad tracks and Central Avenue divide the city into quadrants.

Old Town, Downtown, EDo (East Downtown), and Barelas. Old Town, Downtown, EDo, and Barelas each represent distinct moments in the city's growth, and you're not likely to find a richer range of architecture in such a small area anywhere. Each of these historic enclaves—spanning the early 1800s through modern times—carries the charms of cultures past and a sense of respect for their place in Albuquerque's future.

University of New Mexico & Nob Hill. Off-campus life is focused directly to the south and east of school, stretching along Central Avenue from University Boulevard east through the Nob Hill neighborhood. Low-budget eateries, specialty shops, and music and arts venues are tightly clustered within the college-named streets just to the south of Central; things get more upscale as you head farther east.

North Valley & Northeast Heights. The North Valley (and its sister South Valley) are the agrarian heart of Albuquerque. It is here, where generations of Hispanic families have resided, that you will experience the deepest sense of tradition. The Northeast Heights, however, is all about growth, and can feel like a town apart. Homes here often belong to New Mexico transplants, and continue to spread to within startling proximity of the Sandias.

ALBUQUERQUE PLANNER

WHEN TO GO

Fall is the season of choice. On just about any late-August day through November, big balloons sail across the sharp blue sky, and the scent of freshly roasting green chiles permeates the air. Balloon Fiesta does bring crowds in early October. But shortly after, the weather's still great, and hotel and restaurant prices plummet. Albuquerque's winter days (usually 10°F warmer than those in Santa Fe) are often mild enough for most outdoor activities. The occasional frigid spike is usually gone by morning. Spring brings winds, though it's lovely, too, and rates stay low until the summer crowds flock in. Avoid late June through July when days can be brutally hot. August brings cooler temperatures, humidity, and the spectacular cloud formations that herald the brief "monsoon" season.

GETTING HERE & AROUND

BY AIR   The major gateway to New Mexico is Albuquerque International Sunport (ABQ), which is 65 mi southwest of Santa Fe and 130 mi south of Taos.

BY BUS   Buses are practical for getting between Old Town, Downtown, Nob Hill, and Uptown; the bus system's expedited RapidRide service plies these routes and runs until about 8 PM Sunday–Thursday, and until about 2 AM on Friday and Saturday. You can obtain a customized trip plan at the city's public bus service, ABQ Ride. The Alvarado Transportation Center downtown is ABQ Ride's central hub and offers direct connections to the NM Rail Runner train service north to Bernalillo and Santa Fe, as well as points south. Buses accept bicycles, although space is limited. Service is free on the "Downtown Circulator" shuttle route, or if you are transferring (to any route) from the Rail Runner; otherwise, fare is $1 (bills or coins, exact change only; 25¢ transfers may be requested on boarding). Bus stops are well marked. *See also Bus Travel in the Essentials chapter.*

BY CAR   Although the city's public bus service, ABQ Ride, provides good coverage, a car is the easiest and most convenient way to get around. Albuquerque sprawls in all directions, but getting around town is not difficult. The main highways through the city, north–south Interstate 25 and east–west Interstate 40, converge just northeast of downtown and generally offer the quickest access to outlying neighborhoods and the airport. Rush-hour jams are common in the mornings and late afternoons, but they're still far less severe than in most big U.S. cities. All the major car-rental agencies are represented at Albuquerque's Sunport Airport.

BY TAXI   Taxis are metered in Albuquerque, and service is around-the-clock. Given the considerable distances around town, cabbing it can be expensive; figure about $9 from downtown to Nob Hill, and about $20 from the airport to an Uptown hotel. There's also a $1 airport fee.

BY TRAIN   In summer 2006 the City of Albuquerque launched the state's first-ever commuter-train line, the *New Mexico Rail Runner.* As of this writing, service from Downtown Albuquerque to Santa Fe is on schedule for completion in early winter 2009. Currently service is from Bernalillo south through the city of Albuquerque, continuing south through Los Lunas to the suburb of Belén, covering a distance of about 50 mi. In-town stops are Downtown, at the Alvarado Transportation Center, and at the north end of town at Journal Center / Los Ranchos. Service is limited to commuting hours Monday–Friday, including late nights and weekends for special events (such as Balloon Fiesta). Plans include adding Saturday service in 2009, and eventual Sunday service. Fares are zone based (one way, from $1 to $7); discounted multi-day passes ($2–$9) are available; bicycles ride free. Connections to local bus service are available at most stations. *For information on Amtrak service, see Train Travel in New Mexico Essentials.*

TOURS   The Albuquerque Museum of Art and History leads free, hour-long historical walks through Old Town at 11 AM Tuesday to Sunday, March through November.

Backcountry and local-history expert Roch Hart, owner of **NM Jeep Tours,** offers jeep tours and guided hikes that start from Albuquerque and go as far as time—and permits—allow. He can suggest an itinerary (ghost towns, rock formations, petroglyphs), or tailor one to your interests and time frame.

ESSENTIALS   **Air Contact Albuquerque International Sunport** (☎ *505/244–7700* ⊕ *www. cabq.gov/airport*).

Bus Contact ABQ Ride (☎ *505/243–7433 [RIDE]* ⊕ *www.cabq.gov/transit*).

Taxi Contacts **Albuquerque Cab** (☎ *505/883–4888*). **Yellow Cab** (☎ *505/247– 8888*).

Train Contact **New Mexico Rail Runner Express** (☎*505/245–7245* ⊕*www. nmrailrunner.com*).

Tour Contacts **Albuquerque Museum of Art and History** (☎*505/243–7255* ⊕*www. cabq.gov/museum*). **NM Jeep Tours** (☎ *505/252–0112* ⊕*nmjeeptours.com*).

VISITOR INFORMATION

The Albuquerque Convention and Visitors Bureau operates tourism information kiosks at the airport (on the baggage-claim level) and in Old Town on Plaza Don Luis, across from San Felipe de Neri church.

Albuquerque Convention and Visitors Bureau (✉ *20 1st Plaza NW, Suite 601,* ☎*505/842–9918 or 800/284–2282* ⊕*www.itsatrip.org*). **State Information Center** (✉*Indian Pueblo Cultural Center, 2401 12th St. NW* ☎*505/843–7270* ⊕*www.newmexico.org*).

PLANNING YOUR TIME

Although the city sprawls, it does break down into a few distinct regions. Start at the Rio Grande River corridor, where many of the best museums are clustered near Rio Grande Boulevard. A trip across the river takes you to Petroglyph National Monument. With a car, neighborhoods just east such as Old Town and Downtown are easily traversed.

Interstate 25 defines a central north-south route. If you're going to start with the University of New Mexico area, consider parking the car (The Cornell Parking Structure, off Central Ave. on the eastern edge of the campus, is your best bet if you're stuck for a space and don't mind a fee) and switching to Central Avenue's RapidRide bus. It's just a short spin east to Nob Hill and its shops and restaurants, or west to EDo. From downtown, it's a short ride due south on 4th Street to the National Hispanic Cultural Center. For sights north of UNM, get in the car and take Interstate 25 toward Interstate 40. Consider a shopping tour to Indian Jewelers or, farther north, take in the Gruet Winery, then venture a bit west for the Balloon Museum, or east to the Bien Mur Indian Market. Head farther east to catch the breathtaking sunset from the Sandia Peak Tram.

Running through the Sandia foothills is Tramway Boulevard, the access for side trips to the crest; the Turquoise Trail to Santa Fe; Mountainair to the south; and to the Sandia Tram base terminal. A day's worth of hiking and mountain-bike trails and wooded picnic grounds (Elena Gallegos is especially nice) pepper this area, which is part of the Cibola National Forest. From here you are ideally situated to visit a place that explores another essential component of Albuquerque's history, the National Museum of Nuclear Science and History, nearby on Eubank Boulevard.

EXPLORING ALBUQUERQUE

Albuquerque's terrain is diverse. Along the river in the North and South valleys, the elevation hovers at about 4,800 feet. East of the river, the land rises gently to the foothills of the Sandia Mountains, which rise to over 6,000 feet; the 10,378-foot summit is a grand spot from which to view the city below. West of the Rio Grande, where much of Albu-

GREAT ITINERARY

Most visitors to Albuquerque combine a stay here with some explorations of the entire northern Rio Grande Valley. If you're looking for the perfect regional tour, combine either of the short Albuquerque itineraries here with those provided in the Side Trips from the Cities chapter, which covers several great areas within a 60- to 90-minute drive of Albuquerque as well as covering Isleta Pueblo and the towns of Corrales and Bernalillo, just on the outskirts of Albuquerque.

One of the best places to kick off the day is the Gold Street Caffe, where you can enjoy breakfast in the heart of downtown before checking out the shops and galleries on Gold and Central avenues. From here, it's a short drive or 30-minute walk west along Central to reach Old Town, where you can explore the shops and museums of the neighborhood. Definitely be sure to check out the Albuquerque Museum of Art and History, and also try to make your way over to the Albuquerque Biological Park, which contains the aquarium, zoo, and botanic park. For lunch, try the atmospheric Monica's or the sophisticated St. Clair Winery and Bistro, both near the Old Town center.

Later in the afternoon, you'll need a car to head east a couple of miles along Central to reach the University of New Mexico's main campus and the nearby Nob Hill District. Start with a stroll around the UNM campus with its many historic adobe buildings; if you have time, pop inside either the Maxwell Museum of Anthropology or the University Art Museum. When you're finished here, walk east along Central into Nob Hill and check out the dozens of offbeat shops. If it's summer, meaning that you still have some time before the sun sets, it's worth detouring from Old Town to Far Northeast Heights (a 15-minute drive), where you can take the Sandia Peak Aerial Tramway 2.7 mi up to Sandia Peak for spectacular sunset views of the city. Either way, plan to have dinner back in Nob Hill, perhaps at Graze or Flying Star. If you're still up for more fun, check out one of the neighborhood's lively lounges or head back downtown for a bit of late-night barhopping.

querque's growth is taking place, the terrain rises abruptly in a string of mesas topped by five volcanic cones. The changes in elevation from one part of the city to another result in corresponding changes in temperature, as much as 10°F at any time. It's not uncommon for snow or rain to fall on one part of town but for it to remain dry and sunny in another.

Numbers in the margin correspond to the Albuquerque and Albuquerque Old Town maps.

OLD TOWN, DOWNTOWN, EDO & BARELAS

Albuquerque's social and commercial anchor since the settlement was established in 1706, Old Town and the surrounding blocks contain the wealth of the city's top cultural attractions, including several excellent museums. The action extends from the historic Old Town Plaza for several blocks in all directions—most of the museums are north and east of the Plaza. In this area you'll also find a number of restaurants and scads of shops. Some of these places are touristy and can be missed, but the better ones are included in the Where to Eat and Shopping sections of this chapter. The artsy Saw Mill and Wells Park/Mountain Road neighborhoods extend just east of Old Town's museum row; the Duranes section, where the Indian Pueblo Cultural Center commands attention, is just a bit beyond walking distance to the northeast of Old Town.

To reach Albuquerque's up-and-coming downtown from Old Town, it's a rather drab (though quick) 1¼-mi bus ride, walk, or drive southeast along Central Avenue. Although downtown doesn't have many formal attractions short of its anchor (and destination-worthy) art gallery scene, this bustling neighborhood is one of the West's great urban-comeback stories. It's a diverting place to wander, gallery-hop, shop, snack (or dine), or simply soak in some fine remnants from its Route 66–era boom years for a couple of hours (⇨ *Going Downtown box below*). From here, you're a skip away from the historic Barelas neighborhood to the south, and its superb must-see, the National Hispanic Cultural Center. To the east is another revitalizing section of town: now known as EDo (East Downtown) and encompassing the historic Huning Highland District, this is where Albuquerque's Old Main Library—an architectural gem—and Gothic Revival high school (now condos) still stand, and restaurants and shops seem to sprout up daily.

WHAT TO SEE

❺ **Albuquerque BioPark.** The city's foremost outdoor attraction and nature center, the park comprises the recently restored Tingley Beach as well as three distinct attractions, Albuquerque Aquarium, Rio Grande Botanic Garden, and Rio Grande Zoo. The garden and aquarium are located together (admission gets you into both facilities); the zoo is a short drive southeast. You can also ride the scenic *Rio Line* vintage narrow-gauge railroad between the zoo and gardens and aquarium complex; rides are free if you purchase a combination tickets to all of the park's facilities.

Two main components of the Albuquerque Bio Park, **Albuquerque Aquarium** and **Rio Grande Botanic Garden** (✉ *2601 Central Ave. NW ✛ West of Old Town, north of Central Ave. and just east of the Central Ave. bridge*) are a huge draw with kids but also intrigue adult visitors. At the aquarium, a spectacular shark tank with floor-to-ceiling viewing is among the most popular of the marine exhibits. The Spanish-Moorish garden is one of three walled gardens near the entrance of the 36-acre botanic garden. The exquisite Sasebo Japanese Garden joins other specialty landscapes including the Curandera Garden, exhibiting herbs used by traditional Spanish folk-medicine practitioners, and the Children's Fantasy Garden, complete with walk-through pumpkin, a 14-foot dragon, and giant bees. The seasonal PNM Butterfly Pavilion is open late May through late September, and, year-round, the glass conservatory holds desert and Mediterranean plantings. In summer there are concerts given on Thursday at the botanic garden. From late November through late December, the botanic garden comes alive each

A GOOD TOUR

Soak up the history in **Old Town Plaza ❶**, and then cross the street and visit **San Felipe de Neri Catholic Church ❷**. Then take a five-minute (or longer if the shops or smaller museums beckon) stroll over to two of the city's grandest cultural institutions, the **Albuquerque Museum of Art and History ❻** and the **New Mexico Museum of Natural History and Science ❼**. Kids also enjoy **¡Explora! ❾**, which is next door.

From here, choose one of these options (all short rides away—the first two are on primary bus routes):

1. West on Central, along a historic section of Route 66 lined with shabby vintage motels, is the **Albuquerque BioPark ❺**, which consists of the Albuquerque Aquarium, Botanic Garden, Rio Grande Zoo, and Tingley Beach.

2. East on Central to Downtown, and a gawk at (or tour of) the **KiMo Theatre ⓫** and some neon-viewing and gallery-hopping. **516 Arts** is the place to start (⇨ *Art Galleries in Shopping, below.*) Detour farther east to EDo and take in the old main library (now **Special Collections & the Center for the Book**) and its exhibits, or go directly south on 4th Street to the **National Hispanic Cultural Center ⓭**.

3. Drive east along Mountain Road and enjoy a taste of old Albuquerque neighborhoods. Stop at **Harwood Art Center,** then backtrack a few blocks turning north on 12th Street to the **Indian Pueblo Cultural Center ❿**.

TIMING

The best time to visit Old Town is in the morning, before the stores open at 10 and the daily rush of activity begins. In the beaming morning light, the echoes of the past are almost palpable (and you might find parking). Plan to spend an hour in the Plaza area, and, depending on your interests, another hour or two in the Albuquerque Museum of Art and History and the New Mexico Museum of Natural History and Science. If you try to do it all, the BioPark easily fills an afternoon by itself (allow about two hours for the gardens and aquarium; an hour or so for the zoo). Two hours is reasonable for a basic sense of downtown. The National Hispanic Cultural Center also warrants up to two hours, as does the Indian Pueblo Cultural Center. It's impractical to see everything here in one day, so consider mixing and matching your tour over a couple days if you wish to see every attraction. None of these estimates account for food stops, so plan accordingly.

evening from 6 to 9 PM for the River of Lights festival, a walk-through display of holiday lights and decorations.

The 64-acre **Rio Grande Zoo** (⊠ *903 10th St. SW*) is an oasis of waterfalls, cottonwood trees, and naturalized animal habitats. More than 250 species of wildlife from around the world live here, including giraffes, camels, polar bears, elephants, zebras, and koalas. The Tropical America exhibit offers a bit of contrast for dry Albuquerque, replicating a jungle rain forest and containing toucans, spider monkeys, and brilliant orchids and bromeliads. The zoo has established captive-breeding programs for more than a dozen endangered species. Concerts are performed on the grounds on summer Friday evenings. There's a café on the premises. The *Thunderbird Express* is a ¾-scale train that runs in a nonstop loop within the zoo, and during the 20-minute ride, conductors talk in depth about the creatures and their habitats. Running Tuesday–Sunday, it's free with combo tickets, or $2 otherwise (buy tickets onboard or at the Africa exhibit). **Tingley Beach** (⊠ *1800 Tingley Dr. SW, south of Central Ave. and just east of Central Ave. bridge*) is a recreational arm of the biological park that consists of three ponds, created in the 1930s by diverting water from the Rio Grande. You can rent paddleboats (or bicycles; both seasonally), fish the trout-stocked ponds (gear and fishing licenses can be purchased at the fishing-tackle shop on-site), or sail your model electric or wind-powered boats. To the west of the ponds, the cottonwood Bosque (wetlands forest) fringes the river. Ecological tours of the Bosque are given in summer. It's part of the popular 16-mi Paseo del Bosque bike path that is open year-round. There's also a snack bar and a *Rio Line* station; the ¾-scale passenger trains make a stop here en route between the aquarium and garden complex and the zoo. ⊠ *903 10th St. SW* ☎ *505/764–6200* ⊕ *www. cabq.gov/biopark* ⊠ *Free Tingley Beach and grounds, $7 Albuquerque Aquarium and Rio Grande Botanic Garden (combined ticket), $7 Rio Grande Zoo, $12 combination ticket for all attractions is available for entries Tues.–Sun. 9–noon, and includes unlimited rides on the Rio Line and Thunderbird Express trains* ☉ *Daily 9–5, until 6 on weekends from June–Aug. No trains Mon.*

❻ Albuquerque Museum of Art and History. This modern structure houses the largest collection of Spanish colonial artifacts in the nation, along with a superb photo archive and other relics of the city's birth and development. The "Common Ground" galleries represent an important permanent collection of primarily 20th-century paintings, all by world-renowned artists with a New Mexico connection. Changing exhibits also reveal a commitment to historically important artists and photographers of the 20th and 21st centuries. The centerpiece, "Four Centuries: A History of Albuquerque," is a pair of life-size models of Spanish conquistadors in original chain mail and armor. Perhaps the one on horseback is Francisco Vásquez de Coronado, who, in search of gold, led a small army into New Mexico in 1540—a turning point in the region's history. A multimedia presentation chronicles the development of the city since 1875. The sculpture garden contains more than 50 contemporary works by Southwestern artists that include Glenna Goodacre, Michael Naranjo, and Luís Jiménez. Visitors may also take advantage of three tours, all offered at no additional charge with admission. Each takes 45 minutes to an hour. ⊠ *2000 Mountain Rd. NW, Old Town* ☎ *505/243–7255, 505/242–0434 shop, 505/242–5316 café* ⊕ *www.albuquerquemuseum.com* ⊠ *$4 (NM residents $3); all tours included with admission. Free Sun. 9–1* ☉ *Tues.–Sun. 9–5*

Fodor's Choice ★

NEED A BREAK?

At the Museum of Art and History an intimate outdoor amphitheater is home to live jazz and other musical programming on summer evenings. And year-round, perhaps after a bit of shopping in the sunlit Gallery Store, visitors can dine inside or out at the museum's **City Treats Café** (☉ *Tues.–Sun. 10:30–4*).

The wood-lined café is very pleasant, and fresh offerings—grilled chicken salad with spinach and snap peas, and a homemade Mexican brownie—make this a good refueling stop at the north end of Old Town.

❸ American International Rattlesnake Museum. Included in the largest collection of different species of living rattlers in the world are such rare and unusual specimens as an albino western diamondback. Looking for all the world like a plain old shop from the outside, inside the museum's labels, its engaging staff, and a video supply visitors with the lowdown on these venomous creatures—for instance, that they can't hear their own rattles and that the human death rate from rattlesnake bites is less than 1%. The mission here is to educate the public on the many positive benefits of rattlesnakes, and to contribute to their conservation. ⊠ *202 San Felipe St. NW, just off the southeast corner of the Plaza, Old Town* ☎ *505/242–6569* ⊕ *www.rattlesnakes.com* ⊡ *$3.50* ⊙ *Mon.–Sat. 10–6, Sun. noon–5 (hrs sometimes shorter in winter, call ahead).*

❾ ¡Explora! Albuquerque's cultural corridor received another jewel in 2003, when this imaginatively executed science museum—its driving concept is "Ideas You Can Touch"—opened right across from the New Mexico Museum of Natural History and Science. ¡Explora! bills itself as an all-ages attraction (and enthralled adults abound), but there's no question that many of the innovative hands-on exhibits such as a high-wire bicycle and a kinetic sculpture display are geared to children. They offer big fun in addition to big science (and a good dose of art as well). While its colorful Bucky dome is immediately noticeable from the street, ¡Explora! also features a playground, theater, and a freestanding staircase that appears to "float" between floors. ⊠ *1701 Mountain Rd. NW, Old Town* ☎ *505/224–8300, 505/224–8349 shop* ⊕ *www. explora.us* ⊡ *$7* ⊙ *Mon.–Sat. 10–6, Sun. noon–6.*

❿ Indian Pueblo Cultural Center. The multilevel semicircular design at this museum was inspired by Pueblo Bonito, the prehistoric ruin in Chaco Canyon in northwestern New Mexico. A 2008 renovation emphasizes the relationship between the two sites, with the museum entryway moved to the east-facing (and sacred) exposure. Start by watching the museum's video about the region's Pueblo culture. Then move to the upper-level alcove, where changing exhibits feature aspects of the arts and crafts of each of the state's 19 pueblos. Lower-level exhibits trace the history of the Pueblo people. Youngsters can touch Native American pottery, jewelry, weaving, tools, and dried corn at the Hands-On Corner, draw petroglyph designs, and design pots. Paintings, sculptures, jewelry, leather crafts, rugs, souvenir items, drums, beaded necklaces, painted bowls, and fetishes are for sale. Ceremonial dances are performed on weekends at 11 and 2, and there are arts-and-crafts demonstrations each weekend. The **Pueblo Harvest Café** has been spruced up and is a great spot where you can try such Native American fare as blue-corn pancakes and Indian tacos, or Native Fusion items like Picuris Pasta. ⊠ *2401 12th St. NW, Los Duranes* ☎ *505/843–7270 or 800/766–4405* ⊕ *www.indianpueblo.org* ⊡ *$6* ⊙ *Daily 9–5.*

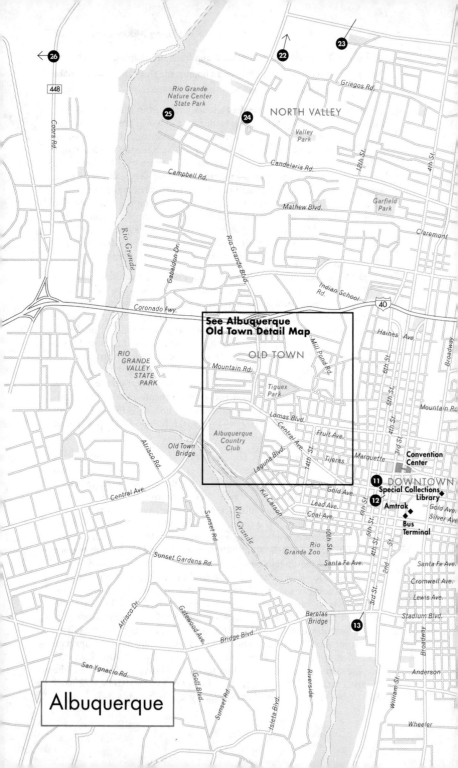

Albuquerque

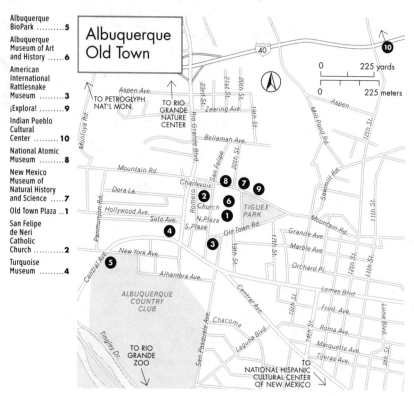

Albuquerque Old Town

❿ **KiMo Theatre.** When the KiMo was built, in 1927, Route 66 was barely

Fodor's Choice established and running on its original alignment: north–south on 4th

★ Street. Downtown was the center of activity, and movie palaces were the national rage. Local merchant Oreste Bachechi saw his moment, and hired architect Carl Boller to design a theater that would reflect the local zeitgeist. And that he did. Decorated with light fixtures made from buffalo skulls (the eye sockets glow amber in the dark), Navajo symbols, and nine spectacular Western-themed wall murals by Carl Von Hassler, the KiMo represents Pueblo Deco at its apex. Luckily, it was saved from the wrecking ball in 1977, and now, fully restored, it stands—one of the few notable early-20th-century structures in downtown Albuquerque remaining. The self-guided tour is a must, or even better, catch a live performance. ⊠ *423 Central Ave. NW, at 5th St., Downtown* ☏ *505/768–3522, 505/768–3544 event info* ⊕ *www.cabq.gov/kimo* 🖼 *Free self-guided tours* ⊙ *Tues.–Fri. 8:30–4:30, Sat. 11–5.*

❽ **National Museum of Nuclear Science & History (aka National Atomic Museum).**

🖐 Renamed after a move from its temporary location in Old Town, this popular museum traces the history of the atomic age and how nuclear science has dramatically influenced the course of modern history. Exhibits include replicas of Little Boy and Fat Man (the bombs dropped on Japan at the end of World War II), and there are children's programs and an exhibit about X-ray technology. With its renaming—and much larger facility—come even bigger changes. A B-29 and other mega-airships are again on display after being removed because of September 11 security issues. All-new exhibits are also on view. A notable one is the restored 1942 Plymouth that was used to transport the plutonium core of the "Gadget" (as that first weapon was known) down from Los Alamos to the Trinity Site for testing. ⌗ *601 Eubank Blvd. SE, ⊹a few blocks south of the Eubank Blvd. exit from I–40* ☎*505/245–2137* ⊕*www.atomicmuseum.org* ⌑*$5* ⊙*Daily 9–5.*

NEED A BREAK?

On the eastern fringe of Old Town, in a nascent arts district, **Golden Crown Panaderia** (⌗ *1103 Mountain Rd. NW, Old Town* ☎ *505/243–2424 or 877/382–2924*) is an aromatic, down-home-style bakery known for two things: the ability to custom-design and bake artful breads in the likeness of just about any person or place, and hearty green-chile bread (made with tomatoes, cilantro, Parmesan, green chile, and onions). You can order hot cocoa, cappuccino, bizcochito (the official state cookie, also known as New Mexican wedding cookies), pumpkin-filled empanadas, and plenty of other sweets and sandwiches (ask what bread is fresh and hot). There's seating on a small patio. Closed Sun. and Mon.

⓭ National Hispanic Cultural Center. A showpiece for the city, and a showcase for Latino culture and genealogy in Albuquerque's old Barelas neighborhood, this exciting contemporary space contains a museum and art galleries, multiple performance venues, a 10,000-volume genealogical research center and library, a restaurant, and an education center. Exhibits include dynamic displays of photography and paintings by local artists as well as by internationally known names. The center mounts performances of flamenco dancing, bilingual theater, traditional Spanish and New Mexican music, world music, the symphony, and more. This is the largest Latino cultural center in the country, and with a $10 million programming endowment (Rita Moreno and Edward James Olmos are among the notables on the national board), the center provides top-notch entertainment in its stunning and acoustically superb Roy E. Disney Center for Performing Arts and smaller Albuquerque Journal Theatre, and hosts major traveling art exhibits in its first-rate museum, which also houses an esteemed permanent collection. Architecturally, the center borrows from a variety of Spanish cultures, from Moorish Spain (including a re-creation of a defensive tower, or Torreón; the finely detailed fresco that embellishes the interior's 45-foot-tall walls and ceiling depicts Hispanic cultural heritage through time) to Mexico and the American Southwest. There's a vintage WPA-era school that now contains the research library and **del Bosque restaurant** ($$, no dinner), which serves solid New Mexican fare indoors and out on the patio; Sunday brunch, live music included, draws a big family crowd. The gift shop, La Tiendita, has a well-chosen and impeccably sourced selection of books, pottery, and artwork. ⌗ *1701 4th St. SW, at Avenida César Chavez (Bridge Blvd), Barelas* ☎*505/246–2261, 505/247–9480 restaurant, 505/766–6604 gift shop, 505/724–4771 box office* ⊕*www.nhccnm.org* ⌑*$3* ⊙*Tues.–Sun. 10–5.*

*Fodor's*Choice ★

Going Downtown

Albuquerque continues to grow into one of the Southwest's most dynamic cities, and downtown continues its renaissance, morphing from a somewhat dicey yet bland district of office buildings and run-down remnants of its Route 66–era heyday into a vibrant, mixed-use neighborhood of upscale condos, historic residential blocks, funky shops, world-class art galleries, hip if somewhat rowdy nightclubs, and increasingly sophisticated restaurants.

During the four or five decades following World War II, Albuquerque, like many American cities, witnessed the death of its Downtown. In the 1920s and '30s, it had been a bona fide retail and entertainment district and mixed-use neighborhood. But through the 1950s and '60s, demographic patterns shifted. Middle- and upper-income residents moved farther from downtown, and Albuquerque sprawled, with much of the city taking on the almost suburban appearance that prevails today. By the 1980s, most people had stopped shopping and playing downtown, and most of the largely abandoned blocks were razed in favor of office towers and parking garages. Into the late '90s, downtown was an empty and occasionally unsafe streetscape on weekends and after 6 PM.

Fast-forward to the present. Many U.S. cities have experienced downtown renaissances, and the traditional rec-

ipe has been to anchor the neighborhood with a sports and entertainment complex, a few cultural attractions, and a slew of high-profile shopping and restaurant franchises. Albuquerque's downtown planners have largely shunned this quick-fix approach. Local developers have attracted independently owned shops, restaurants, and nightclubs and converted former schools and manufacturing buildings into residential lofts and condos. The Spanish colonial–style Alvarado Transportation Center—designed after the old Fred Harvey–run Alvarado Hotel that once stood here—with car rentals, a taxi stand, Greyhound, Amtrak, and local city buses, is a bustling enterprise. The transportation center is also the hub for the state's spanking-new commuter-rail service, the Rail Runner Express.

Downtown's transformation has been gradual, but people have begun to notice. Visitors now wander along Central and Gold avenues, appreciating the architectural and neon holdouts from the area's retro roots, checking out the numerous new galleries, bars, and restaurants, walking over to the restored KiMo Theatre or the snazzy 14-screen movie palace. You're no longer warned to stay off downtown streets at night. It's exciting to watch this neighborhood come back to life.

—by Lynne Arany

⑫ **New Mexico Holocaust & Intolerance Museum.** Although it occupies a rather modest (especially when compared to the over-the-top KiMo Theatre next door) storefront in downtown Albuquerque, this moving museum packs plenty of punch with its low-budget but poignant exhibits that document genocide and persecution throughout history, with special emphasis placed upon the Holocaust carried out by the Nazis before and during World War II. Exhibits inside touch on child slave labor, the rescue of Bulgarian and Danish Jews, a re-created gate from a concentration camp, the Nuremburg Trials, and many artifacts related to Holocaust survivors and the Nazis. There are also exhibits describing genocides throughout history such as the infamous Bataan Death March. ✉*415 Central Ave. NW, Downtown* ☎*505/247–0606* ⊕*www.nmholocaust-museum.org* ✍*Donation suggested* ☉*Tues.–Sat. 11–3:30.*

❼ New Mexico Museum of Natural History and Science. The wonders at Albuquerque's most popular museum include the simulated volcano (with a river of bubbling hot lava flowing beneath the see-through glass floor), the frigid Ice Age cave, and, new in 2008, "Dawn of the Dinosaurs." The only Triassic exhibit in North America, this permanent hall features some of the state's own rare finds. The Evolator—short for Evolution Elevator—a six-minute high-tech ride, uses video, sound, and motion to whisk you through 35 million years of New Mexico's geological history. A film in the Extreme Screen DynaTheater makes viewers feel equally involved. Arrive via the front walkway, and you'll be greeted by life-size bronze sculptures of a 21-foot-long horned Pentaceratops and a 30-foot-long carnivorous Albertosaur. Then, on the flip side of time, the Paul Allen–funded "Start-Up!" galleries explore the silicon age. Detailing of the birth of the PC here in the Duke City (Allen and a very young Bill Gates came here in the mid-1970s to create software for the Altair kits that Ed Roberts designed on the south end of town, and the rest, well, you know), these exhibitions are a fascinating tour through the early garage days of many such start-ups. It's also done a fair job with the Apple side of the story. Also at the museum is the LodeStar Science Center, which features a state-of-the-art planetarium; it's also used for the wildly popular First Friday Fractals program (tickets available online only). ✉*1801 Mountain Rd. NW, Old Town* ☎*505/841–2800* ⊕*www.nmnaturalhistory.org* ✍*Museum $7, DynaTheater $7, planetarium $7; combination ticket for any 2 attractions $12, for any 3 attractions $15* ☉*Daily 9–5.*

❶ Old Town Plaza. Don Francisco Cuervo y Valdés, a provincial governor of New Mexico, laid out this small plaza in 1706. No slouch when it came to political maneuvering, he named the town after the duke of Alburquerque, viceroy of New Spain. He hoped flattery would induce the duke to waive the requirement that a town have 30 families before a charter was issued—there were only 15 families living here in 1706. The duke acquiesced. (Albuquerque is nicknamed "The Duke City," so he's hardly been forgotten.) Today the plaza is tranquil, with shade trees, wrought-iron benches, and a graceful white gazebo. Roughly 200 shops, restaurants, cafés, galleries, and several cultural sites in *placitas* (small plazas) and lanes surround Old Town Plaza. During fiestas Old Town comes alive with mariachi bands and dancing señoritas. ■TIP➔**Seasonally, the Albuquerque Museum (⇨above) offers an excellent guided walking tour that details local history and the historic architecture that remains intact here.** Mostly dating back to the late 1800s, styles from Queen Anne to Territorial and Pueblo Revival, and even Mediterranean, are apparent in the one- and two-story (almost all adobe) structures. Event schedules and maps, which contain a list of public restrooms and many Old Town shops and sights (but by no means all), are available at the **Old Town**

Visitors Center (✉ *303 Romero St. NW, Old Town* ☎ *505/243–3215* ⊕ *www.itsatrip.org*), which is somewhat hidden in the rear of Plaza Don Luis, across the street from the San Felipe de Neri Catholic Church. The center, an outpost of the Albuquerque Convention & Visitors Bureau, offers a wide selection of brochures for attractions citywide and beyond. It is open daily, typically 9–4:30 but usually a bit later in summer.

❷ San Felipe de Neri Catholic Church. More than two centuries after it first welcomed worshippers, this structure, erected in 1793, is still active. The building, which replaced Albuquerque's first Catholic church, has been expanded several times, but its adobe walls and other original features remain. Small gardens front and flank the church; the inside is a respite from the tourism bustle beyond its doorstep—the painting and iconography is simple, authentic, and lovely, the atmosphere hushed. Next to it is a shop and small museum that displays relics—vestments, paintings, carvings—dating from the 17th century. ■ TIP→ There's a hidden treasure behind the church: inside the gnarled tree is a statue that some speculate depicts the Virgin Mary. ✉ *2005 Plaza NW, Old Town* ☎ *505/243–4628* ⊙ *Church open to public daily 8 AM–dusk; museum Mon.–Sat. 1–4. Call ahead to confirm hrs.*

❹ Turquoise Museum. Just west of the hubbub of Old Town, this strip-mall museum focuses on the beauty, mythology, and physical properties of turquoise, a semiprecious but adored gemstone that many people associate with the color of New Mexico's skies. A self-guided tour, entered via a simulated mine shaft, leads to one-of-a-kind showpieces and examples from more than 65 mines on four continents. Displays show how turquoise is formed, the importance of individual mines, and highlight its uses by Native Americans in prehistoric times. At the education center you can learn to distinguish the real McCoy from plastic. The museum's proprietors are a multigenerational family of longtime traders, and know whereof they speak; if you retain nothing else, do remember that only turquoise specified as "natural" is the desirable, unadulterated stuff. There is an active silversmith's shop adjacent to the display area; a small gift shop offers historic and contemporary pieces. ✉ *2107 Central Ave. NW, on the west side of Rio Grande Blvd., in a modern shopping center across the street from the main Plaza area, Old Town* ☎ *505/247–8650* ▭ *$4* ⊙ *Weekdays 9:30–5, Sat. 9:30–4 (last tour entries are one hour before closing).*

NEED A BREAK?

On the east side of downtown in the historic Huning Highland district (though this stretch along Central Avenue is now commonly called EDo), the temptations of **The Grove Cafe & Market** (✉ *600 Central Ave. SE, EDo* ☎ *505/248–9800*) await you. Perfect for breakfast or lunch (sorry, no dinner), among a flock of interesting options in this short strip, it's a good stop as you continue east to the University of New Mexico and Nob Hill districts. This airy, modern establishment is a local favorite that features locally grown, seasonal specials at reasonable prices. Enjoy such fresh, quality treats as Grove Pancakes with fresh fruit, crème fraîche, local honey, and real maple syrup; or a Farmers Salad with roasted golden beets, marcona almonds, goat cheese, and lemon-basil vinaigrette; or an aged Genoa salami sandwich with olive tapenade, arugula, and provolone on an artisanal sourdough bread. You can dine on the arbored patio. Or come by for a loose-leaf tea or latte with a cupcake.

EN ROUTE

Special Collections Library & Center for the Book. Designed by Arthur Rossiter in 1925 in a Spanish–Pueblo Revival style (renowned Santa Fe woodblock artist Gustav Baumann contributed the lovely interior embellishments), this was the main Albuquerque library for some 50 years. Repurposed as the Special Collections division in 1975 when the main library moved to its new digs downtown, the old library now houses an important genealogy center as well as a small museum comprised of historic printing presses and related ephemera, known as the Center for the Book. Changing exhibits in the dramatic double-story, viga-lined, main reading room are always well presented and have included "300 Years of Albuquerque History" (in honor of the recent tricentennial observations), and a look at art, politics, and public works in New Mexico during the New Deal era. ✉ *423 Central Ave. NE, at Edith Blvd., EDo* ☎ *505/848–1376* ⊕ *www.cabq.gov/library* 🖼 *Free* ⊗ *Tues.–Sat. 10–6.*

UNIVERSITY OF NEW MEXICO & NOB HILL

Established in 1889, the University of New Mexico is the state's leading institution of higher education, with internationally recognized programs in anthropology, biology, Latin American studies, and medicine. Its many outstanding galleries and museums are open to the public free of charge. The university's Pueblo Revival–style architecture is noteworthy, particularly the old wing of Zimmerman Library and the Alumni Chapel, both designed by John Gaw Meem, a Santa Fe–based architect whose mid-20th century work dominates the campus.

WHAT TO SEE

⑮ Jonson Gallery. The home and studio of Raymond Jonson (1891–1982) house the abstract, colorful works of this pioneering modernist (and founder, in 1938, of the Transcendental Painting Group) whose paintings and drawings focus on mass and form. The gallery was designed by John Gaw Meem in 1950 to show off the then-new modernism in an appropriately tailored setting. Each summer it mounts a major Jonson retrospective and also exhibits 21st-century works of sculpture, video, and photography, as well as maintaining an important archive on the founding artist and his contemporaries. The Jonson is expected to relocate to a space within the UNM Art Museum by early 2010. ✉ *1909 Las Lomas Rd. NE, mid-campus, to the east of Yale Blvd., University of New Mexico* ☎ *505/277–4967* ⊕ *www.unm.edu/~jonsong* 🖼 *Free* ⊗ *Tues.–Fri. 9–4 and by appointment.*

⑭ Maxwell Museum of Anthropology. Many of the more than 2½ million artifacts at the Maxwell, the first public museum in Albuquerque (established in 1932), come from the Southwest. Two permanent exhibitions chronicle 4 million years of human history and the lifeways, art, and cultures of 11,500 years of human settlement in the Southwest. The photographic archives contain more than 250,000 images, including some of the earliest photos of Pueblo and Navajo cultures. The museum shop sells traditional and contemporary Southwestern Native American jewelry, rugs, pottery, basketry, and beadwork, along with folk art from around the world. In the children's section are inexpensive books and handmade tribal artifacts. Parking permits for adjacent UNM lots are available inside the museum. ⊠ *Redondo West Dr., on the west end of campus, just east of University Blvd. NE, between Las Lomas Rd. NE and Dr. Martin Luther King Blvd. NE, University of New Mexico* ☎ *505/277–4405* ⊕ *www.unm.edu/~maxwell* ⊠ *Free* ⊗ *Tues.–Fri. 9–4, Sat. 10–4.*

⑱ Nob Hill. The heart of Albuquerque's Route 66 culture and also its hippest, funkiest retail and entertainment district, Nob Hill is the neighborhood just east of UNM, with its commercial spine extending along Central Avenue (old Route 66). Along this stretch you'll find dozens of offbeat shops, arty cafés, and student hangouts, and on the blocks just north and south of Central Avenue, you'll see an eclectic assortment of building styles. Most of the hipper and more gentrified businesses are along the stretch of Central between UNM and Carlisle Boulevard, but the activity is gradually moving east. Old art deco strip malls and vintage motels along this stretch are slowly being transformed into new restaurants and shops. The neighborhood was developed during the 1930s and '40s, peaked in prosperity and popularity during the 1950s, and then fell into a state of decline from the 1960s through the mid-'80s. It was at this time that a group of local business and property owners formed a neighborhood group and banded together to help turn the neighborhood around, and Nob Hill has been enjoying great cachet and popularity ever since. ⊠ *Central Ave., from University of New Mexico campus east to Washington St., Nob Hill.*

OFF THE BEATEN PATH

Ernie Pyle Library. After several visits to New Mexico, Ernie Pyle, a Pulitzer prize–winning news reporter, built a house in 1940 that now contains the smallest branch of the Albuquerque Public Library. On display are photos, handwritten articles by Pyle, and news clippings about his career as a correspondent during World War II and his death from a sniper's bullet on April 18, 1945, on the Pacific island of Ie Shima. ⊠ *900 Girard Blvd. SE, University of New Mexico* ☎ *505/256–2065* ⊕ *www.cabq. gov/library* ⊠ *Free* ⊗ *Tues. and Thurs.–Sat. 10–6, Wed. 11–7.*

⑰ Tamarind Institute. This world-famous institution played a major role in reviving the fine art of lithographic printing, which involves working with plates of traditional stone and modern metal. Tamarind certification is to a printer what a degree from Juilliard is to a musician. A small gallery within the facility exhibits prints and lithographs by well-known masters like Jim Dine, and up-and-comers in the craft as well. Guided tours (reservations essential) are conducted on the first

A GOOD WALK

The impeccably landscaped grounds of the University of New Mexico surround a central area containing knolls, a duck pond, fountains, waterfalls, and benches. As you begin a counterclockwise route from the school's southeast corner, your first stop is for a map at the nearby Welcome Center. Then stroll north past the Student Union Building, then left into the plaza (formerly the school's football field). Zimmerman Library will be on your right; stop in and take a look at the old section, yet another one of John Gaw Meem's memorable campus buildings. Directly ahead is the oasis-like Duck Pond. From here, bear right onto Yale Boulevard past the lovely gardens of University House. You will shortly come to a four-way stop, at Las Lomas Road. The **Jonson Gallery** ⑮ is the second building on the northeast corner of this intersection. Backtrack to the Duck Pond, and loop around it to the west. The Alumni Chapel comes into view, and just beyond it is the **Maxwell Museum of Anthropology** ⑭, in the Anthropology Building on the western edge of the campus. Meander southeast now to Northrup Hall and the Meteoritics Museum within. A short distance farther east you will find yourself at the Center for the Arts, just across from the parking structure where you began.

Stop in at the Center, heading past Popejoy Hall to the **UNM Art Museum** ⑯. As you exit, turn right past the UNM bookstore (Lobo gear alert!) and cross Central Avenue. A half-block down on Cornell Drive is the **Tamarind Institute** ⑰. Detour nine blocks south of Central along Girard Boulevard (five blocks east of Cornell) to the **Ernie Pyle Branch Library**. Back on Central, you're a two-minute walk from campus to the edge of **Nob Hill** ⑱, where you can shop, café-hop, and admire the historic residential and commercial architecture.

TIMING

Seeing the University of New Mexico could take as little as an hour or two for the basics, and a solid half day if you visit all the museums. If you've driven here, park the car in the Cornell Parking Structure near the southeast end of campus; it's the side adjacent to Nob Hill and is the ideal place to start—and end—a loop around the university. Spend an hour strolling the grounds, maybe catching some rays by the duck pond. Allot up to an hour for each subsequent stop. All facilities are open year-round, but some are closed from Saturday to Monday. Save Nob Hill for late afternoon or evening, when this neighborhood really comes alive.

Friday of each month at 1:30. Plans are in place for Tamarind to move around the corner to freshly outfitted space in the old UNM architecture building in time for its 50th anniversary in 2010. ✉ *110 Cornell Dr. SE, University of New Mexico* ☎ *505/277–3901* ⊕ *tamarind.unm. edu* 🖾 *Free* ⊘ *By appt. Tues.–Fri. 9–5.*

⑯ **UNM Art Museum.** A handsome facility inside the UNM Center for the Arts, the museum holds New Mexico's largest collection of fine art. Works of old masters share wall space with the likes of Picasso and O'Keeffe, and many photographs and prints are on display. Lectures and symposia, gallery talks, and guided tours are regularly scheduled. ⊠ *University of New Mexico Center for the Arts (north of Central Ave. entrance opposite Cornell Dr. SE)* ☎ *505/277–4001* ⊕ *unmartmuseum. unm.edu* ☒ *Free* ⊙ *Tues. 9–4 and 5–8, Wed.–Fri. 9–4, weekends 1–4.*

NORTH VALLEY & INTO THE HEIGHTS

Most of the other attractions in the city lie north of downtown, Old Town, and the University of New Mexico. Quite a few, including the Anderson and Casa Rodeña wineries and the Rio Grande Nature Center, are clustered in two of the city's longest-settled areas: the more rural and lush cottonwood-lined North Valley, and Los Ranchos, along the Rio Grande. Early Spanish settlers made their homes here, building on top of even earlier Pueblo homesteads. Historic adobe houses abound. This area is a natural gateway to the West Side. Drive across the lovely Montaño Road bridge and Petroglyph National Monument is moments away, as is the highly recommended side-trip destination, Corrales (⇨ *Side Trips from the Cities chapter*). In Northeast Heights you are in the foothills of the Sandia Mountains, in upscale neighborhoods that surprise you with the sudden appearance piñon and ponderosa, which are seen nowhere else in the city. Trips to this area are best combined with more north-central venues like the Bien Shur market or the Balloon museum.

WHAT TO SEE

㉑ **Anderson-Abruzzo International Balloon Museum.** This dramatic museum
★ celebrates the city's legacy as the hot-air ballooning capital of the world. The dashing, massive facility is named for Maxie Anderson and Ben Abruzzo, who pioneered ballooning in Albuquerque and were part of a team of three aviators who made the first manned hot-air balloon crossing of the Atlantic Ocean in 1978. You'll understand why this museum is so large when you see the exhibits—including several historic balloons, and both large- and small-scale replicas of balloons and zeppelins. You'll also see vintage balloon baskets, china and flatware from the ill-fated *Hindenburg* and an engaging display on that tragic craft, and dynamic displays that trace the history of the sport, dating back to the first balloon ride, in 1783. Kids can design their own balloons at one creative interactive exhibit. There's a large museum shop offering just about any book or product you could imagine related to hot-air ballooning.

The museum anchors Albuquerque's Balloon Fiesta Park, home to the legendary **Albuquerque International Balloon Fiesta** (☎ *505/821–1000 or 888/422–7277* ⊕ *www.balloonfiesta.com*), which began in 1972 and runs for nearly two weeks in early October. Albuquerque's history of ballooning dates from 1882, when Professor Park A. Van Tassel, a saloon keeper, ascended in a balloon at the Territorial Fair. During the fiesta, the largest hot-air-balloon gathering anywhere, you can watch the Special Shapes Rodeo, when hundreds of unusual balloons, including depictions of the old lady who lived in the shoe, the pink pig, and dozens of other fanciful characters from fairy tales and popular cul-

CLOSE UP

The Mother Road: Neon and Nostalgia on Rt. 66

Mid-20th-century American motorists came to know their country firsthand via Route 66. Today, frequent flyers yearn for the romance of the open road. Long before the prosperous age of the two-car family, the 2,400 mi of Route 66 opened in 1926 to link eight states, from Chicago to Los Angeles. It came to be known by the nickname John Steinbeck gave it—"The Mother Road." The nation's outlet for movement and change has become enveloped in nostalgia. Today in New Mexico, from Texas to the Arizona border, it's still possible to experience vestiges of the old Route 66.

Built in part to aid rural communities and the transportation of agricultural goods, Route 66 evolved into a farmer's escape from the Dust Bowl of the 1930s, and then a tryst for the love affair between Americans and their automobiles. The route's other nickname, "America's Main Street," was given because it incorporated towns' main streets, and so these communities thrived. Along the highway that ran as vividly through the imagination as through the landscape, many discovered an ability to move beyond the confines of their own hometown. They found places along the road that appeared to offer opportunity to prosper and a way to reinvent themselves.

The 1940s and '50s were the heyday of the highway, as Nat King Cole crooned the lyrics to Bobby Troup's song of the road. The road's adventure was overplayed in the '60s television series *Route 66,* and by 1970, nearly all of the two-laner was trumped by four-lane interstate highways. Along Route 66, the possibility of connection with America's people and places lived beyond every bend in the road.

By contrast, the interstate would dampen travel with franchised monotony. Most of the bypassed Route 66 communities dried up and blew away like tumbleweeds. In many of these ghost towns, only a few crumbling buildings and fading signs remain as markers to a vanished age.

By hopping on and off Interstate 40, it's possible to find the quieter, slower two-laner that's held on to its name. The sense of adventure still flickers in Tucumcari at twilight, when the neon signs of the Buckaroo Motel, the Westerner Drive-In, and the Blue Swallow light up the cobalt sky. In Santa Rosa, at Joseph's Cafe, the Fat Man continues to beckon. In Albuquerque, you can drive down Central Avenue, stopping at the Route 66 Diner or the Route 66 Malt Shop and heading past the vintage El Vado Motor Court just before you cross the Rio Grande. In Gallup, dine at Earl's Restaurant or the Eagle Cafe, and book a room where the stars of yesteryear stayed, El Rancho Hotel. Between Albuquerque and Gallup, this ribbon of road takes you through dusty towns with names like poetry: Budville, Cubero, McCartys, Thoreau. These places once offered the traveler the filling stations, motor courts, curio shops, and cafés that gave comfort on a long drive, and every road tripper today hopes to happen upon such an undiscovered (but really just forgotten) place.

■ TIP→Look for the City of Albuquerque's excellent "Historic Route 66 Map & Guide" brochure at the many visitor kiosks around town (☎ *505/924–3860* ⊕ *www.cabq.gov*) or contact the NM Route 66 Association for recent updates (☎ *505/924–3860* ⊕ *www.rt66nm.org*).

2

ture, soar high above more than a million spectators. There are night flights, obstacle races, and many other surprising balloon events. Book your hotel far in advance if you plan to attend, and note that hotel rates also rise during the fiesta. ⊠ *9201 Balloon Museum Dr. NE, off Alameda Blvd. west of I–25, Northeast Heights* ☏ *505/768–6020* ⊕ *www.balloonmuseum. com* ⊠ *$4* ⊙ *Tues.–Sun. 9–5.*

> **DID YOU KNOW?**
>
> Franciscan monks first planted their grapevines in New Mexico before having more success in northern California.

㉓ Anderson Valley Vineyards. A low-key winery that was established in 1973 and enjoys a dramatic, pastoral North Valley setting not far from the Rio Grande, Anderson Valley specializes in chardonnay and cabernet sauvignon. The staff in the intimate tasting room is friendly and knowledgeable, and you can sip your wine while relaxing on an enchanting patio with wonderful views of the Sandia Mountains in the distance. In this agrarian, tranquil setting, it's hard to imagine that you're just a little more than 3 mi north of the bustle of Old Town and downtown. ⊠ *4920 Rio Grande Blvd. NW, between Montaño and Chavez Rds. NW, North Valley* ☏ *505/344–7266* ⊕ *www.nmwine. com* ⊠ *Free* ⊙ *Tues.–Sun. noon–5.*

㉔ Casa Rondeña Winery. Perhaps the most architecturally stunning of New
★ Mexico's wineries, Casa Rondeña—which is technically in Los Ranchos de Albuquerque, not the Duke City proper—resembles a Tuscan villa, with its green-tile roof and verdant grounds laced with gardens and fountains. It's hard to believe that most of the structures here went up with the winery's founding in 1995. Casa Rondeña produces a superb cabernet franc, one of the most esteemed vintages in New Mexico. You can see a vintage oak fermentation tank and a great hall with soaring ceilings, where tastings are conducted. The winery hosts many events including a chamber music festival with wine receptions and dinners. ⊠ *733 Chavez Rd. NW, between Rio Grande Blvd. and 4th St. NW, North Valley* ☏ *505/344–5911 or 800/706–1699* ⊕ *www. casarondena.com* ⊠ *Free* ⊙ *Wed.–Sat. 10–6, Sun. noon–6.*

⑲ Gruet Winery. It's hard to imagine a wine-tasting venue with less curb
★ appeal. Gruet Winery sits along an ugly access road paralleling Interstate 25, sandwiched between an RV showroom and a lawn-furniture store. But behind the vaguely chalet-like exterior of this otherwise modern industrial building, you're afforded the chance to visit one of the nation's most acclaimed producers of sparkling wines (to see its actual vineyards you'll have to head south to Truth or Consequences). Gruet had been famous in France since the 1950s for its champagnes. In New Mexico, the Gruet family has been producing wine since 1984, and it's earned nationwide kudos for its Methode Champenoise, as well as for impressive pinot noirs, syrahs, and chardonnays. Many of the state's top restaurants now carry Gruet vintages. Tastings include five wines and a souvenir glass. ⊠ *8400 Pan American Freeway NE (north frontage road for I–25), on the east side of I–25, between Alameda*

Blvd. and Paseo del Norte, Northeast Heights ☎*505/821–0055 or 888/857–9463* ⊕*www.gruetwinery.com* ⌨*Free; $6 for a 5-wine tasting* ⊙ *Weekdays 10–5, Sat. noon–5; tours Mon.–Sat. at 2.*

㉖ **Petroglyph National Monument.** Beneath the stumps of five extinct volca-
★ noes, this park encompasses more than 25,000 ancient Native American rock drawings inscribed on the 17-mi-long West Mesa escarpment
overlooking the Rio Grande Valley. For centuries, Native American
hunting parties camped at the base, chipping and scribbling away.
Archaeologists believe most of the petroglyphs were carved on the lava
formations between 1100 and 1600, but some images at the park may
date back as far as 1000 BC. A paved trail at **Boca Negra Canyon** (north
of the visitor center on Unser Boulevard, beyond Montaño Road) leads
past several dozen petroglyphs. The trail at **Rinconado Canyon** (south
of the visitor center on Unser) is unpaved. The rangers at the visitor
center will supply maps and help you determine which trail is best for
the time you have. ⊠ *Visitor center, 6001 Unser Blvd. NW, at Western
Trail Rd.,* ⊹ *3 mi north of I–40 Exit 154; from I–25 take Exit 228 and
proceed west on Montaño Rd. across the bridge, then south on Unser 1
mi, West Side* ☎*505/899–0205* ⊕*www.nps.gov/petr* ⌨*$1 weekdays,
$2 weekends* ⊙*Daily 8–5.*

㉕ **Rio Grande Nature Center State Park.** Along the banks of the Rio Grande,
ᖶ this year-round 170-acre refuge in a portion of the Bosque (about midway up on the Paseo del Bosque trail) is the nation's largest cottonwood forest. If bird-watching is your thing, you've come to the right
place: this is home to all manner of birds and migratory waterfowl.
Constructed half aboveground and half below the edge of a pond,
the park's glass-walled interpretive center (an interesting small-scale
building by noted New Mexico architect Antoine Predock) has viewing windows that provide a look at what's going on at both levels, and
speakers that broadcast the sounds of the birds you're watching into
the room. You may see birds, frogs, ducks, and turtles. The park has
active programs for adults and children and trails for biking, walking,
and jogging. ■TIP➜ **Keep your eye out for what appears to be a game
of jacks abandoned by giants: these jetty jacks were built in the 1950s to
protect the Rio Grande levees from flood debris.** ⊠*2901 Candelaria Rd.
NW, 1½ mi north on Rio Grande Blvd. from I–40 exit 157A, North
Valley* ☎*505/344–7240* ⊕*www.rgnc.org or www.nmparks.com* ⌨*$3
per vehicle; grounds free* ⊙*Nature center daily 10–5, park daily 8–5.*

㉒ **Sandia Peak Aerial Tramway.** Tramway cars climb 2.7 mi up the steep
ᖶ western face of the Sandias, giving you a close-up view of red rocks and
★ tall trees—it's the world's longest aerial tramway. From the observation
deck at the 10,378-foot summit you can see Santa Fe to the northeast
and Los Alamos to the northwest—about 11,000 square mi of spectacular scenery. Tram cars leave from the base at regular intervals for
the 15-minute ride to the top. You may see birds of prey soaring above
or mountain lions roaming the cliff sides. An exhibit room at the top
surveys the wildlife and landscape of the mountain. Narrators point
out what you're seeing below, including the barely visible remnants
of a 1953 plane crash that killed all 16 passengers onboard. If you

want to add a meal to the excursion, there's the upscale **High Finance Restaurant** (☎505/243–9742 ⊕ *www.highfinancerestaurant.com*) on top of the mountain (serving steaks, lobster tail, and good burgers at lunch), and a more casual spot, **Sandiago's** (☎505/856–6692 ⊕*www. sandiagos.com*), at the tram's base. High Finance affords clear views from every table, making it a favorite destination for a romantic dinner—the food isn't bad, but it's more about the scenic experience here. ■TIP→ **It's much colder and windier at the summit than at the tram's base, so pack a jacket.** You can also use the tram as a way to reach the Sandia Peak ski and mountain-biking area (⇨*the Sandia Park section of the Side Trips from the Cities chapter).* ⊠*10 Tramway Loop NE, Far Northeast Heights* ☎*505/856–7325* ⊕*www.sandiapeak.com* ⊠*$15* ⊙*Memorial Day–Labor Day, daily 9–9; Sept.–May, daily 9–8.*

㉒ **Unser Racing Museum.** Albuquerque is home to the illustrious auto-racing family, the Unsers, whose four generations of drivers have dominated the sport since the early 20th century—the most famous members include Bobby Unser Sr. and Al Unser Sr. Exhibits at this spiffy museum include a display on Pikes Peak, Colorado, and the legendary hairpins where the Unser family first got serious about racing; a study of their legacy at the Indianapolis 500; and a good selection of vintage racers, including a few you can test-drive (virtually, that is). ⊠*1776 Montaño Rd. NW, just east of the Rio Grande Blvd. overpass, near the Montaño Rd. Bridge, North Valley* ☎*505/341–1776* ⊕*www.unserracing museum.com* ⊠*$7* ⊙*Daily 10–4.*

WHERE TO EAT

The Duke City has long been a place for hearty home-style cooking in big portions, and to this day, it's easy to find great steak-and-chops houses, barbecue joints, retro diners, and authentic New Mexican restaurants. The trick is finding them amid Albuquerque's miles of chain options and legions of dives, but if you look, you'll be rewarded with innovative food, and generally at prices much lower than in Santa Fe or other major Southwestern cities.

Albuquerque's dining scene has been evolving for the past ten years. In Nob Hill, downtown, and Old Town many hip new restaurants have opened, offering swank decor and complex and artful variations on modern Southwest, Mediterranean, Asian, and other globally inspired cuisine. A significant Vietnamese population has made that cuisine a star, but Indian, Japanese, Thai, and South American traditions all have a presence, making this New Mexico's best destination for ethnic fare.

WHAT IT COSTS				
	¢	$	$$	$$$	$$$$
Restaurants	under $10	$10–$17	$18–$24	$25–$30	over $30

Prices are per person for a main course at dinner, excluding 8.25% sales tax.

BEST BETS FOR ALBUQUERQUE DINING

With hundreds of restaurants to choose from, how will you decide where to eat? Fodor's writers and editors have selected their favorite restaurants by price, cuisine, and experience in the Best Bets lists below. Find specific details about a restaurant in the full reviews, listed alphabetically.

2

FODOR'S CHOICE ★

Artichoke Café $$$
Duran's Central Pharmacy ¢
El Patio ¢
Gold Street Caffè $
Sophia's Place $

By Price

¢

Duran's Central Pharmacy
El Camino Dining Room
Mary & Tito's

$

City Treats Café (in the Albuquerque Museum of Art & History)
Gold Street Caffè
Il Vicino
La Fonda del Bosque
Sadie's
Sophia's Place
Viet Taste

$$

Brasserie La Provençe
Pueblo Harvest Café (in the Indian Pueblo Cultural Center)
Slate Street Café
Standard Diner

$$$

Artichoke Café
Seasons Rotisserie & Grill
Zinc Wine Bar & Bistro

$$$$

Bien Shur
Rancher's Club

By Cuisine

AMERICAN

66 Diner $
Grove St. Market & Café $
Standard Diner $$

CAFÉ

Flying Star $
Gold St. Caffè $

Golden Crown Panadería $
Grove St. Market & Café $
Sophia's Place $

ASIAN

May Café ¢
Viet Taste $

CONTEMPORARY

Artichoke Café $$$
Il Vicino $
Seasons Rotisserie & Grill $$$
Slate St. Café $$
Zinc Wine Bar & Bistro $$$

ITALIAN

Il Vicino $

NEW MEXICAN

Church St. Café $
Duran's Central Pharmacy $
El Camino Dining Room ¢
Mary & Tito's ¢
Sadie's $

By Experience

BEST BURGER

66 Diner $
Standard Diner $$

BREAKFAST

Frontier $$
Gold St. Caffè $
La Fonda del Bosque $$
Sophia's Place $

HOT SPOTS

Season's Rotisserie & Grill $$$
Slate St. Café $$
Sophia's Place $
Zinc Wine Bar & Bistro $$$

SPECIAL OCCASION

Artichoke Café $$$
Bien Shur $$$$
Gruet Steakhouse $$$
Seasons Rotisserie & Grill $$$

PATIO/OUTDOOR SEATING

Barelas Coffee House ¢
Church St. Café $$
Casa de Benavidez $$
La Fonda del Bosque $$
Seasons Rotisserie & Grill $$$
St. Clair Winery & Bistro $

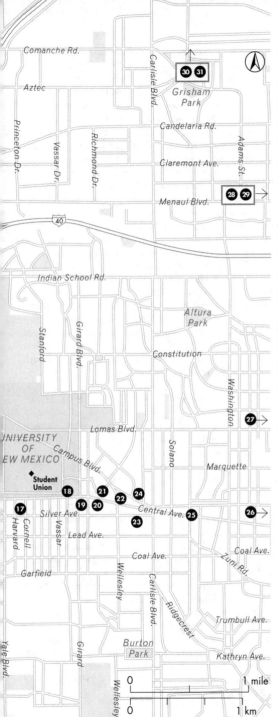

2

$ ╳**66 Diner.** Dining at this '50s-style art-deco diner is a must for fans
AMERICAN of Route 66 nostalgia, and the upbeat decor and friendly service also
make it a hit with families. The specialties here are many: chicken-
fried steak, burgers, malted milk shakes, enchiladas. Plenty of breakfast
treats are available, too. ⊠*1405 Central Ave. NE, University of New
Mexico* 🕾*505/247–1421* ⊕*www.66diner.com* ⊟*AE, D, MC, V.*

$$$ ╳**Artichoke Café.** Locals praise the Artichoke for its service and French,
CONTEMPORARY contemporary American, and Italian dishes prepared, whenever pos-
Fodor's Choice sible, with organically grown ingredients. Specialties include house-
★ made ravioli stuffed with ricotta and butternut squash with a white
wine, sage, and butter sauce; and pan-seared sea scallops wrapped in
prosciutto with red potatoes, haricots verts, and wax beans. The appe-
tizers are so tasty you may want to make a meal out of them. The build-
ing is about a century old, in the historic Huning Highland district on
the eastern edge of downtown, but the decor is uptown modern. The
two-tier dining room spills out into a small courtyard. ⊠*424 Central
Ave. SE, EDo* 🕾*505/243–0200* ⊕*www.artichokecafe.com* ⊟*AE, D,
DC, MC, V* ⊘*Closed Sun. No lunch Sat.*

¢ ╳**Barelas Coffee House.** Barelas may look like a set in search of a script,
NEW MEXICAN but it's the real deal: diners come from all over the city to sup in this
★ old-fashioned chili parlor in the Hispanic Historic Route 66 neighbor-
hood south of downtown. You may notice looks of quiet contentment
on the faces of the many dedicated chili eaters as they dive into their
bowls of Barelas's potent red. There's also tasty breakfast fare. The staff
treats everybody like an old friend—indeed, many of the regulars who
come here have been fans of Barelas for decades. ⊠*1502 4th St. SW,
Barelas* 🕾*505/843–7577* ◭*Reservations not accepted* ⊟*D, MC, V*
⊘*Closed Sun. No dinner.*

$$$$ ╳**Bien Shur.** The panoramic city and mountain views are an essential
CONTEMPORARY part of this quietly refined restaurant on the ninth floor of the San-
dia Casino complex, but Bien Shur also aspires to be one of the most
sophisticated restaurants in the city. Alas, the service can be as uneven
as its contemporary fare. You might start with black mission figs and
Brie, before moving on to pan-roasted sea bass with edamame, shii-
take mushrooms, jasmine rice, and celery-root mousse, or char-grilled
buffalo tenderloin with roasted yellow pepper–onion confit. ⊠*San-
dia Resort & Casino, Tramway Rd. NE, east of I–25, Far Northeast
Heights* 🕾*505/796–7500 or 800/526–9366* ⊕*www.sandiacasino.com*
⊟*AE, D, MC, V* ⊘*Closed Mon. and Tues. No breakfast or lunch.*

$ ╳**Brasserie La Provençe.** You'll find classic French bistro dishes—*moules
FRENCH frites*, couscous merguez, and croque Madame—and a nice wine list in
this pleasant corner spot on the west edge of Nob Hill. Service is good,
and the food—which is very good, but not superior—is improved by
the congenial atmosphere. Try the patio when the weather is fair, or
the lemon-colored back room when it's not. There are specials each
day, and the less-expected menu items such as *Poulet du Midi* (seared
chicken breast stuffed with chèvre and figs) are palate- and budget-
pleasing as well. ⊠ *3001 Central Ave. NE, Nob Hill* 🕾*505/254–7644*
⊕*www.laprovencenobhill.com* ⊟*AE, D, MC, V.*

$$ **NEW MEXICAN** ✕**Casa de Benavidez.** The fajitas at this sprawling local favorite with a romantic patio are among the best in town, and the chili is faultless; the burger wrapped inside a sopaipilla is another specialty, as are the chimichangas packed with beef. The charming restaurant occupies a late-19th-century Territorial-style house. ✉ *8032 4th St. NW, North Valley* ☎ *505/897–7493* ⊕ ⊟ *AE, D, MC, V* ⊗ *No dinner Sun.*

$ **NEW MEXICAN** ★ ✕**Church Street Café.** Built in the early 1700s, this structure is among the oldest in New Mexico. Renovations have preserved the original adobe bricks to ensure that this spacious eatery remains as authentic as its menu, which features

WORD OF MOUTH

"We had a lovely dinner at La Provence Brasserie in Nob Hill.…My husband and his friend split an order of Moules, which they loved. I had Steak Frites with Bordelaise sauce and pommes frites; a classic and well prepared.

"Il Vicino was great as always. I went there way too many times this trip. Frontier, Flying Star, Bumblebee's all saw me on a frequent basis too. Check these places out, they are really worthwhile."

—DebitNM

family recipes spanning four generations—with fresh, local ingredients and spirits employed to satiate streams of hungry tourists and locals. Request the courtyard for alfresco dining amid trellises of sweet grapes and flowers, and where classical and flamenco guitarist José Salazar often performs. Buttery guacamole, with just a bit of bite, is the perfect appetizer to prep one's palate for tender carne asada, redolent and sumptuously spiced. Try house specialty chiles rellenos, stuffed with beef and cheese, or a portobello-and-bell-pepper fajita. Traditional desserts and hearty breakfast choices are also offered. ✉ *2111 Church St. NW, Old Town* ☎ *505/247–8522* ⊕ *www.churchstreetcafe.com* ⊟ *AE, D, MC, V* ⊗ *No dinner Sun.*

$ **JAPANESE** ✕**Crazy Fish.** A good bet for relatively straightforward sushi and sashimi, Crazy Fish is an attractive, upbeat storefront space with minimal fuss and gimmickry—just clean lines and a black-and-gray color scheme. Friendly young servers whisk out plates of fresh food to a mix of students and yuppies. In addition to sushi, the kitchen prepares such favorites as crispy chicken, and seared-albacore salad with a ginger-soy dressing. Tempura-fried bananas make for a sweet ending. ✉ *3015 Central Ave. NE, Nob Hill* ☎ *505/232–3474* ⊟ *AE, D, MC, V* ⊗ *Closed Sun. and Mon.*

¢ **NEW MEXICAN** **Fodor's Choice** ★ ✕**Duran's Central Pharmacy.** This expanded Old Town lunch counter with a dozen tables and a tiny patio just might serve the best tortillas in town. A favorite of old-timers who know their way around a blue-corn enchilada, Duran's is an informal place whose patrons give their food the total attention it deserves. Be sure to leave some browsing time for the pharmacy's book section: Duran's has a good selection of not easily found history and coffee-table volumes covering the Duke City and its storied environs. ✉ *1815 Central Ave. NW, Old Town* ☎ *505/247–4141* ⊟ *No credit cards* ⊗ *No dinner.*

¢ **NEW MEXICAN** ✕**El Camino Dining Room.** Dating back to 1950, after Route 66 had been moved to Central, El Camino seems virtually unchanged, and, if you didn't know better, you'd think it had been built to cater to travelers on the Mother Road. Come here for a fix of perfectly balanced red- (rumor is Sadie of Sadie's even gets a regular dose here) or fine green-chile stew, light and airy sopaipillas, and a setting that evokes another era with its vintage counter, booths, linoleum, and warm and speedy service. It closes at 2 PM. ⊠ *6800 4th St. NW, North Valley* ☎ *505/344–0448* ⚇ *Reservations not accepted* ⊟ *AE, D, MC, V* ⊗ *No dinner.*

¢ ✕ **El Patio.** A university-area hangout, this sentimental favorite has good— sometimes great—food served on the funky patio (the service itself could be described as a student-ghetto gamble). Go for the green-chile-chicken enchiladas or any of the heart-healthy and vegetarian selections. But watch out for the fiery green chiles served at harvesttime. Note that liquor isn't served, but beer and wine are—you can get decent-tasting "margaritas" made with wine. ⊠ *142 Harvard St. NE, University of New Mexico* ☎ *505/268–4245* ⚇ *Reservations not accepted* ⊟ *MC, V.*

NEW MEXICAN
Fodor's Choice
★

$$ ✕ **Frontier Restaurant.** This definitive student hangout across from UNM is open daily for inexpensive diner-style American and New Mexican chow. A notch up from a fast-food joint, it's open later than most such spots in town, and the breakfast burritos are terrific. Featured along with the John Wayne and Elvis artwork in this sprawling '70s spot are oversize cinnamon buns. We won't fault you if you cave and order one. ⊠ *2400 Central Ave. SE (at Cornell Dr. SE)* ☎ *505/266–0550* ⊟ *AE, D, MC, V*

$ ✕ **Flying Star.** Flying Star has become a staple and mini-phenom here, and although it's a chain, it's locally owned and—just like at its Satellite Coffee spots around town—each outpost offers something a little different. The cavernous downtown branch is a favorite for its striking setting inside the historic Southern Union Gas Co. building and its unexpected modernist motif; the North Valley locale is notable for its comfy and shaded outdoor patio. At Nob Hill the crowd is hip, and the space tighter. The concept works on many levels: it's a newsstand, late-night coffeehouse (there's free Wi-Fi), and an order-at-the-counter restaurant serving a mix of creative Asian, American, and New Mexican dishes (plus several types of wine and beer). Options include Greek pasta with shrimp, green-chile cheeseburgers, Thai-style tofu salad with tangy lime dressing, turkey-and-Jack-cheese-melt sandwiches, and an egg- and chile-packed "*graburrito.*" Desserts change often, but count on a tantalizing array. For a winning pick-me-up, employ some strong hot coffee to wash down a tall slice of the fantastic coconut cream pie. We list a few of our favorite locations. ⊠ *723 Silver Ave., Downtown* ☎ *505/244–8099* ⊠ *3416 Central Ave. SE, Nob Hill* ☎ *505/255–6633* ⊠ *4026 Rio Grande NW, North Valley* ☎ *505/344–6714* ⊟ *AE, D, MC, V.*

CAFÉ
★

$ ✕ **Gold Street Caffè.** A culinary cornerstone of downtown Albuquerque's renaissance, this dapper storefront café with exposed-brick walls and high ceilings serves breakfast fare that is a cut above, plus equally satisfying lunch and dinner entrées. In the morning, go with eggs Eleganza (two poached eggs atop a green-chile brioche with local goat cheese), along with a side of chile-glazed bacon. Later in the day, consider polenta-dusted tilapia with a sun-dried-tomato cream sauce, or seared-beef chopped salad with fried rice noodles and chile-lime vinaigrette. You can also just hang out among the hipsters and office workers, sipping a caramel latte

CAFÉ
Fodor's Choice
★

and munching on one of the tasty desserts, or enjoy a glass of wine from the short but well-selected list. ✉*218 Gold Ave. SW, Downtown* ☎*505/765–1633* ➡*MC, V* ⊘*No dinner Sun. and Mon.*

GOOD TERM

Kiva fireplace: A corner fireplace whose round form resembles that of a kiva, a ceremonial room used by Native Americans of the Southwest.

2

$$$
STEAK
✕**Gruet Steakhouse.** The acclaimed Gruet wine-making family operates this chic but casual steak house inside the historic Monte Vista Fire Station, a 1930s WPA-built beauty in the heart of Nob Hill. More than a showcase for promoting Gruet's outstanding sparkling wines, pinot noirs, and chardonnays, the steak house presents consistently good food (including an addictive side dish, lobster-whipped potatoes). Among the apps, try the panfried Dungeness crab cake with a traditional rémoulade sauce. The flat-iron steak topped with chunky Maytag blue cheese is a favorite main dish, along with the rare ahi tuna Wellington with wild mushroom duxelles and seared foie gras. Finish with a distinctive rose-water-infused ricotta cheesecake topped with candied oranges and toasted-almond sugar. A kiva fireplace warms the patio in back. The same owners run Gruet Grille, a contemporary bistro in Northeast Heights. ✉*3201 Central Ave. NE, Nob Hill* ☎*505/256–9463* ⊕*www.gruetsteakhouse.com* ➡*AE, D, MC, V* ⊘*No lunch.*

$
PIZZA
✕**Il Vicino.** The pizzas at Il Vicino are baked in a European-style wood-fired oven. If a suitable combination of the 25 possible toppings eludes you, try the rustica pie, a buttery cornmeal crust topped with roasted garlic, artichokes, kalamata olives, and capers. The competent kitchen also turns out Caesar salad, spinach lasagna, and designer sandwiches. One of the house-brewed beers, say, the Wet Mountain India Pale Ale—which consistently wins awards at the Great American Beer Festival—rounds out the experience. There's another branch, usually less crowded, in a shopping center not too far from Sandia Peak Aerial Tramway. ✉*3403 Central Ave. NE, Nob Hill* ☎*505/266–7855* ✉*11225 Montgomery Blvd., Far Northeast Heights* ☎*505/271–0882* ⊕*www.ilvicino.com* ⌖*Reservations not accepted* ➡*MC, V.*

$
NEW MEXICAN
✕**Los Cuates.** A short drive northeast of Nob Hill and UNM, Los Cuates (a three-location local minichain) doesn't get as much attention as some of the city's more touristy New Mexican restaurants, but the food here is reliable, and prepared with pure vegetable oil rather than lard, which is one reason it's never as greasy as at some competitors. The green-chile stew is vegetarian (unless you request meat). All the usual favorites are served here, but top picks include the roast-beef burrito covered with melted cheese, and the tostada *compuesta* (a corn tortilla stuffed with beef, beans, rice, potatoes, carne adovada, and chili con queso). ✉*4901 Lomas Blvd. NE, near Nob Hill* ☎*505/255–5079* ⊕*www.loscuates restaurants.com* ⌖*Reservations not accepted* ➡*AE, D, MC, V.*

¢
NEW MEXICAN
✕**Mary & Tito's.** Locals do go on about who's got the best chili, red or green. What they don't dispute is that Mary & Tito's, an institution for decades, and run by the same family since it opened, is as tasty as it comes. It's casual, friendly, and the real deal. Grab a booth and try

the rellenos or the enchiladas. A bonus: the chili is vegetarian, and the red is always sm-o-o-o-th. ⊠ *2711 Fourth St. NW, 2 blocks north of Menaul Blvd. NW, North Valley* ☎ *505/344–6266* ⚕ *Reservations not accepted* ▱ *AE, D, MC, V.*

¢   ✗ **May Café.** Few tourists make it to this inexpensive and authentic
VIETNAMESE   Vietnamese restaurant a short drive east of Nob Hill, in an uninspired
★   neighborhood just off old Route 66. Favorites from the extensive menu include rare-beef noodle soup; stir-fried noodles with veggies, fish balls, chicken, barbecue pork, and pork; spicy fish baked in a hot pot; and catfish with lemongrass sauce. You'll also find plenty of vegetarian options, including knockout spring rolls. Friendly, prompt service and a simple, attractive dining room add to the experience. ⊠ *111 Louisiana Blvd. SE, Southeast* ☎ *505/265–4448* ▱ *AE, MC, V* ⊙ *Closed Sun.*

$ ✗ **Monica's El Portal.** Locals in the know favor this rambling, authen-
NEW MEXICAN   tic New Mexican restaurant on the west side of Old Town over the
★   more famous, though less reliable, standbys around Old Town Plaza. Monica's has a prosaic dining room plus a cute tiled patio, and the service is friendly and unhurried yet efficient. If you've never had *chicharrones* (fried pork skins), try them here with beans stuffed inside a flaky sopaipilla. Or consider the traditional blue-corn chicken or beef enchiladas, and the savory green-chile stew. This is honest, home-style food, and lunch here may just fill you up for the rest of the day. ⊠ *321 Rio Grande Blvd. NW, Old Town* ☎ *505/247–9625* ▱ *AE, D, MC, V* ⊙ *Closed Mon. No dinner weekends.*

$ ✗ **Quarters BBQ.** This Albuquerque institution, going strong since the
SOUTHERN   early '70s, certainly has its devoted followers. Their sauce is more tangy than sweet, and slow smoking with a secret recipe makes for a winning combination. Whatever your preference—be it smoky ribs, chicken, brisket, or sausage—you will need a fistful of napkins, that's for sure. Top steaks and Alaskan king crab legs are also available. ⊠ *801 Yale Blvd. SE, University of New Mexico* ☎ *505/843–7505* ▱ *AE, MC, V* ⊙ *Closed Sun.*

$$$$ ✗ **Rancher's Club.** Hotel restaurants in Albuquerque aren't generally
STEAK   special dining destinations, but this clubby, old-world steak house in the Albuquerque Hilton earns raves among deep-pocketed carnivores for its delicious aged steaks and ribs. The dining room is hung with saddles, mounted bison heads, and ranching-related art. If you want to impress a date or clients, order the fillet of Kobe beef with creamed spinach, lobster-mashed potatoes, and morel-mushroom jus. Other standbys include elk chops, fillet of ostrich, porterhouse steak, and the Hunter's Grill of antelope, venison, and wild-boar sausage. ⊠ *Albuquerque Hilton, 1901 University Blvd. NE* ☎ *505/889–8071* ⊕ *the ranchersclubofnm.com* ▱ *AE, D, DC, MC, V* ⊙ *No lunch weekends.*

$ ✗ **Sadie's.** One of the city's longtime favorites for simple-but-spicy, no-
NEW MEXICAN   nonsense, New Mexican fare, Sadie's—remembered fondly by old-timers for the era when it made its home in the Lucky 66 bowling alley next door—now occupies a long, fortresslike adobe building. Specialties include carne adovada, spicy beef burritos, and chiles rellenos. The service is always prompt, though sometimes there's a wait for a table. While you're waiting, try one of the excellent margaritas. Sadie's salsa is locally

renowned and available by the jar for takeout. ⊠*6230 4th St. NW, North Valley* ☎*505/345–5339* ⊕*www.sadiessalsa.com* ▤*AE, D, MC, V.*

$$$ ✕ **Seasons Rotisserie & Grill.** Upbeat yet elegant, this Old Town eatery
CONTEMPORARY is an easy place to have a business lunch or a dinner date, and oeno-philes will revel in its well-chosen cellar. The kitchen serves innovative grills and pastas, such as wood-roasted duck breast with Gorgonzola-sweet potato gratin and grilled prime New York strip steak with garlic-mashed potatoes and black-truffle butter; great starters include seared raw tuna with cucumber-ginger slaw, and pecan-crusted three-cheese chiles rellenos with butternut squash coulis. The rooftop patio and bar provides evening cocktails and lighter meals. ⊠*2031 Mountain Rd. NW, Old Town* ☎*505/766–5100* ⊕*www.seasonsonthenet.com* ▤*AE, D, DC, MC, V* ⊘*No lunch weekends.*

$$ ✕ **Slate Street Cafe.** An airy, high-ceiling dining room with a semicircular,
CONTEMPORARY central wine bar and modern lighting, this stylish restaurant sits amid
★ pawn shops and bail-bond outposts on a quiet, unprepossessing side street downtown. But once inside, you'll find a sophisticated, colorful space serving memorable, modern renditions of classic American fare, such as fried chicken and meat loaf. The starters are notable, including Japa-nese-style fried rock shrimp with orange habañero sauce, and bruschetta topped with honey-cured ham and Brie. Banana-stuffed brioche French toast is a favorite at breakfast and Saturday brunch. More than 30 wines by the glass are served. ⊠*515 Slate St. NW, Downtown* ☎*505/243–2210* ⊕*www.slatestreetcafe.com* ▤*AE, D, MC, V* ⊘*Closed Sun.*

$ ✕ **Sophia's Place.** You'll enjoy *muy buenos* berry pancakes (with real
NEW MEXICAN maple syrup), breakfast burritos (with the *papas* inside, so ask if you'd
Fodor'sChoice like them out instead), enchiladas (sprinkled with *cojita*), and just about
★ anything the kitchen whips up. Dishes range from creative and gener-ous salads and chipotle-chile bacon cheeseburgers to udon noodles and fish tacos. In Los Ranchos de Albuquerque, in the heart of the North Valley, Sophia's (named after the Alice Waters–trained chef-owner's daughter) is a simple neighborhood spot, yet one that people drive out of their way for—especially for the weekend brunch. Everything is fresh, often organic, prettily presented, and always made-to-order. ⊠*6313 4th St. NW, 2 blocks north of Osuna/Chavez Rd. NW, North Valley* ☎*505/345–3935* ⌁*Reservations not accepted* ▤*AE, D, MC, V* ⊘*No dinner Sun.–Wed.*

$ ✕ **St. Clair Winery & Bistro.** The state's largest winery, located in the south-
CONTINENTAL ern New Mexico town of Deming, St. Clair Winery has a charming and affordable restaurant and tasting room in Old Town. It's part of a small shopping center on the west side of the neighborhood, just south of Interstate 40. You enter a shop with a bar for wine tasting and shelves of wines and gourmet goods, which leads into the dark and warmly lighted dining room. There's also a large, attractive patio. At lunch, sample the panini sandwich of New Mexico goat cheese and roasted peppers. Din-ner treats include crab-and-artichoke dip, garlic chicken slow-cooked in chardonnay, and pork tenderloin with merlot and raspberry-chipotle sauce. On weekends, St. Clair serves a popular Sunday brunch. ⊠*901 Rio Grande Blvd., Old Town* ☎*505/243–9916 or 888/870–9916* ⊕*www.stclairvineyards.com* ▤*AE, D, MC, V.*

$$
CONTEMPORARY

✗**Standard Diner.** In the historic Huning Highland district just east of downtown, the Standard opened in 2006 inside a 1930s Texaco station with high ceilings, massive plate-glass windows, and rich tile floors—it's at once elegant yet casual, serving upscale yet affordable takes on traditional diner

standbys. The extensive menu dabbles in meal-size salads (try the chicken-fried-lobster Caesar salad), burgers (including a terrific one topped with crab cakes and hollandaise sauce), sandwiches, and traditional diner entrées given nouvelle flourishes (Moroccan-style pot roast, mac and cheese with smoked salmon and green chiles, flat-iron steak with poblano cream sauce and bell pepper–ginger puree). Kick everything up with a side of wasabi-mashed potatoes, and save room for the twisted tiramisu (espresso-soaked lady fingers, dulce de leche mascarpone, agave-poached pears, and candied pine nuts). ⊠*320 Central Ave. SE, EDo* ☎*505/243–1440* ▤*AE, D, MC, V.*

$
THAI

✗**Thai Crystal.** In a state that's lacked good Thai restaurants until recently, this beautiful space filled with Thai artwork and decorative pieces has been a welcome addition to the downtown scene. The extensive menu includes a mix of typical Thai specialties (pineapple fried rice, chicken satay, beef panang curry) as well as some less predictable items, such as steamed mussels topped with red coconut curry, and pork sautéed with a spicy mint, chile, and onion sauce. ⊠*109 Gold Ave. SW, Downtown* ☎*505/244–3344* ▤*AE, MC, V.*

$
BRAZILIAN

✗**Tucanos Brazilian Grill.** There isn't much point in going to Tucanos if you don't love meat. Sure, they serve some vegetables, but the real focus is on *churrascos*, South American–style grilled skewers of beef, chicken, pork, and turkey that parade endlessly out of the open kitchen on the arms of enthusiastic waiters. Carnivore-centrism aside, one unexpected treat, if it's available, is the grilled pineapple. The noisy, high-ceiling spot next to the Century 14 Downtown movie theater is a good place to go for drinks, too, and if you're looking for either a stand-alone cooler or a liquid partner for your hearty fare, look no further than a bracing *caipirinha,* the lime-steeped national cocktail of Brazil. ⊠*110 Central Ave. SW, Downtown* ☎*505/246–9900* ⊕*www.tucanos.com* ▤*AE, D, MC, V.*

$
VIETNAMESE

✗**Viet Taste.** Come here for another side of spicy hot. Excellent, authentic Vietnamese food is served up in this compact, modern, bamboo-accented restaurant. Ignore the fact that it's within one of Albuquerque's ubiquitous strip malls. Consider the popular pho variations, order the tofu (or chicken or shrimp) spring rolls with tangy peanut sauce, dig into the spicy lemongrass with chicken, and all will be well. ⊠ *5721 Menaul Blvd. NE, on the north side, west of San Pedro NE, between Cardenas and Valencia Rds. NE, Uptown* ☎*505/888– 0101* ▤*AE, D, MC, V.*

$$
GREEK

✗**Yanni's Mediterranean Grill.** Yanni's is a popular place where the food can run second to its refreshing azure-tiled ambience. Serving mari-

2

nated grilled lamb chops with lemon and oregano, grilled yellowfin sole encrusted with Parmesan, pastitsio (a Greek version of mac and cheese), and spinach, feta, and roasted garlic pizzas, Yanni's also offers a vegetarian plate with good meatless moussaka, tabbouleh, spanako-pita, and stuffed grape leaves. There's a huge patio off the main dining room, and next door you can sip cocktails and mingle with locals at Opa Bar. ✉*3109 Central Ave. NE, Nob Hill* ☎*505/268–9250* ⊕*www.yannisandopabar.com* ▭*AE, D, MC, V.*

$$$ ✕ **Zinc Wine Bar & Bistro.** A snazzy spot in lower Nob Hill, fairly close to
CONTEMPORARY UNM, Zinc captures the essence of a San Francisco neighborhood bistro
★ with its high ceilings, hardwood floors, and white tablecloths and dark-wood straight-back café chairs. You can sample wine from the long list or listen to live music downstairs in the Blues Cellar. Consider the starter of asparagus-and-artichoke tart with baby greens and spicy dried-fruit tapenade; or the main dish of over-roasted wild Alaskan halibut with a Parmesan-asparagus risotto cake, braised leek, and fennel, with a roasted-red-pepper vinaigrette. The kitchen uses organic ingredients whenever available. ✉*3009 Central Ave. NE, Nob Hill* ☎*505/254–9462* ⊕*www.zincabq.com* ▭*AE, D, MC, V* ⊘*No lunch Sat.*

WHERE TO STAY

With a few exceptions, Albuquerque's lodging options fall into two categories: modern chain hotels and motels, and distinctive and typically historic inns and B&Bs. You won't find many larger hotels that are independently owned, historic, or rife with personality, although Central Avenue—all across the city—is lined with fascinating old motor courts and motels from the 1930s through the '50s, many with original neon signs and quirky roadside architecture. Alas, nearly all of these are run-down and substandard; they should be avoided unless you're extremely adventurous and can't resist the super-low rates (often as little as $18 a night).

If you're seeking charm and history, try one of the many excellent inns and B&Bs (including those in Corrales and Bernalillo, just north of Albuquerque, listed in the Side Trips from the Cities chapter). Two parts of the city with an excellent variety of economical, plain-Jane, franchise hotels (Hampton Inn, Comfort Inn, Courtyard Marriott, etc.) are the Airport and the north Interstate 25 corridor. Albuquerque's airport is convenient to attractions and downtown, and the north Interstate 25 corridor offers easy access to sightseeing, dining, and Balloon Fiesta Park. Wherever you stay in Albuquerque, you can generally count on finding rates considerably lower than the national average, and much cheaper than those in Santa Fe and Taos.

WHAT IT COSTS					
	¢	$	$$	$$$	$$$$
Hotels	under $70	$70–$130	$130–$190	$190–$260	over $260

Prices are for two people in a standard double room in high season, excluding 12%–13% tax.

BEST BETS FOR ALBUQUERQUE LODGING

Fodor's offers a selective listing of quality lodging experiences in every price range, from the city's best budget beds to its most sophisticated luxury hotels. Here, we've compiled our top recommendations by price and experience. The very best properties—in other words, those that provide a particularly remarkable experience in their price range—are designated in the listings with the Fodor's Choice logo.

FODOR'S CHOICE ★

Embassy Suites Hotel Albuquerque $$$

Inn Sandia Resort & Casino $$

Los Poblanos Inn $$$$

Mauger Estate B&B $$

Hyatt Regency $$

By Price

$

Casa de Sueños

Holiday Inn Select Airport

Hotel Blue

$$

Albuquerque Marriott

Embassy Suites

Hotel Albuquerque

Hyatt Regency

Mauger Estate B&B

Nativo Lodge

$$$

Andaluz

Sandia Resort

$$$$

Los Poblanos Inn

By Experience

BEST HOTEL BAR

Albuquerque Marriott $$

Hotel Albuquerque $$

BEST FOR KIDS

Best Western Rio Grande $

Embassy Suites $$

BEST LOCATION

Albuquerque Marriott $$

Casa de Sueños $

Embassy Suites $$

Hampton Inn Airport $

Hyatt Regency $$

Mauger B&B $$

Nativo Lodge $$

BEST FOR ROMANCE

Cinnamon Morning B&B $$

Hotel Albuquerque $$

Los Poblanos Inn $$$$

BEST SERVICE

Los Poblanos Inn $$$$

Sandia Resort $$$

BEST VIEWS

Albuquerque Marriott $$

Hyatt Regency $$

Sandia Resort $$$

BEST-KEPT SECRET

Casa de Sueños $

Mauger B&B $$

Nativo Lodge $$

BEST SPA

Hyatt Regency $$

Isleta Casino & Resort $$$

Los Poblanos Inn $$$$

DOWNTOWN & OLD TOWN

$ **Best Western Rio Grande Inn.** Although part of the Best Western chain, this contemporary four-story low-rise just off Interstate 40—a 10-minute walk from Old Town's plaza—has an attractive Southwestern design and furnishings, plus such modern touches as free high-speed Internet. The heavy, handcrafted wood furniture, tin sconces, and artwork in the rooms come from local suppliers and artisans. That locals are familiar with the Albuquerque Grill is a good indicator of the restaurant's reputation. It's a good value. **Pros:** 100% nonsmoking; airport shuttle. **Cons:** It's a hike from the rear rooms to the front desk. ✉*1015 Rio Grande Blvd. NW, Old Town* ☎*505/843–9500 or 800/959–4726* 🖷*505/843–9238* ⊕*www.riograndeinn.com* ✍*173 rooms* ⚒*In-room: refrigerator, Wi-Fi (some), Internet (some). In-hotel: restaurant, room service, bar, pool, gym, laundry facilities, parking (free), some pets allowed* ▤*AE, D, DC, MC, V.*

$ **Böttger Mansion of Old Town.** Charles Böttger, a German immigrant, built this pink two-story mansion in 1912. The lacy, richly appointed rooms vary greatly in size and decor; some have four-poster beds, slate floors, claw-foot tubs, or pressed-tin ceilings. All have down comforters, fluffy pillows, and terry robes—and a few are said to be haunted by a friendly ghost or two. The Wine Cellar Suite, in the basement, can accommodate up to six guests and has a kitchenette. A grassy courtyard fronted by a patio provides an escape from the Old Town crowds. Breakfast might consist of stuffed French toast or perhaps burritos smothered in green chile, which you can also enjoy in your room. **Pros:** Balloon, golf, and tour packages are available. **Cons:** Not for the floral-and-frilly phobic. ✉*110 San Felipe St. NW, Old Town* ☎*505/243–3639 or 800/758–3639* ⊕*www.bottger.com* ✍*7 rooms, 1 2-bedroom suite* ⚒*In-room: kitchen (some). In-hotel: parking (paid), no-smoking rooms* ▤*AE, MC, V* ¶*BP.*

$ **Casas de Sueños.** This historic compound of 1930s- and '40s-era
★ adobe casitas is perfect if you're seeking seclusion and quiet, yet seek proximity to museums, restaurants, and shops. Casas de Sueños (*sueños* means dreams in Spanish) is a few blocks south of Old Town Plaza, but on a peaceful residential street fringing the lush grounds of Albuquerque Country Club. The individually decorated units, which open onto a warren of courtyards and gardens, come in a variety of shapes and configurations. Typical features include Saltillo-tile floors, wood-burning kiva-style fireplaces, leather or upholstered armchairs, skylights, and contemporary Southwestern furnishings. Many rooms have large flat-screen TVs with DVD players and CD stereos, and some sleep as many as four adults. The full breakfast is served outside in the garden when the weather permits, and inside a lovely artists' studio at other times. **Pros:** Charming and tucked away; some private patios. **Cons:** Ask which rooms have the newest beds and which have full baths. ✉*310 Rio Grande Blvd. SW, on the south side of Central Ave., Old Town* ☎*505/247–4560 or 800/665–7002* 🖷*505/242–2162* ⊕*www.casasdesuenos.com* ✍*21 casitas* ⚒*In-room: kitchen (some), DVD (some). In-hotel: parking (free)* ▤*AE, MC, V* ¶*BP.*

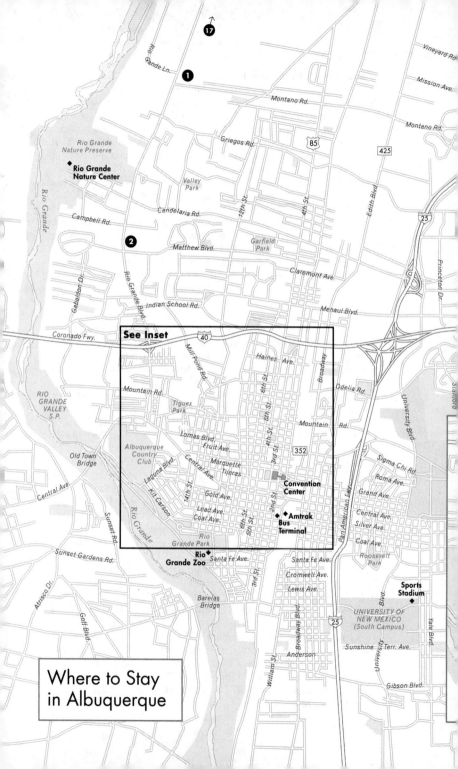

Where to Stay in Albuquerque

2

$ **Doubletree Hotel.** A two-story waterfall splashes down a marble backdrop in the lobby of this 15-story downtown hotel, with attractive, pale-gold rooms that contain mid-century-inspired furnishings and art. The restaurant at the foot of the waterfall is called, appropriately, La Cascada (The Cascade). Breakfast, a lunch buffet, and dinner, from fresh seafood to Southwestern specialties, are served. **Pros:** Old Town shuttle service available; recent renovation brought Sweet Dreams beds to each room and sleek upgrades throughout. **Cons:** Not all rooms have mountain views. ✉ *201 Marquette Ave. NW, Downtown* ☎ *505/247–3344 or 800/222–8733* 🖷 *505/247–7025* 🌐 *www.doubletree.com* *295 rooms* *In-room: Internet. In-hotel: Wi-Fi, restaurant, room service, bar, pool, laundry service, parking (paid)* *AE, D, DC, MC, V.*

$$ Fodor's Choice ★ **Embassy Suites Hotel Albuquerque.** This all-suites high-rise with a striking contemporary design sits on a bluff alongside Interstate 25, affording guests fabulous views of the downtown skyline and vast desert mesas to the west, and the verdant Sandia Mountains to the east. Rooms are large and done in soothing Tuscan colors; the living areas have pull-out sleeper sofas, refrigerators, dining and work areas, microwaves, and coffeemakers. You'll also find two phones and two TVs in each suite. Included in the rates is a nightly reception with hors d'oeuvres and cocktails, and a full breakfast each morning. With so much living and sleeping space and a great location accessible to downtown, Nob Hill, and the airport, this is a great option if you're staying in town for a while or traveling with a family. **Pros:** Quiet but convenient location adjacent to Interstate 25 and just south of Interstate 40; congenial staff. **Cons:** Suites attract families in addition to business travelers; the occasional child running rampant may not appeal to all. ✉ *1000 Woodward Pl. NE, Downtown* ☎ *505/245–7100 or 800/362–2779* 🖷 *505/247–1083* 🌐 *www.embassysuitesalbuquerque.com* *261 suites* *In-room: refrigerator, Wi-Fi. In-hotel: restaurant, bar, gym, spa, parking (free)* *AE, D, MC, V* *BP.*

$$ **Hotel Albuquerque at Old Town.** This 11-story Southwestern-style hotel rises distinctly above Old Town's ancient structures. The large rooms have desert-color appointments, hand-wrought furnishings, and tile bathrooms; most rooms have a small balcony with no patio furniture but nice views. Cristobal's serves commendable Spanish-style steaks and seafood; Café Plazuela & Cantina offers more casual American and New Mexican food; and a fine flamenco guitarist entertains in the Q-Bar & Gallery Lounge. Treatments and facials are available. **Pros:** The high-ceiling, rustically furnished, Territorial-style lobby is a comfy place to hang out. **Cons:** Room décor is a somewhat tired desert motif. ✉ *800 Rio Grande Blvd. NW, Old Town* ☎ *505/843–6300 or 877/901–7666* 🖷 *505/842–8426* 🌐 *www.hotelabq.com* *168 rooms, 20 suites* *In-room: Wi-Fi, refrigerator (some). In-hotel: 2 restaurants, room service, bar, pool, gym, spa, parking (free)* *AE, D, DC, MC, V.*

$ **Hotel Blue.** The reasonable rates here draw a party crowd, and the art deco–inspired rooms can pick up street noise as well; based on the (decidedly basic) services alone it would be a stretch to call this place hip or boutique. Still, people rave about the beds, and it is ideally located, especially for those with business downtown. It overlooks a small park, is a short stroll from downtown's music clubs and restaurants, and it's a short drive, bus ride, or 15-minute walk from Old Town. In summer, a lively Saturday growers' market (including arts vendors, music, and more) sets up in Robinson Park next door. **Pros:** Comfortable Tempurpedic beds; complimentary shuttle to the airport, convention center, and Old Town from 7 AM until 10 PM. **Cons:** This can be a fringe neighborhood by night. ⊠ *717 Central Ave. NW, Old Town* ☎ *505/924–2400 or 877/878–4868* ☎ *505/924–2465* ⊕ *www. thehotelblue.com* ↬ *125 rooms, 10 suites* ⚷ *In-hotel: Wi-Fi, restaurant, bar, pool, gym, parking (free)* ⊟ *AE, D, MC, V* ⦿ *CP.*

$$ 🛏 **Hyatt Regency Albuquerque.** Adjacent to the Albuquerque Convention Center, the city's most sumptuous hotel comprises a pair of soaring, desert-color towers that figure prominently in the city's skyline. The gleaming art deco–inspired interior benefited from a 2008 top-to-bottom renovation; the ambience is refined and not overbearing. The contemporary rooms in mauve, burgundy, and tan combine Southwestern style with all the amenities you'd expect of a high-caliber business-oriented hotel, including Wi-Fi, iPod docking stations, flat-screen TVs, plush pillow-top mattresses, and fluffy bathrobes. McGrath's Bar and Grill serves steaks, chops, chicken, and seafood (and breakfast to the power crowd), and there's also a Starbucks on-site. Bigwigs of all stripes stay in the penthouse. **Pros:** Easy walking distance from the KiMo Theatre and downtown's art galleries and restaurants, and a quick cab (or bus) ride elsewhere; the views, lap pool, and well-equipped 24/7 fitness center (massage service is available there or in rooms). **Cons:** Until you get your bearings, the layout can seem somewhat mazelike. No views on lower floors. ⊠ *330 Tijeras Ave. NW, Downtown* ☎ *505/842–1234 or 800/233–1234* ☎ *505/766–6710* ⊕ *albuquerque.hyatt.com* ↬ *395 rooms, 14 suites* ⚷ *In-room: Wi-Fi. In-hotel: restaurant, bars, pool, gym, parking (paid)* ⊟ *AE, D, DC, MC, V.*

$$ 🛏 **Mauger Estate B&B Inn.** This 1897 Queen Anne–style mansion—on
Fodor's Choice the National Register of Historic Places—was the first home in Albu-
★ querque to have electricity. While the mercantile Mauger (pronounced "major") family is long gone (and the electric long since upgraded, along with a detailed restoration throughout), this well-run B&B has retained many of the building's original architectural elements, including oval windows with beveled and "feather-pattern" glass, hardwood floors, high ceilings, a redbrick exterior, and a front veranda. Rooms—clean and contemporary with a restrained Victorian touch (seen best in the dark woods)—have refrigerators and baskets stocked with munchies, triple-sheeted beds with soft feather duvets, irons and boards, and fresh flowers. There's also a two-bedroom, two-bathroom town house next door. Guests have access to a full-service health club a few blocks away. **Pros:** Pleasant common room, with a library and a late-afternoon cookies-and-wine spread; responsive and informed innkeeper; good breakfasts, which they will pack to go if needed; convenient location. **Cons:** Rooms could use more task lighting; at night, on the northern fringe of downtown, it can feel a bit sketchy for walking, but parking is secure. ⊠ *701 Roma Ave. NW, Downtown* ☎ *505/242–8755 or*

800/719–9189 🖨*505/842–8835* ⊕*www.maugerbb.com* 🛏*8 rooms, 1 2-bedroom town house* 🖧*In-room: Wi-Fi, refrigerator. In-hotel: parking (free), some pets allowed* ▭*AE, D, MC, V* ❏*BP.*

UPTOWN

$$ 🏨**Albuquerque Marriott.** This 17-story, upscale, uptown property draws a mix of business and leisure travelers; it's close to three shopping malls and not too far from Nob Hill. Kachina dolls, Native American pottery, and other regional artworks decorate the elegant public areas. The rooms are traditional American, with walk-in closets, armoires, and crystal lamps, but have Southwestern touches. Rooms on all but the first few floors enjoy staggering views, either of Sandias to the east or the vast mesas to the west. Cielo Sandia specializes in steaks and contemporary New Mexican fare. **Pros:** A top-to-bottom renovation completed in 2007 spruced the place up quite nicely; cozy lobby lounge. **Cons:** Fee for Internet access in rooms. ✉*2101 Louisiana Blvd. NE, Uptown* ☎*505/881–6800 or 800/228–9290* 🖨*505/888–2982* ⊕*www.marriott.com/abqnm* 🛏*405 rooms, 6 suites* 🖧*In-room: refrigerator, Internet. In-hotel: Wi-Fi, restaurant, room service, bar, pool, gym, laundry facilities, laundry service, parking (free)* ▭*AE, D, DC, MC, V.*

$ 🏨**Sheraton Albuquerque Uptown.** Within easy distance of the airport and Albuquerque's newest shopping malls, this 2008-renovated property meets the consistent Sheraton standard with a pleasant lobby with a cozy bar area and a gift shop. Earthy and muted reds, oranges, and sand-shaded colors accent the lobby and functional but ample rooms, whose nicer touches include a second sink outside the bathroom, comfy mattresses, and bathrobes. **Pros:** Central location with easy highway (and shopping) access. **Cons:** At a busy intersection. ✉*2600 Louisiana Blvd. NE, Uptown* ☎*505/881–0000 or 800/252–7772* 🖨*505/881–3736* ⊕*sheratonabq.com* 🛏*294 rooms* 🖧*In-room: refrigerator, Wi-Fi. In-hotel: restaurant, room service, pool, gym* ▭*AE, D, DC, MC, V.*

CAMPING

🛆**Albuquerque Central KOA.** At town's edge, in the foothills of the Sandia Mountains, this well-equipped campground has expansive views, a dog run, and wireless Internet, but only a few trees. Reservations are essential during Balloon Fiesta in October. ✉*12400 Skyline NE, Exit 166 off I–40, Northeast Heights* ☎*505/296–2729 or 800/562–7781* ⊕*www.koakampgrounds.com* 🖧*Flush toilets, full hookups, partial hookups (electric and water), dump station, drinking water, guest laundry, showers, fire grates, grills, picnic tables, electricity, public telephone, general store, play area, service station, swimming (pool)* 🛏*206 sites, 100 with full hookups* ▭*AE, D, MC, V.*

NORTH SIDE

$$ 🏨**Cinnamon Morning B&B.** A private, beautifully maintained, pet-friendly
★ compound set back from the road and a 10-minute drive north of Old Town, Cinnamon Morning is just south of Rio Grande Nature Center

State Park and a perfect roost if you want to be close to the city's wineries and the launching areas used by most hot-air-ballooning companies. Three rooms are in the main house, a richly furnished adobe home with colorful decorations and a lush garden patio. There's also a secluded two-bedroom guesthouse with a bath, full kitchen, private entrance, living room, and fireplace; and a colorfully painted one-bedroom casita with a private patio, Mexican-style furnishings, a viga ceiling, and a living room with a sleeper sofa. The full breakfasts here are filling and delicious, served by a roaring fire in winter or in the courtyard in summer. **Pros:** Hosts will gladly help with travel ideas and planning. **Cons:** Cancellations must be made 14 days ahead. ✉ *2700 Rio Grande Blvd. NW, North Valley* ☎ *505/345–3541 or 800/214–9481* 🖷 *505/342– 2283* ⊕ *www.cinnamonmorning.com* 🛏 *3 rooms, 1 casita, 1 guest house* ⚘ *In-room: kitchen (some), Wi-Fi. In-hotel: some pets allowed* ▭ *AE, D, MC, V* ⥥ *BP.*

$ 🖫 **Inn at Paradise.** Near the first tee of the lush Paradise Hills Golf Club, this pleasant, well-priced B&B resort atop the West Mesa is a golfer's dream: the 6,895 yards of bluegrass fairways and bent-grass greens challenge players of all levels. Works by local artists and craftspeople decorate the large rooms, which are filled with attractive, if functional, contemporary furnishings; the two suites have fireplaces. Many rooms have balconies overlooking the golf course. Golf packages are available. It's a good bet if you want to be close to Petroglyphs National Monument or Corrales. **Pros:** Special rates available during Balloon Fiesta. **Cons:** Bridge traffic back to town can be slow. ✉ *10035 Country Club La. NW, West Side* ☎ *505/898–6161 or 800/938–6161* 🖷 *505/890–1090* ⊕ *www.innatparadise.com* 🛏 *16 rooms, 2 suites, 1 apartment* ⚘ *In-room: kitchen. In-hotel: golf course, parking (free)* ▭ *AE, D, MC, V* ⥥ *CP.*

$$$$ 🖫 **Los Poblanos Inn.** Designed by acclaimed architect John Gaw Meem,
Fodor's Choice this rambling, historic inn lies outside of Albuquerque's sprawl, on 25
★ acres of organic farm fields, lavender plantings, and gardens in Los Ranchos on the town's north side, near the Rio Grande and just across the street from Anderson Valley Vineyards—with all the greenery and the quiet pace of life here, you'd never know you're in the desert, or in the middle of one of the Southwest's largest cities. You reach the inn via a spectacular tree-lined lane. Every accommodation has a private entrance and contains folk paintings, painted viga ceilings, and high-quality linens. Rooms also contain bath products made on-site, including lavender soap and oils; all have kiva fireplaces, too. The property also includes the 15,000-square-foot La Quinta Cultural Center, a conference space available for meetings that contains a dramatic fresco by Peter Hurd. There's also a library with beautiful artwork. **Pros:** The lavender fields are especially lovely; personal trainer and day spa service available. **Cons:** Spa service is off-site, a short drive away. ✉ *4803 Rio Grande Blvd. NW, North Valley* ☎ *505/344–9297 or 866/344– 9297* 🖷 *505/342–1302* ⊕ *www.lospoblanos.com* 🛏 *3 rooms, 4 suites, 2 guesthouses* ⚘ *In-room: kitchen (some), refrigerator (some), DVD (some), Wi-Fi (some). In-hotel: parking (free)* ▭ *AE, MC, V* ⥥ *BP.*

$$ ⬚**Marriott Pyramid.** This curious ziggurat-shaped 10-story building fits in nicely with the other examples of postmodern architecture that have sprung up in northern Albuquerque. It's the most upscale of the slew of chain hotels in the area, and it's an excellent base for exploring the North Valley, or for easier access to Santa Fe than from downtown or airport hotels. Rooms have sponge-painted walls and dapper country-French decor and open onto a soaring atrium lobby. Perks include evening turndown service and newspapers delivered to the room each morning. **Pros:** Easy access to Interstate 25. **Cons:** Service is uneven; the lobby is mazelike and confusing, as you might expect inside a pyramid. ⊠*5151 San Francisco Rd. NE, Journal Center* ☎*505/821–3333 or 800/466–8356* ⊟*505/828–0230* ⊕*www.albuquerquemarriottnorth. com* ⟳*248 rooms, 54 suites* ⌂*In-room: refrigerator, Wi-Fi. In-hotel: restaurant, room service, bar, pool, gym, laundry facilities, laundry service, parking (free)* ⊟*AE, D, DC, MC, V.*

$$ ⬚**Nativo Lodge Hotel.** Although it's priced similarly to a number of
★ generic midrange chain properties on the north side, this five-story property has more character than most, especially in the expansive public areas, bar, and restaurant, which have an attractive Southwestern motif that includes hand-carved panels depicting symbols from Native American lore and river-rock walls. Rooms have wing chairs, work desks, Wi-Fi, and dual-line phones. The hotel is just off Interstate 25, but set back far enough to avoid highway noise; several movie theaters and a bounty of restaurants are nearby. **Pros:** Nice scale, relaxing atmosphere. **Cons:** If your primary business is downtown, this is a bit far north. ⊠*6000 Pan American Freeway NE, Northeast* ☎*505/798–4300 or 888/628–4861* ⊕*hhandr.com/nativo* ⟳*147 rooms, 3 suites* ⌂*In-room: refrigerator, Wi-Fi. In-hotel: restaurant, room service, bar, pool, gym, laundry facilities, parking (free)* ⊟*AE, D, DC, MC, V.*

$$$ ⬚**Sandia Resort & Casino.** Completed in early 2006 after much antici-
Fodor's Choice pation, this seven-story casino-resort set a new standard for luxury in
★ Albuquerque; unfortunately the service here doesn't always quite match the promise. Nevertheless, appointments like 32-inch plasma TVs, handcrafted wooden furniture, louvered wooden blinds, and muted, natural-color palettes lend elegance to the spacious rooms, most of which have sweeping views of the Sandia Mountains or the Rio Grande Valley. The 700-acre grounds, which are in the Far Northeast Heights, just across Interstate 25 from Balloon Fiesta Park, ensure privacy and quiet and include a superb golf course and an amphitheater that hosts top-of-the-line music and comedy acts. The Green Reed Spa offers a wide range of treatments, many using local clay and plants. One of the city's best restaurants for mountain views, Bien Shur, occupies the casino's top floor, and there are three other places to eat on-site. The casino is open 24 hours. **Pros:** 24/7 room service. **Cons:** Smoking is allowed on premises; pool not open year-round. ⊠*Tramway Rd. NE just east of I–25, Northeast Heights* ☎*505/796–7500 or 800/526–9366* ⊕*www. sandiacasino.com* ⟳*198 rooms, 30 suites* ⌂*In-room: Wi-Fi. In-hotel: 4 restaurants, room service, bars, golf course, pool, gym, spa, laundry service, parking (free)* ⊟*AE, D, DC, MC, V.*

AIRPORT

$ 🏨**Hampton Inn Airport.** One of the better midprice options near the airport, the Hampton Inn can be counted on for clean, updated rooms with plenty of perks (free Wi-Fi, a pool, on-the-run breakfast bags to take with you to the airport or wherever you're off to that day). **Pros:** Easy in, easy out. **Cons:** Outdoor-facing rooms. ⊠*2231 Yale Blvd. SE, Airport* 🕿*505/246–2255 or 800/426–7866* 🖷*505/246–2255* ⊕*www. hamptoninn.com* ⤺*62 rooms, 9 suites* ﴾*In-room: Wi-Fi. In-hotel: restaurant, bar, pool, gym, laundry facilities, parking (free)* ▤*AE, D, DC, MC, V.*

$ 🏨**Holiday Inn Select Albuquerque Airport.** Opened just west of the airport in 2006, this upscale, four-story hotel sits high on a bluff, affording nice views of downtown and the western mesa as well as the Sandia Mountains. Some suites have whirlpool tubs. The indoor pool and a small, 24/7 fitness room, along with a 24-hour business center, make this a favorite with business travelers. **Pros:** Work areas are well lit, another plus for the business traveler. **Cons:** Off-site dining is your best bet. ⊠*1501 Sunport Pl. SE, Airport* 🕿*505/944–2255 or 800/315–2621* ⊕*www.holidayinnabq.com* ⤺*110 rooms, 20 suites* ﴾*In-room: Wi-Fi. In-hotel: restaurant, room service, bar, pool, gym, laundry facilities, parking (free)* ▤*AE, D, DC, MC, V.*

$$ 🏨**Sheraton Albuquerque Airport Hotel.** Only 350 yards from the airport,
★   this newly renovated 15-story hotel sits up high on a mesa with vast views of the Sandia Mountains to the east and downtown Albuquerque to the northwest. It's handy being so close to the terminal, and the Southwest-accented rooms have excellent beds, large work desks, Wi-Fi and data ports, and coffeemakers. Rojo Grill ranks among the better hotel restaurants in town. Ask for a room with a view. ⊠*2910 Yale Blvd. SE, Airport* 🕿*505/843–7000 or 800/996–3426* 🖷*505/843–6307* ⊕*www.albuquerquegrandairporthotel.com* ⤺*276 rooms, 2 suites* ﴾*In-room: Wi-Fi. In-hotel: restaurant, room service, bar, tennis courts, pool, gym, parking (free)* ▤*AE, D, DC, MC, V.*

NIGHTLIFE & THE ARTS

For the 411 on arts and nightlife, consult the Venue section of the Sunday edition of the *Albuquerque Journal* (⊕*www.abqjournal.com*), the freebie weekly *Alibi* (⊕*www.alibi.com*), and the Arts Alliance's inclusive Arts & Cultural Calendar (⊕*www.abqarts.org/calendar.htm*). For highlights on some of the best music programming in town, go to ⊕*ampconcerts.org.*

NIGHTLIFE

BARS & LOUNGES

Atomic Cantina (⊠*315 Gold Ave. SW, Downtown* 🕿*505/242–2200*), a funky-hip downtown lounge popular for its cool juke box and extensive happy hours, draws a mix of students, yuppies, and music fans. Many nights there's live music, from punk to rockabilly to trance.

Like its neighbor, Atomic Cantina, **Burt's Tiki Lounge** (✉*313 Gold Ave. SW* ☎*505/247–BURT*) is a place to mingle with unpretentious locals.

Graham Central Station (✉*4770 Montgomery Blvd. NE, Northeast Heights* ☎*505/883–3041*), part of a rowdy regional chain of massive nightclubs, consists of four distinct bars under one roof: country-western, rock, dance, and Latin. It's open Wednesday–Saturday.

Martini Grille (✉*4200 Central Ave. SE, Nob Hill* ☎*505/242–4333*) offers live piano in a swank setting; this gay-popular spot is also a respectable restaurant serving burgers, sandwiches, pastas, and salads.

O'Niell's Pub (✉*4310 Central Ave. SE, Nob Hill* ☎*505/256–0564*) moved into a handsome new space in summer 2006, where it continues to serve good Mexican and American comfort food and present jazz, bebop, and other music in a cheery neighborhood bar near the University of New Mexico.

CASINOS

If you love to gamble, the Albuquerque area has a surfeit of options, including Santa Ana, San Felipe, Sandia, Isleta, Laguna, and Acoma pueblos.

Isleta Casino & Resort (✉*11000 Broadway SE, Exit 215 from I–25, Isleta Pueblo* ☎*877/747–5382* ⊕*www.isleta-casino.com*) is located "7 lucky minutes" south of the Albuquerque airport. Here you can belly up to over 30 table games, sit down at one of 1,600 slots (reel and video styles), or join a high-stakes bingo or poker tournament. The smoke is thick wherever you go (despite designated nonsmoking zones), but you can seek respite in the swank new hotel (or spurn it all and take in a show). Live music here ranges from cabaret acts in the Showroom, and headliners like the Neville Brothers and Dr. John in the 2,500-seat outdoor amphitheater. (⇨ *see Side Trips from Albuquerque for more on Isleta Pueblo*).

Sandia Resort & Casino (✉*Tramway Rd. NE at I–25, Far Northeast Heights* ☎*505/796–7500 or 800/526–9366* ⊕*www.sandiacasino. com*) is a light, open, airy resort with an enormous gaming area brightened by soaring ceilings and big windows. In addition to 1,700 slot machines, you'll find craps, blackjack, mini baccarat, and several versions of poker. The 4,200-seat casino amphitheater hosts rock-circuit stalwarts such as Earth, Wind & Fire; Kenny Rogers; Chicago; the occasional big-name comedian; and other acts.

COMEDY CLUB

Laff's Comedy Club (✉*6001 San Mateo Blvd. NE, Northeast Heights* ☎*505/296–5653*) serves up the live laughs (and dinner) Wednesday–Sunday.

LIVE MUSIC

People are always surprised to hear what a rich and varied music scene Albuquerque has—and at reasonable prices to boot. With world-class world-music festivals like ¡Globalquerque! and the NM Jazz Festival, to *norteño* roots, heartstring-tearing country, blues, folk, and the latest rock permutations—and all manner of venues in which to hear (or dance to) them—there's even room for the big-arena warhorses, who mostly play the casinos these days.

¡Globalquerque! (⊕*www.globalquerque.com or ampconcerts.org*), a two-day world-music festival held at the National Hispanic Cultural Center, has been running annually in late September since 2005, and the acts and auxiliary programming just keep getting better. Festival producer AMP Concerts is also the organization that lures acts like David Byrne and the Cowboy Junkies to intimate venues downtown.

The 12,000-seat **Journal Pavilion** (⊠*5601 University Blvd. SE, Mesa del Sol* ☎*505/452–5100 or 505/246–8742* ⊕*www.journalpavilion. com*) amphitheater attracts big-name acts such as Green Day, Nine Inch Nails, Stevie Nicks, and the Dave Matthews Band.

Outpost Performance Space (⊠*210 Yale Blvd. SE, University of New Mexico* ☎*505/268–0044* ⊕*www.outpostspace.org*) programs an inspired, eclectic slate, from local nuevo-folk to techno, jazz, and traveling East Indian ethnic. Some big names—especially in the jazz world—show up at this special small venue.

THE ARTS

Albuquerque has a remarkable wealth of local talent, but it also draws a surprising number of world-class stage performers from just about every discipline imaginable. Check the listings mentioned at the introduction to this section for everything from poetry readings, impromptu chamber music recitals, folk, jazz, and blues festivals, and formal symphony performances to film festivals, Flamenco Internacional, and theater.

MUSIC

The well-respected **New Mexico Symphony Orchestra** (☎*505/881–8999 or 800/251–6676* ⊕*www.nmso.org*) plays pops, Beethoven, and, at Christmas, Handel's *Messiah*. Most performances are at 2,000-seat Popejoy Hall.

Popejoy Hall (⊠*University of New Mexico Center for the Arts, Central Ave. NE at Stanford Dr. SE* ☎*505/277–4569 or 800/905–3315* ⊕*www.popejoyhall.com*) presents concerts, from rock and pop to classical, plus comedy acts, lectures, and national tours of Broadway shows. UNM's Keller Hall, also in the Center for the Arts, is a small venue with fine acoustics, a perfect home for the University's excellent chamber music program.

THEATER

Albuquerque Little Theatre (✉224 *San Pasquale Ave. SW, Old Town* ☎*505/242–4750* ⊕*www.albuquerquelittletheatre.org*) is a nonprofit community troupe that's been going strong since 1930. Its staff of professionals teams up with local volunteer talent to produce comedies, dramas, musicals, and mysteries. The company theater, across the street from Old Town, was built in 1936 and designed by John Gaw Meem. It contains an art gallery, a large lobby, and a cocktail lounge.

★ The stunning **KiMo Theatre** (✉*423 Central Ave. NW, Downtown* ☎*505/768–3522 or 505/768–3544* ⊕*www.cabq.gov/kimo*), an extravagantly ornamented 650-seat Pueblo Deco movie palace, is one of the best places in town to see anything. Jazz, dance—everything from traveling road shows to local song-and-dance acts—might turn up here. Former Albuquerque resident Vivian Vance of *I Love Lucy* fame once performed on the stage; today you're more likely to see Wilco or a film-festival screening.

While Popejoy Hall draws them in with huge Broadway touring shows, UNM's **Rodey Theater** (✉*University of New Mexico Center for the Arts, Central and Stanford SE* ☎*505/277–4569 or 800/905–3315*), a smaller house in the same complex, stages experimental and niche works throughout the year, including student and professional plays and dance performances such as the acclaimed annual Summerfest Festival of New Plays during July and the June Flamenco Festival.

Often working in conjunction with the National Hispanic Cultural Center (NHCC), the **Teatro Nuevo México** (✉*107 Bryn Mawr SE, University of New Mexico* ☎*505/265–5200* ⊕*www.teatronm.com*) is dedicated to presenting works created by Latino artists. In addition to plays by the likes of Federico García Lorca and Nilo Cruz, notable in their production roster is a revival of the Spanish operetta form known as zarzuela. These crowd-pleasing pieces may be comedies or drama, and are presented in collaboration with NHCC and the New Mexico Symphony Orchestra.

In January and February, theater fans of the fresh and new flock to the **Tricklock Company**'s (✉*1705 Mesa Vista Dr. NE, Nob Hill* ☎*505/254–8393* ⊕*www.tricklock.com*) REVOLUTIONS International Theatre Festival. Recognized internationally, Tricklock's productions tour regularly and emphasize works that take it—and the audience—to the edge of theatrical possibility.

SPORTS & THE OUTDOORS

Albuquerque is blessed with an exceptional setting for outdoor sports, backed by a favorable, if unpredictable, climate. Usually 10°F warmer than Santa Fe's, Albuquerque's winter days are often mild enough for most outdoor activities. The Sandias tempt you with challenging mountain adventures (⇨ *See the Sandia Park section of the Side Trips from the Cities chapter for details on mountain biking and skiing in the Sandia Mountains above Albuquerque*); the Rio Grande and its

Cottonwood forest, the Bosque, provide settings for additional outdoors pursuits.

PARTICIPANT SPORTS

The **City of Albuquerque** (☎505/768–5300 ⊕*www.cabq.gov/living.html*) maintains diverse cultural and recreational programs. Among the city's assets are more than 20,000 acres of open space, four golf courses, 200 parks, 68 paved tracks for biking and jogging, as well as swimming pools, tennis courts, ball fields, playgrounds, and a shooting range.

AMUSEMENT PARK

Drive down San Mateo Northeast in summer and you may see a roller coaster smack in the middle of the city. **Cliff's Amusement Park** (⊠4800 *Osuna Rd. NE, off I–25 at San Mateo Blvd. NE, Northeast Heights* ☎505/881–9373 ⊕*www.cliffsamusementpark.com*) is a clean, well-run attraction for everyone from two-year-olds on up. It features a wooden-track roller coaster as well as rides for all ages and state fair–type games of chance. The park also has a large water-play area. Cliff's is open early April through September, but days and hours vary, so call first.

BALLOONING

Albuquerque's high altitude, mild climate, and steady but manageable winds, make it an ideal destination for ballooning. A wind pattern known as the "Albuquerque Box," created by the city's location against the Sandia Mountains, makes Albuquerque a great place to fly.

If you've never been ballooning, you may picture a bumpy ride, where changes in altitude produce the queasy feeling you get in a tiny propeller plane. But the experience is far calmer than that. The balloons are flown by licensed pilots (don't call them operators) who deftly turn propane-fueled flames on and off, climbing and descending to find winds blowing the way they want to go—there's no real "steering" involved, which makes the pilots' control that much more admirable. Pilots generally land balloons where the wind dictates, so "chase vehicles" pick you up and return you to your departure point, but particularly skilled pilots can use conditions created by the Box to land precisely where you started. Even without door-to-door service, many visitors rank a balloon ride over the Rio Grande Valley as their most memorable experience.

Several reliable companies around Albuquerque offer tours. A ride costs about $160–$180 per person. One of the best is **Rainbow Ryders** (☎505/823–1111 or 800/725–2477 ⊕*www.rainbowryders.com*), an official ride concession for the Albuquerque International Balloon Fiesta. As part of the fun, you get to help inflate and pack away the balloon. In case you missed breakfast prior to your flight, a Continental breakfast and glass of champagne await your return.

FodorsChoice
★

BICYCLING

With the creation of many lanes, trails, and dedicated bike paths, Albuquerque's city leaders are recognized for their bike-friendly efforts—a serious challenge given the committed car culture of its residents. The city's public works department produces a detailed **bike map,** which can be obtained free by calling ☏505/768–3550 or downloaded from ⊕www.cabq.gov/bike.

Albuquerque has miles of bike lanes and trails through and around the city as well as great mountain-biking trails at Sandia Peak Ski Area (⇨ *See the Sandia Park section of the Side Trips from the Cities chapter).*

Although mountain bikes may be rented in the Sandias, bike-rental sources are scarce around town. **Northeast Cyclery** (⊠*8305 Menaul Blvd. NE, Northeast Heights* ☏*505/299–1210*) has a good range of road and mountain bikes for rent. Most are unisex styles, and they carry kid sizes as well.

★ Seasonally, at **Tingley Beach** (⊕*www.cabq.gov*) balloon-tire and mountain bikes are available by the hour (⇨ *see What to See, under Albuquerque BioPark).* The **Paseo del Bosque Bike Trail** (⊕*www.cabq.gov*) runs right through Tingley. It's flat for most of its 16-mi run, and it's one of the loveliest rides in town.

BIRD-WATCHING

The Rio Grande Valley, one of the continent's major flyways, attracts many migratory bird species. Good bird-viewing locales include the **Rio Grande Nature Center State Park** (⊠*2901 Candelaria Rd. NW, North Valley* ☏*505/344–7240* ⊕*www.nmparks.com*).

GOLF

Most of the better courses in the region—and there are some outstanding ones—are just outside town (⇨ *See the North-Central New Mexico chapter for details).* The four courses operated by the city of Albuquerque have their charms, and the rates are reasonable. Each course has a clubhouse and pro shop, where clubs and other equipment can be rented. Weekday play is first-come, first-served, but reservations are taken for weekends. Contact the **Golf Management Office** (☏*505/888–8115* ⊕*www.cabq.gov/golf*) for details. Of the four city courses, **Arroyo del Oso** (⊠*7001 Osuna Rd. NE, Northeast Heights* ☏*505/884–7505*) earns high marks for its undulating 27-hole layout; greens fees are $26 for 18 holes. The 18-hole **Los Altos Golf Course** (⊠*9717 Copper Ave. NE, Northeast Heights* ☏*505/298–1897*), one of the region's most popular facilities, has $26 greens fees. There's also a short, par-3, 9-hole executive course.

★ **Sandia Golf Club** (⊠*Tramway Rd. NE just east of I–25, Far Northeast Heights* ☏*505/798–3990* ⊕*www.sandiagolf.com*), opened in 2005 at the swanky Sandia Resort & Casino, offers 18 holes set amid lush hilly fairways, cascading waterfalls, and desert brush. Greens fees are $51–$61. The University of New Mexico has two superb courses. Both are open daily and have full-service pro shops, instruction, and snack

bars. Greens fees for out-of-staters run about $60 to $70, with cart.
UNM North (✉ *Tucker Rd. at Yale Blvd., University of New Mexico*
☎ *505/277–4146*) is a first-class 9-hole, par-36 course on the north
side of campus. The 18-hole facility at **UNM South** (✉ *3601 University
Blvd., just west of airport off I–25, Southeast Heights* ☎ *505/277–
4546* ⊕ *www.unmgolf.com*) has garnered countless awards from major
golf magazines and hosted PGA and LPGA qualifying events; there's
also a short par-3 9-hole course.

HIKING

In the foothills in Albuquerque's Northeast Heights, you'll find great
hiking in **Cibola National Forest,** which can be accessed from Tramway
Road Northeast, about 4 mi east of Interstate 25 or 2 mi north of Paseo
del Norte. Just follow the road into the hillside, and you'll find several
parking areas (there's a daily parking fee of $3). This is where you'll
★ find the trailhead for the steep and challenging **La Luz Trail,** which rises
some 9 mi (an elevation gain of more than 3,000 feet) to the top of Sandia Crest. You can take the Sandia Peak Aerial Tram (⇨ *see Exploring
Albuquerque, above*) to the top and then hike down the trail, or vice
versa (keep in mind that it can take up to six hours to hike up the trail,
and four to five hours to hike down). Spectacular views of Albuquerque
and many miles of desert and mountain beyond that are had from the
trail. You can also enjoy a hike here without going the whole way—if
your energy and time are limited, just hike a mile or two and back. No
matter how far you hike, however, pack plenty of water.

SPECTATOR SPORTS

BASEBALL

Since 2003, the city has hosted Triple A minor league baseball's **Albuquerque Isotopes** (✉ *University Ave. SE at Avenida Cesar Chavez SE,
Southeast* ☎ *505/924–2255* ⊕ *www.albuquerquebaseball.com*), the
farm club of the major league Florida Marlins; the season runs April
through August.

BASKETBALL

It's hard to beat the excitement of home basketball games of the **University of New Mexico Lobos** (✉ *University Ave. at Avenida Cesar Chavez,
Southeast* ☎ *505/925–5626* ⊕ *golobos.cstv.com*), when 18,000 rabid
fans crowd into the school's arena, "the Pit," from November to
March. Both the women's and men's teams have enjoyed huge success
in past years.

FOOTBALL

The competitively ranked **University of New Mexico Lobos** (✉ *University
Ave. at Avenida César Chavez, Southeast* ☎ *505/925–5626* ⊕ *golobos.
cstv.com*) play at the 40,000-seat University Stadium in the fall.

SHOPPING

Albuquerque's shopping strengths include a handful of cool retail districts, such as Nob Hill, Old Town, and the rapidly gentrifying downtown. These are good neighborhoods for galleries, antiques, and home-furnishing shops, bookstores, and offbeat gift shops. Otherwise, the city is mostly the domain of both strip and indoor malls, mostly filled with ubiquitous chain shops, although you can find some worthwhile independent shops even there.

SHOPPING NEIGHBORHOODS & MALLS

The **Uptown** (⊠ *Louisiana Blvd. NE, between I–40 and Menaul Blvd. NE)* neighborhood is Albuquerque's mall central. From worst to best the big three are: Winrock (on the east side of Louisiana Blvd., just north of Interstate 40), which is in a major slump; Coronado (at Louisiana Blvd. NE and Menaul Blvd. NE), which has a big Barnes & Noble and new Sephora; and the newest and best of the lot, ABQ Uptown (east side, closer to Menaul), which is all outdoors and sports an Apple Store, M.A.C. cosmetics shop, and Williams-Sonoma.

On the far northwest outskirts of town, **Cottonwood Mall** (⊠ *Coors Blvd. NW at Coors Bypass, West Side* ☎ *505/899–7467*) is anchored by Dillard's, Foley's, Mervyn's, JCPenney, and Sears, and has about 130 other shops, including Williams-Sonoma, Aveda, Cache, and Abercrombie & Fitch. There are a dozen restaurants and food stalls, plus a 14-screen theater.

Albuquerque's **Downtown** (⊠ *Central and Gold Aves. from 1st to 10th Sts.*) has had its highs and lows, but local developers are only renting to independent businesses in an effort to keep downtown from turning into a collection of chain outlets. Stroll along Central and Gold avenues (and neighboring blocks) to admire avant-garde galleries, cool cafés, and curious boutiques.

Funky **Nob Hill** (⊠ *Central Ave. from Girard Blvd. to Washington St.*), just east of University of New Mexico and anchored by old Route 66, pulses with colorful storefronts and kitschy signs. At night, neon-lighted boutiques, galleries, and performing-arts spaces encourage foot traffic. Many of the best shops are clustered inside or on the blocks near Nob Hill Business Center, an art deco structure containing several intriguing businesses and La Montañita Natural Foods Co-op, an excellent spot for a snack.

Old Town (⊠ *Central Ave. and Rio Grande Blvd.*) has the city's largest concentration of one-of-a-kind retail shops, selling clothing, home accessories, Native American art, and Mexican imports—and the predictable schlock targeted at tourists.

ART GALLERIES

In addition to Tamarind Institute and Jonson Gallery, both at UNM (⇨ *University of New Mexico & Nob Hill "What to See" section, above*), Albuquerque has a solid and growing gallery scene. For comprehensive gallery listings, pick up a copy of the free annual *Collector's Guide* (⊕*www.collectorsguide.com*); for current shows and ArtsCrawl schedules, look up the Arts & Cultural Calendar online (⊕*www.abqarts. org/calendar.htm or www.artscrawlabq.org*).

516 Arts (⊠*516 Central Ave. SW, Downtown* ☎*505/242–1445* ⊕*www.516arts.org*) holds a special place in the Duke City's art world. They offer world-class contemporary art in changing shows that often cross media boundaries—witness their 2008 Guerrilla Girls performance, a collaboration with AMP Concerts and the KiMo. Exhibits mine the work of local and national artists, and are as likely to speak to issues as they are offer to a powerfully appealing visual presence. LAND/ART, a 2009 series on site-specific environmental art, and the recent "Trappings: Stories of Women, Power, and Clothing," which combined gallery pieces with projections on buses and buildings, are a few examples of 516's commitment.

Every few weeks the exhibits at **Artspace 116** (⊠*116 Central Ave. SW, 2nd fl., Downtown* ☎*505/245–4200* ⊕*www.artspace116.org*) are switched in order to display the work of another New Mexico artist. The small gallery's mission is to present selective one-time shows—of prints, oils, sculpture, and any other media—that will help expose an artist to a new audience. Geometric clay vessels by Elizabeth Fritzsche, moody black-and-white photographs by Steven M. Williams, and Allan Rosenfield's large-scale color-driven acrylic and mixed-media pieces are highlights of recent years.

★ **Coleman Gallery Contemporary Art** (⊠*4115 Silver Ave. SE, Nob Hill* ☎*505/232–0224* ⊕*www.colemancontemporary.com*) has emerged as one of Nob Hill's leading art spaces, showing works by a number of the state's top contemporary talents who work largely in an abstract vein.

DSG (⊠*510 14th St. SW, Old Town* ☎*505/266–7751 or 800/474–7751* ⊕*www.dsg-art.com*), owned by John Cacciatore, handles works of paint, tapestry, sculpture, and photography by leading regional artists, including Frank McCulloch, Carol Hoy, Leo Neufeld, Larry Bell, Angus Macpherson, Jim Bagley, Nancy Kozikowski, and photographer Nathan Small.

Harwood Art Center (⊠*1114 7th St. NW, off Mountain Rd., Old Town* ☎*505/242–6367* ⊕*www.harwoodartcenter.org*), on the fringe of Downtown and Old Town in the Sawmill/Wells Park neighborhood, is a remarkable resource for its huge roster of community-oriented art classes, and a gallery in its own right. Shows—predominantly of New Mexico–based artists working in nontraditional forms—take place in their historic brick school building and change monthly.

Mariposa Gallery (✉*3500 Central Ave. SE, Nob Hill* ☎*505/268–6828* ⊕*www.mariposa-gallery.com*) sells contemporary fine crafts, including jewelry, sculptural glass, works in mixed media and clay, and fiber arts. The changing exhibits focus on upcoming artists; its buyer's sharp eyes can result in real finds for the serious browser.

★ **Weyrich Gallery** (✉*2935–D Louisiana Blvd. NE, Uptown* ☎*505/883–7410* ⊕*www.weyrichgallery.com*) carries distinctive jewelry, fine art, Japanese tea bowls, woodblocks, hand-colored photography, and other largely Asian-inspired pieces.

SPECIALTY STORES

ANTIQUES

Fodor's Choice
★ **Classic Century Square Antique Mall** (✉*4516 Central Ave. SE, Nob Hill* ☎*505/268–8080*) is a three-story emporium of collectibles and antiques. The emphasis is on memorabilia from the early 1880s to the 1950s. (When the set designers for the television miniseries *Lonesome Dove* needed props, they came here.) Items for sale include art deco and art nouveau objects, retro-cool '50s designs, Depression-era glass, Native American goods, quilts and linens, vintage clothes, and Western memorabilia.

Cowboys & Indians (✉*4000 Central Ave. SE, Nob Hill* ☎*505/255–4054*) carries Native American and cowboy art and artifacts.

BOOKS

One of the last of the great independents, **Bookworks** (✉*4022 Rio Grande Blvd. NW, one block north of Griegos Rd. NW, North Valley* ☎*505/344–8139* ⊕*www.bkwrks.com*), maintains an eclectic stock of regional coffee-table books, a well-culled selection of modern fiction and nonfiction, architecture and design titles, and a (small) playground's worth of kids' books. Regular signings and readings draw some very big guns to this tiny treasure.

Massive **Page One** (✉*11018 Montgomery Blvd. NE, Far Northeast Heights* ☎*505/294–2026*), arguably the best bookstore in Albuquerque, specializes in technical and professional titles, maps, globes, children's titles, and 150 out-of-state and foreign newspapers. Book signings, poetry readings, and children's events are frequently scheduled.

GIFTS, FOOD & TOYS

Beeps (✉*Nob Hill Shopping Center, 3500 Central Ave. SE, Nob Hill* ☎*505/262–1900*), a Nob Hill favorite, carries cards, T-shirts, and amusing, if bawdy, novelties.

Candy Lady (✉*Mountain Rd. at Rio Grande Blvd., Old Town* ☎*505/224–9837 or 800/214–7731*) is known as much for its scandalous adult novelty candies as for its tasty red- and green-chile brittle, plus the usual fudge, chocolates, piñon caramels, and candies. A small room, to the right as you enter, displays the "adult" candy, so you can pilot any kids in your party past it.

La Casita de Kaleidoscopes (✉*Poco A Poco Patio, 326–D San Felipe St. NW, Old Town* ☎*505/247–4242*) carries both contemporary and vintage kaleidoscopes of all styles, by more than 80 top artists in the field.

Theobroma Chocolatier (✉*12611 Montgomery Blvd. NE, Far Northeast Heights* ☎*505/293–6545*) carries beautiful, handcrafted, high-quality chocolates, truffles, and candies (most of them made on premises), as well as Taos Cow ice cream.

HISPANIC IMPORTS & TRADITIONS

An Old Town stalwart since the late 1970s, **Casa Talavera** (✉*621 Rio Grande Blvd., Old Town* ☎*505/243–2413* ⊕*www.casatalavera.com*) is just outside the Plaza area, across Rio Grande Boulevard. Do go peruse the wide selection of hand-painted Mexican Talavera tiles. Prices are reasonable, making the colorful geometrics, florals, mural patterns, and solids, close to irresistible. Tin lighting fixtures as well as ceramic sink and cabinet knobs fill in the rest of the space in this DIY-inspiring shop (staff can hook you up with installation information, too).

Hispanaie (✉*410 Romero St. NW, Old Town* ☎*505/244–1533*) is like the Jackalope of yore, and then some. Sure it has every permutation of Our Lady of Guadalupe imaginable (on switch plates, tin tokens, etc.), but Nuestra Señora is just the tip of it. This long narrow space is packed with finds of the Latino craft kind, from inexpensive cake toppers in the shape of sweet little pigs to painted tin Christmas ornaments and hand-carved hardwood furnishings.

La Piñata (✉*No. 2 Patio Market, 206 San Felipe St. NW, Old Town* ☎*505/242–2400*) specializes in piñatas and papier-mâché products, plus Native American jewelry and leather goods.

Saints & Martyrs (✉*404 San Felipe NW, Old Town* ☎*505/224–9323* ⊕*www.saints-martyrs.com*) has almost a gallery feel. Its hand-painted retablos and other saintly images are displayed so well that it's easy to imagine how one might look in your house. This is an excellent place to lay in a supply of milagros; it carries a high-quality selection in sterling.

HOME FURNISHINGS

FodorśChoice
★
A (✉*3500 Central Ave. SE, Nob Hill* ☎*505/266–2222*) is a Nob Hill stop for housewares, soaps, candles, body-care products, and jewelry.

A branch of a popular regional chain, **El Paso Import Co.** (✉*3500 Central Ave. SE, Nob Hill* ☎*505/265–1160*) carries distressed and "peely-paint" antique-looking chests and tables loaded with character. If you love the shabby-chic look, head to this Nob Hill furniture shop.

Hey Jhonny (✉*3418 Central Ave. SE, Nob Hill* ☎*505/256–9244*) is an aromatic store full of exquisite candles, soaps, pillows, fountains, and other soothing items for the home; there's also a branch that carries more furniture and larger pieces around the corner, at 118 Tulane Street.

Objects of Desire (✉ *3225 Central Ave. NE, Nob Hill* ☎ *505/232–3088*) is the place to find that special lamp or table from a whimsical and worldly collection of furnishings.

Peacecraft (✉ *3215 Central Ave. NE, Nob Hill* ☎ *505/255–5229*) supports fair trade and stocks handmade folk art and crafts from around the world—wooden boxes from Kenya, clothing from Guatemala, hats from Honduras. The store employs university students in work-study programs.

MUSIC

Natural Sound (✉ *3422 Central Ave. SE, Nob Hill* ☎ *505/255–8295*) is an eclectic record store with a large selection of new and used CDs.

NATIVE AMERICAN ARTS & CRAFTS

Andrews Pueblo Pottery (✉ *303 Romero St. NW, Suite 116, Old Town* ☎ *505/243–0414*) carries a terrific selection of Pueblo pottery, fetishes, kachina dolls, and baskets for the beginning and seasoned collector.

Bien Mur Indian Market Center (✉ *Tramway Rd. NE east of I–25, Northeast Heights* ☎ *505/821–5400 or 800/365–5400*) in Sandia Pueblo showcases the best of the best in regional Native American rugs, jewelry, and crafts of all kinds. You can feel very secure about what you purchase at this trading post, and prices are fair.

Gertrude Zachary (✉ *1501 Lomas Blvd. NW, Old Town* ☎ *505/247–4442* ✉ *3300 Central Ave. SE, Nob Hill* ☎ *505/766–4700* ✉ *416 2nd St. SW, Downtown* ☎ *505/244–1320*) dazzles with its selection of Native American jewelry. Don't let the screaming billboards around town deter you—this may be the best place to get a bargain on a good bracelet or ring. Locals buy here, too. The 2nd Street branch carries antiques.

To understand what it takes to make Native American jewelry (or if you want to learn the craft yourself), a stop at the fascinating **Indian Jewelers Supply** (✉ *2105 San Mateo Blvd. NE, 1 block south of Indian School Rd. NE, at Haines Ave. NE, Uptown* ☎ *505/265–3701* ⊕ *www.ijsinc. com*) is a must. Trays of gemstones (finished and not), silver sold by weight, findings, and the tools to work them with, fill this large space. It's open 8 to 6—go midmorning to avoid the early rush.

★ **Margaret Moses Gallery** (✉ *326 San Felipe St. NW, Old Town* ☎ *505/842–1808 or 888/842–1808*) stocks Pueblo pottery, including the black earthenware pottery of San Ildefonso, as well as the work of potters from Acoma, Santa Clara, Isleta, and Zía. Rare Zuni and Navajo jewelry is on display, as are Navajo weavings from 1900 to the present.

Santa Fe

WORD OF MOUTH

"Santa Fe is one of my all time favorite cities to visit. We've enjoyed the food at Tia Sophia's on San Francisco Street just off the Plaza, Geronimo (expensive), and Santacafe (excellent with outdoor dining if you like). If you enjoy al fresco dining, go to La Posada Hotel...and check out their restaurant Fuego in the lovely courtyard. Bliss!"

–schoolmarm

Updated by
Georgia de
Katona

WITH ITS CRISP, CLEAR AIR and bright, sunny weather, Santa Fe couldn't be more welcoming or more unique. On a plateau at the base of the Sangre de Cristo Mountains—at an elevation of 7,000 feet—the city is brimming with reminders of nearly four centuries of Spanish and Mexican rule, and of the Pueblo cultures that have been here for hundreds more. The town's placid central Plaza, which dates from the early 17th century, has been the site of bullfights, public floggings, gunfights, political rallies, promenades, and public markets over the years. A one-of-a-kind destination, Santa Fe is fabled for its rows of chic art galleries, superb restaurants, and diverse shops selling everything from Southwestern furnishings and cowboy gear, to Tibetan textiles and Moroccan jewelry.

La Villa Real de la Santa Fe de San Francisco de Asísi (the Royal City of the Holy Faith of St. Francis of Assisi) was founded in the early 1600s by Don Pedro de Peralta, who planted his banner in the name of Spain. After years of oppression, the region's Pueblo people rose in revolt in 1680, burning homes and churches and killing hundreds of Spaniards. After an extended siege in Santa Fe, the Spanish colonists were driven out of New Mexico. The tide turned 12 years later, when General Don Diego de Vargas returned with a new army from El Paso and recaptured Santa Fe. To commemorate de Vargas's recapture of the town in 1692, Las Fiestas de Santa Fe have been held annually since 1712. The nation's oldest community celebration takes place on the weekend after Labor Day, with parades, mariachi bands, pageants, and the burning of *Zozóbra*—a must-see extravaganza held in Fort Marcy Park just blocks north of the Plaza.

Following de Vargas's defeat of the Pueblos, the then-grand Camino Real (Royal Road), stretching from Mexico City to Santa Fe, brought an army of conquistadors, clergymen, and settlers to the northernmost reaches of Spain's New World conquests. In 1820 the Santa Fe Trail—a prime artery of U.S. westward expansion—spilled a flood of covered wagons from Missouri onto the Plaza. A booming trade with the United States was born. After Mexico achieved independence from Spain in 1821, its subsequent rule of New Mexico further increased this commerce.

The Santa Fe Trail's heyday ended with the arrival of the Atchison, Topeka & Santa Fe Railway in 1880. The trains, and later the nation's first highways, brought a new type of settler to Santa Fe—artists who fell in love with its cultural diversity, history, and magical color and light. They were especially drawn to the area because eccentricity was embraced not discouraged, as it often was in the social confines of the East Coast. Their presence attracted tourists, who quickly became a primary source of income for the proud, but largely poor populace.

Santa Fe is renowned for its arts, vibrant tricultural (Native American, Hispanic, and Anglo) heritage, and adobe architecture. The Pueblo people built their homes using a "puddled-mud" method (liquid mud poured between upright wooden frames), which melded well with the adobe brick construction introduced to the Spanish by the Moors. The Hispanic culture, still deeply rooted in its ancient ties to Spain and Catholicism,

TOP EXPERIENCES

■ **A winter stroll on Canyon Road.** There are few experiences to match walking this ancient street when it's covered with snow, scented by piñon fires burning in luminarias along the road, and echoing with the voices of carolers and happy families. It's particularly magical on Christmas Eve.

■ **A culinary adventure.** Start with rellenos for breakfast and try tapas for dinner. Enjoy some strawberry habañero gelato or sip an Aztec Warrior Chocolate Elixir. Take a cooking lesson. Try things you've never heard of and won't find anywhere else.

■ **Into the Wild.** Follow the lead of locals and take any one of the many easy access points into the incredible, and surprisingly lush, mountains that rise out of Santa Fe. Raft the Rio Grande, snowboard, snowshoe, or try mountain biking.

■ **Market Mashup.** Summer offers the phenomenal International Folk Art Market, the famed Indian Market, and the two-for-one weekend of Traditional Spanish Market and Contemporary Hispanic Market. The offerings are breathtaking and the community involvement yet another aspect of Santa Fe to fall in love with.

remains a strong influence on the easier pace of this city. Cosmopolitan visitors from around the world are consistently surprised by the city's rich and varied cultural offerings despite its relatively small size. Often referred to as the "City Different," Santa Fe became the first American city to be designated a UNESCO Creative City, acknowledging its place in the global community as a leader in art, crafts, design, and lifestyle.

ORIENTATION & PLANNING

GETTING ORIENTED

Humorist Will Rogers said on his first visit to Santa Fe, "Whoever designed this town did so while riding on a jackass, backwards, and drunk." The maze of narrow streets and alleyways confounds motorists, but with shops and restaurants, a flowered courtyard, or an eye-catching gallery at nearly every turn, it's a delight for pedestrians. By all means, park your car, grab a map, and explore the town on foot.

Interstate 25 cuts just south of Santa Fe, which is 62 mi northeast of Albuquerque. U.S. 285/84 runs north–south through the city. The NM 599 bypass, also called the Santa Fe Relief Route, cuts around the city from Interstate 25's Exit 276, southwest of the city, to U.S. 285/84, north of the city; it's a great shortcut if you're heading from Albuquerque to Española, Abiquiu, Taos, or other points north of Santa Fe. The modest flow of water called the Santa Fe River runs west, parallel to Alameda Street, from the Sangre de Cristo Mountains to the open prairie southwest of town, where it disappears into a narrow canyon before joining the Rio Grande. There's a *dicho*, or saying, in New Mexico: "*agua es vida*"—water is life—and every little trickle counts.

Santa Fe Plaza. The heart of historic Santa Fe, the Plaza has been the site of a bullring, fiestas, and fandangos. Despite the buildup of tourist shops, the Plaza retains its old-world feel and is still the center of many annual festivities and much of the town's activity.

Canyon Road. One of the city's oldest streets, Canyon Road is lined with galleries, shops, and restaurants housed in adobe compounds, with thick walls, and lush courtyard gardens. The architectural influence of Old Mexico and Spain, and the indigenous Pueblo cultures, makes this street as historic as it is artistic.

Lower Old Santa Fe Trail. In the 1800s wagon trains from Missouri rolled into town from the Old Santa Fe Trail, opening trade into what had been a very insular Spanish colony and forever changing Santa Fe's destiny. This street joins the Plaza on the south side after passing the state capitol and some of the area's oldest neighborhoods.

Upper Old Santa Fe Trail & Museum Hill. What used to be the outskirts of town became the site of gracious, neo-Pueblo style homes in the mid-20th century, many of them designed by the famed architect John Gaw Meem. Old Santa Fe Trail takes you to Camino Lejo, aka Museum Hill, where you'll find four excellent museums and a café.

Guadalupe District. Also known as the Railyard, this bustling area has undergone a major transformation in the last decade. The brand-new Railyard Park is a model for urban green space and houses the vibrant Farmers' Market. The redevelopment along Guadalupe Street has added dozens of shops, galleries, and restaurants to the town's already rich assortment.

SANTA FE PLANNER

WHEN TO GO

The city's population, an estimated 70,000, swells to nearly double that figure in summer. In winter the skiers arrive, lured by the challenging slopes and fluffy, powdery snow of Ski Santa Fe and Taos Ski Valley (⇨ *Chapter 4*). Prices are highest June–August. Between September and November and in April and May they're lower, and (except for the major holidays) from December to March they're the lowest. Santa Fe has four distinct seasons, though the sun shines nearly every day of the year. June through August temperatures are high 80s to low 90s during the day, 50s at night, with afternoon rain showers—monsoons—cooling the air. During this season it's advisable to keep a lightweight, waterproof jacket with you. The monsoons come suddenly and can quickly drench you. September and October bring beautiful weather and a marked reduction in crowds. Temperatures, and prices, drop significantly after Halloween. December through March is ski season. Spring comes late at this elevation. April and May are blustery, with daily warm weather (70s and above) finally arriving in May. ■TIP→ **The high elevation here catches people unawares and altitude sickness can utterly ruin a day of fun. Drink water, drink more water, and then have a little more.**

GETTING HERE & AROUND

BY AIR — Among the smallest state capitals in the country, Santa Fe has no major airport (Albuquerque's is the nearest, about an hour away). Tiny Santa Fe Municipal Airport offers limited services, although there's some talk of expanding the facility and its runways to help lure additional airlines. The airport is 9 mi southwest of downtown.

BY BUS — The city's bus system, Santa Fe Trails, covers 10 major routes through town and is useful for getting from the Plaza to some of the outlying attractions. Route M is most useful for visitors, as it runs from downtown to the museums on Old Santa Fe Trail south of town, and Route 2 is useful if you're staying at one of the motels out on Cerrillos Road and need to get into town (if time is a factor for your visit, a car is a much more practical way to get around). Individual rides cost $1, and a daily pass costs $2. Buses run about every 30 minutes on weekdays, every hour on weekends. Service begins at 6 AM and continues until 11 PM on weekdays, 8–8 on Saturday, and 10–7 (limited routes) on Sunday.

> ### PEDICABS
>
> **Santa Fe Pedicabs** offer a great alternative to getting around the heart of town, especially if your restaurant is a ways from your hotel. Friendly drivers can regale you with all sorts of information and trivia about Santa Fe as the whisk you along in bicycle carriages. Sit back and enjoy watching the crowds and the sights go by. ⊠ *Santa Fe Plaza, Canyon Rd., Guadalupe District* ☎ *505/577–5056* ⊕ *www.santafepedicabs.com.*

BY CAR — Santa Fe is served by several national rental car agencies, including Avis, Budget, and Hertz. Additional agencies with locations in Santa Fe include Advantage, Classy Car Rentals (which specializes in luxury and sports vehicles), Enterprise, Sears, and Thrifty. *See Car Rental in New Mexico Essentials for national rental agency phone numbers.*

BY TAXI — Capital City Cab Company controls all the cabs in Santa Fe. The taxis aren't metered; you pay a flat fee based on how far you're going, usually $6–$10 within the downtown area. There are no cab stands; you must phone to arrange a ride.

BY TRAIN — Amtrak's *Southwest Chief* stops in Lamy, a short drive south of Santa Fe, on its route from Chicago to Los Angeles via Kansas City; other New Mexico stops include Raton, Las Vegas, Albuquerque, and Gallup daily. In summer 2006, the City of Albuquerque launched the state's first-ever commuter train line, the *New Mexico Rail Runner Express.* As of this writing, service is from Bernalillo south through the city of Albuquerque, continuing south through Los Lunas to the suburb of Belén, covering a distance of about 50 mi. The second and final phase of the project, expected to be completed by late 2008, will extend the service north to Santa Fe.

ESSENTIALS — **Air Contacts Santa Fe Municipal Airport (SAF)** (⊠ *Airport Rd. and NM 599* ☎ *505/473–4118*). **Albuquerque International Sunport** (☎ *505/244–7700* ⊕ *www.cabq.gov/airport*).

Bus Contacts Greyhound/Texas, New Mexico & Oklahoma Coaches

(☎ *505/243–4435 or 800/231–2222* ⊕ *www.greyhound.com*). **Santa Fe Trails** (☎ *505/955–2001* ⊕ *www.santafenm.gov*).

Car Rental Contacts **Advantage** (☎ *505/983–9470*). **Enterprise** (☎ *505/473–3600*). **Sears** (☎ *505/984–8038*). **Thrifty** (☎ *505/474–3365 or 800/367–2277*).

Taxi Contacts **Capital City Cab** (☎ *505/438–0000*).

Train Contacts **Amtrak** (☎ *800/872–7245* ⊕ *www.amtrak.com*). **New Mexico Rail Runner Express** (☎ *505/245–7245* ⊕ *www.nmrailrunner.com*).

VISITOR
INFORMATION

New Mexico Department of Tourism visitor center (✉ *Lamy Bldg., 491 Old Santa Fe Trail* ☎ *505/827–7400 or 800/733–6396 Ext. 0643* ⊕ *www.newmexico. org*). **Santa Fe Convention and Visitors Bureau** (✉ *201 W. Marcy St., Box 909* ☎ *505/955–6200 or 800/777–2489* ⊕ *www.santafe.org*).

TOUR INFORMATION

GENERAL
INTEREST

Aboot About has been walking groups through the history, art, and architecture of Santa Fe since the late 1970s. Tours leave daily at 9:45 and 1:45 from the Hotel St. Francis, and Saturday and Monday at 9:45 from La Posada Resort. Tours take about two hours; no reservations are required. The Ghost Tours happen Friday, Saturday, and Monday at 5:30 PM, but reservations are required. The company offers a variety of additional tours on everything from Georgia O'Keeffe Country to local culinary rambles. **Great Southwest Adventures** conducts guided tours in 7- to 35-passenger van and bus excursions to Bandelier, O'Keeffe country, the High Road & Taos, and elsewhere in the region. **Santa Fe Detours** offers a more limited selection of tours, by reservation only. **Custom Tours by Clarice** are guided open-air tram excursions that run five times a day from the corner of Lincoln Avenue and West Palace Avenue. These 90-minute tours offer a nice overview of downtown; the company also gives bus and shuttle tours of Bandelier and Taos, and shuttle services from town to the Santa Fe Opera.

Rojo Tours designs specialized trips—to view wildflowers, pueblo ruins and cliff dwellings, galleries and studios, Native American arts and crafts, and private homes—as well as adventure activity tours. **Santa Fe Guides** is an organization of about 15 respected independent tour guides—its Web site lists each member and his or her specialties.

Information **Aboot About** (☎ *505/988–2774 or 866/614–8404* ⊕ *www. abootabout.com*). **Custom Tours By Clarice** (☎ *505/438–7116* ⊕ *www.santa fecustomtours.com*). **Great Southwest Adventures** (☎ *505/455–2700* ⊕ *www. swadventures.com*). **Rojo Tours** (☎ *505/474–8333* ⊕ *www.rojotours.com*). **Santa Fe Detours** (☎ *505/983–6565 or 800/338–6877* ⊕ *www.sfdetours.com*). **Santa Fe Guides** (☎ *505/466–4877* ⊕ *www.santafeguides.org*).

LEARNING
EXPERIENCES

Art Adventures in the Southwest takes you into the New Mexico landscape for outdoor art classes with Jane Shoenfeld. All materials are supplied, and all experience levels are welcome. **Bohemian Jet Set** offers custom-tailored tours for people wanting a more in-depth experience of Santa Fe and northern New Mexico. It offers an insider's connection to the town as well as engaging, entertaining, and intellectual tours that bring the influences in this fascinating region into perspective. This is the haute couture of tours. They're expensive but designed just for you. ☎ *505/982–2836* ⊕ *www.bohemianjetset.com.*

Santa Fe Art Institute is housed in the Visual Arts Center designed by Mexican architect Ricardo Legorreta (a modernist break from Santa Fe style). The institute (not part of the College of Santa Fe) offers week-long workshops that have been led by such renowned artists as Phoebe Adams and Richard Diebenkorn. Dormitory quarters are available and studio space is provided. Workshops are offered year-round.

Santa Fe Photographic Workshops offers workshops in photographic processes, including digital imaging, platinum, and travel photography. The workshops have an excellent reputation, and many instructors return year after year.

Information **Art Adventures in the Southwest** (☎ *505/986–1108* ⊕ *www. skyfields.net*). **Bohemian Jet Set** (☎ *505/982–2836* ⊕ *www.bohemianjetset. com*).**Santa Fe Art Institute** (✉ *1600 St. Michael's Dr., College of Santa Fe campus* ☎ *505/424–5050* ⊕ *www.sfai.org*). **Santa Fe Photographic Workshops** (☎ *505/983–1400* ⊕ *www.sfworkshop.com*).

PLANNING YOUR TIME

To make the most of your time it's helpful to think of Santa Fe in zones and to arrange your activities within each. If you've got more than a day or two, be sure to explore the northern Rio Grande Valley. For the best tour, combine your adventures in Santa Fe with some from the Side Trips chapter (⇨ *Chapter 5*), which highlights several trips within a 60- to 90-minute drive of town. Your experience of Santa Fe will gain even more depth once you've gotten out of town to absorb the land and cultures that surround the city.

Plan on spending a full day wandering around downtown Santa Fe, strolling down narrow streets, under *portals*, and across ancient cobbled streets. Sip coffee on the Plaza, take in a museum or two (or three) and marvel at the cathedral. **The New Mexico History Museum** and **Palace of the Governors** are great places to start to gain a sense of the history and cultures influencing this area. ■TIP➔**Take one of the docent-led tours offered by the museums.** Almost without exception the docents are engaging and passionate about their subjects. You gain invaluable insight into the collections and their context by taking these free tours. Inquire at the front desk of the museums for more information.

On a stretch called Museum Hill you'll find four world-class museums, all quite different and all highly relevant to the culture of Santa Fe and northern New Mexico. Start at the intimate gem, the **Museum of Spanish Colonial Art**, where you'll gain a real sense of the Spanish empire's influence on the world beyond Spain. **The Museum of International Folk Art** is thoroughly engaging for both young and old. If you have the stamina to keep going, have lunch at the tasty Museum Café and then visit the **Museum of Indian Arts and Culture** and then move on to the **Wheelwright Museum of the American Indian.** There is a path linking all of these museums together and the walk is easy. The museum shops at these four museums are outstanding—if you're a shopper you could easily spend an entire day in the shops alone.

An easy walk from any of the downtown lodgings, Canyon Road should definitely be explored on foot. Take any of the side streets and stroll amongst historical homes and ancient *acequias* (irrigation ditches). If you really enjoy walking, keep going up Canyon Road past Cristo Rey Church, where the street gets even narrower and is lined with residential compounds. At the top is the **Randal Davey Audubon Center**, where bird-watching abounds.

Another enjoyable day can be spent exploring the hip Guadalupe District, which is bursting with energy and development from the new Railyard Park and the various businesses surrounding it. **The Santuario de Guadalupe** is a great place to start. Head south from there and enjoy shops, cafés, art galleries, the farmers' market, and the fun new Railyard Park. If you enjoy ceramics, don't miss a stop at **Santa Fe Clay**, an amazing gallery, supply store, and studio where dozens of artists are busy at work. The venerable **SITE Santa Fe** is also here, with its cutting-edge modern art installations.

There are more galleries and shops in downtown Santa Fe than can be handled in one day. If you've got the time, or if you don't want to spend hours in multiple museums, take a look at our shopping recommendations (⇨ *Shopping below*) and go from there.

EXPLORING SANTA FE

Five Santa Fe museums participate in the Museum of New Mexico pass (four state museums and the privately run Museum of Spanish Colonial Art) and it is by far the most economical way to visit them all. The four-day pass costs $18 and is sold at all five of the museums, which include the New Mexico History Museum/Palace of the Governors, Museum of Fine Arts, Museum of Indian Arts and Culture, Museum of International Folk Art, and Museum of Spanish Colonial Art.

SANTA FE PLAZA

Much of the history of Santa Fe, New Mexico, the Southwest, and even the West has some association with Santa Fe's central Plaza, which New Mexico governor Don Pedro de Peralta laid out in 1607. The Plaza, already well established by the time of the Pueblo revolt in 1680, was the site of a bullring and of fiestas and fandangos. Freight wagons unloaded here after completing their arduous journey across the Santa Fe Trail. The American flag was raised over the Plaza in 1846, during the Mexican War, which resulted in Mexico's loss of all its territories in the present southwestern United States. For a time the Plaza was a tree-shaded park with a white picket fence. In the 1890s it was an expanse of lawn where uniformed bands played in an ornate gazebo. Particularly festive times on the Plaza are the weekend after Labor Day, during Las Fiestas de Santa Fe, and at Christmas, when all the trees are filled with lights and rooftops are outlined with *farolitos,* votive candles lit within paper-bag lanterns.

Numbers in the margin correspond to the Downtown Santa Fe map.

WHAT TO SEE

3 **Georgia O'Keeffe Museum.** One of many East Coast artists who visited
★ New Mexico in the first half of the 20th century, O'Keeffe returned to
live and paint here, eventually emerging as the demigoddess of Southwestern art. O'Keeffe's innovative view of the landscape is captured in
From the Plains, inspired by her memory of the Texas plains, and *Jim-
son Weed,* a study of one of her favorite plants. Special exhibitions with
O'Keeffe's modernist peers are on view throughout the year—many of
these are exceptional, sometimes even more interesting than the permanent collection. ⊠*217 Johnson St.* ☎*505/946–1000* ⊕*www.okeeffe
museum.org* ⊠*$8, free Fri. 5–8 PM* ☉*Sat.–Thurs. 10–5, Fri. 10–8.*

4 **Institute of American Indian Arts (IAIA).** Containing the largest collection
of contemporary Native American art in the United States, this museum's paintings, photography, sculptures, prints, and traditional crafts
were created by past and present students and teachers. The school was
founded as a one-room studio classroom in the early 1930s by Dorothy Dunn, a beloved art teacher who played a critical role in launching
the careers of many Native American artists. In the 1960s and 1970s it
blossomed into the nation's premier center for Native American arts and
its alumni represent almost 600 tribes around the country. Artist Fritz
Scholder taught here, as did sculptor Allan Houser. Among their disciples
was the painter T.C. Cannon. The gift shop is good enough to warrant a
visit all on its own. ⊠*108 Cathedral Pl.* ☎*505/983–1777* ⊕*www.iaia.
edu* ⊠*$5 (under 16 yrs old free)* ☉*Mon.–Sat. 10–5, Sun. noon–5.*

5 **La Fonda.** A *fonda* (inn) has stood on this site, southeast of the Plaza,
for centuries. Architect Isaac Hamilton Rapp, who put Santa Fe style
on the map, built this area landmark in 1922. Remodeled in 1926 by
architect John Gaw Meem, the hotel was sold to the Santa Fe Railway
in 1926 and remained a Harvey House hotel until 1968. Because of its
proximity to the Plaza and its history as a gathering place for everyone
from cowboys to movie stars (Errol Flynn stayed here), it's referred to
as "The Inn at the End of the Trail." Major social events still take place
here. Have a drink at the fifth-floor Bell Tower Bar (open late spring–
early fall), which offers tremendous sunset views. ⊠*E. San Francisco
St. at Old Santa Fe Trail* ☎*505/982–5511.*

**NEED A
BREAK?** **Ecco Gelato** (⊠*105 E. Marcy St.* ☎*505/986–9778)* is a clean, contemporary
café across from the downtown public library with large plate-glass windows, and brushed-metal tables inside and out on the sidewalk under the
portal. Try the delicious and creative gelato flavors (strawberry-habañero,
saffron-honey, minty white grape, chocolate-banana) or some of the espres-
sos and coffees, pastries, and sandwiches (roast beef and blue cheese, tuna
with dill, cucumber, and sprouts).

1 **The New Mexico History Museum.** The new museum is the anchor of a cam-
☺ pus that encompasses the Palace of the Governors, the Palace Press, the
Fodor's Choice Fray Angélico Chávez History Library, and Photo Archives (an assem-
★ blage of more than 750,000 images dating from the 1850s). Located

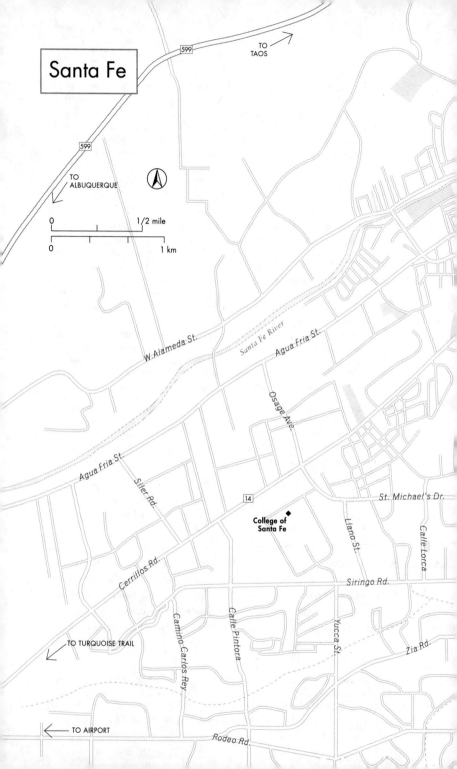

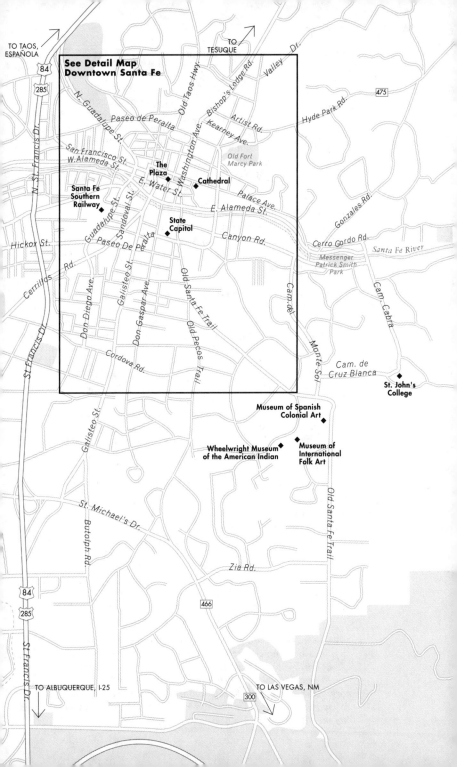

behind the Palace on Lincoln Avenue, the museum thoroughly encompasses the early history of indigenous people, Spanish colonization, the Mexican Period, and travel and commerce on the legendary Santa Fe Trail. Opened in May 2009, the museum has permanent and changing exhibits, such as "Jewish Pioneers of New Mexico," which explores the vital role Jewish immigrants played during the late 19th and early 20th centuries in the state's civic, economic, and cultural development. With advance permission, students and researchers have access to the comprehensive **Fray Angélico Chávez Library** and its rare maps, manuscripts, and photographs (more than 120,000 prints and negatives). The **Museum of New Mexico Press**, which prints books, pamphlets, and cards on antique presses, also hosts bookbinding demonstrations, lectures, and slide shows. The **Palace of the Governors** is a humble one-story neo-Pueblo adobe on the north side of the Plaza, and is the oldest public building in the United States. Its rooms contain period furnishings and exhibits illustrating the building's many functions over the past four centuries. Built at the same time as the Plaza, circa 1610 (scholars debate the exact year), it was the seat of four regional governments—those of Spain, Mexico, the Confederacy, and the U.S. territory that preceded New Mexico's statehood, which was achieved in 1912. The building was abandoned in 1680, following the Pueblo Revolt, but resumed its role as government headquarters when Don Diego de Vargas successfully returned in 1692. It served as the residence for 100 Spanish, Mexican, and American governors, including Governor Lew Wallace, who wrote his epic *Ben Hur* in its then drafty rooms, all the while complaining of the dust and mud that fell from its earthen ceiling.

> **FLAME ON!**
>
> Every weekend after Labor Day thousands gather to watch a groaning, flailing, 50-foot bogey-man-puppet known as Zozóbra go up in flames amidst an incredible display of fireworks—taking troubles of the past year with him. Wildly pagan and utterly Santa Fe.

Dozens of Native American vendors gather daily under the portal of the Palace of the Governors to display and sell pottery, jewelry, bread, and other goods. With few exceptions, the more than 500 artists and craftspeople registered to sell here are Pueblo or Navajo Indians. The merchandise for sale is required to meet strict standards: all items are handmade or hand-strung in Native American households; silver jewelry is either sterling (92.5% pure) or coin (90% pure) silver; all metal jewelry bears the maker's mark, which is registered with the Museum of New Mexico. Prices tend to reflect the high quality of the merchandise but are often significantly less that what you'd pay in a shop. Please remember not to take photographs without permission.

There's an outstanding gift shop and bookstore with many high-quality, locally produced items and books from local authors. ⊠*Palace Ave., north side of Plaza, Lincoln Ave., west of the Palace* ☎*505/476–5100* ⊕*www.palaceofthegovernors.org or www.nmhistorymuseum.org* ⊠*$8, 4-day pass $18 (good at all 4 state museums and Museum of Spanish Colonial Art in Santa Fe), free Fri. 5–8* ☉*Tues.–Thurs. and weekends 10–5, Fri. 10–8.*

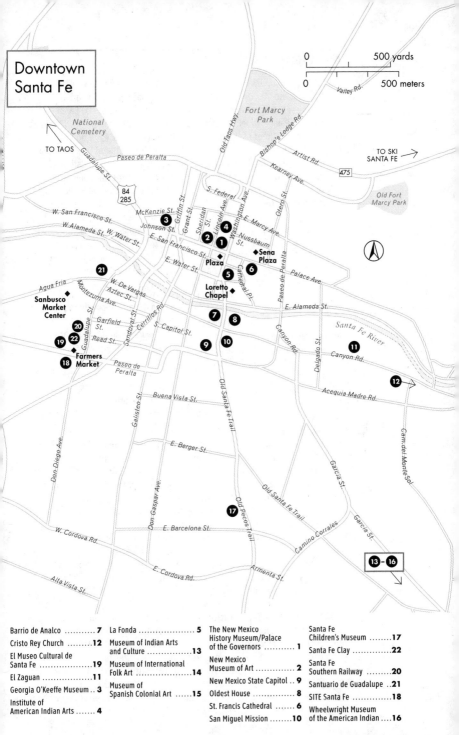

Downtown Santa Fe

A GOOD WALK

To get started, drop by the information booth at the Plaza's northwest corner, across the street from the clock, where Palace Street meets Lincoln Street (in front of the bank) to pick up a free map. From there, begin your walk around the Plaza. You can get an overview of the history of Santa Fe and New Mexico at the **Palace of the Governors** in the just-opened New Mexico History Museum campus ❶, which borders the northern side of the Plaza on Palace Avenue. Outside, under the palace portal, dozens of Native American artisans sell handcrafted wares. From the Palace, cross Lincoln Street to the **New Mexico Museum of Art** ❷, where the works of regional masters are on display. The **Georgia O'Keeffe Museum** ❸, on nearby Johnson Street, exhibits the works of its namesake, New Mexico's best-known painter.

From the O'Keeffe Museum, return to the Plaza and cut across to its southeast corner to Old Santa Fe Trail, where you can find the town's oldest hotel, **La Fonda** ❺, a good place to soak up a little of bygone Santa Fe. One block east on Cathedral Place looms the imposing facade of **St. Francis Cathedral Basilica** ❻. Across from the cathedral is the **Institute of American Indian Arts** ❹, with its wonderful museum. A stone's throw from the museum is cool, quiet Sena Plaza, accessible through two doorways on Palace Avenue.

TIMING

It's possible to zoom through this compact area in about five hours—two hours exploring the Plaza and the Palace of the Governors, two hours seeing the Museum of Fine Arts and the Museum of the Institute of American Indian Arts, and an hour visiting the other sites.

❷ **New Mexico Museum of Art** (*Museum of Fine Arts*). Designed by Isaac Hamilton Rapp in 1917, the museum contains one of America's finest regional collections. It's also one of Santa Fe's earliest Pueblo Revival structures, inspired by the adobe structures at Acoma Pueblo. Split-cedar *latillas* (branches set in a crosshatch pattern) and hand-hewn vigas form the ceilings. The 8,000-piece permanent collection, of which only a fraction is exhibited at any given time, emphasizes the work of regional and nationally renowned artists, including the early modernist Georgia O'Keeffe; realist Robert Henri; the "Cinco Pintores" (five painters) of Santa Fe (including Fremont Elis and Will Shuster, the creative mind behind Zozobra); members of the Taos Society of Artists (Ernest L. Blumenschein, Bert G. Philips, Joseph H. Sharp, and E. Irving Couse, among others); and the works of noted 20th-century photographers of the Southwest, including Laura Gilpin, Ansel Adams, and Dorothea Lange. Rotating exhibits are staged throughout the year. Many excellent examples of Spanish colonial–style furniture are on display. An interior *placita* (small plaza) with fountains, WPA murals, and sculpture, and the St. Francis Auditorium are other highlights. Concerts and lectures are often held in the auditorium. ⊠ *107 W. Palace Ave.* ☎ *505/476–5072* ⊕ *www.mfasantafe.org* ⊠ *$8, 4-day pass $18 (good at 4 state museums and the Museum of Spanish Colonial Art in Santa Fe), free Fri. 5–8 PM* ☉ *Tues.–Thurs. and weekends 10–5, Fri. 10–8.*

❻ St. Francis Cathedral Basilica. This magnificent cathedral, a block east of
★ the Plaza, is one of the rare significant departures from the city's ubiquitous Pueblo architecture. Construction was begun in 1869 by Jean
Baptiste Lamy, Santa Fe's first archbishop, working with French architects and Italian stonemasons. The Romanesque style was popular in
Lamy's native home in southwest France. The circuit-riding cleric was
sent by the Catholic Church to the Southwest to change the religious
practices of its native population (to "civilize" them, as one period document puts it) and is buried in the crypt beneath the church's high altar.
He was the inspiration behind Willa Cather's novel *Death Comes for
the Archbishop* (1927). In 2005 Pope Benedict XVI declared St. Francis the "cradle of Catholicism" in the Southwestern United States, and
upgraded the status of the building from mere cathedral to cathedral
basilica—it's one of just 36 in the country.

A small adobe chapel on the northeast side of the cathedral, the remnant of an earlier church, embodies the Hispanic architectural influence
so conspicuously absent from the cathedral itself. The chapel's *Nuestra
Señora de la Paz* (Our Lady of Peace), popularly known as *La Conquis-
tadora,* the oldest Madonna statue in the United States, accompanied
Don Diego de Vargas on his reconquest of Santa Fe in 1692, a feat
attributed to the statue's spiritual intervention. Take a close look at the
keystone in the main doorway arch: it has a Hebrew tetragram on it.
Bishop Lamy had this carved and placed to honor the Jewish merchants
of Santa Fe who helped provide necessary funds for the construction of
the church. Every Friday the faithful adorn the statue with a new dress.
Just south of the cathedral, where the parking lot meets Paseo de Peralta,
is the **Archdiocese of Santa Fe Museum** (☎*505/983–3811*), a small museum
where many of the area's historic, liturgical artifacts are on view. ⊠*231
Cathedral Pl. ☎505/982–5619 ⊙Mon.–Sat. 6–6, Sun. 7–7, except during mass. Mass Mon.–Sat. at 7* AM *and 5:15* PM; *Sun. at 8 and 10* AM,
noon, and 7 PM. *Museum weekdays 8:30–4:30.*

Sena Plaza. Two-story buildings enclose this courtyard, which can be
entered only through two small doorways on Palace Avenue. Surrounding the oasis of flowering fruit trees, a fountain, and inviting benches are
unique, locally owned shops. The quiet courtyard is a good place for
repose. The buildings, erected in the 1700s as a single-family residence,
had quarters for blacksmiths, bakers, farmers, and all manner of help.
⊠*125 E. Palace Ave .*

CANYON ROAD

Once a trail used by indigenous people to access water and the lush forest above, and an early-20th-century route for woodcutters and their
burros, Canyon Road is now lined with art galleries, shops, and restaurants. The narrow road begins at the eastern curve of Paseo de Peralta
and stretches for about 2 mi at a moderate incline toward the base of
the mountains. Lower Canyon Road is where you'll find the galleries,
shops, and restaurants. Upper Canyon Road (above East Alameda) is
narrow and residential, with access to hiking and biking trails along the
way, and the Randall Davey Audubon Center at the very top.

CLOSE UP

New Mexico Art & Architecture: A Glossary of Terms

Perhaps more than any other region in the United States, New Mexico has its own distinctive cuisine and architectural style, both heavily influenced by Native American, Spanish-colonial, Mexican, and American frontier traditions. The brief glossary that follows explains terms used frequently in this book.

ART & ARCHITECTURE

Adobe: A brick of sun-dried earth and clay, usually stabilized with straw; a structure made of adobe.

Banco: A small bench, or banquette, often upholstered with handwoven textiles, that gracefully emerges from adobe walls.

Bulto: Folk-art figures of a santo (saint), usually carved from wood.

Camposanto: A graveyard.

Capilla: A chapel.

Casita: Literally "small house," this term is generally used to describe a separate guesthouse.

Cerquita: A spiked, wrought-iron, rectangular fence, often marking grave sites.

Coyote fence: A type of wooden fence that surrounds many New Mexico homes; it comprises branches, usually from cedar or aspen trees, arranged vertically and wired tightly together.

Farolito: Small votive candles set in paper-bag lanterns, farolitos are popular at Christmastime. The term is used in northern New Mexico only. People in Albuquerque and points south call the lanterns *luminarias,* which in the north is the term for the bonfires of Christmas Eve.

Heishi: Shell jewelry.

Hornos: Outdoor domed ovens.

Kiva: A ceremonial room, rounded and built at least partially underground, used by Native Americans of the Southwest. Entrance is gained from the roof.

Kiva fireplace: A corner fireplace whose round form resembles that of a kiva.

Nicho: A built-in shelf cut into an adobe or stucco wall.

Placita: A small plaza.

Portal: A porch or large covered area adjacent to a house.

Pueblo Revival (also informally called Pueblo-style): Most homes in this style, modeled after the traditional dwellings of the Southwest Pueblo Indians, are cube or rectangle shaped. Other characteristics are flat roofs, thick adobe or stucco walls, small windows, rounded corners, and viga beams.

Retablo: Holy image painted on wood or tin.

Santero: Maker of religious images.

Terrones adobes: Adobe cut from the ground rather than formed from mud.

Viga: Horizontal roof beam made of logs, usually protruding from the side of the house.

A GOOD WALK

Begin on Paseo de Peralta at the **Gerald Peters Gallery**, which has an enormous collection. Continue a half-block north to Canyon Road. Turn right (east) and follow the road, which unfolds in shadows of undulating adobe walls. Street parking is at a premium, but there's a city-owned pay lot at the corner of Camino del Monte Sol, a few blocks up. Between visits to galleries and shops, take a break at one of the courtyards or fine restaurants. Be sure to stop by the beautiful gardens outside **El Zaguan** ⓫. At the intersection of Upper Canyon and Cristo Rey you'll find the massive

Cristo Rey Church ⓬. Wear good walking shoes and watch out for the irregular sidewalks, which can get icy in winter.

TIMING

A tour of Canyon Road could take a whole day or as little as a few hours. If art is more than a curiosity to you, you may want to view the Gerald Peters Gallery apart from your Canyon Road tour. There's so much to see there that visual overload could hit before you get halfway up the road. Even on a cold day the walk is a pleasure, with massive, glistening icicles hanging off roofs and a silence shrouding the side streets.

Most establishments are in authentic, old adobe homes with thick, undulating walls that appear to have been carved out of the earth. Within those walls is art ranging from cutting-edge contemporary to traditional and even ancient works. Some artists are internationally renowned, like Fernando Botero, others' identities have been lost with time, like the weavers of magnificent Navajo rugs.

There are few places as festive as Canyon Road on Christmas Eve, when thousands of farolitos illuminate walkways, walls, roofs, and even trees. In May the scent of lilacs wafts over the adobe walls, and in August red hollyhocks enhance the surreal color of the blue sky on a dry summer day.

WHAT TO SEE

⓬ **Cristo Rey Church.** Built in 1940 and designed by legendary Santa Fe architect John Gaw Meem to commemorate the 400th anniversary of Francisco Vásquez de Coronado's exploration of the Southwest, this church is the largest Spanish adobe structure in the United States and is considered by many the finest example of Pueblo-style architecture anywhere. The church was constructed in the old-fashioned way by parishioners, who mixed the more than 200,000 mud-and-straw adobe bricks and hauled them into place. The 225-ton stone *reredos* (altar screen) is magnificent. ⊠*Canyon Rd. at Cristo Rey* ☎*505/983–8528* ☉*Daily 8–7.*

NEED A BREAK?

Kakawa (*1050 Paseo de Peralta, across the street from Gerald Peters Gallery* ☎*505/982–0388* ⊕*www.kakawachocolates.com*) is the place to go if chocolate, very good chocolate, is an essential part of your day. Proprietor Mark Sciscenti is a self-described chocolate historian and chocolate alchemist and you're unlikely to ever have tasted anything like the divine, agave-sweetened, artisanal creations that emerge from his kitchen. Historically accurate chocolate drinks, like the Aztec Warrior Chocolate Elixir, delicious coffees, and gluten-free chocolate baked goods are served in this cozy, welcoming shop that's as much a taste experience as an educational one.

⑪ **El Zaguan.** Headquarters of the **Historic Santa Fe Foundation (HSFF)**, this 19th-century Territorial-style house has a small exhibit on Santa Fe architecture and preservation, but the real draw is the small but stunning garden abundant with lavender, roses, and 160-year-old trees. You can relax on a wrought-iron bench and take in the fine views of the hills northeast of town. An HSFF horticulturist often gives free tours and lectures in the garden on Thursday at 1 in summer (call to confirm). Tours are available of many of the Foundation's properties on Mother's Day. ✉ *545 Canyon Rd.* ☎ *505/983–2567* ⊕ *www.historicsantafe.org* ✉ *Free* ⊙ *Foundation office weekdays 9–noon and 1:30–5; gardens Mon.–Sat. 9–5.*

Gerald Peters Gallery. While under construction, this 32,000-square-foot building was dubbed the "ninth northern pueblo," its scale rivaling that of the eight northern pueblos around Santa Fe. The suavely designed Pueblo-style gallery is Santa Fe's premier showcase for American and European art from the 19th century to the present. It feels like a museum, but all the works are for sale. Pablo Picasso, Georgia O'Keeffe, Charles M. Russell, Deborah Butterfield, George Rickey, and members of the Taos Society are among the artists represented, along with nationally renowned contemporary ones. ✉ *1011 Paseo de Peralta* ☎ *505/954–5700* ⊕ *www.gpgallery.com* ✉ *Free* ⊙ *Mon.–Sat. 10–5.*

NEED A BREAK?

Locals congregate in the courtyard or on the front portal of **Downtown Subscription** (✉ *376 Garcia St.87501* ☎ *505/983–3085*), a block east of Canyon Road. A great, friendly spot to people-watch, this café-newsstand sells coffees, snacks, and pastries, plus one of the largest assortments of newspapers and magazines in New Mexico. It has lovely outdoor spaces to sit and sip during warm weather. A delightful spot toward the end of gallery row on Canyon Road, right at the intersection with East Palace Avenue, the **Teahouse** (✉ *821 Canyon Rd.87501* ☎ *505/992–0972*) has several bright dining rooms throughout the converted adobe home, and a tranquil outdoor seating area in a rock garden. In addition to fine teas from all over the world, you can find extremely well-prepared breakfast and lunch fare. The service tends to be leisurely but friendly.

LOWER OLD SANTA FE TRAIL

It was along the Old Santa Fe Trail that wagon trains from Missouri rolled into town in the 1800s, forever changing Santa Fe's destiny. This street, off the south corner of the Plaza, is one of Santa Fe's most historic and is dotted with houses, shops, markets and the state capitol several blocks down.

A GOOD WALK

The **Loretto Chapel**, facing the Old Santa Fe Trail, behind the La Fonda hotel, is a good place to start your walk. After visiting the chapel, head southeast on Old Santa Fe Trail to the **San Miguel Mission** ➓. Across from the mission, on De Vargas Street, is the **Oldest House** ➑. Up and down narrow De Vargas stretches the **Barrio de Analco** ➐. Across Old Santa Fe Trail on the west side of De Vargas, check out the historic Santa Fe Playhouse. In the early art colony days, literary luminaries like Mary Austin and Wit-

ter Bynner would stage shows here. Walk farther away from downtown until you come to the **New Mexico State Capitol** ➒, with grounds showcasing some fantastic sculpture and interesting rotating art exhibits in the Governor's Gallery inside.

TIMING
Plan on spending half an hour at each of the churches and the New Mexico State Capitol and another half hour exploring the Barrio de Analco. The entire walk can be done in about two hours.

WHAT TO SEE

➐ **Barrio de Analco.** Along the south bank of the Santa Fe River, the barrio—its name means "district on the other side of the water"—is one of America's oldest neighborhoods, settled in the early 1600s by the Tlaxcalan Indians (who were forbidden to live with the Spanish near the Plaza) and in the 1690s by soldiers who had helped recapture New Mexico after the Pueblo Revolt. Plaques on houses on East De Vargas Street will help you locate some of the important structures. Check the performance schedule at the **Santa Fe Playhouse** on De Vargas Street, founded by writer Mary Austin and other Santa Feans in the 1920s.

Loretto Chapel. A delicate Gothic church modeled after Sainte-Chapelle in Paris, Loretto was built in 1873 by the same French architects and Italian stonemasons who built St. Francis Cathedral. The chapel is known for the "Miraculous Staircase" that leads to the choir loft. Legend has it that the chapel was almost complete when it became obvious that there wasn't room to build a staircase to the choir loft. In answer to the prayers of the cathedral's nuns, a mysterious carpenter arrived on a donkey, built a 20-foot staircase—using only a square, a saw, and a tub of water to season the wood—and then disappeared as quickly as he came. Many of the faithful believed it was St. Joseph himself. The staircase contains two complete 360-degree turns with no central support; no nails were used in its construction. The chapel closes for services and special events. Adjoining the chapel are a small museum and gift shop. ✉ *207 Old Santa Fe Trail* ☎ *505/982–0092* ⊕ *www.lorettochapel.com* 💵 *Donation suggested* ⊙ *Mon.–Sat. 9–6, Sun. 10:30–5.*

➒ **New Mexico State Capitol.** The symbol of the Zía Pueblo, which repre-
★ sents the Circle of Life, was the inspiration for the capitol, also known as the Roundhouse. Doorways at opposing sides of this 1966 structure symbolize the four winds, the four directions, and the four seasons. Throughout the building are artworks from the outstanding collection of the Capitol Art Foundation, historical and cultural displays, and

handcrafted furniture—it's a superb and somewhat overlooked array of fine art. The **Governor's Gallery** hosts temporary exhibits. Six acres of imaginatively landscaped gardens shelter outstanding sculptures. ⊠*Old Santa Fe Trail at Paseo de Peralta* ☎*505/986–4589* ⊕*www. newmexico.gov* ⊠*Free* ⊙ *Weekdays 7–6; tours weekdays by appt.*

⑧ The Oldest House. More than 800 years ago, Pueblo people built this structure out of "puddled" adobe (liquid mud poured between upright wooden frames). This house, which contains a gift shop, is said to be the oldest in the United States. ⊠*215 E. De Vargas St.*

⑩ San Miguel Mission. The oldest church still in use in the United States, this simple earth-hue adobe structure was built in the early 17th century by the Tlaxcalan Indians of Mexico, who came to New Mexico as servants of the Spanish. Badly damaged in the 1680 Pueblo Revolt, the structure was restored and enlarged in 1710. On display in the chapel are priceless statues and paintings and the San José Bell, weighing nearly 800 pounds, which is believed to have been cast in Spain in 1356. In winter the church sometimes closes before its official closing hour. Mass is held on Sunday at 5 PM. Next door in the back of the Territorial-style dormitories of the old St. Michael's High School, a **Visitor Information Center** can help you find your way around northern New Mexico. ⊠*401 Old Santa Fe Trail* ☎*505/983–3974* ⊠*$1* ⊙*Mission Mon.–Sat. 9–5, Sun. 9–4.*

FodorśChoice
★

UPPER OLD SANTA FE TRAIL & MUSEUM HILL

WHAT TO SEE

⑬ Museum of Indian Arts and Culture. An interactive, multimedia exhibition tells the story of Native American history in the Southwest, merging contemporary Native American experience with historical accounts and artifacts. The collection has some of New Mexico's oldest works of art: pottery vessels, fine stone and silver jewelry, intricate textiles, and other arts and crafts created by Pueblo, Navajo, and Apache artisans. Changing exhibitions feature arts and traditions of historic and contemporary Native Americans. You can also see art demonstrations and a video about the life and work of Pueblo potter Maria Martinez. ⊠*710 Camino Lejo* ☎*505/476–1250* ⊕*www.indianartsand culture.org* ⊠*$8, 4-day pass $18, good at all 4 state museums and the Museum of Spanish Colonial Art in Santa Fe* ⊙*Tues.–Sun. 10–5.*

★

⑭ Museum of International Folk Art (MOIFA). A delight for adults and children alike, this museum is the premier institution of its kind in the world. In the Girard Wing you'll find thousands of amazingly inventive handmade objects—a tin Madonna, a devil made from bread dough, dolls from around the world, and miniature village scenes galore. The Hispanic Heritage Wing contains art dating from the Spanish colonial period (in New Mexico, 1598–1821) to the present. The 5,000-piece exhibit includes religious works—particularly *bultos* (carved wooden statues of saints) and *retablos* (holy images painted on wood or tin), as well as textiles and furniture. The exhibits in the Neutrogena Wing rotate, showing subjects ranging from outsider art to the magnificent quilts of

A GOOD TOUR

This museum tour begins 2 mi south of the Plaza, an area known as Museum Hill that's best reached by car or via one of the city buses that leaves hourly from near the Plaza. Begin at the **Museum of Indian Arts and Culture** ⓭, which is set around **Milner Plaza,** an attractively landscaped courtyard and gardens with outdoor art installations. On some summer days the Plaza hosts Native American dances, jewelry-making demonstrations, kids' activities, and other interactive events; there's also the Museum Hill Cafe, which is open for lunch (and Sunday brunch) and serves delicious and reasonably priced salads, quiche, burgers, sandwiches and wraps, ice cream, and other light fare. To get here from downtown, drive uphill

on Old Santa Fe Trail to Camino Lejo. Across Milner Plaza is the **Museum of International Folk Art (MOIFA)** ⓮. From Milner Plaza, a pedestrian path leads a short way to the **Museum of Spanish Colonial Art** ⓯. Return to Milner Plaza, from which a different pedestrian path leads a short way to the **Wheelwright Museum of the American Indian** ⓰. To reach the **Santa Fe Children's Museum** ⓱ you need to drive back down the hill or ask the bus driver to let you off near it.

TIMING

Set aside a full day to see all the museums on the Upper Santa Fe Trail/Museum Hill. Kids usually have to be dragged from the Children's Museum, even after an hour or two.

Gee's Bend. Lloyd's Treasure Chest, the wing's innovative basement section, provides a behind-the-scenes look at this collection. You can rummage through storage drawers, peer into microscopes, and, on occasion, speak with conservators and other museum personnel. Check the Web site or call to see if any of the excellent children's activities are scheduled for the time of your visit. Save time to visit the incredible gift shop and bookstore. ⊠ *706 Camino Lejo* ☎ *505/476–1200* ⊕ *www.moifa.org* ☞ *$8, 4-day pass $18, good at all 4 state museums and the Museum of Spanish Colonial Art in Santa Fe* ☉ *Tues.–Sun. 10–5.*

⓯ **Museum of Spanish Colonial Art.**
Fodor'sChoice Opened in 2002, this 5,000-
★ square-foot adobe museum occupies a building designed in 1930 by acclaimed architect John Gaw Meem. The Spanish Colonial Art Society formed in Santa Fe in 1925 to preserve traditional Spanish-colonial art and culture. The museum, which sits next to the Museum of New Mexico complex, displays the fruits of the society's labor—one of the most comprehensive collections of Spanish colonial art in the world. The Hale Matthews Library contains a 1,000-volume collection

IFAM

The **International Folk Art Market** (☎ *505/476–1197* ⊕ *www. folkartmarket.org*), held the second full weekend in July on Milner Plaza, is the grassroots art gathering. Master folk artists from every corner of the planet come together to sell their work amidst a festive array of huge tents, colorful banners, music, food, and delighted crowds. There is a feeling of fellowship and celebration here that enhances the satisfaction of buying wonderful folk art.

of books relating to this important period in art history. Objects here, dating from the 16th century to the present, include retablos, elaborate santos, tinwork, straw appliqué, furniture, ceramics, and ironwork. There's also a fine collection of works by Hispanic artists of the 20th century. ⊠ *750 Camino Lejo* 🕾 *505/982–2226* ⊕ *www.spanish colonial.org* ⊠ *$6, 4-day pass $18, good at all 4 state museums and the Museum of Spanish Colonial Art in Santa Fe* ☉ *Daily 10–5.*

⑰ Santa Fe Children's Museum. Stimulating hands-on exhibits, a solar greenhouse, oversize geometric forms, and a simulated 18-foot mountain-climbing wall all contribute to this museum's popularity with kids. Outdoor gardens with climbing structures, forts, and hands-on activities are great for whiling away the time in the shade of big trees. Puppeteers and storytellers perform often. ⊠ *1050 Old Pecos Trail* 🕾 *505/989–8359* ⊕ *www.santafechildrensmuseum.org* ⊠ *$8* ☉ *Sept.–May, Wed.–Sat. 10–5, Sun. noon–5; June–Aug., Tues.–Sat. 10–5, Sun. noon–5.*

⑯ Wheelwright Museum of the American Indian. A private institution in a building shaped like a traditional octagonal Navajo hogan, the Wheelwright opened in 1937. Founded by Boston scholar Mary Cabot Wheelwright and Navajo medicine man Hastiin Klah, the museum originated as a place to house ceremonial materials. Those items were returned to the Navajo in 1977, but what remains is an incredible collection of 19th- and 20th-century baskets, pottery, sculpture, weavings, metalwork, photography, paintings, including contemporary works by Native American artists, and typically fascinating changing exhibits. The Case Trading Post on the lower level is modeled after the trading posts that dotted the southwestern frontier more than 100 years ago. It carries an extensive selection of books and contemporary Native American jewelry, kachina dolls, weaving, and pottery. ⊠ *704 Camino Lejo* 🕾 *505/982–4636 or 800/607–4636* ⊕ *www.wheelwright.org* ⊠ *Free* ☉ *Mon.–Sat. 10–5, Sun. 1–5; gallery tours weekdays at 2, Sat. at 1.*

GUADALUPE DISTRICT

The historic warehouse and Railyard District of Santa Fe is commonly referred to as the Guadalupe District. After the demise of the train route through town, the low-lying warehouses were converted to artists' studios and antiques shops, and bookstores, specialty shops, and restaurants have sprung up. The restored scenic train line puts the town's old Mission-style depot to use, and eventually this station will be the Santa Fe terminus of the *Railrunner* commuter train service that's planned from Albuquerque sometime in 2008.

In September 2008 the Railyard Park, at the corner of Cerrillos Road (sir ee ohs) and Guadalupe Street, was unveiled after a decade-long redevelopment effort. The new park, with permaculture landscaping and extensive water-catchment and irrigation systems, was designed to highlight native plants and provide citizens with a lush, urban park. The adjoining buildings to the park house the vibrant Santa Fe Farmers' Market, the teen-oriented community art center Warehouse21, SITE Santa Fe, art galleries, shops, restaurants, and live-work spaces for artists. It is the most significant development Santa Fe has seen for decades and represents the fascinating way Santa Feans have worked to meet the needs of an expanding city while paying strict attention to the city's historic relevance.

WHAT TO SEE

⑲ El Museo Cultural de Santa Fe. As much an educational and community gathering space as a museum, the Santa Fe Cultural Museum celebrates Santa Fe's—and New Mexico's—rich Hispanic heritage by presenting a wide range of events, from children's theater, to musical concerts, to a great Dia de Los Muertos celebration at the beginning of November. The museum sponsors the Contemporary Hispanic Market just off the Plaza each July (held the same time as Spanish Market), and the Contemporary Hispanic Artists Winter Market, held at El Museo Cultural in late November. There's a gallery that exhibits contemporary art by Hispanic artists. A great resource to visitors are the many classes and workshops, which are open to the public, and touch on everything from guitar and Mexican folkloric dance to children's theater and art. The museum occupies what had been a dilapidated liquor warehouse before El Museo took over the space in the late '90s. ⊠ *1615 Paseo de Peralta* ☎ *505/992–0591* ⊕ *www.elmuseocultural.org* ⊠ *Free; prices vary for events and shows* ☉ *Tues.–Fri. 1–5, Sat. 10–5; additionally for events and shows.*

㉒ Santa Fe Clay. Occupying 10,000 square feet of space, this combination clay studio, supply shop, and gallery has, for the past 14 years, become more and more respected in the community for the artists producing works and the quality of the classes taught. Regular classes and studio space are available for adults and children alike, and classes are taught by highly respected ceramic artists. Gallery shows change regularly and are worth stopping in for a look. ⊠ *1615 Paseo de Peralta* ☎ *505/984–1122* ⊕ *www.santafeclay.com* ☉ *Call for classes Mon.–Sat.*

⑳ Santa Fe Southern Railway. For a leisurely tour across the Santa Fe plateau and into the vast Galisteo Basin, where panoramic views extend for up to 120 mi, take a nostalgic ride on the antique cars of the Santa Fe Southern Railway. The train once served a spur of the Atchison, Topeka & Santa Fe Railway. Today the train takes visitors on 36-mi round-trip scenic trips to Lamy, a sleepy village with the region's only Amtrak service, offering picnics under the cottonwoods (bring your own or buy one from the caterer that meets the train) at the quaint rail station. Shorter runs travel down to the scenic Galisteo Basin. Aside from day trips, the railway offers special events such as a Friday-night "High Desert High Ball" cash bar with appetizers and a Saturday Night Barbecue Train ($58). Trains depart from the Santa Fe Depot, rebuilt in 1909 after the original was destroyed in a fire. There's talk of eventually opening a regional transportation and rail museum here, as part of the efforts to redevelop this part of the Guadalupe District. ⊠ *410 S. Guadalupe St.* ☎ *505/989–8600 or 888/989–8600* ⊕ *www.sfsr.com* ⚲ *Reservations essential* ⊠ *Day trips from $32* ☉ *Call for schedule.*

㉑ Santuario de Guadalupe. A humble adobe structure built by Franciscan missionaries between 1776 and 1795, this is the oldest shrine in the United States to Our Lady of Guadalupe, Mexico's patron saint. The

A GOOD TOUR

From the Plaza, head west on San Francisco Street, and then take a left onto Guadalupe Street toward **Santuario de Guadalupe** ㉑, a block up on your right. After you visit the Santuario, take your time browsing through the shops and eating lunch in one of the restaurants lining Guadalupe Street or around the corner, to the right on Montezuma St., at the **Sanbusco Market Center,** a massive, converted warehouse. Check out the great shops and the photographic history on the walls near the market's main entrance. Back on Guadalupe, head south to the historic Gross Kelly Warehouse, one of the earliest Santa Fe–style buildings. Note Santa Fe's two train depots—one is now the site of popular, but touristy, Tomasita's Restaurant; the other, set farther back, is the Santa Fe Depot, where the **Santa Fe Southern Railway** ⓴ departs. Continue a short distance south on Guadalupe until you reach **SITE Santa Fe** ⓲ gallery and performance space, set inside a former bottling warehouse. Spend some time wandering the aisles, or picking up picnic supplies, at the friendly, bustling Santa Fe Farmers' Market. You are likely to be amazed at the amount of produce and goods coming from this high desert region. Just beyond the Farmers' Market is the Railyard Park, where you can stroll, or lounge, and enjoy your edible goodies amidst green grass, lovely trees, and great stonework. Cater-corner from SITE Santa Fe, **El Museo Cultural de Santa Fe** ⓳ is one of the state's more unusual museums, a combination performance space, classroom, gallery, and event venue that promotes Hispanic culture and education in the City Different.

TIMING
A visit to the Santuario de Guadalupe can take 15 minutes to an hour, depending on whether or not there's an art show in progress. If you like shopping and visiting art galleries, and decide to eat in this area, you might spend hours in this diverse and exciting neighborhood.

sanctuary, now a nonprofit cultural center, has adobe walls nearly 3 feet thick. Among the sanctuary's religious art and artifacts is a priceless 16th-century work by Venetian painter Leonardo de Ponte Bassano that depicts Jesus driving the money changers from the Temple. Also of note is a portrait of Our Lady of Guadalupe by the Mexican colonial painter José de Alzíbar. Other highlights are the traditional New Mexican carved and painted altar screen, an authentic 19th-century sacristy, a pictorial-history archive, a library devoted to Archbishop Jean Baptiste Lamy that is furnished with many of his belongings, and a garden with plants from the Holy Land. ✉ *100 Guadalupe St.* ☎ *505/988–2027* ✉*Donation suggested* ⊙*May–Oct., Mon.–Sat. 9–4; Nov.–Apr., weekdays 9–4.*

⓲ ★ **SITE Santa Fe.** The events at this nexus of international contemporary art include lectures, concerts, author readings, performance art, and gallery shows. The facility hosts a biennial exhibition every even-numbered year. There are always provocative exhibitions here, however, and the immense, open space is ideal for taking in the many larger-than-life installations. ✉*1606 Paseo de Peralta* ☎*505/989–1199* ⊕*www.sitesantafe.org* ✉*$10, free Fri.* ⊙ *Wed., Thurs., and Sat. 10–5, Fri. 10–7, Sun. noon–5.*

WHERE TO EAT

Eating out is a major pastime in Santa Fe and it's well worth coming here with a mind to join in on the fun. Restaurants with high-profile chefs stand beside low-key joints, each offering unique and intriguing variations on regional and international cuisine. You'll find restaurants full of locals and tourists alike all over the downtown and surrounding areas. People often comment that food prices rival those in San Francisco or New York. Don't fret. There is wonderful food available for reasonable prices if you look around a bit. Waits for tables are very common during the busy summer season, so it's a good idea to call ahead even when reservations aren't accepted, if only to get a sense of the waiting time. Reservations for dinner at the better restaurants are a must for much of the year.

So-called Santa Fe–style cuisine has so many influences that the term is virtually meaningless. Traditional, old-style Santa Fe restaurants serve New Mexican fare, which combines both Native American and Hispanic traditions and is quite different from Americanized or even authentic Mexican cooking. Many of the better restaurants in town serve a contemporary regional style of cooking that blends New Mexican ingredients and preparations with those of interior and coastal Mexico, Latin America, the Mediterranean, East Asia, and varied parts of the United States. For a city this small, there is a delightful array of cuisines available aside from the delicious and spicy food of northern New Mexico; Middle Eastern, Spanish, Japanese, Italian, East Indian and French, to name just a few. More and more restaurants, from casual lunch joints to the finest dining establishments, are focusing on using local and regional ingredients, from meats, to cheeses, to produce. Smoking was recently banned in all bars and restaurants in the city, infuriating some and thrilling many.

WHAT IT COSTS					
	¢	$	$$	$$$	$$$$
Restaurants	under $10	$10–$17	$18–$24	$25–$30	over $30

Prices are per person for a main course at dinner, excluding 8.25% sales tax.

$$$
CONTEMPORARY
★
✕ **315 Restaurant & Wine Bar.** As if it were on a thoroughfare in Paris rather than on Old Santa Fe Trail, 315 has a Continental, white-tablecloth sophistication, but the offbeat wall art gives it a contemporary feel. Chef-owner Louis Moskow, who also owns the popular Railyard Restaurant (⇨ *below*), prepares refreshingly uncomplicated fare using organic vegetables and locally raised meats. Seasonal specialties on the ever-evolving menu might include squash blossom beignets with local goat cheese, basil-wrapped shrimp with apricot chutney and curry sauce, or grilled boneless lamb loin with crispy polenta, spring vegetables, and green peppercorn sauce. The garden patio opens onto the street scene. There's also a wine bar with an exceptional list of vintages. ⊠ *315 Old Santa Fe Trail* ☎ *505/986–9190* ⊕ *www.315santafe.com* ☐ *AE, MC, V* ☺ *Closed Sun. No lunch Mon.*

BEST BETS FOR SANTA FE DINING

With hundreds of restaurants to choose from, how will you decide where to eat? Fodor's writers and editors have selected their favorite restaurants by price, cuisine, and experience in the Best Bets lists below. Find specific details about a restaurant in the full reviews, listed alphabetically later in the chapter.

FODOR'S CHOICE

Aqua Santa $$$
Bobcat Bite ¢
Bumble Bee's Baja Grill $
Cafe Pasqual's $$$$
The Compound $$$$
Geronimo $$$$
Harry's Roadhouse $
Inn of the Anasazi $$$$
La Boca $$
La Choza ¢
The Shed $$

By Price

¢

Bobcat Bite
Clafoutis
La Choza

$

Andiamo
Bumble Bee
Tune Up

$$

La Boca
Pyramid
The Shed
Zia Diner

$$$

Aqua Santa
El Farol
El Meson
Ristra
Shohko

$$$$

315 Restaurant and Wine Bar
Café Pasqual's
Fuego
Geronimo

By Cuisine

AMERICAN

Bobcat Bite ¢
Railyard Restaurant & Saloon $$
Zia Diner $$

CAFÉ

Aztec ¢
Chocolate Maven $
Clafoutis ¢
Mission Café ¢

ASIAN

Mu Du Noodles $$

CONTEMPORARY

315 Restaurant & Wine Bar $$$$
Aqua Santa $$$
Café Pasqual's $$$
Ristra $$$

ITALIAN

Andiamo $
Trattoria Nostrani $$$$

NEW MEXICAN

La Boca $$
La Choza ¢
Maria's $
Tia Sophia's ¢

By Experience

BAR MENU

El Farol $$$
El Mesón $$$
Railyard $$
Zia Diner $$

BEST BURGER

Bobcat Bite ¢
Compound $$$$
Ristra (Bar) $$$
Tune Up ¢

BREAKFAST

Café Pasqual's $$$$
Harry's $
Tecolote ¢
Tia Sophia's ¢

CHILD-FRIENDLY

Cowgirl $
Harry's $
Plaza Café $
San Francisco Street Bar & Grill $
Zia Diner $$

HISTORIC INTEREST

Compound $$$$
El Farol $$$
Mission Café ¢
Railyard $$

$ | **Andiamo.** Produce from the farm-
ITALIAN | ers' market down the street adds to
★ | the seasonal surprises of this inti-
mate northern Italian restaurant set inside a sweet cottage in the Guadalupe District. Start with the delectable crispy polenta with rosemary and Gorgonzola sauce; move on to the white pizza with roasted garlic, fontina, grilled radicchio, pancetta, and rosemary; and consider such hearty entrées as crispy duck legs with grilled polenta, roasted turnips, and sautéed spinach. ⊠*322 Garfield St.* ☎*505/995–9595* ⊕*www.andiamoonline.com* ⊟*AE, DC, MC, V* ⊘*No lunch.*

$$$ | **Aqua Santa.** Brian Knox, the
CONTEMPORARY | charming, gregarious chef at the
Fodor'sChoice | helm of this locals' favorite, is a
★ | devotee of the slow-food philosophy. His love and appreciation of food is palpable; some of the finest,

WORD OF MOUTH

"I've read many of the Santa Fe/Taos threads about all of the wonderful restaurants/cafes....If you could have dinner at only one, which would you choose?"
  –hikrchick

"Dinner or lunch at El Farol....I liked it so much I ate twice there in my 4 days in Santa Fe. Also, they have a lively bar w/ great live music 7 nights a week." –emd

"Check out Plaza Cafe when you are wandering through the plaza area. Delicious, inexpensive, fresh food that should give you plenty of options—in a historic setting, to boot! I never go to Santa Fe without eating there." –jayne1973

simplest, yet most sophisticated dishes in town come from the open kitchen in this tiny, one-room gem of a restaurant. The creamy, plastered walls of the intimate dining room are hung with art from local artists, and the ramada-covered patio open in summer feels like dining at a chic friend's house. Diners enjoy dishes like the fabulously tangy Caesar salad, panfried oysters with bitter honey and a balsamic reduction, Tuscan bean soup with white-truffle oil, and braised organic New Mexico lamb with olives and summer squash. Brian can be spotted shopping around town for fresh, local ingredients, and the menu changes regularly based on his gastronomic discoveries. Save room for dessert; the silky panna cotta may be the best on the continent. There's an extensive, reasonable wine list, too; ask the friendly staff for their current favorites. ⊠*451 W. Alameda St. (entrance off Water St.)* ☎*505/982–6297* ⊟*MC, V* ⊘*Closed Sun. and Mon. No lunch Tues. or Sat.*

¢ | **Atomic Grill.** Burgers, salads, pizzas, sandwiches, and other light fare are
AMERICAN | served at this tiny late-night café a block off the Plaza. The food is decent but the service can be brusque. The best attributes are the comfy patio overlooking pedestrian-heavy Water Street, the huge list of imported beers, and the late hours (it's open until 3 most nights)—an extreme rarity in Santa Fe. You'll be glad this place exists when the bars let out and you're famished. ⊠*103 Water St.* ☎*505/820–2866* ⊟*MC, V.*

¢ | **Aztec.** If a cup of really tasty, locally roasted, noncorporate coffee in a
CAFÉ | funky, creaky-wood-floored old adobe sounds like nirvana to you, then
★ | this is the place. Cozy, colorful rooms inside are lined with local art (and artists), the staff is laid-back and friendly, and the little patio outside is a busy meeting ground for locals. Food is homemade, healthy, and flavorful. The menu includes sandwiches such as the Martin-roast turkey,

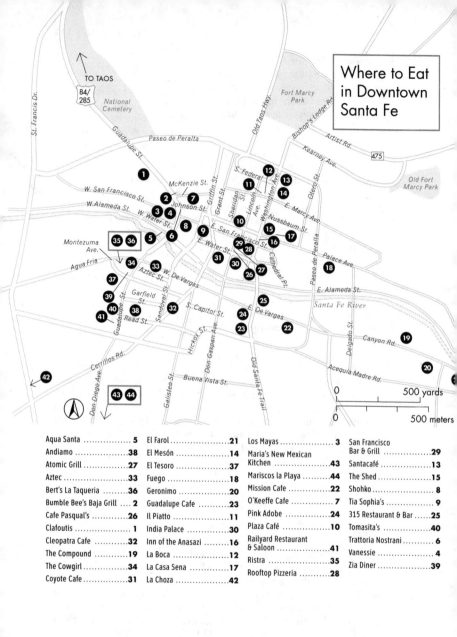

Where to Eat in Downtown Santa Fe

green apples, and Swiss cheese; fabulous, fluffy quiches; soups, breakfast burritos, and ice cream in the warm season. It's open until 7 (6 PM Sundays) in case you get late-afternoon munchies. There's free Wi-Fi and a public computer with Internet access. ✉ *317 Aztec St., Guadalupe District* ☎ *505/820–0025* ⌕ *Reservations not accepted* ▭ *AE, MC, V.*

$ ✕ **Bert's la Taqueria.** Fans of interior-Mexican cuisine love this upbeat spot
MEXICAN with multiple rooms in an old adobe building that was once the nun's cloister for the Santuario de Guadalupe across the street. Colorful paintings hang on the whitewashed walls. The menu mixes the expected Mexican fare—enchiladas, excellent soft tacos—with more unusual regional recipes, such as *chapulines* (grasshoppers—yes, you read that correctly—sautéed with garlic butter) on tostaditas, or cuitlacoche (a delicious mushroomlike fungus that grows on corn) with black beans and fresh corn tortillas. The margaritas are made from scratch and are muy delicioso. ✉ *416 Agua Fria St.* ☎ *505/474–0791* ▭ *AE, MC, V* ✪ *Closed Sun.*

¢ ✕ **Bobcat Bite.** It'll take you 15 easy minutes from Downtown to drive to
AMERICAN this tiny roadhouse southeast of town and it's worth it. Folks drive a lot
Fodor's Choice farther for Bobcat Bite's steaks and chops ($17) but come especially for
★ one thing: the biggest and juiciest burgers in town. Locals prefer them topped with cheese and green chiles. Only early dinners are available, as the place closes by 8 most nights, and you'll want to arrive early to get a seat. No desserts and no credit cards. ✉ *Old Las Vegas Hwy., 4½ mi south of Old Pecos Trail exit off I-25* ☎ *505/983–5319* ⌕ *Reservations not accepted* ▭ *No credit cards* ✪ *Closed Sun.–Tues.*

$ ✕ **Body Cafe.** There is a world of things to do inside the contemporary,
CAFÉ Asian-inspired Body. At this holistically minded center five minutes from downtown, you'll find a spa offering a full range of treatments, a yoga studio (with a good range of classes open to visitors), a childcare center, and a boutique selling a wide range of beauty, health, and lifestyle products, plus jewelry, clothing, music, tarot cards, and all sorts of interesting gifts. The café uses mostly organic, local ingredients and serves three meals a day, with an emphasis on vegan and raw dishes. The breakfast smoothies and homemade granola are delicious. At lunch try soba noodles with peanuts and ginger-soy vinaigrette, and at dinner there's an unbelievably good vegan lasagna layered with basil-sunflower pesto, portobello mushrooms, spinach, squash, tomatoes, nut cheese, and marinara sauce. Beer and wine are served. ✉ *333 Cordova Rd.* ☎ *505/986–0362* ▭ *AE, D, MC, V.*

$ ✕ **Bumble Bee's Baja Grill.** A bright, vibrantly colored restaurant with
MEXICAN closely spaced tables, piñatas, and ceiling fans wafting overhead, Bumble
Fodor's Choice Bee's (it's the nickname of the ebullient owner, Bob) delights locals with
★ its super-fresh Cal-Mex–style food. If you like fish tacos, the mahimahi ones with creamy, nondairy slaw are outstanding; try them with a side of salad instead of beans and rice and *hijole*. What a meal! Mammoth burritos with a wide range of fillings (including asparagus—yum!), roasted chicken with cilantro-lime rice, char-grilled trout platters, and a wide variety of vegetarian options keep folks pouring through the doors. You order at the counter, grab some chips and any one of a number of freshly made salsas from the bar, and wait for your number to come up. Beer, wine, and Mexican soft drinks are served. Try a homemade Mexi-

can chocolate brownie for dessert. There's live jazz on Saturday nights. ✉*301 Jefferson St.* ☎*505/820–2862* ⊕*www.bumblebeesbajagrill.com* ✉*3701 Cerrillos Rd.* ☎*505/988–3278* ▤*AE, D, MC, V.*

$$$$
CONTEMPORARY
Fodor'sChoice
★

✕ **Cafe Pasqual's.** A perennial favorite, this cheerful cubbyhole dishes up Southwestern and Nuevo Latino specialties for breakfast, lunch, and dinner. Don't be discouraged by lines out front—it's worth the wait. The culinary muse behind it all is Katharine Kagel, who championed organic, local ingredients, and whose expert kitchen staff produces mouthwatering breakfast and lunch specialties like chile relleno picadillo (cheese-stuffed chile with eggs and a smoky tomato salsa served with beans and tortillas), huevos motuleños (eggs in a tangy tomatillo salsa with black beans and fried bananas), and the sublime grilled free-range chicken sandwich. Dinner is a more formal, though still friendly and easygoing, affair: char-grilled lamb with pomegranate-molasses glaze, steamed sugar-snap peas, and pan-seared potato cakes is a pleasure; the kicky starter of spicy Vietnamese squid salad with tamarind, garlic, and tomato over arugula is also fantastic. Mexican folk art, colorful tiles, and murals by Oaxacan artist Leovigildo Martinez create a festive atmosphere. Try the chummy communal table, or go late morning or after 1:30 PM to (hopefully) avoid the crush. ✉*121 Don Gaspar Ave.* ☎*505/983–9340* ⊕*www.pasquals.com* ▤*AE, MC, V* ☻ *No reservations for breakfast and lunch.*

$
CAFÉ
★

✕ **Chocolate Maven.** Although the name of this cheery bakery suggests sweets, and it does sweets especially well, Chocolate Maven produces impressive savory breakfast and lunch fare. Favorite treats include wild-mushroom-and-goat-cheese focaccia sandwiches, eggs ménage à trois (one each of eggs Benedict, Florentine, and Madison—the latter consisting of smoked salmon and poached egg), and Caprese salad of fresh mozzarella, basil, and tomatoes. Pizzas are thin-crusted and delicate. Some of the top desserts include Belgian chocolate fudge brownies, mocha-buttercream torte with chocolate-covered strawberries, and French lemon-raspberry cake. Don't let the industrial building put you off; the interior is light, bright, and cozy. Try the Mayan Mocha, espresso mixed with steamed milk and a delicious combo of chocolate, cinnamon, and red chiles—heavenly! ✉*821 W. San Mateo St.* ☎*505/984–1980* ⊕ *www.chocolatemaven.com* ▤*AE, D, MC, V* ☻*No dinner.*

¢
CAFÉ
★

✕ **Clafoutis.** Undeniably French, this bustling café serves authentic, delicious food. Walk through the door of this bright, open space and you'll almost certainly be greeted with a cheery "bon jour" from Anne Laure, who owns it with her husband, Philippe. Start your day with a crepe, one of their fluffy omelets, or les gauffres (large house waffles). Lunch offers quiches with perfectly flaky crusts, an enticing selection of large salads (the salade de la maison has pears, pine nuts, blue cheese, Spanish chorizo, tomatoes, and cucumbers atop mixed greens), and savory sandwiches, like the classic croque madame, on homemade bread. The classic onion soup is amazingly comforting on a cold day. The café's namesake dessert, clafoutis, is worth saving room for. Fantastic espresso. ✉ *402 N. Guadalupe St., near Santa Fe Plaza* ☎*505/988–1809* ⊸*Reservations not accepted* ▤*AE, MC, V* ☻*No dinner Closed Sun.*

¢

MIDDLE
EASTERN

✕**Cleopatra Cafe.** A no-fuss, order-at-the-counter Middle Eastern café inside the Design Center home-furnishings mall, Cleopatra serves up ultrafresh Egyptian, Lebanese, and Greek food at bargain prices. You might start with *besara* (fava beans with cilantro, garlic, fried onion, and pita bread). Popular entrées include the falafel plate, with hummus and tabbouleh salad, and grilled organic-lamb kebabs with onions, bell peppers, rice, tahini, and Greek salad. Tangy fresh-squeezed lemonade and potent Turkish coffee are also offered. The friendly owner, Jack, greets everyone as though they are friends. He's opened a new, sit-down restaurant on the south side of town at 3482 Zafarano Street. ✉*418 Cerrillos Rd.* ☎*505/820–7381* ▭*MC, V* ⊗*Closed Sun.*

$$$$

CONTEMPORARY

Fodor's Choice

★

✕**The Compound.** Chef Mark Kiffin has transformed this gracious, folk-art-filled old restaurant into one of the state's culinary darlings. No longer white-glove formal, it's still a fancy place, thanks to decor by famed designer Alexander Girard and a highly attentive staff, but maintains an easygoing feel. From chef Kiffin's oft-changing menu, devoted to ingredients based on those introduced to the area by the Spanish, consider a starter of warm flan of summer sweet corn, with lobster succotash and radish sprouts. Memorable entrées include Alaskan halibut with orange lentils, summer squash, and piquillo peppers in a smoked ham hock broth; and buttermilk roast chicken with creamed fresh spinach and foie gras pan gravy. The extensive and carefully chosen wine list will please the most discerning oenophile. Lunch is as delightful as dinner, while considerably less expensive—about $14 per person. ✉*653 Canyon Rd.* ☎*505/982–4353* ⊕*www.compoundrestaurant. com* ▭*AE, D, DC, MC, V* ⊗*No lunch weekends.*

$

AMERICAN

☾

✕**The Cowgirl Hall of Fame (aka The Cowgirl).** A rollicking, popular bar and grill with several rooms overflowing with Old West memorabilia, Cowgirl has reasonably priced Southwestern, Tex-Mex, barbecue, and Southern fare. Highlights include barbecue, buffalo burgers, chiles rellenos, and salmon tacos with tomatillo salsa. A real treat for parents is the outdoor-but-enclosed Kiddie Corral where kids have swings, a climbing structure, and various games to entertain themselves. So what's the bad news? Frequently subpar service and food that doesn't stand out in a town of stellar food. Nevertheless, the crowd is friendly and diverse, the drinks are cold, and if you catch one of the nightly music acts—usually rock or blues—you're likely to leave smiling. Grab a seat on the spacious patio in warm weather. The attached pool hall has a great juke box to keep toes tapping. ✉*319 S. Guadalupe St.* ☎*505/982–2565* ▭*AE, D, MC, V.*

$$$$

CONTEMPORARY

✕**Coyote Cafe.** Santa Fe went through a culinary shake-up in 2007 with several celebrity chefs changing restaurants. Eric DiStefano, formerly of Geronimo, took over Coyote Café with three other local industry veterans, and the results have been mixed so far. The famed locus of Southwestern cuisine, the restaurant is still the place to go to taste variations on the beloved green chile, but the menu has evolved to include the flavors of French and Asian cuisine. Menu offerings include griddled buttermilk corn cakes with chipotle prawns, DiStefano's signature dish, a peppery elk tenderloin, and the five-spice rotisserie rock hen with green chile "mac 'n' cheese." Service and food quality have varied widely, both in the main dining room and at the Rooftop Cantina, the fun outdoor gathering spot next door where cocktails and under-$15 fare is served April through October. ⊠*132 W. Water St.* ☎*505/983–1615* ⊕*www.coyotecafe.com* ⊟*AE, D, DC, MC, V* ⊘*No lunch except at Rooftop Cantina.*

$$$
SPANISH
✕ **El Farol.** In this crossover-cuisine town, owner David Salazar sums up his food in one word: "Spanish." Order a classic entrée like paella or make a meal from the nearly 30 different tapas—from tiny fried squid to wild mushrooms. Dining is indoors and out. Touted as the oldest continuously operated restaurant in Santa Fe, El Farol (built in 1835) has a relaxed ambience, a unique blend of the Western frontier and contemporary Santa Fe. People push back the chairs and start dancing at around 9:30. The restaurant books outstanding live entertainment seven nights a week, from blues and Latin to border-reggae, and there's a festive flamenco performance on Wednesday. ⊠*808 Canyon Rd.* ☎*505/983–9912* ⊟*AE, D, MC, V*

$$$
SPANISH
★
✕ **El Mesón & Chispa Tapas Bar.** This place is as fun for having drinks and tapas or catching live music (from tango nights to Sephardic music) as for enjoying a full meal. The dignified dining room with an old-world feel has simple dark-wood tables and chairs, white walls, and a wood-beam ceiling—unpretentious yet elegant. Livelier but still quite handsome is the Chispa bar. The delicious tapas menu includes Serrano ham and fried red potatoes with garlic aioli. Among the more substantial entrées are a stellar paella as well as cannelloni stuffed with veal, smothered with béchamel sauce, and served with manchego cheese au gratin. ⊠*213 Washington Ave.* ☎*505/983–6756* ⊟*AE, MC, V* ⊘*Closed Sun. and Mon. No lunch.*

¢
LATIN
✕ **El Tesoro.** One of the Guadalupe District's better-kept secrets, this small café occupies a spot in the high-ceilinged center of the Sanbusco Center, steps from several chic boutiques. The tiny kitchen turns out a mix of Central American, New Mexican, and American dishes, all of them using super-fresh ingredients. Grilled tuna tacos with salsa fresca, black beans, and rice; and Salvadorian chicken tamales wrapped in banana leaves are among the tastiest treats. El Tesoro also serves pastries, gelato, lemon bars, hot cocoa, and other snacks, making it a perfect break from shopping. ⊠*Sanbusco Market Center, 500 Montezuma Ave.* ☎*505/988–3886* ⊟*MC, V* ⊘*No dinner.*

$$$$
CONTEMPORARY
✕ **Fuego.** An elegant yet comfortable dining room inside the oasis of La Posada resort, Fuego has become a local favorite for fantastic, inventive food and flawless service. It is one of Santa Fe's top culinary secrets, albeit with sky-high prices. You might start with seared foie gras with apple pie au poivre, before trying free-range *poussin* (young chicken) over a nest of braised leeks and salsify, or roast rack of Colorado elk with parsnip dumplings and a dried-cherry mole. Perhaps the most astounding offering is the artisanal cheese plate—Fuego has one of the largest selections of cheeses west of Manhattan. The wine list is similarly impressive and the helpful sommelier is always on hand to advise. Le Menu Découverte allows you to sample a five-course meal of chef's specialties for $125 (additional $65 for wine pairing). The spectacular Sunday brunch, at $45 per person, is a bargain. ⊠*330 E. Palace Ave.* ☎*505/986–0000* ⊕*www.laposadadesantafe.com* ⊟*AE, D, DC, MC, V.*

$ ✕**Gabriel's.** This restaurant has location (convenient for pre-opera and NEW MEXICAN post-high-road tours), a gorgeous setting (the Spanish colonial–style art, the building, the flower-filled courtyard, and those mountain views!), and the made-to-order guacamole going for it. The margaritas are stellar. The caveat? The quality of the entrées tends to be wildly uneven. Service is friendly, but as uneven as the food. If you're content with a gorgeous setting and making the stellar guacamole and margaritas your mainstay, with little care as to whether or not the entrée is memorable, this is a great place to go for sunset. Prices are reasonable and the setting truly is spectacular. ⊠ *U.S. 285/84, Exit 176, just north of Camel Rock Casino, 5 mi north of Santa Fe Opera* ☎*505/455–7000* ⊕*www. gabrielsrestaurante.com* ⊟*AE, D, DC, MC, V.*

$$$$ ✕**Geronimo.** Renowned chef Martin Rios (formerly at the Inn of the CONTEMPORARY Anasazi) and two seasoned managing partners took over one of New Fodor'sChoice Mexico's most-celebrated restaurants in 2008. Bringing classical French ★ training, a fondness for Asian and Southwestern flavors, and an eye on molecular gastronomy, Rios changes his menu frequently. Dishes range from coriander-cured semiboneless quail, served with seared foie gras, harissa French toast, and Pedro Jiminez roasted grapes, to the New York strip, served with a gratin of crushed golden potato, carrot confit, pearl onions, and sauce Bordelaise. Desserts are artful and rich and the Sunday brunch is impressive. Located in the Borrego House, a massive-walled adobe dating from 1756, the intimate, white dining rooms have beamed ceilings, wood floors, fireplaces, and cushioned *bancos*. The new team is easier going and Rios clearly enjoys experimenting with new flavors and techniques. In summer you can dine under the front portal; in winter the bar with fireplace is inviting. ⊠*724 Canyon Rd.* ☎*505/982–1500* ⊕*www.geronimorestaurant.com* ⊟*AE, MC, V* ◷*No lunch Mon.*

$ ✕**Guadalupe Cafe.** Come to this informal café for hefty servings of New NEW MEXICAN Mexican favorites like enchiladas—vegetarian options are delicious— and quesadillas, or burritos smothered in green or red chile, topped off with sopaipilla and honey. The seasonal raspberry pancakes are one of many breakfast favorites as are eggs Benedict with green chile hollandaise sauce. Service is hit-or-miss and the wait for a table considerable—but the food keeps 'em coming back for more. ⊠*422 Old Santa Fe Trail* ☎*505/982–9762* ♨*Reservations not accepted* ⊟*DC, MC, V* ◷*Closed Mon. No dinner Sun.*

$ ✕**Harry's Roadhouse.** This busy, friendly, art-filled compound just south- ECLECTIC east of town consists of several inviting rooms, from a diner-style space ☾ with counter seating to a cozier nook with a fireplace—there's also an Fodor'sChoice enchanting courtyard out back with juniper trees and flower gardens. ★ The varied menu of contemporary diner favorites, pizzas, New Mexican fare, and bountiful salads is supplemented by a long list of daily specials—which often include delicious ethnic dishes. Favorites include smoked-chicken quesadillas and grilled-salmon tacos with tomatillo salsa and black beans. Breakfast is fantastic. On weekends, if you're there early, you might just get a chance at one of owner–pastry chef Peyton's phenomenal cinnamon rolls. Desserts here are homey favorites, from the chocolate pudding to the blueberry cobbler. ⊠*96-B Old Las Vegas Hwy., 1 mi east of Old Pecos Trail exit off I–25* ☎*505/989– 4629* ⊟*AE, D, MC, V.*

$
ITALIAN
✕ **Il Piatto.** Creative pasta dishes like pappardelle with braised duckling, caramelized onions, sun-dried tomatoes, and mascarpone-duck au jus, and homemade pumpkin ravioli with pine nuts and brown sage butter grace the seasonally changing menu here. Entrées include grilled salmon with spinach risotto and tomato-caper sauce, and a superb pancetta-wrapped trout with rosemary, wild mushrooms, and polenta. It's a crowded but enjoyable trattoria with informal ambience, reasonable prices, and a snug bar. ✉ *95 W. Marcy St.* ☎ *505/984–1091* ▤ *AE, D, MC, V* ⊘ *No lunch weekends.*

$$
INDIAN
★
✕ **India Palace.** Even seasoned veterans of East Indian cuisine have been known to rate this deep-pink, art-filled restaurant among the best in the United States. The kitchen prepares fairly traditional recipes—tandoori chicken, lamb vindaloo, *saag paneer* (spinach with Farmers' cheese), shrimp *biryani* (tossed with cashews, raisins, almonds, and saffron rice)—but the presentation is always flawless and the ingredients fresh. Meals are cooked as hot or mild as requested. Try the Indian buffet at lunch. ✉ *227 Don Gaspar Ave., enter from parking lot on Water St.* ☎ *505/986–5859* ⊕ *www.indiapalace.com* ▤ *AE, MC, V.*

$$$$
CONTEMPORARY
Fodor's Choice
★
✕ **Inn of the Anasazi.** The romantic, 90-seat restaurant with hardwood floors, soft lighting, and beam ceilings feels slightly less formal than the other big-ticket dining rooms in town. A patio is open during the summertime and makes for fun street-side people-watching. New executive chef Oliver Ridgeway has redone the menu using a global approach to local and seasonally available ingredients, serving dishes like mole-glazed veal medallions with white and green asparagus, Oregon morels and elephant garlic, and Hawaiian tuna with wasabi-nut crust. Patio fare is lighter and just as interesting—the ahi tuna gyro and fennel salad with a kalamata tapenade are just two of the terrific dishes. Sunday brunch is a sure bet. ✉ *113 Washington Ave.* ☎ *505/988–3030* ▤ *AE, D, DC, MC, V.*

$$
SPANISH
Fodor's Choice
★
✕ **La Boca.** This little restaurant, a clean, bright room within an old adobe building, has quickly gained rave reviews and become a local favorite for its intriguingly prepared Spanish food and excellent wine list. Chef James Campbell Caruso has created a menu just right for Santa Fe's eating style; a wide, changing array of delectable tapas and an edited selection of classic entrées, like the paella. The friendly, efficient staff is happy to advise on wine and food selections. The chef's tasting menu for $55 per person (additional $25 for wine or sherry pairings) is a fun way to experience Caruso's well-honed approach to his food. Desserts, like the rich chocolate pot au feu, are sumptuous. The room tends to be loud and can get stuffy during winter when the Dutch door and windows are closed, but crowds are friendly and you never know who you'll end up next to in this town of low-key luminaries and celebrities. Half-price Tapas en la Tarde from 3 to 5 during the week make a perfect late lunch. ✉ *72 W. Marcy St, Santa Fe Plaza* ☎ *505/982–3433* ▤ *AE, D, DC, MC, V* ⊘ *No lunch Sun.*

$$$
CONTEMPORARY
✕ **La Casa Sena.** The Southwestern-accented and Continental fare served at La Casa Sena is beautifully presented if not consistently as delicious as it appears. Weather permitting, get a table on the patio surrounded by hollyhocks, flowering shrubs, and centuries-old adobe walls. A favorite entrée is the braised Colorado lamb shank with huitlacoche-chipotle demi-glace,

roasted purple-and–Yukon gold potatoes, braised cippolini onions, and orange gremolata. There's a knockout lavender crème brûlée on the dessert menu. For a musical meal (evenings only), sit in the restaurant's adjacent, less-pricey Cantina ($$), where the talented and perky staff belt out Broadway show tunes. There's also a wineshop, which sells many of the estimable vintages offered on the restaurant's wine list. ⊠*Sena Plaza, 125 E. Palace Ave.* ☎*505/988–9232* ⊕*www.lacasasena.com* ☰*AE, D, DC, MC, V.*

¢ ✗ **La Choza.** The less touristy, harder-to-find, and less expensive sister to the Shed, La Choza (which means "the shed" in Spanish), serves super-tasty, super-traditional New Mexican fare. Chicken or pork *carne adovada* burritos, white clam chowder spiced with green chiles, huevos rancheros, and wine margaritas are specialties. The dining rooms are dark and cozy, with vigas set across the ceiling and local art on the walls. The staff is friendly and competent. ⊠*905 Alarid St. , near Cerrillos Rd. at St. Francis Dr., around the corner from the Railyard Park* ☎*505/982–0909* ☰*AE, DC, MC, V* ⊗*Closed Sun.*

NEW MEXICAN
Fodor'sChoice
★

$$ ✗ **Los Mayas.** Owners Fernando Antillas and Reyes Solano brought the spirit of Latin America with them when they opened this restaurant. They've transformed a nondescript building into a cozy, tile-floored space with a shady patio—albeit with plastic patio chairs. The menu mixes New Mexican, Latin American, and South American recipes. The guacamole made table-side is a sure bet, as is the chile en nogada, a stuffed pepper in a smooth, rich, and slightly sweet walnut sauce. Entrées, such as the charbroiled skirt steak and cheese rellenos with rice and black beans, or shrimp sautéed with butter and garlic, are equally reliable. There's guitar music every night, including flamenco on Saturday. ⊠*409 W. Water St.* ☎*505/986–9930* ⊕*www.losmayas. com* ☰*AE, D, DC, MC, V* ⊗*No lunch.*

LATIN

$ ✗ **Maria's New Mexican Kitchen.** Serving more than 100 kinds of margaritas is but one of this rustic restaurant's claims to fame. The house margarita is one of the best in town (and you may have surmised that we take our margaritas seriously here). Get the silver coin if you want to go top-shelf and leave the rest of the super tequilas to sip on without intrusion of other flavors. The place holds its own as a reliable, super-tasty source of authentic New Mexican fare, including chiles rellenos, blue-corn enchiladas, and green-chile tamales. The Galisteo chicken, parboiled and covered in red chiles, is simple and satisfying. ⊠*555 W. Cordova Rd.* ☎*505/983–7929* ⊕*www.marias-santafe.com* ☰*AE, D, DC, MC, V.*

NEW MEXICAN
★

$ ✗ **Mariscos la Playa.** Yes, even in landlocked Santa Fe, it's possible to find incredibly fresh and well-prepared seafood served in big portions. This cheery, colorful Mexican restaurant surrounded by strip malls is just a

SEAFOOD
★

SANTA FE COOKING

If you'd like to bring the flavors of the Southwest to your own kitchen, consider taking one or more of the wildly popular and fun cooking classes at the **Santa Fe School of Cooking** (✉116 W. San Francisco St., Santa Fe Plaza ☎505/983–4511 ⊕www.santafeschoolofcooking.com). Regular classes are taught during days and evenings, and more elaborate courses include the Insider's Culinary Adventure, a meeting-and-eating tour with some of Santa Fe's most notable chefs, or the multiday New Mexico Culture & Cuisine Tour that introduces participants to the chefs, restaurants, and farmers whose passionate devotion to food has made Santa Fe the culinary hot spot that it is. It offers courses that are kid-friendly, too. Reservations are a must.

short hop south of downtown. Favorite dishes include the absolutely delicious shrimp wrapped in bacon with Mexican cheese and *caldo vuelve a la vida,* a hearty soup of shrimp, octopus, scallops, clams, crab, and calamari. There's also shrimp soup in a tomato broth, fresh oysters on the half shell, and grilled salmon with pico de gallo. The staff and service are delightful. ✉537 W. Cordova St. ☎505/982–2790 🗀AE, DC, MC, V

¢ ✕**Mission Cafe.** Tucked down the alley behind the San Miguel Mission, this sunny, art-filled gem of a café inside an 1850s adobe serves super-tasty and satisfying breakfast and lunch fare. The food is American- and New Mexican–inspired, with excellent breakfast burritos, delicious pies and cakes from Josie's (hard to come by, longtime local favorites), strong espresso drinks, and locally produced Taos's Cow Ice Cream. Local, natural, and organic meats and ingredients are used. During the warmer months, dine on the big front patio, shaded with leafy trees. ✉237 E. DeVargas St. ☎505/983–3033 🗀MC, V ⊗No dinner. Closed Sun.

CAFÉ

★

$$ ✕**Mu Du Noodles.** This warm and cozy eatery on busy stretch of Cerrillos Road excels both in its friendly and helpful staff and its interesting pan-Asian fare. Book ahead on weekends—this place fills up fast. Dinner specials are always good, though if you're fond of spicy food be sure to ask for "hot" as their food tends to the mild.–Sample sweet-and-sour rockfish with water chestnuts, smoked bacon, and jasmine rice; Vietnamese spring rolls with peanut-hoisin sauce; or stir-fried tenderloin beef with whole scallions, sweet peppers, bean sprouts, and fat rice noodles. Mu, the proprietor, is a strong advocate of cooking with local, organic ingredients. ✉1494 Cerrillos Rd. ☎505/988–1411 ⊕www.mudunoodles.com 🗀AE, MC, V ⊗Closed Sun. and Mon. No lunch.

ASIAN

$$$$ ✕**O'Keeffe Cafe.** This swanky but low-key restaurant next to the Georgia O'Keeffe Museum turns out some delicious and creative fare, including what may be the town's best soups. This is much more than a typical museum café, although the lunches do make a great break following a jaunt through the museum. Dinner is the main event, however, showcasing such tempting and tasty selections as sweetbreads with shallots and cherry demi-glace; cashew-encrusted mahimahi over

CONTEMPORARY

garlic-mashed potatoes with a mango-citrus–butter sauce; and Colorado lamb chops with red chile–honey glaze; and mint-infused couscous. Chef Laurent Rea's tasting menu with wine pairing for $120 is a very good deal. Patios shaded by leafy trees are great dining spots during warm weather. ⊠*217 Johnson St.* ☎*505/946–1065* ⊕*www. okeeffecafe.com* ⊟*AE, D, MC, V.*

$$$ ✕**Pink Adobe.** Rosalea Murphy opened this restaurant in 1944, and
ECLECTIC the place still reflects a time when fewer than 20,000 people lived here. The intimate, rambling rooms of this late-17th-century house have fireplaces and artwork and are filled with conversation made over special-occasion meals. The ambience of the restaurant, rather than the mediocre food and spotty service, accounts for its popularity. The steak Dunigan, smothered in green chile sauce and mushrooms, the lobster, crab, and shrimp enchiladas in green chile lobster bisque, and the Southern fried chicken are among the eclectic dishes served. The apple pie drenched in rum sauce is a favorite. Excellent, top-shelf margaritas are mixed in the adjacent Dragon Room bar. ⊠*406 Old Santa Fe Trail* ☎*505/983–7712* ⊕*www.thepinkadobe.com* ⊟*AE, D, DC, MC, V* ⊗*No lunch weekends.*

$ ✕**Plaza Café.** Run with homespun care by the Razatos family since
ECLECTIC 1947, this café has been a fixture on the Plaza since 1918. The decor—
★ red leather banquettes, black Formica tables, tile floors, a coffered tin ceiling, and a 1940s-style service counter—hasn't changed much in the past half century. The food runs the gamut, from cashew mole enchiladas to New Mexico meat loaf to Mission-style burritos, but the ingredients tend toward Southwestern. You'll rarely taste a better tortilla soup. You can cool it off with an old-fashioned ice-cream treat from the soda fountain. It's a good, tasty stop for breakfast, lunch, or dinner. ⊠*54 Lincoln Ave.* ☎*505/982–1664* ≜*Reservations not accepted* ⊟*AE, D, MC, V.*

$ ✕**Pyramid Cafe.** Tucked into a strip mall five minutes south of down-
MIDDLE town, this restaurant, with photos of Tunisia, kilim rugs, and North
EASTERN African textiles on the walls, delights locals with flavors not available
★ anywhere else in town. The Tunisian owner and his staff are adept at preparing classic dishes with the Mediterranean flavors of Lebanon and Greece, but when they turn their attention to home flavors, and those of neighboring Morocco, your taste buds will sing. Try the specials, like the Moroccan *tajin* with chicken, prunes, raisins, and spices served with rice in a domed, terra-cotta dish. The *brik a l'oeuf*, a turnover-like Tunisian specialty in phyllo dough with an egg and creamy herbed mashed potatoes tucked inside, is as wonderful as it is unusual. The Tunisian plate, a sampler, is incredible. Local, organic ingredients are used, and there are excellent vegetarian options. The lunch buffet is fresh and satisfying. ⊠ *505 W. Cordova, near Sav-On, south of Guadalupe District* ☎*505/989–1378* ⊟*AE, MC, V.*

$$ ✕**Railyard Restaurant & Saloon.** Set inside a bustling, handsome ware-
AMERICAN house in the Railyard at the Guadalupe District, this trendy spot operated by the same talented management that runs 315 Restaurant & Wine Bar serves relatively affordable, well-prepared American favorites that have been given nouvelle twists. Good bets include steamed black

mussels in fresh tomato-and-basil broth, fried buttermilk-chicken strips with Creole rémoulade dipping sauce, sesame-and-panko-crusted tuna with a soy-honey sauce, and barbecued baby back ribs. If the soft-shell crab is available, order it. Many patrons sit in the casual bar, where both the full and lighter menus are available, and sip on pomegranate margaritas or well-chosen wines by the glass. The patio out front, with breathtaking views of the Sangre de Cristo mountains, is a great spot to sit in the summer. Lunch prices average about $10. ⊠ *530 S. Guadalupe St.* ☎ *505/989–3300* ▤ *AE, D, MC, V* ⊘ *No lunch Sun.*

$$$
CONTEMPORARY
★

✕ **Ristra.** This unprepossessing restaurant in the trendy Guadalupe District presents a first-rate menu of Southwestern-influenced country French cooking. You might start with chorizo-stuffed calamari with watercress and smoked-tomato sauce; roasted rack of lamb with couscous, minted tomatoes, preserved lemon, and Niçoise olives is a tempting main dish. Top off your meal with an almond-butter cake served with warm spiced apples and a mascarpone-caramel sauce. The wines are well selected, and the service is swift and courteous. Navajo blankets hang on stark white walls, and Pueblo pottery adorns the handful of niches. There's a hip, stylish cocktail bar with its own menu of lighter dishes, including a great burger. ⊠ *548 Agua Fria St.* ☎ *505/982–8608* ⊕ *www.ristrarestaurant.com* ▤ *AE, MC, V* ⊘ *No lunch.*

$
PIZZA
★

✕ **Rooftop Pizzeria.** Santa Fe got its first truly sophisticated pizza parlor in 2006 with the opening of this slick indoor-outdoor restaurant atop the Santa Fe Arcade. The kitchen here scores high marks for its rich and imaginative pizza toppings: consider the one topped with lobster, shrimp, mushrooms, apple-smoked bacon, caramelized leeks, truffle oil, Alfredo sauce, and four cheeses on a blue-corn crust. Antipasti and salads are impressive, too, as there's a wonderful smoked-duck confit–and–peppercorn spread, or the smoked-salmon Caesar salad. There's also an extensive beer and wine list. Although the Santa Fe Arcade's main entrance is on the Plaza, it's easier to access the restaurant from the arcade's Water Street entrance, a few doors up from Don Gaspar Avenue. ⊠ *60 E. San Francisco St.* ☎ *505/984–0008* ▤ *AE, D, MC, V.*

$
AMERICAN

✕ **San Francisco Street Bar & Grill.** Occupying a sun-filled, second-floor space just off the Plaza, this convivial spot offers inexpensive, well-prepared American fare with New Mexican flourishes, along with a nice selection of wines, beers, and cocktails. It's a family-friendly place with comfy booths and smaller hardwood tables and chairs, and walls adorned with fine local art. Popular starters include fried calamari or pan-seared shrimp salad. The half-pound burger here is superb, along with such reliable standbys as asiago-basil-garlic ravioli and grilled ruby trout with grilled-pineapple salsa. ⊠ *50 E. San Francisco St. (look for the sign and head up the somewhat-hidden staircase)* ☎ *505/982–2044* ▤ *AE, D, MC, V.*

$$$
CONTEMPORARY
★

✕ **Santacafé.** Minimalist elegance marks the interior of Santacafé, one of Santa Fe's vanguard "food as art" restaurants, two blocks north of the Plaza in the historic Padre Gallegos House. Seasonal ingredients are included in the inventive dishes, which might include Alaskan halibut with English peas, saffron couscous, capers, and preserved lemon. Shiitake-and-cactus spring rolls with ponzu sauce make a terrific starter, as does the sublime crispy-fried calamari with a snappy lime-chile dipping sauce—which is big; add a salad for a couple of dollars and you've got a meal. The patio is a joy in summer, and the bar makes a snazzy spot to meet friends for drinks just about any time of year. If you're on a tight budget, consider the reasonably priced lunch menu. Sunday brunch is a favorite among locals. ⊠ *231 Washington Ave.* ☎ *505/984–1788* ⊕ *www.santacafe.com* ▤ *AE, MC, V* ⊘ *No lunch Sun.*

> **WORD OF MOUTH**
>
> "We had lunch at The Shed and had the famous mocha cake for dessert, worth every rave word anyone has ever uttered about it....Thank goodness we got one to share though. That is one intense cake!"
>
> —J62

$$ ✕ **The Shed.** The lines at lunch attest to the status of this downtown New
NEW MEXICAN
FodorsChoice
★
Mexican eatery. The rambling, low-doored, and atmospheric adobe dating from 1692 is decorated with folk art, and service is downright neighborly. Even if you're a devoted green chile sauce fan, you must try the locally grown red chile the place is famous for; it is rich and perfectly spicy. Specialties include red-chile enchiladas, green-chile stew with potatoes and pork, comforting posole, and their charbroiled Shedburgers. The mushroom bisque is a surprising and delicious offering. Homemade desserts, like the mocha cake, are fabulous. There's a full bar, too. ⊠ *113½ E. Palace Ave.* ☎ *505/982–9030* ▤ *AE, DC, MC, V* ⊘ *Closed Sun.*

$$ ✕ **Shohko.** After a brief hiatus Shohko and her family have returned and
JAPANESE
★
once again this is the place for the freshest, best-prepared sushi and sashimi in town. On any given night there are two dozen or more varieties of fresh fish available. The soft-shell crab tempura is feather-light, and the Kobe beef with Japanese salsa is tender and delicious. Sit at the sushi bar and watch the expert chefs work their magic, or at one of the tables in this old adobe with whitewashed walls, dark-wood vigas, and Japanese decorative details. Table service is friendly, but can be slow. ⊠ *321 Johnson St., near Santa Fe Plaza* ☎ *505/982–9708* ▤ *AE, D, DC, MC, V* ⊘ *No lunch weekends.*

¢ ✕ **Tecolote Cafe.** The mantra here is "no toast" and you won't miss it.
ECLECTIC
★
Since 1980, owners Alice and Bill Jamison have filled the bellies of locals and tourists alike with their delicious breakfasts and lunches founded, primarily, on northern New Mexican cuisine. The simple rooms and comfortable seating allow you to focus on such dishes as the sheepherder's breakfast (red potatoes browned with jalapeños and topped with red and green chiles and two eggs), delicious carne adovada (lean pork slow-cooked in their homemade red chile), and a green-chile stew that locals swear by to cure colds. French toast is prepared with homemade breads. When the server asks if you'd like a tortilla or the bakery basket, go for the basket—it's full of warm, fresh muffins and biscuits that are heavenly. ⊠ *1203 Cerrillos Rd.* ☎ *505/988–1362* ⌯ *Reservations not accepted* ▤ *AE, D, DC, MC, V* ⊘ *No dinner.*

¢ ✕ **Tia Sophia's.** This downtown joint serves strictly New Mexican break-
NEW MEXICAN
★
fasts and lunches (open until 2 PM). You're as likely to be seated next to a family from a remote village in the mountains as you are to a legislator or lobbyist from the nearby state capitol. Tia's ("Auntie's") delicious homemade chorizo disappears fast on Saturdays; if you're an aficionado,

Where to
Stay & Eat in
Greater Santa Fe

0   1/2 mile

0   1 km

TO TAOS, ESPAÑOLA

84/285

See Detail Maps:
**Where to Stay in
Downtown Santa Fe
Where to Eat in
Downtown Santa Fe**

N. Guadalupe St.

San Francisco St.
W. Alameda St.

Old
Santa Fe
Station

Guadalupe St.

Sandoval St.

Galisteo St.

Hickox St.

Cerrillos   Rd.

N. St. Francis Dr.

Don Diego Ave.

Don Gaspar Ave.

Cordova Rd.

St. Francis Dr.

W. Alameda St.

Santa Fe River

Agua Fria St.

Osage Rd.

Galisteo St.

Cerrillos Rd.

14

College
of Santa Fe

Llano St.

St. Michael's Dr.

Calle Lorca

Butolph Rd.

St. Michael's Dr.

TO TURQUOISE TRAIL

Siringo Rd.

84/285

Camino Carlos Rey

Yucca St.

Zia Rd.

TO ALBUQUERQUE

1

2

3

4

5

6

6

7

4 5

Restaurants ▼

Hotels & Campgrounds ▼

3

KEY

① Restaurant

① Hotel

get there early. Order anything and expect a true taste of local tradition. Mammoth chile-smothered breakfast burritos will hold you over for hours on the powdery ski slopes during winter. Be warned, though: the red and green chiles are spicy and you're expected to understand this elemental fact of local cuisine. No alcohol. ⊠*210 W. San Francisco St.* ☎*505/983–9880* ⊟*MC, V* ⊘*No dinner. Closed Sun.*

> ## WORD OF MOUTH
>
> "For us, nothing beats Tia Sophia's on a Saturday morning. Well, Tesuque Village Market is right up there, too."
>
> —BeachGirl247

$
NEW MEXICAN

✕**Tomasita's.** An evergreen local favorite, yet in the scheme of the amazing New Mexican food available in this town, it's not a standout, though everything is reliable. Located in one of the old railroad depots, the interior is nondescript, though the yellow-glass windows cast a strange light over the place. It's almost always busy, full of locals and tourists who line up at the door for spicy green-chile dishes. The full bar is an interesting place to watch a local, not-for-tourists, scene unfold. ⊠ *500 S. Guadalupe St., Guadalupe District* ☎*505/983–5721* ⚐*Reservations not accepted* ⊟*A, D, DC, MC, V.*

$$$$
ITALIAN

✕**Trattoria Nostrani.** This restaurant earns kudos for such stellar seasonal northern Italian fare as fried squash blossoms and baby artichokes with salsa verde and griddled montasio cheese, and taglierini with shaved summer truffles. The cozy dining room occupies a late-19th-century Territorial-style house a few blocks from the Plaza; dining on the front porch is especially pleasant. The wine list is extensive and meticulously selected. The caveat: despite excellent service, widespread complaints about the arrogant management persist, and there are extremely rigid no-scent and no-cell-phone policies. ⊠*304 Johnson St.* ☎*505/983–3800* ⊕*www.trattorianostrani.com* ⊟*AE, DC, MC, V* ⊘*Closed Sun. No lunch.*

¢
ECLECTIC
★

✕**Tune Up.** The local favorite formerly known as Dave's Not Here has become Tune Up. After a fairly extensive renovation of what is still a very small space, the new room has a cozier feel with colorful walls and wood details, booths, a few tables, and a community table. The shaded patio out front is a great summertime spot to enjoy the toothsome breakfasts and lunches served. Start the day with savory, and surprisingly delicate, breakfast rellenos, fluffy buttermilk pancakes, or the huevos Salvadoreños (eggs scrambled with scallions and tomatoes, served with refried beans, panfried bananas, and a tortilla). Lunch offerings include the super-juicy Dave Was Here burger served with crispy home-cut fries, a ginger-chicken sandwich on ciabatta bread, and Salvadoran treats called pupusas, which are most like griddled, flattened, soft tamales—delicious! Homemade baked goods include a peanut-butter-cookie sandwich filled with Nutella. The staff is friendly and efficient and the care taken by the new owners, Chuy and Charlotte Rivera, is evident. ⊠ *115 Hickox St.* ☎*505/983–7060* ⚐*Reservations not accepted* ⊟*AE, MC, V* ⊘*No dinner.*

$$
STEAK

✕**Vanessie.** This classy, lodgelike space with high ceilings and a tremendously popular piano cabaret serves hefty portions of well-prepared chops and seafood to a well-heeled, older clientele. New Zealand rack of lamb, tenderloin of elk, and dry-aged steaks are among the specialties. There's lighter fare—burgers, onion loaf, salads—served in the piano bar, where noted musicians Doug Montgomery and Charles Tichenor perform classical and Broadway favorites well into the evening (no cover). ⊠*434 W. San Francisco St.* ☎*505/982–9966* ⊟*AE, DC, MC, V* ⊘*No lunch.*

$$
AMERICAN
★
✕ **Zia Diner.** Located in a renovated coal warehouse from the 1880s, this slick diner with a low-key, art deco–style interior serves comfort food with a twist (green chile–piñon meat loaf, for example). Stop in for a full meal or just snack on their classic banana split with homemade hot fudge sauce. Zia's Cobb salad is one of the best in town, and the amazingly fluffy corn, green chile, and asiago pie served with a mixed green salad is hard to match. Service is friendly, and the food is fresh with lots of local ingredients. There's a small patio and a friendly bar known for its tasty mixed drinks and personable bartenders. Breakfast here is great start to the day: try the Nutty New Mexican, a take on eggs Benedict with green-chile corned beef hash, poached eggs, and hollandaise sauce. Yum! ⊠*326 S. Guadalupe St.* ☎*505/988–7008* ⊕*www.ziadiner.com* ⊟*AE, MC, V.*

WHERE TO STAY

Depending on how much you spend, you can ensconce yourself in quintessential Santa Fe style or anonymous hotel-chain decor. Cheaper options are available on Cerrillos (pronounced sir-*ee*-yos) Road, the rather unattractive business thoroughfare southwest of downtown. You pay more as you get closer to the Plaza, but for many visitors it's worth it to be within walking distance of many attractions. Some of the best deals are offered by B&Bs—many of those near the Plaza offer much better values than the big, touristy hotels. Rates drop, often from 30% to 50%, from November to April (excluding Thanksgiving and Christmas).

Santa Fe also has a wide range of long- and short-term vacation rentals, some of them available through the **Management Group** (☎*866/982–2823* ⊕*www.santaferentals.com*). Rates generally range from $100 to $300 per night for double-occupancy units, with better values at some of the two- to four-bedroom properties. Many have fully stocked kitchens. Another route is to rent a furnished condo or casita at one of several compounds geared to travelers seeking longer stays. The best of these is the luxurious **Campanilla Compound** (☎*505/988–7585 or 800/828–9700* ⊕*www.campanillacompound.com*), just north of downtown; rates run from about $1,400 to $1,800 per week in summer. Another good, similarly priced bet is **Fort Marcy Suites** (☎ *888/570–2775* ⊕*www.fortmarcy. com*), on a bluff just northeast of the Plaza with great views. The individually furnished units accommodate two to six guests and come with full kitchens and wood fireplaces—these can be rented nightly or weekly.

WHAT IT COSTS				
¢	$	$$	$$$	$$$$
Hotels	under $70	$70–$130	$131–$190	$191–$260	over $260

Prices are for a standard double room in room in high season, excluding 13.5%–14.5% tax.

BEST BETS FOR SANTA FE LODGING

Fodor's offers a selective listing of quality lodging experiences in every price range, from the city's best budget beds to its most sophisticated luxury hotels. Here, we've compiled our top recommendations by price and experience. The very best properties—in other words, those that provide a particularly remarkable experience in their price range—are designated in the listings with the Fodor's Choice logo.

FODOR'S CHOICE

Don Gaspar Inn $$
El Rey Inn $
Hacienda Nicholas $$
Hotel Santa Fe $$
Inn of the Anasazi $$$$
Inn of the Five Graces $$$$
Inn on the Alameda $$$
Madeleine Inn $$
Ten Thousand Waves $$$$

By Price

$

El Rey
Santa Fe Courtyard by Marriott
Bobcat Inn $

$$

Don Gaspar Inn
Hacienda Nicholas
Old Santa Fe Inn
Madeleine Inn

$$$

El Farolito
Inn on the Alameda
Water St. Inn

$$$$

Inn of the Anasazi
Inn of the Five Graces
Ten Thousand Waves

By Experience

BEST HOTEL BAR

Hotel St. Francis $$$
Inn of the Anasazi $$$$
Inn of the Governors (Del Charro) $$$
La Fonda $$$$

BEST FOR KIDS

El Rey $
La Posada $$$$
Inn at Loretto $$$$

BEST LOCATION

La Fonda $$$$
Inn on the Alameda $$$
Inn of the Anasazi $$$$

BEST FOR ROMANCE

Inn of the Five Graces $$$$
La Posada $$$$
Madeleine Inn & Absolute Nirvana Spa $$
Ten Thousand Waves $$$$

BEST SERVICE

Inn of the Anasazi $$$$
Inn on the Alameda $$$
Inn of the Five Graces $$$$

BEST VIEWS

Inn at Loretto $$$$
La Fonda $$$$

BEST-KEPT SECRET

El Farolito $$$
Don Gaspar $$
Hacienda Nicholas $$

DOWNTOWN VICINITY

$$$
★
🏨**Alexander's Inn.** Once a B&B, Alexander's now rents two two-story cottages. It remains an excellent lodging option. Located just a few blocks from the Plaza and Canyon Road, it exudes the charm of old Santa Fe. Cottages are cozy, with Southwest- and American country–style furnishings, ethnic heirlooms, skylights, tall windows, and fireplaces. Each has a kitchen, fireplace, full bathroom, and private bedroom upstairs. The grounds are dotted with tulips, hyacinths, lilac, and apricot trees. Guests receive discounts at the nearby Absolute Nirvana Spa (⇨ *Spa box*) and full access to El Gancho Health Club, a 15-minute drive away. You'll find a generous welcome basket with wine and snacks, and attentive service. **Pros:** Private, homey retreat in the heart of historic Santa Fe, an excellent value. **Cons:** Shares open yard with private home. ⊠ *529 E. Palace Ave.* ☎ *505/986–1431 or 888/321–5123* ⊕ *www.alexanders-inn. com* ⇨ *2 cottages* ⟨ *In-room: kitchen. In-hotel: parking (free), Wi-Fi, some pets allowed* ⊟*D, MC, V* ⊺⊘⋈*CP.*

$$
Fodor's Choice
★
🏨**Don Gaspar Inn.** One of the city's best-kept secrets, this exquisitely landscaped and decorated compound is on a pretty residential street a few blocks south of the Plaza. Its three historic houses have three distinct architectural styles: Arts and Crafts, Pueblo Revival, and Territorial. Floral gardens and aspen and cottonwood trees shade the tranquil paths and terraces, and both Southwest and Native American paintings and handmade furnishings enliven the sunny rooms and suites. The Arts and Crafts main house has two fireplaces, two bedrooms, and a fully equipped kitchen. Staff is attentive without hovering. Considering the setting and amenities, it's a great value. **Pros:** Beautiful decor, generous breakfasts, lush gardens. **Cons:** Some rooms close to elementary school can be noisy in the morning when school is in. ⊠ *623 Don Gaspar Ave.* ☎ *505/986–8664 or 888/986–8664* 🖷 *505/986–0696* ⊕ *www.dongaspar.com* ⇨ *5 rooms, 5 suites, 1 cottage* ⟨ *In-room: kitchen (some), refrigerator, Wi-Fi. In-hotel: parking (free), no-smoking rooms* ⊟*AE, MC, V* ⊺⊘⋈*CP.*

$$
🏨**Eldorado Hotel & Spa.** Because it's the closest thing Santa Fe has to a convention hotel, the Eldorado sometimes gets a bad rap, but it's actually fairly inviting, with individually decorated rooms and stunning mountain views. Rooms are stylishly furnished with carved Southwestern-style desks and chairs, large upholstered club chairs, and art prints; many have terraces or kiva-style fireplaces. The rooftop pool and gym are great fun, and there's music nightly, from classical Spanish guitar to piano, in the comfortable lobby lounge. A full slate of treatments, from Vichy rain showers to High Mesa salt scrubs, is offered by the hotel's luxe Nidah Spa. **Pros:** Serviceable accommodations three blocks from Santa Fe Plaza. **Cons:** Staff's attention to service varies wildly. ⊠ *309 W. San Francisco St.* ☎ *505/988–4455 or 800/955–4455* 🖷 *505/995–4555* ⊕ *www.eldoradohotel.com* ⇨ *213 rooms* ⟨ *In-room: kitchen (some), Wi-Fi. In-hotel: 2 restaurants, room service, bar, pool, gym, spa, laundry service, parking (paid)* ⊟*AE, D, DC, MC, V.*

$$$
🏨**El Farolito.** All the beautiful Southwestern and Mexican furniture in this small, upscale compound is custom-made, and all the art and photography original. Rooms are spacious and pleasant with fireplaces

and separate entrances; some are in their own little buildings. El Farolito has a peaceful downtown location, just steps from the capitol and a few blocks from the Plaza. Some have CD players. The same owners run the smaller Four Kachinas inn, which is close by and has one handicapped-accessible room (rare among smaller Santa Fe properties). The Continental breakfast here is a real treat, featuring a tempting range of delicious baked goods. **Pros:** Attentive service; special dietary requests accommodated. **Cons:** No on-site pool or hot tub. ⊠*514 Galisteo St.* ☎*505/988–1631 or 888/634–8782* ⊕*www.farolito.com* ☞*7 rooms, 1 suite* ♿*In-room: Wi-Fi. In-hotel: no-smoking rooms* ⊟*AE, D, MC, V* ⦿*CP.*

> **WORD OF MOUTH**
>
> "We enjoyed our stay at Hacienda Nicholas. It is in the adobe style, very comfortable rooms, reasonably priced, and close to both the Plaza and the Canyon Road galleries."
>
> —PJTravels

$$ **Garrett's Desert Inn.** This sprawling, U-shaped motel may surround
★ a parking lot and offer relatively little in the way of ambience, but it's fairly well maintained and you can't beat its location two blocks from the Plaza, smack in the middle of historic Barrio de Analco. The clean, no-frills rooms are done in earthy tones with a smattering of Southwest touches, and there's a pleasant pool and patio as well as an inviting bar that serves cocktails and light food and has a pool table. **Pros:** Ongoing updates of rooms continue to improve this downtown bargain. **Cons:** $8 per night parking fee. ⊠*311 Old Santa Fe Trail* ☎*505/982–1851 or 800/888–2145* ⊕*www.garrettsdesertinn.com* ☞*83 rooms* ♿*In-room: Wi-Fi. In-hotel: restaurant, pool, gym, laundry facilities, parking (paid)* ⊟*AE, DC, MC, V.*

$$ **Hacienda Nicholas.** It is rare to find classic Santa Fe accommoda-
Fodor'sChoice tions—this actually *is* an old hacienda—blocks from the Plaza for rea-
★ sonable prices. This is one such place. The thick adobe walls surrounding the building create a peace and solitude that belies its central location. Southwest decor mixes with French country and Mexican details to create an ambience perfectly suited to this city. Homemade, organic breakfasts are deluxe; afternoon snacks will leave you begging for the recipes (which they'll cheerfully provide). The rooms are extremely comfortable and quiet, with details like plush comforters and sheets, and cozy robes. Several rooms open on to the interior courtyard, which has a kiva fireplace and offers a perfect respite after a long day of exploring. This is a real find. **Pros:** Rates are significantly lower than one would expect for the level of service and amenities here; the inn is one of the most "eco-friendly" in town. **Cons:** No hot tub or pool, though guests have privileges at El Gancho Health & Fitness Club 15 minutes away. ⊠*320 E. Marcy St., Santa Fe Plaza* ☎*888/284–3170* ⊕*www.haciendanicholas. com* ☞*7 rooms* ♿*In-hotel: Wi-Fi* ⊟*AE, D, MC, V.*

$$ **Hotel Santa Fe.** Picurís Pueblo has controlling interest in this hand-
Fodor'sChoice some Pueblo-style three-story hotel on the Guadalupe District's edge
★ and a short walk from the Plaza. The light, airy rooms and suites are traditional Southwestern, with locally handmade furniture, wooden

blinds, and Pueblo paintings; many have balconies. The hotel gift shop, Santa Fe's only tribally owned store, has lower prices than many nearby retail stores. The 35 rooms and suites in the posh Hacienda wing have corner fireplaces and the use of a London-trained butler. Amaya is one of the better hotel restaurants in town. Informal talks about Native American history and culture are held in the lobby, and Native American dances take place May–October. **Pros:** Professional, helpful staff, lots of amenities. **Cons:** Some rooms are cramped; standard rooms only slightly above chain-hotel decor. ✉ *1501 Paseo de Peralta* ☎ *505/982–1200 or 800/825–9876* 🖷 *505/984–2211* ⊕ *www. hotelsantafe.com* 🛏 *40 rooms, 91 suites* ⚲ *In-hotel: restaurant, bar, pool, laundry service, parking (free)* ☰ *AE, D, DC, MC, V.*

$$$ 🛏 **Hotel St. Francis.** Listed on the National Register of Historic Places, this three-story building, parts of which were constructed in 1923, has walkways lined with turn-of-the-20th-century lampposts and is one block south of the Plaza. The simple, elegant rooms with high ceilings, casement windows, brass-and-iron beds, marble and cherry antiques, and original artworks suggest a refined establishment, though this isn't always the case. Afternoon tea, with scones and finger sandwiches, is served daily (not complimentary) in the huge lobby, which rises 50 feet from a floor of blood-red tiles. **Pros:** The hotel bar is among the few places in town where you can grab a bite to eat until midnight. **Cons:** Service can be spotty and many of the rooms (and especially bathrooms) are quite tiny. ✉ *210 Don Gaspar Ave.* ☎ *505/983–5700 or 800/529–5700* 🖷 *505/989–7690* ⊕ *www.hotelstfrancis.com* 🛏 *80 rooms, 2 suites* ⚲ *In-room: refrigerator, Wi-Fi. In-hotel: restaurant, room service, bar, gym, concierge, laundry service, parking (paid)* ☰ *AE, D, DC, MC, V.*

$$$ 🛏 **Inn on the Alameda.** Near the Plaza and Canyon Road is one of the
Fodor's Choice   Southwest's best small hotels. Alameda means "tree-lined lane," and
★   this one perfectly complements the inn's location by the gurgling Santa Fe River. The adobe architecture and enclosed courtyards strewn with climbing rose vines combine a relaxed New Mexico country atmosphere with the luxury and amenities of a top-notch hotel, from afternoon wine and cheese to free local and toll-free calls to triple-sheeted beds with 300-count Egyptian bedding. Rooms have a Southwestern color scheme, handmade armoires and headboards, and ceramic lamps and tiles—many have patios and kiva fireplaces. **Pros:** The solicitous staff is first-rate; excellent breakfasts. **Cons:** No pool. ✉ *303 E. Alameda St.* ☎ *505/984–2121 or 888/984–2121* 🖷 *505/986–8325* ⊕ *www. innonthealameda.com* 🛏 *59 rooms, 10 suites* ⚲ *In-room: refrigerator (some). In-hotel: bar, gym, laundry facilities, parking (free), some pets allowed, Wi-Fi* ☰ *AE, D, DC, MC, V* ⧉*CP.*

$$$$ 🛏 **Inn of the Anasazi.** Unassuming from the outside, this first-rate bou-
Fodor's Choice   tique hotel is one of Santa Fe's finest, with superb architectural detail.
★   The prestigious Rosewood Hotel group took over the property in 2005, carefully upgrading the already sumptuous linens and furnishings. Each room has a beamed viga-and-latilla ceiling, kiva-style gas fireplace, antique Indian rugs, handwoven fabrics, and organic toiletries (including sunblock). Other amenities include full concierge services, twice-

daily maid service, exercise bikes upon request, and a library. Especially nice touches in this desert town are the humidifiers in each guest room. A few deluxe rooms have balconies. The restaurant is excellent. **Pros:** The staff is thorough, gracious, and highly professional. **Cons:** Few rooms have balconies to take advantage of the lovely views; no hot tub or pool. ⊠ *113 Washington Ave.* ☎ *505/988–3030 or 800/688–8100* 🖷 *505/988–3277* ⊕ *www.innoftheanasazi.com* 🛏 *58 rooms* ⟵ *In-room: safe, Wi-Fi. In-hotel: restaurant, bar, parking (paid), some pets allowed* ⊟ *AE, D, DC, MC, V.*

$$$$
Fodor'sChoice
★

🔝 **Inn of the Five Graces.** There isn't another property in Santa Fe to compare to this sumptuous yet relaxed inn with an unmistakable East-meets-West feel. The management and staff at this hotel have created a property that fits right in with the kind of memorable properties you hear about in Morocco and Bali. The decor differs from the cliché Santa Fe style, yet locals would tell you that this melding of styles is what true Santa Fe style is all about. The suites have Asian and Latin American antiques and art, kilim rugs, jewel-tone throw pillows, and mosaic-tile bathrooms; most have fireplaces, and many have soaking tubs or walk-in steam showers. The personal service stands out: dream catchers and ghost stories are left on your pillow, refrigerators are stocked, and afternoon margarita and wine-and-cheese spreads, an exquisite breakfast, and even daily walking tours are all available. A new spa treatment room has been added with several luxe treatments to salve the skin from the high, dry mountain climate. **Pros:** Tucked into a quiet, ancient neighborhood, the Plaza is only minutes away; fantastic staff, attentive but not overbearing. **Cons:** The cost of a room limits a stay here to all but the very fortunate. ⊠ *150 E. DeVargas St.* ☎ *505/992–0957 or 866/992–0957* 🖷 *505/955–0549* ⊕ *www.fivegraces.com* 🛏 *22 suites* ⟵ *In-room: kitchen (some), refrigerator, Wi-Fi. In-hotel: parking (free), some pets allowed* ⊟ *AE, MC, V* ⦾ *BP.*

$$$
★

🔝 **Inn of the Governors.** This rambling hotel by the Santa Fe River received a major makeover in 2004, and is staffed by a polite, enthusiastic bunch. Rooms have a Mexican theme, with bright colors, hand-painted folk art, feather pillows, Southwestern fabrics, and handmade furnishings; deluxe rooms also have balconies and fireplaces. Perks include a complimentary tea-and-sherry social each afternoon and a quite extensive breakfast buffet along with free Wi-Fi and newspapers. New Mexican dishes and lighter fare like wood-oven pizzas are served in the very popular and very reasonably priced (¢) bar-restaurant, Del Charro. **Pros:** Close to Plaza; friendly, helpful staff. **Cons:** Standard rooms tend to be small and cramped. ⊠ *101 W. Alameda St.* ☎ *505/982–4333 or 800/234–4534* 🖷 *505/989–9149* ⊕ *www.innofthegovernors.com* 🛏 *100 rooms* ⟵ *In-room: refrigerator, Wi-Fi. In-hotel: restaurant, room service, bar, pool, parking (free)* ⊟ *AE, D, DC, MC, V* ⦾ *BP.*

$$$$

🔝 **Inn at Loretto.** This plush, oft-photographed, pueblo-inspired property attracts a loyal clientele, many of whom swear by the friendly staff and high decorating standards. The lobby opens up to the gardens and large pool, and leather couches and high-end architectural details make the hotel a pleasure to relax in. Rooms are among the largest of any downtown property and contain vibrantly upholstered, handcrafted furnishings and sumptuous slate-floor bathrooms—many have large balconies overlooking downtown. Other nice touches include an iPod dock and a complimentary newspaper each day. The new restaurant, Luminaria, serves creative Southwestern fare. The spa offers a wide range of Balinese and Thai-style treatments and services. **Pros:** The location, two blocks from the Plaza, is ideal. **Cons:** Fairly expensive parking and resort fees. ⊠*211 Old Santa Fe Trail* ☎*505/988–5531 or 800/727–5531* 🖷*505/984–7988* ⊕*www.hotelloretto.com* 💬*134 rooms, 5 suites* ⌂*In-room: Mini-bar, Wi-Fi. In-hotel: restaurant, bar, pool, gym, spa, parking (paid)* ⊟*AE, D, DC, MC, V.*

$$ 🖫 **Inn on the Paseo.** This inn is on a busy road, but at least this stretch of Paseo de Peralta is two lanes wide and is in a semi-residential neighborhood a short walk from the Plaza. Rooms are fairly simple, and can be small, but clean and light, some with hardwood floors and all with pleasing Southwestern furnishings and color schemes—some have fireplaces and private patios. The staff is laid-back and friendly. The two historic main buildings are joined by a modern lobby with a pitched ceiling, where Continental breakfast is served—in warm weather you can dine on the sundeck. **Pros:** Located just a few blocks from the Plaza. **Cons:** Try to get a room away from the road to avoid traffic noise. ⊠*630 Paseo de Peralta* ☎*505/984–8200 or 800/457–9045* ⊕*www.innonthepaseo.com* 💬*16 rooms, 2 suites* ⌂*In-hotel: parking (free), no kids under 8, no-smoking rooms* ⊟*MC, V* ⊙*CP.*

$$ 🖫 **Inn of the Turquoise Bear.** In the 1920s, poet Witter Bynner played host
★ to an eccentric circle of artists and intellectuals, as well as some wild parties in his mid-19th-century Spanish–Pueblo Revival home, which is now a B&B. Rooms are simple but have plush linens. The inn's style preserves the building's historic integrity, and there's plenty of ambience and a ranchlike lobby. You might sleep in the room where D.H. Lawrence slept, or perhaps Robert Oppenheimer's room. The terraced flower gardens provide plenty of places to repose away from the traffic on Old Santa Fe Trail, which borders the property. This is the quintessential Santa Fe inn. **Pros:** Gorgeous grounds and a house steeped in local history; gracious, knowledgeable staff. **Cons:** No pool or hot tub on-site. ⊠*342 E. Buena Vista* ☎*505/983–0798 or 800/396–4104* ⊕*www.turquoisebear.com* 💬*8 rooms, 2 with shared bath; 3 suites* ⌂*In-room: Wi-Fi. In-hotel: parking (free), some pets allowed* ⊟*AE, D, MC, V* ⊙*CP.*

$$$$ 🖫 **La Fonda.** History and charm are more prevalent in this sole Plaza-front hotel than first-class service and amenities. The pueblo-inspired structure was built in 1922 and enlarged many times. Antiques and Native American art decorate the tiled lobby, and each room has hand-decorated wood furniture, wrought-iron light fixtures, beamed ceilings, and high-speed wireless. Some suites have fireplaces. The 14 rooftop rooms are the most luxurious and include Continental breakfast and private concierge services; there's also an exercise room, garden, and outdoor hot tub there. La Plazuela Restaurant, with its hand-painted glass tiles, serves good and creative Southwestern food. Folk and R&B bands rotate nightly in the bar. **Pros:** Great building and location,

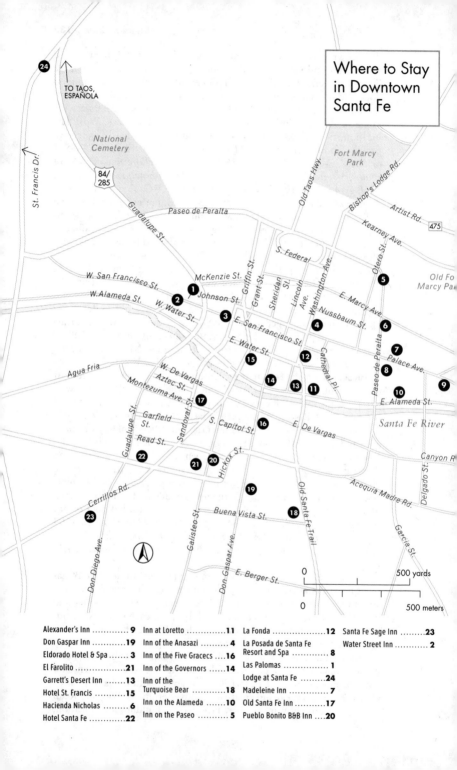

Where to Stay in Downtown Santa Fe

Santa Fe: Spa Mecca of the Southwest

Santa Fe has established itself as a major spa destination. From day spas to resorts where you can spend days ensconced in beautiful surroundings with endless treatment options, there is a spa and a specialty for everyone in this town. There are spas at most of the better hotel resorts, but the spas listed here stand out for their highly trained therapists, specialized treatments, and overall experience.

Absolute Nirvana lives up to its name with its lush, peaceful Indo-Asian setting and the sumptuous treatments it offers. Master-level massage therapists use all-organic, delectable food-grade ingredients. Most treatments finish with homemade snacks and a rose-petal bath in a massive stone tub. A certified Green Spa, it doesn't get better than Nirvana. ⊠ *106 Faithway St., on the grounds of Madeleine Inn, Santa Fe Plaza* ☎ *505/983–7942* ⊕ *www.absolute nirvana.com.*

Body is a day spa just south of the Guadalupe District offering Thai, Swedish, and Japanese massage in addition to Rolfing, Reiki, and prenatal massage. Facials focus on rehydrating skin. Café, boutique, and child-care on the premises. ⊠ *333 Cordova Rd.* ☎ *505/986–0362* ⊕ *www.bodyof santafe.com.*

La Posada Resort & Spa offers a wide range of treatments, many with regional ingredients, in this historic downtown resort. Hair and nail services and a fitness center are also in the spa complex. ⊠ *330 E. Palace Ave., Santa Fe Plaza* ☎ *505/986–0000* ⊕ *www.laposadadesantafe.com.*

Spa Samadhi at Sunrise Springs Resort offers art-strewn walls and waterfalls, fruit and tea, and a profusion of treatments to move one's chi. Earthy cedar sauna and outdoor hot tubs are at your disposal. Transformative sessions, such as holographic and polarity therapies, sound healing, nutritional counseling, and lymphatic release are also available. This eco-resort unfolds over 70 green and serene acres, 15 mi southwest of downtown Santa Fe. ⊠ *242 Los Piños Rd.* ☎ *505/471–3600* ⊕ *www.sunrise springs.com.*

Ten Thousand Waves is a renowned Japanese-style spa with outstanding facilities and treatments, 10 minutes north of Santa Fe toward the ski basin. Primarily a day spa—the hot tubs are a popular option—it has a limited number of suites available for longer stays. ⊠ *3451 Hyde Park Rd.* ☎ *505/992–5025* ⊕ *www.ten thousandwaves.com.*

steeped in history. **Cons:** For the price, facilities don't stand up to comparison with other downtown properties. ⊠ *100 E. San Francisco St.* ☎ *505/982–5511 or 800/523–5002* 🖶 *505/988–2952* ⊕ *www.lafondasantafe.com* 🛏 *143 rooms, 24 suites* ⚷ *In-room: Wi-Fi. In-hotel: restaurant, bars, pool, gym, laundry service, parking (paid)* 🚻 *AE, D, DC, MC, V.*

$$$$ 🏨 **La Posada de Santa Fe Resort and Spa.** Rooms on the beautiful, quiet grounds of this hotel vary, but extensive renovations have enhanced all rooms to a level of luxury previously lacking. Many have fireplaces, all have flat-screen TVs, CD players, leather couches, marble bathrooms, and Navajo-inspired rugs. The main building contains a handful of

luxurious, high-ceiling Victorian rooms. The property boasts excellent bar, spa, and common areas, including the fantastic contemporary restaurant Fuego (⇨ *Where to Eat*) and the Staab House Lounge. Guests are offered numerous complimentary events throughout the week, like Margarita Monday, wine-and-cheese pairings on Wednesday, and chef's receptions on Friday. **Pros:** Numerous amenities, two blocks from the Santa Fe Plaza. **Cons:** Resort can sometimes feel overrun with tour-bus crowds. ⊠*330 E. Palace Ave.* ☎*505/986–0000 or 866/331–7625* 🖷*505/982–6850* ⊕*www.laposadadesantafe.com* ✒*120 rooms, 39 suites* ⚘*In-room: Wi-Fi. In-hotel: restaurant, bar, pool, gym, spa, parking (paid)* ▤*AE, D, DC, MC, V.*

$$$ 🏨**Las Palomas.** It's a pleasant 10-minute walk west of the Plaza to reach this group of properties, consisting of two historic, luxurious compounds, one of them Spanish Pueblo–style adobe, the other done in the Territorial style, with a Victorian ambience, as well as the 15 rooms in the recently acquired La Tienda & Duran House compound. A network of brick paths shaded by mature trees leads past the casitas, connecting them with secluded courtyards and flower gardens. Each casita has a bedroom, full kitchen, living room with pull-out sofa, and fireplace, and each opens onto a terrace or patio. Locally handcrafted wood-and-leather sofas, desks, and tables fill these spacious accommodations, along with Native American artwork and sculptures. It's an elegant alternative to the city's upscale full-service hotels, affording guests a bit more privacy and the feel of a private cottage rental—though it is managed by the Hotel Santa Fe. **Pros:** Kid-friendly, with swings and a play yard; on-site fitness center. **Cons:** Big variation in accommodations; no hot tub or pool on-site (guests may use pool at the Hotel Santa Fe). ⊠*460 W. San Francisco St.* ☎*505/982–5560 or 877/982–5560* 🖷*505/982–5562* ⊕*www.laspalomas.com* ✒*38 units* ⚘*In-room: kitchen, Wi-Fi. In-hotel: gym* ▤*AE, D, DC, MC, V* ⏸*CP.*

$$ 🏨**Lodge at Santa Fe.** Rooms at this former Radisson have pleasant Southwestern furnishings and earth-tone fabrics, though some of the furnishings and facilities are showing wear. The hilltop location offers spectacular views east toward the Sangre de Cristo Mountains and south toward the Sandias—but only from certain rooms, so ask when reserving. The Plaza is a five-minute drive (they offer free shuttle service), the Santa Fe Opera just a bit farther. Las Mañanitas restaurant serves decent Spanish and Southwestern fare, and the adjacent cabaret is home in summer to flamenco dancer Maria Benitez's troupe. The bar hosts some of the town's better DJs for dancing. **Pros:** Guests have free access to the Santa Fe Spa next door, which has a full health club. **Cons:** Service is lackluster; no restaurants or attractions within walking distance. ⊠*750 N. St. Francis Dr.* ☎*505/992–5800 or 888/563–4373* 🖷*505/842–9863* ⊕*www.hhandr.com* ✒*103 rooms, 25 suites* ⚘*In-room: Wi-Fi. In-hotel: restaurant, room service, bar, pool, parking (free)* ▤*AE, D, DC, MC, V.*

$$ 🏨**Madeleine Inn.** Santa Fe hasn't always been a town of pseudo-pueblo buildings and this lovely Queen Anne Victorian is living proof. Built by a railroad tycoon in 1886, this beautifully maintained B&B is nestled amongst mature trees and gardens just four blocks from the Plaza.

Fodor's Choice
★

Plush beds, lovely antiques and art adorn the rooms. Fireplaces grace four rooms and the smells of freshly baked goodies welcome you in the afternoon. Organic breakfasts here are worth sticking around for, and the staff is professional and gracious. The amazing Absolute Nirvana spa is on the premises. Guests have privileges to El Gancho Health & Tennis Club 15 minutes away. **Pros:** Like its companion inn, Hacienda Nicholas, the rates at this committed "eco-friendly" business are a bargain for the services and amenities provided. **Cons:** Steep stairs, no elevators in this three-story Victorian. ⊠ *106 Faithway St. Santa Fe Plaza* ☎ *505/982–3465 or 888/877–7622* ⊕ *www.madeleineinn.com* ⤶ *7 rooms* ⚐ *In hotel: Wi-Fi* ⊟ *AE, D, MC, V.*

\$\$ ⚿ **Old Santa Fe Inn.** About four blocks south of the Plaza, in the hip ★ Guadalupe District, this contemporary inn, which opened in 2001 and looks like an attractive, if fairly ordinary, adobe motel, has stunning and spotless rooms with elegant Southwestern furnishings. Tile baths, high-quality linens, and upscale furnishings fill every room, along with two phone lines and CD stereos; many have kiva fireplaces, or balconies and patios. A small business center and gym are open 24 hours. Most rooms open onto a gravel courtyard parking lot, although chile ristras hanging outside each unit brighten things up. The make-your-own-breakfast-burrito buffet is a nice touch. **Pros:** Rooms are more inviting than several more-expensive downtown hotels and it's a short walk to the Plaza. **Cons:** Minimal, though friendly and professional, staffing. ⊠ *320 Galisteo St.* ☎ *505/995–0800 or 800/745–9910* 🖷 *505/995–0400* ⊕ *www.oldsantafeinn.com* ⤶ *34 rooms, 9 suites* ⚐ *In-room: refrigerator (some), Wi-Fi. In-hotel: gym, parking (free)* ⊟ *AE, D, DC, MC, V* ⦿*CP.*

\$\$ ⚿ **Pueblo Bonito B&B Inn.** Rooms in this 1873 adobe compound have handmade and hand-painted furnishings, Navajo weavings, brick and hardwood floors, sand paintings and pottery, locally carved santos (Catholic saints), and Western art. All have kiva fireplaces and private entrances, and many have kitchens. Breakfast is served in the main dining room. Afternoon tea also offers complimentary margaritas. The Plaza is a five-minute walk away. **Pros:** Intimate, cozy inn on peaceful grounds. **Cons:** Bathrooms tend to be small; breakfast is Continental, not home-cooked. ⊠ *138 W. Manhattan Ave.* ☎ *505/984–8001 or 800/461–4599* 🖷 *505/984–3155* ⊕ *www.pueblobonitoinn.com* ⤶ *13 rooms, 5 suites* ⚐ *In-room: kitchen (some), refrigerator (some). In-hotel: restaurant, laundry facilities, parking (free), no-smoking rooms* ⊟ *AE, DC, MC, V* ⦿*CP.*

\$ ⚿ **Santa Fe Sage Inn.** On the southern edge of the Guadalupe District, ★ this motel offers affordable low-frills comfort and surprisingly attractive (given the low rates) Southwestern decor within walking distance of the Plaza (six blocks). Special packages are available for three- and four-day stays during peak-season events. Get a room upstairs and in one of the rear buildings for the most privacy and quiet. Continental breakfast is served. **Pros:** Comfortable, affordable, and close to downtown. **Cons:** Rooms on corner of Cerrillos and Don Diego can be noisy; unrenovated rooms lackluster. ⊠ *725 Cerrillos Rd.* ☎ *505/982–5952 or 866/433–0335* ⊕ *www.santafesageinn.com* ⤶ *162 rooms* ⚐ *In-*

room: Wi-Fi. In-hotel: restaurant, pool, parking (free), some pets allowed ▭*AE, DC, MC, V* ¶◎¶*CP.*

$$$ **Water Street Inn.** The large rooms in this restored adobe 2½ blocks from the Plaza are decorated with reed shutters, antique pine beds, viga-beam ceilings, hand-stenciled artwork, and a blend of cowboy, Hispanic, and Native American art and artifacts. Most have fireplaces, and all have flat-screen TVs with DVD players and CD stereos. Afternoon hors d'oeuvres are served in the living room. A patio deck is available for relaxing. **Pros:** Close to restaurants, Plaza; gracious staff. **Cons:** Inn overlooks a parking lot. ✉*427 W. Water St.* ☎*505/984–1193 or 800/646–6752* 🌐*www.waterstreetinn.com* *8 rooms, 4 suites* *In-room: DVD, Wi-Fi. In-hotel: parking (free)* ▭*AE, DC, MC, V* ¶◎¶*CP.*

SOUTH OF DOWNTOWN

$ ★ **Bobcat Inn.** A delightful, affordable, country hacienda that's a 15-minute drive southeast of the Plaza, this adobe B&B sits amid 10 secluded acres of piñon and ponderosa pine, with grand views of the Ortiz Mountains and the area's high-desert mesas. John and Amy Bobrick run this low-key retreat and prepare expansive full breakfasts as well as high tea on Saturday during the summer high season (these are by reservation only). Arts and Crafts furniture and Southwest pottery fill the common room, in which breakfast is served and guests can relax throughout the day. The unpretentious rooms are brightened by Talavera tiles, folk art, and colorful blankets and rugs; some have kiva fireplaces. The Lodge Room is outfitted with handcrafted Adirondack furniture, and its bathroom has a whirlpool tub. Guests have access to El Gancho Health & Fitness center (fee) nearby. **Pros:** Gracious, secluded inn; wonderful hosts. **Cons:** Located outside town, a drive is required for all activities except eating at Bobcat Bite, which is right next door; no pets; no children under age 6. ✉*442 Old Las Vegas Hwy.* ☎*505/988–9239* 🌐*www.nm-inn.com* *5 rooms* *In-room: no TV, Wi-Fi. In-hotel: parking (free)* ▭*D, MC, V* ¶◎¶*BP.*

$$ Fodor'sChoice ★ **El Rey Inn.** The kind of place where Lucy and Ricky might have stayed during one of their cross-country adventures, the El Rey was built in 1936 but has been brought gracefully into the 21st century, its rooms and bathrooms handsomely updated without losing any period charm. Rooms are individually decorated and might include antique television armoires, beamed ceilings, upholstered wing chairs and sofas; some have kitchenettes. Each unit has a small covered front patio with wrought-iron chairs. Beautifully landscaped grounds are covered with flowers in the summer and towering trees shade the parking lot. There's a landscaped courtyard with tables and chairs by the pool. **Pros:** Excellent price for a distinctive, charming property. **Cons:** Rooms closest to Cerrillos can be noisy; some rooms are quite dark. ✉*1862 Cerrillos Rd.* ☎*505/982–1931 or 800/521–1349* 📠*505/989–9249* 🌐*www.elreyinnsantafe.com* *86 rooms* *In-room: kitchen (some), Wi-Fi. In-hotel: pool, laundry facilities, parking (free), no-smoking in rooms, gym* ▭*AE, DC, MC, V* ¶◎¶*CP.*

$$$ **Residence Inn.** This compound consists of clusters of three-story adobe town houses with pitched roofs and tall chimneys. Best bets

for families or up to four adults traveling together are the one-room suites, which each have a loft bedroom and a separate sitting area (with a curtain divider) that has a Murphy bed. All units have wood-burning fireplaces. It's right off a major intersection about 3 mi south of the Plaza, but it's set back far enough so that there's no traffic noise. Ask for one of the second-floor end units for the best mountain views. **Pros:** Complimentary full breakfast, evening socials, and grocery-shopping service are provided. **Cons:** Not within walking distance of any restaurants or attractions. ⊠ *1698 Galisteo St.* ☎ *505/988–7300 or 800/331–3131* ⊟ *505/988–3243* ⊕ *www.marriott.com/safnm* ⬦ *120 suites* ⚬ *In-room: kitchen. In-hotel: Wi-Fi, parking (free)* ⊟ *AE, D, DC, MC, V* ❍|*BP.*

3

$ 🏨 **Santa Fe Courtyard by Marriott.** Of the dozens of chain properties along gritty Cerrillos Road, this is the only bona fide gem, even though it looks like all the others: clad in faux adobe and surrounded by parking lots and strip malls. Don't fret—it's easy to forget about the nondescript setting once inside this glitzy miniature resort, which comprises several buildings set around a warren of lushly landscaped interior courtyards. Aesthetically, the rooms look Southwestern, with chunky carved-wood armoires, desks, and headboards reminiscent of a Spanish colonial hacienda. **Pros:** Rooms have the usual upscale-chain doodads: mini-refrigerators, coffeemakers, hair dryers, clock radios—there's also high-speed Internet. **Cons:** Hotel lacks character; need to drive to Downtown. ⊠ *3347 Cerrillos Rd.* ☎ *505/473–2800 or 800/777–3347* ⊟ *505/473–4905* ⊕ *www.santafecourtyard.com* ⬦ *213 rooms* ⚬ *In-room: refrigerator, Wi-Fi. In-hotel: restaurant, room service, bar, pool, gym, laundry facilities, laundry service, parking (free)* ⊟ *AE, D, DC, MC, V.*

¢ 🏨 **Silver Saddle Motel.** Something of an exception to the other seedy and sketchy old motels along Cerrillos Road, this low-slung adobe property transcends the genre, if barely. There's a kitschy, quirky aspect to the place. Rooms are named for icons of the West (Annie Oakley, Wyatt Earp) and contain related plaques with colorful biographies. Furnishings range from motel drab to quirky Southwest: Mexican-tile bathrooms, serape tapestries, built-in bancos, and equipale chairs are present in most. The wildly popular home-furnishings and gift emporium, Jackalope, is next door. The motel is across the street from the town's one strip club, which could be either a pro or a con. **Pros:** Super-affordable, good-sized rooms, some with refrigerators. **Cons:** The facility is aging, mattresses tend to sag, walls are thin. ⊠ *2810 Cerrillos Rd.* ☎ *505/471–7663* ⬦ *27 rooms* ⚬ *In-room: kitchen (some). In-hotel: parking (free)* ⊟ *AE, D, MC, V* ❍|*CP.*

NORTH OF SANTA FE

$$$$ 🏨 **Bishop's Lodge Resort and Spa.** Although this historic resort is just five minutes from the Plaza, its setting in a bucolic valley at the foot of the Sangre de Cristo Mountains makes it feel worlds apart. Outdoor activities abound including hiking, horseback riding, skeet-shooting, tennis (professional lessons available) and trapshooting. History runs deep here with the nearly 150-year-old chapel built by Archbishop Jean Baptiste Lamy—a figure lionized by writer Willa Cather—at the resort's

center. Rooms have antique and reproduction Southwestern furnishings—shipping chests, Mexican tinwork, and Native American and Western art. Many offer balconies or patios with spectacular mountain vistas. The Las Fuentes Restaurant & Bar specializes in inventive Nuevo Latino fare. Locals often descend on the excellent Sunday brunch. **Pros:** Service with a smile—every member of the staff is trained in the art of hospitality, and it shows in their genuine eagerness to please. The tranquil ShâNah Spa and the beautiful grounds make this place a special getaway only minutes from downtown. **Cons:** Resort is spread out over 700 acres and some rooms seem rather far flung. The narrow, windy roads throughout make driving around the property a bit precarious, especially after heavy summer rains. ⊠*Bishop's Lodge Rd., 2½ mi north of downtown* ☎*505/983–6377 or 800/419–0492* ⊕*www.bishopslodge.com* ⇆*92 rooms, 19 suites* ♿*In-room: refrigerator. In-hotel: 2 restaurants (one open during summer only), bar, tennis courts, pool, fitness center, spa, children's programs (ages 5–13), airport shuttle, parking (no fee)* ⊟*AE, D, MC, V.*

$$$$ ⬚**Encantado Auberge Resort.** Sister to famed Auberge du Soleil and Esperanza Resort, Encantado embraces five-star luxury while respecting the region's Native American spirit. Taking advantage of Santa Fe's endless supply of sunshine, villa-style casitas are contemporary, airy and earthy. Kitted with adobe fireplaces, deep soaking tubs, heated bathroom floors and spacious dressing areas, rooms exemplify comfortable luxury. Local Colorado products in the mini-bar (Cap Rock Organic Grape Vodka and C.G. Higgins Caramel Corn) are a thoughtful touch. Detox at The Spa with regionally inspired treatments like Mountain Spirit Purification or take a Pilates class in the movement studio before enjoying a sunset cocktail at The Bar and a sumptuous globe-spanning culinary adventure at Terra. Complimentary shuttles run regularly into town and guests have access to Encantado's downtown concierge center. **Pros:** free-standing couples spa suites; Terra was recently announced as one of *Esquire's* "Best New Restaurants 2008;" complimentary mini-bar (non-alcoholic beverages only). **Cons:** several of the private terraces overlook parking lots; service isn't consistently up to five star standards; landscaping is not mature. ⊠*198 State Road 592* ☎*877/262-4666* ⊕*www.encantadoresort.com* ⇆*65 rooms* ♿*In-room: safe, refrigerator, DVD, Wi-Fi. In-hotel: 1 restaurant, room service, bar, pool, gym, spa treatments, no elevator, laundry service, concierge, public Wi-Fi, parking (no fee), some pets allowed (fee), no-smoking rooms* ⊟*AE, MC, V.*

$$$$ ⬚**Ten Thousand Waves.** Devotees appreciate the Zenlike atmosphere of
FodorśChoice   this Japanese-style health spa and small hotel above town. Twelve light
★   and airy hillside cottages are settled down a piñon-covered hill below the first-rate spa, which is tremendously popular with day visitors. The sleek, uncluttered accommodations have marble or stone wood-burning fireplaces, CD stereos, fine woodwork, low-slung beds or futons, and courtyards or patios; two come with full kitchens. There's also a cozy, vintage Airstream Bambi trailer available at much lower rates ($139 nightly)—it's a kitschy, fun alternative to the much pricier cottages. The facility has private and communal indoor and outdoor hot

tubs and spa treatments. Overnight guests can use the communal tubs for free. The snack bar serves sushi and other healthful treats. Ask about the Japanese movie nights. **Pros:** This is a delightfully sensuous experience all the way around. **Cons:** You might not want to leave the premises, but you'll have to because there is no on-site restaurant. ✉ *3451 Hyde Park Rd., 4 mi northeast of the Plaza* 🕾 *Box 10200, 87504* 🕾 *505/982–9304* 🕾 *505/989–5077* ⊕ *www.tenthousandwaves. com* 🛏 *12 cottages, 1 trailer* 🕭 *In-room: no a/c, kitchen (some), refrigerator, no TV (some), Wi-Fi (some). In-hotel: spa, parking (free), some pets allowed* ▭ *D, MC, V.*

CAMPING

🛆 **Los Campos RV Resort.** The only full-service RV park in town lies between a car dealership on one side and open vistas on the other. Poplars and Russian olive trees, a dry riverbed, and mountains rise in the background. ✉ *3574 Cerrillos Rd.* 🕾 *505/473–1949 or 800/852–8160* 🕭 *Flush toilets, full hookups, dump station, drinking water, guest laundry, grills, picnic tables, electricity, public telephone, play area, swimming (pool), free Wi-Fi* 🛏 *95 sites* ▭ *MC, V.*

★ 🛆 **Rancheros de Santa Fe Campground.** This 22-acre camping park is on a hill in the midst of a piñon forest. Bring your tent or RV, or rent a cabin. You can get LP gas service here. Amenities include free Wi-Fi and cable TV hookups, nightly movies in summer, a hiking trail, a fenced-in dog run, and a recreation room. ✉ *736 Old Las Vegas Hwy., Exit 290 from I–25, 10½ mi south of the Plaza* 🕾 *505/466–3482 or 800/426–9259* ⊕ *www.rancheros.com* 🕭 *Flush toilets, full hookups, dump station, drinking water, guest laundry, showers, grills, picnic tables, electricity, public telephone, general store, play area, swimming (pool)* 🛏 *37 tent sites, 95 RV sites, 5 cabins* ▭ *MC, V.*

🛆 **Santa Fe KOA.** In the foothills of the Sangre de Cristo Mountains, 20 minutes southeast of Santa Fe, this large campground with tent sites, RV sites, and cabins is covered with piñons, cedars, and junipers. Wi-Fi is available; activities include basketball, ring toss, video games, and free movies. ✉ *Old Las Vegas Hwy., Box 95–A* 🕾 *505/466–1419 or 800/562–1514* ⊕ *www.koa.com/where/nm/31159.htm* 🕭 *Flush toilets, partial hookups (electric), drinking water, guest laundry, showers, fire grates, fire pits, picnic tables, electricity, public telephone, general store* 🛏 *44 RV sites, 20 tent sites, 10 cabins* ▭ *D, MC, V* ⊗ *Mar.–Oct.*

NIGHTLIFE & THE ARTS

Few, if any, small cities in America can claim an arts scene as thriving as Santa Fe's—with opera, symphony, and theater in splendid abundance. The music acts here tend to be high-caliber, but rather sporadic. Nightlife, as in dance clubs, is considered fairly "bleak." When popular acts come to town the whole community shows up and dances like there's no tomorrow. A super, seven-week series of music on the Plaza bandstand runs through the summer with performances four nights a week. Gallery openings, poetry readings, plays, and dance concerts take place year-round, not to mention the famed opera and chamber-music festivals. Check the arts and entertainment listings in Santa Fe's daily newspaper, the *New Mexican* (⊕ *www.santafenewmexican.com*), particularly on Friday, when the arts and entertainment section, "Pasatiempo," is included, or check the weekly *Santa Fe Reporter* (⊕ *www.sfreporter.com*) for shows and events. As you suspect by now, activities peak in the summer.

NIGHTLIFE

Culturally endowed though it is, Santa Fe has a pretty mellow nightlife scene; its key strength is live music, which is presented at numerous bars, hotel lounges, and restaurants. Austin-based blues and country groups and other acts wander into town, and members of blockbuster bands have been known to perform unannounced at small clubs while vacationing in the area. But on most nights your best bet might be quiet cocktails beside the flickering embers of a piñon fire or under the stars out on the patio.

Catamount Bar (⊠ *125 E. Water St.* ☏ *505/988–7222*) is popular with the postcollege set; jazz and blues-rock groups play on weekends and some weeknights. The dance floor is small, but there's an enjoyable second-story balcony with seating. The pool tables are a big draw.

★ **The Cowgirl** (⊠ *319 S. Guadalupe St.* ☏ *505/982–2565*) is one of the most popular spots in town for live blues, country, rock, folk, and even comedy, on occasion. The bar is friendly and the drinks are great. The pool hall is fun and can get wild as the night gets late.

Dragon Room (⊠ *406 Old Santa Fe Trail* ☏ *505/983–7712*), at the Pink Adobe restaurant (⇨ Where to Eat above), long a hot spot in town, has been tidied up and, consequently, it's no longer the fun, lively destination for colorful locals and curious tourists. Good drinks and bar food, though.

Eldorado Court and Lounge (⊠ *309 W. San Francisco St.* ☏ *505/988–4455*), in the lobby of the classy Eldorado Hotel, is a gracious lounge where classical guitarists and pianists perform nightly. It has the largest wines-by-the-glass list in town.

★ **El Farol** (⊠ *808 Canyon Rd.* ☏ *505/983–9912*) is where locals go to have a drink at the end of the day; the front porch is a particularly choice spot to enjoy the afternoon and evenings of summer. The roomy, rustic bar has a true Old West atmosphere, and you can order some fine Spanish brandies and sherries in addition to cold beers and tasty mixed drinks (particularly those margaritas locals are so fond of). It's a great place to see a variety of music; the dance floor fills up with a friendly crowd.

Evangelo's (⊠ *200 W. San Francisco St.* ☏ *505/982–9014*) is an old-fashioned, street-side bar, with pool tables downstairs, 200 types of imported beer, and rock bands on many weekends.

★ **Matador** (⊠*116 W. San Francisco St., Suite 113, enter down stairs on Galisteo St., Santa Fe Plaza* ☎*No phone*) is exactly what Santa Fe needed: a dark, subterranean dive bar right downtown. Owners Frank and César, both entertaining characters, have banished any notions of Southwest-style decor by painting the place black and covering the walls with old punk posters, and locals love it. You'll find a decent selection of beers, stiff mixed drinks, and some fine tequilas (this is Santa Fe, after all). The music is all-over-the-place-loud, with local DJs spinning on various nights, and campy flicks play on a wall screen. The early crowd is older, and gets younger and hipper as the night goes on. **Cash only!**

Santa Fe Brewing Company (⊠*35 Fire Pl., on NM 14, the Turquoise Trail* ☎*505/424–3333* ⊕*www.santafebrewing.com*) hosts all sorts of music and serves fine microbrews and food (and Taos's Cow ice cream!) from its location about 15 minutes south of downtown. Recent acts have included X, Sierra Leone Refugee All-Stars, Taj Mahal, and local stars Hundred-Year Flood and Goshen. Very kid-friendly, the venue has an indoor room for the cold months, and a great outdoor stage where the performers, and the sunset, are on full view.

Second Street Brewery (⊠*1814 2nd St.* ☎*505/982–3030*), a short drive south of downtown, packs in an eclectic, easygoing bunch for its own microbrewed ales, pretty lackluster pub fare, live rock, folk, and some great local DJs. There's an expansive patio, and the staff is friendly.

Tin Star Saloon (⊠*411B W. Water St., near Santa Fe Plaza* ☎*505/984–5050* ⊕*www.tinstarsaloon.com*) is a welcome addition to Santa Fe's nightlife, with a great bar in a cozy room and live music almost every night. They book a wide range of music, from hard rock to R&B. The crowd here likes to dance.

Tiny's (⊠*Cerrillos Rd. and St. Francis Dr.* ☎*505/983–9817*), a retro-fabulous restaurant serving steaks and New Mexican fare, is a legend in this town with politicos, reporters, and deal-makers. The real draw is the kitsch-filled '50s cocktail lounge.

WilLee's Blues Club (⊠*401 S. Guadalupe St.* ☎*505/982–0117*) presents poundin' blues, rock and hip-hop shows several nights a week in an intimate, often-packed space in the Guadalupe District.

THE ARTS

The performing arts scene in Santa Fe blossoms in summer. Classical or jazz concerts, Shakespeare on the grounds of St. John's campus, experimental theater at Santa Fe Stages, or flamenco—"too many choices!" is the biggest complaint. The rest of the year is a bit quieter, but an increasing number of off-season venues have developed in recent years. The Pasatiempo section of the *Santa Fe New Mexican*'s Friday edition or the *Santa Fe Reporter*, released on Wednesday, are great sources for current happenings.

The city's most interesting multiuse arts venue, the **Center for Contemporary Arts (CCA)** (⊠*1050 Old Pecos Trail* ☎*505/982–1338* ⊕*www. ccasantafe.org*) presents indie and foreign films, art exhibitions, provocative theater, and countless workshops and lectures.

CONCERT VENUES

A 10-minute drive north of town, **Camel Rock Casino** (⊠*U.S. 285/84* ☎*800/462–2635* ⊕*www.camelrockcasino.com*) hosts a fairly wide variety of performers such as Buju Banton, the Marshall Tucker Band, and Chubby Checker.

Santa Fe's vintage downtown movie house was fully restored and converted into the 850-seat **Lensic Performing Arts Center** (⊠*211 W. San Francisco St.* ☎*505/988–1234* ⊕*www.lensic.com*) in 2001. The grand 1931 building, with Moorish and Spanish Renaissance influences, hosts the Santa Fe Symphony, theater, classic films, lectures and readings, noted world, pop, and jazz musicians, and many other noteworthy events.

On the campus of the Santa Fe Indian School, the **Paolo Soleri Outdoor Amphitheater** (⊠*1501 Cerrillos Rd.* ☎*505/989–6318*) is a fantastic venue and hosts pop, blues, rock, reggae, and jazz concerts spring–fall; past performers have included Ozomatli, Bonnie Raitt, and Chris Isaak. Watching the sunsets play across the sky is as spectacular as the shows onstage.

The **St. Francis Auditorium** (⊠*Museum of Fine Arts, northwest corner of Plaza*) is the scene of cultural events such as theatrical productions and varied musical performances.

DANCE

The esteemed **Aspen Santa Fe Ballet** (☎*505/983–5591 or 505/988–1234* ⊕*www.aspensantafeballet.com*) presents several ballet performances throughout the year at the Lensic Performing Arts Center.

Fans of Spanish dance should make every effort to see **Maria Benitez Teatro Flamenco** (⊠ *1050 Old Pecos Trail in the back of the Children's Museum Bldg.* ☎*505/955–8562 or 888/435–2636* ⊕*www.maria benitez.com*), who performs from late June through August. Maria Benitez is one of the world's premier flamenco dancers, and her performances often sell out well in advance.

FILM

Santa Fe Film Center (⊠*1616 St. Michaels Dr.* ☎*505/988–7414* ⊕*www. santafefilmfestival.com*) is a project of the increasingly well-attended Santa Fe Film Festival. It screens independent films regularly, and sometimes hosts filmmakers for discussions. Call or check its Web site for current showings.

The Screen (⊠*1600 St. Michael's Dr.* ☎*505/473–6494* ⊕*www.the screen.csf.edu* 🎫*$9*) is an intimate art-house theater on the campus of the College of Santa Fe. This relatively small town supports very good film. If you need a reprieve from the sunlight, it's worth checking out its schedule.

MUSIC

★ The acclaimed **Santa Fe Chamber Music Festival** (☎*505/983–2075* ⊕*www. sfcmf.org*) runs mid-July through late August, with performances nearly every night at the St. Francis Auditorium, or, occasionally, the Lensic Performing Arts Center. There are also free youth-oriented concerts given on several summer mornings. You can also attend many rehearsals for free; call for times.

Performances by the **Santa Fe Desert Chorale** (☎*505/988–2282 or 800/244–4011* ⊕*www.desertchorale.org*) take place throughout the summer at a variety of intriguing venues, from the Cathedral Basilica St. Francis to Loretto Chapel. This highly regarded singing group, which was started in 1982, also performs a series of concerts during the December holiday season.

Fodor's Choice **Santa Fe Opera** (☎*505/986–5900 or 800/280–4654* ⊕*www.santafe* ★ *opera.org*) performs in a strikingly modern structure—a 2,126-seat, indoor-outdoor amphitheater with excellent acoustics and sight lines. Carved into the natural curves of a hillside 7 mi north of the city on U.S. 285/84, the opera overlooks mountains, mesas, and sky. Add some of the most acclaimed singers, directors, conductors, musicians, designers, and composers from Europe and the United States, and you begin to understand the excitement that builds every June. The company, which celebrated its 60th anniversary in 2006, presents five works in repertory each summer—a blend of seasoned classics, neglected masterpieces, and world premieres. Many evenings sell out far in advance, but inexpensive standing-room tickets are often available on the day of the performance. A favorite pre-opera pastime is tailgating in the parking lot before the evening performance—many guests set up elaborate picnics of their own, but you can also preorder picnic meals ($32 per meal) by calling (☎*505/983–2433*) 24 hours in advance; pick up your meal up to two hours before the show, at the Angel Food Catering kiosk on the west side of the parking lot. Or you can dine at the Preview Buffet, set up 2½ hours before each performance by the Guilds of the Santa Fe Opera. These meals include a large spread of very good food along with wine, held on the opera grounds. During dessert, a prominent local expert on opera gives a talk about the evening's performance. The Preview Buffet is by reservation only, by calling the opera box office number listed above, and the cost is $50 per person.

Orchestra and chamber concerts are given at St. Francis Auditorium and the Lensic Performing Arts Center by the **Santa Fe Pro Musica** (☎*505/988–4640 or 800/960–6680* ⊕*www.santafepromusica.com*) from September through April. Baroque and other classical compositions are the normal fare; the annual Christmas performance is a highlight.

The **Santa Fe Symphony** (☎*505/983–1414 or 800/480–1319* ⊕*www. sf-symphony.org*) performs seven concerts each season (from October to April) in the Lensic Performing Arts Center.

THEATER

The **Greer Garson Theatre Company** (⊠*College of Santa Fe, 1600 St. Michael's Dr.* ☎*505/473–6511 or 800/456–2673* ⊕*www.csf.edu*) stages student productions of comedies, dramas, and musicals from October to May.

Santa Fe Performing Arts (☎*505/984–1370* ⊕*www.sfperformingarts. org*), running since 1986, has become a local favorite for its professional productions and adult resident company as well as its commitment to outreach education in the schools and for community youth in its after-school programs. The theater is committed to developing new works; call or check the Web site for the current schedule.

The oldest extant theater company west of the Mississippi, the **Santa Fe Playhouse** (⊠*142 E. De Vargas St.* ☎*505/988–4262* ⊕*www.santafe playhouse.org*) occupies a converted 19th-century adobe stable and has been presenting an adventurous mix of avant-garde pieces, classical drama, and musical comedy since 1922. The Fiesta Melodrama—a spoof of the Santa Fe scene—runs late August–mid-September.

Theaterwork (⊠*James A. Little Theater at the New Mexico School for the Deaf, 1060 Cerrillos Rd.* ☎*505/471–1799* ⊕*www.theaterwork. org*) is a well-respected community theater group that performs five plays each season, which run from September through May.

SPORTS & THE OUTDOORS

The Santa Fe National Forest is right in the city's backyard and includes the Dome Wilderness (5,200 acres in the volcanically formed Jémez Mountains) and the Pecos Wilderness (223,333 acres of high mountains, forests, and meadows at the southern end of the Rocky Mountain chain). The 12,500-foot Sangre de Cristo Mountains (the name translates as "Blood of Christ," for the red glow they radiate at sunset) fringe the city's east side, constant and gentle reminders of the mystery and power of the natural world. To the south and west, sweeping high desert is punctuated by several less formidable mountain ranges. The dramatic shifts in elevation and topography around Santa Fe make for a wealth of outdoor activities. Head to the mountains for fishing, camping, and skiing; to the nearby Rio Grande for kayaking and rafting; and almost anywhere in the area for bird-watching, hiking, and biking.

PARTICIPANT SPORTS

For a report on general conditions in the forest, contact the **Santa Fe National Forest Office** (⊠*1474 Rodeo Rd.* ☎*505/438–7840* ⊕*www. fs.fed.us/r3/sfe*). For a one-stop shop for information about recreation on public lands, which include national and state parks, contact the **New Mexico Public Lands Information Center** (⊠*1474 Rodeo Rd.,* ☎*505/438–7542* 🖷*505/438–7582* ⊕*www.publiclands.org*). It has maps, reference materials, licenses, permits—just about everything you need to plan an adventure in the New Mexican wilderness.

○ The huge **Genoveva Chavez Community Center** (✉*3221 Rodeo Rd.*
★ ☎*505/955–4001* ⊕*www.chavezcenter.com*) is a reasonably priced
(adults $4 per day) facility with a regulation-size ice rink (you can
rent ice skates for the whole family), an enormous gymnasium, indoor
running track, 50-meter pool, leisure pool with waterslide and play
structures, aerobics center, fitness room, two racquetball courts, and a
child-care center.

For gear related to just about any outdoors activity you can think of,
check out **Sangre de Cristo Mountain Works** (✉*328 S. Guadalupe St.*
☎*505/984–8221*), a well-stocked shop that both sells and rents hiking,
climbing, camping, trekking, snowshoeing, and skiing equipment. The
staff here can also advise you on the best venues for these activities.

BICYCLING

You can pick up a map of bike trips—among them a 30-mi round-trip
ride from downtown Santa Fe to Ski Santa Fe at the end of NM 475—
from the New Mexico Public Lands Information Center, or at the bike
shops listed below. One excellent place to mountain bike is the Dale
Ball Trail Network, which is accessed from several points.

Bike N' Sport (✉*530 W. Cordova Rd.* ☎*505/820–0809*) provides rentals and information about guided tours.

Mellow Velo (✉*638 Old Santa Fe Trail , Lower Old Santa Fe Trail*
☎*505/995–VELO[8356]*) is a friendly, neighborhood bike shop offering group tours, privately guided rides, bicycle rentals ($35.50 per
day—make reservations), and repairs. These guys offer a great way
to spend a day.

Santa Fe Mountain Sports (✉*607 Cerrillos Rd., Ste. A* ☎*505/988–3337*
⊕*www.santafemountainsports.com* ⊙*Mon.–Sat. 9–6, Sun. 9–5*) has
a good selection of bikes for rent (⇨ *Skiing below*).

BIRD-WATCHING

At the end of Upper Canyon Road, at the mouth of the canyon as
○ it wends into the foothills, the 135-acre **Randall Davey Audubon Cen-**
Fodor's Choice **ter** harbors diverse birds and other wildlife. Guided nature walks are
★ given many weekends; there are also two major hiking trails that you
can tackle on your own. The home and studio of Randall Davey, a
prolific early Santa Fe artist, can be toured on Monday afternoons in
summer. There's also a nature bookstore. ✉*1800 Upper Canyon Rd.*
☎*505/983–4609* ⊕*www.audubon.org/chapter/nm/nm/rdac* 🎟*$2,*
house tour $5 ⊙ *Weekdays 9–5, weekends 10–4; grounds daily dawn-*
dusk; house tours Mon. at 2.

For a knowledgeable insider's perspective, take a tour with **WingsWest**
Birding Tours (☎*800/583–6928* ⊕ *home.earthlink.net/~wingswestnm/*).
Gregarious and knowledgeable guide Bill West leads four- to eight-hour
early-morning or sunset tours that venture into some of the region's
best bird-watching areas, including Santa Fe Ski Basin, Cochiti Lake,
the Jémez Mountains, the Upper Pecos Valley, and Bosque del Apache
National Wildlife Refuge.

FISHING

There's excellent fishing spring through fall in the Rio Grande and the mountain streams that feed into it, as well as a short drive away along the Pecos River. **High Desert Angler** (⊠*453 Cerrillos Rd.* ☎*505/988–7688 or 888/988–7688* ⊕*www.highdesertangler.com*) is a superb fly-fishing outfitter and guide service. This is your one-stop shop for equipment rental, fly-fishing tackle, licenses, and advice.

GOLF

Marty Sanchez Links de Santa Fe (⊠*205 Caja del Rio Rd., off NM 599, the Santa Fe Relief Rte.* ☎*505/955–4400* ⊕*www.linksdesantafe.com*), an outstanding municipal facility with beautifully groomed 18- and 9-hole courses, sits on high prairie west of Santa Fe with fine mountain views. It has driving and putting ranges, a pro shop, and a snack bar. The greens fees are $31 for the 18-hole course, $22 on the par-3 9-holer.

HIKING

Hiking around Santa Fe can take you into high-altitude alpine country or into lunaresque high desert as you head south and west to lower elevations. For winter hiking, the gentler climates to the south are less likely to be snow packed, while the alpine areas will likely require snowshoes or cross-country skis. In summer, wildflowers bloom in the high country, and the temperature is generally at least 10 degrees cooler than in town. The mountain trails accessible at the base of the Ski Santa Fe area (end of NM 475) stay cool on even the hottest summer days. Weather can change with one gust of wind, so be prepared with extra clothing, rain gear, food, and lots of water. Keep in mind that the sun at 10,000 feet is very powerful, even with a hat and sunscreen. *See the Side Trips from the Cities chapter (Chapter 4) for additional hiking areas near Santa Fe.*

For information about specific hiking areas, contact the New Mexico Public Lands Information Center. Any of the outdoor gear stores in town can also help with guides and recommendations. The **Sierra Club** (⊕*www.riogrande.sierraclub.org*) organizes group hikes of all levels of difficulty; a schedule of hikes is posted on the Web site.

Aspen Vista is a lovely hike along a south-facing mountainside. Take Hyde Park Road (NM 475) 13 mi, and the trail begins before the ski area. After walking a few miles through thick aspen groves you come to panoramic views of Santa Fe. The path is well marked and gently inclines toward Tesuque Peak. The trail becomes shadier with elevation—snow has been reported on the trail as late as July. In winter, after heavy snows, the trail is great for intermediate-advanced cross-country skiing. The round-trip is 12 mi and sees an elevation gain of 2,000 feet, but it's just 3½ mi to the spectacular overlook. The hillside is covered with golden aspen trees in late September.

A favorite spot for a ramble, with a vast network of trails, is the **Dale Ball Foothills Trail Network,** a network of some 20 mi of paths that winds and wends up through the foothills east of town and can be accessed at a few points, including Hyde Park Road (en route to the ski valley) and the upper end of Canyon Road, at Cerro Gordo. There are trail maps and signs at these points, and the trails are very well marked.

★ Spurring off the Dale Ball trail system, the steep but rewarding (and dog-friendly) **Atalaya Trail** runs from the visitor parking lot of St. John's College (off Camino de Cruz Blanca, on the east side), up a winding, ponderosa pine–studded trail to the peak of Mt. Atalaya, which affords incredible 270-degree views of Santa Fe. The nearly 6-mi round-trip hike climbs nearly 2,000 feet (to an elevation of 9,121 feet), so pace yourself. The good news: the return to the parking area is nearly all downhill.

HORSEBACK RIDING

New Mexico's rugged countryside has been the setting for many Hollywood westerns. Whether you want to ride the range that Gregory Peck and Kevin Costner rode or just head out feeling tall in the saddle, you can do so year-round. Rates average about $20 an hour. *See the Side Trips from the Cities chapter (Chapter 5) for additional horseback listings in Cerrillos, Galisteo, and Ojo Caliente.*

Bishop's Lodge (⊠*1297 Bishop's Lodge Rd.* ☏*505/983–6377*) provides rides and guides year-round. Call for reservations.

JOGGING

Because of the city's altitude (7,000–7,500 feet), you may feel heavy-legged and light-headed if you start running shortly after you arrive. Once you become acclimated, though, you can find that this is a great place to run. There's a jogging path along the Santa Fe River, parallel to Alameda, and another at Fort Marcy on Washington Avenue. The winding roads and paths up near the scenic campus of St. John's College are also ideal, although the terrain is quite hilly. Pick up gear and running advice at **Running Hub** (⊠*527–B W. Cordova Rd.* ☏*505/820–2523*); the store hosts informal group runs many days and a store run on Thursday at 6 PM. Excellent staff of expert runners and triathletes.

RIVER RAFTING

If you want to watch birds and wildlife along the banks, try the laid-back Huck Finn floats along the Rio Chama or the Rio Grande's White Rock Canyon. The season is generally between April and September. Most outfitters have overnight package plans, and all offer half- and full-day trips. Be prepared to get wet, and wear secure water shoes. For a list of outfitters who guide trips on the Rio Grande and the Rio Chama, write the **Bureau of Land Management (BLM), Taos Resource Area Office** (⊠*226 Cruz Alta Rd., Taos* ☏*505/758–8851* ⊕*www.nm.blm. gov*), or stop by the BLM visitor center along NM 68, 16 mi south of Taos in Pilar.

Kokopelli Rafting Adventures (⊠*551 W. Cordova Rd.* ☏*505/983–3734 or 800/879–9035* ⊕*www.kokopelliraft.com*) will take you on half-day to multiday river trips down the Rio Grande and Rio Chama. **New Wave Rafting** (⊠*Mi 21, Hwy. 68; 70 CR 84B* ☏*800/984–1444* ⊕*www.new waverafting.com*) conducts full-day, half-day, and overnight river trips, as well as fly-fishing trips, from its new location in Embudo, 21 mi north of Española. **Santa Fe Rafting Company and Outfitters** (⊠ *1000 Cerrillos Rd.* ☎ *505/988–4914 or 888/988–4914* ⊕ *www.santaferafting.com*) customizes rafting tours. Tell them what you want—they'll do it.

SKIING

To save time during the busy holiday season you may want to rent skis or snowboards in town the night before hitting the slopes so you don't waste any time waiting during the morning rush. **Alpine Sports** (⊠ *121 Sandoval St.* ☎ *505/983–5155* ⊕ *www.alpinesports-santafe.com*) rents downhill and cross-country skis and snowboards. **Cottam's Ski Rentals** (⊠ *Hyde Park Rd., 7 mi northeast of downtown, toward Ski Santa Fe* ☎ *505/982–0495 or 800/322–8267*) rents the works, including snowboards, sleds, and snowshoes.

★ **Santa Fe Mountain Sports** (⊠ *607 Cerrillos Rd., Guadalupe District* ☎ *505/988–3337* ⊕ *www.santafemountainsports.com*) is a family-owned specialty mountain shop that rents boots, skis, and snowboards for the whole family in the winter, as well as bicycles in the summertime. The super-helpful staff is great to work with.

Ski Santa Fe (⊠ *End of NM 475, 18 mi northeast of downtown* ☎ *505/982–4429, 505/983–9155 conditions* ⊕ *www.skisantafe.com*), open roughly from late November through early April, is a fine, mid-size operation that receives an average of 225 inches of snow a year and plenty of sunshine. It's one of America's highest ski areas—the 12,000-foot summit has a variety of terrain and seems bigger than its 1,700 feet of vertical rise and 660 acres. There are some great powder stashes, tough bump runs, and many wide, gentle cruising runs. The 44 trails are ranked 20% beginner, 40% intermediate, and 40% advanced; there are seven lifts. Snowboarders are welcome, and there's the Norquist Trail for cross-country skiers. Chipmunk Corner provides day care and supervised kids' skiing. The ski school is excellent. Rentals, a good restaurant, a ski shop, and Totemoff Bar and Grill round out the amenities.

SNOWSHOEING

You can always snowshoe on your own in Santa Fe National Forest, which also has fine cross-country ski trails, by renting poles and shoes at **Alpine Sports** *(see above)*, but it's more fun and interesting to take a guided tour. **Outspire Santa Fe** (☎ *505/660–0394* ⊕ *www.outspire.com*) offers guided snowshoe tours in Santa Fe National Forest. No experience is necessary to enjoy this relaxing, wintertime version of hiking. They guide hiking and fishing trips during the summer.

SHOPPING

Santa Fe has been a trading post for eons. Nearly a thousand years ago the great pueblos of the Chacoan civilizations were strategically located between the buffalo-hunting tribes of the Great Plains and the Indians of Mexico. Native Americans in New Mexico traded turquoise and other valuables with Indians from Mexico for metals, shells, parrots, and other exotic items. After the arrival of the Spanish and the West's subsequent development, Santa Fe became the place to exchange silver from Mexico and natural resources from New Mexico for manufactured goods, whiskey, and greenbacks from the United States. With the building of the railroad in 1880, Santa Fe had access to all kinds of manufactured goods as well as those unique to the region via the old trade routes.

The trading legacy remains, but now downtown Santa Fe caters to those looking for handcrafted goods. Sure, T-shirt outlets and a few major retail clothing shops have moved in, but shopping in Santa Fe consists mostly of one-of-a-kind independent stores. Canyon Road, packed with art galleries, is the perfect place to find unique gifts and collectibles. The downtown district, around the Plaza, has unusual gift shops, clothing, and shoe stores that range from theatrical to conventional, curio shops, and art galleries. The funky, up-and-coming Guadalupe District, less touristy than the Plaza, is on downtown's southwest perimeter and includes the Sanbusco Market Center and the Design Center, both hubs of unique and wonderful boutiques.

ART GALLERIES

The following are only a few of the nearly 200 galleries in greater Santa Fe—with the best of representational, nonobjective, Native American, Latin American, cutting-edge, photographic, and soulful works that defy categorization. The Santa Fe Convention and Visitors Bureau (⇨ *Visitor Information in Essentials, above*) has a more extensive listing. *The Collectors Guide to Santa Fe, Taos, and Albuquerque* is a good resource and is available in hotels and at some galleries, as well as on the Web at ⊕ *www.collectorsguide.com*. Check the "Pasatiempo" pullout in the *Santa Fe New Mexican* on Friday for a preview of gallery openings.

Fodor's Choice ★ **Andrew Smith Gallery** (⊠ *203 W. San Francisco St.* ☎ *505/984–1234*) is a significant photo gallery dealing in works by Edward S. Curtis and other 19th-century chroniclers of the American West. Other major figures are Ansel Adams, Edward Weston, O. Winston Link, Henri Cartier-Bresson, Eliot Porter, Laura Gilpin, Dorothea Lange, Alfred Stieglitz, Annie Liebowitz, and regional artists like Barbara Van Cleve.

Bellas Artes (⊠ *653 Canyon Rd.* ☎ *505/983–2745*), a sophisticated gallery and sculpture garden, has ancient ceramics and represents internationally renowned artists like Judy Pfaff, Phoebe Adams, and Olga de Amaral.

Charlotte Jackson Fine Art (⊠ *200 W. Marcy St.* ☎ *505/989–8688*) focuses primarily on monochromatic "radical" painting. Florence Pierce, Joe Barnes, William Metcalf, Anne Cooper, and Joseph Marioni are among the artists producing minimalist works dealing with light and space.

Fodor's Choice ★ **evo Gallery** (⊠ *554 S. Guadalupe St., Guadalupe District* ☎ *505/982–4610* ⊕ *www.evogallery.org*) is another gallery that affirms Santa Fe's reputation as a leading center of contemporary art. Powerhouse artists like Jenny Holzer, Ed Ruscha, Donald Judd, Jasper Johns, and Agnes Martin are represented in this huge space in the Guadalupe District.

Fodor'sChoice   **Gerald Peters Gallery** (⊠*1011 Paseo de Peralta* ☎*505/954–5700*) is
★   Santa Fe's leading gallery of American and European art from the 19th century to the present. It has works by Max Weber, Albert Bierstadt, the Taos Society, the New Mexico modernists, and Georgia O'Keeffe, as well as contemporary artists.

Fodor'sChoice   **James Kelly Contemporary** (⊠*1601 Paseo de Peralta, Guadalupe District*
★   ☎*505/989–1601* ⊕*www.jameskelly.com*) mounts sophisticated, high-caliber shows by international and regional artists, such as Agnes Martin, Bruce Nauman, Susan Rothenberg, and Richard Tuttle. Located in a renovated warehouse directly across from SITE Santa Fe, James Kelly has been instrumental in transforming the Railyard District into Santa Fe's center for contemporary art.

LewAllen Contemporary (⊠*129 W. Palace Ave.* ☎*505/988–8997*) is a leading center for a variety of contemporary arts by both Southwestern and other acclaimed artists, among them Judy Chicago; sculpture, photography, ceramics, basketry, and painting are all shown in this dynamic space.

Fodor'sChoice   **Linda Durham Gallery** (⊠*1101 Paseo de Peralta, near Canyon Rd.*
★   ☎*505/466–6600* ⊕*www.lindadurham.com*) has showcased paintings, sculpture and photography of, primarily, New Mexico–based artists. This community-minded gallery has become highly regarded and its artists highly sought.

Monroe Gallery (⊠*112 Don Gaspar Ave.* ☎*505/992–0800*) showcases works by the most celebrated black-and-white photographers of the 20th century, from Margaret Bourke-White to Alfred Eisenstaedt.

★   **Nedra Matteucci Galleries** (⊠*1075 Paseo de Peralta* ☎*505/982–4631* ⊠*555 Canyon Rd.* ☎*505/983–2731*) exhibits works by California regionalists, members of the early Taos and Santa Fe schools, and masters of American Impressionism and Modernism. Spanish colonial furniture, Indian antiquities, and a fantastic sculpture garden are other draws of this well-respected establishment.

Peyton Wright (⊠*237 E. Palace Ave.* ☎*505/989–9888*), tucked inside the historic Spiegelberg house, represents some of the most talented emerging and established contemporary artists in the country, as well as antique and even ancient Chinese, pre-Columbian, Russian, and Latin works.

Photo-eye Gallery (⊠*376–A Garcia St.* ☎*505/988–5159*) shows contemporary photography that includes the beautiful and sublime; there's also a stellar bookstore.

Pushkin Gallery (⊠*550 Canyon Rd.* ☎*505/982–1990*) provides yet more evidence that Santa Fe's art scene is about so much more than regional work—here you can peruse works by some of Russia's leading 19th- and 20th-century talents, with an emphasis on impressionism.

Riva Yares Gallery (⌧*123 Grant St.* ☎*505/984–0330*) specializes in contemporary artists of Latin American descent. There are sculptures by California artist Manuel Neri, color field paintings by Esteban Vicente, and works by Santa Feans Elias Rivera, Rico Eastman, and others—plus paintings by such international legends as Hans Hofman, Milton Avery, and Helen Frankenthaler.

Santa Fe Art Institute (⌧*1600 St. Michael's Dr.* ☎*505/424–5050*), a nonprofit educational art organization that sponsors several artists in residence and presents workshops, exhibitions, and lectures, has a respected gallery whose exhibits change regularly. The institute is set inside a dramatic contemporary building. Past artists in residence have included Richard Diebenkorn, Larry Bell, Moon Zappa, Henriette Wyeth Hurd, and and Judy Pfaff.

☺ FodorsChoice ★ **Shidoni Foundry and Galleries** (⌧*Bishop's Lodge Rd., 5 mi north of Santa Fe, Tesuque* ☎*505/988–8001*) casts work for accomplished and emerging artists from all over North America. On the grounds of an old chicken ranch, Shidoni has a rambling sculpture garden and a gallery. Self-guided foundry tours are permitted Saturday 9–5 and weekdays noon–1, but the sculpture garden is open daily during daylight hours; you can watch bronze pourings most Saturday afternoons. This is a dream of a place to expose your kids to large-scale art and enjoy a lovely expanse of green grass at the same time.

SPECIALTY STORES

ANTIQUES & HOME FURNISHINGS

Artesanos (⌧*1414 Maclovia St.* ☎*505/471–8020*) is one of the best Mexican-import shops in the nation, with everything from leather equipale chairs to papier-mâché *calaveras* (skeletons used in Day of the Dead celebrations), and tinware. It specializes in Talavera and other tiles.

At **Asian Adobe** (⌧*310 Johnson St.* ☎*505/992–6846*) browse porcelain lamps, ornate antique baby hats and shoes, red-lacquer armoires, and similarly stunning Chinese and Southeast Asian artifacts and antiques.

Bosshard Fine Art Furnishings (⌧*340 S. Guadalupe St.* ☎*505/989–9150*) deals in African ethnographica, which complement the vast selection of tapestries, architectural elements, statues, and ceramics from the Southwest as well as Asia.

Casa Nova (⌧*530 S. Guadalupe St.* ☎*505/983–8558*) sells functional art from around the world, deftly mixing colors, textures, and cultural icons—old and new—from stylish pewter tableware from South Africa to vintage hand-carved ex-votos (votive offerings) from Brazil.

FodorsChoice ★ The **Design Center** (⌧*418 Cerrillos Rd.*), which occupies a former Chevy dealership in the Guadalupe District, contains some of the most distinctive antique and decorative-arts shops in town, plus a couple of small restaurants. Be sure to browse the precious Latin American antiques at

The Art of Santa Fe

The artistic roots of Santa Fe stretch back to the landscape and the devotion of those who roamed and settled here long before the Santa Fe Trail transplanted goods and people from the East. The intricate designs on Native American pottery and baskets, the embroidery on the ritual dance wear, the color and pattern on Rio Grande weavings, and the delicate paintings and carvings of devotional images called santos all contributed to the value and awareness of beauty that Santa Fe holds as its cultural birthright. The rugged landscape, the ineffable quality of the light, and the community itself continue to draw to Santa Fe a plethora of musicians, writers, and visual artists. The spell of beauty is so powerful here that some people call the town "Fanta Se," but for those who live in Santa Fe the arts are very real (as are economic realities; most artists hold additional jobs—ask your waiter).

With wide-eyed enchantment, visitors often buy paintings in orange, pink, and turquoise that are perfect next to the adobe architecture, blue sky, and red rocks of the New Mexican landscape. When they get home, however, the admired works sometimes end up in a closet simply because it's so hard to integrate the Southwestern look with the tone of the existing furnishings and artwork. Taking the risk is part of the experience. Rather than suffering from buyer's remorse, those who make the aesthetic leap can take the spirit of northern New Mexico home with them. Although it may shake up the home decor, the works are a reminder of a new way of seeing and of all the other values that inspire one to travel in the first place.

Most galleries will send a painting (not posters or prints) out on a trial basis for very interested clients. If looking at art is new to you, ask yourself if your interest is in bringing home a souvenir that says "I was there" or in art that will live in the present and inspire the future, independent of the nostalgia for the "land of enchantment." Santa Fe has plenty of both to offer—use discrimination while you look so you don't burn out on the first block of Canyon Road.

Santa Fe, while holding strong in its regional art identity, emerged in the late 1990s as a more international art scene. Native American and Hispanic arts groups now include the work of contemporary artists who have pressed beyond the bounds of tradition. Bold color and the oft-depicted New Mexico landscape are still evident, but you're just as likely to see mixed-media collages by a Chinese artist currently living in San Francisco. A few Santa Fe outlets, such as the Riva Yares Gallery and evo Gallery, are dedicated to representing artists with Latin American roots. "The world is wide here," Georgia O'Keeffe once noted about northern New Mexico. And just as Santa Fe welcomed early modernist painters who responded to the open landscape and the artistic freedom it engendered, contemporary artists working with edgier media, such as conceptual, performance, and installation art, are finding welcoming venues in Santa Fe, specifically at SITE Santa Fe museum.

Claiborne Gallery (☎505/982–8019), along with the artful contemporary desks, tables, and chairs created by owner Omer Claiborne. **Gloria List Gallery** (☎505/982–5622) specializes in rare 17th- and 18th-century devotional and folk art, chiefly from South America, Italy, Spain, and Mexico. And at **Sparrow & Magpie Antiques** (☎505/982–1446), look mostly for East Coast and Midwest folk art and textiles, although the shop carries some Southwestern pieces, too.

Design Warehouse (✉101 W. Marcy St. ☎505/988–1555), a welcome antidote to Santa Fe's preponderance of shops selling Native American and Spanish colonial antiques, stocks hip, contemporary sofas, kitchenware, lamps, and other sleek knickknacks, such as those made by the Italian firm Alessi.

Doodlet's (✉120 Don Gaspar Ave. ☎505/983–3771) has an eclectic collection of stuff: pop-up books, silly postcards, tin art, hooked rugs, and stringed lights. Wonderment is in every display case, drawing the eye to the unusual. Delightfully quirky, there's something for just about everyone here, and often it's affordable.

Foreign Traders (✉202 Galisteo St. ☎505/983–6441), a Santa Fe institution founded as the Old Mexico Shop in 1927 and still run by the same family, stocks handicrafts, antiques, and accessories from Mexico and other parts of the world.

Jackalope (✉2820 Cerrillos Rd. ☎505/471–8539), a legendary if somewhat overpriced bazaar, sprawls over 7 acres, incorporating several pottery barns, a furniture store, endless aisles of knickknacks from Latin America and Asia, and a huge greenhouse. There's also an area where craftspeople, artisans, and others sell their wares—sort of a mini–flea market.

★ **La Mesa** (✉225 Canyon Rd. ☎505/984–1688 ⊕www.lamesaofsanta fe.com) has become well-known for showcasing contemporary handcrafted works by more than 50, mostly local, artists including Kathy O'Neill, Gregory Lomayesva, and Melissa Haid. Collections include dinnerware, glassware, pottery, lighting, fine art, and accessories.

★ **Montez Gallery** (✉Sena Plaza Courtyard, 125 E. Palace Ave. ☎505/982–1828) sells Hispanic works of religious art and decoration, including retablos (holy images painted on wood or tin), bultos (carved wooden statues of saints), furniture, paintings, pottery, weavings, and jewelry. You'll find works by a number of award-winning local artists here.

Pachamama (✉223 Canyon Rd. ☎505/983–4020) carries Latin American folk art, including small tin or silver *milagros,* the stamped metal images used as votive offerings. The shop also carries weavings and Spanish colonial antiques and other delightful trinkets.

Sequoia (✉201 Galisteo St.87501 ☎505/982–7000) shows the imaginative, almost surreal, furniture creations of its owner, who was born in India. Curvaceous glass shelves, lamps, and candlesticks mix with paintings and fine linens.

BOOKS

More than a dozen shops in Santa Fe sell used books, and a handful of high-quality shops carry the latest releases from mainstream and small presses.

ALLÁ (✉102 W. San Francisco St., upstairs ☎505/988–5416) is one of Santa Fe's most delightful small bookstores. It focuses on hard-to-find Spanish-language books and records, including limited-edition handmade books from Central America. It also carries Native American books and music, as well as English translations.

Collected Works Book Store (✉208B W. San Francisco St. ☎505/988–4226) carries art and travel books, including a generous selection of books on Southwestern art, architecture, and general history, as well as the latest in contemporary literature. The proprietress, Dorothy Massey, and her staff are well-loved for their knowledge and helpfulness.

Garcia Street Books (✉376 Garcia St. ☎505/986–0151) is an outstanding independent shop strong on art, architecture, cookbooks, literature, and regional Southwestern works—it's a block from the Canyon Road galleries. It hosts frequent talks by authors under its portal during the summer.

Nicholas Potter (✉211 E. Palace Ave. ☎505/983–5434) specializes in used, rare, and out-of-print books. The quixotic shop also stocks used jazz and classical CDs.

Photo-eye Books (✉376 Garcia St. ☎505/988–5152) stocks new, rare, and out-of-print photography books.

Travel Bug (✉839 Paseo de Peralta ☎505/992–0418) has a huge array of travel tomes and guidebooks, and USGS and other maps. There's also a cozy coffeehouse with high-speed wireless.

CLOTHING & ACCESSORIES

Many tourists arrive in clothing from mainstream department stores and leave bedecked in Western garb looking like they've stepped from a bygone era. If you simply cannot live without a getup Annie Oakley herself would envy, you will find shopping options beyond your wildest dreams. But take a look around at the striking and highly individualized styles of the locals and you'll see that Western gear is mixed with pieces from all over the globe to create what is the real Santa Fe style. There are few towns where you'll find more distinctive, sometimes downright eccentric, expressions of personal style on every age and every shape. Indians, cowboys, hipsters, students, artists, yogis, immigrants from all over the world, and world travelers all bring something to the style mix of this town and you'll find plenty of shops that will allow you to join in the fun.

It is worth asking specifically to see the work of locals during your wanderings. There are artists of every bent in this town and the surrounding areas, not only putting paint to canvas, but creating jewelry, clothing, accessories, and more. Informed by cultural traditions but as cutting-edge and innovative as anything you'll find in New York or San Francisco, the contemporary jewelry coming from Native American artists like Cody Sanderson and Pat Pruitt is incredible. The shops at IAIA downtown and the Museum of Indian Arts and Culture on Museum Hill are good places to see these artists and many others.

Fodor'sChoice
★ **Back at the Ranch** (⊠ *209 E. Marcy St.* ☎ *505/989–8110 or 888/962– 6687*) is the place for cowboy boots. The cozy space, in an old, creaky-floored adobe is stocked with perhaps the finest handmade cowboy boots you will ever see—in every color, style, and embellishment imaginable. Other finds, like funky ranch-style furniture, 1950s blanket coats, jewelry, and belt buckles are also sold. The staff is top-notch and the boots are breathtaking.

★ **Double Take at the Ranch** (⊠ *321 S. Guadalupe St.* ☎ *505/820–7775*) ranks among the best consignment stores in the West, carrying elaborately embroidered vintage cowboy shirts, hundreds of pairs of boots, funky old prints, and amazing vintage Indian pawn and Mexican jewelry. The store adjoins Santa Fe Pottery, which carries the works of local artists.

Lucchese (⊠ *203 W. Water St.* ☎ *505/820–1883*) has been crafting some of the West's finest handmade cowboy boots since 1883.

Maya (⊠ *108 Galisteo St., Santa Fe Plaza* ☎ *505/989–7590*) is a groovy assemblage of unconventional and fun women's clothing, jewelry, accessories, select books, shoes, handbags, global folk art, hats, and a small selection of housewares. It's a funky shop with many lines from small design houses and local jewelers. Check out the selection of *relicario*-style (tiny images of saints in silver frames) jewelry from Wanda Lobito. The staff isn't always terribly helpful, but they aren't unfriendly.

Mirá (⊠ *101 W. Marcy St.* ☎ *505/988–3585*) clothing for women is hip, eclectic, and funky, combining the adventurous spirit of New Mexico with global contemporary fashion. The shop has jewelry, accessories, and collectibles from Latin America, the Flax line of natural-fiber clothing, and knockout dresses and separates not sold anywhere else in town.

Fodor'sChoice
★ **O'Farrell Hats** (⊠ *111 E. San Francisco St.* ☎ *505/989–9666*) is the domain of America's foremost hat-making family. Founder Kevin O'Farrell passed away in 2006, but the legacy continues with his son Scott and the highly trained staff. This quirky shop custom crafts one-of-a-kind beaver-lined cowboy hats that make the ultimate Santa Fe keepsake. This level of quality comes at a cost, but devoted customers—who have included everyone from cattle ranchers to U.S. presidents—swear by O'Farrell's artful creations.

Origins (⊠ *135 W. San Francisco St.* ☎ *505/988–2323*) borrows from many cultures, carrying pricey women's wear like antique kimonos and custom-dyed silk jackets. One-of-a-kind accessories complete the spectacular look that Santa Fe inspires.

FOOD & COOKERY

In the DeVargas shopping center, **Las Cosas Kitchen Shoppe** (⊠ *N. Guadalupe St. at Paseo de Peralta in the De Vargas Mall* ☎ *505/988–3394 or 877/229–7184*) carries a fantastic selection of cookery, tableware, and kitchen gadgetry and gifts. The shop is also renowned for its cooking classes, which touch on everything from high-altitude baking to Asian-style grilling.

★ **The Spanish Table** (⊠ *109 N. Guadalupe St., Santa Fe Plaza* ☎ *505/986–0243* ⊕ *www.spanishtable.com*) stands out as a destination for all Spanish culinary needs. With its Spanish meats and cheeses, cookware and beautiful Majolica pottery, books, dry goods, and wonderful world-music selection, you will be challenged to leave empty-handed. The staff is always ready to help advise on a recipe or gift idea and will ship your purchases anywhere you like.

Fodor'sChoice **Todos Santos** (⊠ *125 E. Palace Ave.* ☎ *505/982–3855*) is a tiny candy
★ shop in the 18th-century courtyard of Sena Plaza, carrying must-be-seen-to-be-believed works of edible art, including chocolate milagros and altar pieces gilded with 23-karat gold or silver leaf. Truffles come in exotic flavors, like tangerine chile, rose caramel, and lemon verbena. Amidst the taste sensations and quirky folk art are amazing and delightful customized Pez dispensers from Albuquerque folk artist Steve White. Hayward, the proprietor, is delightful, and he'll ship.

JEWELRY

Eidos (⊠ *500 Montezuma Ave., inside Sanbusco Center, Guadalupe District* ☎ *505/992–0020* ⊕ *www.eidosjewelry.com*) features "concept-led" minimalist contemporary jewelry from European designers and Deborah Alexander and Gordon Lawrie, who own the store. Lovely, contemporary space, fascinating array of materials, good range of prices, and helpful staff.

Golden Eye (⊠ *115 Don Gaspar St., Santa Fe Plaza* ☎ *505/984–0040*) is a pint-size shop (even by Santa Fe standards) that features fine, handcrafted jewelry in high-karat gold, often paired with gemstones. Its experienced, helpful staff of artisans can help you pick out something beautiful and unusual.

Jett (⊠ *110 Old Santa Fe Trail, Santa Fe Plaza* ☎ *505/988–1414*) showcases jewelers and artists, many local, who are remarkable for creative, original approaches to their work. Intriguing selection of surprisingly affordable silver and gold jewelry, modern artistic lighting, and delightful miniature objects like vintage trailers and circus tents made from recycled metal.

LewAllen & LewAllen Jewelry (⊠ *105 E. Palace Ave., Santa Fe Plaza* ☎ *800/988–5112* ⊕ *www.lewallenjewelry.com*) is run by father-and-daughter silversmiths Ross and Laura LewAllen. Handmade jewelry ranges from whimsical to mystical inside their tiny shop just off the Plaza. There is something for absolutely everyone in here, including delightful charms for your pet's collar.

Fodor'sChoice **Patina** (⊠*131 W. Palace Ave., Santa Fe Plaza* ☎*505/986–3432 or*
★ *877/877–0827* ⊕*www.patina-gallery.com*) presents outstanding contemporary jewelry, textiles, and sculptural objects of metal, clay, and
wood, in a airy, museum-like space. With a staff whose courtesy is
matched by knowledge of the genre, artists-owners Ivan and Allison
Barnett have used their fresh curatorial aesthetic to create a showplace
for the 112 American and European artists they represent—many of
whom are in permanent collections of museums such as MoMA.

MARKETS

Fodor'sChoice Browse through the vast selection of local produce, meat, flowers,
★ honey, and cheese—much of it organic—at the thriving **Santa Fe Farmers' market** (⊠*Guadalupe St. and Cerrillos Rd.* ☎*505/983–4098*
⊕*www.santafefarmersmarket.com*). The market is now housed in its
new, permanent building in the Railyard and it's open year-round. It's
a great people-watching event, and there's storytelling for kids as well
as a snack bar selling terrific breakfast burritos and other goodies.
With the growing awareness of the importance and necessity of eating
locally grown and organic food, this market offers living testimony to
the fact that farming can be done successfully, even in a high-desert
region like this one.

Tesuque Pueblo Flea Market (⊠*U.S. 285/84, 7 mi north of Santa Fe*
☎*505/983–2667* ⊕*www.tesuquepuebloflealmarket.com*) was once
considered the best flea market in America by its loyal legion of bargain
hunters. The Tesuque Pueblo took over the market in the late '90s and
raised vendor fees, which increased the presence of predictable, often
pricey goods brought in by professional flea-market dealers. In recent
years, however, the pueblo has brought in a nice range of vendors, and
this market with as many as 500 vendors in peak season is again one
of the best shopping events in town. The 12-acre market is next to the
Santa Fe Opera and is open Friday–Sunday, mid-March–December.

NATIVE AMERICAN ARTS & CRAFTS

Frank Howell Gallery (⊠*103 Washington Ave.* ☎*505/984–1074*) stocks
lithographs, serigraphs, prints, and posters of the late Frank Howell as
well as works by other Native American artists.

Morning Star Gallery (⊠*513 Canyon Rd.* ☎*505/982–8187*) is a veritable museum of Native American art and artifacts. An adobe shaded
by a huge cottonwood tree houses antique basketry, pre-1940 Navajo
silver jewelry, Northwest Coast Native American carvings, Navajo
weavings, and art of the Plains Indians. Prices and quality prohibit
casual purchases, but the collection is magnificent.

Niman Fine Arts (⊠*125 Lincoln Ave.* ☎*505/988–5091*) focuses on the
prolific work of contemporary Native American artists–Hopi painters
Arlo Namingha and Michael Namingha.

Packard's on the Plaza (⊠*61 Old Santa Fe Trail* ☎*505/983–9241*), the
oldest Native American arts-and-crafts store on Santa Fe Plaza, also
sells Zapotec Indian rugs from Mexico and original rug designs by
Richard Enzer, old pottery, saddles, kachina dolls, and an excellent

selection of coral and turquoise jewelry. Local favorite Lawrence Baca, whose iconic jewelry has made him a regular prizewinner at Spanish Market, is featured here. Prices are often high, but so are the standards. There's also an extensive clothing selection.

Fodor's Choice ★ The **Rainbow Man** (✉107 E. Palace Ave. ☎505/982–8706), established in 1945, does business in an old, rambling adobe complex, part of which dates from before the1680 Pueblo Revolt. The shop carries early Navajo, Mexican, and Chimayó textiles, along with photographs by Edward S. Curtis, a breathtaking collection of vintage pawn and Mexican jewelry, Day of the Dead figures, Oaxacan folk animals, New Mexican folk art, kachinas, and contemporary jewelry from local artists. The friendly staff possesses an encyclopedic knowledge of the art here.

Fodor's Choice ★ **Robert Nichols Gallery** (✉419 Canyon Rd., Canyon Road ☎505/982–2145 ⊕www.robertnicholsgallery.com) represents a remarkable group of Native American ceramics artists doing primarily nontraditional work. Diverse artists such as Glen Nipshank, whose organic, sensuous shapes would be right at home in MoMA, and Diego Romero, whose Cochiti-style vessels are detailed with graphic-novel-style characters and sharp social commentary, are right at home here. It is a treat to see cutting-edge work that is clearly informed by indigenous traditions.

Trade Roots Collection (✉411 Paseo de Peralta ☎505/982–8168) sells Native American ritual objects, such as fetish jewelry and Hopi rattles. Open by appointment only, this store is an excellent source of fine ethnic crafts materials for artists.

Trader's Collection (✉218 Galisteo St., Santa Fe Plaza ☎505/992–0441 ⊕traderscollection.com) was created by several key staff members when the venerable Shush Yaz gallery closed in August, 2007. In this new showplace of American Indian arts and crafts, antique pieces commingle with contemporary works by artists such as Nocona Burgess and jeweler Kim Knifechief. The staff is friendly and knowledgeable.

Taos

WORD OF MOUTH

"We loved Taos. It has a very eclectic mix which appealed to us and we also appreciated the easy access to trails. Restaurants: we enjoyed Joseph's Table and The Apple Tree. Hikes: we enjoyed a very satisfying hike along the west rim of the Rio Grande (another surprise – I had no idea it would be in such a deep canyon) and a wonderful if strenuous hike in Italianos Canyon part way up to the ski valley."

—Diz01

Updated by
Barbara Floria

TAOS CASTS A LINGERING SPELL. Set on a rolling mesa at the base of the Sangre de Cristo Mountains, it's a place of piercing light and spectacular views, where the desert palette changes almost hourly as the sun moves across the sky. Adobe buildings—some of them centuries old—lie nestled amid pine trees and scrub, some in the shadow of majestic Taos Mountain. The smell of piñon wood smoke rises from the valley in winter; in spring and summer, it gives way to fragrant sage.

The magic of the area has drawn people here for hundreds of years. The earliest inhabitants were Native Americans of the Taos–Tiwa tribe; their descendants still live and maintain a traditional way of life at Taos Pueblo, a 95,000-acre reserve 3 mi north of what is now the town's commercial center. Spanish settlers, who arrived in the 1500s, brought both farming and Catholicism to the area; their influence can still be seen today at Ranchos de Taos, 4 mi south of town, and at the San Francisco de Asís Church, whose massive adobe walls and *camposanto* (graveyard) are among the most photographed in the country.

In the early 20th century, another population—artists—discovered Taos and began making the pilgrimage here to write, paint, and take photographs. The early adopters of this movement were painters Bert Phillips and Ernest Blumenschein, who were traveling from Denver on a planned painting trip into Mexico in 1898 when they stopped to have a broken wagon wheel repaired in Taos. Enthralled with the earthy beauty of the region, they abandoned their plan to journey farther south, settled, and eventually formed the Taos Society of Artists in 1915. Over the following years, many illustrious artists, including Georgia O'Keeffe, Ansel Adams, and D. H. Lawrence also took up residence in the area, and it is still a mecca for creative types today. The downtown area is now filled with galleries and shops that display the work of local artists, and museums that document Taos's artistic history.

These days, Taos has a variable population of about 6,500 (the 2000 U.S. Census officially places it at 4,700, but there's always an influx during the summer and the winter ski season, and these numbers don't include Arroyo Seco, Taos Ski Valley, and other neighboring villages). Many come here for a break from the urban sprawl of larger U.S. cities; actress Julia Roberts is among the escapees.

ORIENTATION & PLANNING

GETTING ORIENTED

Taos is small and resolutely rustic, and the central area is highly walkable. Sociable Taoseños make the town a welcoming place to explore. You need a car to reach the Rio Grande Gorge and other places of interest beyond Taos proper. Traffic can be heavy in the peak summer and winter seasons (an accident on the main route through town, Paseo del Pueblo, can back up traffic for miles); ask locals about back roads that let you avoid the busy street.

TOP REASONS TO GO

■ **Southwestern style.** The simple elegance of adobe architecture balances the vibrancy of Southwestern art. The result? Aesthetic perfection.

■ **American roots.** The Taos Pueblo and the proud Navajo Indians that call the area home provide a unique perspective on pre-Columbian culture and accomplishments.

■ **Desert solitaire.** Bask in the ultimate stress-reducer of the empty high desert and pine-covered hills.

■ **Green chiles.** Piquant, but not overly hot, the ubiquitous green chile shows up in everything from breakfast burritos to stacked blue corn enchiladas to lobster bisque. Smokey and smooth, it's an apt corollary to Proust's madeleine.

4

Downtown Taos. More than four centuries after it was laid out, the Taos Plaza and adjacent streets remain the center of tourist activity in Taos. Bent Street, where New Mexico's first American governor lived and died, is an upscale shopping area and gallery enclave, and many of the best restaurants and bars are within walking distance.

South of Taos. The first Spanish settlers were farmers and many families continue to till the fertile land south of Taos. Ranchos de Taos is a small village a few miles south of the Plaza centered around the iconic church memorialized by Georgia O'Keeffe and photographer Ansel Adams.

Taos Pueblo to Rio Grande Gorge. The Pueblo is the virtual beating heart of the entire valley, setting historic precedents and architectural reference points for everything that Taos has become. The casino aside, the area has been spared commercial development and remains a neighborhood of modest homes and farms. High desert scrub and wide-open spaces fall away beneath the elegance of the Rio Grande Gorge Bridge.

TAOS PLANNER

WHEN TO GO

With more than 300 days of sunshine annually, Taos typically yields good weather year-round. The summer high season brings hot days (80s) and cool nights (50s), as well as afternoon thunderstorms. A packed arts and festival schedule in summer means the hotels and B&Bs are filled, lodging rates are high, restaurants are jammed, and traffic anywhere near the Plaza is often at a standstill. Spring and fall are stunning and favor milder temperatures, fewer visitors, and shoulder-season prices. If the snow is plentiful, skiers arrive en masse but are likely to stay close to the slopes, only venturing into town for a meal or two.

GETTING HERE & AROUND

BY AIR Albuquerque International Sunport is the nearest (130 mi) major airport to Taos. Taos Municipal Airport is 12 mi west of the city but ceased offering commercial service in 2005 and is just open to charters and private planes. Faust's Transportation offers shuttle service between Albuquerque's airport and Taos, as well as to Taos Ski Valley, Angel Fire, and Red River. The cost is $50 to $60 per person, and the ride takes 2¾–3 hours.

BY BUS Greyhound Lines runs buses once a day from Albuquerque to Taos.

BY CAR The main route from Santa Fe to Taos is NM 68, also known as the Low Road, which winds between the Rio Grande and red-rock cliffs before rising to a spectacular view of the plain and river gorge. You can also take the wooded High Road to Taos. From points north of Taos, take NM 522; from points east or west, take U.S. 64. **Cottam Walker** rents cars by the day, week, and month.

BY TAXI Taxi service in Taos is sparse, but Faust's Transportation, based in nearby El Prado, has a fleet of radio-dispatched cabs.

ESSENTIALS **Air Contact Albuquerque International Sunport** (☎505/244–7700 ⊕www. cabq.gov/airport).

Air Shuttle Contact Faust's Transportation (☎575/758–3410 or 888/830–3410 ⊕www.newmexiconet.com/trans/faust/faust.html).

Bus Contacts Greyhound (☎800/231–2222 ⊕www.greyhound.com).

Car Rental Contacts Cottam Walker Ford (✉1320 Paseo del Pueblo Sur ☎575/751–3200 ⊕www.forddetaos.com).

Taxi Contacts Faust's Transportation (☎575/758–3410 or 888/231–2222).

VISITOR
INFORMATION **Taos Visitors Center** (✉1139 Paseo del Pueblo Sur ✑Drawer I, Taos 87571 ☎505/758–3873 ⊕www.taosvacationguide.com). **Taos Ski Valley Chamber of Commerce** (☎575/776–1413 or 800/517–9816 ⊕www.taosskivalley.com).

PLANNING YOUR TIME

Whether you've got an afternoon or a week in the area, begin by strolling around Taos Plaza and along Bent Street, taking in the galleries, Native American crafts shops, and eclectic clothing stores. Take Ledoux Street south from west Plaza and go two blocks to the Harwood Museum, then walk back to the Plaza and cross over to Kit Carson Road, where you can find more shops and galleries as well as the Kit Carson Home and Museum. Continue north on Paseo del Pueblo to the Taos Art Museum at the Fechin House and you'll have enjoyed much of the best Taos has to offer. If you have time to venture a bit farther afield, head north on Paseo del Pueblo out to the Taos Pueblo, then west to the magnificent Millicent Rogers Museum. If you're headed south, stop at La Hacienda de los Martínez for a look at early life in Taos and then on to Ranchos de Taos to see the stunning San Francisco de Asís Church and channel your inner artist.

IF YOU LIKE

ARTS & CRAFTS

If your idea of fun is museum-going and gallery-hopping, you'll love Taos. The creative spirit is strong here, and it's contagious. Even if you begin by just browsing, you might find that you can't go home without a certain painting or pot that captures the unique enchantment of the place. When browsing for art, you often have the opportunity to meet the artists themselves, an eclectic and almost universally free-thinking collection of individuals, some of whom might wear cowboy boots and speak with drawl. You can even join in the flow of creative energy by participating in art workshops yourself. It's easy to visit a lot of galleries in a short time; many are side by side on a few streets around the Plaza. Southwestern landscapes and Native American themes are frequent subjects. Look for outstanding weaving, jewelry, tinwork, and other crafts, too.

NEW MEXICAN CUISINE

Taos is a great place for New Mexican fare, prepared with locally grown chiles and homemade tortillas, but the town also draws raves for outstanding contemporary restaurants with award-winning wine lists. The many New Agers who live in and frequent the area mean that fresh, organic, and vegetarian dishes abound here. Pan-Asian and Middle Eastern flavors are also influences in the increasingly sophisticated cuisines finding their way to this small town with a big attitude.

OUTDOOR ACTIVITIES & SPORTS

The glorious landscape around Taos draws serious athletes as well as those who just want to wander under the huge skies and gaze at the mountains. Cycling is popular, with rallies and races held in late summer. The vast Carson National Forest is an excellent spot for most any outdoor pursuit. The rivers and lakes are excellent for trout fishing; you can arrange for outings with local expert guides. The waters also invite rafters, especially when spring runoff fills the rivers with white water. There are innumerable trails for hiking for all levels of fitness, up into alpine reaches and down into rocky gorges. If you're really after a thrill or something different, try a hot-air balloon ride into the Rio Grande Gorge or llama trekking in the wilderness. And of course winter brings skiers from all over to the world-class slopes of Taos Ski Valley and other nearby resorts.

EXPLORING TAOS

The Museum Association of Taos includes five properties. Among them are the Harwood Museum, Taos Art Museum at the Fechin House, the Millicent Rogers Museum, the E.L. Blumenschein Home and Museum, and La Hacienda de los Martínez. Each of the museums charges $8–$10 for admission, but you can opt for a combination ticket—$25 for all five, valid for one year.

Numbers correspond to the Taos map.

A GOOD WALK

Begin at the gazebo in the middle of **Taos Plaza ❶**. After exploring the Plaza, head south from its western edge down the small unmarked alley (its name is West Plaza Drive). The first cross street is Camino de la Placita. Across it, West Plaza Drive becomes Ledoux Street. Continue south on Ledoux to the **Blumenschein Home and Museum ❷** and, a few doors farther south, the **Harwood Museum ❸**. (If you're driving, the parking area for the Harwood Foundation is at Ledoux and Ranchitos Road.)

From the Harwood Foundation, walk back north on Ranchitos Road a few blocks, make a left on Camino de la Placita, and go right onto Don Fernando Road. Follow it east along the north side of the Plaza to Paseo del Pueblo Norte (NM 68), which is the main street of Taos. As you cross NM 68, Don Fernando Road changes to Kit Carson Road. On the north side of Kit Carson Road is the **Kit Carson Home and Museum ❹**. After visiting the home, head back to Paseo del Pueblo Norte and walk north past the Taos Inn to browse through Bent Street's shops, boutiques, and galleries.

In a tiny plaza is the **Governor Bent Museum ❺**, the modest home of

the first Anglo governor of the state. Across the street is the John Dunn House. Once the homestead of a colorful and well-respected Taos gambling and transportation entrepreneur, the Dunn House is now a small shopping plaza. At the western end of Bent Street, head north on Camino de la Placita. In about 2½ blocks you'll come to the Taos Volunteer Fire Department building, which doubles as a fire station and the **Firehouse Collection ❻** exhibition space.

Head east on Civic Plaza and cross Paseo del Pueblo Norte. To the north will be **Kit Carson Park ❼** and the **Taos Art Museum at the Fechin House ❽**, named for the iconoclastic artist Nicolai Fechin.

TIMING

The entire walk can be done in a half day, a whole day if you stop to lunch along the way and browse in the shops and galleries. The Taos Art Museum at the Fechin House is closed Monday. Hours vary by season, but visits by appointment are welcomed. Some museums are closed on the weekend, so you may want to do this walk on a Wednesday, Thursday, or Friday. You can tour each of the museums in less than an hour.

DOWNTOWN TAOS

WHAT TO SEE

❷ **Blumenschein Home and Museum.** For an introduction to the history of the Taos art scene, start with Ernest L. Blumenschein's residence, which provides a glimpse into the cosmopolitan lives led by the members of the Taos Society of Artists, of which Blumenschein was a founding member. One of the rooms in the adobe-style structure dates from 1797. On display are the art, antiques, and other personal possessions of Blumenschein and his wife, Mary Greene Blumenschein, who also painted, as did their daughter Helen. Several of Ernest Blumenschein's vivid oil paintings hang in his former studio, and works by other early

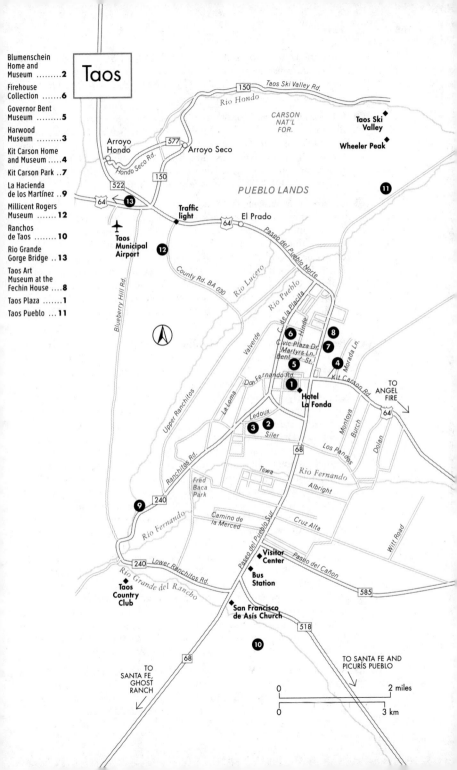

Taos

Taos artists are also on display. ⊠*222 Ledoux St.* ☎*575/758–0505* ⊕*www.taoshistoricmuseums.org* ⌦*$8, $25 with Museum Association of Taos combination ticket* ⊙*May–Dec., daily 10–5; call for winter hours.*

❻ Firehouse Collection. More than 100 works by well-known Taos artists ♻ like Joseph Sharp, Ernest L. Blumenschein, and Bert Phillips hang in the Taos Volunteer Fire Department building. The exhibition space adjoins the station house, where five fire engines are maintained at the ready and an antique fire engine is on display. ⊠*323 Camino de la Placita* ☎*575/758–3386* ⌦*Free* ⊙*Weekdays 9–4:30.*

❺ Governor Bent Museum. In 1846, when New Mexico became a U.S. pos- ♻ session as a result of the Mexican War, Charles Bent, a trader, trapper, and mountain man, was appointed governor. Less than a year later he was killed in his house by an angry mob protesting New Mexico's annexation by the United States. Governor Bent was married to María Ignacia, the older sister of Josefa Jaramillo, the wife of mountain man Kit Carson. A collection of Native American artifacts, Western Americana, and family possessions is squeezed into five small rooms of the adobe building where Bent and his family lived. ⊠*117 Bent St.* ☎*575/758–2376* ⌦*$3* ⊙ *Daily 10–5.*

❸ Harwood Museum. The Pueblo Revival former home of Burritt Elihu ★ "Burt" Harwood, a dedicated painter who studied in France before moving to Taos in 1916, is adjacent to a museum dedicated to the works of local artists. Traditional Hispanic northern New Mexican artists, early art-colony painters, post–World War II modernists, and contemporary artists such as Larry Bell, Agnes Martin, Ken Price, and Earl Stroh are represented. Mabel Dodge Luhan, a major arts patron, bequeathed many of the 19th- and early-20th-century works in the Harwoods' collection, including *retablos* (painted wood representations of Catholic saints) and *bultos* (three-dimensional carvings of the saints). In the Hispanic Traditions Gallery upstairs are 19th-century tinwork, furniture, and sculpture. Downstairs, among early-20th-century art-colony holdings, look for E. Martin Hennings's *Chamisa in Bloom,* which captures the Taos landscape particularly beautifully. A tour of the ground-floor galleries shows that Taos painters of the era, notably Oscar Berninghaus, Ernest Blumenschein, Victor Higgins, Walter Ufer, Marsden Hartley, and John Marin, were fascinated by the land and the people linked to it. An octagonal gallery exhibits works by Agnes Martin. Martin's seven large canvas panels (each 5 feet square) are studies in white, their precise lines and blocks forming textured grids. Operated by the University of New Mexico since 1936, the Harwood is the second-oldest art museum in the state. ⊠*238 Ledoux St.* ☎*575/758–9826* ⊕*www.harwoodmuseum.org* ⌦*$8, $25 with Museum Association of Taos combination ticket* ⊙*Tues.–Sat. 10–5, Sun. noon–5.*

❹ Kit Carson Home and Museum. Kit Carson bought this low-slung 12-room ♻ adobe home in 1843 for his wife, Josefa Jaramillo, the daughter of a powerful, politically influential Spanish family. Three of the museum's rooms are furnished as they were when the Carson family lived here.

The rest of the museum is devoted to gun and mountain man exhibits, such as rugged leather clothing and Kit's own Spencer carbine rifle with its beaded leather carrying case, and early Taos antiques, artifacts, and manuscripts. ⊠ *113 Kit Carson Rd.* ☎ *575/758–0505* ⊕ *www.kitcarson home.com* ⊠ *$8* ⊙ *Tues.–Sat. 10–4, Sun. noon–4.*

NEED A BREAK?

Let the aroma of fresh-ground coffee draw you into the tiny **World Cup** (⊠ *102-A Paseo del Pueblo Norte* ☎ *575/737–5299*), where you can sit at the counter or wander outside to a bench on the porch. Locals engage in political rhetoric here, often slanted toward the left, so be prepared for a rousing debate if you dare to dissent.

❼ Kit Carson Park. The noted pioneer is buried in the park that bears his name. His grave is marked with a *cerquita* (a spiked, wrought-iron, rectangular fence), traditionally used to outline and protect burial sites. Also interred here is Mabel Dodge Luhan, the pioneering patron of the early Taos art scene. The 32-acre park has swings and slides for recreational breaks. It's well marked with big stone pillars and a gate. ⊠ *211 Paseo del Pueblo Norte* ☎ *575/758–8234* ⊠ *Free* ⊙ *Late May–early Sept., daily 8–8; early Sept.–late May, daily 8–5.*

❽ Taos Art Museum at the Fechin House. The interior of this extraordinary adobe house, built between 1927 and 1933 by Russian émigré and artist Nicolai Fechin, is a marvel of carved Russian-style woodwork and furniture. Fechin constructed it to showcase his daringly colorful paintings. The house has hosted the Taos Art Museum since 2003, with a collection of paintings from more than 50 Taos artists, including founders of the original Taos Society of Artists, among them Joseph Sharp, Ernest Blumenschein, Bert Phillips, E. I. Couse, and Oscar Berninghaus. ⊠ *227 Paseo del Pueblo Norte* ☎ *575/758–2690* ⊕ *www.taosart museum.org* ⊠ *$8, $25 with Museum Association of Taos combination ticket* ⊙ *Tues.–Sun. 10–5.*

FodorśChoice ★

❶ Taos Plaza. The first European explorers of the Taos Valley came here with Captain Hernando de Alvarado, a member of Francisco Vásquez de Coronado's expedition of 1540. Basque explorer Don Juan de Oñate arrived in Taos in July 1598 and established a mission and trading arrangements with residents of Taos Pueblo. The settlement developed into two plazas: the Plaza at the heart of the town became a thriving business district for the early colony, and a walled residential plaza was constructed a few hundred yards behind. It remains active today, home to a throng of gift and coffee shops. The covered gazebo was donated by heiress and longtime Taos resident Mabel Dodge Luhan. On the southeastern corner of Taos Plaza is the **Hotel La Fonda de Taos.** Some infamous erotic paintings by D. H. Lawrence that were naughty in his day but are quite tame by present standards can be viewed ($3 entry fee for nonguests) in the former barroom beyond the lobby.

NEED A BREAK?

Join the locals at the north or south location of the **Bean** (⊠ *900 Paseo del Pueblo Norte* ☎ *No phone* ⊠ *1033 Paseo del Pueblo Sur* ☎ *575/758–5123*). The Bean roasts its own coffee, and the south-side location (where

A GOOD DRIVE

Head south 3 mi on NM 240 (also known as Ranchitos Road) to **La Hacienda de los Martínez** ❾. As you pass by the adobe cottages and modest homes dotting the landscape, you get a sense of the area's rural roots. From the hacienda continue south and east another 4 mi to NM 68 and the small farming village of **Ranchos de Taos** ❿. Watch for signs for **San Francisco de Asís Church,** which is on the east side of NM 68. The small plaza here con-tains several galleries and gift shops worth checking out.

TIMING
Set aside about two hours to tour the hacienda, a bit of Ranchos de Taos, and San Francisco de Asís Church.

you can dine on an outside patio) offers good breakfast and lunch fare. The north location, in an adobe building, displays local artwork and is the more atmospheric of the two.

SOUTH OF TAOS

WHAT TO SEE

❾ **La Hacienda de los Martínez.** Spare and fortlike, this adobe structure built between 1804 and 1827 on the bank of the Rio Pueblo served as a community refuge during Comanche and Apache raids. Its thick walls, which have few windows, surround two central courtyards. Don Antonio Severino Martínez was a farmer and trader; the hacienda was the final stop along El Camino Real (the Royal Road), the trade route the Spanish established between Mexico City and New Mexico. The restored period rooms here contain textiles, foods, and crafts of the early 19th century. There's a working blacksmith's shop, usually open to visitors on Saturday, and weavers create beautiful textiles on reconstructed period looms. ⊠ *708 Hacienda Rd., off Ranchitos Rd., NM 240* ☎ *575/758–1000 www.taoshistoricmuseums.org* ⊠ *$8, $25 with Museum Association of Taos combination ticket* ☉ *May–Dec., daily 10–4; call for winter hours.*

❿ **Ranchos de Taos.** A few minutes' drive south of the center of Taos, this village still retains some of its rural atmosphere despite the highway traffic passing through. Huddled around its famous adobe church and dusty plaza are cheerful, remodeled shops and galleries standing shoulder to shoulder with crumbling adobe shells. This ranching, farming, and budding small-business community was an early home to Taos Native Americans before being settled by Spaniards in 1716. Although many of the adobe dwellings have seen better days, the shops, modest galleries, taco stands, and two fine restaurants point to an ongoing revival.

★ The massive bulk of **San Francisco de Asís Church** ($\boxtimes NM$ 68, 500 *yards south of NM 518, Ranchos de Taos* $\textcircled{\scriptsize\faPhone}575/758–2754$) is an enduring attraction. The Spanish Mission–style church was erected in 1815 as a spiritual and physical refuge from raiding Apaches, Utes, and Comanches. In 1979 the deteriorated church was rebuilt with traditional adobe bricks by community volunteers. Every spring a group gathers to re-mud the facade. The earthy, clean lines of the exterior walls and supporting bulwarks have inspired generations of painters and photographers. The late-afternoon light provides the best exposure of the heavily buttressed rear of the church—though today's image-takers face the challenge of framing the architecturally pure lines through rows of parked cars and a large, white sign put up by church officials; morning light is best for the front. Bells in the twin belfries call Taoseños to services on Sunday and holidays. Monday through Saturday from 9 to 4 you can step inside. In the parish hall just north of the church (and for a $3 fee) you can view a 15-minute video presentation every half hour that describes the history and restoration of the church and explains the mysterious painting *Shadow of the Cross,* on which each evening the shadow of a cross appears over Christ's shoulder (scientific studies made on the canvas and the paint pigments cannot explain the phenomenon). The fee also allows you to view the painting.

TAOS PUEBLO TO RIO GRANDE GORGE

WHAT TO SEE

⓬ Millicent Rogers Museum. More than 5,000 pieces of spectacular Native American and Hispanic art, many of them from the private collection of the late Standard Oil heiress Millicent Rogers, are on display here. Among the pieces are baskets, blankets, rugs, kachina dolls, carvings, paintings, rare religious artifacts, and, most significantly, jewelry (Rogers, a fashion icon in her day, was one of the first Americans to appreciate the turquoise-and-silver artistry of Native American jewelers). Other important works include the pottery and ceramics of Maria Martinez and other potters from San Ildefonso Pueblo (23 mi north of Santa Fe). Docents conduct guided tours by appointment, and the museum hosts lectures, films, workshops, and demonstrations. The two-room gift shop has exceptional jewelry, rugs, books, and pottery. $\boxtimes 1504$ *Millicent Rogers Rd., from Taos Plaza head north on Paseo del Pueblo Norte and left at sign for CR BA030, also called Millicent Rogers Rd.* $\textcircled{\scriptsize\faPhone}575/758–2462$ ⊕*www.millicentrogers.com* $\textcircled{\scriptsize\$}$\$8, \$25 *with Museum Association of Taos combination ticket* $\circlearrowright$ *Daily 10–5; Closed Mon. in November*

FodorsChoice
★

⓭ Rio Grande Gorge Bridge. It's a dizzying experience to see the Rio Grande 650 feet underfoot, where it flows at the bottom of an immense, steep rock canyon. In summer the reddish rocks dotted with green scrub contrast brilliantly with the blue sky, where you might see a hawk lazily floating in circles. The bridge is the second-highest expansion bridge in the country. Hold on to your camera and eyeglasses when looking down, and watch out for low-flying planes. The Taos Municipal Airport is close by, and daredevil private pilots have been known to

A GOOD DRIVE

Drive 2 mi north on Paseo del Pueblo Norte (NM 68), and keep your eyes peeled for the signs on the right, beyond the post office, directing you to **Taos Pueblo** ⓫. To reach the **Millicent Rogers Museum** ⓬ next, return to NM 68 to head north and make a left onto County Road BA030. If you find yourself at the intersection with U.S. 64 and 150, you've gone too far. Continue down the county road to the big adobe wall; the sign for the museum is on the right. This rural road eventually connects back onto Upper Ranchitos Road. After exploring the museum, return to NM 68 north; then make a left on U.S. 64 west to the **Rio Grande Gorge Bridge** ⓭, a stunning marriage of natural wonder and human engineering. Bring along sturdy hiking shoes and plenty of water and snacks for an invigorating walk down into the gorge. But remember, what goes down must come up, and it's an arduous path.

TIMING

Plan on spending 1½ hours at the pueblo. Taos can get hot in summer, but if you visit the pueblo in the morning, you'll avoid the heat and the crowds. Winters can be cold and windy, so dress warmly. If your visit coincides with a ceremonial observance, set aside several hours, because the ceremonies, though they are worth the wait, never start on time. Two hours should be enough time to take in the museum and the grandeur of the Rio Grande Gorge Bridge.

challenge one another to fly under the bridge. Shortly after daybreak, hot-air balloons fly above and even inside the gorge. ⊠ *U.S. 64, 12 mi west of town.*

⓫ **Taos Pueblo.** For nearly 1,000 years the mud-and-straw adobe walls of Taos Pueblo have sheltered Tiwa-speaking Native Americans. A United Nations World Heritage Site, this is the largest collection of multistory pueblo dwellings in the United States. The pueblo's main buildings, Hlauuma (north house) and Hlaukwima (south house), are separated by a creek. These structures are believed to be of a similar age, probably built between 1000 and 1450. The dwellings have common walls but no connecting doorways—the Tiwas gained access only from the top, via ladders that were retrieved after entering. Small buildings and corrals are scattered about.

The pueblo today appears much as it did when the first Spanish explorers arrived in New Mexico in 1540. The adobe walls glistening with mica caused the conquistadors to believe they had discovered one of the fabled Seven Cities of Gold. The outside surfaces are continuously maintained by replastering with thin layers of mud, and the interior walls are frequently coated with thin washes of white clay. Some walls are several feet thick in places. The roofs of each of the five-story structures are supported by large timbers, or vigas, hauled down from the mountain forests. Pine or aspen *latillas* (smaller pieces of wood) are placed side by side between the vigas; the entire roof is then packed with dirt.

Even after 400 years of Spanish and Anglo presence in Taos, inside the pueblo the traditional Native American way of life has endured. Tribal custom allows no electricity or running water in Hlauuma and Hlaukwima, where varying numbers (usually fewer than 100) of Taos Native Americans live full-

> **DID YOU KNOW?**
>
> The privilege of setting up an easel and painting all day at a pueblo will cost you as little as $35 or as much as $150 (at Taos Pueblo).

time. About 2,000 others live in conventional homes on the pueblo's 95,000 acres. The crystal-clear Rio Pueblo de Taos, originating high above in the mountains at the sacred Blue Lake, is the primary source of water for drinking and irrigating. Bread is still baked in *hornos* (outdoor domed ovens). Artisans of the Taos Pueblo produce and sell (tax-free) traditionally handcrafted wares, such as mica-flecked pottery and silver jewelry. Great hunters, the Taos Native Americans are also known for their work with animal skins and their excellent moccasins, boots, and drums.

Although the population is about 80% Catholic, the people of Taos Pueblo, like most Pueblo Native Americans, also maintain their native religious traditions. At Christmas and other sacred holidays, for instance, immediately after Mass, dancers dressed in seasonal sacred garb proceed down the aisle of St. Jerome Chapel, drums beating and rattles shaking, to begin other religious rites.

The pueblo **Church of San Geronimo**, or St. Jerome, the patron saint of Taos Pueblo, was completed in 1850 to replace the one destroyed by the U.S. Army in 1847 during the Mexican War. With its smooth symmetry, stepped portal, and twin bell towers, the church is a popular subject for photographers and artists (though the taking of photographs inside is discouraged).

The public is invited to certain ceremonial dances held throughout the year: January 1, Turtle Dance; January 6, Buffalo or Deer Dance; May 3, Feast of Santa Cruz Foot Race and Corn Dance; June 13, Feast of San Antonio Corn Dance; June 24, Feast of San Juan Corn Dance; second weekend in July, Taos Pueblo Powwow; July 25 and 26, Feast of Santa Ana and Santiago Corn Dance; September 29 and 30, Feast of San Geronimo Sunset Dance; December 24, Vespers and Bonfire Procession; December 25, Deer Dance or Matachines. While you're at the pueblo, respect the RESTRICTED AREA signs that protect the privacy of residents and native religious sites; do not enter private homes or open any doors not clearly labeled as curio shops; do not photograph tribal members without asking permission; do not enter the cemetery grounds; and do not wade in the Rio Pueblo de Taos, which is considered sacred and is the community's sole source of drinking water.

The small, rather prosaic, and smoke-free Taos Mountain Casino (open daily) is just off Camino del Pueblo after you turn right off Paseo del Pueblo on your way to the main pueblo. ⊠*Head to right off Paseo del Pueblo Norte just past Best Western Kachina Lodge* ☎575/758–

1028 ⊕ *www.taospueblo.com* ✉ *Tourist fees $10. Guided tours by appt. Still-camera permit $5; note: cameras that may look commercial, such as those with telephoto lenses, might be denied a permit; video-camera permit $5. Commercial photography, sketching, or painting only by prior permission from governor's office (575/758–1028); fees vary; apply at least 10 days in advance ☉ Mon.–Sat. 8–5, Sun. 8:30–5. Closed for funerals, religious ceremonies, and for 2-month quiet time in late winter or early spring, and last part of Aug.; call ahead before visiting at these times.*

| NEED A BREAK? | Look for signs that read FRY BREAD on dwellings in the pueblo: you can enter the kitchen and buy a piece of fresh bread dough that's flattened and deep-fried until puffy and golden brown and then topped with honey or powdered sugar. You also can buy delicious bread that's baked daily in the clay hornos (outdoor adobe ovens) that are scattered throughout the pueblo. |

WHERE TO EAT

For a place as remote as Taos, the dining scene is surprisingly varied. You can find the usual coffee shops and Mexican-style eateries but also restaurants serving creatively prepared Continental, Asian, and Southwestern cuisine.

WHAT IT COSTS				
	¢	$	$$	$$$	$$$$
AT DINNER	under $10	$10–$17	$17–$24	$24–$32	over $32

Prices are for a main course, excluding 8.25% sales tax.

¢
CAFÉ
✗**Abe's Cantina y Cocina.** Family-owned and -operated since the 1940s, Abe's is both store and restaurant. You can have your breakfast burrito, rolled tacos, or homemade tamales at one of the small tables crowded next to the canned goods, or take it on a picnic. ✉ *489 NM 150, Taos Ski Valley Rd., Arroyo Seco* ☎ *575/776–8643* ☰ *AE, D, MC, V* ☉ *Closed Sun.*

$$
ECLECTIC
★
✗**Apple Tree.** Named for the large tree in its umbrella-shaded courtyard, this terrific lunch and dinner spot is in a historic adobe just a block from the Plaza. Among the well-crafted dishes are mango-chicken enchiladas, vegetarian calabaza quesadillas, and barbecued duck fajitas. The restaurant has an outstanding wine list. Sunday brunch is great fun here—dig into a plate of Papas Tapadas (two eggs any style over seasoned home fries, with red or green chiles, and topped with white cheddar. Expect a bit of a wait if you don't have a reservation. ✉ *123 Bent St.* ☎ *575/758–1900* ⊕ *www.appletreerestaurant.com* ☰ *AE, D, DC, MC, V.*

$
CAFÉ
★
✗**Bent Street Cafe & Deli.** Try for a seat on the cheery, covered outdoor patio next to giant sunflowers. You can enjoy a breakfast burrito, homemade granola, fresh baked goods, dozens of deli sandwiches, tortilla soup, and homemade chili. Your meal can be topped off with

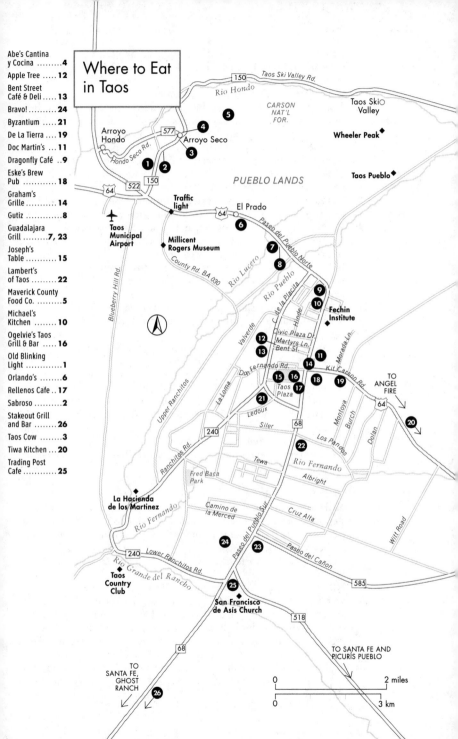

Where to Eat in Taos

a chocolate-nut brownie and accompanied by beer, wine, and gourmet coffees. Friendly service is rendered in an old-fashioned country-kitchen atmosphere, complete with frilly curtains. ⊠ *120–M Bent St.* ☎ *575/758–5787* ▤ *MC, V* ⊙ *No Dinner*

$ ╳**Bravo!** This restaurant and full bar inside an upscale grocery, beer,
AMERICAN and wineshop, is a great stop for gourmet picnic fixings or an on-site meal on the outdoor patio. You can feast on anything from a turkey sandwich to lobster-and-shrimp ravioli to well-prepared pizzas. The beer and wine selection is formidable. ⊠ *1353–A Paseo del Pueblo Sur* ☎ *575/758–8100* ⊕ *www.bravotaos.com* ⚑ *Reservations not accepted* ▤ *AE, MC, V* ⊙ *Closed Sun.*

$$ ╳**Byzantium.** Off a grassy courtyard near the Blumenschein and Har-
CONTEMPORARY wood museums, this traditional-looking adobe restaurant offers an
★ eclectic menu. Asian, European, and Middle Eastern influences can be tasted in dishes like Chilean sea bass poached in coconut lemongrass, tandoori quail, and sizzling mussels on the half shell. Service is friendly, and the vibe is low-key—this is a spot relatively few tourists find out about. ⊠ *11–C La Placita* ☎ *575/751–0805* ▤ *AE, MC, V* ⊙ *Closed Tues. and Wed. No lunch.*

$$$ ╳**De La Tierra.** A dashing, dramatic, high-ceiling restaurant inside the
CONTEMPORARY fancifully plush El Monte Sagrado resort, this chic spot presents dar-
★ ing, globally influenced cuisine. Top starters include roasted garlic soup and tandoori chicken and a butter lettuce salad with stone fruit and sherry vinaigrette. Among the mains, you can't go wrong with the roasted duck with black bean pilaf and mango mole or the pistachio-crusted pork tenderloin with red chile demi-glace. Buttermilk churros with pistachio anglaise makes for a happy ending. It's dressy by Taos standards, but you'll still fit in wearing smartly casual threads. ⊠ *317 Kit Carson Rd., El Monte Sagrado Resort* ☎ *575/758–3502* ⊕ *www. elmontesagrado.com* ▤ *AE, D, DC, MC, V.*

$$ ╳**Doc Martin's.** The restaurant of the Historic Taos Inn takes its name
CONTEMPORARY from the building's original owner, a local physician who saw patients in the rooms that are now the dining areas. The creative menu includes wild salmon with roasted-pepper sauce, pepper-crusted buffalo strip steak with bourbon demi-glace, and a pan-seared halibut with mint-chipotle vinaigrette. There's an extensive wine list, and the adjoining Adobe Bar serves up some of the best margaritas in town. In winter ask for a table near the cozy kiva fireplace. ⊠ *Historic Taos Inn, 125 Paseo del Pueblo Norte* ☎ *575/758–1977* ⊕ *www.taosinn.com* ▤ *AE, D, MC, V.*

$ ╳**Dragonfly Café.** This charming café bakes its own bread and serves
CAFÉ a variety of ethnic specialties including organic Asian salads, Middle Eastern lamb served with a Greek salad, hummus and pita bread, curried chicken salad, bison burgers, and Vietnamese chicken salad. You can sit out front on a shaded outdoor patio with a fountain when it's warm and watch the tourists go by. Dragonfly also does a brisk mail-order business with its red-chile–infused truffles, delicious granola, and many other tasty products. ⊠ *402 Paseo del Pueblo Norte* ☎ *575/737–5859* ⊕ *www.dragonflytaos.com* ▤ *MC, V* ⊙ *No dinner Sun. Closed Mon. and Tues.*

$ ✕**Eske's Brew Pub.** This casual, dining-and-quaffing pub is favored by
AMERICAN off-duty ski patrollers and river guides. The menu mostly covers hearty
sandwiches (try the grilled bratwurst and sauerkraut sandwich), soups,
and salads. The microbrewery downstairs produces everything from
nutty, dark stout to light ales, but you shouldn't leave without sampling the house specialty—Taos green-chile beer. There's live music on
weekends, and in good weather you can relax on the patio. ⌂ *106 Des
Georges La.* ☎*575/758–1517* ⊕*www.eskesbrewpub.com* ▭*MC, V.*

$ ✕**Guadalajara Grill.** Some of the tastiest Mexican food this side of the
MEXICAN border makes the well-priced menu of this relaxed and friendly estab-
★ lishment so popular there's a location on both the north and south ends
of town. It's ultracasual here (you select your own beer from a cooler,
and order from the counter). The extensive menu includes grilled fish
tacos served in soft homemade tortillas, shrimp with garlic sauce, bulg-
ing burritos smothered in red or green chiles, and for the adventurous,
shark enchiladas. ⌂ *822 Paseo del Pueblo Norte* ☎*575/737–0816*
✉*1384 Paseo del Pueblo Sur* ☎*575/751–0063* ▭*MC, V.*

$ ✕**Graham's Grille.** The folks who frequent this upscale bar and eatery
CONTEMPORARY tend to be hip and sophisticated—just like the artful food served in
this minimalist environment. Local, seasonal produce, cage-free chick-
ens, and homemade stocks are key to the fresh flavors and creative
combinations prepared by chef Leslie Fay, a long-time Taos restaura-
teur. Small plates worth sampling include grilled artichoke with lemon
aioli, creole crab cakes with green chile rémoulade, and corn-and-crab
chowder. Main courses range from buffalo burgers to fancy grilled
salmon topped with pink grapefruit, orange, and avocado salsa. Worthy desserts include a coconut cake with mango cream and a lemon-
and-piñon pound cake with blueberry coulis. ⌂ *106 Paseo del Pueblo
Norte* ☎*575/751–1350* ▭*AE, MC, V* ⊙ *Closed Sun.*

$ ✕**Gutiz.** When French, Spanish, and South American culinary influ-
FUSION ences combine, the result is the menu at Gutiz, a casual eatery on the
north end of town. Best bets for breakfast include cinnamon French
toast made with thick homemade bread or a baked omelet topped
with a green tapenade. Lunch favorites might include a warm salad
Niçoise and *chicharon de pollo*—fried chicken tenders topped with
hot aji Amarillo sauce. Dinner is served Wednesday through Sunday
and includes nightly specials. Meals are served on a gravel patio or
inside the small lilac-hued dining room with views of the open kitchen.
⌂ *812B Paseo del Pueblo Norte* ☎*575/758–1226* ⌲*Reservations not
accepted* ▭*No credit cards* ⊙*Closed Mon.*

$$$ ✕**Joseph's Table.** Locally renowned chef Joseph Wrede has moved
CONTEMPORARY around the area a bit in recent years, but has settled into what he does
★ best—overseeing his own swank yet friendly restaurant in La Fonda
Hotel on the Taos Plaza. Amid artful surroundings of giant flowers
hand-painted on walls, you can sample some of the most innovative
and masterfully prepared cuisine: try tuna tartare with fresh-mango-
and-avocado salsa before moving on to ruby trout with pinot noir
reduction and fried capers. But the masterpiece here is pepper-crusted
beef tenderloin with Madeira-mushroom sauce. Lighter fare, including
addictive duck-fat fries, is available at the bar, and there's an astound-

4

ing wine list. ⊠*108–A S. Taos Plaza, La Fonda Hotel* ☎*575/751–4512* ⊕*www.josephstable.com* ⊟*AE, D, DC, MC, V.*

$$$
CONTINENTAL
Fodor's Choice
★

✕**Lambert's of Taos.** Superb service and creative cuisine define this Taos landmark located 2½ blocks south of the Plaza. Don't miss the marinated roasted-beet salad with warm goat cheese and pumpkin seeds, Dungeness crab cakes with Thai curry, or corn-and-applewood-smoked-bacon chowder appetizers. Or have all three and call it a night. The signature entrees include pepper-crusted lamb with a red-wine demi-glace and roasted duck with an apricot-chipotle glaze. Memorable desserts are a warm-apple-and-almond crisp topped with white-chocolate ice cream and a dark-chocolate mouse with raspberry sauce. A small-plate bistro menu is available in the cozy bar or in the spacious dining rooms. The lengthy wine list includes some of California's finest vintages. ⊠*309 Paseo del Pueblo Sur* ☎*575/758–1009* ⊟*AE, D, DC, MC, V* ◷*No lunch.*

$
AMERICAN

✕**Maverick County Food Co.** If you like casual and friendly eateries with unfussy fare and great desserts you'll feel right at home in this out-of-the-way local's choice. Chef Sheila Guzman serves up masterful buffalo and beef burgers, curries, Asian bowls, and simple salads. Save room for the mile-high coconut cake, fresh seasonal fruit pies, and bourbon-chocolate cake. ⊠ *480 State Road 150, Arroyo Seco* ☎*575/776–0900* ⌂*Reservations not accepted* ⊟*No credit cards* ◷*No Dinner. Closed Sun. and Mon.*

$
AMERICAN

✕**Michael's Kitchen.** This casual, homey restaurant serves up a bit of everything—you can have a hamburger while your friend who can't get enough chile sauce can order up vegetarian cheese enchiladas garnished with lettuce and tomatoes. Brunch is popular with the locals (dig into a plate of strawberry-banana-pecan pancakes), and amusing asides to the waitstaff over the intercom contribute to the energetic buzz. Breakfast, lunch, and dinner are served daily, but you must order dinner by 8:30 PM. ⊠*304 Paseo del Pueblo Norte* ☎*575/758–4178* ⊕*www.michaels kitchen.com* ⌂*Reservations not accepted* ⊟*AE, D, MC, V.*

$$
AMERICAN

✕**Ogelvie's Taos Grill and Bar.** On the second floor of an old two-story adobe building, touristy but festive Ogelvie's is the perfect spot for people-watching from on high, especially from the outdoor patio in summer. You won't find any culinary surprises here, just dependable meat-and-potato dishes. The sure bets are filet mignon with brandy-cream sauce, lamb sirloin with rosemary aioli, and blue-corn enchiladas stuffed with beef or chicken. There's live music many nights. ⊠*103 E. Plaza* ☎*575/758–8866* ⊕*www.ogelvies.com* ⌂*Reservations not accepted* ⊟*AE, D, MC, V.*

$$
NEW MEXICAN

✕**Old Blinking Light.** Just past the landmark "old blinking light" (now a regular stoplight at Mile Marker 1), this rambling adobe is known for its steaks, ribs, and enormous (and potent) margaritas. There's also a long list of tasty appetizers, such as posole stew and chipotle-shrimp quesadillas. Several huge burgers are available, plus first-rate chicken mole. In summer you can sit out in the walled garden and take in the spectacular mountain view. There's a wineshop on the premises. ⊠*Mile Marker 1, Taos Ski Valley Rd., between El Prado and Arroyo Seco* ☎*575/776–8787* ⊕*www.oldblinkinglight.com* ⊟*AE, MC, V* ◷*No lunch.*

¢ ✕**Orlando's.** This family-run local favorite is likely to be packed dur-
NEW MEXICAN ing peak hours, while guests wait patiently to devour favorites such as
★ *carne adovada* (red chile–marinated pork), blue-corn enchiladas, and
scrumptious shrimp burritos. You can eat in the cozy dining room, outside on the front patio, or call ahead for takeout if you'd rather avoid
the crowds. ✉*114 Don Juan Valdez La., off Paseo del Pueblo Norte*
☎*575/751–1450* ⊟*MC, V.*

$ ✕**Rellenos Cafe.** Touted as the only organic New Mexican restaurant in
NEW MEXICAN town, this casual eatery also serves wheat-free, gluten-free, and vegan
menu options on request. Popular specialties served on the casual outdoor patio include killer chiles rellenos topped with a brandy-cream
sauce, grilled garlic shrimp, and seafood paella. Service is friendly, the
clientele largely local. The house drink, a fruity sangria, is served in
gargantuan Mexican glasses. ✉ *135 Paseo del Pueblo Sur* ☎*575/758–*
7001 ⚠*Reservations not accepted* ⊟*MC, V* ⊘ *Closed Sun.*

$$$ ✕**Sabroso.** Reasonably priced, innovative cuisine and outstanding
CONTEMPORARY wines are served in this 150-year-old adobe hacienda, where you can
★ also relax in lounge chairs near the bar, or on a delightful patio sur-
rounded by plum trees. The Mediterranean-influenced contemporary
menu changes regularly, but an evening's entrée might be pan-seared
sea scallops, risotto cakes, and ratatouille, or rib-eye steak topped with
a slice of Stilton cheese. There's live jazz and cabaret in the piano bar
several nights a week. Order from the simpler bar menu if you're seek-
ing something light—the antipasto plate and white-truffle-oil fries are
both delicious. ✉*470 NM 150, Taos Ski Valley Rd.* ☎*575/776–3333*
⊕*www.sabrosotaos.com* ⊟*AE, MC, V* ⊘ *No lunch.*

$$$$ ✕**Stakeout Grill and Bar.** On Outlaw Hill in the foothills of the Sangre
STEAK de Cristo Mountains, this old adobe homestead has 100-mi-long views
Fodor'sChoice and sunsets that dazzle. The outdoor patio encircled by a piñon forest
★ has kiva fireplaces to warm you during cooler months. The decadent
fare is well prepared, fully living up to the view it accompanies—try
filet mignon with béarnaise sauce, buffalo rib eye with chipotle-cilan-
tro butter, almond-crusted wild sockeye salmon with shaved fennel, or
kurobuta pork rack with red-wine sauce. Don't miss the tasty Kentucky
bourbon pecan pie and crème brûlée with toasted coconut for dessert.
✉*Stakeout Dr., 8 mi south of Taos Plaza, east of NM 68, look for cow-*
boy sign ☎*575/758–2042* ⊟*AE, D, DC, MC, V* ⊘*No lunch.*

¢ ✕**Taos Cow.** Locals, travelers headed up to Taos Ski Valley, and visitors
CAFÉ to funky Arroyo Seco rejoiced when the famed Taos Cow ice-cream
★ company opened this cozy storefront café in 1994. This isn't merely a
place to sample amazing homemade ice cream (including such innova-
tive flavors as piñon-caramel, lavender, and Chocolate Rio Grande—
chocolate ice cream packed with cinnamon-chocolate chunks). You can
also nosh on French toast, omelets, turkey-and-Brie sandwiches, black-
bean-and-brown-rice bowls, organic teas and coffees, natural sodas,
homemade granola, and more. The friendly staff and burning incense
lend a hippie-dippie vibe to the place. ✉*485 NM 150* ☎*575/776–*
5640 ⊕*www.taoscow.com* ⊟*MC, V* ⊘*No dinner.*

4

¢   ✕ **Tiwa Kitchen.** This one-of-a-kind restaurant, even for Taos, serves
NATIVE   authentic Native American food in a casual setting. Ben White Buffalo
AMERICAN   and his wife Debbie Moonlight Flowers organically grow many of the
restaurant's ingredients themselves and use traditional beehive wood-
fired ovens just outside the back door for baking corn and roasting pep-
pers. Try the blue-corn taco made with blue-corn fry bread or grilled
buffalo sausage served with red or green chile. ⊠ *328 Veterans Hwy.*
(Taos Pueblo Rd.) ☎*575/751–1020* ⌲ *Reservations not accepted*
⊟*No credit cards* ⊘*Closed Tues. and 6 weeks in spring during the*
Pueblo's traditional "quiet time."

$$ ✕ **Trading Post Cafe.** Local hipsters outnumber tourists at this casual
CONTEMPORARY   spot. Intelligent and attentive service along with well-presented con-
★   temporary Southwestern art make any meal a pleasure. For starters try
the signature noodle soup or minestrone with smoked ham before mov-
ing on to an oven-roasted duck with seasonal vegetables and creamy
mashed potatoes or any of the traditional pasta dishes. Superb desserts
include a coconut-cream pie and rich strawberry shortcake. To park,
turn east onto NM 518 (Talpa Road) just north of the restaurant, and
then walk back along Talpa Road to get to the entrance. ⊠*4179 Paseo*
del Pueblo Sur, NM 68, Ranchos de Taos ☎*575/758–5089* ⊟*AE, D,*
MC, V ⊘*Closed Mon. No lunch Sun.*

WHERE TO STAY

The hotels and motels along NM 68 (Paseo del Pueblo Sur and Norte)
suit every need and budget; with a few exceptions, rates vary little
between big-name chains and smaller establishments. Make advance
reservations and expect higher rates during the ski season (usually from
late December to early April) and in the summer. Skiers have many
choices for overnighting, from accommodations in the town of Taos to
spots snuggled up right beside the slopes, although several of the hotels
up at Taos Ski Valley have been converted to condos in recent years,
eroding the supply of overnight accommodations. Arroyo Seco is a
good alternative if you can't find a room right up in the Ski Valley.

The best deals in town are the bed-and-breakfasts. Mostly family-
owned, they provide personal service, delicious breakfasts, and many
extras that hotels charge for. The B&Bs are often in old adobes that
have been refurbished with style and flair. Many have "casitas," private
cottages or lodges separate from the main building.

WHAT IT COSTS				
¢	$	$$	$$$	$$$$
FOR TWO PEOPLE	under $70	$70–$130	$130–$190	$190–$260	over $260

Prices are for a standard double room in high season, excluding 10%–12% tax.

DOWNTOWN TAOS

$$ ⊡**Adobe & Pines Inn.** Native American and Mexican artifacts decorate the main house of this B&B, which has expansive mountain views. Part of the main adobe building dates from 1830. The rooms and suites contain Mexican-tile baths, kiva fireplaces, and fluffy goose-down pillows and comforters, plus such modern touches as flat-screen TVs, DVD players, Wi-Fi, and CD players. Separate casitas and suites are more spacious and offer plenty of seclusion, with private entrances and courtyard access. The owners serve gourmet breakfasts in a sunny glass-enclosed patio. **Pros:** Quiet rural location; fantastic views. **Cons:** Not in town; some bedrooms are small. ⊠*NM 68* ⌂*Box 837, Ranchos de Taos 87557* ☎*575/751–0947 or 800/723–8267* ⊕*www.adobepines.com* ⟳*4 rooms, 2 suites, 2 casitas* ⌂*In-room: refrigerator (some), kitchen (some), DVD, Wi-Fi. In-hotel: some pets allowed* ⊟*MC, V* ⧖*BP.*

$$ ⊡**American Artists Gallery House Bed & Breakfast.** Each of the immacu-
★ late adobe-style rooms and suites here is called a "gallery," and owners LeAn and Charles Clamurro have taken care to decorate them with local arts and crafts. Some have Jacuzzis and all have kiva fireplaces; one family-friendly suite has a full kitchen; and all have private entrances, wood-burning fireplaces, and front porches where you can admire the view of Taos Mountain. Sumptuous hot breakfasts—along with conversation and suggestions about local attractions—are served up at a community table in the main house each morning, where you can often see the resident peacock, George, preening outside the windows. **Pros:** Private entrances; true gourmet breakfast. **Cons:** Some rooms have small bathrooms; small common room. ⊠*132 Frontier La., Box 584* ☎*575/758–4446 or 800/532–2041* ☎*575/758–0497* ⊕*www.taosbedandbreakfast.com* ⟳*7 rooms, 3 suites* ⌂*In-room: Wi-Fi, kitchen (some), refrigerator (some). In-hotel: some pets allowed* ⊟*AE, D, DC, MC, V* ⧖*BP.*

$$$ ⊡**Casa de las Chimeneas.** Tile hearths, French doors, and traditional
★ viga ceilings grace the "House of Chimneys" B&B, two-and-a-half blocks from the Plaza and secluded behind thick walls. Each room in the 1912 structure has a private entrance, a fireplace, handmade New Mexican furniture, bathrooms with Talavera tiles, and a bar stocked with complimentary beverages. All rooms overlook the gardens, and facilities include a small but excellent spa offering a wide range of treatments. Two-course breakfasts are included, as are full evening meals. **Pros:** Private setting; in-house spa. **Cons:** 30-day cancellation policy. ⊠*405 Cordoba Rd., Box 5303* ☎*575/758–4777 or 877/758–4777* ☎*575/758–3976* ⊕*www.visittaos.com* ⟳*6 rooms, 2 suites* ⌂*In-room: refrigerator (some). In-room: refrigerator. In-hotel: gym, spa, laundry facilities, no-smoking rooms, Wi-Fi* ⊟*AE, D, DC, MC, V* ⧖*MAP.*

> ### WORD OF MOUTH
>
> "We absolutely loved Casa de las Chimneas when we went to Taos. Close enough to walk to downtown and a beautiful setting."
>
> —patandhank

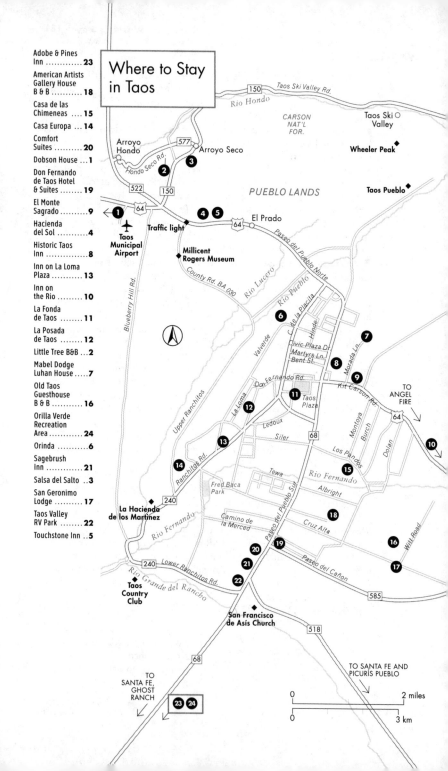

Where to Stay in Taos

$$ **Casa Europa.** The main part of this exquisite 18th-century adobe
Fodor'sChoice   estate has been tastefully expanded to create an unforgettable B&B
★   with old-world romance. Each room is furnished with hand-picked
European antiques accented with Southwestern accessories. The two
main common areas are light and airy, with comfortable chairs to relax
in while the fireplace crackles. Breakfasts are elaborate, and compli-
mentary homemade afternoon baked treats are served. Although the
property is less than 2 mi from the Plaza, its pastoral setting makes
it feel a world away. Innkeepers Lisa and Joe McCutcheon take per-
sonal pride in offering their guests every courtesy and assistance. **Pros:**
Attentive service; memorable setting and sophisticated style. **Cons:** No
elevator to second floor; short drive to town. ⊠ *840 Upper Ranchitos
Rd.* ⌂*HC 68, Box 3F, 87571* ☎*888/758–9798* ☎☎*575/758–9798*
⊕*www.casaeuropanm.com* ⌂*5 rooms, 2 suites* ⌂*In-hotel: bars,
some pets allowed* ▤*AE, D, MC, V* ⎟⊙⎟*BP.*

$ **Comfort Suites.** Clean and comfortable rooms make this property
one of the better chain options in town. The units are large (techni-
cally they're not full suites but rather rooms with large sitting areas)
and have a sense of Southwestern style. The lobby has a kiva fireplace
surrounded by *nichos*—enclaves where statues are placed. Guests have
access to the Sagebrush Inn (⇨ *below*) facilities next door. **Pros:** One of
the newest chains in town; good value. **Cons:** Cookie-cutter decor; con-
crete patio around the pool. ⊠ *1500 Paseo del Pueblo Sur, Box 1268*
☎*575/751–1555 or 888/751–1555* ⊕*www.taoshotels.com/comfort
suites* ⌂*60 rooms* ⌂*In-room: Internet, refrigerator. In-hotel: pool,
Wi-Fi* ▤*AE, D, DC, MC, V* ⎟⊙⎟*CP.*

$$ **Dobson House.** Guests who book one of the two private suites at this
eco-tourist destination can help preserve the environment in style. This
eclectic B&B relies primarily on passive heating and cooling and electricity is provided by solar panels. In addition, the 6,000-square-foot
residence, within walking distance of the Rio Grande gorge, was built
by hand by innkeepers Joan and John Dobson using 2,000 old tires,
20,000 recycled aluminum cans, and 28,000 pounds of dry cement
and packed earth. Even so, guests live luxuriously with Ralph Lauren
linens, and Joan's full breakfasts of Texas pecan biscuits, chicken-apple
sausage, and Mexican baked eggs. The couples' sophisticated art collection adorns the home's authentic adobe walls. **Pros:** Environmentally
friendly; one-of-a-kind accommodation; serene and private. **Cons:** A
long drive to town for dinner; hard to find. ⊠ *475 Tune Dr., El Prado*
☎*575/776–5738* ⊕ *www.new-mexico-bed-and-breakfast.com* ⌂*2
suites* ⌂*In-room: no a/c, no phone, no TV. In-hotel: no kids under 14*
▤*No credit cards* ⎟⊙⎟ *BP.*

$ **Don Fernando de Taos Hotel.** The accommodations at this hotel are
grouped around central courtyards and connected by walkways. The
hotel-style rooms are appointed with Southwestern furnishings, and
some rooms have fireplaces. A glassed-in atrium with sliding side doors
and roof panels surrounds the pool. There's a free shuttle to take guests
to the town center. **Pros:** Large rooms; indoor pool. **Cons:** Spread
out; highway noise. ⊠ *1005 Paseo del Pueblo Sur* ☎*575/758–4444
or 800/759–2736* ☎*575/758–0055* ⊕*www.donfernandodetaos.com*

4

◻110 rooms, 14 suites ♿In-room: Wi-Fi, refrigerator (some). In-hotel: restaurant, bar, pool, laundry service ▤AE, D, DC, MC, V.

$$$$ ☖**El Monte Sagrado.** Pricey but classy (although the resort has lowered its rates a bit in recent years), El Monte Sagrado is an eco-sensitive New Age haven offering all manner of amenities, from alternative therapies like milk-and-honey body wraps to cooking and wine classes. A short drive away, the property has an expansive ranch property that's available for you to explore on horseback or on foot. Suites and casitas are accented with exotic themes, ranging from Native American designs to foreign flourishes from faraway lands including Japan or Tibet. A popular outdoor area dubbed the Sacred Circle is a patch of grassy land encircled by cottonwoods. The on-site restaurant, De la Tierra, serves daring cuisine. **Pros:** Eco-friendly; exotic and sophisticated. **Cons:** Sprawling property not easily walkable. ⊠317 Kit Carson Rd. ☎575/758-3502 or 800/828-8267 ▤575/737-2980 ⊕www.elmontesagrado.com ◻48 rooms, 6 casitas, 30 suites ♿In-room: kitchen (some), refrigerator (some), Wi-Fi. In-hotel: 2 restaurants, room service, bar, pool, gym, spa, bicycles, children's programs (ages 4–12), laundry service, some pets allowed ▤AE, D, DC, MC, V.

$$$ ☖**Hacienda del Sol.** Art patron Mabel Dodge Luhan bought this house
★   in the 1920s and lived here with her husband, Tony Luhan, while building their main house. It was also their private retreat and guesthouse for visiting notables; Frank Waters wrote *People of the Valley* here— other guests have included Willa Cather and D. H. Lawrence. Most of the rooms contain kiva fireplaces, Southwestern handcrafted furniture, and original artwork, and all have CD players. Certain adjoining rooms can be combined into suites. Breakfast is a gourmet affair that might include huevos rancheros or Belgian waffles. Perhaps above all else, the "backyards" of the rooms and the secluded outdoor hot tub have a view of Taos Mountain. **Pros:** Cozy public rooms, private setting. **Cons:** Traffic noise; some rooms are less private than others. ⊠109 Mabel Dodge La., Box 177 ☎575/758-0287 or 866/333-4459 ▤575/758-5895 ⊕www.taoshaciendadelsol.com ◻11 rooms ♿In-room: Wi-Fi, refrigerator (some), no TV ▤AE, D, MC, V ⊙⎸BP.

$$ ☖**Historic Taos Inn.** Mere steps from Taos Plaza, the inn is listed on the
★   National Register of Historic Places. Spanish colonial–style architecture, including decorative alcoves in rooms, provides an authentic feel to this atmospheric property that consists of four buildings, including the upscale Helen's House, which was added in 2006 and contains eight posh rooms. Many rooms have been updated and the older ones have thick adobe walls, viga ceilings, and other elements typical of vintage Taos architecture. In summer there's dining alfresco on the patio. The lobby, which also serves as seating for the Adobe Bar, is built around an old town well from which a fountain bubbles forth.

The Plaza and many shops and eateries are within walking distance of the inn, and the restaurant, Doc Martin's, is popular with locals. **Pros:** Across from the Plaza; lushly furnished rooms. **Cons:** Street noise; bar noise. ✉ *125 Paseo del Pueblo Norte* ☎*575/758–2233 or 888/518– 8267* 🖷*575/758–5776* ⊕*www.taosinn.com* 📱*43 rooms, 3 suites* ⚘*In-hotel: restaurant, bar* ▤*AE, DC, MC, V.*

$$$$ 🏨**Inn on La Loma Plaza.** The walls surrounding this Pueblo Revival build-
★   ing date from the early 1800s; the inn itself is listed on the National Register of Historic Places. The rooms have kiva fireplaces, CD ste-reos, coffeemakers, and Mexican-tile bathrooms, and many have pri-vate patios or decks. The living room has a well-stocked library with books on Taos and art. Owners Jerry and Peggy Davis provide help-ful advice about the area and serve a generous breakfast, afternoon snacks, and evening coffee. Guests have privileges at the nearby health club (but the inn has its own hot tub). **Pros:** Towering trees; inspiring views. **Cons:** Lots of stairs; on a busy street. ✉*315 Ranchitos Rd., Box 4159* ☎*575/758–1717 or 800/530–3040* 🖷*575/751–0155* ⊕*www. vacationtaos.com* 📱*5 rooms, 1 suite, 2 studios* ⚘*In-room: kitchen (some), DVD, Wi-Fi* ▤*AE, D, MC, V* ⦿*BP.*

$ 🏨**Inn on the Rio.** This property started as a strip motel, but over the years it has been transformed with adobe-style architecture and hand-painted murals into a charming B&B. The overall feel of the rooms can't quite escape its motel roots, but rooms are tastefully furnished with Southwestern art and linens. A well-tended garden overflowing with wildflowers and herbs surrounds the pool and hot tub area. Inn-keepers Robert and Julie Cahalane prepare homemade bread, green-chile-and-egg casseroles, and cinnamon-infused coffee for breakfast. **Pros:** One of the few outdoor heated pools in town; private entrance to each room. **Cons:** Traffic noise; small bathrooms. ✉*910 E. Kit Car-son Rd.* ☎ *575/758–7199 or 800/859–6752.* ⊕ *www.innontherio. com* 📱*12 rooms* ⚘*In-room: no a/c, Wi-Fi. In-hotel: pool, some pets allowed* ▤*AE, D, MC, V* ⦿ *BP.*

$$$ 🏨**La Fonda de Taos.** A much-needed interior and exterior renovation has brought this historic property (there's been a hotel on this loca-tion since 1840) up to snuff. Its Plaza location, upscale rooms, and no-children-under-8 policy make this a great choice for a romantic getaway. The rooms are rustic yet elegant and are furnished in neutral colors with luxury linens and hand-tiled bathrooms. It also houses the award-winning Joseph's Table restaurant. **Pros:** Location, loca-tion, location. **Cons:** Street noise; not family-friendly. ✉*108 S. Plaza* ☎ *575/758–2211 or 800/833–2211* ⊕ *www.lafondataos.com* 📱*19 rooms, 5 suites, 1 penthouse* ⚘*In-room: refrigerator, Wi-Fi. In-hotel: 2 restaurants, bar, parking (free), no kids under 8, no-smoking rooms* ▤*AE, D, MC, V*

$$ 🏨**La Posada de Taos.** A couple of blocks from Taos Plaza, this fam-ily-friendly 100-year-old inn has beam ceilings, a decorative arched doorway, and the intimacy of a private hacienda. Five guest rooms are in the main house; the sixth is a separate cottage with a king-size bed, sitting room, and fireplace. The rooms all have mountain or courtyard garden views, and some open onto private patios. Almost

all have kiva-style fireplaces. Breakfasts are hearty. **Pros:** A few blocks from the Plaza; historic building. **Cons:** Small rooms; not much privacy in the main house. ✉309 Juanita La., Box 1118 ☎575/758–8164 or 800/645–4803 🖷575/751–4694 ⊕www.laposadadetaos.com ♥5 rooms, 1 cottage ⚐In-room: no a/c, no phone. In hotel: Wi-Fi ⊟AE, MC, V ⓘBP.

\$\$ ★ ☷ **Mabel Dodge Luhan House.** Quirky and offbeat—much like Taos—this National Historic Landmark was once home to the heiress who drew illustrious writers and artists—including D. H. Lawrence, Willa Cather, Georgia O'Keeffe, Ansel Adams, Martha Graham, and Carl Jung—to Taos. The main house, which has kept its simple, rustic feel, has nine guest rooms; there are eight more in a modern building, as well as two two-bedroom cottages. The house exudes early-20th-century elegance and the grounds offer numerous quiet corners for private conversations or solo meditation. Guests can stay in what was Mabel's room, in her hand-carved double bed to be precise; or in the solarium, an airy room at the top of the house which is completely surrounded by glass (and accessible by a ladder). For art groupies, nothing can quite compare with sleeping in the elegant room Georgia O'Keeffe stayed in while visiting. The inn is frequently used for artistic, cultural, and educational workshops—hence the tiny, but exceptional, bookstore in the lobby specializing in local authors and artists. **Pros:** Historical relevance; rural setting just blocks from the Plaza. **Cons:** Lots of stairs and uneven paths. ✉240 Morada La. ☎575/751–9686 or 800/846–2235 🖷575/737–0365 ⊕www.mabeldodgeluhan.com ♥16 rooms, 1 suite, 2 casitas ⚐In-room: no phone, no TV. In-hotel: Wi-Fi ⊟AE, MC, V ⓘBP.

\$\$ ☷ **Old Taos Guesthouse B&B.** Once a ramshackle 180-year-old adobe hacienda, this homey B&B on 7½ acres has been completely and lovingly outfitted with the owners' hand-carved doors and furniture, Western artifacts, and antiques. There are 80-mi views from the outdoor hot tub and a shady veranda surrounds the courtyard. The owners welcome families. Breakfasts are healthy and hearty. **Pros:** Beautifully appointed; private entrance to each room. **Cons:** Very small bathrooms; some rooms are dark. ✉1028 Witt Rd., Box 6552 ☎575/758–5448 or 800/758–5448 ⊕www.oldtaos.com ♥7 rooms, 2 suites ⚐In-room: no phone (some), kitchen (some), VCR (some) . In-hotel: Wi-Fi, some pets allowed (fee) ⊟D, MC, V ⓘBP.

\$\$\$ ☷ **Orinda.** Built in 1947, this adobe estate has spectacular views and country privacy. The rustic rooms have separate entrances, kiva-style fireplaces, traditional viga ceilings, and Mexican-tile baths. Some of the rooms can be combined with a shared living area into a large suite. One has a Jacuzzi. The hearty breakfast is served family-style in the soaring two-story sun atrium amid a gallery of artworks, all for sale. **Pros:** Most rooms are spacious; gorgeous views of Taos Mountain. **Cons:** Rooms are a little bland; a bit pricey for what is offered. ✉461 Valverde ☎575/758–8581 or 800/847–1837 🖷575/751–0534 ⊕www.orindabb.com ♥5 rooms ⚐In-room: no a/c (some), refrigerator. In-hotel: no-smoking rooms, some pets allowed ⊟AE, MC, V ⓘBP.

$$ 🏨**Sagebrush Inn.** Georgia O'Keeffe once lived and painted in a third-story room of the original inn. These days it's not as upscale—or expensive—as many other lodging options in Taos, but it has a shaded patio with large trees, a good restaurant, and a collection of antique Navajo rugs. Many of the guest rooms have kiva-style fireplaces; some have balconies. There's country-western music nightly. **Pros:** Good value; nightly music. **Cons:** Very spread out; many of the rooms are dark; traffic noise. ⊠*1508 Paseo del Pueblo Sur, Box 557* ☎*575/758–2254 or 800/428–3626* 🖷*575/758–5077* ⊕*www.sagebrushinn.com* ☏*68 rooms, 32 suites* ♿*In-hotel: 2 restaurants, bar, Wi-Fi, pool* ☐*AE, D, DC, MC, V* �*BP.*

$$ 🏨**San Geronimo Lodge.** Built in 1925, this property was one of the
★ first resort hotels in Taos and sits on 2½ acres that front majestic Taos Mountain and adjoin the Carson National Forest. New owners Charles and Pam Montgomery are upgrading the rooms as needed, while preserving the property's historical charm and appeal. An extensive library, attractive grounds, rooms with fireplaces and private decks, two rooms designed for people with disabilities, and five rooms for guests with pets are among the draws. Hanging Navajo rugs, Talavera-tile bathrooms, and high viga ceilings provide an authentic Southwestern experience. **Pros:** Serene inside and out; extensive common rooms. **Cons:** Hard to find; some rooms have small bathrooms. ⊠*1101 Witt Rd.* ☎*575/751–3776 or 800/894–4119* 🖷*575/751–1493* ⊕*www.san geronimolodge.com* ☏*18 rooms* ♿*In-room: Wi-Fi. In-hotel: pool, some pets allowed* ☐*AE, D, MC, V* modifier*BP.*

$$$ 🏨**Touchstone Inn.** D. H. Lawrence visited this house in 1929; accord-
★ ingly, the inn's owner, Taos artist Bren Price, has named many of the antique-filled rooms after famous Taos literary figures. The grounds overlook part of the Taos Pueblo lands, all within a mile of Taos Plaza. Some rooms have fireplaces. The enormous Royale Suite has a second-story private deck and large bathroom with Jacuzzi, walk-in shower, and skylight. Early-morning coffee is available in the living room, and breakfasts with inventive vegetarian presentations (such as blueberry pancakes with lemon sauce) are served in the glassed-in patio. The adjacent Spa offers a wide range of beauty and skin treatments. **Pros:** Extensive common rooms; impeccably furnished rooms. **Cons:** Highway noise; lots of stairs. ⊠*110 Mabel Dodge La.* ☎*575/758–0192 or 800/758–0192* 🖷*575/758–3498* ⊕*www.touchstoneinn.com* ☏*6 rooms, 3 suites* ♿*In-hotel: Wi-Fi, spa* ☐*MC, V* modifier*BP.*

CAMPING

★ 🏕**Orilla Verde Recreation Area.** You can hike, fish, and picnic among trees and sagebrush at this beautiful area along the banks of the Rio Grande, 10 mi south of Ranchos de Taos, off NM 68 at NM 570. The area has four developed campgrounds with running water, flush toilets, and showers. Three primitive campgrounds have vault toilets only. To pay the camping fee, leave cash in an envelope provided, drop it in a tube, and the rangers will collect it (or a volunteer sometimes is on hand to collect payments). *Bureau of Land Management, 226 Cruz Alta Rd., Taos 87571* ☎*575/758–4060* ♿*Flush toilets, drinking* *water, fire grates, picnic tables* ↻*9 RV sites with hookups, 70 developed sites (tent and RV)* ☰*No credit cards.*

⚠ **Taos Valley RV Park and Campground.** The sites are grassy, with a few shade trees, in this park 2½ mi from Taos Plaza near the junction of NM 68 and NM 518. Some RV supplies are for sale. ✉*120 Estes Rd., off Paseo del Pueblo Sur, behind Rio Grande Ace Hardware* ⌂*Box 7204, Taos 87571* ☎*575/758–2524 or 800/999–7571* ⊕*www.taos net.com/rv* ♿*Flush toilets, full hookups, drinking water, showers, picnic tables, electricity, public telephone, Wi-Fi, general store, play area* ↻*92 RV sites, 24 tent sites* ☰*AE, MC, V. 575/758–2524*

ARROYO SECO

$$ ⊡ **Little Tree B&B.** In an authentic adobe house in the open country
★ between Taos and the ski valley, Little Tree's rooms are built around a garden courtyard and have magnificent views of Taos Mountain and the high desert that spans for nearly 100 mi to the west. Some have kiva fireplaces and Jacuzzis, and all are decorated in true Southwestern style. **Pros:** Rare opportunity to stay in a real adobe (not stucco) home; spotless and beautifully maintained. **Cons:** 15-minute drive to Taos; isolated. ✉*226 Hondo Seco Rd., Arroyo Hondo* ⌂*Box 509, 87571* ☎*575/776–8467 or 800/334–8467* ⊕*www.littletreebandb.com* ↻*4 rooms* ♿*In-room: Wi-Fi, no TV (some)* ☰*MC, V* ⦿*BP.*

$$ ⊡ **Salsa del Salto.** Rooms at this handsome compound set back from the road to the Ski Valley, just a short drive up from the funky village of Arroyo Seco, are either in the sunny, contemporary, main inn building or in separate units with private entrances and a bit more seclusion. The master suite affords panoramic views of the mountains and has a huge bathroom. The Lobo and Kachina rooms are a great value, not as large as some but with romantic glass-brick showers, high-beam ceilings, and Saltillo-tile floors with radiant heating. Friendly and helpful owners Pam and Jim Maisey worked for Marriott hotels for 25 years, and it shows. Breakfast is a substantial affair, where you might enjoy a shrimp, mushroom, and provolone omelet or salmon eggs Benedict, and there's always a hearty soup or snack presented in the afternoon. **Pros:** Spacious rooms; good access for skiers. **Cons:** Far from cultural attractions in Taos; feels more like a hotel than a B&B. ✉*543 NM 150, Box 1468, El Prado* ☎*575/776–2422 or 800/530–3097* 🖷*575/776–5734* ⊕*www.bandbtaos.com* ↻*10 rooms* ♿*In-room: DVD (some), Wi-Fi. In-hotel: pool* ☰*AE, MC, V* ⦿*BP.*

NIGHTLIFE & THE ARTS

Evening entertainment is modest in Taos. Some motels and hotels present solo musicians or small combos in their bars and lounges. Everything from down-home blues bands to Texas two-step dancing blossoms on Saturday and Sunday nights in winter. In summer things heat up during the week as well. For information about what's going on around town pick up *Taos Magazine.* The weekly *Taos News,* pub-

The Taos Hum

Investigations into what causes a mysterious low-frequency sound dubbed the "Taos Hum" are ongoing, although the topic was more popular during a worldwide news media frenzy in the 1990s. Taos isn't the only place where the mysterious hum has been heard, but it's probably the best-known locale for the phenomenon. (The Taos Hum, for example, now has been officially documented in Encyclopaedia Britannica.)

Scientists visited Taos during the 1990s in unsuccessful good-faith efforts to trace the sound, which surveys indicated were heard by about 2% of the town's population. Described as a frequency similar to the low, throbbing engine of a diesel truck, the Taos Hum has reportedly created disturbances among its few hearers from mildly irritating to profoundly disturbing. In the extreme, hearers say they experience constant problems including interrupted sleep and physical effects such as dizziness and nosebleeds.

Speculation about the Taos Hum abounds. Conspiracy theorists believe the sound originates from ominous, secret, government testing, possibly emanating from the federal defense establishment of Los Alamos National Laboratory 55 mi southwest of Taos. The theory correlates with reports of some hearers that the sound began suddenly, as though something had been switched on.

Some investigators say the hearers may have extraordinary sensitivity to low-frequency sound waves, which could originate from all manner of human devices (cell phones, for one) creating constant sources of electromagnetic energy. Still other theorists postulate that low-frequency sound waves may originate in the Earth's lower atmosphere. One intriguing theory says that the hum could be explained by vibrations deep within the Earth, as a sort of precursor to earthquakes (although earthquakes are extremely rare in New Mexico).

Although many believe there's something to the mysterious Taos Hum, less kindly skeptics have dismissed the phenomenon as New Age nonsense linked to mass hysteria. But while you're here, you may as well give it a try (no one need know what you're up to). Find yourself a peaceful spot. Sit quietly. And listen.

lished on Thursday, carries arts and entertainment information in the "Tempo" section. The arts scene is much more lively, with festivals every season for nearly every taste.

NIGHTLIFE

Fodor's Choice ★ The **Adobe Bar** (⊠ *Taos Inn, 125 Paseo del Pueblo Norte* ☎ *575/758– 2233*), a local meet-and-greet spot known as "Taos's living room," books talented acts, from solo guitarists to small folk groups and, two or three nights a week, jazz musicians.

★ **Alley Cantina** (⊠ *121 Teresina La.* ☎ *575/758–2121*) has jazz, folk, and blues—as well as shuffleboard, pool, and board games for those not moved to dance. It's housed in the oldest structure in downtown Taos.

Caffe Tazza (⊠ *122 Kit Carson Rd.* ☎ *575/758–8706*) presents free evening performances throughout the week—folk-singing, jazz, belly dancing, blues, poetry, and fiction readings.

Fernando's Hideaway (⊠ *Don Fernando de Taos Hotel & Suites, 1005 Paseo del Pueblo Sur* ☎ *575/758–4444*) occasionally presents live entertainment—jazz, blues, hip-hop, R&B, salsa, and country music. Complimentary happy-hour snacks are laid out on weekday evenings, 5–7.

The **Kachina Lodge Cabaret** (⊠ *413 Paseo del Pueblo Norte* ☎ *575/758–2275*) usually brings in an area radio DJ to liven up various forms of music and dancing.

The piano bar at **Sabroso** (⊠ *470 CR 150, Arroyo Seco* ☎ *575/776–3333*) often presents jazz and old standards.

The **Sagebrush Inn** (⊠ *1508 Paseo del Pueblo Sur* ☎ *575/758–2254*) hosts musicians and dancing in its lobby lounge. There's usually no cover charge for country-western dancing.

THE ARTS

Long a beacon for visual artists, Taos is also becoming a magnet for touring musicians, especially in summer, when performers and audiences are drawn to the heady high-desert atmosphere. Festivals celebrate the visual arts, music, poetry, and film.

The **Taos Center for the Arts** (⊠ *133 Paseo del Pueblo Norte* ☎ *575/758–2052* ⊕ *www.taoscenterforthearts.org*), which encompasses the Taos Community Auditorium, presents films, plays, concerts, and dance performances.

The **Taos Fall Arts Festival** (☎ *575/758–21063 or 800/732–8267* ⊕ *www.taosfallarts.com*), from late September to early October, is the area's major arts gathering, when buyers are in town and many other events, such as a Taos Pueblo feast, take place.

The **Taos Spring Arts Celebration** (☎ *575/758–3873 or 800/732–8267*), held throughout Taos in May, is a showcase for the visual, performing, and literary arts of the community and allows you to rub elbows with the many artists who call Taos home. The Mother's Day Arts and Crafts weekend during the festival always draws an especially large crowd.

MUSIC

From mid-June to early August the Taos School of Music fills the evenings with the sounds of chamber music at the **Taos School of Music Program and Festival** (☎ *705/776–2388* ⊕ *www.taosschoolofmusic.com*). Running strong since 1963, this is America's oldest chamber music summer program and possibly the largest assembly of top string quartets in the country. Concerts are presented a couple of times a week from mid-June to August, at the Taos Community Auditorium and at Taos Ski Valley. Tickets cost $10–$20. The events at Taos Ski Valley are free.

Solar energy was pioneered in this land of sunshine, and each year in late June the flag of sustainability is raised at the three-day **Taos Solar Music Festival** (⊕ *www.solarmusicfest.com*). Top-name acts appear, and booths promote alternative energy, permaculture, and other eco-friendly technologies.

> **DID YOU KNOW?**
>
> Anyone over the age of 12 who wishes to fish must buy a New Mexico fishing license. Many sporting goods stores in the state sell them.

SPORTS & THE OUTDOORS

Whether you plan to cycle around town, jog along Paseo del Pueblo Norte, or play a few rounds of golf, keep in mind that the altitude in Taos is higher than 7,000 feet. It's best to keep physical exertion to a minimum until your body becomes acclimated to the altitude—a full day to a few days, depending on your constitution.

BALLOONING

Hot-air ballooning has become nearly as popular in Taos as in Albuquerque, with a handful of outfitters offering rides, most starting at about $200 per person. **Paradise Balloons** (☎ *575/751–6098* ⊕ *www. taosballooning.com*) will thrill you with a "splash and dash" in the Rio Grande River as part of a silent journey through the 600-foot canyon walls of Rio Grande Gorge. **Pueblo Balloon Company** (☎ *575/751–9877* ⊕ *www.puebloballoon.com*) conducts balloon rides over and into the Rio Grande Gorge.

BICYCLING

Taos-area roads are steep and hilly, and none have marked bicycle lanes, so be careful while cycling. The West Rim Trail offers a fairly flat but view-studded 9-mi ride that follows the Rio Grande canyon's west rim from the Rio Grande Gorge Bridge to near the Taos Junction Bridge.

Gearing Up Bicycle Shop (⊠ *129 Paseo del Pueblo Sur* ☎ *575/751–0365*) is a full-service bike shop that also has information about tours and guides. **Native Sons Adventures** (⊠ *1033–A Paseo del Pueblo Sur* ☎ *575/758–9342 or 800/753–7559*) offers guided tours on its mountain bikes.

FISHING

Carson National Forest has some of the best trout fishing in New Mexico. Its streams and lakes are home to rainbow, brown, and native Rio Grande cutthroat trout.

In midtown Taos, **Cottam's Ski & Outdoor** (⊠ *207–A Paseo del Pueblo Sur* ☎ *575/758–2822 or 800/322–8267* ⊕ *www.cottamsoutdoor.com*) provides fishing and bike trips and ski and snowboard rentals. **Solitary Angler** (⊠ *204–B Paseo del Pueblo Norte* ☎ *575/758–5653 or 866/502–1700* ⊕ *www.thesolitaryangler.com*) guides fly-fishing expeditions that search out uncrowded habitats. Well-known area fishing guide Taylor Streit of **Taos Fly Shop & Streit Fly Fishing** (⊠ *308–C Paseo del Pueblo Sur* ☎*575/751–1312* ⊕*www.taosflyshop.com*) takes individuals or small groups out for fishing and lessons.

GOLF

The greens fees at the 18-hole, PGA-rated, par-72 championship course at **Taos Country Club** (⊠ *54 Golf Course Dr., Ranchos de Taos* ☎*575/758–7300*) are $59–$75.

HEALTH CLUBS & FITNESS CENTERS

☾ The **Northside Health & Fitness Center** (⊠ *1307 Paseo del Pueblo Norte* ☎*575/751–1242*) is a spotlessly clean facility with indoor and outdoor saltwater pools, a hot tub, tennis courts, and aerobics classes. Nonmembers pay $8.50 per day. The center provides paid child care with a certified Montessori teacher. The **Taos Youth and Family Center** (⊠ *407 Paseo del Cañon E* ☎*575/758–4160*) has an outdoor Olympic-size ice arena, where rollerblading, volleyball, and basketball take place in summer. There's also a large swimming pool. Admission is $2 per day.

LLAMA TREKKING

☾ As one of the most offbeat outdoor recreational activities in the Taos area, llama trekking is offered by **Wild Earth Llama Adventures** (☎*575/586–0174 or 800/758–5262* ⊕*www.llamaadventures.com*) in a variety of packages, from one-day tours to excursions lasting several days in wilderness areas of the nearby Sangre de Cristo Mountains. Llamas, relatives of the camel, are used as pack animals on trips that begin at $89 for a day hike. Gourmet lunches eaten on the trail are part of the package, along with overnight camping and meals for longer trips.

RIVER RAFTING

The Taos Box, at the bottom of the steep-walled canyon far below the Rio Grande Gorge Bridge, is the granddaddy of thrilling white water in New Mexico and is best attempted by experts only—or on a guided trip—but the river also offers more placid sections such as through the Orilla Verde Recreation Area. Spring runoff is the busy season, from mid-April through June, but rafting companies conduct tours March to November. Shorter two-hour options usually cover the fairly tame section of the river. The **Bureau of Land Management, Taos Resource Area Office** (⊠ *226 Cruz Alta* ☎*575/758–8851*) has a list of registered river guides and information about running the river on your own.

Big River Raft Trips (☎*575/758–9711 or 800/748–3760* ⊕*www.bigriver rafts.com*) offers dinner float trips and rapids runs. **Far Flung Adventures** (☎*575/758–2628 or 800/359–2627* ⊕*www.farflung.com*) operates half-day, full-day, and overnight rafting trips along the Rio Grande and the Rio Chama. **Los Rios River Runners** (☎*575/776–8854 or 800/544–1181* ⊕*www.losriosriverrunners.com*) will take you to your choice of spots—the Rio Chama, the Lower Gorge, or the Taos Box. **Native Sons Adventures** (⊠ *1335 Paseo del Pueblo Sur* ☎*575/758–9342 or 800/753–7559* ⊕*www.nativesonsadventures.com*) offers several trip options on the Rio Grande.

SHOPPING

Retail options in Taos Plaza consist mostly of T-shirt emporiums and souvenir shops that are easily bypassed, though a few stores carry quality Native American artifacts and jewelry. The more upscale galleries and boutiques are two short blocks north on Bent Street, including the John Dunn House Shops. Kit Carson Road, also known as U.S. 64, has a mix of the old and the new. There's metered municipal parking downtown, though the traffic can be daunting. Some shops worth checking out are in St. Francis Plaza in Ranchos de Taos, 4 mi south of the Plaza near the San Francisco de Asís Church. Just north of Taos off NM 522 you can find Overland Ranch (including Overland Sheepskin Co.), which has gorgeous sheepskin and leather clothing, along with other shops, galleries, restaurants, and an outdoor path winding through displays of wind sculptures.

4

ART GALLERIES

For at least a century, artists have been drawn to Taos's natural grandeur. The result is a vigorous art community with some 80 galleries, a lively market, and an estimated 1,000 residents producing art full- or part-time. Many artists explore themes of the Western landscape, Native Americans, and adobe architecture; others create abstract forms and mixed-media works that may or may not reflect the Southwest. Some local artists grew up in Taos, but many—Anglo, Hispanic, and Native Americans—are adopted Taoseños.

Envision Gallery (✉ *Overland Ranch Complex, NM 522 north of Taos* ☎ *505/751–1344*) has contemporary art and an outdoor exhibit of wind sculptures.

Farnsworth Gallery Taos (✉ *133 Paseo del Pueblo Norte* ☎ *575/758–0776*) contains the work of artist John Farnsworth, best known for his finely detailed paintings of horses, and also includes colorful local landscapes, large-scale still-lifes, and scenes of Native American kiva dancers.

Fenix Gallery (✉ *208–A Ranchitos Rd.* ☎ *575/758–9120*) is a showcase for contemporary art, exhibiting paintings, sculpture, ceramics, and lithography by established Taos artists.

Gallery Elena (✉ *111 Morada La.* ☎ *575/758–9094*) shows the symbolic and impressionistic works of Veloy, Dan, and Michael Vigil.

Inger Jirby Gallery (✉ *207 Ledoux St.* ☎ *575/758–7333*) displays Jirby's whimsically colored landscape paintings.

★ **J.D. Challenger Gallery** (✉ *221 Paseo del Pueblo Norte* ☎ *575/751–6773 or 800/511–6773*) is the home base of personable painter J.D. Challenger, who has become famous for his dramatically rendered portraits of Native Americans from tribes throughout North America.

Las Comadres (✉ *228–A Paseo del Pueblo Norte* ☎ *575/737–5323*) is a women's cooperative gallery showing arts and crafts.

Lumina Fine Art & Sculpture Gardens (✉ *11 NM 230* ☎ *575/776–0123 or 877/558–6462*) exhibits paintings by worldwide artists and has 3 acres of sculpture gardens, including works of Japanese stone carvers.

Michael McCormick Gallery (✉106–C Paseo del Pueblo Norte ☎575/758–1372 or 800/279–0879) is home to the sensual, stylized female portraits of Miguel Martinez and the iconic portraits of Malcolm Furlow. The gallery also has an extensive collection of Rembrandt etchings.

Mission Gallery (✉138 E. Kit Carson Rd. ☎575/758–2861) carries the works of early Taos artists, early New Mexico modernists, and important contemporary artists. The gallery is in the former home of painter Joseph H. Sharp.

Navajo Gallery (✉210 Ledoux St. ☎575/758–3250) shows the works of the internationally renowned Navajo painter and sculptor R. C. Gorman, who died in 2005 and who was known for his ethereal imagery—especially his portraits of Native American women.

Nichols Taos Fine Art Gallery (✉403 Paseo del Pueblo Norte ☎575/758–2475) has exhibits of oils, watercolors, pastels, charcoal, and pencils from artists representing many prestigious national art organizations.

Parks Gallery (✉127–A Bent St. ☎575/751–0343) specializes in contemporary paintings, sculptures, and prints. Mixed-media artist Melissa Zink shows here, as does painter Jim Wagner.

R. B. Ravens Gallery (✉4146 NM 68, Ranchos de Taos ☎575/758–7322 or 866/758–7322) exhibits paintings by the founding artists of Taos, pre-1930s Native American weavings, and ceramics in a spare museum-quality setting.

Robert L. Parsons Fine Art (✉131 Bent St. ☎575/751–0159 or 800/613–5091) shows early Taos art colony paintings, antiques, and authentic antique Navajo blankets.

Six Directions (✉129B N. Plaza ☎575/758–5844) has paintings, alabaster and bronze sculpture, Native American artifacts, silver jewelry, and pottery. Bill Rabbit and Robert Redbird are among the artists represented here.

Spirit Runner Gallery (✉303 Paseo del Pueblo Norte ☎575/758–1132) exhibits colorful acrylic and gold-leaf paintings by Taos native Ouray Meyers.

Studio de Colores Gallery (✉119 Quesnel, El Prado near Taos ☎575/751–3502 or 888/751–3502) is home to the work of two artists, Ann Huston and Ed Sandoval, who are married to one another but have extremely distinctive styles. Sandoval is known for his trademark *Viejito* (Old Man) images and swirling, vibrantly colored landscapes; Ann specializes in soft-hue still lifes and scenes of incredible stillness.

★ At **Two Graces Gallery** (✉San Francisco Plaza ☎575/758–4639) owner and artist Robert Cafazzo displays an astonishing assortment of traditional Indian pottery and kachinas, contemporary art by local artists, old postcards, and rare books on area artists.

SPECIALTY STORES

BOOKS

Brodsky Bookshop (✉ *226–A Paseo del Pueblo Norte* ☎ *575/758–9468*) has new and used books—contemporary literature, Southwestern classics, children's titles—piled here and there, but amiable proprietor Rick Smith will help you find what you need.

G. Robinson Old Prints and Maps (✉ *John Dunn House, 124–D Bent St.* ☎ *575/758–2278*) stocks rare books, maps, and prints from the 16th to 19th century.

Moby Dickens (✉ *John Dunn House, 124–A Bent St.* ☎ *575/758–3050*), a full-service book store, specializes in rare and out-of-print books and carries a wide selection of contemporary fiction and nonfiction.

Sustaining Cultures (✉ *114 Doña Luz* ☎ *575/751–0959*) stocks spiritual and New Age books and tapes and offers tarot readings.

CLOTHING

Artemisia(✉ *115 Bent St.* ☎ *575/737–9800*) has a wide selection of one-of-a-kind wearable art by local artists.

Aventura (✉ *129-D Kit Carson Rd. 87571* ☎ *575/758–2144*), which opened in 2005, produces stylish (and super-warm), contemporary blanket "wraps" as well as other winter-oriented outdoor wear.

Clarke & Co. (✉ *120–E Bent St.* ☎ *575/758–2696*)is the only store in Taos that sells contemporary, upscale men's clothing.

Coactemalan Art Import (✉ *108 Kit Carson* ☎ *575/751–3775*) has Central and South American handmade clothing and gifts.

The Little Place Boutique (✉ *124–H Bent St.* ☎ *575/758–0440*) sells distinctive women's resort clothing, jewelry, and gifts.

Lollipops(✉ *120–D Bent St.* ☎ *575/758–8477*) carries designer children's clothing and accessories.

Mariposa Boutique Inc. (✉ *120–F Bent St.* ☎ *575/758–9028*) has handmade women's and children's specialty clothing.

Overland Sheepskin Company (✉ *NM 522, Overland Ranch, 4 mi north of Taos* ☎ *575/758–8820 or 888/754–8352*) carries high-quality sheepskin coats, hats, mittens, and slippers, many with Taos beadwork.

Steppin' Out (✉ *120–K Bent St.* ☎ *575/758–4487*) carries European footwear, distinctive clothing, handmade handbags, and unique accessories.

COLLECTIBLES & GIFTS

Arroyo Seco Mercantile (✉ *488 State Rd. 15, Arroyo Seco* ☎ *575/776–8806* ⊕ *www.secomerc.com*) carries a varied assortment of 1930s linens, handmade quilts, candles, organic soaps, vintage cookware, hand-thrown pottery, decorated crosses, and souvenirs.

Casa Mia Gift Shop (✉ *San Franciso Plaza* ☎ *575/758–1185*) carries authentic Indian jewelry, weavings, drums, and pottery.

Coyote Moon (✉ *120–C Bent St.* ☎ *575/758–4437*) has a great selection of south-of-the-border folk art, painted crosses, jewelry, and Day of the Dead figurines, some featuring American rock stars.

Horse Feathers (✉ *109–B Kit Carson Rd.* ☎ *575/758–7457*) is a fun collection of cowboy antiques and vintage Western wear—boots, hats, buckles, jewelry, and all manner of paraphernalia.

Letherwerks (⊠*124–B Bent St.* ☎*575/758–2778*) makes and sells handmade leather belts, bags, wallets, and backpacks.

San Francisco de Asis Parish Gift Shop (⊠*San Francisco Plaza* ☎*575/758–2754*) has a wide range of religious art including handmade retablos, rosaries, crosses painted by local artists, and traditional pottery.

Taos Drums (⊠*NM 68, 5 mi south of Plaza* ☎*575/758–9844 or 800/424–3786*) is the factory outlet for the Taos Drum Factory. The store, 5 mi south of Taos Plaza (look for the large tepee), stocks handmade Pueblo log drums, leather lamp shades, and wrought-iron and Southwestern furniture.

White Lotus (⊠*122–A/B Paseo del Pueblo Sur* ☎*751/758–0040*) expatriate Tibetans own this festive shop that has clothing, jewelry, Eastern spiritual books, and crafts from India, Nepal, Tibet, Thailand, and Indonesia.

HOME FURNISHINGS

Abydos (⊠*7036 SR 518, Talap, near Ranchos de Taos* ☎*575/758–0483 or 888/900–0863*) sells fine handmade New Mexican–style furniture.

★ **Alhambra** (⊠*124 Paseo del Pueblo Sur* ☎*575/758–4161*) carries rare antique furniture, rugs, and textiles from India, Tibet, Nepal, Thailand, and China.

At **Antiquarius Imports** (⊠*487 State Road 150,87514 Arroyo Seco* ☎*575/776–8381* ⊕*www.antiquariusimports.com*) Ivelisse Brooks's eclectic shop, you'll find rare Indian, Afghan, and African antiques and furniture along with contemporary, naturally dyed carpets made in Pakistan.

Casa Cristal Pottery (⊠*1306 Paseo del Pueblo Norte* ☎*575/758–1530*), 2½ mi north of the Taos Plaza, has a huge stock of stoneware, serapes, clay pots, Native American ironwood carvings, fountains, sweaters, ponchos, clay fireplaces, Mexican blankets, tiles, piñatas, and blue glassware from Guadalajara.

★ **Country Furnishings of Taos** (⊠*534 Paseo del Pueblo Norte* ☎*575/758–4633*) sells folk art from northern New Mexico, handmade furniture, metalwork lamps and beds, and colorful accessories.

EC-LEK-TIC (⊠*401 Paseo del Pueblo Norte* ☎*575/758–7232*) imports rare Indian, Tibetan, and Chinese antique furniture, sculpture, rugs, and home furnishings.

Starr Interiors (⊠*117 Paseo del Pueblo Norte* ☎*575/758–3065*) has a striking collection of Zapotec Indian rugs and hangings.

Taos Blue (⊠*101–A Bent St.* ☎*575/758–3561*) carries jewelry, pottery, and contemporary works by Native Americans (masks, rattles, sculpture), as well as Hispanic *santos* (bultos and retablos).

The **Taos Company** (⊠*124–K Bent St.* ☎*575/758–1141 or 800/548–1141*) sells magnificent Spanish-style furniture, chandeliers, rugs, and textiles; Mexican *equipal* (wood and leather) chairs; and other accessories.

Taos Tin Works (⊠*1204–D Paseo del Pueblo Norte* ☎*575/758–9724*) sells handcrafted tinwork such as wall sconces, mirrors, lamps, and table ornaments by Marion Moore. **Weaving Southwest** (⊠*216–B Paseo del Pueblo Norte 8* ☎*575/758–0433*) represents 20 tapestry artists who make beautiful rugs and blankets. The store also sells supplies for weavers, including hand-dyed yarn.

> **DID YOU KNOW?**
>
> Your best guarantee of authenticity, particularly involving Navajo blankets, is to purchase directly from a reputable reservation outlet.

NATIVE AMERICAN ARTS & CRAFTS

Buffalo Dancer (⊠*103–A E. Plaza* ☎*575/758–8718*) buys, sells, and trades Native American arts and crafts, including pottery, belts, kachina dolls, hides, and silver-coin jewelry. **El Rincón Trading Post** (⊠*114 E. Kit Carson Rd.* ☎*575/758–9188*) is housed in a large, dark, cluttered century-old adobe. Native American items of all kinds are bought and sold here: drums, feathered headdresses, Navajo rugs, beads, bowls, baskets, shields, beaded moccasins, jewelry, arrows, and spearheads. The packed back room contains Native American, Hispanic, and Anglo Wild West artifacts. **Taos General Store** (⊠*223–C Paseo del Pueblo Sur* ☎*575/758–9051*) stocks a large selection of furniture and decorative items from around the world, as well as American Indian pots, rugs, and jewelry.

SPORTING GOODS

Cottam's Ski & Outdoor (⊠*207–A Paseo del Pueblo Sur* ☎*575/758–2822*) carries hiking and backpacking gear, snowboarding and skateboarding equipment, maps, fishing licenses and supplies, and ski equipment, along with related clothing and accessories. **Mudd 'n' Flood Mountain Shop** (⊠*134 Bent St.* ☎*575/751–9100*) has gear and clothing for rock climbers, backpackers, campers, and backcountry skiers. **Taos Mountain Outfitters** (⊠*114 S. Plaza* ☎*575/758–9292*) has supplies for kayakers, skiers, climbers, and backpackers, as well as maps, books, and handy advice.

TAOS SKI VALLEY

NM 150, 22 mi northeast of Taos.

A trip to Taos Ski Valley begins at the traffic light where you turn right onto NM 150 (Taos Ski Valley Road) from U.S. 64. Along the way, the hamlet of Arroyo Seco, some 5 mi up NM 150 from the traffic light, is worth a stop for lunch (try Maverick County Food Co.) and a look at crafts and antiques shops. Beyond Arroyo Seco the road crosses a high plain, then plunges into the Rio Hondo Canyon to follow the cascading brook upstream through the forest to Taos Ski Valley, where NM 150 ends. (It docs not continue to Red River, as some disappointed motorists discover.)

Skiers from around the world return to the slopes and hospitality of the Village of Taos Ski Valley every year. This world-class area is known for its alpine-village atmosphere, perhaps the finest ski school in the country, and the variety of its 72 runs—it's also slowly but surely becoming more of a year-round destination, as the valley attracts outdoors enthusiasts with spectacular, and often challenging, hiking in summer and fall. Many of the few hotels at the ski valley have been converted to ski-in ski-out condos since the early 2000s, further evidence that the once funky ski area is becoming more of a Colorado-style full-scale resort town. Some of the best trails in Carson National Forest begin at the Village of Taos Ski Valley and go though dense woodland up to alpine tundra. There aren't many summer visitors, so you can have the trails up to Bull-of-the-Woods, Gold Hill, Williams Lake, Italianos, and Wheeler Peak nearly all to yourself. Easy nature hikes are organized by the Bavarian hotel, guided by Shar Sharghi, a botanist and horticulturist. Special events like barn dances and wine tastings occur throughout the nonskiing seasons.

WHERE TO EAT

$$
AMERICAN
✕**Rhoda's Restaurant.** Rhoda Blake founded Taos Ski Valley with her husband, Ernie. Her slope-side restaurant serves pasta, burgers, and sandwiches for lunch. Dinner fare is a bit more substantive, such as veal medallions with pancetta and seafood chiles rellenos with ancho-chile sauce. ⊠*Resort Center, on the slope* ☎*575/776–2005* ▤*AE, MC, V Closed June–Aug.*

$$
SOUTHWESTERN
✕**Tim's Stray Dog Cantina.** This wildly popular spot occupies a chalet-style building in the heart of the Taos ski area, and it's a favorite spot for lunch, dinner, and après-ski cocktails. Favorites include rainbow trout with lemon butter, chiles rellenos, and green-chile burgers (both beef and veggie). ⊠*105 Sutton Pl.* ☎*575/776–2894* ▤*MC, V.*

WHERE TO STAY

$$$
★
▥**Austing Haus.** Owner Paul Austing constructed much of this handsome, glass-sheathed building, 1½ mi from Taos Ski Valley, along with many of its furnishings. The breakfast room has large picture windows, stained-glass paneling, and an impressive fireplace. Aromas of fresh-baked goods, such as Paul's apple strudel, come from the kitchen. Guest rooms are pretty and quiet with harmonious, peaceful colors; some have four-poster beds and fireplaces. In winter the inn offers ski packages. ⊠*NM 150* ✉*Box 8, Village of Taos Ski Valley 87525* ☎*575/776–2649 or 800/748–2932* 🖷*575/776–8751* ⊕*www.austinghaus.net* 🛏*22 rooms, 3 chalets* ♿*In-hotel: restaurant* ▤*AE, DC, MC, V* ❙◎❙*CP.*

$$$$
★
▥**The Bavarian.** This luxurious, secluded re-creation of a Bavarian lodge has the only midmountain accommodations in the Taos Ski Valley. The King Ludwig suite has a dining room, kitchen, marble bathroom, and two bedrooms with canopied beds. Three suites have whirlpool tubs. The restaurant ($$$$) serves contemporary Bavarian-inspired cuisine, such as baked artichokes and Gruyère, and braised pork loin with garlic-mashed potatoes and red cabbage. Summer activities include hiking, touring with the resident botanist, horseback riding, rafting, and

fishing. Seven-night ski packages are offered. ✉ *100 Kachina Rd. ⌂ Box 653, Taos Ski Valley 87525* ☎ *575/776–8020* 🖷 *575/776–5301* ⊕ *www.thebavarian.net* ➟ *4 suites* ♿ *In-room: kitchen. In-hotel: restaurant* ▭ *AE, MC, V* ☉ *Closed May and early Nov.* ❢❶*BP.*

> **DID YOU KNOW?**
>
> Compared with other notable ski areas, New Mexico is more susceptible to extended periods of dry weather that can create meltdowns.

$$$$ ☷ **Inn at Snakedance.** This modern condominium resort is right on the slopes. The inn has a handsome library where guests can enjoy an après-ski coffee or after-dinner drink next to a fieldstone fireplace. Some rooms have fireplaces. In summer the hotel offers weeklong vacation packages, including a cooking school and fitness adventure courses. Hondo Restaurant ($; closed in summer) turns out esteemed contemporary American cooking, such as smoked Memphis-style ribs. ✉ *110 Sutton Place Rd. ⌂ NM 150; Box 89, Village of Taos Ski Valley 87525* ☎ *575/776–2277 or 800/322–9815* 🖷 *575/776–1410* ➟ *33 condo units* ♿ *In-room: kitchen, Wi-Fi. In-hotel: restaurant* ▭ *AE, DC, MC, V* ☉ *Closed mid-Apr.–Memorial Day* ❢❶*CP.*

SPORTS & THE OUTDOORS

Wheeler Peak is a designated wilderness area of Carson National Forest, where travel is restricted to hiking or horseback riding. Part of the Sangre de Cristo Mountains, this 13,161-foot peak is New Mexico's highest. The 8-mi trail to the top begins at the Village of Taos Ski Valley. Only experienced hikers should tackle this strenuous trail. Dress warmly even in summer, take plenty of water and food, and pay attention to *all* warnings and instructions distributed by the forest rangers. Quite a few shorter and less taxing trails also depart from the ski valley and points nearby; trailheads are usually marked with signs. ✉ *Twining Campground, next to ski area parking lot* ☎ *575/758–6200.*

Fodor's Choice
★ With 72 runs—more than half of them for experts—and an average of more than 320 inches of annual snowfall, **Taos Ski Valley** ranks among the country's most respected—and challenging—resorts. The slopes tend to be tough here (the ridge chutes, Al's Run, Inferno), but 25% (e.g., Honeysuckle) are for intermediate skiers, and 24% (e.g., Bambi, Porcupine) for beginners. Until recently it was one of the nation's handful of resorts that banned snowboarding. Taos Ski Valley is justly famous for its outstanding ski schools, one of the best in the country—if you're new to the sport, this is a terrific resort to give a try. ✉ *Village of Taos Ski Valley* ☎ *575/776–2291* ⊕ *www.skitaos.org* 🎟 *Lift tickets $66* ☉ *Late Nov.–early Apr.*

SHOPPING

Andean Softwear (✉ *118 Sutton Pl.* ☎ *575/776–2508*) carries exotic clothing, textiles, and jewelry. Note the deliciously soft alpaca sweaters from Peru.

Side Trips from the Cities

WORD OF MOUTH

"Wednesday we...went to Tent Rocks. I am so very grateful to all who posted about that being the highlight of their trips, as it certainly was one of ours as well, and we would have never known about it if not for folks here [at fodors.com]. We did both trails. There were a couple parts of the one in the high trail that I found challenging, but do-able, and oh so worth it.the views were spectacular. But even for those who don't go up, just entering the beginning of that trail and being right in amongst those rock formations of millions of years...words seem inadequate.

—go_laura

IF YOU'RE PLANNING A TRIP to any of north-central New Mexico's three most important destinations—Albuquerque, Santa Fe, or Taos— it's worth spending an extra day or even just a half day to explore the surrounding area. It's by venturing out of town that you really come to appreciate and understand northern Rio Grande Valley's exceptionally diverse and visually stunning scenery, from dramatic river gorges with sheer basalt walls to the evergreen- and aspen-covered slopes of the highest mountain range in New Mexico, the Sangre de Cristos. Within an hour's drive of Albuquerque, Santa Fe, or Taos are nearly a dozen Indian pueblos, the countryside that inspired Georgia O'Keeffe's artwork, some of the West's finest ski resorts, an emerging crop of prestigious wineries, several insular villages famous for both contemporary and traditional arts and crafts, two villages famous for their curative hot springs, and some of the best hiking, rafting, fly-fishing, and biking terrain you'll ever lay eyes on.

There are at least three road routes to get from Albuquerque to Santa Fe, and then three more from Santa Fe up to Taos. And they all have their charms, even the seemingly mundane trek up Interstate 25 from Albuquerque to Santa Fe. Traveling among the region's three key towns, and opting when time allows for the most scenic and circuitous routing, is one way to experience north-central New Mexico's most alluring off-the-beaten-path scenery. Another is simply to plan a few day trips from Albuquerque, Santa Fe, or Taos, or even to consider spending the night in one of the out-of-the-way communities described in this chapter—the region offers a wealth of lodging options, from funky to five-star elegant, and prices out in the country tend to be considerably lower than in Santa Fe and Taos.

However you go about experiencing the region's smaller communities and less-traveled byways, venture out into the hinterlands as often as you can. You haven't really been to north-central New Mexico until you've explored the cave dwellings at Bandelier National Monument, driven over the dramatic mountain passes of the Enchanted Circle and High Road to Taos, or checked out the acclaimed galleries and funky shops of Madrid and Chimayó. As the old travel cliché goes, in New Mexico, getting there is half the fun.

EXPLORING NORTH-CENTRAL NEW MEXICO

You need a car to embark on any of the side trips described in this chapter. Distances aren't as vast in north-central New Mexico as in the rest of the state: the Turquoise Trail extends only about 70 mi from Albuquerque to Santa Fe and can be managed, if you hustle, in roughly 90 minutes, but to truly appreciate the scenery and attractions along the way, you should really allow anywhere from three to six hours. Same goes for driving the High Road to Taos, the Enchanted Circle, Jémez Country, and Abiquiu. Roads in this part of the state can be windy and even a bit treacherous, especially in snowy winter weather, so take your time and avoid racing around on roads unfamiliar to you.

That being said, virtually every attraction and community covered here can be visited as part of a day trip from Albuquerque, Santa Fe, and/or Taos. If you have only two or three hours, stick with manageable and nearby jaunts. From Albuquerque, head to Isleta Pueblo or Corrales. From Santa Fe, visit some of the towns just south of town or some of the pueblos to the north—you can even visit Los Alamos or Bandelier in a half day if you're quick. From Taos, it's possible to cover part of the Enchanted Circle, and to drive up to the ski valley, in just two or three hours.

Keep in mind that many of the recreation areas, museums, camp-grounds, and even restaurants and lodgings covered in this chapter keep seasonal or limited hours. As it can take a bit of driving to reach some of these places, it's *always* best to phone ahead to avoid disap-pointment. And if you're unfamiliar with the area, always ask about driving times and current weather conditions. A little planning goes a long way when exploring some of the region's more remote towns and villages.

ABOUT THE RESTAURANTS

Somehow, just about any meal tastes a little better when it follows a long, windy road trip through magnificent scenery. North-central New Mexico has no shortage of tantalizing "road food"—simple and hon-est New Mexican fare, diner snacks, juicy burgers, and the like. But in these parts you can also find one of the Southwest's most acclaimed restaurants, Rancho de San Juan, along with several other fine eateries. A number of the restaurants in these parts are informal and operate with seasonal or less-than-regular hours, so it's always best to call first. Most of them serve dinner on the early side, too, so don't expect to find a restaurant open after 9 PM—or even 8 PM on weeknights, and, likely not at all on Sunday. Casual attire is always the norm around here.

ABOUT THE HOTELS

There are several good reasons to consider spending a night in one of the towns covered in this chapter, rather than in Albuquerque, Santa Fe, and Taos. First, distinctive bed-and-breakfasts and inns are the norm when you get out into the countryside—these properties tend to be more personal than big chain hotels, which predominate in Albu-querque and to a lesser extent in Santa Fe and Taos. Also, you pay higher prices for the same amenities in Santa Fe and Taos, if not Albu-querque, which has quite low hotel rates. If you prefer the sounds of coyotes howling and a pitch-black sky illuminated only by bright stars, you're more likely to appreciate one of the off-the-beaten-path lodgings described in this chapter than a place right in the heart of busy and bus-tling Albuquerque, Santa Fe, or even Taos. What you may lose in con-venience to shopping, dining, and nightlife, you often gain in proximity to great outdoorsy attractions, such as ski resorts and hiking trails.

	¢	$	$$	$$$	$$$$
WHAT IT COSTS					
Restaurants	under $10	$10–$17	$17–$24	$24–$30	over $30
Hotels	under $70	$70–$130	$130–$190	$190–$260	over $260

Restaurant prices are per person for a main course at dinner, excluding the 8.25% sales tax. Hotel prices are for two people in a standard double room in high season, excluding 11%–14% tax.

SIDE TRIPS FROM ALBUQUERQUE

Updated by Lynne Arany

It takes only a few minutes of driving in any direction to leave urban Albuquerque behind and experience some of New Mexico's natural and small-town beauty. Rivers, valleys, canyons, and peaks are just outside the city's limits, and amid them are many villages worth a stop. If you're headed up to Santa Fe, definitely consider traveling there by way of the rambling and tortuous Turquoise Trail, a charming alternative to speedy Interstate 25.

SOUTH OF ALBUQUERQUE

When Francisco Vásquez de Coronado arrived in what is now New Mexico in 1540, he found a dozen or so villages along the Rio Grande in the ancient province of Tiguex, between what is now Bernalillo to the north of Albuquerque and Isleta to the south. Of those, only Sandia and Isleta survive today. The Salinas Pueblo Missions ruins, about 65 mi southeast of Albuquerque, remain a striking example of the Spanish penchant for building churches on sites inhabited by native people.

ISLETA PUEBLO
13 mi south of Albuquerque, via I–25 (Exit 213) and NM 47.

Of the pueblos in New Mexico when the Spanish first arrived, Isleta Pueblo is one of two Tiwa-speaking communities left in the middle of the Rio Grande Valley. It was also one of a handful of pueblos that didn't participate in the Pueblo Revolt of 1680, during which Isleta was abandoned. Some of the residents fled New Mexico with the Spanish to El Paso, where their descendants live to this day on a reservation called Ysleta del Sur. Other members went to live with the Hopi of Arizona but eventually returned and rebuilt the pueblo.

Facing the quiet plaza is Isleta's church, **St. Augustine,** built in 1629. One of the oldest churches in New Mexico, it has thick adobe walls, a viga-crossed ceiling, and an austere interior. Legend has it that the ground beneath the floor has the odd propensity to push church and community figures buried under the floor back up out of the ground; bodies have been reburied several times, only to emerge again.

Polychrome pottery with red and black designs on a white background is a specialty here. The pueblo celebrates its feast days on August 28 and September 4, both in honor of St. Augustine. The tribal govern-

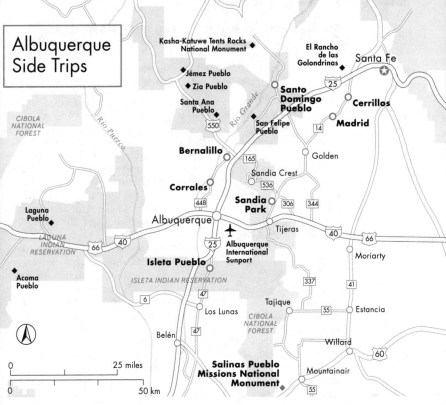

Albuquerque Side Trips

Kasha-Katuwe Tents Rocks
National Monument

El Rancho
de las
Golondrinas

Santa Fe

Jémez Pueblo

Zia Pueblo

Santa Ana
Pueblo

**Santo
Domingo
Pueblo**

Cerrillos

Madrid

San Felipe
Pueblo

CIBOLA
NATIONAL
FOREST

Rio Grande

Rio Puerco

Bernalillo

Golden

Sandia Crest

Corrales

**Sandia
Park**

Albuquerque

Tijeras

Laguna
Pueblo

LAGUNA
INDIAN
RESERVATION

Albuquerque
International
Sunport

Moriarty

Isleta Pueblo

Acoma
Pueblo

ISLETA INDIAN RESERVATION

Tajique

CIBOLA
NATIONAL
FOREST

Los Lunas

Estancia

Belén

Willard

25 miles

**Salinas Pueblo
Missions National
Monument**

Mountainair

50 km

ment maintains picnicking and camping facilities, several fishing ponds, and a renowned 18-hole golf course. It also runs the **Isleta Casino & Resort** (⊠ *11000 Broadway SE [NM 47]* ☎ *505/724–3800 or 877/747–5382* ⊕ *www.isletacasinoresort.com*), which ranks among the state's most popular gaming facilities. It's a large and handsome space with plenty of slots and myriad gaming tables; the concert hall hosts a mix of oldies, pop stars, and country-and-western acts—past numbers have included Tom Jones, Vince Gill, and Tony Bennett. There's also boxing held throughout the year. A full-service, upscale, 201-room hotel and spa opened in 2008, making Isleta more competitive with other high-profile Native American resorts in the Rio Grande region, including Sandia, Santa Ana, and Pojoaque. Although Isleta is wonderfully picturesque—beehive ovens stand beside adobe homes bedecked with crimson chilies—camera use is restricted here. Only the church may be photographed. ⊠ *Tribal Rd. 40* ☎ *505/869–3111* ⊕ *www.isleta pueblo.com* ☑ *Free.*

SPORTS & THE OUTDOORS

One of the most esteemed facilities in the state, **Isleta Eagle Golf Course** (⊠ *4001 NM 47 SE* ☎ *505/848–1900 or 866/475–3822* ⊕ *www.isletaeagle.com*) consists of three 9-hole layouts set around three lakes; greens fees are $40–$55 for 18 holes.

SALINAS PUEBLO MISSIONS NATIONAL MONUMENT

58 mi (to Punta Agua/Quarai) from Albuquerque, east on I–40 (to Tijeras Exit), south on NM 337 and NM 55; 23 mi from Punta Agua to Abó, south on NM 55, west (at Mountainair) on U.S. 60, and north on NM 513; 34 mi from Punta Agua to Gran Quivira, south on NM 55.

Salinas Pueblo Missions National Monument is made up of three sites—**Quarai, Abó, and Gran Quivira**—each with the ruins of a 17th-century Spanish colonial Franciscan missionary church and an associated pueblo. The sites represent the convergence of two Native American peoples, the Anasazi and the Mogollon, who lived here for centuries before the Spanish arrived. Quarai, the nearest to Albuquerque, was a flourishing Tiwa pueblo whose inhabitants' pottery, weaving, and basket-making techniques were quite refined. On the fringe of the Great Plains, all three of the Salinas pueblos were vulnerable to raids by nomadic Plains Indians. Quarai was abandoned about 50 years after its mission church, **San Purísima Concepción de Cuarac,** was built in 1630. If you can arrange it, arrive in time for the late-afternoon light—the church's red sandstone walls still rise 40 feet out of the earth, and are a powerful sight. At Abó are the remains of the three-story church of San Gregorio and a large unexcavated pueblo. (The masonry style at Abó, also built of red stone, bore some similarity to that at Chaco Canyon, which has led some archaeologists to speculate that the pueblo was built by people who left the Chaco Canyon area.) Gran Quivira contains two churches and some excavated Native American structures. There are walking trails and small interpretive centers at each of the pueblos, and expanded exhibits at the monument headquarters in the old cow town–cum–arts center of Mountainair. ■ TIP→ **You'll come to Quarai first via this route, and this is the loveliest of the three**, with Abó—which you can swing by easily enough if you loop back to Albuquerque via U.S. 60 west (through Mountainair), then north on either NM 47 (for the scenic back route through Isleta); or Interstate 25—a close second. Gran Quivira is more a detour, and you might find yourself wanting to take a little time to stroll down Mountainair's quaint main street then getting a bite at Pop Shaffer's Café (⇨ *below*) instead. ⊠*N. Ripley Ave. at W. Broadway (U.S. 60), Mountainair* ☏*505/847–2585* ⊕*www.nps.gov/sapu* ✉*Free* ☉ *Late May–early Sept., daily 9–6; early Sept.–late May, daily 9–5.*

WHERE TO STAY

$ 🏠**Casa Manzano.** Tucked about a mile up a dirt-and-gravel forest road, Casa Manzano rewards its guests with intimate views of the Manzano Mountains, and accommodations that warrant its reputation as a retreat. Designed by cohost Bert Herrman, this thoughtfully laid-out modern property is beautifully detailed with red-tile roofs, saltillo-tile floors, courtyard garden, hand-plastered *nichos*, hand-crafted woodwork, and finely impressed tinwork. And it's as environmentally up-to-date as can be. Its straw-bale construction (a 1-inch-thick layer of cement coated with softly textured plaster, inside and out, renders it fireproof), south-facing Trombe wall, and radiant heating make Casa Manzano a case study of solar-powered elegance. **Pros:** Breakfast is sumptuous—and often includes offerings from the lovingly tended garden. **Cons:** Other meals require a drive, either into town or down to Mountainair. ✉*103 Forest Rd. 321, Tajique* ✛*29 mi south from Tijeras on NM 337 and NM 55* ☎*505/384–9767* ⟲*4 casitas* ♿*In-room: no TV. In-hotel: dial-up, fitness facilities* ▤ *MC, V* ⦿*BP.*

$ ⛫ **Shaffer Hotel.** One of the nation's few remaining structures built in the Pueblo Deco style, the Shaffer was restored and reopened as a hotel in 2005 after many years of neglect. The 1923 building, in the heart of historic—if modest—downtown Mountainair, offers a wide range of accommodations. The simple "cowboy rooms" share a community bathroom, but all others have private baths, some with original claw-foot tubs. All are done with 1920s and '30s deco antiques and tile bath-rooms; they're not fancy, but they are comfortable. Try for a side room facing the park—you'll still hear the freight trains rumbling by much of the night, but it's worse in the back. The lobby's a tin-ceiling period gem (original owner Pop Shaffer himself did all the woodwork), and from it you can step right into **Pop Shaffer's Café** ($). The homemade pie (pecan, mmm), breakfast burritos, and *bizcochitos* are all highly com-mendable, as is the hand-painted true-to-era Native American–inspired decor. **Pros:** Rife with history, this place is a real slice. **Cons:** Service can be a bit spotty, and the rooms a bit sterile. ✉*103 W. Main St., Mountainair* ☎*505/847–2888 or 888/595–2888* ⊕*www.shafferhotel. com* ⟲*11 rooms, 9 with bath; 8 suites* ♿ *In-hotel: restaurant, Wi-Fi* ▤*AE, D, MC, V.*

BEYOND THE NORTH VALLEY

The land north of Albuquerque is a little bit cooler, a little bit greener, and a lot more pastoral than the city. Drive slowly through Bernalillo and Corrales, and you're bound to see lots of horses, cows, and llamas.

CORRALES
2 mi north of Albuquerque. Take Paseo Del Norte (NM 423) or Alam-eda Blvd. (NM 528) west from I–25 and head north on Corrales Rd. (NM 448).

Serene Corrales is an ancient agricultural community now inhabited by artists, craftspeople, and the affluent—plus a few descendants of the old families. Small galleries, shops, and places to eat dot the town, and in fall, roadside fruit and vegetable stands open. Bordered by Albuquerque and Rio Rancho, Corrales makes a pleasant escape to winding dirt roads, fields of corn, and apple orchards. On summer weekends visit the Cor-rales Farmers' Market; in October, the village holds a Harvest Festival. The village's main drag, NM 448, is one of New Mexico's official scenic byways, lined with grand estates and haciendas and shaded by cotton-woods. Just off the byway, you can break for a stroll through Corrales Bosque Preserve, a shaded sanctuary abutting the Rio Grande that's a favorite spot for bird-watching—some 180 species pass through here throughout the year. You can also catch a glimpse of historic hacienda life when you take a tour of the exquisitely restored 19th-century adobe compound of **Casa San Ysidro** (✉ *973 Old Church Rd.* ☎ *505/898–3915* ⊕ *www.cabq.gov* 💲 *$4* ⊙ *Wed.–Sun., call for times*).

WHERE TO EAT & STAY

$$$ ✕**The Old House Gastropub.** Set in a rambling early-18th-century com-
ECLECTIC pound along the Corrales Scenic Byway, this purportedly haunted haci-
enda was, for many years, the esteemed Casa Vieja. It hit a rough
patch after charismatic chef Jim White sold it in 2005, but it seems
to be finding itself again under its new Brit owners. They have repur-
posed it as a casual pub with an unusually meaty twist: you'll find
burgers of yak, ostrich, wild boar, and more—all supposedly not on
the endangered-species list. Stick with the simple dishes and go here
knowing its historic vibe is a key part of your meal. ✉ *4541 Corrales
Rd.* ☎ *505/898–7489* 🚫 *AE, D, MC, V.*

¢ ✕**Village Pizza.** A Chicago native with a knack for baking runs this
PIZZA ordinarily named joint that serves extraordinarily good pizza. Crusts
come in different styles (including Chicago-style deep dish), and a wide
range of toppings is offered, including such gourmet fixings as artichoke
hearts and smoked oysters. In back is an adobe-walled courtyard with
a couple of big leafy trees and lots of seating. You get a 10% discount
if you ride in on horseback. ✉ *4266 Corrales Rd.* ☎ *505/898–0045*
🚫 *AE, D, MC, V.*

$ 🏨**Chocolate Turtle B&B.** Hosts Nancy and Dallas Renner run this light-
★ filled four-room hideaway in a quiet neighborhood in West Corrales. It's
a short drive from Rio Rancho and 20 minutes from downtown Albu-
querque, but the setting is as peaceful as can be. This Territorial-style
home's large windows and neatly landscaped grounds afford sweeping
views of the Sandia Mountains. Fresh flowers further brighten the col-
orfully painted Southwestern-themed rooms, which range from a cozy
single to three more substantial doubles, the most desirable with its
own private terrace. **Pros:** Service is always good. **Cons:** Decor may be
a little too bright for some. ✉ *1098 W. Meadowlark La.* ☎ *505/898–
1800 or 877/298–1800* ⊕ *www.chocolateturtlebb.com* 🛏 *4 rooms*
△ *In-room: no phone, no TV, Wi-Fi* 🚫 *AE, D, MC, V* 🍽*BP.*

BERNALILLO
*17 mi north of Albuquerque via I–25, 8 mi north of Corrales via NM
448 to NM 528.*

Once a rather tranquil Hispanic village, Bernalillo is today one of New
Mexico's fastest-growing towns—it's increasingly absorbing the subur-
ban growth northward from Albuquerque. The town holds a Wine Fes-
tival each Labor Day weekend, but the most memorable annual event is
the Fiesta of San Lorenzo, which has honored the town's patron saint
for nearly 400 years. On August 10, San Lorenzo Day, the entire town
takes to the streets to participate in the traditional masked *matachine*
dance. Matachines, of Moorish origin, were brought to this hemisphere
by the Spanish. In New Mexico various versions are danced to haunt-
ing fiddle music, in both Native American pueblos and old Spanish vil-
lages at different holidays. Though interpretations of the matachines
are inexact, one general theme is that of conquest. One dancer, wearing

a devil's mask and wielding a whip, presides over the others. A young girl, dressed in white, is also present.

The town's leading attraction, **Coronado State Monument,** is named in honor of Francisco Vásquez de Coronado, the leader of the first organized Spanish expedition into the Southwest, from 1540 to 1542. The prehistoric **Kuaua Pueblo,** on a bluff overlooking the Rio Grande, is believed to have been the headquarters of Coronado and his army, who were caught unprepared by severe winter weather during their search for the legendary Seven Cities of Gold. A worthy stop, the monument has a museum in a restored kiva, with copies of magnificent frescoes done in black, yellow, red, blue, green, and white. The frescoes depict fertility rites, rain dances, and hunting rituals. The original artworks are preserved in the small visitor center. Adjacent to the monument is **Coronado State Park,** which has campsites and picnic grounds, both open year-round. In autumn the views at the monument and park are especially breathtaking, with the trees turning russet and gold. There's also overnight camping at the adjacent Coronado Campground (☎505/980–8256). ✉485 Kuaua Rd., off NM 44/U.S. 550 ☎505/867–5351 ⊕www.nmstatemonuments.org ✉$3 ⊙Wed.– Mon. 8:30–5.

WHERE TO EAT & STAY

$$$ ✕**Prairie Star.** Albuquerque residents often make the drive to this 1920s
ECLECTIC Pueblo Revival hacienda, renowned for the sunset views from its patio.
★ The menu combines contemporary American, Southwestern, and classical cuisine, including duck-confit crepes with red-chili-infused blueberries, lemon chèvre, mint, and pistachios, and dry-aged prime New York steak with black truffle potatoes, cheesy collard greens, and roasted garlic–tomato confit. The culinary quality has become consistently outstanding over the years, and the setting is gorgeous. Prairie Star is on the Santa Ana reservation, right beside the Santa Ana Golf Club. ✉288 Prairie Star Rd., Santa Ana Pueblo ☎505/867–3327 ⊕www.santa anagolf.com ☐AE, D, DC, MC, V ⊙Closed Mon. No lunch.

$ ✕**Range Cafe & Bakery.** Banana pancakes, giant cinnamon rolls, Asian
ECLECTIC spinach salad, homemade portobello burgers, homemade meat loaf with
Fodor'sChoice garlic mashed potatoes, steak-and-enchilada platters, and the signature
★ dessert, Death by Lemon, are among the highlights at this quirky spot known for down-home fare with creative touches. All the above, plus a full complement of rich, decadent Taos Cow ice cream, is served in a refurbished mercantile building with a dead-center view of the Sandia Mountains. You can order breakfast fare until 3 PM. There are also two newer branches in Albuquerque, but the original has the best ambience. ✉925 Camino del Pueblo ☎505/867–1700 ⊕www.rangecafe.com ⚠Reservations not accepted ☐AE, D, MC, V.

$$$$ ⌂**Hyatt Regency Tamaya.** This spectacular large-scale resort, on 500
Fodor'sChoice acres on the Santa Ana Pueblo, includes a top-rated golf course, state-
★ of-the-art spa, and cultural museum and learning center. Most rooms, swathed in natural stone, wood, and adobe and filled with pueblo-inspired textiles and pottery, overlook the Sandia Mountains or cottonwood groves; many have balconies or patios. Cultural events include

bread-baking demonstrations (in traditional adobe ovens), storytelling, and live tribal dance and music performances. Other amenities include waterslides over two of the outdoor pools, atmospheric bars, guided nature walks, and hot-air ballooning nearby. The Hyatt's outstanding **Corn Maiden Restaurant** (⊘ *Closed Sun. and Mon. No lunch*) serves outstanding contemporary fare that mixes New Mexican, Asian, regional American influences and ingredients. Try buffalo topped with foie gras and a truffle demi-glace, or crispy-skin duck served with an apple–green chili pancake and orange-whiskey sauce. The Santa Ana Star Casino is a free shuttle ride away. And if you're looking for an exceptional horseback ride, arrange one with the Tamaya stables. As you drink in eyefuls of the spectacular pueblo backcountry and weave among trees and plantings, you'll wonder why you ever settled for the dull nose-to-butt riding experiences of yesteryear. If you're too suave to wear the helmet or gloves offered, by all means do not forego a heavy layer of sunscreen, especially on your face, ears, and neck. **Pros:** This is the place to come to get away. **Cons:** Occasionally quirky front-desk service, but that's it. ⊠ *1300 Tuyuna Trail, Santa Ana Pueblo* ☎ *505/867-1234 or 800/633-7313* 📠 *505/771-6180* ⊕ *www.tamaya.hyatt.com* ⮪ *331 rooms, 19 suites* ⚐ *In-room: Wi-Fi, refrigerator. In-hotel: 3 restaurants, room service, bars, golf course, tennis courts, pools, gym, spa, children's programs (ages 2–14)* ⊟ *AE, D, DC, MC, V.*

CAMPING

⚠ **Albuquerque North Bernalillo KOA.** Cottonwoods, pines, evergreens, and willows shade this park, where morning brings a free pancake breakfast and in summer free outdoor movies are screened. You can play badminton, basketball, croquet, horseshoes, and video games. ⊠ *55 S. Hill Rd.* ☎ *505/867-5227 or 800/562-3616* ⊕ *www.koa. com* ⚐ *Guest laundry, flush toilets, full hookups, showers, grills, picnic tables, swimming (pool)* ⮪ *57 RV sites, 36 tent sites, 6 cabins* ⊟ *D, MC, V.*

SANTO DOMINGO PUEBLO
40 mi northeast of Albuquerque via I–25; exit on NM 22 and drive 4½ mi west.

Santo Domingo Pueblo craftspeople sell outstanding *heishi* (shell) jewelry and pottery, along with other traditional arts and crafts, year-round, but the pueblo's three-day Labor Day Arts and Crafts Fair brings out artists and visitors in full force. The colorful, dramatic Corn Dance, held in honor of St. Dominic, the pueblo's patron saint, on August 4, attracts more than 2,000 dancers, clowns, singers, and drummers. Painter Georgia O'Keeffe supposedly said the Corn Dance was one of the great events in her life. Still and video cameras, tape recorders, and sketching materials are prohibited. It's quite easy to visit the pueblo as part of a trip to Tent Rocks (⇨ *South of Santa Fe section*). ⊠ *Off NM 22, 4½ mi west of I–25* ☎ *505/465-2214* 🏷 *Donations encouraged* ⊘ *Daily dawn–dusk.*

THE TURQUOISE TRAIL

Fodor'sChoice
★

Etched out in the early 1970s and still well traveled is the scenic Turquoise Trail (or more prosaically, NM 14), a National Scenic Byway which follows an old route between Albuquerque and Santa Fe that's dotted with ghost towns now being restored by writers, artists, and other urban refugees. This 70 mi of piñon-studded mountain back road along the eastern flank of the sacred Sandia Mountains is a gentle roller coaster that also affords panoramic views of the Ortiz, Jémez, and Sangre de Cristo mountains. It's believed that 2,000 years ago Native Americans mined turquoise in these hills. The Spanish took up turquoise mining in the 16th century, and the practice continued into the early 20th century, with Tiffany & Co. removing a fair share of the semiprecious stone. In addition, gold, silver, tin, lead, and coal have been mined here. There's plenty of opportunity for picture taking and picnicking along the way. The pace is slow, the talk is about the weather, and Albuquerque might as well be on another planet. The entire loop of this trip takes a day, the drive up the Sandia Crest a half day. Two Web sites offer good information: ⊕*www.turquoisetrail.org* and *www.byways.org*.

SANDIA PARK

7 mi north of Tijeras. From Tijeras, take I–40 east and exit north on the Turquoise Trail (NM 14); proceed 6 mi and turn left onto NM 536.

Driving east from Albuquerque, before you head up the Turquoise Trail, drop down south from Interstate 40 first, and stop at the **Sandia Ranger Station** for a bit of orientation on the Cibola National Forest and the mountains you're about to drive through. Pick up pamphlets and trail maps, and—if there are enough kids in the audience—witness a fire-prevention program with a Smokey the Bear motif. From here you can also embark on a short self-guided tour to the nearby **fire lookout tower** and **Tijeras Pueblo ruins,** and head out on the trails throughout the forest. ⊠*11776 NM 337, Tijeras, south of I–40, off Exit 175* ☎*505/281–3304* ⊕*www.fs.fed.us/r3/cibola/districts/ sandia.shtml* ☞*Free, $3 for parking in Cibola National Forest* ☺*Mon.–Sat. 8–4:30.*

In Cedar Crest, just off NM 14 a couple of miles south of Sandia Park, the modest but nicely laid-out **Museum of Archaeology & Material Culture** chronicles archaeological finds and contains artifacts dating from the Ice Age to the Battle of Wounded Knee. Exhibits shed light on prehistoric man, buffalo hunting, a history of turquoise mining in north-central New Mexico, and the 1930s excavations of Sandia Cave (about 15 mi away) that offered evidence of some of the earliest human life in North America. ⊠*22 Calvary Rd. Turn west 5 mi north of I–40 Exit 175 in Cedar Crest* ☎*505/281–2005* ☞*$3* ☺*May–Oct., daily noon–7.*

☾
Fodor'sChoice
★

It may take months for this odyssey of a place to completely sink in: quirky and utterly fascinating, **Tinkertown Museum** contains a world of miniature carved-wood characters. The museum's late founder, Ross Ward, spent more than 40 years carving and collecting the hundreds of figures that populate this cheerfully bizarre museum, including an animated miniature Western village, a Boot Hill cemetery, and a 1940s circus exhibit. Ragtime piano music, a 40-foot sailboat, and a life-size general store are other highlights. The walls surrounding this 22-room museum have been fashioned out of more than 50,000 glass bottles pressed into cement. This homage to folk art, found art, and eccentric kitsch tends to strike a chord with people of all ages. As you might expect, the gift shop offers plenty of fun oddities. ⊠ *121 Sandia Crest Rd. (NM 536) , take Cedar Crest exit175 north off I-40 east and follow signs on NM 14 to Sandia Crest turnoff* ☎ *505/281–5233* ⊕ *www. tinkertown.com* ⊠ *$3* ⊙ *Apr.–Oct., daily 9–6.*

For awesome views of Albuquerque and half of New Mexico, take NM 536 up the back side of the Sandia Mountains through Cibola
★ National Forest to **Sandia Crest.** At the 10,378-foot summit, explore the foot trails along the rim (particularly in summer) and take in the breathtaking views of Albuquerque down below, and of the so-called Steel Forest—the nearby cluster of radio and television towers. Always bring an extra layer of clothing, even in summer—the temperature at the crest can be anywhere from 15 to 25 degrees cooler than down in Albuquerque. If you're in need of refreshments or are searching for some inexpensive souvenirs, visit the **Sandia Crest House Gift Shop and Restaurant** (☎ *505/243–0605*), on the rim of the crest.

As you continue north up NM 14 from Sandia Park, after about 12 mi you pass through the sleepy village of **Golden,** the site of the first gold rush (in 1825) west of the Mississippi. It has a rock shop and a mercantile store. The rustic adobe church and graveyard are popular with photographers. Be aware that locals are very protective of this area and aren't known to warm up to strangers.

WHERE TO STAY

$$
★ 🏠 **Elaine's, A Bed and Breakfast.** This antique-filled three-story log-and-stone home is set in the evergreen folds of the Sandia Mountain foothills. Four acres of wooded grounds beckon outside the back door. The top two floors have rooms with balconies and big picture windows that bring the lush mountain views indoors. The third-floor room also has cathedral ceilings and a brass bed; some rooms have fireplaces, and one has its own outside entrance. Breakfast, served in a plant-filled room or outside on a patio with a fountain, often includes fresh fruit, pancakes, or waffles with sausage. ⊠ *Snowline Estate, 72 Snowline Rd.* ⊕ *Box 444, Cedar Crest 87008* ☎ *505/281–2467 or 800/821–3092* ⊕ *www. elainesbnb.com* ⊠ *5 rooms* ⅙ *In-room: no phone, no TV. In-hotel: no-smoking rooms* ⊟ *AE, D, MC, V* ⓧ *BP.*

CAMPING

🏕 **Turquoise Trail Campground and RV Park.** Pine and cedar trees dot this 14-acre park in the Sandias, which has hiking trails with access to the Cibola National Forest. Adjacent to the premises is the Museum of Archaeology & Material Culture. Campsite rates are calculated per person; you will need reservations in October when spots fill up quickly. ⊠ *22 Calvary Rd., 5 mi north of I-40 Exit 175 in Cedar Crest*

☎505/281–2005 ♿ *Guest laundry, flush toilets, full hookups, partial hookups (electric and water), dump station, drinking water, showers, fire grates, fire pits, grills, picnic tables, electricity, public telephone, general store, play area* ⇔*57 sites, 45 with hookups.*

SPORTS & THE OUTDOORS

The 18-hole **Paa-Ko Ridge Golf Course** (✉ *1 Club House Dr.* ☎505/281–6000 or 866/898–5987 ⊕*www.paakoridge.com*) has been voted "The Best Place to Play Golf in New Mexico" by *Golf Digest*. Golfers enjoy vistas of the mesas and the Sandia Mountains from any of five tee placements on each hole. Greens fees are $59–$99, and tee-time reservations may be made a month ahead. The course is just off NM 14, 3½ mi north of the turnoff for Sandia Crest (NM 536).

Although less extensive and challenging than the ski areas farther north in the Sangre de Cristos, **Sandia Peak** (✉*NM 536* ☎505/242–9052, 505/857–8977 *snow conditions* ⊕*www.sandiapeak.com*) is extremely popular with locals from Albuquerque and offers a nice range of novice, intermediate, and expert downhill trails; there's also a ski school. Snowboarding is welcome on all trails, and there's cross-country terrain as well, whenever snow is available. Snowfall can be sporadic, so call ahead to check for cross-country; Sandia has snowmaking capacity for about 30 of its 200 acres of downhill skiing. The season runs from mid-December to mid-March, and lift tickets cost $43. Keep in mind that you can also access the ski area year-round via the Sandia Peak Aerial Tramway (⇨*Chapter 2, Albuquerque*), which is faster from Albuquerque than driving all the way around. In summer, the ski area converts into a fantastic mountain-biking and hiking terrain. The ski area offers a number of packages with bike and helmet rentals and lift tickets. Other summer activities at Sandia Peak include sand-pit volleyball, horseshoes, and picnicking.

MADRID

37 mi northeast of Albuquerque, 12 mi north of Golden on NM 14.

Totally abandoned when its coal mine closed in the 1950s, Madrid (locals put the emphasis on the first syllable: *mah*-drid) has gradually been rebuilt and is now—to the dismay of some longtime locals—on the verge of trendiness (some would say it's already there). The entire town was offered for sale for $250,000 back then, but there were no takers. Finally, in the early 1970s, a few artists fleeing big cities settled in and began restoration. Weathered houses and old company stores have been repaired and turned into boutiques and galleries, some of them selling high-quality furniture, paintings, and crafts. Big events here include Old Timers Days on July 4 weekend, and the Christmas open house, held weekends in December, when galleries and studios are open and the famous Madrid Christmas lights twinkle brightly.

NEED A BREAK?

Aged hippies, youthful hipsters, and everyone in between congregate at Java Junction (✉2855 NM 1487010 ☎505/438–2772) for lattes, chai, sandwiches, pastries, and other toothsome treats. Upstairs there's a pleasantly decorated room for rent that can sleep up to three guests.

☺ Madrid's **Old Coal Mine Museum** is a remnant of a once-flourishing industry. Children can explore the old tunnel, climb aboard a 1900 steam train, and poke through antique buildings full of marvelous relics. Museum tickets are available at the Mine Shaft Tavern out front. On weekends at 3 PM from late May to mid-October you can cheer the heroes and hiss the villains of the old-fashioned melodramas performed at the **Engine House Theatre.** The theater, inside a converted roundhouse machine shop, has a full-size steam train that comes chugging onto the stage. ⊠ *2814 NM 14* ☎ *505/438–3780* ⊕ *www.turquoisetrail.org/ oldcoalmine* ⊠ *Museum $4, melodrama $10* ⊙ *Late May–mid-Oct., weekdays 9:30–5, weekends 9:30–6; mid-Oct.–late May, daily 10–4 (weather permitting; call ahead).*

WHERE TO EAT

¢ ✕ **Mineshaft Tavern.** A rollicking old bar and restaurant adjacent to the
CAFÉ Old Coal Mine Museum, this boisterous place was a miners' commis-
★ sary back in the day. Today it serves what many people consider to be the best green-chili cheeseburger in New Mexico, along with ice-cold beer and a selection of other pub favorites and comfort foods. ⊠ *2846 NM 14* ☎ *505/473–0743* ⊟ *D, MC, V* ⊙ *No dinner Mon., Tues., and Thurs.*

SHOPPING

The town of Madrid has only one street, so the three-dozen-or-so shops and galleries are easy to find.

You can watch live glassblowing demonstrations at **Al Leedom Studio** (☎ *505/473–2054*); his vibrant vases and bowls are sold alongside the beautiful handcrafted jewelry of wife Barbara Leedom. The Leedoms' friendly cat and dancing dog are also big crowd pleasers. In a pale-blue cottage in the center of town, the **Ghost Town Trading Post** (☎ *505/471– 7605*) is a great bet for fine Western jewelry fashioned out of local gemstones (not just turquoise but opal, amber, and onyx). **Johnsen & Swan** (☎ *505/473–1963*) stocks fine leather belts, bags, and wallets; beadwork; custom-made chaps; and Western-inspired jewelry and gifts. **Johnsons of Madrid** (☎ *505/471–1054*) ranks among the most prestigious galleries in town, showing painting, photography, sculpture, and textiles created by some of the region's leading artists. You could spend hours browsing the fine rugs and furnishings at **Seppanen & Daughters Fine Textiles** (☎ *505/424–7470*), which stocks custom Zapotec textiles from Oaxaca, Navajo weavings, Tibetan carpets, and fine Arts and Crafts tables, sofas, and chairs.

CERRILLOS

3 mi northeast of Madrid on NM 14.

Cerrillos was a boomtown in the 1880s—its mines brimmed with gold, silver, and turquoise, and eight newspapers, four hotels, and 21 taverns flourished. When the mines went dry the town went bust. Since then, Cerrillos has served as the backdrop for feature-film and television westerns, among them *Young Guns* and *Lonesome Dove.* Today, it might easily be mistaken for a ghost town, which it's been well on the way to becoming for decades. Time has left its streets dry, dusty, and almost deserted, although it is home to a number of artists, and the occasional Amtrak roars through to remind you what century you're in.

Casa Grande (⊠*17 Waldo St.* ☎*505/438–3008*), a 28-room adobe (several rooms of which are part of a shop), has a small museum ($2) with a display of early mining exhibits. There's also a clean and neat, but oddly out-of-place petting zoo ($2) and a genuinely scenic overlook. Casa Grande is open daily 8 AM–sunset.

Pack rats and browsers alike ought not to miss the **What-Not Shop** (⊠*15B 1st St.* ☎*505/471–2744*), a venerable secondhand–antiques shop of a half-century's standing packed floor to ceiling with Native American pottery, cut glass, rocks, political buttons, old postcards, clocks, and who knows what else.

WHERE TO EAT & STAY

$
CAFÉ
Fodor'sChoice
★

✕**San Marcos Cafe.** In Lone Butte, about 6 mi north of Cerrillos, this restaurant is known for its creative fare and nontraditional setting—an actual feed store, with roosters, turkeys, and peacocks running about outside. In one of the two bric-a-brac–filled dining rooms, sample rich cinnamon rolls and such delectables as burritos stuffed with roast beef and potatoes and topped with green chili, and the classic eggs San Marcos, tortillas stuffed with scrambled eggs and topped with guacamole, pinto beans, melted Jack cheese, and red chili. Hot apple pie à la mode with rum sauce is a favorite. Expect a wait on weekends unless you make a reservation. ⊠*3877 NM 14*☎*505/471–9298* ▤*MC, V* ⊗*No dinner.*

$$$
🛏**High Feather Ranch.** A grand adobe homestead opened as a B&B in 2001, plush High Feather Ranch anchors 65 wide-open acres with breathtaking mountain views. It feels completely removed from civilization but is, in fact, within an hour's drive of both Santa Fe and Albuquerque. Although newly built, the sprawling inn contains reclaimed 19th-century timber, antique gates, and fine vintage furnishings. Rooms have high ceilings and plenty of windows, and you're never far from a portal or patio; one room has an outdoor shower in a private courtyard. Rates include an impressive full breakfast. **Pros:** Between Madrid and Cerrillos, you're alone with the scenery and certain to leave relaxed and well fed. **Cons:** There's a 1-mi stretch of dirt road to get to the door, but it's nothing to fret about. ⊠*29 High Feather Ranch 2 mi north of Madrid turn right onto CR 55/Gold Mine Rd.* ☎*505/424–1333 or 800/757–4410* ⊕*www.highfeatherranch.com* ⤢*2 rooms, 1 suite* ⌕*In-room: Wi-Fi, no phone, no TV. In-hotel: no-smoking rooms, some pets allowed* ▤*AE, D, MC, V* ⊠*BP.*

SPORTS & THE OUTDOORS

★ Rides with **Broken Saddle Riding Co.** (⊠*Off NM 14, Cerrillos* ☎*505/424–7774* ⊕*www.brokensaddle.com*) take you around the old turquoise and silver mines the Cerrillos area is noted for. On a Tennessee Walker or a Missouri Fox Trotter you can explore the Cerrillos hills and canyons, 23 mi southeast of Santa Fe. This is not the usual nose-to-tail trail ride.

SIDE TRIPS FROM SANTA FE

Updated by
Georgia de
Katona

Take even a day or two to explore the areas around Santa Fe and you'll start to get a sense of just how ancient this region is and how deeply the modern culture has been shaped by the Pueblo and Spanish people who have been here for centuries. If you're a geology buff or just happy to wander through this dramatic environment, you'll see things you couldn't possibly expect. Each of the excursions below can be accomplished in a day or less. The High Road to Taos trip makes for a very full day, so start early or plan to spend the night near or in Taos.

SOUTH OF SANTA FE

The most prominent side trip south of the city is along the fabled Turquoise Trail, an excellent—and leisurely—alternative route to Albuquerque that's far more interesting than Interstate 25; it's covered in the Side Trips from Albuquerque section. Although the drive down Interstate 25 offers some fantastic views of the Jémez and Sandia mountains, the most interesting sites south of town require hopping off the interstate. From here you can uncover the region's history at El Rancho de las Golondrinas and enjoy one of New Mexico's most dramatic day hikes at Tent Rocks canyon. Conversely, if you leave Santa Fe via Interstate 25 north and then cut down in a southerly direction along U.S. 285 and NM 41, you come to tiny Galisteo, a little hamlet steeped in Spanish colonial history.

PECOS NATIONAL HISTORIC PARK
★ *25 mi east of Santa Fe on I–25.*

Pecos was the last major encampment that travelers on the Santa Fe Trail reached before Santa Fe. Today the little village is mostly a starting point for exploring the Pecos National Historic Park, the centerpiece of which is the **ruins of Pecos**, once a major pueblo village with more than 1,100 rooms. Twenty-five hundred people are thought to have lived in this structure, as high as five stories in places. Pecos, in a fertile valley between the Great Plains and the Rio Grande Valley, was a trading center centuries before the Spanish conquistadors visited in about 1540. The Spanish later returned to build two missions.

The pueblo was abandoned in 1838, and its 17 surviving occupants moved to the Jémez Pueblo. Anglo travelers on the Santa Fe Trail observed the mission ruins with a great sense of fascination (and relief—for they knew it meant their journey was nearly over). A couple of miles from the ruins, **Andrew Kozlowski's Ranch** served as a stage depot, where a fresh spring quenched the thirsts of horses and weary passengers. The ranch now houses the park's law-enforcement corps and is not open to the public. You can view the mission ruins and the excavated pueblo on a ¼-mi self-guided tour in about two hours.

The pivotal Civil War battle of Glorieta Pass took place on an outlying parcel of parkland in late March 1862; a victory over Confederate forces firmly established the Union army's control over the New Mexico Territory. The Union troops maintained headquarters at Kozlowski's

Santa Fe Side Trips/
High and Low Roads to Taos

Chama 17

64/84

Los Ojos
Brazos

Tierra Amarilla 64

CARSON
NATIONAL
FOREST

Questa

522

San Cristobal

El Vado

Cebolla

Arroyo Hondo

519

Rio Grande

Canjilon

Vallecitos

Taos

111

La Madera

Rancho de Taos

Rio Chama

Ghost
Ranch

El Rito

554

Ojo Caliente

Pilar

285

Dixon

Peñasco

518

Abiquiu 84

Medanales

Velarde

Chamisal

SANTA FE
NATIONAL
FOREST

Alcade

Truchas

Española

Chimayó

Santa
Cruz

Cordova

Santa Clara
Pueblo

San Ildefonso
Pueblo

Nambé
Pueblo

SANTA FE
NATIONAL
FOREST

126

Valle Caldera
National Preserve

Los
Alamos 4

Pojoaque
Pueblo

Baldy Peak

Jémez
Springs

Kasha-Katuwe
Tent Rocks
National
Monument

Bandelier
National
Monument

84/
285

Hyde Memorial
State Park

4

Cañon

475

Santa Fe
Ski Area

Tesuque

El Rancho de las
Golondrinas

Santa
Fe

Pecos
National
Historic
Park

Jémez Pueblo

599

San Isidro

La
Cienaga

Glorieta

Pecos

25

14

Lamy

Rowe

Cerrillos

Galisteo

285

Madrid

Rio Grande

41

0   10 miles

Golden

0   20 km

Ranch during the battle. Check out the park visitor center for information about guided park tours (in summer only) and to see exhibits on the region's checkered history. ⊠*NM 63, off I–25 at Exit 307, Pecos* ☎*505/757–7200 park info, 505/757–7241 visitor center* ⊕*www.nps. gov/peco* 🎟*$3* ☉*Late May–early Sept., daily 8–6; early Sept.–late May, daily 8–5.*

GALISTEO

25 mi south of Santa Fe via I–25 north to U.S. 285 to NM 41 south.

South of Santa Fe lie the immense open spaces and subtle colorings of the Galisteo Basin and the quintessential New Mexican village of Galisteo—a blend of multigenerational New Mexicans and recent migrants who protect and treasure the bucolic solitude of their home. The drive from Santa Fe takes about 30 minutes and offers a panoramic view of the low, sculpted landscape of the Galisteo Basin, which is an austere contrast to the alpine country of the Sangre de Cristos. It's a good place to go for a leisurely lunch or a sunset drive to dinner, maybe with horseback riding. Aside from these options, there really isn't anything more to do here except enjoy the surroundings.

Founded as a Spanish outpost in 1614, with original buildings constructed largely with stones from the large pueblo ruin nearby that had once housed 1,000 people, Galisteo has attracted a significant number of artists and equestrians (trail rides and rentals are available at local stables) to the otherwise very traditional community. Cottonwoods shade the low-lying Pueblo-style architecture, a premier example of vernacular use of adobe and stone. The small church is open only for Sunday services.

WHERE TO STAY

$$ 🏨 **The Galisteo Inn.** This rambling old adobe hacienda has been transformed into an idyllic inn. Worn pine floors and massive wood beams rich in patina, and patios from which to enjoy the vistas, add to the romance of this private, upscale refuge, which also has two cozy, economical rooms that share a bath. Many rooms, including one of the inexpensive ones, have fireplaces, and all are decorated with tasteful, understated antiques and hand-crafted newer pieces. The acclaimed La Mancha Restaurant ($$; no dinner Sunday and Monday, reservations essential) serves superb, contemporary, Latin-inspired cuisine and is well worth a visit whether or not you're staying at the inn. If you can, eat out on the lawn under the massive cottonwood trees during the summer. The often-changing menu might feature pistachio-crusted Dungeness crab cakes with pineapple-caper tartar sauce, and an unusual mac-and-cheese with orzo pasta, black truffles, oyster mushrooms, goat cheese, and white-truffle essence. The bar serves light fare and requires no reservation; the Sunday brunch is wonderful and does require reservations. **Pros:** The rustic chic of this congenial, cozy inn is a delightful respite from busy Santa Fe. **Cons:** Not much to do beyond the walls of the inn unless you hire guides to explore. ⊠*9 La Vega St.* ⌖*HC 75, Box 4, 87540* ☎*505/466–8200 or 866/404–8200* 🖷*505/466–4008* ⊕*www.galisteoinn.com* 🛏*11 rooms, 9 with bath;*

Fodor'sChoice
★

1 suite ♿*In-hotel: restaurant, pool, no kids under 10, no-smoking rooms, Wi-Fi* ▭*D, MC, V* ⦿*BP.*

SPORTS & THE OUTDOORS

Galarosa Stable (✉*NM 41, Galisteo* ☎*505/466–4654 or 505/670– 2467* ⊕*www.galarosastables.com*) offers two-hour rides starting at $70 per person, south of Santa Fe in the panoramic Galisteo Basin.

EL RANCHO DE LAS GOLONDRINAS

★ *15 mi south of Santa Fe off I–25's Exit 276 in La Cienega.*

The "Williamsburg of the Southwest," El Rancho de las Golondrinas ("ranch of the swallows") is a reconstruction of a small agricultural village with buildings from the 17th to 19th century. Travelers on El Camino Real would stop at the ranch before making the final leg of the journey north, a half-day ride from Santa Fe in horse-and-wagon time. By car, the ranch is only a 25-minute drive from the Plaza. From Interstate 25, the village is tucked away from view, frozen in time. Owned and operated by the Paloheimo family, direct descendants of those who owned the ranch when it functioned as a *paraje,* or stopping place, the grounds maintain an authentic character without compromising history for commercial gain. Even the gift shop carries items that reflect ranch life and the cultural exchange that took place there.

Self-guided tours survey Spanish colonial lifestyles in New Mexico from 1660 to 1890: you can view a molasses mill, threshing grounds, and wheelwright and blacksmith shops, as well as a mountain village and a *morada* (meeting place) of the order of *Penitentes* (a religious fraternity known for its reenactment during Holy Week of the tortures suffered by Christ). Farm animals roam through the barnyards on the 200-acre complex. Wool from the sheep is spun into yarn and woven into traditional Rio Grande–style blankets, and the corn grown is used to feed the animals. During the spring and harvest festivals, on the first weekends of June and October, respectively, the village comes alive with Spanish-American folk music, dancing, and food and crafts demonstrations. There are ample picnic facilities, and a snack bar serves a limited number of items on weekends only. ✉*334 Los Pinos Rd.* ☎*505/471–2261* ⊕*www.golondrinas.org* ▭*$5* ☉*June–Sept., Wed.– Sun. 10–4; some additional weekends for special events.*

WHERE TO STAY

$$$ 🏨**Sunrise Springs Inn.** Suffused with art and nature, this 70-acre spread is a tranquil home base from which to explore Santa Fe, but enticements such as movement (e.g., yoga, tai chi) and meditation; Asian tea ceremonies and spa treatments (*see Spas Box in Chapter 3*); and cooking, wine-tasting and *raku* pottery classes may compel you to stay put. Gated casitas, with Zen-chic decor and high ceilings, are private, spacious havens that sport private patios, kitchenettes, and fireplaces. Garden View rooms also have private patios, and guests enjoy access to a comfy, communal lounge. The excellent Lotus Champagne Bar and Blue Heron restaurant ($$) are reasons enough to visit. Not only will you find a stunning selection of fine spirits and ceviches, but also impeccable

service and marvelous, sincere cuisine. Live music and fire dancing some evenings. **Pros:** Restaurant uses organic vegetables and herbs grown on-site; free Wi-Fi and luscious, organic toiletries from Taos. **Cons:** Rooms with pond views are small, and you may feel you must tiptoe about because of proximity to spa; located a 20-minute drive away from the Plaza. ⊠*242 Los Pinos Rd., Santa Fe* ☎*505/471–3600 or 800/955–0028* 🖳*505/471–7365* ⊕*www.sunrisesprings.com* ⤸*38 rooms, 20 casitas, 2 suites* ♿*In-room: kitchen (some), refrigerator (some), DVD (some), no TV (some). In-hotel: restaurant, bar, spa* ▭*AE, D, MC, V.*

KASHA-KATUWE TENT ROCKS NATIONAL MONUMENT

Fodor'sChoice
★

40 mi south of Santa Fe via I–25, Exit 264.

This is a terrific hiking getaway, especially if you have time for only one hike. The sandstone rock formations look like stacked tents in a stark, water- and wind-eroded box canyon. Located 45 minutes south of Santa Fe, near Cochiti Pueblo, Tent Rocks offers excellent hiking year-round, although it can get hot in summer, when you should bring extra water. The drive to this magical landscape is equally awesome, as the road heads west toward Cochiti Dam and through the cottonwood groves around the pueblo. It's a good hike for kids. The round-trip hiking distance is only 2 mi, about 1½ hours, but it's the kind of place where you'll want to hang out for a while. Take a camera. There are no facilities here, just a small parking area with a posted trail map and a self-pay admission box; you can get gas and pick up picnic supplies and bottled water at Cochiti Lake Convenience Store. ⊠*I–25 south to Cochiti Exit 264; follow NM 16 for 8 mi, turning right onto NM 22; continue approximately 3½ more mi past Cochiti Pueblo entrance; turn right onto BIA 92, which after 2 mi becomes Forest Service Rd. 266, a rough road of jarring, washboard gravel that leads 5 mi to well-marked parking area* ☎*505/761–8700* ⊕*www.nm.blm.gov* ▭*$5 per vehicle* ☉*Apr.–Oct., daily 7–7; Nov.–Mar., daily 8–5.*

SPORTS & THE OUTDOORS

The 18-hole, par-72 **Pueblo de Cochiti Golf Course** (⊠*5200 Cochiti Hwy., Cochiti Lake* ☎*505/465–2239*), set against a backdrop of steep canyons and red-rock mesas, is a 45-minute drive southwest of Santa Fe. Cochiti was designed by Robert Trent Jones Jr. and offers one of the most challenging and visually stunning golfing experiences in the state. Greens fees are $62 (Friday through Sunday) and include a cart.

PUEBLOS NEAR SANTA FE

For a pleasant side trip, visit several of the state's 19 pueblos, including San Ildefonso, one of the state's most picturesque, and Santa Clara, whose lands harbor a dramatic set of ancient cliff dwellings. Between the two reservations sits the striking landmark called Black Mesa, which you can see from NM 30 or NM 502. The solitary butte has inspired many painters, including Georgia O'Keeffe, and it is from this mesa that deer dancers descend at dawn during winter ceremonial dances. Both of these pueblos are home to outstanding potters and it is well worth visiting open studios to watch the process and see what is available. Plan on spending one to three hours at each pueblo, and leave the day open if you're there for a feast day, when dances are set to an organic rather than mechanical clock. Pueblo grounds and hiking areas do not permit pets.

POJOAQUE PUEBLO
17 mi north of Santa Fe on U.S. 285/84.

There's not much to see in the pueblo's plaza area, but the state visitor center and adjoining **Poeh Cultural Center and Museum** on U.S. 285/84 are well worth a visit. The latter is an impressive complex of traditional adobe buildings, including the three-story Sun Tower; the facility comprises a museum, a cultural center, and artists' studios. The museum holds some 8,000 photographs, including many by esteemed early-20th-century photographer Edward S. Curtis, as well as hundreds of works of both traditional and contemporary pottery, jewelry, textiles, and sculpture. There are frequent demonstrations by artists, exhibitions, and, on Saturday from May through September, traditional ceremonial dances. By the early 20th century the pueblo was virtually uninhabited, but the survivors eventually began to restore it. Pojoaque's feast day is celebrated with dancing on December 12. The visitor center is one of the friendliest and best stocked in northern New Mexico, with free maps and literature on hiking, fishing, and the area's history. The crafts shop in the visitor center is one of the most extensive among the state's pueblos; it carries weaving, pottery, jewelry, and other crafts by both Pojoaque and other indigenous New Mexicans. ⌂ *78 Cities of Gold Rd., off U.S. 285/84, 17 mi north of Santa Fe* ☎*505/455–3334* ⊕*www.poehmuseum.com* ⊠*Donation.*

NAMBÉ PUEBLO
4 mi east of Pojoaque on NM 503, 20 mi north of Santa Fe.

Nambé Pueblo has no visitor center, so the best time to visit is during the October 4 feast day of St. Francis celebration or the very popular July 4 celebration. If you want to explore the landscape surrounding the pueblo, take the drive past the pueblo until you come to **Nambé Falls** and **Nambé Lake Recreation Area** (☎*505/455–2304*). There's a shady picnic area and a large fishing lake that's open March–November (the cost is $10 for fishing, and $20 for boating—no gas motors are permitted). The waterfalls are about a 15-minute hike in from the parking and picnic area along a rocky, clearly marked path. The water pours over a rock precipice—a loud and dramatic sight given the river's modest size. Overnight RV ($35) and tent ($25) camping are also offered. ⌂*Nambé Pueblo Rd. off NM 503* ☎*505/455–4444 (info), 505/455–2304 ranger station* ⊕*www.newmexico.org/native_america/pueblos/nambe.php* ⊠*$8 per car.*

SAN ILDEFONSO PUEBLO
23 mi north of Santa Fe via U.S. 285/84 to NM 502 west.

Maria Martinez, one of the most renowned Pueblo potters, lived here. She first created her exquisite "black on black" pottery in 1919 and in doing so sparked a major revival of pueblo arts and crafts. She died in

5

CLOSE UP

Pueblo Etiquette

When visiting pueblos and reservations, you're expected to follow a certain etiquette. Each pueblo has its own regulations for the use of still and video cameras and video and tape recorders, as well as for sketching and painting. Some pueblos, such as Santo Domingo, prohibit photography altogether. Others, such as Santa Clara, prohibit photography at certain times; for example, during ritual dances. Still others allow photography but require a permit, which usually costs from $10 to $20, depending on whether you use a still or video camera. The privilege of setting up an easel and painting all day will cost you as little as $35 or as much as $150 (at Taos Pueblo). Associated fees for using images also can vary widely, depending on what kind of reproduction rights you might require. **Be sure to ask permission before photographing anyone in the pueblos**; it's also customary to give the subject a dollar or two for agreeing to be photographed. Native American law prevails on the pueblos, and violations of photography regulations could result in confiscation of cameras.

Specific restrictions for the various pueblos are noted in the individual descriptions. Other rules are described below.

■ Possessing or using drugs and/or alcohol on Native American land is forbidden.

■ Ritual dances often have serious religious significance and should be respected as such. Silence is mandatory—that means no questions about ceremonies or dances while they're being performed. Don't walk across the dance plaza during a performance, and don't applaud afterward.

■ Kivas and ceremonial rooms are restricted to pueblo members only.

■ Cemeteries are sacred. They're off-limits to all visitors and should never be photographed.

■ Unless pueblo dwellings are clearly marked as shops, don't wander or peek inside. Remember, these are private homes.

■ Many of the pueblo buildings are hundreds of years old. Don't try to scale adobe walls or climb on top of buildings, or you may come tumbling down.

■ Don't litter. Nature is sacred on the pueblos, and defacing land can be a serious offense.

■ Don't bring your pet or feed stray dogs.

■ Even off reservation sites, state and federal laws prohibit picking up artifacts such as arrowheads or pottery from public lands.

1980, and the 26,000-acre San Ildefonso Pueblo remains a major center for pottery and other arts and crafts. Many artists sell from their homes, and there are trading posts, a visitor center, and a museum where some of Martinez's work can be seen on weekdays. San Ildefonso is also one of the more visually appealing pueblos, with a well-defined plaza core and a spectacular setting beneath the Pajarito Plateau and Black Mesa. The pueblo's feast day is January 23, when unforgettable buffalo, deer, and Comanche dances are performed from dawn to dusk. Cameras are not permitted at any of the ceremonial dances but may be used at other times with a permit. ✉ *NM 502* ☎ *505/455–3549* 💲 *$7 per vehicle, still-camera permit $10, video-recorder permit $20, sketching permit $25* 🕙 *Daily (Apr.–Oct.) 8–5; museum weekdays 8–4:30.*

SANTA CLARA PUEBLO
27 mi northwest of Santa Fe, 10 mi north of San Ildefonso Pueblo via NM 30.

Santa Clara Pueblo, southwest of Española, is the home of a historic treasure—the awesome **Puyé Cliff Dwellings**, believed to have been built in the 13th to 14th centuries. They can be seen by driving 9 mi up a gravel road through a canyon, south of the village off NM 502.

The pueblo also contains four ponds, miles of stream fishing, and picnicking and camping facilities. You can tour the cliff dwellings, topped by the ruins of a 740-room pueblo, on your own or with a guide. Permits for the use of trails, camping, and picnic areas, as well as for fishing in trout ponds, are available at the sites; recreation areas are open April–October, dawn–dusk.

The village's shops sell burnished red pottery, engraved blackware, paintings, and other arts and crafts. All pottery is made via the coil method, not with a pottery wheel. Santa Clara is known for its carved pieces, and *Avanyu*, a water serpent that guards the waters, is the pueblo's symbol. Other typical works include engagement baskets, wedding vessels, and seed pots. The pueblo's feast day of St. Claire is celebrated on August 12. ✉ *Off NM 502 on NM 30, Española* ☎ *505/753–7326* 💲 *Pueblo free, cliff dwellings $5, still-camera permits $5* 🕙 *Daily 9–4:30.*

JÉMEZ COUNTRY

In the Jémez region, the 1,000-year-old ancestral Puebloan ruins at Bandelier National Monument present a vivid contrast to Los Alamos National Laboratory, birthplace of the atomic bomb. You can easily take in part of Jémez Country in a day trip from Santa Fe.

On this tour you can see terrific views of the Rio Grande Valley, the Sangre de Cristos, the Galisteo Basin, and, in the distance, the Sandias. There are places to eat and shop for essentials in Los Alamos and a few roadside eateries along NM 4 in La Cueva and Jémez Springs. There are also numerous turnouts along NM 4, several that have paths leading down to the many excellent fishing spots along the Jémez River.

The 48,000-acre Cerro Grande fire of May 2000 burned much of the pine forest in the lower Jémez Mountains, as well as more than 250 homes in Los Alamos. Parts of the drive are still scarred with charcoaled remains, but most of the vegetation has returned, and many homes have been rebuilt in the residential areas.

LOS ALAMOS

35 mi from Santa Fe via U.S. 285/84 north to NM 502 west.

Look at old books on New Mexico and you rarely find a mention of Los Alamos, now a busy town of 19,000 that has the highest per capita income in the state. Like so many other Southwestern communities, Los Alamos was created expressly as a company town; only here the workers weren't mining iron, manning freight trains, or hauling lumber—they were busy toiling at America's foremost nuclear research facility, Los Alamos National Laboratory (LANL). The facility still employs some 8,000 full-time workers, most living in town but many others in the Española Valley and even Santa Fe. The lab has experienced some tough times in recent years, from the infamous Wen Ho Lee espionage case in the late '90s to a slew of alleged security breaches in 2003 and 2004. The controversies have shed some doubt on the future of LANL.

A few miles from ancient cave dwellings, scientists led by J. Robert Oppenheimer built Fat Man and Little Boy, the atom bombs that in August 1945 decimated Hiroshima and Nagasaki, respectively. LANL was created in 1943 under the auspices of the intensely covert Manhattan Project, whose express purpose it was to expedite an Allied victory during World War II. Indeed, Japan surrendered—but a full-blown Cold War between Russia and the United States ensued for another four and a half decades.

Despite the negative publicity of recent years, LANL works hard today to promote its broader platforms, including "enhancing global nuclear security" but also finding new ways to detect radiation, fighting pollution and environmental risks associated with nuclear energy, and furthering studies of the solar system, biology, and computer sciences. Similarly, the town of Los Alamos strives to be more well-rounded, better understood, and tourist friendly.

The **Bradbury Science Museum** is Los Alamos National Laboratory's public showcase, and its exhibits offer a balanced and provocative examination of such topics as atomic weapons and nuclear power. You can experiment with lasers; witness research in solar, geothermal, fission, and fusion energy; learn about DNA fingerprinting; and view exhibits about World War II's Project Y (the Manhattan Project, whose participants developed the atomic bomb). ⊠ *Los Alamos National Laboratory, 15th St. and Central Ave.* ☎ *505/667–4444* ⊕ *www.lanl. gov/museum* ☑ *Free* ۞ *Tues.–Fri. 9–5, Sat.–Mon. 1–5.*

New Mexican architect John Gaw Meem designed **Fuller Lodge,** a short drive up Central Avenue from the Bradbury Science Museum. The massive log building was erected in 1928 as a dining and recreation hall for a small private boys' school. In 1942 the federal government purchased the school and made it the base of operations for the Manhattan Project. Part of the lodge contains an art center that shows the works of northern New Mexican artists; there's a picturesque rose garden on the grounds. This is a bustling center with drop-in art classes, nine art shows per year, and a gallery gift shop featuring 70 local artisans.

The Web site is updated regularly and is a good reference for current activities. ⊠*2132 Central Ave.* ☎*505/662–9331* ⊕*www.artfulnm.org* ⊠*Free* ☺*Mon.–Sat. 10–4.*

NEED A BREAK?

Join the ranks of locals, Los Alamos National Laboratory employees, and tourists who line up each morning at **Chili Works** (⊠*1743 Trinity Dr.* ☎*505/662–7591*) to sample one of the state's best breakfast burritos. This inexpensive, simple takeout spot is also worth a stop to grab breakfast or lunch before heading off for a hike at Bandelier. The burritos are stellar and the chili is *hot*.

The **Los Alamos Historical Museum,** in a log building beside Fuller Lodge, displays exhibits on the once-volatile geological history of the volcanic Jémez Mountains, the 700-year history of human life in this area, and more on—you guessed it—the Manhattan Project. It's rather jarring to observe ancient Puebloan potsherds and arrowheads in one display and photos of an obliterated Nagasaki in the next. ⊠*1921 Juniper St.* ☎*505/662–4493* ⊕*www.losalamoshistory.org* ⊠*Free* ☺*Mon.–Sat. 9:30–4:30, Sun. 1–4.*

WHERE TO EAT & STAY

$

ECLECTIC

★

✕ **Blue Window Bistro.** Despite its relative wealth, Los Alamos has never cultivated much of a dining scene, which makes this cheerful and elegant restaurant all the more appreciated by foodies. The kitchen turns out a mix of New Mexican, American, and Continental dishes, from a first-rate Cobb salad to steak topped with Jack cheese and green chili to double-cut pork chops with mashed potatoes, applewood-smoked bacon, and red-onion marmalade. In addition to the softly lighted dining room with terra-cotta walls, there are several tables on a patio overlooking a lush garden. ⊠*813 Central Ave.* ☎*505/662–6305* ⊟*AE, D, DC, MC, V* ☺*Closed Sun.*

$

Best Western Hilltop House Hotel. Minutes from the Los Alamos National Laboratory, this well-kept three-story hotel hosts both vacationers and scientists. It's standard chain-hotel decor here: rooms are done with contemporary, functional furniture and have microwaves, refrigerators, and coffeemakers; deluxe ones have kitchenettes. The La Vista Restaurant on the premises serves tasty, if predictable, American fare. The very good Blue Window Bistro is next door. **Pros:** Great proximity to the restaurants and shops in town; friendly, easygoing staff. **Cons:** This isn't a property with much character; but it's a solid bet for business travelers and those wanting to use Los Alamos as a jumping-off point for excursions beyond Santa Fe. ⊠*400 Trinity Dr.* ☎*505/662–2441 or 800/462–0936* ☐*505/662–5913* ⊕*www.bwhill top.com* ⊃*73 rooms, 19 suites* &*In-room: kitchen (some), refrigerator, Wi-Fi. In-hotel: restaurant, room service, bar, pool, gym, laundry facilities, some pets allowed* ⊟*AE, D, DC, MC, V* ⓞ*CP.*

SPORTS & THE OUTDOORS

HIKING

★

Tsankawi (pronounced sank-ah-*wee*) is an ancestral Puebloan ruin that is actually a part of Bandelier National Monument, although it lies 12 mi from the main park area. The pueblo people's daily routines created trails carved into the soft volcanic rock of the Pajarito Plateau in the 1400s as they made their way from their mesa-top homes to the fields and springs in the canyon below. In the 1½-mi loop you can see petroglyphs and south-facing cave dwellings. There is a large, unexcavated, pueblo ruin on top of the mesa. Wear good shoes for the rocky path and a climb on a 12-foot ladder that shoots between a crevasse in the rock and the highest point of the mesa. This is an ideal walk if you don't have time to explore Bandelier National Monument in depth. It's on the road toward White Rock, about a 35-minute drive from Santa Fe. ⊠ *From NM 502, take turnoff for White Rock, NM 4; continue west for about ¼ mi to sign for Tsankawi on left; trail is clearly marked* ☎ *505/672–3861.*

SKIING   **Pajarito Mountain Ski Area**, a small, low-key area near Los Alamos, has some excellent long runs and a good selection of wide-open, intermediate mogul runs, plus a terrain park; the base elevation is 9,200 feet, and there's a vertical drop of 1,410 feet. There's no artificial snowmaking, so the slopes are barely open during dry winters and the season runs according to conditions (usually about mid-December through April). But there's never a wait for the five lifts. In summer there's mountain biking on Pajarito's trails and occasional concerts and events at the base. ⊠ *397 Camp May Rd., off NM 501, just west of downtown Los Alamos* ☎ *505/662–5725* ⊕ *www.skipajarito.com*

BANDELIER NATIONAL MONUMENT

🕙   *10 mi south of Los Alamos via NM 501 south to NM 4 east; 40 mi north*
Fodor's Choice *of Santa Fe via U.S. 285/84 north to NM 502 west to NM 4 west.*
★

Seven centuries before the Declaration of Independence was signed, compact city-states existed in the Southwest. Remnants of one of the most impressive of them can be seen at **Frijoles Canyon** in Bandelier National Monument. At the canyon's base, near a gurgling stream, are the remains of cave dwellings, ancient ceremonial kivas, and other stone structures that stretch out for more than a mile beneath the sheer walls of the canyon's tree-fringed rim. For hundreds of years the ancestral Puebloan people, relatives of today's Rio Grande Pueblo Indians, thrived on wild game, corn, and beans. Suddenly, for reasons still undetermined, the settlements were abandoned.

Wander through the site on a paved, self-guided trail. Steep wooden ladders and narrow doorways lead you to the cave dwellings and cell-like rooms. There is one kiva in the cliff wall that is large, and tall enough to stand in.

Bandelier National Monument, named after author and ethnologist Adolph Bandelier (his novel *The Delight Makers* is set in Frijoles Canyon), contains 23,000 acres of backcountry wilderness, waterfalls, and wildlife. Sixty miles of trails traverse the park. A small museum in the visitor center focuses on the area's prehistoric and contemporary Native American cultures, with displays of artifacts from 1200 to modern times as well as displays on the forest fires that have devastated parts of the park in recent years. There is a small café in the wonderful, 1930s CCC-built stone visitors complex. It is worth getting up early to get here when there are still shadows on the cliff walls because the petroglyphs are fantastic and all but disappear in the bright light of the afternoon. If you are staying in the area, ask about the night walks at the visitor center, they're stellar! Pets are not allowed on any trails. ☎505/672–0343 ⊕ *www.nps.gov/band/index.htm* ✉*$12 per vehicle, good for 7 days* ⊙ *Late May–early Sept., daily 8–6; early Sept.–Oct. and Apr.–late May, daily 8–5:30; Nov.–Mar., daily 8–4:30.*

JÉMEZ SPRINGS
20 mi west of Valles Caldera on NM 4.

The funky mountain village of Jémez (say *hem*-ez) Springs draws outdoorsy types for hiking, cross-country skiing, and camping in the nearby U.S. Forest Service areas. The town's biggest tourist draws are Jémez State Monument and Soda Dam, but many people come here for relaxation at the town's bathhouse.

The geological wonder known as **Soda Dam** was created over thousands of years by travertine deposits—minerals that precipitate out of geothermal springs. With its strange mushroom-shaped exterior and caves split by a roaring waterfall, it's no wonder the spot was considered sacred by Native Americans. In summer it's popular for swimming. ⊠*NM 4, 1 mi north of Jémez State Monument.*

Jémez State Monument contains impressive Spanish and Native American ruins set throughout a 7-acre site and toured via an easy ⅓-mi loop trail. About 700 years ago ancestors of the people of Jémez Pueblo built several villages in and around the narrow mountain valley. One of the villages was *Guisewa*, or "Place of the Boiling Waters." The Spanish colonists built a mission church beside it, San José de los Jémez, which was abandoned by around 1640. ⊠*NM 4* ☎*505/829–3530* ⊕*www.nmstatemonuments.org* ✉*$3* ⊙ *Wed.–Mon. 8:30–5.*

★ Now owned and operated by the village of Jémez Springs, the original structure at the **Jémez Spring Bath House** was erected in the 1870s near a mineral hot spring. Many other buildings were added over the years, and the complex was completely renovated into an intimate Victorian-style hideaway in the mid-1990s. It's a funky, low-key spot that's far less formal and fancy than the several spa resorts near Santa Fe. You can soak in a mineral bath for $10 (30 minutes) or $15 (60 minutes). Massages cost between $37 (30 minutes) and $95 (90 minutes). An acupuncturist is available with advance notice. Beauty treatments include facials, manicures, and pedicures. The Jémez Package ($95) includes a half-hour bath, an herbal blanket wrap, and a one-hour massage. You can stroll down a short path behind the house to see where the steaming hot springs feed into the Jémez River. The tubs are not communal, but individual, and there are no outdoor tubs. Children under 14 are not allowed. ⊠*NM 4 062 Jémez Springs Plaza, Jémez Springs* ☎*505/829–3303 or 866/204–8303* ⊕*www.jemezspringsbathhouse.com* ⊙*June–early Oct., daily 10–8; early Nov.–May, daily 10–6.*

Giggling Springs (⊠ *040 Abousleman Loop* ☎ *505/829–9175* ⊕ *www. gigglingsprings.com* ⊙ *Closed Mon. and Tues.*) offers a large, outdoor, natural-mineral hot spring. Right across the street from the Laughing Lizard, this is a good option for the soakers who want hot water but don't want the individualized treatments at the Bath House. Very accommodating staff; no children under 14. Pool capacity is limited to 8 at a time; reservations are recommended. $15 per hour, $25 for two hours, $35 for the day.

WHERE TO STAY

$ ⊡ **Cañon del Rio.** On 6 acres along the Jémez River beneath towering mesas, this light-filled, contemporary adobe inn (formerly called the Riverdancer) has rooms with cove ceilings, tile floors, and Native American arts and crafts. All have French doors and open onto a courtyard with a natural-spring fountain. Wellness packages include massage, acupuncture, and aromatherapy. Breakfasts are a big deal here and they're delicious. **Pros:** Property has an abundance of water—a real treat in New Mexico. **Cons:** Though comfortable, room decor looks like a Southwestern chain hotel. ⊠ *16445 NM 4* ☎ *505/829–4377* ⊕ *www.canondelrio.com* ⮑ *6 rooms, 1 suite* ♿ *In-room: kitchen (some), no TV. In-hotel: Wi-Fi* ⊟ *AE, D, MC, V* ⊠ *CP.*

¢ ⊡ **Laughing Lizard Inn and Cafe.** Consisting of a simple four-room motel-
★ style inn and a cute adobe-and-stone café with a corrugated-metal roof, the Laughing Lizard makes for a sweet and cheerful diversion—it's right in the center of the village. Rooms are cozy and simple with white linens, dressers, books, and porches that look out over the rugged mesa beyond the river valley. Healthful, eclectic fare—apple-walnut sandwiches, sweet potato–and–spinach salads, raspberry-chipotle-chicken burritos, veggie pizzas, herbal teas, offbeat beers, homemade desserts—is served in the homey café (limited hours off-season; call first), which has a saltillo-tile screened porch and an open-air wooden deck. **Pros:** Great staff, beautiful location. **Cons:** Rooms are on the worn side, and fairly small; no a/c. ⊠ *NM 4* ☎ *505/829–3108* ⊕ *www.thelaughing lizard.com* ⮑ *4 rooms* ♿ *In-room: no a/c. In-hotel: restaurant, some pets allowed* ⊟ *D, MC, V.*

JÉMEZ PUEBLO

12 mi south of Jémez Springs via NM 4; 85 mi west of Santa Fe via U.S. 285/84 and NM 4; 50 mi north of Albuquerque via I–25, U.S. 550, and NM 4.

As you continue southwest along NM 4, the terrain changes from a wooded river valley with high mesas on either side to an open red-rock valley, the home of the Jémez Pueblo, which is set along the Jémez River. After the pueblo at Pecos (⇨ *Chapter 6*) was abandoned in 1838, Jémez was the state's only pueblo with residents who spoke Towa (different from Tiwa and Tewa). The Jémez Reservation encompasses 89,000 acres, with two lakes, Holy Ghost Springs and Dragonfly Lake (off NM 4), open for fishing by permit only, April to October on weekends and holidays. The only part of the pueblo open to the public is the **Walatowa Visitor Center,** a fancy Pueblo Revival building that contains a small museum, an extensive pottery and crafts shop, and rotating art and photography exhibits; there's a short nature walk outside. The pueblo is sometimes open to the public for special events, demonstrations, and ceremonial dances—call for details. The pueblo is noted for its polychrome pottery. The Walatowa gas and convenience store, on NM 4 next to the visitor center, is one of the few such establishments between Los Alamos and Bernalillo. Photographing, sketching, and video recording are prohibited. ☒*7413 NM 4* ☎*505/834–7235* ⊕*www.jemezpueblo.org* ☒*Free* ☉*Daily 8–5.*

GEORGIA O'KEEFFE COUNTRY

It's a 20-minute drive north of Santa Fe to reach the Española Valley, where you head west to the striking mesas, cliffs, and valleys that so inspired the artist Georgia O'Keeffe—she lived in this area for the final 50 years of her life. You first come to the small, workaday city of Española, a major crossroads from which roads lead to Taos, Chama, and Abiquiu. The other notable community in this area is tiny Ojo Caliente, famous for its hot-springs spa retreat.

ESPAÑOLA
20 mi north of Santa Fe via U.S. 285/84.

This small but growing city midway along the Low Road from Santa Fe to Taos is a business hub for the many villages and pueblos scattered throughout the region north of Santa Fe. The area at the confluence of the Rio Grande and Rio Chama was declared the capital for Spain by Don Juan de Oñate in 1598, but wasn't more than a collection of small settlements until the town was founded in 1880s as a stop on the Denver & Rio Grande Railroad. Lacking the colonial charm of either Santa Fe or Taos, Española is known for being pretty rough-and-tumble. There are many cheap burger joints, New Mexican restaurants, and a few chain motels, but few reasons to stick around for more than a quick meal. The city has become known as the "lowrider capital of the world" because of the mostly classic cars that have been retrofitted with lowered chassis and hydraulics that allow the cars to bump and grind as they cruise the streets on perpetual parade. The cars are often painted spectacularly, with religious murals, homages to dead relatives, and other spectacular scenes adorning them.

You may see a number of people wearing white (and sometimes orange or blue) turbans; they are members of the large American Sikh community that settled on the south end of town in the late 60s. Initially viewed with suspicion by the provincial Hispanics of the area, the Sikhs have become integral members of the community, teaching Kundalini yoga, establishing businesses and medical practices, and influencing many local restaurants to add vegetarian versions of New Mexican dishes to their menus.

All of the main arteries converge in the heart of town amidst a series of drab shopping centers, so watch the signs on the town's south side. Traffic moves slowly, especially on weekend nights when cruisers bring car culture alive.

Lovin' Oven serves delicious homemade donuts, apple fritters and turnovers, and hot coffee amidst all the latest news and gossip shared amongst the hordes of locals who pour through the doors at this sweet little shop on Española's south end. Get there early, once the goodies are gone they're gone. ⊠ *107 N. Riverside Dr.* ☎ *505/753–5461.*

The region is known for its longstanding weaving traditions, and one place you can learn about this heritage is the **Española Valley Fiber Arts Center** (⊠ *325 Paseo de Oñate* ☎ *505/747–3577* ⊕ *www.evfac.org* ▣ *Free* ☉ *Mon. 9–8, Tues.–Sat. 9–5, Sun. noon–5*), a nonprofit facility set inside an adobe building in the city's historic section. Here you can watch local weavers working with traditional materials and looms and admire (and purchase) their works in a small gallery. There are also classes offered on spinning, weaving, and knitting, which are open to the public and range from one day to several weeks. Emphasis here is placed on the styles of weaving that have been practiced here in the northern Rio Grande Valley since the Spaniards brought sheep and treadle looms here in the late 16th century. The center also celebrates the ancient traditions of New Mexico's Navajo and Pueblo weavers.

WHERE TO EAT & STAY

$$
MEXICAN
★
✕ **El Paragua Restaurant.** With a dark, intimate atmosphere of wood and stone, this historic place started out as a lemonade-cum-taco stand in the late 1950s but is now known for some of the state's most authentic New Mexican and regional Mexican cuisine. Steaks and fish are grilled over a mesquite-wood fire; other specialties include chorizo enchiladas, panfried breaded trout amandine, and menudo. This restaurant is still a family affair; service is gracious and the food is worth the drive. If you don't have time to sit down for a meal, stop at El Parasol taco stand in the parking lot next door for excellent, cheap Mexican–New Mexican. Vegetarians, ask for the Khalsa special, a superdelicious veggie quesadilla created for the local Sikhs. ⊠ *603 Santa Cruz Rd., NM 76 just east of NM 68* ☎ *505/753–3211 or 800/929–8226* ⊕ *www.elparagua. com* ▤ *AE, DC, MC, V.*

$$$$
Fodor's Choice
★
▦ **Rancho de San Juan.** This secluded 225-acre Relais & Châteaux compound hugs Black Mesa's base. Many of the inn's rooms are self-contained suites, some set around a courtyard and others amid the wilderness. All rooms have Southwestern furnishings, Frette robes, Aveda bath products, and CD stereos; nearly all have kiva fireplaces. The top units have such cushy touches as two bedrooms, 12-foot ceilings, Mexican marble showers, kitchens, Jacuzzis, and private patios. The à la carte menu in the restaurant (dinner Tuesday through Saturday, by reservation only) featuring spectacular contemporary cuisine, changes weekly. Past fare has included Texas quail stuffed with corn bread, green chilies, and linguica sausage, and Alaskan halibut with tomatillo-lime salsa, caramelized butternut squash, and creamed spinach. Hike to a beautiful hand-carved sandstone shrine on a bluff above the property. In-suite spa and massage services are available. ⊠ *U.S. 285, 3½ mi north of U.S. 84* ✆ *Box 4140, 87533* ☎ *505/753–6818* ⊕ *www. ranchodesanjuan.com* ✑ *4 suites, 9 casitas* ☟ *In-room: no a/c (some),*

kitchen (some), no TV. In-hotel: restaurant, no kids under 8, no-smoking rooms ▭*AE, D, DC, MC, V.*

ABIQUIU

24 mi northwest of Española via U.S. 84.

This tiny, very traditional Hispanic village was originally home to freed *genizaros,* indigenous and mixed-blood slaves who served as house servants, shepherds, and other key roles in Spanish, Mexican, and American households well into the 1880s. Genizaros now make up a significant population of the state. Many descendants of original families still live in the area, although since the late 1980s Abiquiu and its surrounding countryside have become a nesting ground for those fleeing big-city life, among them actresses Marsha Mason and Shirley MacLaine. Abiquiu—along with parts of the nearby Española Valley—is also a hotbed of organic farming, with many of the operations here selling their goods at the Santa Fe Farmers Market and to restaurants throughout the Rio Grande Valley. Newcomers or visitors may find themselves shut out by locals; it's best to observe one very important local custom: no photography is allowed in and around the village.

A number of artists live in Abiquiu, and several studios showing traditional Hispanic art as well as contemporary works and pottery, are open regularly to the public; many others open each year over Columbus Day weekend for the **Annual Abiquiu Studio Tour** (☎*505/685–4454* ⊕*www.abiquiustudiotour.org).*

You can visit **Georgia O'Keeffe's home** through advance reservation (at least four months is recommended if you come during high season) with the **Georgia O'Keeffe Museum** (☎*505/685–4539* ⊕*www.okeeffe museum.org*), which conducts one-hour tours Tuesday, Thursday, and Friday, mid-March–November, with additional tours on Wednesday in July and August, for $30. In 1945 Georgia O'Keeffe bought a large, dilapidated late-18th-century Spanish colonial adobe compound just off the Plaza. Upon the 1946 death of her husband, photographer Alfred Stieglitz, she left New York City and began dividing her time permanently between this home, which figured prominently in many of her works, and the one in nearby Ghost Ranch. She wrote about the house, "When I first saw the Abiquiú house it was a ruin...As I climbed and walked about in the ruin I found a patio with a very pretty well house and a bucket to draw up water. It was a good-sized patio with a long wall with a door on one side. That wall with a door in it was something I had to have. It took me 10 years to get it—three more years to fix the house up so I could live in it—and after that the wall with the door was painted many times." The patio is featured in *Black Patio Door* (1955) and *Patio with Cloud* (1956). O'Keeffe died in 1986 at the age of 98 and left provisions in her will to ensure that the property's houses would never be public monuments.

SHOPPING

★ **Bode's** (✉*U.S. 84, look for Phillips 66 gas station sign* ☎*505/685– 4422* ⊕*www.bodes.com*), pronounced bow-dees, across from the Abiquiu post office, is much more than a gas station. It's a popular stop for newspapers, quirky gifts, locally made products, cold drinks, supplies, fishing gear (including licenses), amazing breakfast burritos, hearty green-chili stew, sandwiches, and other short-order fare. The friendly, busy station serves as general store and exchange post for news and gossip.

WHERE TO STAY

$$ ☒ **Abiquiu Inn and Cafe Abiquiu.** Deep in the Chama Valley, the inn has a secluded, exotic feel—almost like an oasis—with brightly decorated rooms, including several four-person casitas, with woodstoves or fireplaces and tiled baths; some units have verandas with hammocks and open views of O'Keeffe Country. The café ($$) serves commendable New Mexican, Italian, and American fare, from blue-corn tacos stuffed with grilled trout to lamb-and-poblano stew; it's also known for its seasonal fresh-fruit cobblers. The inn is the departure point for O'Keeffe-home tours, where the O'Keeffe Museum has a small office. It has an exceptional art gallery, crafts shop, and gardens. Two basic but very comfortable rooms are available for $80. The RV park on the property offers full hookups and a dump station for $18 per night. ☒ *U.S. 84* ☏ *Box 120, 87510* ☎ *505/685–4378 or 888/735–2902* ☏ *505/685–4931* ⊕ *www.abiquiuinn.com* ⇌ *12 rooms, 2 suites, 5 casitas* ₺ *In-room: kitchen (some). In-hotel: restaurant, Wi-Fi* ☐ *AE, D, DC, MC, V.*

GHOST RANCH

10 mi northwest of Abiquiu on U.S. 84.

For art historians, the name Ghost Ranch brings to mind Georgia O'Keeffe, who lived on a small parcel of this 20,000-acre dude and cattle ranch. The ranch's owner in the 1930s—conservationist and publisher of *Nature Magazine,* Arthur Pack—first invited O'Keeffe here to visit in 1934; Pack soon sold the artist the 7-acre plot on which she lived summer through fall for most of the rest of her life.

In 1955 Pack donated the rest of the ranch to the Presbyterian Church, which continues to use Pack's original structures and about 55 acres of land as a conference center.

☉
Fodor'sChoice
★
The **Ghost Ranch Education and Retreat Center** (☒ *U.S. 84* ☎ *505/685–4333 or* ⊕ *www.ghostranch.org* ☒ *Suggested donation $3 minimum*), open to the public year-round, is busiest in summer, when the majority of workshops take place. Subjects range from poetry and literary arts to photography, horseback riding, and every conceivable traditional craft of northern New Mexico. These courses are open to the public, and guests camp or stay in semirustic cottages or casitas. If you're here for a day trip, after registering at the main office, you may come in and hike high among the wind-hewn rocks so beloved by O'Keeffe. The **Florence Hawley Ellis Museum of Anthropology** contains Native American tools, pottery, and other artifacts excavated from the Ghost Ranch Gallina digs. Pioneer anthropologist Florence Hawley Ellis conducted excavations at Chaco Canyon and at other sites in New Mexico. Adjacent to the Ellis Museum, the **Ruth Hall Museum of Paleontology** exhibits the New Mexico state fossil, the coelophysis, also known as "the lit-

tlest dinosaur," originally excavated near Ghost Ranch. For the art lover, or the lover of the New Mexican landscape, Ghost Ranch offers guided O'Keeffe & Ghost Ranch Landscape Tours of the specific sites on the ranch that O'Keeffe painted during the five decades that she summered here. Her original house is not part of the tour and is closed to the public. These one-hour tours are available mid-March through mid-October, on Tuesday, Wednesday, Friday, and Saturday at 1:30 and 3; the cost is $25, and you must call first to make a reservation. The landscape tours are timed to coincide with the tours given at her house in Abiquiu, although they have nothing to do with the O'Keeffe studio tours offered there. Here's a little-known tidbit: limited camping is available on Ghost Ranch for both RVs and tents ($16–$26) and full hookups are available for RVs.

The **Ghost Ranch Piedra Lumbre Education and Visitor Center,** which is part of the Ghost Ranch organization, has a gallery with rotating art presentations, exhibits on New Mexico's natural history, a gift shop, and two museums. ⊠ *U.S. 84, just north of main Ghost Ranch entrance* ☎ *505/685–4312* ⊕ *www.ghostranch.org* ☜ *Donation* ⊙ *Visitor center: Mar.–Oct., daily 9–5. Hawley Ellis and Hall museums: late May–early Sept., Tues.–Sat. 9–5, Sun. and Mon. 1–5; early Sept.–late May, Tues.–Sat. 9–5.*

OFF THE BEATEN PATH

Monastery of Christ in the Desert. Designed by renowned Japanese-American architect and wood carver George Nakashima, this remote rock-and-adobe church—with one of the state's most spectacular natural settings—can be visited for daily prayer or silent overnight retreats (if requested in advance by mail or e-mail); there are basic accommodations for up to 16 guests (10 single and 3 double rooms), and there's a two-night minimum, with most visitors staying for several days. A suggested per-night donation of $50 to $125 is requested, depending on the room, and none have electricity. Day visitors can come anytime and stroll the grounds, visit the gift shop, and participate in different prayer services throughout the day, but are asked to respect the silence practiced at the monastery. The road is rutted in places and becomes impassable during rainy weather—you can definitely get stuck here for a day, or even a few days, during particularly wet periods, such as summer monsoon season. Check weather forecasts carefully if you're only intending to visit for the day. ⊠ *Guestmaster, Christ in the Desert; pass Ghost Ranch visitor center and turn left on Forest Service Rd. 151; follow dirt road 13 mi to monastery* ✆ *Box 270, Abiquiu 87510* ☎ *801/545–8567 messages only* ⊕ *www.christdesert.org.*

The best and most interesting way to reach Ojo Caliente from Ghost Ranch is to return down U.S. 84 just past Abiquiu and then make a left turn (north) onto NM 554 toward El Rito, 12 mi away. This small, rural community known for its crafts making (especially weaving) has a ★ funky general store and **El Farolito** (⊠ *1212 Main St.* ☎ *505/581–9509* ⊟ *No credit cards* ⊙ *Closed Mon.*), a cubbyhole of a restaurant on the town's tree-shaded Main Street that serves State Fair blue-ribbon green chili and other New Mexican specialties, including a terrific *posole.* This place celebrated its 25th year in 2008 and has something of a cult following, so don't be surprised if you have to wait for dinner. The ride here offers a stunning view back east toward the Sangre de Cristos.

OJO CALIENTE

28 mi northeast of Abiquiu by way of El Rito via NM 554 to NM 111 to U.S. 285, 50 mi north of Santa Fe on U.S. 285.

Ojo Caliente is the only place in North America where five different types of hot springs—iron, lithium, arsenic, salt, and soda—are found side by side. The town was named by Spanish explorer Cabeza de Vaca, who visited in 1535 and believed he had stumbled upon the Fountain of Youth. Modern-day visitors draw a similar conclusion about the restorative powers of the springs. The spa itself, built in the 1920s, is a no-frills establishment that is in the process of extensive renovations; it comprises a hotel and cottages, a restaurant, a gift shop, massage rooms, men's and women's bathhouses, a chlorine-free swimming pool, and indoor and outdoor mineral-water tubs. The hotel, one of the original bathhouses, and the springs are all on the National Register of Historic Places, as is the adjacent and recently restored Round Barn (the only adobe one in the nation), from which visitors can take horseback tours and guided hikes to ancient Pueblo dwellings and petroglyph-etched rocks. Spa services include wraps, massage, facials, and acupuncture. The setting at the foot of sandstone cliffs topped by the ruins of ancient Indian pueblos is nothing short of inspiring.

WHERE TO STAY

$ ⬚ **Ojo Caliente Mineral Springs Spa and Resort.** Accommodations here run the gamut from spartan in the unfussy 1916 hotel (no TVs, simple furnishings) to rather upscale in the elegant suites, which were added in summer 2006. Rooms in the hotel have bathrooms but no showers or tubs—bathing takes place in the mineral springs (it's an arrangement that pleases most longtime devotees but doesn't sit well with others). The cottages are quite comfy, with refrigerators and TVs; some have kitchenettes, with tile showers in the bathrooms. The 12 spacious suites have such luxury touches as kiva fireplaces and patios; half have private, double soaking tubs outside, which are filled with Ojo mineral waters. All lodgers have complimentary access to the mineral pools and *milagro* (miracle) wraps, and the bathhouse has showers. Horseback tours can be prearranged. The Artesian Restaurant ($$) serves worldbeat fare in a charming dining room. Four-day and overnight packages are available, from $700 per person. There's also camping on-site, beside the cottonwood-shaded Rio Ojo Caliente—double-occupancy camping rates are $20 for tents, $40 for RVs. **Pros:** This place can feel like a real getaway for fairly reasonable rates. **Cons:** Service and treatments can be disappointing; ask about the construction-renovation—it can be loud and unrelaxing. ⊠ *50 Los Baños Dr., off U.S. 285, 30 mi north of Española* ⌂*Box 68, 87549* ☎*505/583–2233 or 800/222–9162* ᵬ*505/583–2464* ⊕*www.ojocalientesprings.com* ⬞*19 rooms, 19 cottages, 12 suites, 3 3-bedroom houses* ⌂*In-room: no a/c, no phone, kitchen (some), refrigerator (some), no TV (some). In-hotel: restaurant, spa* ▭*AE, D, DC, MC, V.*

LOW ROAD TO TAOS

Widely considered to be the less scenic route to Taos, the Low Road actually offers plenty of dazzling scenery once you get through traffic-clogged Española and into the Rio Grande Gorge. As you emerge from the gorge roughly 25 minutes later, NM 68 cuts up over a plateau that affords stupendous views of Taos and the surrounding mountains. Note that whether you take the Low Road or the High Road (⇨ *below*), you first follow U.S. 285/84 north from Santa Fe for about 20 mi—this somewhat dull stretch of road was vastly improved in 2004 with a major road-widening project. Whereas you exit the highway just north of Pojoaque in order to travel the High Road, you remain on U.S. 285/84 all the way to Española to follow the Low Road; once there, you pick up NM 68 north. Just before you enter into the Rio Grande Gorge, where you parallel the river for several scenic miles, you pass through tiny Velarde, which has a number of fruit and vegetable stands worth checking out. Without stops, it takes 80 to 90 minutes to make it from Santa Fe to Taos via the Low Road, whereas the High Road takes 2 to 2½ hours.

DIXON
45 mi north of Santa Fe via U.S. 285/84 and NM 68, 20 mi south of Taos via NM 68.

The small village of Dixon and its surrounding country lanes are home to a surprising number of artists. Artistic sensitivity, as well as generations of dedicated farmers, account for the community's well-tended fields, pretty gardens, and fruit trees—a source of produce for restaurants and farmers' markets such as the one in Santa Fe. It's simple to find your way around; there's only one main road.

The Dixon Arts Association has some four dozen members, many represented in a cooperative gallery attached to **Métier Weaving & Gallery** (⊠*NM 75* ☎*505/579–4111*), which also has also has a showroom that sells the textiles and weavings of artists and owners Irene Smith and Lezlie King. Dixon also hosts a popular studio tour (⊕*www. dixonarts.org*) the first full weekend in November, when area artists open up their home studios to the public.

WHERE TO EAT & STAY

$ ✕**Embudo Station.** Set inside an 1880s railroad station, historic Embudo
AMERICAN Station comprises a casual restaurant with a riverside patio; a smokehouse that cures delicious ham, turkey, pheasant, and rainbow trout; a winery open for tastings; and a cabin available for nightly or weekly rentals ($). The restaurant serves traditional New Mexican fare and barbecue; many dishes incorporate the house-smoked meats. Limited sandwich fare, beers, and wine are available on weekends during the off-season, but it's always best to call first. ⊠*NM 68, Embudo* ☎*505/852–4707 or 800/852–4707* ⊕*www.embudostation.com* ⊟*AE, MC, V* ⊘*Closed Nov.–Mar. and Mon.*

$ ⊞**Rock Pool Gardens.** This private guesthouse has two warmly furnished two-bedroom suites, one with a kitchenette and a bathroom connecting the bedrooms, the other with a full kitchen. Each has its own access

5

and patio. The rustic walls, Mexican tile work, and country furnishings lend a cozy air to these otherwise contemporary suites, and lush gardens surround the building. There's a Jacuzzi under the trees and an indoor heated pool set in natural rock. Both suites can be rented for a group for $160 per night. **Pros:** Rock Pool is one of the few accommodations between Española and Taos, and it's also a good value. **Cons:** There aren't restaurants or sights within walking distance. ⊠*NM 75, Dixon* ☎*505/579–4602* ⬅*2 suites* ⚫*In-room: kitchen, refrigerator, Wi-Fi. In-hotel: pool, some pets allowed* ⊟*No credit cards* ⦿*CP.*

THE HIGH ROAD TO TAOS

Fodor's Choice
★
The main highway to Taos (NM 68) is a good, even scenic, route if you've got limited time, but by far the most spectacular route is what is known as the High Road. Towering peaks, lush hillsides, orchards, and meadows surround tiny, ancient Hispanic villages that are as picturesque as they are historically fascinating. The High Road follows U.S. 285/84 north to NM 503 (a right turn just past Pojoaque), to County Road 98 (a left toward Chimayó), to NM 76 northeast to NM 75 east, to NM 518 north. The drive takes you through the badlands of stark, weathered rock—where numerous westerns have been filmed—quickly into rolling foothills, lush canyons, and finally into pine forests. Although most of these insular, traditional Hispanic communities offer little in the way of shopping and dining, the region has become a haven for artists.

From Chimayó to Peñasco, you can find mostly low-key but often high-quality art galleries, many of them run out of the owners' homes. During the final two weekends in September each year, more than 100 artists show their work in the **High Road Art Tour** (☎*866/343–5381* ⊕*www.highroadnewmexico.com*); call or visit the Web site for a studio map.

Depending on when you make this drive, you're in for some of the state's most radiant scenery. In mid-April the orchards are in blossom; summer turns the valleys into lush green oases; and in fall the smell of piñon adds to the sensual overload of golden leaves and red-chile ristras hanging from the houses. In winter the fields are covered with quilts of snow, and the lines of homes, fences, and trees stand out like bold pen-and-ink drawings against the sky. But the roads can be icy and treacherous—if in doubt, stick with the Low Road to Taos. If you decide to take the High Road just one way between Santa Fe and Taos, you might want to save it for the return journey—the scenery is even more stunning when traveling north to south.

CHIMAYÓ
28 mi north of Santa Fe, 10 mi east of Española on NM 76.

From U.S. 285/84 north of Pojoaque, scenic NM 503 winds past horse paddocks and orchards in the narrow Nambé Valley, then ascends into the red-sandstone canyons with a view of Truchas Peaks to the northeast before dropping into the bucolic village of Chimayó. Nestled into hillsides where gnarled piñons seem to grow from bare bedrock, Chimayó is famed for its weaving, its red chiles, and its two chapels.

Fodor'sChoice **El Santuario de Chimayó,** a small, frontier, adobe church, has a fantasti-
★ cally carved and painted *reredos* (wood altar) and is built on the site where, believers say, a mysterious light came from the ground on Good Friday in 1810 and where a large wooden crucifix was found beneath the earth. The chapel sits above a sacred *pozito* (a small hole), the dirt from which is believed to have miraculous healing properties. Dozens of abandoned crutches and braces placed in the anteroom—along with many notes, letters, and photos—testify to this. The Santuario draws a steady stream of worshippers year-round—Chimayó is considered the Lourdes of the Southwest. During Holy Week as many as 50,000 pilgrims come here. The shrine is a National Historic Landmark, and its altar and artwork underwent an ambitious and much-needed restoration in 2004. It's surrounded by small adobe shops selling every kind of religious curio imaginable, and some very fine traditional Hispanic work from local artists. ⊠*Signed lane off CR 98* ☎*505/351–4889* ⊕*www. archdiocesesantafe.org/AboutASF/Chimayo.html* ⊠*Free* ☉*June–Sept., daily 9–5; Oct.–May, daily 9–4.*

A smaller chapel 200 yards from El Santuario was built in 1857 and dedicated to **Santo Niño de Atocha.** As at the more famous Santuario, the dirt at Santo Niño de Atocha's chapel is said to have healing properties in the place where the *Santo Niño* was first placed. The little boy saint was brought here from Mexico by Severiano Medina, who claimed Santo Niño de Atocha had healed him of rheumatism. San Ildefonso pottery master Maria Martinez came here for healing as a child. Tales of the boy saint's losing one of his shoes as he wandered through the countryside helping those in trouble endeared him to the people of northern New Mexico. It became a tradition to place shoes at the foot of the statue as an offering. Many soldiers who survived the Bataan Death March during World War II credit Santo Niño for saving them, adding to his beloved status in this state where the percentage of young people who enlist in the military remains quite high. ⊠*Free* ☉*Daily 9–5.*

WHERE TO EAT & STAY

¢ ✕**Leona's Restaurante.** This fast-food-style burrito and chili stand under
SOUTHWESTERN a massive catalpa tree at one end of the Santuario de Chimayó park-
★ ing lot has only a few tables, and in summer it's crowded. Delicious dishes from the kitchen include homemade posole stew, *carne adovada*, and green-chili-and-cheese tamales. The specialty is flavored tortillas—everything from jalapeño to butterscotch. The tortillas have become so legendary that owner Léona Medina-Tiede opened a tortilla factory in Chimayó's Manzana Center and now does a thriving mail-order business. ⊠*Off CR 98, behind Santuario de Chimayó* ☎*505/351–4569 or 888/561–5569* ⊕*www.leonasrestaurante.com* ▤*AE, D, DC, MC, V* ☉*Closed Tues. and Wed. No dinner.*

$ ▦**Casa Escondida.** Intimate and peaceful, this adobe inn has sweeping
★ views of the Sangre de Cristo range. The setting makes it a great base for mountain bikers. The scent of fresh-baked strudel wafts through

the rooms, which are decorated with antiques and Native American and other regional arts and crafts. Ask for the Sun Room, in the main house, which has a private patio, viga ceilings, and a brick floor. The separate one-bedroom Casita Escondida has a kiva-style fireplace, tile floors, kitchenette, and a sitting area. A large hot tub is hidden in a grove behind wild berry bushes, there are several covered porches, and a massive bird-feeding station that draws dozens and dozens of birds. In-room massage is available by appointment, and special packages—romance or birthday, for example—are also available. **Pros:** This B&B is a very good value, with gracious hosts and in beautiful surroundings; there's not a TV on the entire property. **Cons:** Remote setting means you must drive to sights. ⊠ *CR 0100, off NM 76* ⌂ *Box 142, 85722* ☎ *505/351–4805 or 800/643–7201* ☐ *505/351–2575* ⊕ *www. casaescondida.com* ⏃ *In-room: no phone, kitchen (some), no TV, Wi-Fi. In-hotel: no-smoking rooms, some pets allowed, Wi-Fi* ⟡ *7 rooms, 1 suite* ☐ *MC, V* ⧖ *BP.*

SHOPPING

Centinela Traditional Arts-Weaving (⊠ *NM 76, 1 mi east of junction with CR 98* ☎ *505/351–2180 or 877/351–2180* ⊕ *www.chimayoweavers. com*) continues the Trujillo family weaving tradition, which started in northern New Mexico more than seven generations ago. Irvin Trujillo and his wife, Lisa, are both gifted, award-winning master weavers, creating Rio Grande–style tapestry blankets and rugs, many of them with natural dyes that authentically replicate early weavings. Most designs are historically based, but the Trujillos contribute their own designs as well. The shop and gallery carries these heirloom-quality textiles, with a knowledgeable staff on hand to demonstrate or answer questions about the weaving technique.

Ortega's Weaving Shop (⊠ *NM 76 at CR 98* ☎ *505/351–2288 or 877/351–4215* ⊕ *www.ortegasdechimayo.com*) sells Rio Grande– and Chimayó-style textiles made by the family whose Spanish ancestors brought the craft to New Mexico in the 1600s. The Galeria Ortega, next door, sells traditional New Mexican and Hispanic and contemporary Native American arts and crafts. In winter the shop is closed on Sunday.

In the plaza just outside the Santuario, **Highroad Marketplace** (⊠ *Off CR 98* ☎ *505/351–1078 or 866/343–5381*) stocks a variety of arts and crafts created all along the High Road, from Chimayó to Peñasco. Be sure to stop into **El Potrero**, a treasure trove of trinkets as well as high-quality arts and crafts from local artists.

CORDOVA
4 mi east of Chimayó via NM 76.

A picturesque mountain village with a small central plaza, a school, a post office, and a church, Cordova is the center of the regional wood-carving industry. The town supports more than 30 full-time and part-time carvers. Many of them are descendants of José Dolores López, who in the 1920s created the village's signature unpainted "Cordova style" of carving. Most of the *santeros* (makers of religious images) have signs outside their homes indicating that *santos* are for sale. Many pieces are fairly expensive, a reflection of the hard work and fine craftsmanship involved—ranging from several hundred dollars for small ones to several thousand for larger figures—but there are also affordable and delightful small carvings of animals and birds. The St. Anthony of Padua Chapel, which is filled with handcrafted *retablos* (wood tablets painted with saints) and other religious art, is worth a visit.

TRUCHAS
4 mi northeast of Cordova via NM 76.

Truchas (Spanish for "trout") is where Robert Redford shot the movie *The Milagro Beanfield War* (based on the novel written by Taos author John Nichols). This village is perched dramatically on the rim of a deep canyon beneath the towering Truchas Peaks, mountains high enough to be almost perpetually capped with snow. The tallest of the Truchas Peaks is 13,102 feet, the second-highest point in New Mexico. This is an insular town, and locals aren't always welcoming to visitors, so be discreet especially when taking pictures. Truchas has been developing cachet with artsy, independent-minded transplants from Santa Fe and Taos, who have come for the cheaper real estate and the breathtaking setting. There are several galleries in town, most open by chance, as well as a small general store that sells snacks and a few gifts.

Continue 7 mi north on NM 76, toward Peñasco, and you come to the marvelous San José de Gracia Church in the village of Trampas. It dates from circa 1760.

SHOPPING
In the heart of Truchas, **Cordova's Handweaving Workshop** (✉ *Country Rd. 75* ☎ *505/689–2437*) produces vibrant and colorful contemporary and traditional rugs.

PEÑASCO
15 mi north of Truchas on NM 76.

Although still a modest-size community, Peñasco is one of the larger towns along the High Road and a good bet if you need to fill your tank with gas or pick up a snack at a convenience store.

WHERE TO EAT
$ ✕**Sugar Nymphs Bistro.** It's taken a little time for people to learn about, CONTEMPORARY let alone find, this delightful little place set inside a vintage theater Fodor's Choice in sleepy Peñasco. You can't miss the vivid murals on the building, ★ it's right on the High Road, and it is hands down the best restaurant along this entire route. If you get an early start from Santa Fe and get through Chimayó in the morning, you'll get here right in time for a fabulous lunch, or an early dinner if you've meandered. Chef-owner Kai Harper Leah earned her stripes at San Francisco's famed vegetarian restaurant, Greens, and presents an eclectic menu of reasonably priced, inspired food: creatively topped pizzas, bountiful salads, juicy bacon cheeseburgers, butternut-squash ravioli. Desserts are also memorable—consider the chocolate pecan pie. You can dine on the patio

in warm weather. The Sunday brunch is excellent. ✉ *15046 NM 75* ☎ *505/587–0311* ▭ *MC, V* ⊘ *Closed Mon.*

SIDE TRIPS FROM TAOS

Surrounded by thousands of acres of pristine Carson National Forest and undeveloped high desert, Taos makes an ideal base for road-tripping. Most of the nearby adventures involve the outdoors, from skiing to hiking to mountain biking, and there are several noteworthy campgrounds in this part of the state. Although these side trips can be done in a day, several of the ski-resort communities mentioned in this section have extensive overnight accommodations.

THE ENCHANTED CIRCLE

Fodor's Choice ★ The Enchanted Circle, an 84-mi loop north from Taos and back, rings Wheeler Peak, New Mexico's highest mountain, and takes you through glorious panoramas of alpine valleys and the towering mountains of the lush Carson National Forest. You can see all the major sights in one day, or take a more leisurely tour and stay overnight.

From Taos, head north about 15 mi via U.S. 64 to NM 522, keeping your eye out for the sign on the right that points to the D.H. Lawrence Ranch and Memorial. You can visit the memorial, but the other buildings on the ranch are closed to the public. Continue north a short way to reach Red River Hatchery, and then go another 5 mi to the village of Questa. Here you have the option of continuing north on NM 522 and detouring for some hiking at Wild Rivers Recreation Area, or turning east from Questa on NM 38 and driving for about 12 mi to the rollicking ski town of Red River. From here, continue 16 mi east along NM 38 and head over dramatic Bobcat Pass, which rises to just under 10,000 feet. You'll come to the sleepy, old-fashioned village of Eagle Nest, comprising a few shops and down-home restaurants and motels. From here, U.S. 64 joins with NM 38 and runs southeast about 15 mi to one of the state's fastest-growing communities, Angel Fire, an upscale ski resort that's popular for hiking, golfing, and mountain biking in summer. It's about a 25-mi drive west over 9,000-foot Palo Flechado Pass and down through winding Taos Canyon to return to Taos.

Leave early in the morning and plan to spend the entire day on this trip. During ski season, which runs from late November to early April, you may want to make it an overnight trip and get in a day of skiing. In spring, summer, and fall your drive

> **WORD OF MOUTH**
>
> "We drove the Enchanted Circle as a day trip from Taos. It's a beautiful drive that takes you up through the Sangre de Cristo mountains, passing Red River, Wheeler Peak (highest in NM), and Eagle Nest, before coming back down to Taos. We also loved our day trip to Bandelier National Monument, an abandoned cliff dwelling in a beautiful little valley."
>
> —beach_dweller

should be free of snow and ice. A sunny winter day can yield some lovely scenery (but if it's snowy, don't forget your sunglasses).

Carson National Forest surrounds Taos and spans almost 200 mi across northern New Mexico, encompassing mountains, lakes, streams, villages, and much of the Enchanted Circle. Hiking, cross-country skiing, horseback riding, mountain biking, backpacking, trout fishing, boating, and wildflower viewing are among the popular activities here. The forest is home to big-game animals and many species of smaller animals and songbirds. For canyon climbing, head into the rocky Rio Grande Gorge. The best entry point into the gorge is at the Wild Rivers Recreation Area, north of Questa. You can drive into the forest land via NM 522, NM 150, NM 38, and NM 578. Carson National Forest also has some of the best trout fishing in New Mexico. Its streams and lakes are home to rainbow, brown, and native Rio Grande cutthroat trout.

The forest provides a wealth of camping opportunities, from organized campgrounds with restrooms and limited facilities to informal roadside campsites and sites that require backpacking in. If mountains, pines, and streams are your goal, stake out sites in Carson National Forest along the Rio Hondo or Red River; if you prefer high-desert country along the banks of the Rio Grande, consider Orilla Verde or Wild Rivers Recreation Area. Backcountry sites are free; others cost up to $7 per night.

If you're coming from a lower altitude, you should take time to acclimatize, and all hikers should follow basic safety procedures. Wind, cold, and wetness can occur any time of year, and the mountain climate produces sudden storms. Dress in layers and wear sturdy footwear; carry water, food, sunscreen, hat, sunglasses, and a first-aid kit. Contact the Carson National Forest's visitor center for maps, safety guidelines, camping information, and conditions (it's open weekdays 8–4:30). ⊠ *Forest Service Bldg., 208 Cruz Alta Rd., Taos* ☎ *575/758–6200* ⊕ *www.fs.fed.us/r3/carson.*

The Enchanted Circle Bike Tour takes place in mid-September. The rally loops through the entire 84-mi Enchanted Circle, revealing a brilliant blaze of fall color. In summer you can head up the mountainside via ski lift in Red River and Angel Fire.

QUESTA

25 mi north of Taos via U.S. 64 to NM 522.

Literally "hill," in the heart of the Sangre de Cristo Mountains, Questa is a quiet village nestled against the Red River and amid some of New Mexico's most striking mountain country. **St. Anthony's Church,** built of adobe with 5-foot-thick walls and viga ceilings, is on the main street. Questa's **Cabresto Lake,** in Carson National Forest, is about 8 mi from town. Follow NM 563 northeast to Forest Route 134, then 2 mi of a primitive road (134A)—you'll need a four-wheel-drive vehicle. You can trout fish and boat here from about June to October.

Although it's only a few miles west of Questa as the crow flies, you have to drive about 15 mi north of Questa via NM 522 to NM 378 to reach

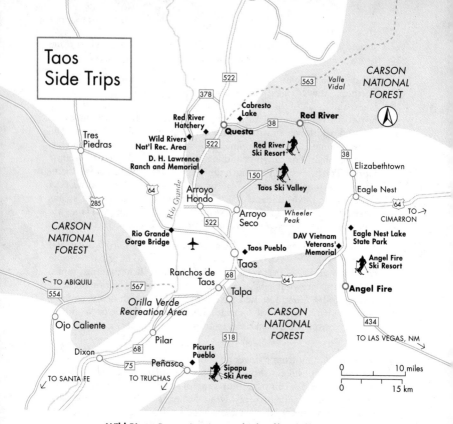

Taos Side Trips

Red River Hatchery
Cabresto Lake
Red River
Questa
522
563
Valle Vidal
CARSON NATIONAL FOREST
522
378
Tres Piedras
Wild Rivers Nat'l Rec. Area
Red River Ski Resort
38
D. H. Lawrence Ranch and Memorial
150
Elizabethtown
64
Arroyo Hondo
Taos Ski Valley
Eagle Nest
64
TO CIMARRON
285
Rio Grande
522
Arroyo Seco
Wheeler Peak
Eagle Nest Lake State Park
CARSON NATIONAL FOREST
Rio Grande Gorge Bridge
Taos Pueblo
DAV Vietnam Veterans' Memorial
Angel Fire Ski Resort
Taos
68
64
Angel Fire
← TO ABIQUIU
554
Ranchos de Taos
567
Talpa
Orilla Verde Recreation Area
CARSON NATIONAL FOREST
434
TO LAS VEGAS, NM
Ojo Caliente
Pilar
518
Dixon
68
Picuris Pueblo
75
Peñasco
Sipapu Ski Area
TO SANTA FE
TO TRUCHAS
0   10 miles
0   15 km

Wild Rivers Recreation Area, which offers hiking access to the dramatic confluence of two national wild and scenic rivers, the Rio Grande and Red River. There are some fairly easy and flat trails along the gorge's rim, including a ½-mi interpretive loop from the visitor center out to La Junta Point, which offers a nice view of the river. But the compelling reason to visit is a chance to hike down into the gorge and study the rivers up close, which entails hiking one of a couple of well-marked but steep trails down into the gorge, a descent of about 650 feet. It's not an especially strenuous trek, but many visitors come without sufficient water and stamina, have an easy time descending into the gorge, and then find it difficult to make it back up. There are also 29 basic campsites, some along the rim and others along the river. ✉NM 522, follow signed dirt road from highway, Cerro ☎575/770–1600 camping information ✆$3 per vehicle; camping $7 per vehicle ⏱Daily 6 AM–10 PM; visitor center late May–early Sept., daily 10–4.

NEED A BREAK?

Hip coffeehouses are something of a rarity in rural New Mexico, but funky **Paloma Blanca** (✉2322 S. NM 522 ☎575/586–2261) is a hit, not only because of its excellent coffee drinks but also due to its excellent sandwiches, pizza, pastries, homemade bread, and Taos Cow ice cream. It's the perfect place to stock up on food before hiking at Wild Rivers Recreation Area.

At the **Red River Hatchery,** freshwater trout are raised to stock waters in Questa, Red River, Taos, Raton, and Las Vegas. You can feed them and learn how they're hatched, reared, stocked, and controlled. The visitor center has displays and exhibits, a fishing pond, and a machine that dispenses fish food. The self-guided tour can last anywhere from 20 minutes to more than an hour, depending on how enraptured you become. There's a picnic area and camping on the grounds. ✉*NM 522, 5 mi south of Questa* ☎*575/586–0222* 🏷*Free* 🕐*Daily 8–5.*

The influential and controversial English writer David Herbert Lawrence and his wife, Frieda, arrived in Taos at the invitation of Mabel Dodge Luhan, who collected famous writers and artists the way some people collect butterflies. Luhan provided them a place to live, Kiowa Ranch, on 160 acres in the mountains. Rustic and remote, it's now known as the **D. H. Lawrence Ranch and Memorial,** though Lawrence never actually owned it. Lawrence lived in Taos on and off for about 22 months during a three-year period between 1922 and 1925. He wrote his novel *The Plumed Serpent* (1926), as well as some of his finest short stories and poetry, while in Taos and on excursions to Mexico. The houses here, owned by the University of New Mexico, are not open to the public, but you can enter the small cabin where Dorothy Brett, the Lawrences' traveling companion, stayed. You can also visit the D. H. Lawrence Memorial, a short walk up Lobo Mountain. A white shed-like structure, it's simple and unimposing. The writer fell ill while in France and died in a sanatorium there in 1930. Five years later Frieda had Lawrence's body disinterred and cremated and brought his ashes back to Taos. Frieda Lawrence is buried, as was her wish, in front of the memorial. ✉*NM 522, follow signed dirt road from highway, San Cristobal* ☎*575/776–2245* 🏷*Free* 🕐*Daily dawn–dusk.*

RED RIVER
12 mi east of Questa via NM 38.

Home of a major ski resort that has a particularly strong following with visitors from Oklahoma and the Texas panhandle, Red River (elevation 8,750 feet) came into being as a miners' boomtown during the 19th century, taking its name from the river whose mineral content gives it a rosy color. When the gold petered out, Red River died, only to be rediscovered in the 1920s by migrants escaping the dust storms in the Great Plains. An Old West flavor remains: Main Street shootouts, an authentic melodrama, and square dancing and two-stepping are among the diversions. Because of its many country dances and festivals, Red River is affectionately called "The New Mexico Home of the Texas Two-Step." The bustling little downtown area contains souvenir shops and sportswear boutiques, casual steak and barbecue joints, and a number of motels, lodges, and condos. There's good fishing to be had in the Red River itself, and excellent alpine and Nordic skiing in the surrounding forest.

NEED A BREAK? In Red River stop by the **Sundance** (✉ *401 E. High St.* ☎ *575/754–2971*) for Mexican food or a fresh-fruit sangria. The stuffed sopapillas here are particularly good. **Texas Red's Steakhouse** (✉ *111 E. Main St.* ☎ *575/754–2964*) has charbroiled steaks, chops, buffalo burgers, and chicken. There's also a branch in Eagle Nest, in the heart of downtown.

About 16 mi southeast of Red River, NM 38 leads to the small village of Eagle Nest, the home of New Mexico's most recently designated state park, **Eagle Nest Lake State Park** (⊠ *42 Marina Way, south of town* ☎ *575/377–1594* ⊕ *www.emnrd.state.nm.us* ⊠ *$5*), which became part of the park system in 2004. This 2,400-acre lake is one of the state's top spots for kokanee salmon and rainbow trout fishing as well as a favorite venue for boating; there are two boat ramps on the lake's northwest side. You may also spy elk, bears, mule deer, and even reclusive mountain lions around this rippling body of water, which in winter is popular for snowmobiling and ice fishing. The park is open daily 6 AM–9 PM, and camping is not permitted.

Thousands of acres of national forest surround rustic Eagle Nest, population 189, elevation 8,090 feet. The shops and other buildings here evoke New Mexico's mining heritage, while a 1950s-style diner, Kaw-Lija's, serves up a memorable burger; you can also grab some takeout food in town and bring it to Eagle Nest Lake for a picnic.

WHERE TO STAY

🏕️ **Roadrunner Campground.** The Red River runs right through this woodsy mountain campground set on 25 rugged acres. There are two tennis courts and a video-game room. ⊠ *1371 E. Main St., Box 588* ☎ *575/754–2286 or 800/243–2286* ⊕ *www.redrivernm.com/roadrunnerrv* ⸖ *Guest laundry, flush toilets, full hookups, drinking water, showers, picnic tables, electricity, public telephone, general store, play area, swimming (river)* ⇥ *141 RV sites, 2 cabins* ☉ *Closed mid-Sept.–Apr.*

SPORTS & THE OUTDOORS

★ At the **Enchanted Forest Cross-Country Ski Area,** 24 mi of groomed trails loop from the warming hut, stocked with snacks and hot cocoa, through 600 acres of meadows and pines in Carson National Forest, 3 mi east of Red River. ⊠ *417 W. Main St.* ☎ *575/754–2374 or 800/966–9381* ⊕ *www.enchantedforestxc.com* ⊠ *$14* ☉ *Late Nov.– Easter, weather permitting.*

The **Red River Ski Area** is in the middle of the historic gold-mining town of Red River, with lifts within walking distance of restaurants and hotels. Slopes for all levels of skiers make the area popular with families, and there's a snowboarding park. There are 58 trails served by seven lifts, and the vertical drop is about 1,600 feet. Red River has plenty of rental shops and accommodations. ⊠ *400 Pioneer Rd., off NM 38* ☎ *575/754–2223* ⊕ *www.redriverskiarea.com* ⊠ *Lift tickets $58* ☉ *Late Nov.–late Mar.*

ANGEL FIRE

30 mi south of Red River and 13 mi south of Eagle Nest via NM 38 and U.S. 64.

Named for its blazing sunrise and sunset colors by the Ute Indians who gathered here each autumn, Angel Fire is known these days primarily as a ski resort, generally rated the second best in the state after Taos. In summer there are arts and music events as well as hiking, river rafting, and ballooning. A prominent landmark along U.S. 64, just northeast of town, is the **DAV Vietnam Veterans Memorial,** a 50-foot-high wing-shaped monument built in 1971 by D. Victor Westphall, whose son David was killed in Vietnam.

WHERE TO STAY

$$$ Angel Fire Resort. The centerpiece of New Mexico's fastest-growing and most highly acclaimed four-season sports resort, this upscale hotel is set at the mountain's base, a stone's throw from the chairlift. Indeed, winter is the busiest season here, but during the warmer months it's a popular retreat with hikers, golfers, and other outdoorsy types who appreciate retiring each evening to spacious digs. Even the standard rooms are 500 square feet, and the larger deluxe units have feather pillows, ski-boot warmers, and fireplaces. The resort also manages a variety of privately owned condo units, from studios to three-bed-rooms, which are available nightly or long-term. **Pros:** Slope-side loca-tion; fantastic views. **Cons:** Some rooms are in need of an upgrade. ⊠*10 Miller La., Box Drawer B* ☎*575/377–6401or 800/633–7463* 🖶*575/377–4200* ⊕*www.angelfireresort.com* ⬎*139 rooms* ⌂*In-room: refrigerator, Wi-Fi. In-hotel: 4 restaurants, bars, golf course, tennis courts, bicycles* ⊟*AE, D, MC, V.*

CAMPING

⚠ **Enchanted Moon Campground.** In Valle Escondido, off U.S. 64 near Angel Fire, this wooded area with a trout pond has views of the San-gre de Cristos. Features include horse stalls, a chuckwagon, and an indoor recreation area with video games. ⊠*7 Valle Escondido Rd., Valle Escondido* ☎*575/758–3338* ⊕*www.emooncampground.com* ⌂*Flush toilets, full hookups, Wi-Fi, drinking water, showers, grills, picnic tables, electricity, play area* ⬎*27 RV sites, 22 tent sites* ☉*Closed mid-Oct.–Apr.*

NIGHTLIFE & THE ARTS

Music from Angel Fire (☎*575/377–3233 or 888/377–3300* ⊕*www. musicfromangelfire.org*) is a nightly series of classical (and occasional jazz) concerts presented at venues around Angel Fire and Taos for about three weeks from late August to early September. Tickets cost $20–$30 per concert, and the festival—begun in 1983—continues to grow in popularity and esteem each year.

SPORTS & THE OUTDOORS

The 18-hole golf course at the **Angel Fire Country Club** (⊠*Country Club Dr. off NM 434* ☎*575/377–3055*), one of the highest in the nation, is open May to mid-October, weather permitting. The challenging front 9 runs a bit longer than the back and takes in great views of aspen- and pine-shaded canyons; the shorter back 9 has more water play and somewhat tighter fairways. Greens fees are $75–$85.

★ The fast-growing and beautifully maintained **Angel Fire Resort** is a busy ski destination, with 70 runs for all levels of skiers, five lifts, 19 mi of

246

cross-country trails, and four terrain parks; the vertical drop is about 2,100 feet. Other amenities include a 1,000-foot snow-tubing hill, a well-respected ski and snowboard school, snow biking (also taught at the school), ice fishing, a children's ski-and-snowboard center, and superb snowmaking capacity. ⊠ *N. Angel Fire Rd. off NM 434* ☎ *575/377–6401, 800/633–7463, 575/377–4222 snow conditions* ⊕ *www.angel fireresort.com* ✉ *Lift tickets $59* ⊗ *Mid-Dec.–early Apr.*

Northwestern New Mexico

WORD OF MOUTH

"We...went to see Chaco It is amazing! It is so big and the site is awe-inspiring. I am used to seeing cliff dwellings like this in our neighboring Mesa Verde NP. These structures are free standing and are so different. I urge you take the turn off and drive down the long and dusty road to see a unique piece of our history. Go early, it gets hot and there are no real "creature comforts" at the info center other than water and restrooms."

—Debit_NM

Updated by
Lynne Arany

WHEN NEW MEXICANS GLIBLY SAY they are "on Indian time," they're referring to a certain relaxed approach to schedules and numbers that is simply part of the way of life in their home state. But once you leave the urban areas of Albuquerque or Santa Fe and start winding your way through the red canyons of the northwestern New Mexican desert, the phrase seems to take on a new significance. The enormous, silent sweep of plateaus and sky really does seem to form a landscape that's impervious to time—one that conjures the spirits of those who lived here long before recorded history. As you stand on the edge of a sandstone cliff overlooking the San Juan River, enter Pueblo Bonito in Chaco Canyon, or study the pattern of a handwoven Navajo rug, don't be surprised if you sense the presence of the ancient cultures that inhabited these places, and lived their lives based on the cycles of nature rather than the clock.

The countryside here has a stark and powerful beauty that has been recognized for centuries. The Anasazi people (whose name in Navajo means "Ancient Enemies") first built their cities and roads here more than 1,000 years ago. Today, the region is dominated by the Navajo in the northwest, and the Puebloan descendants of the Anasazi, who live closer to the Rio Grande. The two largest cities in the northwest today, Gallup and Farmington, are the legacy of even later arrivals—the traders, soldiers, homesteaders, and prospectors who made this area their home beginning in the 19th century. Today Gallup is a prime destination for Native American art and jewelry, and Farmington, at the crossroads of the entire Four Corners area, is a hub of energy exploration.

ORIENTATION & PLANNING

GETTING ORIENTED

Broadly referred to as Indian Country, New Mexico's northwestern region is for most travelers the next stop after Albuquerque, Santa Fe, or Taos. This beautiful high-desert area extends about two hours west from Albuquerque on Interstate 40 to Gallup and then the Arizona border, and four hours northwest to Farmington via U.S. 550. Many consider most of the region to be part of the Four Corners area. While drive times between stops may be long—and the roads can be rugged if you venture off the beaten path (as we recommend you do)—these lands will reward you with stunning natural settings of terrain, sky, and cloud; a diversity of cultures; a sense of the sacred; and a timeless sense of history.

Heading West on Route 66. The scent of smoldering piñon, the hypnotic chant of dancers, and the quiet intensity of ancient pueblos combine to make this stretch of the legendary highway a truly multisensory journey. Under vibrantly blue skies the pueblos of Laguna, Acoma, and Zuni follow one another as you head into Navajo territory, and remnants of Route 66's storied past (seen in storefronts and signage) punctuate the landscape.

TOP REASONS TO GO

■ **Chaco Canyon:** Wander through the ruins in Chaco Canyon and feel a mystic connection to ancient Puebloan cultures.

■ **Route 66:** Fugitive remnants of signage once brightly painted, now barely visible on a crumbling adobe building in Cubero; the old Puerco bridge; a lunch joint in Grants—these are a few of the fascinating relics of historic Route 66 that await you.

■ **Ancient Way Trail:** The Ancient Way Trail of NM 53 compresses many of northwestern New Mexico's scenic wonders into one journey: Los

Gigantes sandstone formations, ponderosa forest, El Malpais badlands, artisans along the trail—and then there's Zuni.

■ **Bisti Wilderness:** Hoodoos and some of the strangest and most wonderful rock formations in the American Southwest can be found in this multicolored, crumbling landscape.

■ **Acoma:** This remarkably picturesque high-mesa landscape is the site of what many archaeologists agree is the oldest continually inhabited city in America.

The Four Corners Area. Traveling northwest on the four-lane curves of U.S. 550 through volcanic formations and sandstone striations instills a delicious sense of anticipation. Awaiting the intrepid traveler are monumental ancestral Pueblo ruins, the surreal Bisti Badlands (for hoodoos and hiking), historic trading posts purveying Navajo silverwork and rugs, and a magical countryside that changes with every shift in light.

NORTHWESTERN NEW MEXICO PLANNER

WHEN TO GO

The best months to tour the Anasazi ruins are from April to early June and from late August to October, but there's no bad time. On rare occasions the roads to Chaco Canyon (or other back-roads locations, like El Malpais or the De-Na-Zin Wilderness area) are closed because of snow or mud in winter (though rain can make the roads extra-slick in summer as well), and cold winds can make the going rough in late fall and early spring. The best seasons for attending Pueblo Indian dances are summer and fall, when harvest celebrations take place, and from Thanksgiving through early January. Late June through July are the hottest months, but by August afternoon thunderstorms, called monsoons, begin cooling things down. The trick, as elsewhere in the Southwest, is to simply slow down and relax, Zen-like, into the dry heat.

When visiting pueblos and reservations you are expected to follow a certain etiquette (⇨ *"Pueblo Etiquette" box in Chapter 5*). Check the pueblos and monuments for dates of feast-day celebrations and fairs; some pueblos are open only on specific days.

GETTING HERE AND AROUND

BY AIR Most major airlines provide service to the state's main airport in Albuquerque, 145 mi east of Gallup and 185 mi southeast of Farmington. Some regional carriers fly in and out of Four Corners Regional Airport in Farmington; Great Lakes Aviation flies from Denver. There are currently no airlines flying into Gallup.

BY BUS   Texas, New Mexico & Oklahoma Coaches, affiliated with Greyhound Lines, provides service to Grants, Gallup, Farmington, and other towns in northwestern New Mexico.

BY CAR   A car is your best bet for getting to and around the region. Interstate 40 heads due west from Albuquerque toward Arizona. U.S. 64 leads west from Taos into northwestern New Mexico and east from Arizona. U.S. 550 travels to the northwest from Interstate 25 (15 mi north of Albuquerque), intersecting with U.S. 64 at Bloomfield, 14 mi east of Farmington. Road conditions vary with the seasons. Winter can create snowy, icy roads; summer can bring ferocious thunderstorms, hailstorms, and flash-flood warnings. Any back-roads driving warrants a vehicle with high clearance. You can rent a car from Avis, Budget, or Hertz at the Farmington airport. Budget and Enterprise have offices at the Gallup airport. *See Car Rental in New Mexico Essentials for national rental agency phone numbers.*

BY TRAIN   Amtrak has daily service between Gallup and Albuquerque (a guide accompanies the ride), as well as service from Lamy, near Santa Fe, on the *Southwest Chief.* Taking a train into Gallup and renting a car there to explore western New Mexico is an alternative.

ESSENTIALS   **Air contacts City of Gallup Airport** (✉ *2111 W. NM 66, Gallup* ☎ *505/722–4896*). **Four Corners Regional Airport** (✉ *1300 W. Navajo St., Farmington* ☎ *505/599–1285*). **Great Lakes Aviation** (☎ *800/554–5111* ⊕ *www.greatlakesav.com*). **Mesa Airlines** (☎ *800/637–2247* ⊕ *www.mesa-air.com*).

Bus Contact Texas, New Mexico & Oklahoma Coaches (☎ *505/325–1009 or 800/231–2222*).

Train Contact Amtrak (☎ *800/872–7245* ⊕ *www.amtrak.com*).

VISITOR INFORMATION   **Indian Country/NM Tourism** (⊕ *www.indiancountrynm.org*). **Acoma–Sky City Cultural Center** (✉ *Box 310, Acoma 87034* ☎ *505/552–6604 or 800/747–0181* ⊕ *www.acomaskycity.org*). **Farmington Convention and Visitors Bureau** (✉ *3041 E. Main St. 87402* ☎ *505/326–7602 or 800/448–1240* ⊕ *www.farmingtonnm.org*). **Gallup Convention and Visitors Bureau** (✉ *701 Montoya St. 87301* ☎ *505/863–3841 or 800/242–4282*). **Grants/Cibola County Chamber of Commerce** (✉ *100 N. Iron Ave. 87020* ☎ *800/748–2142* ⊕ *www.grants.org*). **Indian Pueblo Cultural Center** (✉ *2401 12th St. NW, Albuquerque 87104* ☎ *505/843–7270 or 866/855–7902* ⊕ *www.indianpueblo.org*). **Jicarilla Apache Tribe, Tourism Department** (✉ *Box 507, Dulce 87528* ☎ *505/759–3242* ⊟ *505/759–3005* ⊕ *www.jicarilla.net*). **Laguna Pueblo** (*Box 194, Laguna 87026* ☎ *505/552–6654* ⊕ *www.lagunapueblo.org*). **Navajo Nation Tourism Office** (✉ *Box 633, Window Rock, AZ 86515* ☎ *520/871–6436 or 520/871–7371* ⊕ *www.discovernavajo.com*). **Zuni Tourism** (*1203 NM 53, Box 339, Zuni 87327* ☎ *505/782–7238* ⊕ *www.ashiwi.org or www.zunitourism.com*).

PLANNING YOUR TIME

This region covers an immense territory—give yourself five to seven days for a thorough exploration. Begin by heading west out of Albuquerque on Interstate 40, planning a night or two in western pueblo country, and then heading north toward Farmington for another night in the Four Corners Region. Allow most of a day for touring Chaco Canyon. On your way back to Albuquerque, take an hour or so to visit the Jémez area. If you're daunted by squeezing so much into a short period, remember that it's easy to visit Acoma, Laguna, and Grants at other times as day trips from Albuquerque or Santa Fe. Some tackle Chaco as a day trip from the Rio Grande Valley, but it's far more practical to spend the night closer by, if not in Cuba then in Abiquiu, Bloomfield, or Farmington, or even Grants or Gallup (the last two towns being relatively near Chaco's southern entrance). *See also "Great Itineraries" feature below.*

ABOUT THE RESTAURANTS

Fast-food and familiar franchise restaurants thrive in this region, but there are also lots of reputable homegrown establishments. The B&Bs here serve uniformly delicious, homemade breakfasts (and some serve equally tasty dinners). Western favorites like rib-eye steak and barbecue pork and chicken are common menu items, breakfast burritos are ubiquitous, and, as elsewhere in New Mexico, topping everything is red and green chile sauce, commonly referred to simply as "chili." *Vegetarians take note*: chili is often cooked with pork in its green incarnation, and beef with red; ask about it when you order. Posole is another dish in which it is more common to find pork than not. Other local specialties include Navajo fry bread, which can be served plain, or topped with honey and powdered sugar, or taco-style with meat, beans, lettuce, and cheese; and mutton stew such as you would be served at a pueblo's feast day. Delicious bread and pies, baked in beehive-shaped outdoor *hornos* (ovens), are sold at roadside stands at some pueblos.

ABOUT THE HOTELS

Farmington, Grants, and Gallup are well supplied with chain motels; Cuba also has a couple decent motels, but Bloomfield has the nicest chain option and is even closer to Chaco. There are several appealing B&Bs in the region. Rooms in the areas surrounding Chaco Canyon can fill quickly during the spring and fall seasons when weather is ideal, but booking ahead in summer, especially for busy Farmington and Bloomfield, is a good idea. Definitely book in advance if attending a special event.

WHAT IT COSTS					
	¢	$	$$	$$$	$$$$
Restaurants	under $10	$10–$15	$16–$22	$23–$30	over $30
Hotels	under $70	$70–$120	$121–$175	$176–$250	over $250

Restaurant prices are per person for a main course at dinner. Hotel prices are for two people in a standard double room in high season, excluding 5%–12% tax.

GREAT ITINERARIES

IF YOU HAVE 2 OR 3 DAYS

The only way to tour this region adequately in two days is if you're incorporating your trip into a journey west into Arizona (via Gallup or Farmington), northwest into Utah (via Farmington), or north into Colorado (via Farmington). In three days, however, you can make a nice loop of the region's top sites: drive west from Albuquerque on Interstate 40, stopping in **Acoma Pueblo** before continuing west to **Gallup**. Spend the late afternoon shopping the old trading posts there, have dinner at Earl's, and stay overnight at the atmospheric El Rancho—or, if it's not too late, head south to spend a night in Zuni at the stellar **Inn at Halona**. On Day 2, head south on NM 602 to **Zuni**, before heading east on NM 53 to **El Morro National Monument** and then the **Ice Cave and Bandera Volcano**. If you've got a third day, spend the night in **Grants**, get up early and head north to spend as much time as you can manage in **Chaco Culture National**

Historical Park before heading back (exiting via the north entrance) to **Albuquerque.**

IF YOU HAVE 5 TO 7 DAYS

In five to seven days you can get a real sense for the past and present of northwestern New Mexico. On Day 1, drive west on Interstate 40, pause at **Laguna Pueblo,** then continue on to **Acoma Pueblo**, then loop down along NM 53 for short hikes at the **Ice Cave and Bandera Volcano**, and stay the night at one of the B&Bs in the area. The next day, explore **El Morro National Monument** before stopping at **Zuni Pueblo** en route to **Gallup**. Spend the remainder of the day wandering the trading posts and book a night at **El Rancho**. Next, follow U.S. 491 (via Shiprock) to **Farmington**, or backtrack to NM 371, visiting the Bisti Wilderness Area en route. Plan to spend at least a day exploring **Chaco Culture National Historical Park** from your base in Farmington, and you may find it surprisingly easy to go back for another day or more.

HEADING WEST ON ROUTE 66

Old Route 66 may be mostly subsumed by the interstate these days, but there are plenty of opportunities for drivers traveling west from Albuquerque to jump off Interstate 40 and explore the remaining sections of the Mother Road.

Drive due west past the historic Puerco River Bridge and the turnoff to the To'hajilee-he Navajo reservation, and soon the red-rock bluffs loom. If you're lucky, you might catch a glimpse of the *Southwest Chief* as it wends its way around the pueblo at Old Laguna on its daily run from Chicago to Los Angeles—this passenger train dates back to the early days and still makes stops in Gallup and Albuquerque. Secluded Acoma Pueblo is next, but not before you pass the remnants of an old Route 66 tourist outpost in Cubero.

Approaching Grants there's the La Ventana Arch and El Malpais badlands, both to the south, to consider. And almost immediately after that little 66 hub you can choose to stay on Interstate 40 and steamroll to

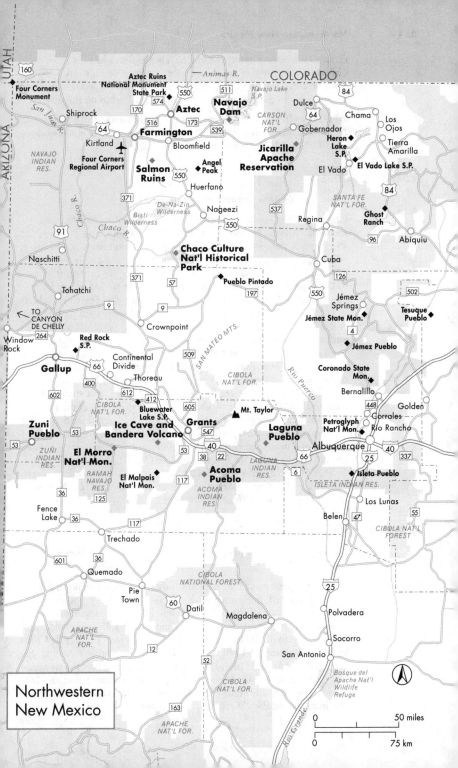

Gallup and Navajo lands (or exit at Thoreau and head up to Chaco Canyon via its rougher south entrance), or drop down south onto the Ancient Way Trail (NM 53), and instead take this gorgeous loop route around—passing through El Morro and Zuni Pueblo on the way.

■TIP→**Excellent guides accompany the well-planned full-day tours to Zuni and Acoma offered by the Indian Pueblo Cultural Center in Albuquerque** (☎505/843–7270 ⊕www.indianpueblo.org).

LAGUNA PUEBLO

50 mi west of Albuquerque on I–40 (Exit 114).

Laguna Pueblo actually comprises six villages, all traditionally Keres-speaking: Mesita, Seama, Encinal, Paraje, Laguna, and Paguate. (In 1953 one of the world's largest open-pit uranium mines, the Jackpile, began operation in Paguate, bringing with it income and health issues. The mine was shut down in 1982.) But visitors are especially drawn to **Old Laguna**, capped by the eye-catching white facade of San José de Laguna Church, which is visible from Interstate 40. The church, built in 1699, is a National Historic Landmark; its lovely hand-painted and embellished interior may be accessed by special permission. In shops and artists' homes (the latter identified by signs)—and occasionally in front of the church, or at the scenic overview just west of the Laguna exit—you can buy silver jewelry and fine pottery decorated with traditional geometric designs. The pueblo's villages enjoy many feast days, including St. Ann (July 26, Seama), Virgin Mary (September 8, Encinal), and St. Margaret Mary (October 17, Paraje). Most of the pueblo's residents (and the welcome public) gather at Old Laguna on September 19 to grandly honor St. Joseph with dances and a fair. No photographs are allowed inside the church; other photography rules vary—contact the governor's office for information. ⊠*Old Laguna: Exit 114 from I–40* ☎*505/552–6654 governor's office, 505/552–9330 church access, 505/331–6683 tours* ⊠*Free; fee for tours varies* ⊙*Daily 8–4:30 (church until 3:30), village tours by appt.*

ACOMA PUEBLO

★ *63 mi west of Albuquerque on I–40 (Exit 102) and Indian Route 32/38 south.*

Atop a 367-foot mesa that rises abruptly from the valley floor, Acoma Pueblo's terraced, multistory, multiunit Sky City is like no other pueblo structure. It's one of the oldest continually inhabited spots in North America, with portions believed to be more than 1,500 years old. Captain Hernando de Alvarado, a member of Francisco Vásquez de Coronado's expedition of 1540, was the first European to see Acoma. He reported that he had "found a rock with a village on top, the strongest position ever seen in the world." The Spanish eventually conquered the Acoma people and brutally compelled them to build **San Estéban del Rey**, the immense adobe church that stands to this day. Native American laborers cut the massive vigas for the church's ceiling 30 mi away on Mt. Taylor and physically carried them back to the mesa.

About a dozen families live at the mesa-top pueblo full time, with most other Acomas living on Native American land nearby and returning only in summer and for celebrations, such as the feast day of St. Stephen (September 2), and Christmas mass (both are open to the public). Acoma's artisans are known for their thin-walled pottery, hand-painted with intricate black-and-white or polychrome geometrical patterns.

Once you park at the mesa base, plan to spend time in the superb **Haak'u Museum at the Sky City Cultural Center**. Changing exhibits explore traditional and contemporary arts, and are perfectly set in this modernist interpretation of traditional pueblo forms, with fine sandstone detailing and glass panels prepared to evoke historic mica windows. Visitation on the mesa top is by an hour-long guided tour; you're whisked by van up a steep road from behind the Center and then led about the mesa community on foot (allow extra time if you choose to walk back down instead, via the ancient staircase carved into the side of the mesa). An Acoma guide will point out kivas, hornos, and unforgettable views toward their sacred sites of Enchanted Mesa and **Mt. Taylor**, and describe pueblo history in-depth, as well as direct you to artisan displays throughout the village. (Note: the terrain can be uneven; heeled shoes or flip-flops are not advised.) There's no electricity or running water in the village, but you can see cars parked outside many homes—one wonders what it must have been like to visit Acoma before the road was constructed in 1969. Open hours vary slightly, depending on the weather. Videotaping, sketching, and painting are prohibited, and a permit is required for still photography. Note that the pueblo prohibits photography of the church interior and exterior as well as the adjoining cemetery. As at all indigenous locales, ask permission before photographing residents or their artwork. Regroup back at Haak'u and browse the bookstore or enjoy blue-corn pancakes or a grilled chicken wrap with green-chile guacamole at the cozy **Yaak'a** (Corn) **Café**. There is shuttle service available if you are staying at the **Sky City Hotel/Casino** (☎888/Sky–City). For day tours from Albuquerque, contact the **Indian Pueblo Cultural Center** (☎505/843–7270). ⊠16 mi south of I-40 Exit 102, on Indian Route 32/38 ☎505/552–6604 or 800/747–0181 ⊕www.acomaskycity.org ☜Sky City Tour: $12; Haak'u Museum: $4 ☉Apr.– Oct., daily 8–6:30, tours daily 8–5:30; Nov.–Mar., daily 8–5, tours daily 8–4. The café closes 1 hr before the museum.

GRANTS

34 mi west of Laguna Pueblo, 29 mi northwest of Acoma via NM 38 north and I–40 west.

The largest community on old Route 66 between Albuquerque and Gallup, little Grants has an intriguing museum and enough chain hotels and inexpensive restaurants to make it a fair base for exploring the eastern half of this region. The night skies here are said to be some of the clearest in the world, making it a worthwhile stop for stargazers.

FODOR'S FIRST PERSON

Georgia de Katona
Writer, avid motorist

So much has been written about Route 66 that I'm almost embarrassed to admit my fascination with it. Almost involuntarily I turn onto its crumbling asphalt, cruising slowly past countless broken-down establishments in remote parts of New Mexico and beyond. From my abiding curiosity grows a hope that I'll see signs of life reemerging in some of the sweetest old towns you're ever likely to see.

I'm happy to report that Albuquerque's stretch of Route 66 is, for the most part, a treasure trove of vitality and variety. Hip restaurants and shops, the huge University of New Mexico, brewpubs, groovy thrift stores, and art galleries populate the route across the city. Multiple lifestyles, ethnicities, and eccentricities are on full display. Route 66 as it exists in Albuquerque today is the one place in the state that might possibly live up to the nostalgic language referring to the route as the "embodiment of all that makes this nation great." But, wow, that's a lot to live up to.

The stretch of 66 from Albuquerque through most of eastern New Mexico is a reminder that the transition from highway to freeway was rough on many little towns whose lifeblood was the motorists themselves. Places like San Jon (pronounced "hone"), Montoya, Cuervo, San Fidel, and Bluewater provide homes for just a few remaining residents these days. This is where the route is missed. Tucumcari's lovely old downtown, just a few blocks north of Route 66, is all but abandoned, its ornate and intriguing early-20th-century buildings succumbing to age and neglect.

At many points on the road, the memory of what's no longer there is less troubling than what is: in Gallup, Santa Rosa, and parts of Albuquerque the road is sprinkled with pedestrian big-box stores, an almost boundless variety of mediocre restaurants, vendors of pseudo-Western and "Indian" trinkets made in China, and other schlock that's bound to make passing motorists and born-and-bread Westerners (like yours truly) lament the state of an American icon.

In such moments of despair about Route 66, there is often a simple antidote: neon. Amid the decay and blandness is an abundance of neon in crazy, kitschy themes and otherworldly colors. It outlives the attention span of property owners, tourists, and highway planners. Its glow draws folks like Connie and Jean (who I met at the Blue Swallow in Tucumcari, and again in Santa Rosa when they saved me from a terrible restaurant). It tempts them with the allure of driving from Chicago all the way to Santa Monica on a road that really has shaped the American psyche.

The seat of Cibola County, Grants started out as a farming and ranching center, grew into a rail transport hub, and boomed during the 1950s when uranium was discovered in the nearby mountains. The city has struggled since then to find its economic niche.

In the center of sleepy downtown Grants, the small **New Mexico Mining Museum** shares quarters with the chamber of commerce off Santa Fe Avenue. On the ground level are charts, photos, gems, and minerals, and depictions of uranium-mining life in the region—this area is free. After paying admission, you can ride the elevator down into a realistic, re-created mine in the building's basement, where you can take a self-guided tour of the equipment and exhibits. ⊠*100 N. Iron Ave.* ☎*505/287–4802 or 800/748–2142* ⊕*www.grants.org* ✉*Museum free, mine exhibit $3* ☉*Mon.–Sat. 9–4.*

Looming 11,301 feet above Grants to the northeast, **Mt. Taylor** is the highest peak in northwestern New Mexico. Its stark presence on the horizon gives a sense of why the mountain is considered sacred not just to the Acoma, but the Zuni, Laguna, and Navajo as well. You can drive fairly far up the mountain for fine views and hop out to hike on marked trails. On the main road to the peak, about 10 mi northeast of Grants off NM 547, Coal Mine and Lobo Canyon campgrounds, both at 7,400 feet elevation, offer first-come, first-served campsites (and restrooms, but no drinking water) amidst ponderosa pines. The campground is closed September 30–May 15; call the Cibola National Forest/Mt. Taylor Ranger District station (☎*505/287–8833*) for information. The annual **Mt. Taylor Winter Quadrathlon** (☎*505/287–4802 or 800/748–2142* ⊕*www.mttaylorquad.org*) takes place in mid-February, when 600 unbelievably fit athletes compete in a highly challenging bicycle, foot, ski, and snowshoe race near the summit.

6

WHERE TO EAT & STAY

¢ ╳**El Cafecito.** Nothing fancy, just big helpings of tasty regional favor-
NEW MEXICAN ites like enchiladas, stuffed sopaipillas, burgers, and the breakfast of Southwest champions: huevos rancheros. Chili is rich and hot. Kids are welcome and happily accommodated. ⊠*820 E. Santa Fe Ave.* ☎*505/285–6229* ▤*AE, DC, MC, V* ☉*Closed Sun.*

¢ ▥**Ancient Way Café/El Morro RV Park & Cabins.** This pleasant oasis is made up of log-style cabins, a campground, and a café with a great front porch overlooking a gorgeous valley. The old-time wood-lined café, which serves breakfast, lunch, and dinner—including vegetarian plates such as a tasty lasagna and the gamut of New Mexican favorites—is one of the better eateries in the Grants–Gallup area. The cabins come in three sizes and provide adequate shelter with private baths, coffeemakers, and refrigerators, and camping is available for tents and RVs. **Pros:** Ideal location right off the Trail of the Ancients. **Cons:** Cabin decor ranges from '50s frowsy to quaint; no cooking in cabins. ⊠ *On NM 53 at Hwy. Marker 46, 1 mi east of El Morro Nat'l Monument, between Ramah and Grants* ☎☎*505/783–4612* ⊕*www. elmorro-nm.com* ⇥*6 cabins* ⚲ *Wi-Fi; full RV hookups, showers for campers* ▤*AE, DC, MC, V.*

$$ ▥**Cimarron Rose.** Rustic Southwestern comfort is the specialty of the house at this B&B, on 20 ponderosa pine–laden acres. Proprietor Sheri McWethy has created a "green" inn, with natural-fiber sheets, no perfumes or dyes in the cleaning products, absolutely no smoking allowed in rooms or anywhere on-site, and a conscientious approach to water

use. Full breakfasts are delivered to your door each morning—banana–blue corn pancakes (with real maple syrup) and Mexican hot chocolate are favorites—and special dietary requests are accommodated with notice. Day packs and picnic baskets are supplied for those wanting to explore the area. Reservations are required. **Pros:** Each accommodation is a suite (including a complete kitchen) with private entry; daily rates decrease for stays over two nights. **Cons:** Guests heat up their pre-cooked breakfasts in their rooms; not all pets allowed; an extra fee is charged if accepted. ⊠*689 Oso Ridge Rte., 30 mi southwest of Grants on NM 53* 🖀🖀*505/783–4770 or 800/856–5776* ⊕*www.cimarronrose.com* ➡*3 suites* ⟵*In-room: kitchens, Wi-Fi, no phone, DVD, no TV* ⊟*No credit cards* ⦾*BP.*

$$ 🏠**The Mission at Riverwalk.** How about sleeping in the former parsonage, now guest house, of the first Protestant church built in this heavily Catholic region (1920)? Fact is, in addition to all its intriguing historical tidbits, interesting architecture (adobe, but not Pueblo-style), and on-site gallery, the Mission is a gracious and comfortable B&B. A complimentary bottle of wine awaits your arrival and a Jacuzzi tub will soak travel-tired muscles. The guest house is perfect for families, and management will roll extra beds (up to two, no charge) into the living room at your request. **Pros:** Special weekly and monthly rates are available. **Cons:** Minimum stay is three nights; can fit four people max. ⊠*422 W. Santa Fe Ave.* 🖀*505/285–4632* ⊕*www.grantsmission.com* ➡*1 house* ⟵*In-room: kitchen, Wi-Fi* ⊟*AE, D, MC, V* ⦾*BP.*

$ 🏠**Zuni Mountain Lodge.** Airy and tranquil, this white wood-framed lodge lies at the edge of the Zuni Mountain Range, 1 mi from Bluewater Lake State Park, south of Thoreau (pronounced "through"). Simply furnished rooms with private baths are quiet and surrounded by views of the lake and Cibola National Forest. The proprietor is a wellspring of area history and suggestions for places to explore. Included in your stay are a full breakfast and delicious dinners of hearty home-style favorites. **Pros:** A broad program (Chaco Canyon, Canyon de Chelly, and more) of guided day tours is available; TV, video library, and games in common room. **Cons:** Dinner is served only at 7 PM. ⊠*40 Perch Dr., between Grants and Gallup; from I–40 Exit 53, head south 13 mi on NM 612* ⟐*Box 5114, Thoreau 87323* 🖀 🖀*505/862–7616* ⊕*www.zuniml.com* ➡*7 rooms* ⟵*In-room: no phone, no TV. In-hotel: some pets allowed, Internet (some)* ⊟*No credit cards* ⦾*MAP.*

EN ROUTE   Traveling west on Interstate 40, along the south side of the freeway in the last 10 mi or so before you hit Grants, you'll catch your first glimpse of the stark, volcanic-rock-strewn **El Malpais National Monument and Conservation Area** (⊠ *NM 117, 10 mi east of Grants; NM 53, 23 mi south of Grants* 🖀*505/287–7911 BLM, 505/783–4774 NPS* ⊕*www.nps.gov/elma*). Take Exit 89, on the east edge of the flow, and travel south on NM 117 7 mi to La Ventana, New Mexico's largest natural arch. Before you get to that sandstone wonder, you might pull off at the BLM's El Malpais Ranger Station for maps and information about the conservation area's miles of hiking trails; the nearby Sandstone Bluffs overlook offers a grand view across El Malpais ("the Badlands"). Alternatively, proceed into Grants, stopping at the National Park Service's visitor center for maps and info, then continue west on Interstate 40 to Exit 81, then south on NM 53 to the monument area. El Malpais is not much of an attraction for the just-passing-through visitor, but it's well worth spending a full day or two exploring the park in depth. Popular for hiking as well as caving in the miles of lava tubes, its some 40 volcanoes dot 114,000 acres. (A quick snapshot of the volcanic landscape may be gained from the Ice Cave and Bandera Crater.) Backcountry camping permits are available at the visitor center, though camping is *very* primitive—no facilities exist.

ICE CAVE & BANDERA VOLCANO

🕙 *25 mi southwest of Grants, 1 mi west of El Malpais via NM 53.*

Despite its unabashed commercialism (announced by its many somewhat-over-the-top, retro-style billboard advertisements), this roadside curiosity, set squarely on the Continental Divide, easily merits an hour of your time—the short trail from the 1930s trading post (now the gift shop) just off NM 53 affords unusual vistas of blackened lava fields and gnarled juniper and ponderosa stands. It's about a 20-minute moderately strenuous jaunt up to the 1,200-foot-diameter crater of **Bandera Volcano**, which last unleashed a torrent of lava 10,000 years ago. An even shorter walk leads to an old wooden staircase that descends 100 feet into the bowels of a collapsed lava tube, where the **Ice Cave** remains 31°F year-round and has a perpetual floor of blue-green ice. The ice remains year after year because of the combination of the air flow patterns in the lava tube and the insulating properties of the lava itself. ⊠ *NM 53 (12000 Ice Caves Rd.)* ☎ *888/423–2283* ⊕ *www.icecaves.com* 🎟 *$9* ⊙ *Late May–early Sept., daily 8–7; early Sept.–late May, daily 8–5.*

OFF THE BEATEN PATH

Wild Spirit Wolf Sanctuary. The mystique of wolves is powerful and Wild Spirit is one of the few places where you can see them up close, in large enough enclosures that allow them to behave somewhat naturally. The staff at Wild Spirit are focused on educating the public about the dangers of trying to keep these animals, even hybrid wolf dogs, as pets. Camping is allowed on the premises, if you have a hankering to listen to wolf howls; it's primitive and only $10 a night. The gift shop closes after the last tour, about 4:30. If you'll arrive later than that, you *must* call ahead to make arrangements. ⊠ *Candy Kitchen. 50 mi southwest of Grants, or 10 mi east of Ramah on NM 53, turn south onto Rte. 125. Follow Rte. 125 8 mi south through Mountainview. Turn right onto Rte. 120. Sanctuary is 4 mi down on left* ☎ *505/775–3304* ⊕ *www.wildspiritwolfsanctuary.org* 🎟 *$5* ⊙ *Tues.–Sun., tours at 11, 12:30, 2, and 3:30.*

EL MORRO NATIONAL MONUMENT

★ *43 mi southwest of Grants, 36 mi east of Zuni, via NM 53.*

When you see the imposing 200-foot-high sandstone bluff that served as a rest stop for Indians, explorers, soldiers, and pioneers, you can understand how El Morro ("the Headlands") got its name. The bluff is the famous **Inscription Rock,** where wayfarers stopped to partake of a waterhole at its base and left behind messages, signatures, and petroglyphs carved into the soft sandstone. The **Inscription Trail** makes a quick ½-mi round-trip from the visitor center. Although El Morro is justly renowned for Inscription Rock, try to allow an extra 90 minutes or so to venture along the spectacular, moderately strenuous 2-mi (round-trip) **Mesa Top Trail,** which meanders past the excavated edge of an extensive field of pueblo ruins, cuts along the precarious rim of a deep box canyon, and affords panoramic views of the region. The monument's **museum** chronicles 700 years of human history in this region. ⊠ *Visitor center: NM 53* ☎ *505/783–4226* ⊕ *www.nps.gov/elmo* ☑ *$3 per person* ⊙ *Late May–early Sept., daily 8–7; early Sept.–late May, daily 9–5. Trails close 1 hr before monument; in winter, ice and snow may close them altogether. Call ahead.*

WHERE TO STAY

⚠ **El Morro National Monument.** The park has a primitive campground amid the trees ¼ mi from the visitor center. Tap water is turned off between approximately November and April; at those times camping is free. ⊠ *NM 53* ☎ *505/783–4226* ⬧ *Pit toilets, drinking water, picnic tables, public telephone* ⤵ *9 sites* ⚠ *Reservations not accepted.*

ZUNI PUEBLO

36 mi west of El Morro National Monument on NM 53; 42 mi southwest of Gallup.

Zuni Pueblo has been occupied continuously since at least the year 700, and its language is unrelated to that of any other pueblo. Hawikuh, a Zuni-speaking settlement now 12 mi south of the pueblo, was the first to come in contact with the Spaniards, in 1539. Francisco Vásquez de Coronado came here seeking one of the Seven Cities of Gold. He'd been tipped off by his guide, Estéban, who had seen the setting sun striking the walls of the dwellings and thought the multistoried villages were made of gold.

With a population of more than 10,000, Zuni Pueblo is the largest of New Mexico's 19 Indian pueblos. Zuni has a mix of buildings: modern ones in addition to traditional adobes, along with some beautifully hewn red sandstone structures more than 100 years old. The artists and craftspeople here are renowned for their masterful stone inlay, Zuni "needlepoint" turquoise and silver jewelry, carved stone animal fetishes, pottery, and kachina figures. Weavings are becoming increasingly difficult to find as old weavers pass on and younger Zunis don't take up the craft, but it's fine work and worth looking for if textiles are your passion.

The **Zuni Visitor Center,** where the helpful staff will tell you what your options are for exploring Zuni (and about any special events that might be going on), is also a tribally required stop before you begin to explore this most traditional of the New Mexico pueblos. It is here that you must inquire about photography permits and guidelines (cultural and religious activities are always off-limits). ⊠ *1239 NM 53, on south side* *of the road as you enter pueblo from east, in Zuni Tribal Government complex* ☎*505/782–7238* ⊕*www.ashiwi.org or www.zunitourism. com* ⊙ *Weekdays 9–5.*

The original **Our Lady of Guadalupe Mission,** built in 1629, was destroyed during the Pueblo Revolt of 1680 when Native Americans ousted the Spanish. In 1699 the mission was rebuilt, and in 1966 it was excavated and reconstructed in the simple late-colonial adobe style prevalent throughout New Mexico. ⊠*Old Mission Dr.* ☎*505/782–4403* 🎫*Free* ⊙ *Weekdays 9–noon; hrs sometimes vary, call ahead.*

A:shiwi A:wan Museum and Heritage Center, which celebrates Zuni history and culture, is housed in a historic trading post. The museum gives a basic orientation to the Zuni culture, which tends to be lesser known than other pueblos because of its remoteness in the region. Artifacts, baskets, and pottery are displayed, as well as a beautiful mural depicting the peoples' history. ⊠*On the south side of NM 53, at Pia Mesa and Ojo Caliente Rds.* ☎*505/782–4403* ⊕*www.ashiwi-museum. org or www.zunitourism.org* 🎫*Free* ⊙*Nov.–Apr., weekdays 9–5:30; May–Oct., Mon.–Sat. 9–5:30.*

WHERE TO STAY

$ 🏨**The Inn at Halona.** Your only opportunity to stay right in the heart of Zuni, this bright and cheery inn is decorated with handwoven rugs, fine Zuni arts and crafts, and locally made furniture. Six of the rooms have private baths, two share a bath. Outside you can relax in the tree-shaded, enclosed, flagstone courtyard or walk a short distance to the village plaza and several art galleries. Limited room service is available if you order ahead, or you may purchase ingredients at the tribe-staffed Halona Plaza market next door—which is also where Inn guests must go to check in—and prepare a meal in the communal kitchen. The breakfasts (homemade blue-corn pancakes) are not to be missed. Between the host, the staff, and the comfortable (if a little over-stuffed) rooms laden with Indian blankets and pottery, this is a Southwestern standout. **Pros:** A one-of-a-kind lodging experience. **Cons:** Dinner is takeout from the adjacent market, or a drive up to Gallup or back toward El Morro. ⊠*23 Pia Mesa Rd., off NM 53* 🖃*Box 446, Zuni 87327* ☎*505/782–4547 or 800/752–3278* 🖷*505/782–2155* ⊕*www. halona.com* 🛏*8 rooms* 🖳*In-room: no TV. In-hotel: no-smoking rooms, Wi-Fi (some)* ☰*MC, V* ⦿*BP.*

Fodor'sChoice ★

SHOPPING

Pueblo of Zuni Arts & Crafts (⊠*1222 NM 53, on south side of the road as you enter pueblo from east* ☎*505/782–5531*), next to the Visitor Center, is a tribally operated shop that carries authentic Zuni products of all kinds. In addition to an excellent selection of books on Zuni history, arts, and culture, you can find jewelry, fetishes, and pottery. Also sold here are beautifully crafted furnishings from the Zuni Furniture Enterprise, a woodworking cooperative on the pueblo. Handcrafted from pine and exotic woods like wormwood maple, and decorated with distinctive, highly stylized traditional motifs, these pieces are different from anything you'll find in mainstream furniture stores.

GALLUP

42 mi north of Zuni on NM 602, 138 mi west of Albuquerque on I–40.

With a population mix of Navajo, Anglo, and Hispanic—plus a Mormon influence, a strong presence of other tribes, and a richly intertwined culture and history that reflects that mix—Gallup is a place like nowhere else. Known as both the Heart of Indian Country and the Indian Jewelry Capital of the World, with more than 100 trading posts that deal in Native American jewelry, pottery, rugs, and all manner of other arts and crafts, Gallup might just be the best place to acquire that concho belt or squash-blossom necklace you've always wanted. Prices are often better than those you can find in Santa Fe, and the selection is just short of overwhelming. Many of the Navajos selling their wares (and here to shop for more mundane goods themselves) have come in from Window Rock, Arizona, the Navajo Nation's capital, 25 mi northwest of town, or from less accessible rural spots on the surrounding reservation lands. The Navajo Veteran's Memorial Park and the Navajo Nation Museum, both in Window Rock, are an easy drive from Gallup.

Gallup originated in the 1880s as a coal-mining town, and the railroad that followed encouraged a boom. Long strings of freight cars still rumble along the tracks paralleling Historic Route 66, and train whistles hoot regularly. During the late 1920s and '30s, Gallup became a fabled stop along Route 66. When you drive down its neon-illuminated main street, you enter a retro world of pop-culture nostalgia.

The 12-block downtown section bounded by Historic Route 66, 1st Street, Hill Avenue, and 4th Street is made for a walking tour. You can browse through the trading posts and get a fine glimpse of modern murals and 19th-century and WPA-vintage architecture (notably, the **McKinley County Courthouse**). West Coal Avenue, parallel to and one block south of Route 66, is the main culture strip.

The small but lively contemporary arts scene is best enjoyed on the second Saturday of every month during the **Arts Crawl** (☎ *505/863–3841 or 505 722–2258*). Downtown galleries such as **Crashing Thunder** (✉ *226 W. Coal Ave.*) and **GPAC Art Gallery** (✉ *1500 S. Second St.* ☎ *505/722–2258* ⊕ *www.gpac.info*) open their doors with new shows, while coffeehouses and shops offer snacks and entertainment.

The renovated 1928 "Pueblo Deco" **El Morro Theater** (✉ *207 W. Coal Ave.* ☎ *505/726–0050*) is a shining example of a unique regional building style. El Morro tends to be open sporadically for events and the occasional film fest, call to find out what's on the schedule. Walk one block south of Route 66 to have a look.

NEED A BREAK?

The **Coffee House** (✉ *203 W. Coal Ave., 1 block south of Rte. 66* ☎ *505/726–0291*) serves delicious coffees, teas, and Italian sodas in addition to salads, sandwiches, and sweet treats. This friendly, family-run community house of sorts is also a gallery, with exhibits of local artists' works changing monthly.

Buying Smart: Native Arts & Crafts

When you visit northwestern New Mexico, you'll have numerous opportunities to buy Native American arts, crafts, and souvenirs. But how can you be sure the pieces you buy are authentic? There's a lot of fake merchandise out there, and it's sold by Native Americans and non–Native Americans alike.

Although quality arts and crafts aren't necessarily expensive, if a price for a piece seems too good to be true, it probably is. Still, knowing what you're looking for—and most important, what questions to ask—can help you determine what's worth buying and what isn't. Here are some good rules of thumb:

Goods carrying the IACA (Indian Arts & Crafts Association) symbol are reliably authentic.

When buying jewelry, ask the vendor to tell you about the stones you're looking at and where they came from. The first thing to ask about turquoise is whether it is natural or not ("genuine" won't do—it does not confirm that the stone is its natural color, nor whether it has been treated in any other way). Ask if the turquoise is stabilized, from block, or injected. Hand-polished American turquoise (or Chinese, which is quite common these days and not generally considered a negative by fine artisans—unless it has been treated, of course) is more costly if it hasn't been stabilized or injected with dye to enhance the color, and is uniquely beautiful. Matrix, the brown or black veins in turquoise, is not a flaw, but it often provides clues as to the quality of the stone. Also ask if the jewelry settings, usually silver, are hand fabricated or precast; the former will be more expensive.

If you're interested in pottery, start looking at the wares offered by the renowned potters at Acoma, although the Laguna and Zuni pueblos also have fine potters. Ask whether you're looking at "greenware," precast commercial ceramics that come ready for the artist to apply paint, or hand-coiled pottery. Hand-coiled pots start as coils of hand-gathered clay and are built from the bottom up; feel inside a pot and for the tell-tale unevenness that distinguishes a hand-coiled pot. You can also ask what kind of paintbrush was used to embellish the pottery; traditionally, yucca-fiber brushes are used for this intricate work.

In the market for a rug? Beware of imported, foreign-made rugs with Navajo designs. These rugs may be nicely made, but they are entirely different from handwoven Navajo textiles. Authentic pieces usually have tags that identify the weaver; but you can also ask if the yarn is hand spun, hand dyed, and what types of dye were used (commercial or natural or both). A rug that is entirely hand processed will be the most expensive, but it will also be an heirloom. And before complaining about the $5,000 price of a Two Gray Hills rug, remember that it probably took several months to weave.

6

On weekend evenings you're likely to catch a poetry reading or an open-mike night.

Clothing, furniture, tools, and typewriters are among the artifacts of the coal-mining era on display at the **Rex Museum,** operated by the Gallup Historical Society inside the former Rex Hotel. ✉*300 W. Historic Rte. 66* ☎*505/863–1363* 💰*$2* ☉*Weekdays (and some Sat.) 9–3:30*

Part of the **Gallup Cultural Center,** a project of the Southwest Indian Foundation, is inside the restored almost century-old Atchison, Topeka & Santa Fe Railway station. (A quintessential Fred Harvey House—architect Mary Colter's fabulous El Navajo hotel and restaurant—was added on to the depot in 1923, but has long since been demolished.) Buses and trains still run in and out of the station (this is where riders pickup Amtrak's historic *Southwest Chief* on its twice-daily run). The cultural center includes a café (where you can lunch or sip coffee out of replicas of the china used on AT&S trains), a cinema that screens documentaries about the Southwest, changing art exhibits, and two dozen dioramas that relate the history of area native peoples, Western expansion, and the building of the railroads. In summer there are Native American dances in the courtyard at 7 every night. ✉*201 E. Historic Rte. 66* ☎*505/863–4131* 💰*Free* ☉*Late May–early Sept., daily 9–9; early Sept.–late May, daily 9–4.*

In spring, summer, and early fall, wildflowers add brilliance to the landscape of **Red Rock State Park,** which has two popular hiking trails (the 3-mi Pyramid Rock Trail hits an elevation of 7,487 feet, and has knockout views of the formation to go with it), campgrounds, and a museum.The park's red-rock amphitheater holds the ever-growing **Gallup Inter-Tribal Indian Ceremonial** (☎ *505/863–3896* ⊕*www.gallup-ceremonial.org*). Gallup's premier event since it began in 1922, over the course of four or five days every August some 50,000 people come to see the dances of more than 50 tribes from across the Americas, watch rodeo events and parades, munch on fry bread, and stroll the native-arts marketplaces. In early December the park hosts a **Balloon Rally** ☎*505/863–3743 or 800/380–4989* ⊕*www.redrockballoonrally.com*); although it's smaller in scale than Albuquerque's international extravaganza, the setting here makes this one special. The **Red Rock Museum** contains well-mounted exhibits of jewelry, pottery, rugs, architecture, and tools of the Anasazi, Zuni, Hopi, and Navajo, as well as native plantings. ✉*NM 566, Exit 26 or 31 from I-40, 7 mi east of Gallup* ☎*505/722–3839 park, 505/863–1337 museum* 💰*Park free, museum (suggested donation) $1* ☉*Park Nov.–Feb., daily 8–4:30; Mar.–mid-May, daily 8–6; mid-May–mid-Sept., daily 7:30 AM–10 PM; mid-Sept.–Oct., daily 7:30–6. Museum weekdays 8:30–4:30.*

Window Rock Monument & Navajo Veteran's Memorial Park, at the base of an immense, red-sandstone, natural arch—truly a window onto the Navajo landscape—is a compelling exhibit dedicated to all Navajo war veterans, but in particular to the Code Talkers of World War II. Designed in the shape of a sacred Medicine Wheel, the spiritual aspect of this profound memorial is apparent to all. ✉*On Rte. 12 at NM/AZ*

264, ¼ mi west of Arizona border (23 mi northwest of Gallup), Window Rock, AZ 86515 ☎*928/871–6647, guided tours 928/871–6417* ⊕*navajonationparks.org* ▣*Free* ⊙*Daily 8–5.*

Close by the memorial park sits the modern hogan-inspired form of the **Navajo Nation Museum.** Inside visitors will find a complete authentic hogan, as well as small and changing exhibits that explore the culture and history of the tribe. (✉*Loop Rd. at NM/AZ 264, ¼ mi west of Arizona border (23 mi northwest of Gallup), Window Rock, AZ 86515* ☎*928/871–7941* ⊕*www.discovernavajo.com* ▣*Free* ⊙*Tues.–Sat. 8–5.*

OFF THE
BEATEN
PATH
Canyon de Chelly National Monument. Ninety-eight miles northwest of Gallup, past Window Rock on AZ Route 264, Canyon de Chelly—pronounced de-*shay*—is well worth the drive and a day of exploring. Amid its fascinating pueblo ruins, Navajo residents farm and raise sheep in the canyon. The visitor center and museum are open all year, and from there, or at nearby **Thunderbird Lodge** (☎*928/674–5841*) you can book tours on the canyon bottom—by vehicle or, even more memorably, by horseback—with Navajo guides, or drive the canyon rim and take the self-guided hikes. A guide will cost about $15 per hour, per vehicle, and is well worth doing if your budget allows. Campgrounds and lodging are available in Chinle. ✉*NM/AZ Rte. 264 west (through Window Rock), then north on U.S. 191 30 mi to Chinle , Chinle, AZ* ☎*928/674–5500* ⊕*www.nps.gov/cach* ▣*Free* ⊙*Daily 8–5.*

Directly en route to Canyon de Chelly, **Hubbell Trading Post**, in operation since 1878, is still active (though operated by the National Park Service now). With its creaking wood floors, dim lighting, and goods hanging from the rafters, Hubbell provides a palpable sense of what a post was like back in the day. ✉*NM/AZ Rte. 264, 1 mi west of U.S. 191S, Ganado, AZ 86505* ☎*520/755–3475* ⊕*www.nps.gov/hutr* ▣*Free; Hubbell home tours $2* ⊙*Late Apr.–early Sept., daily 8–6; early Sept.–late Apr., daily 8–5.*

⚠ **Canyon de Chelly National Monument/Cottonwood Campgrounds.** Rustling cottonwood trees shade campsites that serve both RVs and tents. ✉*AZ Rte. 264, 3 mi east of AZ Rte. 191, Chinle, AZ* ☎*928/674–5501* ⚒*Flush toilets, dump station, drinking water, fire pits, picnic tables, public telephone* ⏏*104 tent and RV sites* ⚑*Reservations not accepted.*

SPORTS & THE OUTDOORS

In addition to its panoramic Pyramid Rock and Church Rock trails at Red Rock State Park, Gallup is a growing resource for mountain bikers, hikers, and rock climbers. The **High Desert Trail System** begins at Gamerco, a former coal town just north of Gallup, and courses from east to west offer increasingly difficult terrain along a single track. ✉*High Desert Trail System, east trailhead: 3 mi north of Gallup off U.S. 491.*

Mentmore Rock Climbing Area challenges even the nonvertiginous with bolted top-rope and sports climbs that range from 25 to 45 vertical feet ✉ *Mentmore Rd., on the west end of Gallup, ½ mi from I–40 Exit 16 to CR 1* ⊕*www.adventuregallup.org.*

WHERE TO EAT

¢ ✕**Coal Street Pub.** Gallup's first pub has arrived at long last. There are
AMERICAN plenty of bars in this town, for sure, but this is a friendly, relaxed pub,
locally owned by the Chavez family. A good selection of beer is backed
up with tasty Western favorites: burgers, bratwurst, steaks, salads, fish,
and crispy, gooey appetizers. ⊠*303 W. Coal Ave.* ☎*505/722–0117*
▤*MC, V.*

¢ ✕**Earl's Restaurant.** If you have time for only one meal in Gallup, do as
SOUTHWESTERN most people do and head to Earl's. The home-style rib-sticking daily
★ specials here include meat loaf and fried chicken with mashed potatoes, as well as some of the best green chile in all New Mexico. This is
a classic Southwestern diner, down to the Naugahyde booths and the
Western Americana objects hanging on the walls. It's a custom here
for Native American jewelry vendors to go table to table displaying
their wares. Simply say "No, thank you" if you're not interested and
the vendor will leave. ⊠*1400 E. Historic Rte. 66* ☎*505/863–4201*
▤*AE, D, DC, MC, V.*

¢ ✕**El Sombrero.** Open daily, and serving up fine traditional New Mexi-
NEW MEXICAN can–style enchiladas, and the like, it's the cozy alternative to Earl's.
⊠*1201 W. Historic Rte. 66* ☎*505/863–4554* ⌕*Reservations not
accepted* ▤*AE, MC, V.*

WHERE TO STAY

$ ▥**El Rancho.** For a combination of aging '50s-era nostalgia and Old
Fodor'sChoice West glamour, book a night in El Rancho's Katharine Hepburn or Ron-
★ ald Reagan room. All units at this 1937 National Register historic
property are named for vintage movie stars, many of whom stayed here
back when Hollywood westerns were shot in the region (the connection goes deeper—El Rancho was built by R.E. Griffith, D.W. Griffith's
brother). Rooms are basic, accented with Western prints and a few
other flourishes. The restaurant ($), open all day, is cozy and serves
acceptable American and Mexican food. You can browse through
the on-site shop for pottery, kachinas, and sand paintings. **Pros:** Gor-
geously appointed Western-rustic lobby; at Christmas the lights—and
two-story tree—are a serious throwback, and an assuredly warming
sight. **Cons:** Rooms do vary—don't be shy about asking to see a few; no
reason to stay in the attached motel portion of the complex. ⊠*1000 E.
Historic Rte. 66* ☎*505/863–9311 or 800/543–6351* ⎙*505/722–5917*
⊕*www.elranchohotel.com* ⇆*73 rooms, 3 suites* ⌕*In-hotel: restaurant, bar, no-smoking rooms* ▤*AE, D, MC, V.*

$ ▥**Sleep Inn.** Stay here and you get a reasonably priced motel room with
all the basics: chairs, a dresser, TV with remote, Internet service, and a
phone. The pool offers the expected respite from the dry desert climate.
Pros: Next to a Denny's; easy highway access; pets allowed. **Cons:**
Stripped-down basic, and the walls are thin; pets allowed. ⊠*3820 E.
Historic Rte. 66* ☎*505/863–3535 or 800/753–3746* ⎙*505/722–3737*
⇆*61 rooms* ⌕*In-room: Internet. In-hotel: pool, no-smoking rooms*
▤*AE, D, DC, MC, V.*

CAMPING

🏕 **Red Rock State Park.** Red rocks loom 500 feet over the park's paved campsites, which are surrounded by red sand and shady trees. ✉*NM 566, Exit 26 or 31 from I–40, 7 mi east of Gallup* ☎*505/722–3839* ♿*Flush toilets, partial hookups, dump station, drinking water, showers, fire pits, picnic tables, public telephone, ranger station* ⟿*160 RV sites* ▤*MC, V.*

SHOPPING

As elsewhere, you should be careful when buying in Gallup. Generally, if a deal seems too good to be true, it is. To assure yourself of authenticity and quality, shop at a reputable, established dealer and ask lots of questions (⇨ *"Buying Smart: Native Arts & Crafts" above*).

At **Richardson's Trading Company** (✉*222 W. Historic Rte. 66* ☎*505/722–4762* ⊕*www.richardsontrading.com*), the great-granddaddy of trading posts, the wooden floors creak under your feet as you gawk at the knockout array of Navajo and Zuni turquoise and silver earrings, squash blossoms, concho belts, bracelets, natural-dye handwoven rugs, and beadwork. Richardson's is also a veritable museum of old pawn (the often valuable, unclaimed items pawned by local Native Americans). Coming up from Zuni on NM 602, travelers will come upon **Ellis Tanner Trading** (✉*1980 NM 602, on the south side of Gallup. Take I–40 Exit 20* ☎*505/863–4434 or 800/469–4434* ⊕*www.etanner. com*), a venerable fourth-generation family operation. Another branch of the Tanner trading family runs **Shush Yaz Trading Co.** (✉*1304 W. Lincoln Ave., off U.S. 491 just north of I–40 Exit 20* ☎*505/722–0130* ⊕*www.shushyaz.com*), which stocks all manner of Native American arts and crafts, including locally made Navajo squaw skirts. The store sells traditional and contemporary jewelry and is a great source of old pawn. The on-site restaurant serves native foods. **Perry Null Trading Co.** (✉*1710 S. 2nd St.* ☎*505/863–5249* ⊕*perrynulltrading.com*) bought out the 80-year-old Tobe Turpen post in 2005; Perry Null, himself a trader since the 1970s, continues to sell kachinas, sand paintings, jewelry, folk art, and more.

EN ROUTE

Heading east on Interstate 40? Usually held on the third Friday of every month, the **Crownpoint Rug Auction** (✉*Crownpoint Elementary School, NM 371, 26 mi north of Thoreau at I–40, Exit 53* ☎*505/786–7386 or 505/786–5302* ⊕*www.crownpointrugauction.com*) is the foremost place to buy handwoven Navajo rugs—you're bidding with a mix of collectors and dealers, so prices on the some 300 to 400 rugs are sometimes well below what you'd pay at a store. Viewing begins at 4, with the actual auction running from 7 usually until midnight or later. Keep in mind there are no overnight facilities in Crownpoint, though there is a food and drink concession at the auction. Call ahead to confirm auction dates. Cash, traveler's checks, personal checks *only*; no credit cards. ■**TIP→If Chaco Canyon is your next stop (via the south entrance, which is also off NM 371), do not drive there after dark. Backtrack 26 mi to Interstate 40 and stay overnight in Grants (30 mi east). Note: NM 371 is also a direct route to Farmington (80 mi north of Crownpoint).**

THE FOUR CORNERS AREA

To gain a sense of the beauty, power, and complexity of the ancient civilizations of the Americas, you can do no better than to travel to Chaco Canyon, sometimes called the "Stonehenge of the West," and the more accessible Salmon Ruins and Aztec Ruins. Discoveries of the past 30 or 40 years have increased interest in ancient roadways and archaeoastronomy—the study of the ways in which ancient peoples surveyed the skies, kept track of the movement of the planets and stars, and marked their passage within the construction of elaborate stone structures. And it is likely that if you are up this way, you already have it in mind to visit Mesa Verde, in nearby southern Colorado, or Canyon de Chelly (Arizona) in addition to these New Mexico sites.

But the Four Corners region is more than the Ancestral Pueblo ruins of the 12 and 13th centuries. The Navajo reservation covers much of the western portion of the area; the Jicarilla Apache are on the east, the Southern Ute to the north. Near the trout-fishing mecca of Navajo Dam, the Gobernador area, with its striking sandstone formations, is also home to a host of Navajo, or Dinetah, pueblitos which date back to the late 17th and 18th centuries. And everywhere, spectacular hiking, biking, camping, and fishing can be had, along with the opportunity to poke through small towns that are the products of northwestern New Mexico's homesteading era. The best shopping is for antiques, Navajo rugs, and Native American jewelry and pottery.

FARMINGTON

142 mi north of Gallup via I–40 east to NM 371 north.

A rough-and-tumble, unpretentious town full of pickup trucks, whose radio dial is loaded with country-and-western stations, Farmington sits in the heart of the Four Corners region (so called because four different states intersect here at one point). Archaeological, recreational, and scenic wonders are within easy driving distance, and its reasonable prices and friendly ways make it an ideal base for exploring the area. (Farmington is also big for the energy biz and major summertime events like the Connie Mack World Series and the National High School Rodeo finals; book ahead accordingly.)

The Navajo gave the name *Totah* ("among the waters") to the land around what is now Farmington, which lies at the confluence of three rivers—the Animas, La Plata, and San Juan. For both travelers and locals, the presence of these flowing waters gives welcome respite from the surrounding region's dry mesas. Homesteaders began planting farms and orchards on the fertile land in 1879, and the "farming town" eventually became Farmington.

The agricultural economy shifted to one based on oil and gas in the early 1920s, beginning a boom-and-bust cycle tied to the fluctuation of fuel prices. Diversification didn't come until the past decade or so, when Farmington began promoting its historic past with more gusto. Even more revitalizing overall—though it's had a mixed effect on the

BISTI BADLANDS

Dinosaurs roamed the **Bisti Badlands** and **De-Na-Zin Wilderness areas** when they were part of a shallow sea some 70 million years ago. Hoodoos (mushroom-shaped rock formations in subtle shades of brown, gray, and white) lend the 45,000 acres an eerie, lunar appearance. De-Na-Zin (pronounced *duh-nah*-zen and named for a petroglyph found nearby) is the much larger and less visited of the two sections, and here you can find hillier and more challenging terrain, plus numerous fossils and petrified logs. At Bisti (pronounced *biss*-tye), you can encounter deeply eroded hoodoos whose striations represent layers of sandstone, shale, mudstone, coal, and silt. In many spots you'll climb over mounds of crumbly clay and silt that look a bit like the topping of a coffee cake (but gray). Both sections are ideal for photography, and backcountry camping is permitted—and not to be missed during

a full moon, if your timing is good. The Bureau of Land Management (BLM), which administers the land, asks that you remove nothing from either area, preserving its magical appearance for those who follow. The most fascinating terrain is 2 to 3 mi from the parking areas, and there are no trails (or water facilities), so bring a compass and be alert about your surroundings and where you are in relation to the sun—it's relatively easy to get lost in this vast, incredible place. And how 'bout bringing some more water? ⊠ *Bisti: NM 371, 36 mi south of Farmington; De-Na-Zin: unpaved CR 7500, off either NM 371 8 mi south of Bisti entrance or NM 550 at Huerfano, 34 mi south of Bloomington. Roads can be impassable in wet weather, and high-clearance vehicles are advised in all conditions. Contact the BLM Field Office in Farmington for complete information.* ☎ *505/599–8900* ⊕ *www.blm.gov.*

fortunes of the historic downtown—was the creation of a regional shopping center, which swells the population by thousands on weekends. People from miles around make their weekly or monthly trip to town to stock up on supplies.

WHAT TO SEE

You can get an inkling of what the Four Corners area was like during the trading-post days at the **Farmington Museum and Visitor Center,** in a modern sandstone building whose stonework is fashioned to echo that found at Aztec and Chaco ruins. Landscaped grounds behind the building extend down to the Animas River—an ideal spot for a picnic. The museum presents art, science, Native American, and regional history exhibits throughout the year (the "Geovator," goofy as it is, simulates a trip deep into the subsurface stratigraphy of limestone, sandstone, and shale that yields oil and natural gas wealth for the region). Occasionally a traveling exhibit will require an entrance fee; otherwise, admission is free. There's a summertime music series on the terrace; 6–7:30 PM, call for dates and performers. And the visitor center will supply you with all the maps and brochures you need for ventures farther into the Four Corners. ⊠ *3041 E. Main St., at Gateway Park on the east side of Browning Pkwy.* ☎ *505/599–1174* *museum, 800/448–1240 visitor center* ✉*Free, $2 donation requested* ⏰*Mon.–Sat. 8–5* ⊕*www.farmingtonmuseum.org.*

☾ **Riverside Nature Center**, with its immense colony of Gunnison's prairie dogs and family activities most weekends, anchors the east end of the city's lovely and revivifying **River Corridor.** A 3¼-mi walkway and bike path meanders along the Animas River; hidden, yet right in the center of town, it passes through Animas and Berg parks and ends just behind the Scott Avenue hotel strip on the west. The corridor contains 5½ additional mi of side trails for walkers, runners, cyclists, and wildlife- and bird-watchers, as well as a man-made, 300-yard-long white-water course. ⊠*Riverside Nature Center: in Animas Park off Browning Pkwy. at U.S. 64* ☎*505/599–1422* ⏰*Tues.–Sat. 1–6, Sun. 1–5.*

☾ If the kids need some indoor fun, try stopping by the **E³ Children's Museum & Science Center.** The interactive exhibits here include a shadow room, a magnet table, giant floor puzzles, and a role-play area. It's a low-key spot for the younger set to rest and regroup. ⊠*302 N. Orchard Ave.87401* ☎*505/599–1425* ✉*Free* ⏰*Tues.–Sat. noon–5.*

Bolack Electromechanical Museum is the legacy of former state governor Tom Bolack, who collected wildlife of the taxidermic kind. His son Tommy carries on the collecting tradition, but his museum on the family's B-Square Ranch is a wonder of large-scale, unexpected, electrical items, from aged radio-station transmitters and all the car speakers from the old Rincon Drive-In in Aztec, to a three-stage compressor from a Nevada uranium testing site, a 16-foot-diameter drill bit, and an entire electrical substation. Set back into the bluffs on the south side of town, the spread itself is a sight even if all the objects here don't appeal. Keep an eye out for the peacocks on the road in. **Note:** You must stop and register at the first buildings you see. ⊠*3901 Bloomfield Hwy.* ☎*505/325–4275* ⊕*www.bolackmuseum.com* ✉*Free* ⏰*Appointment only, 1–2 hour guided tours, Mon.–Sat. 9–3.*

▌ **OFF THE BEATEN PATH**

Shiprock Peak. West of Farmington, at U.S. 491 (though the odd map will still refer to this road by its old number, 666) and U.S. 64, just southwest of the town of Shiprock, 1,700-foot Shiprock Peak rises from the desert floor like a massive schooner. It's sacred to the Navajo, who call it Tse'Bit'Ai, or "rock with wings." No climbing or hiking is permitted. The formation—sometimes referred to as a pinnacle—is composed of igneous rock flanked by upright walls of solidified lava.

Four Corners Monument. About 30 mi west of Shiprock you can reach the only place in the United States where you can stand in four states at the same time—at the intersection of New Mexico, Arizona, Colorado, and Utah. There's no view to speak of at this popular attraction, though Native American artisans do sell their wares here nearly every day of the year. ⊠*U.S. 160, north from U.S. 64* ☎*928/871–6647* ✉*$3* ⏰*May–Aug., daily 7 AM–8 PM; Sept.–Apr., daily 8–5.*

WHERE TO EAT

¢ ✕**Andrea Kristina's Bookstore & Kafé.** Right downtown, Andrea Kristina's
AMERICAN is a rare find for Farmington: the consummate cozy bookstore-cum-
Internet café (free Wi-Fi) that serves great—read: healthy, fresh, creative, *and* tasty—food throughout the day. Coffee, too, of course, or
Oregon chai latte if you prefer. Chef Ira's veggie breakfast burrito is
special (the version with chorizo is as well); the lunch-and-dinner menu
covers territory like a hot Anaïs Nin sandwich (broiled chicken with
pesto, on ciabatta), a range of custom pizzas, and a flock of substantial
salads, from Mediterranean spinach to avocado shrimp. Live entertainment Thursday through Saturday evenings. ✉*218 W. Main St. 87401*
☎*505/327–3313* ⊕*www.andreakristinas.com* ⌨*Reservations not
accepted* ▭*AE, MC, V* ✛*Closed Sun.*

$$ ✕**Emilio's Grill & Bar.** Sit outside on the patio, or ask for a booth inside
MEXICAN and settle in. Order up an ice-cold Steam Works microbrewed ale, and
Fodor'sChoice try not to get full on the fresh chips and uniquely tangy cilantro-laced
★ salsa. Plates here are more like serving platters, and traditional *maris-
cos* dishes like *camarones ala diablo* are so good that it's hard not to
eat past the stuffing point. Sharing is good. Landlocked or not, Emilio's
serves up Mexican-style seafood items like stuffed red snapper or a
whole deep-fried tilapia. New Mexican dishes are available, too. Spe-
cials can be quite pricey, but items off the regular menu keep the budget
in check. There's pop-rock music on the patio on summer weekends.
✉*525 E. Broadway* ☎*505/327–2270* ▭*AE, MC, V.*

$$ ✕**K. B. Dillon's.** The punched-tin ceiling and dark-wood furnishings
STEAK feed the appeal of this clubby steak house. The steak-averse can make
do with another house specialty, Shrimp Dillon, or a decent pasta, but
really, the local grass-fed beef's the thing—and a cold one from the
selection of over 30 local microbrews. There's live music on weekend nights. ✉*101 W. Broadway* ☎*505/325–0222* ▭*AE, MC, V*
✛*Closed Sun.*

¢ ✕**The Spare Rib.** The decor here is nothing fancy—just plastic table-
SOUTHERN cloths over picnic tables—but the whole family can fill up on generous
portions of delicious smoked pork and beef barbecue. Ribs and brisket are as tender as they come, all slow-cooked in house-made sauce.
✉*1700 E. Main St.* ☎*505/325–4800* ⌨*Reservations not accepted*
▭*AE, D, MC, V* ✛*Closed Sun.*

$ ✕**Three Rivers Eatery & Brewhouse.** In a 1912 one-time drugstore with
AMERICAN a gorgeous pressed-tin ceiling, exposed air ducts, and walls lined with
★ vintage photos, this microbrewery whips up more than 10 kinds of beer
(also available to go) with names like Roustabout Stout and Chaco
Nut Brown Ale. The brews go well with the enormous portions of
tasty soups, salads, burgers, ribs, and other basic pub grub served here.
Stroll down the block a bit to find a friendly local scene at its **Tap Room**
and pool-hall outpost. Respectably dingy (some of the patina from its
original incarnation as Fred Carson's Trading Post remains), occasional
live music draws a diverse crowd. ✉*101 E. Main St.* ☎*505/324–2187*
⊕*www.threeriversbrewery.com* ⌨*Reservations not accepted* ▭*AE,
MC, V* ✛*Closed Sun.*

6

WHERE TO STAY

$$ ☷ **Casa Blanca Inn.** Luxury without pretense is the trademark at this Mission-style inn, which stands atop a bluff overlooking Farmington. You can relax in the Southwestern-style den or near the patio's fountain, or watch city lights twinkle from the solarium. One room has a two-person hot tub, another has a fireplace, most have porches that face the lovely gardens, some face the bluffs, and all are beautifully appointed. Breakfast is a gourmet affair, and fresh-baked goodies are served in the afternoon. Business travelers seeking a homey atmosphere make it a point to stay in this little oasis. **Pros:** The innkeepers are well-informed on local doings; they are also rightfully proud of their hand-tended gardens that reap heirloom tomatoes and lavender. **Cons:** The hosts' attentiveness might seem intrusive to some. ⊠ *505 E. La Plata St.* ☏ *505/327–6503 or 800/550–6503* ⊕ *www.casablancanm.com* ↩ *4 rooms, 1 suite* ⟜ *In-room: kitchen (some). In-hotel: no-smoking rooms, gym, laundry facilities, Wi-Fi* ⊟*AE, MC, V* ⦿*BP.*

$$$ ☷ **Kokopelli's Cave.** Carved into the cliff side 250 feet above the La Plata
★   River and surrounded by distant mountains (on a clear day you can see Shiprock and the Chuskas), this man-made cave's exposed sandstone walls trace 70 million years of erosion history. Blasted out in the 1980s and '90s—and originally intended as a getaway office for a local geologist—the decor is generally modern, with a bit of a 1960s "conversation pit" feel. It's laid out like a home, with a fireplace in the den, full kitchen, and a rustic shower that trickles into a hot tub. Two terraces provide breathtaking views, and a trail on the cliff face runs some 70 vertical feet to the parking area. The cave accommodates up to six people and remains a temperate 72°F year-round. Book at least one month in advance. Note: Guests are instructed to stop at the manager's home to check in before going to the cave. Lindy Poole, the congenial manager, will accompany all visitors on their first time out—and fill them in on some of the antics it took to outfit the place. **Pros:** The space is immaculate, and more spacious—tall people will be comfortable—than photos indicate; it is a truly unique experience to stay inside a cave on a cliff dwelling. **Cons:** Caves aren't easy to access, especially with large luggage; food supplied is supermarket-deli caliber. ⊠ *The cave parking area is about 20 minutes northwest from downtown Farmington* ☏ *505/325–7855, 505/326–2461 manager* ⊕*www. bbonline.com/nm/kokopelli* ↩ *1 unit* ⟜ *In-room: no a/c. In-hotel: no kids under 12, no-smoking rooms* ⊟*AE, MC, V* ⦿*CP.*

$ ☷ **The Region Inn.** The Region is plain-Jane from the front, and inside the rooms are a bit dark, but all are updated and comfortable. The three-story motel is independently owned, and the staff's accessibility and responsiveness reflects that. Tequila's restaurant off to the side is quite serviceable and fun for a drink at least. ⊠ *601 E. Broadway* ☏*505/325–1191 or 888/325–1911* ⊕*www.theregioninn.com* ↩*75 rooms, 2 suites* ⟜ *In-room: Internet, Wi-Fi, refrigerator. In-hotel: pool, no-smoking rooms, Wi-Fi* ⊟*AE, D, MC, V* ⦿*CP.*

$$ ☷ **Silver River Adobe Inn.** Take a deep breath and relax at this red-roof adobe. It's perched on a cottonwood-covered sandstone cliff 30 feet above the junction of the San Juan River and the La Plata. Rough-hewn timbers, fluffy quilts, and complete privacy make this rustic getaway ideal for romance or rumination, though the property and the proprietors are definitely kid-friendly. The proprietors, Diana Ohlson and David Beers, are smart, down-to-earth, and excellent sources of information about adventures and explorations in the area. Organic, home-style breakfasts such as light and puffy Dutch Babies, waffles, crepes, peach clafouti, pumpkin bread, or Tuscan apple cake are a great start to the day. Those interested in sustainability will appreciate the inn's use of solar collectors and the heat-holding adobe construction. **Pros:** Diana maintains a massage practice on-site; all rooms have private entrances, baths, and river views. **Cons:** No TV, phone, or Internet. ⊠*3151 W. Main St., Box 3411* ☎*505/325–8219 or 800/382–9251* ⊕*www.silveradobe.com* ⇆*2 rooms, 1 suite* ♻*In-room: kitchen (some), no TV, no phone* ⊟*AE, MC, V* ⊚*BP.*

NIGHTLIFE & THE ARTS

Several Farmington restaurants are popular for cocktails, notably K. B. Dillon's, Three Rivers Eatery & Brewhouse, and Emilio's. All have live music on weekend nights; the last offers good sunset views from its street-front patio as you listen. Andrea Kristina's Bookstore & Kafé is a more intimate (though booze-free) setting for acoustic country and jazz on Friday and Saturday nights; there is also an occasional movie on the program.

Summer stock rules at the **Lions Wilderness Amphitheater** (⊠ *Lions Wilderness Park, College Blvd. at Piñon Hills Blvd.* ☎*877/599–3311 or 505/599–1140* ⊕*www.fmtn.org/sandstone*) between mid-June and mid-August. Broadway shows are the usual fare of the Sandstone Theatre's series, which is presented outdoors here in a natural sandstone amphitheater. Performances are usually in the evening, Thursday–Sunday; prior to each show, guests may enjoy an optional Southwestern-style dinner. **San Juan College Theater** (⊠*4601 College Blvd.* ☎*505/566–3430 or 505/327–0076*) presents performances by the San Juan Symphony and other concerts, student recitals, and theatrical performances.

SPORTS & THE OUTDOORS

Fly-fishing is the pre-eminent sport in the San Juan River region. The heart of this prime fishing is at Navajo Dam, about 30 mi east of Farmington (⇨ *Navajo Dam below*). Farmington itself draws a goodly group of mountain bikers and golfers, and with good reason.

BIKING **Cottonwood Cycles** is a good local source for mountain- (and road-) bike equipment and guidance. ⊠*4370 E. Main St. 87402* ☎*505/326–0429* ☉*Mon.–Sat. 10–5.*

Glade Run Recreation Area. The 30-mi Road Apple Rally—around since 1981, it was one of the first of its kind for mountain bikes—runs here every October. During the rest of the year, bikers can traverse over 19,000 challenging acres of slick rock and sandy washes. Trails in the north end of the Glade are marked for mountain- and dirt-bike use only; the more southerly trails are shared with ATVs. Check at the BLM office or local bike stores for maps and information. ⊠*1235*

La Plata Hwy. ☎*505/599–8900* ⊕*www.nm.blm.gov* ▣*Free* ⊙*daily, dawn–dusk.*

GOLF   Consistently rated one of the best municipal courses in the country, **Piñon Hills Golf Course** (✉*2101 Sunrise Pkwy. 87402* ☎*505/326–6066* ⊕*www.fmtn.org/pinonhills* ▣*18 holes, residents $21 Mon.–Fri., $25 Sat. & Sun; nonresidents $40 Mon.–Fri, $46 Sat. & Sun.* ⊙*Mar.–Oct., daily dawn–dusk; Nov.–Feb., daily 9–5*) offers striking desert views and very low greens fees.

WATER   **Farmington Aquatic Center**, an indoor water wonderland, has a 150-foot-
SPORTS   long waterslide and three pools. Prices for the pool and slide are $5 for adults, $3.25–$4.50 for children; 2 and under free. ✉*1151 N. Sullivan St.* ☎*505/599–1167* ⊙ *Mon. and Fri. 4:30–7:30, Wed. and Sat. 1–7:30*

SHOPPING

The historic trading-post district along Main Street downtown (about a five-block stretch from Auburn Avenue east to Orchard Avenue, at Three Rivers Brewhouse) is a good place to look for antiques, especially 20th-century Southwestern Americana, and native arts.

In a town with two super-sized Wal-Marts and a Target, a shopping round-up would not be complete without mentioning the gargantuan **Animas Valley Mall** (✉*4601 E. Main St.* ☎*505/326–5465*). Expect the usual chain suspects, plus a multiplex movie theater. To break the chain step out to Dad's Diner next door (✉*4395 Largo St.* ☎*505/564–2516*); it's fun, open on Sunday—not much else is—and a major cut above mall food.

Emerson Gallery (✉*121 W. Main St.* ☎*505/599–8597* ⊕*www.emerson gallery.com*) highlights the modern, appealing paintings and prints of Anthony Chee Emerson. His bright yet harmonious palette is decidedly nontraditional, yet his themes speak—sometimes in the same piece—to Indian history and contemporary issues.

Detour one block south to **Fifth Generation Trading Co.** (✉*232 W. Broadway* ☎*505/326–3211*), an old trading post run by the Tanner family since 1875. Big and distinctly tourist-driven these days, it has a wealth of Native American wares and is known for sand paintings. About a half-hour drive west of town, in Waterflow, are a number of old-time posts, including the **Hogback Trading Co.** (✉*3221 U.S. 64, in Waterflow* ☎*505/598–5154 or 505/598–9243*). A fourth-generation operation in business since 1871, it is especially known for fine, hand-woven Navajo rugs.

An intriguing spread of vintage goods—from mid-century lamp shades and signed, original, hand-painted pottery with Old Mexico themes, to sweet hankies, 1930s and '40s printed tablecloths and aprons, deco jewelry—all at surprisingly good prices, make **Old Faithful** (✉*108 W. Main St.* ☎*505/326–3641*) a worthy stop.

The Shiprock Trading Co. (✉*301 W. Main St.* ☎*505/324–0881 or 800/210–7847* ⊕*www.shiprocktrading.com*), established in 1894, came to Farmington in 2007. What sets this location off from its brethren in Santa Fe and Albuquerque is its direct connection to the Navajo artisans who come here to buy the richly dyed skeins of wool that collectors will eventually see in their finished rugs. Stop here to view a good selection of topical books, outstanding jewelry from Indian artists creating contemporary designs from traditional materials, rare Chieftain rugs, and almost as rare Zuni and Navajo pawn.

BLOOMFIELD/SALMON RUINS

★ *10 mi east of Farmington on U.S. 64.*

Little Bloomfield sits at the crossroads of the Four Corners. It's a great place to stay if you're heading south to Chaco Canyon; it's equally good as a stepping-off point to Farmington, Aztec, Navajo Lake, and Mesa Verde. Pick up supplies here, refuel at one of the locally run cafés, and absolutely leave time to tour Salmon Ruins.

Salmon (pronounced *sol*-mon) **Ruins**, which dates from the 11th century, is a large Chacoan Anasazi living complex on the northern edge of the San Juan River. It's a stunning example of pre-Columbian Pueblo architecture and stonework—the masonry is much finer than that at Aztec; the Chaco connection is immediately clear here. The site is named for a homesteader whose family protected the ruins for nearly a century. **Heritage Park** contains the restored Salmon Homestead, a root cellar, bunkhouse, sweat lodge, hogan, and other types of native housing structures. Salmon also runs off-road tours, all guided by field experts; check with them about routes through Chaco Canyon, Bisti Badlands, and Dinétah pueblitos, their extraordinary specialty. ⊠*6131 U.S. 64, 2 mi west of U.S. 550* ☎*505/632–2013* ⊕*www.salmonruins.com* ⊠*$3* ☉*Apr.–Oct., daily 9–5; Nov.–Mar., Mon.–Sat. 8–5, Sun. noon–5.*

WHERE TO EAT & STAY

¢ ✕**Triangle Café.** This is "where friends meet to eat," and have been AMERICAN doing so since the late 1950s. Serving three square meals daily (or catch the brunch buffet on weekends), this is the genuine local article. Come for homemade pies (coconut cream, cherry, and more), pork chops, burgers, and solid New Mexican. Sit at the counter, or grab a table or booth. ⊠*506 W. Broadway (U.S. 64), just west of U.S. 550* ☎*505/632–9918* ☰*AE, MC, V.*

$ ⊡**Best Western Territorial Inn & Suites.** Don't confuse this spot with the run-down Best Western in Farmington. Guests here are not only positioned ideally for Chaco access and the rest of the Four Corners' wonders, but can get a good night's sleep in comfortable, mostly quiet quarters, and a nice free breakfast spread to boot. A spacious mural-lined lounge and outdoor patio, plus a well-equipped, if modest, fitness center, Jacuzzi, and lap-style pool complete the scene. ⊠*415 S. Bloomfield Blvd, on U.S. 550 just south of U.S. 64* ☎*505/632–9100* ⊕*www.bestwesternnewmexico.com* ⇆*65* ♺*In-room: Wi-Fi. In-hotel: gym, pool* ☰*AE, MC, V* ⋈*CP.*

CAMPING

⚠**Angel Peak Scenic Area.** The heavenly form of this 7,000-foot-high sandstone formation is visible for miles, but an up-close view is even more rewarding. Get the feel of the canyon rim country and enjoy a hike through badlands formed by an ancient seabed before you pitch your tent. The last 6 mi of road leading to this primitive site are gravel. Wood must be brought in; no electrical hook ups or water. ✉ *County Rd. 7175, off U.S. 550, 15 mi south of Bloomfield* ☎ *505/599–8900* ⊕ *www.blm.gov* ♿ *Pit toilets, picnic tables, fire grate* ⛺*9 tent sites.*

AZTEC

14 mi northeast of Farmington on NM 516, 10 mi north of Bloomfield on U.S. 550.

The many Victorian brick buildings and quaint outlying residential blocks give charming Aztec, the seat of San Juan County, the feeling of a picture-book hometown. Adding to the allure are the views of the far-distant snowcapped mountains north of Durango, Colorado.

Ⓒ The village part of the **Aztec Museum & Pioneer Village** contains more than a dozen late-19th-century buildings—a blacksmith shop, a schoolhouse, a wooden oil derrick, and a log cabin, among others—that convey a sense of life as it used to be lived in these parts. ✉*125 N. Main Ave. (U.S. 550)* ☎*505/334–9829* ⊕*aztecmuseum.org* 💲*$3* ⊙ *Wed.–Sat. 10–4.*

★ Dating from the early 1100s, North America's largest reconstructed Great Kiva (a partially submerged, circular earthen structure used for ceremonial and community-wide activities) and a pueblo dwelling that once contained more than 500 rooms, **Aztec Ruins National Monument and Museum,** makes for a fun stop. The ruins have been designated a World Heritage Site because of their significance in what is known as the Chaco Phenomenon, the extensive multitribal social and economic system that reached far beyond Chaco Canyon. This pueblo was abandoned by the mid-1200s. Early homesteaders thought they'd come across an ancient Aztec ruin, hence the odd name. You only need an hour or so to tour the ruin, which is less spectacular but considerably more accessible than those at Chaco. ✉ *Ruins Rd., ½ mi north of NM 516* ☎*505/334–6174* ⊕*www.nps.gov/azru* 💲*$5* ⊙*Late May–early Sept., daily 8–6; early Sept.–late May, daily 8–5.*

WHERE TO EAT & STAY

$
AMERICAN
✕**Hiway Grill.** There's a blue '50s-era car suspended high on signpost outside; inside, the vintage-car photos, art-deco tables, red-vinyl booths, and super-friendly staff give this decades-old place the feel of an old-time malt shop. Many of the American and New Mexican dishes, like the Mustang Melt (a burger with grilled onions and melted Swiss on rye with Thousand Island dressing), are named for classic cars. Only order a shake if you've really got an appetite or someone to share it with; chocolate is the local favorite. ✉*401 N.E. Aztec Blvd. (NM 516)* ☎*505/334–6533* ▭*AE, D, MC, V* ⊙*Closed Sun.*

ON TO COLORADO: MESA VERDE NATIONAL PARK

If you are up in the Four Corners area, **Mesa Verde National Park** should be on your list of must-sees. Known for its cliff dwellings (spectacular doesn't even begin to describe them), Balcony House, Cliff Palace, and Spruce House are the biggies. Visitors to these ancestral Puebloan ruins are also in for a rare scenic treat—and the hairpin turns that go with it; weather can shut this place down. On-site accommodations include **Far View Lodge** (☎ *800/449–2288*), near the visitor center, and **Morefield Campground** (☎ *800/449–2288*), 4 mi inside the park. ✉ *Off U.S. 160, between Cortez and Mancos in CO* ✛ *about 95 mi from Aztec (via U.S. 550) or from Farmington (via NM 170 or U.S. 491)* ☎ *970/529–4465* ⊕ *www. nps.gov/meve* ✉ *Per vehicle: May 25–Sept. 27 $15 (good for 7 days), $10. rest of year; Ranger-guided tours: $3* ⊙ *Visitor center: daily 8–5; All facilities, museum, and tours vary seasonally—check ahead.*

¢ ✕**Main Street Bistro.** When just the thought of one more plate of heavy
AMERICAN food in hot weather makes you want to *cry*, forestall a meltdown by coming here. Quiches, soups, frittatas, and delicious sandwiches will set you straight, as will their excellent coffee. The Bistro Special is a grilled portobello mushroom sandwich with mixed greens, tomato, sprouts, and a homemade Italian feta dressing. Also worthwhile is the Ultimate, a croissant with thin-sliced turkey, avocado, greens, red onion, crispy bacon, provolone, and creamy avocado dressing. Fresh pastries and desserts are available daily. And there's free Wi-Fi. ✉*122 N. Main Ave. (U.S. 550), across from Aztec Museum* ☎*505/334–0109* ▭*D, MC, V* ⊙*No dinner. Closed Sun.*

$ ☷**Step Back Inn.** Though technically a standard motor hotel, this Victorian-style clapboard structure on the north edge of downtown offers a more distinctive experience than you can have at any of the countless chain properties in nearby Farmington, and at similar prices. The public areas are inviting, and individually decorated rooms have a mix of newer pieces and reproduction antiques, floral wallpaper, and cozy chenille bedspreads. **Pros:** Friendly staff; quiet—it's set-back from the road. **Cons:** It's getting worn on the edges; Wi-Fi doesn't reach all rooms. ✉*123 W. Aztec Blvd. (NM 516) , 1 mi west of U.S. 550, near intersection with NM 574* ☎*505/334–1200 or 800/334–1255* 🖷*505/334–9858* ⇌*40 rooms In-hotel: Wi-Fi (some) AE, MC, V* ⊙|*CP.*

NAVAJO DAM

26 mi east of Aztec on NM 173, or 25 mi east of Bloomfield via NM 64 and NM 511.

Navajo Dam is the name of a tiny town a few miles below Navajo Lake State Park, as well as the name of the dam itself. At the base of the dam lie the legendary "Quality Waters" of the San Juan River. Exceeding the hype, this restricted ¾-mi stretch—a portion of which is catch-and-release only—is one of the country's top five trophy-trout streams. The next 12 mi of the San Juan are open waters with year-round fishing for trout, as well as kokanee salmon, and largemouth and smallmouth bass. The wildlife-friendly river carves a scenic gorge of stepped cliffs along cottonwood-lined banks that attract elk, Barbary sheep, golden and bald eagles, blue herons, and not a few fly fishers in waders.

As you drive up over the dam you will be rewarded with panoramic views down into the valley.

Created in 1962 when the dam was built, the eponymous lake at **Navajo Lake State Park** is a popular boating and fishing spot; you can rent boats at two marinas. Short trails lead to the lakeshore, and the 3-mi-long cottonwood-shaded San Juan River Trail parallels the river down below the dam. Driving the narrow road across the top of the dam, with no guardrails, is a slightly hair-raising, memorable experience. A fishing permit is required. ✉*1448 NM 511, off NM 173 or NM 64* ☎*505/632–2278 or 888/451–2541, reservations 877/664–7787* ⊕*www.nmparks.com* ✍*$5 per vehicle.*

WHERE TO STAY

$$$$
★
🏨 **Soaring Eagle Lodge.** A haven for fly fishers who want casual but upscale accommodations, this lodge houses guests in cabins that are fully furnished, complete with kitchenettes and rod-and-wader racks. You can step out of your cabin to a mile and a half of private river access, or take advantage of the on-site guide service and full fly shop. The food here is excellent, and the location remote, so the package that includes breakfast and dinner is a good choice. **Pros:** Fine chefs, comfortably appointed, and fully wired, with an on-site conference center. **Cons:** Three guests max per cabin; pro guides, but they can triple cost. ✉*48 CR 4370, off NM 511, 7 mi south of Navajo Dam* ☎*505/632–3721 or 800/866–2719* ⊕*www.soaringeaglelodge.net* ✍*11 cabins* ⚷*In-room: kitchen, Wi-Fi* ❏*MAP.*

CAMPING

⛺ **Navajo Lake State Park.** At the park's three campgrounds some sites sit among piñon and juniper trees and overlook the lake. Hot showers are available at Sims Mesa and Pine campgrounds but not at Cottonwood Campground. ✉*1448 NM 511, off NM 173 or NM 64* ☎*505/632–2278 or 888/451–2541,reservations 877/664–7787* ⊕*www.nmparks. com* ⚷*Flush toilets, dump station, drinking water, fire pits, picnic tables* ✍*200 sites.*

SPORTS & THE OUTDOORS

Stop by **Abe's Motel & Fly Shop/Born 'n' Raised on the San Juan** (✉*1791 NM 173* ☎*505/632–2194* ⊕*www.sanjuanriver.com*) to find out what flies you need to snare the wily San Juan rainbows, book a wade or float trip, or just to pick up a cold drink and snacks. There's also lodging here, although it's nothing fancy ($68–$74 per room, some with kitchenettes—but they are BYO for utensils and cookware; there are 59 rooms, all with Wi-Fi). If you're hungry for more than chips, El Pescador's Restaurant & Lounge is next door. At the revered **Rizuto's Fly Shop & San Juan River Lodge** (✉*1796 NM 173* ☎*505/632–3893,* *lodge 505/632–1411)*, you can pick up fishing tips or book a guide; or stay overnight in a very basic room ($78 per, each with refrigrator, microwave—and a fly-tying table).

CHACO CULTURE NATIONAL HISTORICAL PARK

Fodor's Choice *90 mi south of Farmington via U.S. 550 to CR 7900 (paved) / CR 7950*
★ *(unpaved) south; 144 mi west of Abiquiu via NM 96 to U.S. 550, then north to CR 7900 (paved) / CR 7950 (unpaved) south; 78 mi north of Grants via I–40, Exit 53 to NM 57 (rough dirt) north.*

The roads accessing **Chaco Canyon**, home to Chaco Culture National Historical Park, do a fine job of deterring exploration: they are mostly unpaved and can be very muddy and/or icy during inclement weather (particularly Route 57 from the south). The silver lining is that the roads leading in—and the lack of gas stations, food concessions, or hotels once you get off the highway—keep this archaeological treasure free from the overcrowding that can mar other national park visits: only about 85,000 people visit annually, compared with at least 10 times that number to Canyon de Chelly, which is 80 mi away as the crow flies.

6

Once past the rough roads you'll see one of the most amazingly well-preserved and fascinating ruin sites on the continent. The excavations here have uncovered what was once the administrative and economic core of a vast community—the locus of a system of over 400 mi of ancient roads that have been identified to date. While there is evidence that people lived in the canyon at least since 400 AD, the majority of these roads, and the buildings and dwellings that make up the canyon site, were constructed from 850 to 1250 AD. Several of the ancient structures—such as an immense Great Kiva, Casa Rinconada, or Pueblo Bonito—are simply astounding, if only for the extreme subtlety and detail of their precisely cut and chinked sandstone masonry. But there's still a shroud of mystery surrounding them. Did 5,000 people really once live here, as some archaeologists believe? Or was Chaco maintained solely as a ceremonial and trade center? The more that's learned about the prehistoric roadways and the outlying sites that they connect, or wondrous creations such as the **Sun Dagger**—an arrangement of stone slabs positioned to allow a spear of sunlight to pass through and bisect a pair of spiral petroglyphs precisely at each summer solstice—the more questions arise about the sophistication of the people that created them.

At the **visitor center** you can meander through a small museum on Chaco culture, peruse the bookstore, buy bottled water (but no food), and inquire about hiking permits. From here you can drive (or bike) along the 9-mi paved inner loop road to the various trailheads for the ruins; at each you can find a small box containing a detailed self-guided tour brochure (a 50¢ donation per map is requested). Many of the 13 ruins at Chaco require a significant hike, but a few of the most impressive are just a couple hundred yards off the road. The stargazing here is spectacular: there is a small observatory and numerous telescopes, which are brought out for star parties; ask about the schedule at the front desk. **Pueblo Bonito** is the largest and most dramatic of the Chaco Canyon ruins, a massive semicircular "great house" that once stood four stories in places and held some 600 rooms (*and* 40 kivas). The park trail runs alongside its fine outer mortar-and-sandstone walls, up a hill that allows a great view over the entire canyon, and then right through the ruin and several rooms. It's the most substantial of the structures—the ritualistic and cultural center of a Chacoan culture that may once have comprised some 150 settlements. *Box 220, Nageezi, NM 87037* ⊹ *North entrance: Take U.S. 550 3 mi east of Nageezi, then turn south onto CR 7900; continue 5 mi to CR 7950 (16 mi, unpaved), follow signs to the visitor center. South entrance: Take I–40 to Thoreau, Exit 53, then north on NM 371; just past Crownpoint (26 mi) turn east onto Navajo 9 to Seven Lakes (12 mi), then north on NM 57 (20 mi, rough dirt) to visitor center* ☎ *505/786–7014* ⊕ *www.nps.gov/chcu* ✉ *$8 per vehicle* ⊙ *Park: Daily dawn to dusk; visitor center: daily 8–5.*

WHERE TO STAY

⚠ **Chaco Culture National Historical Park.** Not far from the visitor center is a park service–operated campground. The site's primitiveness is its greatest asset: at night the skies come alive with stars, and the only noises you can hear are those of nature. The primary advantage of staying here is waking up in the canyon and having a full day to explore the ruins and perhaps hike some of the backcountry trails. Camping is limited to seven days; vehicles up to 30 feet can park here. Drinking water is available at the visitor center. Starting in early May it's best to arrive as early in the day as possible; the campground fills quickly. Reservations are not accepted, except for groups. ⊹ *North entrance: Take U.S. 550 3 mi east of Nageezi, then turn south onto CR 7900; continue 5 mi to CR 7950 (16 mi, unpaved), follow signs to the visitor center. South entrance: Take I–40 to Thoreau, Exit 53, then north on NM 371; just past Crownpoint (26 mi) turn east onto Navajo 9 to Seven Lakes (12 mi), then north on NM 57 (20 mi, rough dirt) to visitor center* ☎ *505/786–7014* ⚐ *Flush toilets, fire grates, picnic tables* ⤳ *47 sites.*

EN ROUTE Whether you're coming or going from Chaco's north entrance, or simply heading south on U.S. 550, **Cuba** is a good place to stop for gas and, depending on your inclination and the season, hot coffee or a cold soda. Remnants of when this route was the notoriously unsafe—and much narrower—NM 44, there are gas stations, a convenience store, and **El Bruno's** (✉ *U.S. 550 at NM 126* ☎ *505/289–9429*), a decent Mexican restaurant that's right on the highway, plus a handful of inexpensive motels that could serve for a pre- or post-Chaco overnighter; your best bet in this regard is the **Cuban Lodge** (✉ *6332 U.S. 550* ☎ *505/289–3475*). If you've got some time to spare, visit **Pueblo Pintado,** about 60 mi west, on Navajo Route 9 via NM 197 from Cuba. The village is little more than a few houses and a convenience store, but the Chacoan ruins are spectacular and easy to find (you can also do the reverse and get here by sneaking out of Chaco the south way, but turn east on Navajo 9 instead of west). Continue south on U.S. 550 in daylight if at all possible (late afternoon is perfect): the views only get more spectacular as you go. Watch for Cabezon Peak on your right.

JICARILLA APACHE RESERVATION

55 mi east of Navajo Dam on U.S. 64; 36 mi west of Chama on U.S. 64.

The Spanish named the Jicarilla tribe (pronounced "hick-uh-*ree*-ya," meaning little basket), for their beautiful basketry. For centuries before the arrival of the Spanish, these Native Americans, who were related to the Navajo and Apache, were a nomadic people who roamed across northeastern New Mexico, southeastern Colorado, and the Oklahoma and Texas panhandles. Their tribe of 10,000 was decimated to 330 by 1897. The federal government relocated the tribe to this isolated area of almost a million acres a century ago. Since then, the tribe has made something of a comeback with the sale of timber, oil, and gas development, casino gambling, and savvy investing.

Dulce (pronounced "*dull*-say," meaning "sweet" in Spanish) on U.S. 64 is the capital of the reservation. The free **Arts & Crafts Museum** (⊠¼ *mi west of downtown, U.S. 64* ☎*505/759–3242 Ext. 274*) remains the best place to see the fine historic Jicarilla baskets, beadwork, and pottery. It's also the place to inquire about tours, events, and any tourism restrictions in place because of ceremonial activities. The **Cultural Center** (⊠*Basket La. and U.S. 64* ☎*505/759–1343*) is a small gift shop that sells mostly beadwork and some basketry. This country is known for fishing, particularly at Stone Lake, and for hunting; contact the **Game & Fish Department** (☎*505/759–3442*) for information. You may also hike and camp. As on many other pueblos in New Mexico, the casino has become a big draw as well. Some Jicarilla celebrations are open to the public. The Little Beaver Roundup, the third weekend in July, entails a rodeo, powwow, and carnival and draws participants from Native American tribes and pueblos throughout the United States.

WHERE TO STAY

$ ☷ **Best Western Jicarilla Inn.** This is the only place to stay in Dulce. The room furnishings preserve the flavor of the cultural and natural setting, with dark woods, Native American art, and stone fireplaces. The restaurant, the Hill Crest, is a favorite gathering spot for celebration dinners. **Pros:** Small fitness center. **Cons:** Only 21 nonsmoking rooms. ⊠*Jicarilla Blvd. (U.S. 64), 12 mi west of Junction 84* ☐*Box 233, Dulce 87528* ☎*505/759–3663 or 800/528–1234* ⊕*www.bestwestern newmexico.com* ➴*42 rooms* ⌂*In-room: kitchen (some). In-hotel: restaurant, some pets allowed, Wi-Fi* ☰*AE, D, MC, V.*

Northeastern
New Mexico

WORD OF MOUTH

"Is Las Vegas worth taking the time to see?"

—Betsyp

"It is a very small town with many interesting houses and buildings... The Rough Riders museum is small, but well done. I would agree... that it's probably not worth the trip from Santa Fe, but it's an interesting place to stop if you're going that way. If you do decide to go, check the hours on the museum as I seem to remember them keeping odd hours."

—jbee

Updated by
Barbara Floria

YOU'LL BATTLE NEITHER CROWDS NOR hype in northeastern New Mexico, truly one of the best-kept secrets in the state. You can have a wildflower-strewn trail through alpine meadows and forests of aspen and ponderosa pine all to yourself, or step back in time in small towns that treasure their past but do not exploit it. The sheer variety of terrain and climate, and the combination of natural and social history, make the region an ideal destination, whether as a short side trip or part of a journey from New Mexico toward the Plains states.

The northeastern region of New Mexico has been inhabited for centuries by such Native American tribes as the Apaches, Comanches, and Utes, but it wasn't until about 1835 that non-Native American populations moved in in any significant numbers. Hispanic settlers moved up into the area at that time from San Miguel del Vado, which is just south of Interstate 25, and established the Las Vegas Land Grant; Las Vegas has remained a Hispanic stronghold ever since. William Becknell had established Las Vegas as the Mexican port of entry when he brought the first packtrain west from Missouri to Santa Fe in 1821, in turn creating a pathway for Americans to spread west. The railroad's arrival in the 1870s and '80s brought streams of people and goods into northeastern New Mexico, as did the coal mines. Italians, Mexicans, Greeks, Slavs, Spaniards, and Irish all headed to Raton to harvest coal in mines that first opened in 1879. German-Jewish merchants opened shops in Las Vegas to serve the miners, the railroads, and the local Hispanic population.

In 1908, an African-American cowboy named George McJunkin found a collection of arrowheads in an arroyo near Folsom where he was looking for lost cattle. They looked different from the other arrowheads he'd seen—and indeed they were. Archaeologists eventually determined that the arrowheads had been made by ancient hominids, now known as Folsom Man, who inhabited northeastern New Mexico at least 10,000 years ago.

During the railroad heyday, Civil War veterans homesteaded in the region, some working for Lucien Maxwell, onetime mountain man and fur trader who came to control the largest landholding (1,714,765 acres) in the western hemisphere. Many of New Mexico's large ranches date from the era of the Maxwell Land Grant, territory awarded to the father of Maxwell's wife and another man by the Mexican government in 1841. Modern-day land baron Ted Turner now owns an enormous chunk of open land in these parts. The historic Bell Ranch near Solano still maintains an active cattle operation (as well as a beautiful guest hacienda) on 292,000 acres near Solano, though it originally held 655,468 acres as the Pablo Montoya Land Grant of 1824.

History is very much alive in northeastern New Mexico, in the stories and the way of life of the people who live here, in the architecture, and in the landscape itself. Exploring this land of vast plains, rugged mesas, and wild, crystalline streams may well be the best way to immerse yourself in the American West.

TOP REASONS TO GO

■ **Wild West.** History comes alive around every bend in the road. Following the Santa Fe Trail, spending the night at Cimarron's St. James Hotel, or counting the bullet holes in the ceiling of the Eklund Hotel dining room can put you in an old-timey mood.

■ **Wide-open spaces.** The high plains give a new meaning to lonely. If you're ever feeling crowded or hemmed in by humanity, you can always move to Capulin.

■ **High-mountain majesty.** Rocky cliffs, pine-covered valleys, and clear streams offer respite from big-city life and summer temperatures.

■ **Small-town pleasures.** Raton, Las Vegas, and Springer maintain the best of the past while moving toward the future. To wit: there's not a B&B around that doesn't provide Wi-Fi for guests.

ORIENTATION & PLANNING

GETTING ORIENTED

Interstate 25 heading north from Santa Fe is the fastest route through the region, but you'll want to sample as many local roads as possible to catch the area's true flavor. The destinations below are arranged in a loop from Las Vegas, Springer, and Raton (with an optional side loop over Johnson Mesa to Folsom, Capulin, and Clayton). Either way, the tour continues by heading west to Cimarron and then along U.S. 64 west through Cimarron Canyon; past Eagle Nest Lake and Angel Fire; and then south on NM 434 through stunning Guadalupita Canyon to Mora. Here you can either continue south toward Santa Fe back through Las Vegas or opt for the more dramatic mountain route, skirting over the east face of the Sangre de Cristo range.

NORTHEASTERN NEW MEXICO PLANNER

WHEN TO GO

In a region where the weather is close to perfect, the only months to consider avoiding are March and April, when "Texas blows through" and you find yourself dodging tumbleweeds, though this is applicable to the flatter regions rather than the mountains, which are still quite cool. From late spring, when the wildflowers begin to bloom, into late summer is a wonderful time to visit—an occasional afternoon thunderstorm, or "monsoon," often followed by a rainbow, punctuates days that are mostly sunny. Fall brings the gold of aspens, and fishing and hiking are especially spectacular. Temperatures can remain mild through Thanksgiving, and a crisp winter with good snow is a blessing for cross-country skiers. The wide vistas on snowy days are unforgettable. Roads are well maintained throughout the year, but be alert to storm warnings.

GETTING HERE & AROUND

BY AIR The two closest airports to northeastern New Mexico are Albuquerque (ABQ) and Amarillo, Texas (AMA). Albuquerque is closer to Las Vegas, Cimarron, Mora, and Springer. Amarillo is closer to Clayton, Capulin, Santa Rosa, and Tucumcari. Raton is about equidistant from both.

BY BUS Greyhound makes daily runs between Albuquerque and Raton and between Taos and Raton, with stops in Las Vegas, Springer, Cimarron, and Maxwell.

BY CAR Interstate 25 is the main route into northeastern New Mexico from Santa Fe. U.S. 64 heads east into the region from Taos and west into the region from Oklahoma. U.S. 56/412 heads west from Oklahoma toward Springer, where it connects with Interstate 25. From Interstate 40, take either of two very scenic routes into the northeast: U.S. 84 from west of Santa Rosa, or NM 3 from west of Vaughn.

You can rent a car from one of the majors at Amarillo International Airport and Albuquerque International Sunport.

BY TRAIN Amtrak operates the *Southwest Chief* between Chicago and Los Angeles; Las Vegas and Raton are the train's stops in northeastern New Mexico.

ESSENTIALS **Air Contacts Great Lakes Aviation** (☎800/554-5111 ⊕www.greatlakesav. com). **Albuquerque International Sunport** (✉2200 Sunport Blvd. SE, Albuquerque ☎575/842-4366 ⊕www.cabq.gov/airport). **Amarillo International Airport** (✉10801 Airport Blvd. ✛take I-40 to Airport Blvd. exit Amarillo, TX ☎806/335-1671).

Bus Contact Greyhound (☎800/231-2222 ⊕www.greyhound.com).

Train Contact Amtrak (☎800/872-7245 ⊕www.amtrak.com).

VISITOR INFORMATION **Cimarron Chamber of Commerce** (✉104 N. Lincoln Ave. ☎505/376-2417 ⊕www.cimarronnm.com). **Clayton Chamber of Commerce** (✉1103 S 1st St. ☎505/374-9253 or 800/390-7858 ⊕www.claytonnewmexico.org). **Las Vegas Visitor Center** (✉503 6th St. ⌂Box 128, 87701 ☎505/425-8631 or 800/832-5947 ⊕www.lasvegasnewmexico.com). **New Mexico Department of Tourism** (⊕www.nenewmexico.com). **Raton Chamber of Commerce** (✉100 Clayton Rd. 87740 ☎505/445-3689 or 800/638-6161 ⊕www.raton.com). **Springer Chamber of Commerce** (✉606 Maxwell St. 87747 ☎505/483-2998).

ABOUT THE RESTAURANTS

Food in the northeast is heavily New Mexican and American and dining is casual, just like the region itself. You can continue on the chile tour of the West, but vegetarians should ask whether there is beef in the red or pork in the green before diving in. Reservations are almost unheard of here, but seasonal closings during winter months are common.

ABOUT THE HOTELS

Chain hotels, privately operated lodges, and B&Bs are abundant. Choose a B&B when you can—you can get a real taste of regional character, and delicious breakfasts to boot. Given the amazing natural beauty and generally easy weather from May through late September, it's also no surprise that many visitors to the area choose to camp.

WHAT IT COSTS				
¢	$	$$	$$$	$$$$
Restaurants	under $10	$10–$15	$16–$22	$23–$30	over $30
Hotels	under $70	$70–$120	$121–$175	$176–$250	over $250

Restaurant prices are per person for a main course at dinner. Hotel prices are for two people in a standard double room in high season, excluding 5%–12% tax.

PLANNING YOUR TIME

For a quick tour of the region, stroll around the Plaza and Bridge Street in **Las Vegas**. After you've walked the town, drive north on Interstate 25 to **Raton** and visit the Raton Museum and Historic First Street. Take a picnic up to Lake Maloya in Sugarite Canyon State Park and hike or go fishing. The next day, drive west on U.S. 64 to **Cimarron,** exploring the heart of yesteryear's Wild West. Spend the night in the allegedly haunted St. James Hotel. In the morning continue west on U.S. 64, stopping off to fish or walk along the Cimarron River in Cimarron Canyon, and then head south on NM 434 at Angel Fire, stopping off for a visit to Victory Ranch in **Mora,** before continuing back toward Santa Fe.

IF YOU HAVE 4 TO 5 DAYS

The main routes through northeastern New Mexico follow the path of the original Santa Fe Trail and its shortcut, the Cimarron Route (which passed near Clayton and Springer), enabling you to retrace the steps of the pioneers. Begin in **Las Vegas**, where you can stay at the Plaza Hotel. Detour for an hour or two to **Fort Union National Monument**. Back at Interstate 25, continue north to **Raton**. On Day 3 head east on NM 72 over starkly captivating Johnson Mesa and visit Capulin Volcano National Monument. After viewing four states from the rim of the volcano, have lunch at the Capulin Country Store, at the junction of U.S. 64/87 and NM 325. If you have an extra day, head east to **Clayton** to view the dinosaur tracks at Clayton Lake State Park. Have dinner and stay at the Eklund Hotel Dining Room & Saloon. The following day drive west on U.S. 56 toward **Springer,** a good place to have lunch and browse the antiques shops downtown. With or without the Clayton detour, continue west to **Cimarron** (via U.S. 64 from Capulin, or NM 58 from Springer), and from here do the last day of the three-day itinerary given above.

SANTA FE TRAIL COUNTRY

Native American tribes of the Great Plains and Southwest lived and thrived in resource-rich northeastern New Mexico. Throughout the region you can find reminders of them and the pioneers who traveled the Santa Fe Trail, two sections of which passed through the area. The Mountain Route entered New Mexico from southeastern Colorado, crossed through Raton Pass, and passed Cimarron and Rayado before heading on to Fort Union. Because it was so arduous, this route was less

Northeastern
New Mexico

COLORADO

Sugarite
Canyon
S.P.

NRA
Whittington
Center

Raton

72

551

456

OKLAHOMA

CARSON
NAT'L FOREST

Valle
Vidal

325

Capulin

64
87

370

Cimarron
Canyon
S.P.

Questa

Vermejo R.

522

Eagle
Nest Lake

Cimarron

64

25

Maxwell Nat'l
Wildlife Refuge

Rio Grande

Taos

64

434

Rayado

58

21

Springer

56/
412

Clayton

402

Coyote
Creek S.P.

518

Guadalapita

Canadian R.

39

Kiowa Nat'l
Grasslands

Chimayó

Mora

La Cueva

Wagon
Mound

Kiowa Nat'l
Grasslands

120

562

102

Ute Cr.

SANTA FE
NATIONAL
FOREST

518

Watrous

161

Fort Union
Nat'l Mon.

120

Mosquero Cr.

Amistad

420

Santa
Fe

Pecos
National
Historic
Park

Las
Vegas

Mora R.

Mosquero

419

TEXAS

39

285

25

Las Vegas
Nat'l Wildlife
Refuge

Trujillo

Catalinas R.

Conchas R.

Conchas
Lake

Conchas
Dam

KEY

0   25 miles

0   50 km

TO SUMNER LAKE
STATE PARK

84

Pecos R.

104

·········· Santa Fe Trail,
Cimarron Cutoff

– – – Santa Fe Trail,
Mountain Branch

subject to attack from the Comanches and Apaches, who were on the
defensive warpath because their land was being usurped. The quicker,
flatter Cimarron Route (aka Cimarron Cutoff), entering New Mexico
from Oklahoma and passing across the dry grasslands, left travelers
much more vulnerable. The Mountain Route, which William Becknell
followed 900 mi from Franklin, Missouri, during his first successful
navigation, also provided an excellent source of water—the Arkansas
River—while the Cimarron Route was deathly dry.

LAS VEGAS

64 mi northeast of Santa Fe on I–25.

The antithesis of the Nevada city that shares its name, Las Vegas, elevation 6,470 feet, is a town of 16,000 that time appears to have passed
by. For decades, Las Vegas was actually two towns: East Las Vegas, the
Hispanic community anchored by the Spanish-style plaza, and West
Las Vegas, where German Jews and Midwesterners have established
themselves around a proper town square. Once an oasis for stagecoach
passengers en route to Santa Fe, it became—for a brief period after the
railroad arrived in the late 19th century—New Mexico's major center

of commerce, and its largest town, where more than a million dollars in goods and services were traded annually.

Booming business and near-total lawlessness characterized the 1870s. Famous characters on both sides of the law passed through the town—including Doc Holliday (who practiced dentistry here), Billy the Kid, and Wyatt Earp. Fierce battles for land—often swindled out of the hands of illiterate Hispanic land-grant holders by ruthless American businessmen—and water rights ensued, with the *Gorras Blancos* ("white hoods") appearing in 1889 to begin their campaign of cutting fences and setting fire to buildings on lands that had once been community property of the many land grants of the area. Today, the town is positively sedate, though ethnic tensions still occasionally arise.

The seat of San Miguel County, Las Vegas lies where the Sangre de Cristo Mountains meet the high plains of New Mexico, and its name, meaning "the meadows," reflects its scenic setting. Bookstores, Western-wear shops, restaurants, boutiques, and coffeehouses line the streets near the downtown Plaza and Bridge Street. More than 900 structures here are listed on the National Register of Historic Places, and the town has nine historic districts, many with homes and commercial buildings of ornate Italianate design (a welcome relief if you're experiencing adobe overload). Many of these buildings can be seen easily by taking a walk around town. Exploring on foot will give you a sense of some of the area's rough-and-tumble history—Butch Cassidy is rumored to have tended bar here. You may also recognize some of the streets and facades from films; Las Vegas is where scenes from *Wyatt Earp, The HiLo Country,* and *All the Pretty Horses* were shot and where Tom Mix shot his vintage westerns.

WHAT TO SEE
To gain an appreciation of the town's architecture, try some of the walking tours described in brochures available at the **Las Vegas Visitors Center**. Best bets include Stone Architecture of Las Vegas; the Carnegie Park Historic District, with the Carnegie Library; and the Business District of Douglas–6th Street and Railroad Avenue. The latter includes the famous Harvey House hotel of the railroad chain, La Casteneda, where the grand lobby and dining room are still intact. ⊠ *503 6th Ave.* ☎ *505/425–8631 or 800/832–5947.*

Las Vegas City Museum & Rough Riders Memorial houses historical photos, medals, uniforms, and memorabilia from the Spanish-American War, documents pertaining to the city's history, and Native American artifacts. Theodore Roosevelt recruited many of his Rough Riders—the men the future president led into battle in Cuba in 1898—from northeastern New Mexico, and their first reunion was held here. ⊠ *727 Grand Ave.* ☎ *505/454–1401 Ext. 283* ⊠ *Free* ⊗ *Tues.– Sat. 10–4.*

A favorite fishing hole for rainbow and German brown trout is **Storrie Lake State Park.** The 1,200-acre lake also draws water-skiers, sailboarders, and windsurfers. You can camp in the area. ⊠ *NM 518, 4 mi north of Las Vegas* ☎ *505/425–7278* ⊕ *www.emnrd.state.nm.us* ⊠ *$5 per vehicle.*

Las Vegas National Wildlife Refuge has the best bird-watching around, with 271 known species—including eagles, sandhill cranes, hawks, and prairie falcons—that travel the Central Flyway to this 18,750-acre area of marsh, wetlands, native grasslands, and timber. Here, where the Sangre de Cristo Mountains meet the Great Plains, a ½-mi-long nature trail winds beside sandstone cliffs and ruins. You can get oriented by dropping by the visitor center. ⊠ *Rte. 1, 1 mi east of Las Vegas on NM 104, then 4 mi south on NM 281* ⌂ *Box 399, Las Vegas 87701* ☎ *505/425–3581.*

Las Vegas is the home of **New Mexico Highlands University**, which puts on concerts, plays, sporting events, and lectures. Its tree-shaded campus of largely Spanish colonial and Romanesque Revival buildings anchors the eastern side of downtown. It houses Depression-era murals by painter Lloyd Moylan. ⊠ *901 University Ave.* ☎ *800/338–6648* ⊕ *www.nmhu.edu.*

About 5 mi northwest of town in Montezuma, students from around the world study language and culture at the **Armand Hammer United World College of the American West**. Looming over the school property is the fantastically ornate, vaguely Queen Anne–inspired Montezuma Castle, a former resort hotel developed by the Santa Fe Railroad and designed by the famous Chicago firm of Burnham and Root. The structure that stands today was the third incarnation of the Montezuma Hotel, which opened in 1886. Tours of the castle are available, and you can wander the school's majestic, rolling grounds. Check in with the guard booth at the campus entrance. ⊠ *NM 65* ☎ *505/454–4200* ⊕ *www.uwc-usa.org.*

★ If you continue another ½ mi past the turnoff of the campus on NM 65, you can see the signs to the right for the **hot springs** that inspired Montezuma's tourist boom in the 1880s. Soaking in these relaxing, lithium-laced pools is free, as long as you follow basic rules: no nude bathing, no alcohol, and bathing only between 5 AM and midnight. If crowds allow, try soaking in several different pools; temperatures vary significantly but the view of the Castle and the creek are equally lovely.

OFF THE BEATEN PATH

Madison Vineyards & Winery. If you're driving to or from the northeast on Interstate 25, a side trip down NM 3 is well worth your while. Scenic and loaded with history, the road will also take you to the proud producers of some very fine New Mexico wines, including the crisp, sweet, white Pecos Wildflower. Madison has picked up quite a few awards over the years. The tasting room in El Barranco is open Thursday–Saturday 11–4, Sunday noon–4. ⊠ *NM 3, 6 mi south of I–25, Exit 323, 23 mi southwest of Las Vegas* ☎ *505/421–8028.*

WHERE TO EAT

¢ ✕ **Charlie's Bakery & Café.** Huevos rancheros and burritos smothered with
CAFÉ spicy salsa top the list in this large, simply furnished room that rings with friendly greetings among locals and is a good bet for either breakfast or lunch. You can also pick up cookies, doughnuts, and pastries from the on-site bakery, or a stack of freshly made corn tortillas from the *tortilleria.* ⊠ *715 Douglas* ☎ *505/426–1921* ⊟ *AE, DC, MC, V.*

$ × **El Rialto Restaurant & Lounge.** The margaritas here will put you in the
NEW MEXICAN right mood for fried oyster dinners, huge steaks, stuffed sopaipillas, and
tamales. American dishes, seafood, and the salad bar are other options.
The antique bar and historic photos, in addition to good drinks and an
eclectic jumble of friendly locals, make the attached Rye Lounge a fun
spot for drinks. ⊠ *141 Bridge St.* ☎ *505/454–0037* ☐ *AE, D, MC, V*
⊘ *Closed Sun.*

¢ × **Estella's Restaurant.** An old-fashioned storefront café with a high
SOUTHWESTERN pressed-tin ceiling, vintage photos, and a Formica counter with swivel
★ stools, Estella's serves simple but memorable New Mexican fare—
chicken burritos smothered with green chile, huevos rancheros, stacked
enchiladas—plus a few American favorites like burgers. Pescado Vera-
cruz, snapper simmered in a piquant sauce of spices, tomato, red chile,
and onion, is a good choice for dinner. ⊠ *148 Bridge St.* ☎ *505/454–
0048* ☐ *No credit cards* ⊘ *Closed Sun. No dinner Mon.–Wed.*

WHERE TO STAY

$ ⊞ **Pendaries Village.** The mood here (where the name is pronounced
"panda-ray") is Holiday Inn meets Kit Carson, but the hotel and the
surrounding mountain hamlet of Rociada provide a relaxing place to
enjoy some high-altitude golfing. The **Pendaries Golf Course** begins at
7,500 feet with a par 73, set smack at the eastern edge of the Sangre
de Cristo Mountains. Special golf packages are offered. Greens fees
are $45 weekdays, $55 weekends; optional golf-cart rental is $15. The
rooms here have standard motel-room decor, but are clean and comfortable; the on-site restaurant is usually crowded with locals who come
for the steaks and Southwestern food. **Pros:** Well-priced; plenty of outdoor activities. **Cons:** Some rooms are dark; could use updating. ⊠ *1
Lodge Rd., off NM 105, 26 mi northwest of Las Vegas* ⊙ *Box 820,
Rociada 87742* ☎ *505/425–3561 or 800/733–5267* ⊕ *www.pendaries.
net* ⌂ *18 rooms* ♿ *In-hotel: restaurant, bar, golf course* ☐ *MC, V.*

$$ ⊞ **Plaza Hotel.** Rooms at this three-story Italianate hotel balance the
★ old and the new—they're not fancy, but they've got plenty of space,
painted molding, high stamped-tin ceilings, and a sprinkling of charming
antiques. Each room also has a modern bath, coffeemaker, TV, phone,
and full breakfast included in the rate. The hotel recently doubled in
size, expanding its operations to include 40 more rooms, a ballroom,
and meeting facilities. Reasonably priced packages include dinner at the
Landmark Grill, which serves, among other dishes, filet mignon, piñon-
crusted trout, and Mexican specialties. **Pros:** Best hotel in town; feels
like the Old West. **Cons:** Moderate street noise; an old property with
quirks and minor inconveniences. ⊠ *230 Old Town Plaza,* ☎ *505/425–
3591 or 800/328–1882* ⊟ *505/425–9659* ⊕ *www.plazahotel-nm.com*
⌂ *72 rooms, 4 suites* ♿ *In-hotel: 2 restaurants, room service, bar, some
pets allowed, Wi-Fi* ☐ *AE, D, DC, MC, V* ⦿ *BP.*

CAMPING

⚠ **Las Vegas New Mexico KOA.** Five miles south of Las Vegas you can
camp and cook out near a piñon-juniper hillside with beautiful views.
There's a recreation room, as well as outdoor areas for playing volley-
ball and horseshoes. The pool feels fantastic after a dry, dusty day of

exploring. In addition to the usual KOA accommodations, this site has a one-bedroom apartment available above the main office. ⊠*I–25, Exit 339, at U.S. 84* ⌖*HCR 31, Box 1, Las Vegas 87701* ☎*505/454–0180 or 800/562–3423* ⊕*www.koa.com* ⌂ *Pool, laundry facilities, flush toilets, full hookups, drinking water, showers, picnic tables, general store, play area, Wi-Fi* ⟿*5 cabins, 80 tent sites, 54 hookups* ▭*D, MC, V.*

SPORTS & THE OUTDOORS
Brazos River Ranch and Outfitters (☎*505/425–1509*) can take you on hunting and fishing trips—and they'll do it with the friendliest service this side of the Pecos.

SHOPPING
Shops are located mainly on Bridge Street, off the Plaza. **New Moon Fashions** (⊠*132 Bridge St.* ☎*505/454–0669*) has a well-chosen selection of natural-fiber and imported women's clothing, and comfortable shoes. **Plaza Antiques** (⊠*1805 Old Town Plaza* ☎*505/454–9447*) contains several dealers offering a wide range of antiques from different periods; it's in a stunningly restored hip-roof adobe 1870s Victorian. **Tome on the Range** (⊠*158 Bridge St.* ☎*505/454–9944*) is a well-appointed bookstore with good Southwestern and kids' sections.

FORT UNION NATIONAL MONUMENT

26 mi from Las Vegas, north on I–25 and (past Watrous) northwest on NM 161; 94 mi northeast of Santa Fe on I–25.

The ruins of New Mexico's largest American frontier–era fort sit on an empty windswept plain. It still echoes with the isolation surely felt by the soldiers stationed here between 1851 and 1890, when the fort was established to protect travelers and settlers along the Santa Fe Trail. It eventually became a military supply depot for the Southwest, but with the "taming" of the West it was abandoned. The visitor center provides historical background about the fort and the Santa Fe Trail; guided tours are available when volunteers are on hand. ⊠*Off NM 161, Watrous* ☎*505/425–8025* ▱*$3* ⊙*Early Sept.–late May, daily 8–4; late May–early Sept., daily 8–6.*

WAGON MOUND

40 mi north of Las Vegas on I–25.

As you drive up Interstate 25 from Las Vegas and Fort Union, the high prairie unfolds to the east, an infinite horizon of grassland that's quite breathtaking when the sun sets. Wagon Mound, a butte shaped like a covered wagon, rises just off the road to insert itself into the open vista. The butte is where travelers crossed over from the Cimarron Cutoff to journey south to Fort Union. Local lore tells of mysterious lights, ghosts, and murders committed on top of the butte. The town serves a free barbecue at noon on Labor Day to celebrate its bean-growing heritage. Other events—horseshoe tournaments, a rodeo, and a parade—take place that same weekend in this otherwise sleepy village.

SPRINGER

25 mi north of Wagon Mound on I–25.

A stroll under the shady oaks of Springer's main street is a journey into the past; if it weren't for the modern-day cars driving by, you might think Harry Truman was still president. More than a few locals here still seem a bit rankled about losing the title of county seat to Raton—in 1897. The main industry of this town of 1,262 is the Springer Boys School, an incarceration facility for minors. Long a shipping center for cattle, sheep, and mining machinery, Springer was founded in 1870 when land baron Lucien Maxwell deeded 320 acres to his lawyer, Frank Springer, for handling the sale of the Maxwell Land Grant to the Dutch East India Company.

Crammed with everything you'd expect to find at a five-and-dime, **Springer Drug** is a local hangout and the site of an ongoing gabfest. The highlight is the old (not old-fashioned, this is the original article) soda fountain, where you can order a sundae, malt, shake, or cone. The root-beer float comes in a glass so big you could dive into it. In winter home-made chili is served on Wednesday. ⊠ *825 4th St.* ☎ *505/483–2356.*

When Springer was the Colfax County seat, the 1883 structure that houses the **Santa Fe Trail Museum** served as a courthouse. The museum has a curious jumble of documents, maps, memorabilia, and other artifacts. The setup is not particularly sophisticated—it takes a bit of patience to wade through the assorted bits and pieces of the past. ⊠ *516 Maxwell St.* ☎ *505/483–5554* ☑ *$2* ◷ *Late May–early Sept., Mon.–Sat. 9–4; limited hrs early fall to late spring, call ahead.*

OFF THE BEATEN PATH

Dorsey Mansion. In the middle of nowhere (about 35 mi northeast of Springer) stands this curious 36-room log-and-masonry castle built in 1880 by Stephen Dorsey, a U.S. senator from Arkansas. It was once a social gathering place for the rich and powerful. The career of the ambitious senator, who owned the mansion for 15 years, dissolved in a mail-fraud scandal. It's not open to the public, but history buffs may want to drive by. ⊠ *Off U.S. 56, 25 mi east of Springer; turn north (left) at rest stop at Mile Marker 24 and take dirt road 12 mi.*

Maxwell National Wildlife Refuge. More than 300 species of migratory waterfowl, including many geese and ducks in fall and winter, stop for a spell at this low-key 2,800-acre prairie refuge 12 mi north of Springer. Sightings of great blue herons are not uncommon in midwinter, and bald eagles are fairly plentiful at this time. Sandhill cranes usually drop by in early fall, Canada geese around December. Deer, prairie dogs, long-tail weasels, jackrabbits, coyotes, bears, and elk live here. The fishing season (Lake 13 is a fabled spot to catch rainbows) is between March and October. You can camp (no fee, no facilities) near the fishing areas. ⊠ *Off I–25, take Maxwell Lakes exit at Mile Marker 426; follow NM 445 north ¾ mi, then NM 505 west 2½ mi to unmarked gravel road to refuge* ☎ *505/375–2331* ☑ *Free* ◷ *Daily.*

7

WHERE TO STAY

¢ 🔝 **Brown Hotel & Cafe.** Granny's parlor circa 1924 is the best way to describe the Brown Hotel, where the lobby furnishings include a rocking chair by the fireplace and hooked rugs and doilies. Antiques decorate the basic rooms, some of which have chenille bedspreads. The café's ($) claims to fame include the baked goods and made-from-scratch soups (try the yummy broccoli–cheddar); both New Mexican and standard American dishes are on the menu. **Pros:** Feels like the Wild West; best restaurant in town. **Cons:** Could be better maintained; noise can be an issue. ⊠*302 Maxwell Ave.* ☎*505/483–2269* ⤳*11 rooms* ⚲*In-hotel: restaurant* ▤*AE, MC, V* ⑩*BP.*

SHOPPING

Jespersen's Cache (⊠*403 Maxwell Ave.* ☎*505/483–2349*), a pack rat's paradise, is a place to get lost for a morning or afternoon. The sheer mass of stuff is astounding—boxed Barbies, railroad lanterns, Depression-era glass, carousel horses. If you've got a collector's eye, you could make your lucky find here. Call if the doors are locked between 9 and 5; the proprietor may be around the corner at her house and she'll come right down.

RATON

39 mi north of Springer on I–25, 100 mi northeast of Taos on U.S. 64.

Generally underrated as a destination, Raton occupies an appealing spot at the foot of a lush mountain pass and offers wide-open views of stepped mesas and sloping canyons from the higher points in town. Midway between Albuquerque and Denver, it's an ideal base for exploring northeastern New Mexico. Because Raton was a racetrack town from the 1940s through the early '90s, motels are plentiful. There's always talk of bringing back horse racing.

As it has for more than a century, Raton (population 8,500), the seat of Colfax County, runs on ranching, railroading, and the industry for which it's most famous, mining. In the early 1900s there were about 35 coal camps around Raton, most of them occupied by immigrants from Italy, Greece, and Eastern Europe. It was hard-living in these camps and a tough road out, but a close-knit familial interdependence grew out of mining life—a spirit that still prevails in Raton today. People here are genuinely friendly and have great pride in their town.

Originally a Santa Fe Trail forage station called Willow Springs, Raton was born in 1880 when the Atchison, Topeka & Santa Fe Railway established a repair shop at the bottom of Raton Pass. The town grew up around 1st Street, which paralleled the railroad tracks. Much of the Raton Downtown Historic District, which has 70-odd buildings on the National Register of Historic Places, lies along Historic First Street, which consists of several restored blocks of antiques shops, galleries, and everyday businesses. Much of historic downtown is closed on Sunday; some businesses are closed Monday as well.

The Historic First Street area provides a fine survey of Western architecture from the 1880s to the early 1900s.

WHAT TO SEE

In the early 20th century the **Mission Santa Fe Depot**, a 1903 Spanish Mission Revival structure, serviced several dozen trains daily (Amtrak still stops here). ⊠ *1st St. and Cook Ave.*

The **Wells Fargo Express Building**, also designed in the Spanish Mission Revival style, was erected in 1910. The building houses the **Old Pass Gallery** (☎ *575/445–2052*), which presents exhibits of regional art, books, and jewelry. ⊠ *145 S. 1st St.*

Garlands and female figureheads adorn the 1906 **Abourezk Building**, originally a drugstore, later a dry-goods and grocery store, and now the home of the Heirloom Shop. ⊠ *132 S. 1st St.*

The tiny storefront **Raton Museum,** inside the 1906 Coors Building (the beer manufacturer once used it as a warehouse), brims with artifacts of the coal camps, railroading, ranch life, and the Santa Fe Trail. The museum, which has a large and interesting photo collection, is a good first stop on a visit to the area. The docents enjoy explaining local history. ⊠ *108 S. 2nd St.* ☎ *575/445–8979* ⊑ *Free* ☼ *May–Sept., Tues.–Sat. 10–4; Oct.–Apr., Wed.–Sat. 10–4.*

Just down a couple of blocks from the train station, the **Scouting Museum,** devoted to all things Boy Scout, is a must-see for anyone planning a visit to Philmont Scout Ranch in Cimarron. Amiable curator Dennis Downing has amassed an exhaustive collection of scouting-related books, badges, films of old jamborees, buttons, and *Boys Life* magazines. ⊠ *400 S. 1st St.* ☎ *575/445–1413* ⊑ *Free* ☼ *June–Aug., daily 10–7, or by appt.*

More retro 1930s and '40s than Victorian, 2nd Street—Raton's main commercial drag—also has a number of handsome old buildings. The pride and joy of the neighborhood is the **Shuler Theater**, a 1915 European rococo–style structure whose lobby contains WPA murals depicting local history. The Shuler is one of the few remaining stages where all sets, curtains, and scenery are hand-operated with hemp rope and wooden pulleys. On weekdays between 8 and 5 the staff will happily take you on a free tour. ⊠ *131 N. 2nd St.* ☎ *575/445–4746*

Southern California may have its HOLLYWOOD sign, but northeastern New Mexico has its RATON sign—and this neon-red beauty is completely accessible. From the north end of 3rd Street, head west on Moulton Avenue to Hill Street and follow signs along the twisting road to the parking area at Goat Hill. Here you can walk around the sign, take in 270-degree views of the countryside, or picnic while contemplating the history of Raton Pass—the original Santa Fe Trail ran up Goat Hill clear into Colorado.

★ **Sugarite Canyon State Park,** a gem of a park near the Colorado state line, ☾ has some of the state's best hiking, camping, wildflower viewing, fishing, and bird-watching ("sugarite" is a corruption of the Comanche word *chicorica,* meaning "an abundance of birds," and is pronounced shug-ur-*eet*). The road to Sugarite twists and turns high up into the canyon to Lake Maloya, a trout-stocked body of water from which a spillway carries overflow down into the canyon. From its 7,500-foot elevation hills rise up the eastern and western canyon walls where miners once dug for ore; you can still see gray slag heaps and remnants of the coal camp, which thrived here from 1910 to 1940, along portions of the park road near the visitor center (the former coal-camp post office) and down near the base of the canyon. The center contains exhibits on the mining legacy, and from here you can hike 1½ mi to the original camp.

Hikes elsewhere in the park range from the easy ½-mi Grande Vista Nature Trail to the pleasant 4-mi jaunt around Lake Maloya to the challenging Opportunity Trail. "Caprock" is the name given to the park's striking basaltic rock columns, which were formed millions of years ago when hot lava from a nearby volcano created the 10- to 100-foot-thick rocks. Climbing is permitted on these sheer cliffs, although it's not recommended for the faint of heart. ⊠*NM 526, 7 mi northeast of Raton via NM 72* ☎*575/445–5607* ⊕*www.emnrd.state.nm.us* ⊠*$4 per vehicle* ☉*Daily 6* AM–9 PM.

WHERE TO EAT

¢   ✕ **The Bakery and Coffee Shop.** Also known as Eva's Bakery, this cheerful
BAKERY   sit-down bakery across from the Shuler Theater has fabulous chocolate-cake doughnuts and oatmeal-raisin cookies—as well as a regular crowd of old-timers who gather here to keep up with town gossip. Breakfast burritos, chile fries, burgers, and Frito pies are big sellers. ⊠*134 N. 2nd St.* ☎*575/445–3781* ⊴*Reservations not accepted* ☉*Closed Sun. No dinner.*

$$ ✕ **The Icehouse.** A historic 1909 icehouse is the setting for this restaurant
AMERICAN   serving steaks and seafood. The high-ceiling brick structure is accented with lots of old wood, historic photos of the icehouse in its working days, local cowboys and beautifully groomed prize bulls. If a memorable steak is what you're after, the prime Angus cuts are prepared to perfection by chef and co-owner Bill Ratliff. ⊠*945 S. 2nd St., just south of downtown* ☎*575/445–2339* ⊟*AE, DC, MC, V* ☉*Closed Sun.*

$$ ✕ **Sweet Shop Restaurant.** Don't be put off by the plain storefront; you
AMERICAN   can feel pampered at this restaurant, whose antiques and collectibles exude a sense of history and a pleasant nostalgia for Pappas, the Greek candy maker who founded the place in the 1920s. It's no longer a sweetshop, but it does serve familiar American fare, like Alaskan king crab legs, porterhouse steak, shrimp fettuccine, and a few surf-and-turf combos. ⊠*1201 S. 2nd St.* ☎*575/445–9811* ⊟*AE, D, DC, MC, V* ☉*Closed Sun.*

WHERE TO STAY

$$ ▦ **Best Western Sands.** Some of the good-size rooms at this charming, rather kitschy 1950s-style motel have refrigerators, and all have coffeemakers, queen or king beds, and TVs with premium cable. **Pros:** Centrally located; heated pool. **Cons:** Pricey for a Best Western. ⊠*300 Clayton Rd., NM 87–U.S. 64,* ☎*575/445–2737 or 800/528–1234*

575/445–4053 *50 rooms In-room: refrigerator (some), Wi-Fi. In-hotel: restaurant, pool, no-smoking rooms =AE, D, MC, V.

$ ★ **Hearts Desire Inn Bed & Breakfast.** Gregarious host Barbara Riley, who grew up on a ranch south of Springer, has filled the rooms of her inn with Victorian antiques and collectibles (many for sale). This 1885 former boardinghouse is steps from downtown dining and the historic district. The top-floor hunting-and-fishing-theme suite has a full kitchen, TV and VCR, and two twin beds. In addition to what is likely the best breakfast in town, snacks are served in the evening. **Pros:** Historical 1885 building; convenient downtown location. **Cons:** Lots of stairs; some of the bathrooms are small. ⊠*301 S. 3rd St.* ☎*575/445–1000 *5 rooms, 1 suite In-room: kitchen (some) =AE, D, MC, V *BP.

$$ **Holiday Inn Express.** If you prefer modern rather than rustic lodgings, this is the place for you. Clean rooms, fine views of Johnson Mesa and the vast grasslands, and a location south of downtown are all draws here. An extensive Continental breakfast buffet is included, as are snacks in the lobby from 4 to 8. **Pros:** Beautiful vistas; no surprises. **Cons:** Pricey for a chain motel; no restaurant. ⊠*101 Card Ave., I–25 Exit 450* ☎*575/445–1500 or 800/465–4329* 575/445–7650 *50 rooms In-room: Wi-Fi. In-hotel: pool, laundry facilities, no-smoking rooms =AE, D, DC, MC, V *BP.

$$$$ **Vermejo Park Ranch.** This breathtaking 588,000-acre property, the heart of the famous 2-million-acre Maxwell Land Grant, includes a private hunting and fishing resort. Here you can stay in rustic yet luxurious accommodations; hunt for bison, elk, turkey, and mule deer; skeet shoot; horseback ride; and fish among the property's 21 lakes and countless rivers. The impressive main lodge houses a dining room, bar, gift shop, and guest services desk; a second lodge houses guests in six rooms and has its own private chef, dining room, and bar (room rates here include all meals, as well as activities like horseback riding and fishing). There's no TV on the premises, nor are there hot tubs, swimming pools, or a golf course—this place is all about returning to the land. Media mogul Ted Turner owns the ranch and his attention to land and animal stewardship is both remarkable, and evident. **Pros:** Majestic setting; no distractions. **Cons:** Very expensive; remote. *Drawer E, Raton 87740* ☎*575/445–3097* 575/445–0545 *www.vermejoparkranch.com *21 rooms In-hotel: restaurant, bar, Wi-Fi =AE, D, DC, MC, V *AI.

CAMPING

Sugarite Canyon State Park. Arrive early for the best choice among the fully developed sites at either of this park's two campgrounds, Lake Alice and Soda Pocket. Be sure to follow park warnings regarding the resident brown bears at Soda Pocket. ⊠*NM 526, 6 mi northeast of Raton* *HCR 63, Box 386, 87740* ☎*575/445–5607, 877/664–7787 reservations* *www.emnrd.state.nm.us Flush toilets, full hookups, dump station, drinking water, showers, picnic tables, electricity *41 tent and RV sites, 12 with hookups =MC, V.

NIGHTLIFE & THE ARTS

Shuler Theater (⊠ *131 N. 2nd St.* ☏ *575/445–4746*) presents late-summer concerts, Music from Angel Fire (a program that brings world-class chamber music to various venues in northern New Mexico), and productions by the Creede Repertory Theater. Children's theater, local college productions, and traveling dance, folk dance, and vocal evenings are scheduled throughout the year. For the better part of this century, locals have popped into the rollicking **White House Saloon** (⊠ *133 Cook Ave.* ☏ *575/445–9992*) for drinks after work and late into the evening. If you get hungry, the adjoining restaurant serves well-prepared steaks and seafood from 6 to 9. No credit cards are accepted.

SPORTS & THE OUTDOORS

Raton's playground is **Sugarite Canyon State Park.** Sugarite's alpine **Lake Maloya** (⊠ *NM 526, 10 mi northeast of Raton* ☏ *575/445–5607*) is generously stocked with rainbow trout. The profusion of wildflowers and flocks of bluebirds make the lake a joy to hike around. Boating and ice-fishing are popular as well.

SHOPPING

Hattie Sloan, proprietor of the **Heirloom Shop** (⊠ *132 S. 1st St.* ☏ *575/445–8876*), was one of the key figures involved in the restoration of Historic First Street. Hattie knows her antiques and has packed her highly browsable shop with beautiful selections, from rhinestone necklaces to quilts, china, and linens.

Rubin's Family Clothiers (⊠ *113 S. 2nd St.* ☏ *575/445–9492*) sells Pendleton shirts, woolen skirts, and well-made shoes. Its owners, Kathryn and Leon Rubin, can tell you a thing or two about local history—their store has been in the family for almost a century. Given the quality of some of the merchandise, the prices at **Santa Fe Trail Traders** (⊠ *100 S. 2nd St.* ☏ *575/445–2888 or 800/286–6975*) are reasonable. Items include earrings, sand paintings, dream catchers, Nambé hand-cast bowls, Navajo rugs old and new, beadwork, and kachinas (many by well-known artists). You can enter **Solano's Boot & Western Wear** (⊠ *101 S. 2nd St.* ☏ *575/445–2632*) a city slicker and exit a cowboy or cowgirl. The enormous space, an experience as much as a store, is full of fashionable, practical Western garb. Check out the collection of cowboy hats.

EN ROUTE To reach Capulin from Raton, skip U.S. 64 and instead take **NM 72** past Sugarite Canyon State Park, a stunning road that climbs up over Johnson Mesa, from which you have amazing 100-mi views north over the mesa into the plains of eastern Colorado. It's bare and flat up here, as though you're driving across a table straddling the Colorado–New Mexico border. About halfway across the mesa (15 mi from Raton), note the old stone church to your right, which was built by the early farmsteaders and has since been abandoned—it's a beautiful, lonely little building with a presence that illustrates the life of solitude the mesa's settlers must have endured.

Farther along on the right, a historical marker details the 1908 discovery of Folsom Man by George McJunkin, which established the existence of indigenous inhabitants in the area dating back some 10,000 years. The road trails down the eastern side of the mesa and leads into tiny Folsom. Here make a right turn south on NM 325 to reach Capulin Volcano, 6 mi away.

CAPULIN

46 mi east of Raton via NM 72 and NM 325.

Tiny Capulin has a gas station, a campground, and—well—little else.

If you're in luck—and in season—lunch will be on at the delightful **Capulin Country Store** *(⇨ see below)*, which in addition to fine food sells crafts and gifts (like candlesticks made of elk antlers and dolls sewn from old quilts), snacks, maps, and cold drinks.

From the crest of **Capulin Volcano National Monument,** elevation 8,182 feet, you can see four states: Colorado, New Mexico, Texas, and Oklahoma. To the southeast is the vast section of the Santa Fe Trail that includes the Cimarron Cutoff; to the west are the snowcapped Sangre de Cristo Mountains. Unlike much of the dry surrounding territory, Capulin has enough water to support an oasis of trees, shrubs, and wildflowers. A narrow 2-mi paved road (no trailers, towed vehicles, bicycles, or pedestrians allowed) leads to the rim of the volcano; from there you can walk the final .2 mi into the extinct, and rather uninteresting, crater vent. (An easy-to-hike 1-mi trail circles the rim, so you can see it from different angles.) The cone of Capulin (the word is Spanish for "chokecherry"; these bushes are scattered across the area) rises more than 1,300 feet from its base. The visitor center has books, a brief video about the site, and interpretive exhibits. On busy summer weekends, you may have a short wait to enter the paved road. ⊠ *NM 325, 3 mi north of Capulin off U.S. 64* ☎ *575/278-2201* ⊕ *www.nps. gov/cavo* 🔁 *$5 per vehicle* ⊙ *Late May–early Sept., daily 7:30–6:30; early Sept.–late May, daily 8–4.*

WHERE TO EAT

¢–$ ✕ **Capulin Country Store.** From May to the end of November, seven days
SOUTHWESTERN a week, lunch is the big meal (and big deal) of the day at the Capulin Country Store, where Jenny Lee Pugh sets the tables with chicken-fried steak with mashed potatoes, the volcano burger (smothered in chili and cheese), and excellent desserts. Sunday dinner buffets served on holiday weekends only are not to be missed, as the ranchers who drive from miles in every direction will tell you. Lunch happens from 11 to 3, and the store shuts down at 6. ⊠ *U.S. 64 at NM 325* ☎ *575/278–3900* ⇲ *Reservations not accepted* ▤ *AE, D, MC, V* ⊙ *No lunch Nov.–Apr.*

**EN
ROUTE** If you decide to skip Clayton and drive back west to Cimarron, take U.S. 64 west via Raton, which passes through ranch country underneath the biggest, bluest skies imaginable. Antelope herds graze alongside cattle. This is the classic West, with old windmills jutting into the sky of the rimrock country. The 29-mi stretch from Capulin passes through the **Raton-Clayton volcano field,** where the cones of quiet volcanoes break the flat, green landscape.

CLAYTON

43 mi east of Capulin on U.S. 64–87, 83 mi east of Springer on U.S. 56.

Clayton, which lies flat on the high prairie at an elevation of 5,000 feet, seemingly grew up out of nothing. Downtown is sleepy and sunny, with the old-fashioned retro-veneer typical of little Western towns. It's nowhere near an interstate and so lacks the scads of ubiquitous chain properties found in Las Vegas and Raton; mom-and-pop-owned shops dominate. The town bills itself as the carbon dioxide capital of the world, but the carbon dioxide here isn't hanging in the air but rather underground, embedded in sandstone southwest of town. Cattle graze on the many ranches around Clayton.

WHAT TO SEE

The friendly locals here may look at you cockeyed when they learn you've come to sightsee, but Clayton does have a few notable landmarks.

The 1892 **Eklund Hotel Dining Room & Saloon,** whose splendid Victorian dining room has crystal chandeliers, apricot tufted-velvet booths, gilt-flocked wallpaper, and marble fireplaces is quite a draw in Clayton. The hunting-lodge atmosphere in the saloon is quite different but no less authentic, with a large raw-rock fireplace, wooden booths, mounted game heads, and historic photos and clippings of Clayton's past. The town's most famous historical character, the notorious train robber Black Jack Ketchum, was hanged just out front in 1901. His last words were "I had breakfast in Clayton, but I'll have dinner in hell!" Put your boot up on the brass rail at the bar (won in a poker game) and order a cold one. ⊠*15 Main St.* ☎*877/355–8631* ⊕*www.theeklund.com.*

More than 500 fossilized dinosaur tracks can be observed along the ½-mi wooden **Dinosaur Trackway at Clayton Lake State Park,** making this one of the few sites of its kind in the world. The tracks, estimated to be 100 million years old, were made when the area was the shore of a prehistoric sea. Eight species of dinosaurs, vegetarian and carnivorous, lived here. The sparkling lake that gives the state park its name is ideal for camping, hiking, and fishing. ⊠*NM 370, 12 mi north of Clayton* ☎*575/374–8808* ⊕ *www.emnrd.state.nm.us/prd/Clayton.htm* ▧*$5 per vehicle* ⊗*Daily 6 AM–9 PM.*

There are few better places in New Mexico to soak in wide-open prairie vistas, clear skies, and fresh air than in the 136,000-acre **Kiowa National Grasslands.** One section of the grasslands is near Clayton and spreads east into Oklahoma and Texas. The other is about 80 mi west of Clayton, closer to Springer, south of U.S. 56. In the section near Clayton, if you look carefully, you can see ruts made by the wagons that crossed on the Old Santa Fe Trail. The land was drought-stricken during the Dust Bowl of the 1920s and '30s, when homesteaders abandoned their farms. After that, the government purchased the land and rehabilitated it to demonstrate that it could be returned to the tall grassland native to the region.

For an enjoyable loop drive through the grasslands, head east out of Clayton on U.S. 56; at NM 406 head north to just past Seneca, to where NM 406 makes a sharp turn to the east. Take the county gravel road west 3 mi and north 1 mi, noting the interpretive sign about the Santa Fe Trail. Continue a little farther north to the green gate that leads to the trail (following the limestone markers), where you can see ancient wagon ruts. Except for the occasional house or windmill, the view from the trail is not much different from what the pioneers saw. ⊠*Off U.S. 56, north and south of Clayton* ⌂*Administrative office: 714 Main St., Clayton 88415* ☎*575/374–9652* ☜*Free.*

WHERE TO STAY

$ 📺**Best Western Kokopelli Lodge.** Locals have long used this Southwestern-style Best Western to house out-of-town guests, where the rooms are spacious and pets are allowed (by prior arrangement only). **Pros:** Well maintained; large rooms. **Cons:** Next to railroad tracks; traffic noise. ⊠*702 S. 1st St.* ☎*575/374–2589 or 800/392–6691* 🛏*44 rooms* ♿*In-hotel: pool, some pets allowed* ☰*AE, D, MC, V* ⫶◯⫶*BP.*

$ 📺**Eklund Hotel Dining Room & Saloon.** The renovated rooms of this rustic
★   beauty of a building are comfortable and elegant, and each has custom-made furniture and a modern-but-period-style bathroom. Friendly staff help get you situated and will happily tell you about the hotel's history and things to do in the area. American standards and Southwestern fare are served in the dining room and saloon ($–$$). Old West elegance and the house specialty—hand-cut steaks—please locals and visitors alike. **Pros:** Wild West decor and history; friendly staff. **Cons:** Street noise; some rooms are dark. ⊠*15 Main St.* ☎*575/374–2551 or 877/355–8631* 🖷*575/374–2500* ⊕*www.theeklund.com* 🛏*26 rooms* ♿*In-hotel: no-smoking rooms, Wi-Fi* ☰*MC, V* ⫶◯⫶*CP.*

CIMARRON

108 mi from Clayton via U.S. 56/412 west to Springer, I–25 north, and NM 58 west; 42 mi southwest of Raton on U.S. 64.

As you approach Cimarron from the south or east, you can't help but notice a massive, grayish-white pinnacle perched atop the mountain at the northwest edge of town. Known as the **Tooth of Time,** it indicated to Santa Fe Trail travelers that their journey was nearing an end, for Santa Fe was only seven days away by wagon. Today the Tooth of Time is the emblem of the Philmont Scout Ranch, where 25,000 Boy Scouts assemble each summer.

In a land that was once home to Jicarilla Apaches and Utes, Cimarron later became a refuge for gamblers and outlaws and a stopping point for soldiers, gold seekers, and mountain men. (Its name means "untamed" in Spanish.) Founded in the early 1840s, it was the home of land baron Lucien Maxwell. These days, with a population around 900, it's a sleepy little town with some fine old buildings, and a good base from which to do some great fishing on the Cimarron River or in the various rivers flowing through Valle Vidal. It's common to see deer grazing on the edge of town—and look out for elk if you're driving at dusk or after dark. They are huge and hitting one can be deadly.

With 27 bullet holes in the tin dining-room ceiling, resident ghosts profiled on the TV show *Unsolved Mysteries*, and a guest book signed by Jesse James, the **St. James Hotel** (⊠*NM 21 at 17th St.* ☎*575/376–2664* ⊕*www.stjamescimarron.com* ⊙ *Tours daily between 10 and 4*) epitomizes the Wild West. Every notable outlaw of the late 19th century is said to have visited the place. Chef to presidents Lincoln and Grant, Frenchman Henri Lambert opened the St. James first as a saloon in 1872 and then eight years later developed it into a hotel. The lobby is filled with Western Victoriana: overstuffed sofas; stuffed heads of bison, elk, deer, and bear on the walls; and fringe on the lamp shades.

★ The workers who toiled inside the sturdy stone building that holds the **Old Mill Museum** once processed 300 barrels of flour a day for the Maxwell Ranch and the Jicarilla Apache reservation. Now the mill houses four floors of vintage photos, clothing, tools, and memorabilia depicting life in Colfax County from the 1860s into the 20th century. ⊠*220 W. 17th St., 1 block north of St. James Hotel* ☎*575/376–2417* ▱*$2* ⊙ *Late May–early Sept., Mon. and Wed.–Sat. 10–noon and 1–5. Sun. 1–5. 10–3.*

The largest scouting venue in the world, 137,000-acre **Philmont Scout Ranch** hosts nearly 30,000 Boy Scouts every summer—on any given day about 3,000 of them are out plying the property's miles of rugged trails. Phillips Petroleum magnate and Boy Scouts of American benefactor Waite Phillips established the mountainous ranch. The museums of the Philmont Scout Ranch include **Villa Philmonte,** the restored 1927 Spanish-Mediterranean summer home of Waite Phillips, furnished with European and Southwestern antiques and Native American and Southwestern art. Tours of the mansion are conducted in July and August. Scouting cofounder Ernest Thompson Seton donated most of the holdings of the **Philmont Museum & Seton Memorial Library,** among them New Mexican art and artifacts and books on natural history and the history of the Southwest. ⊠*NM 21, 4 mi south of Cimarron* ☎*575/376–2281* ▱*Museum free, villa tour $5* ⊙ *Museum Sept.–May, weekdays 8–5; June–Aug., daily 8–5:30. Villa tours July and Aug., daily 7:45–4:30; by appt. rest of yr.*

☺ Costumed reenactments at **Kit Carson Museum** demonstrate 19th-century life on what was then the Maxwell Land Grant, but is now part of the incredible Philmont Ranch. Exhibits include a working horno oven, blacksmith shop, and the Maxwell Trading Post—stocked as it might have been during Santa Fe Trail days. Period crafts are also demonstrated. ⊠*NM 21, 11 mi south of Cimarron in Rayado* ☎*575/376–4621* ▱*Free* ⊙ *June–Aug., daily 8–5.*

**OFF THE
BEATEN
PATH**
★

Valle Vidal. One of New Mexico's great scenic routes heads northwest from U.S. 64 toward the town of Costillo (44 mi north of Taos on NM 522), affording great opportunities for sighting elk, deer, wild turkeys, and many other birds. The roughly 80-mi dirt road requires several hours of driving to complete—although it's okay for non–four-wheel-drive vehicles in summer and fall (assuming there hasn't been a major rainfall in a couple days and you're comfortable driving on some pretty rough roads). The trip passes through high-mountain grasslands, ponderosa, aspen, and sandstone cliffs. The fishing (season is July–December) in Valle Vidal is mighty fine—the native Rio Grande cutthroat trout is found only in the rivers here—and there are two campgrounds, Cimarron and McCrystal. The western section of the road is closed May through June for elk-calving season, and the eastern section is closed to protect the elks January through March. ⊠ *Off U.S. 64, turnoff is 8 mi east of Cimarron* ☎ *575/758–6200.*

WHERE TO EAT & STAY

¢ ✕**Colfax Tavern.** Also known as Cold Beer, New Mexico, this little red
AMERICAN roadhouse continues a tradition from the Prohibition era. An ongoing
★ card game, excellent green-chile burgers, Shiner Bock (a beloved beer from Shiner, Texas) on tap, spaghetti Monday, Saturday-night dances, and a winter *Jeopardy!* tournament are among the joint's trademarks. Visitors can walk into this hangout and feel right at home. Wear your cowboy boots. ⊠ *U.S. 64, 11 mi east of Cimarron, Colfax* ☎ *575/376–2229* ⚑ *Reservations not accepted* ☰ *No credit cards.* ☉ *Open 1–close. Closed Tuesday.*

$ ☷**Casa del Gavilan.** On the Santa Fe Trail and directly below the Tooth
★ of Time, this 1912 white adobe compound (the name means "house of the hawk") on 225 acres is a romantic hideaway of the first order. The original owner, industrialist J. J. Nairn, used to entertain artists and other creative types here, and writer Zane Grey wrote "Knights of the Range" while he was holed up here. The rooms here are furnished with Southwestern antiques and artworks by the likes of Frederick Remington and Charles Stewart, and the 12-foot ceilings with huge pine vigas (support beams) lend an airy feel to the massive adobe walls. Breakfasts, which are fabulous, should be taken on the patio when the weather permits. **Pros:** Tranquil setting; large rooms. **Cons:** Remote; no TV. ⊠ *NM 21, 6 mi south of Cimarron* ⬡ *Box 518, 87714* ☎ *575/376–2246 or 800/428–4526* ⬚ *575/376–2247* ⬡ *www.casa delgavilan.com* ⚑ *5 rooms* ⬧ *In-room: no TV. In-hotel: no-smoking rooms* ☰ *D, MC, V* ❙◎❙ *BP.*

$ ☷**St. James Hotel.** Lace curtains and Victorian-era antiques adorn 12 of the rooms here (there are also 10 modern but less distinctive motel rooms). The lodgings aren't particularly luxurious (or soundproofed), and there's a bit of a chill in the air—but that's just what you'd expect in an allegedly haunted hotel. The restaurant ($–$$), with a ceiling full of bullet holes from the old days, serves steaks and pastas, and the café (¢–$$) serves American and Mexican standards. **Pros:** Quaint; rustic. **Cons:** Thin walls; noise can be an issue. ⊠ *NM 21 at 17th St.,* ☎ *575/376–2664 or 866/472–5019* ⬚ *575/376–2623* ⬡ *www.stjames cimarron.com* ⚑ *22 rooms, 1 suite* ⬧ *In-hotel: restaurant, bar* ☰ *AE, D, MC, V.*

7

SCENIC DRIVE

One of the most breathtaking stretches of highway in the state is U.S. 64 west from Cimarron through **Cimarron Canyon State Park** (☎ 575/377–6271 ⊕ www.emnrd. state.nm.us/prd/CimarronCanyon.htm ⌨ $5 per vehicle). The road passes through a steep and lush canyon banked by 400-foot crenellated granite palisades. Paralleling the road is the sparkling Cimarron River, which is known for its superb trout fishing. Wildlife (including elk, deer, and bear), granite cliff formations, a natural spring, an abandoned mine, and a visitor center are also draws. There's a campground beneath the pines, too, with spaces for RVs (no hookups) and tents, picnic tables, and pit toilets.

West of Cimarron Canyon State Park, U.S. 64 passes over a high bald ridge, from which you'll be awarded a magnificent view over **Eagle Nest Lake**, the Moreno Valley, and the eastern slope of the Sangre de Cristo Mountains in the distance. Continue down through Eagle Nest Lake village toward Angel Fire. Then make a left turn (south) onto NM 434, which passes little Black Lake and offers one final view of the valley before narrowing sharply and plum-

meting into dark, deep, ponderosa pine–shrouded Guadalupita Canyon. Drive slowly: the road twists and turns and crosses several one-lane bridges over Coyote Creek.

The Rincon Mountains rise to 9,500 feet to the west of NM 434, and to the east (a left turn off the highway) you can stop for a ramble at **Coyote Creek State Park** (☎ 575/387–2328 ⌨ $5), which also has exceptionally good trout fishing and some campsites.

South of Coyote Creek State Park on NM 434, you'll pass through tiny, insular **El Turquillo.** Here the highway widens as it opens into a broad sunny valley—to the east you'll spy the red-rock cliffs that form the face of Black Mesa, the land barrier between here and the eastern grasslands.

As you come around a bend in NM 434 heading from El Turquillo toward Mora, behold the Sangre de Cristo range, specifically the east side of **Trampas and Truchas peaks,** from an angle few tourists ever see. Just before Mora and the intersection with NM 518 is an intricate network of irrigation ditches that farmers employ to keep this region so fertile.

SHOPPING

Just off the main highway to the north is a street of historic buildings and a few shops. The **Cimarron Art Gallery** (✉ 337 E. 9th St. ☎ 575/376–2614) sells Southwestern odds, ends, and artifacts, and there's a 1930s soda fountain that serves sodas, ice-cream cones, and coffee drinks. **Blue Moon Eclectics** (✉ 333 E. 9th St. ☎ 575/376–9040) has locally made arts and crafts as well as some Navajo and Zuni jewelry.

Tapetes de Lana

There are few fairy-tale stories of revitalized rural economies in America. Tapetes de Lana is one of them.

Tapetes de Lana ("wool tapestry" in Spanish) started as a vocational-training program for weavers in Las Vegas in 1998 with a small grant and the sheer determination of its founder, Carla Gomez. Gomez had supported herself and her three children with her weaving for years and wanted to extend the skill to her community in the hopes that others could do the same rather than leave the area to find work or take minimum-wage jobs in one of the large national chain stores that have begun to populate the area.

What started out as a small group of women working in an old, one-room schoolhouse on the outskirts of Las Vegas has blossomed—considerably. Gomez now runs two weaving centers (one on the Las Vegas plaza, the other in the center of Mora), oversees 40 employees, and is supervising the construction of a spinning mill, theater arts complex, and commercial kitchen on the Mora property.

The weaving centers offer more than the promise of a new economic base in these relatively sleepy areas—they also represent a revitalization of a traditional art form that in many areas of the country is dying out entirely. Weaving has been a mainstay in New Mexico since 1598, when Don Juan de Oñate brought Spanish colonists and churro sheep from Spain. Despite struggling to stay vital since the late 1800s, New Mexico's weavers retain a reputation for high-quality, uniquely beautiful products. Tapetes de Lana has become an essential component of that living tradition.

And the result of all this industriousness? Gorgeous, handwoven shawls, scarves, rugs, and heirloom *jerga* blankets. Custom-made pillows, coasters, and yarns are available. Silk and alpaca, mohair, wool, and chenille textiles all hang gracefully from the walls and racks in the studios. Weavers study and practice their skills in the same studio where the work is sold.

When you're in Las Vegas or Mora, stop and visit the bustling shops and studios of Tapetes de Lana. You're witnessing rural revitalization in action.

7

MORA

72 mi south from Cimarron on U.S. 64 west to Eagle Nest Lake and NM 434 south via Angel Fire; 30 mi northwest of Las Vegas on NM 518; 85 mi northeast of Santa Fe via High Road to Taos north to Peñasco and then NM 518 south.

Originally settled in 1835 by land grantees, Mora was seen by the Mexican government as a buffer between their territory and encroaching Americans. The town grew rapidly from the get-go, but refused to give up loyalty to Mexico when the U.S. troops took over in 1846. Battles for control of the area raged for more than a year, until the United States finally gained the upper hand on its new territory. One hundred years ago, Mora was a bustling center of commerce and politics, and was known as the breadbasket of New Mexico because of its incredible production of wheat and grains. The wide, curbed streets and building fronts, though in need of restoration, attest to the town's past importance.

Today Mora is a small, still mostly Hispanic farming village where you can get gas, pick up snacks at the supermarket, and get your bearings. There are a couple of restaurants on the main road if a New Mexican meal is what you need. **Tapetes de Lana,** the local weaving collaborative, has a spacious studio and shop on the corner of NM 518 and NM 434, where you can purchase beautiful handwoven textiles and help support the local economy and culture. ☎*575/387–2247* ⊕*www. tapetesdelana.com.*

☺ If you've got animal-loving kids with you, stop by **Victory Ranch,** a working 1,100-acre alpaca farm. You can pet and feed the high-altitude–loving creatures as well as visit the gift shop for Peruvian-made hats, sweaters, and mittens. The ranch is handicapped-accessible. ⊠*NM 434, 1 mi north of NM 518* ☎*575/387–2254* ⊕*www.victoryranch. com* ☞*$3* ⊙*Daily 10–4.*

At the junction of NM 434 and NM 518, make a right and head a couple of miles north to **Cleveland Roller Mill,** a fixture in Mora Valley, which served as the region's main flour mill in the late 1800s. Milling demonstrations are held over the Labor Day Millfest, and in summer you can visit the artists' cooperative, where local artisans sell their sculpture, weaving, jewelry, and other crafts. ⊠*NM 518* ☎*575/387–2645* ☞*$2* ⊙*Daily 10–3.*

EN ROUTE

From Cleveland Roller Mill you can either return via NM 518 to Las Vegas (about 30 mi) or continue north on NM 518 over the gorgeous eastern face of the Sangre de Cristo range. You'll eventually come to Peñasco, on the High Road to Taos, from which you can either go south to Santa Fe or north to Taos. **The drive from Mora to Peñasco** offers spectacular mountain views, and passes by old farmsteads and adobe hamlets slowly being worn down by the wind and weather.

★ As you head south on NM 518 toward Las Vegas, be sure to stop in the **La Cueva Historic District.** Among the buildings here, which date to the 1850s, is a stone-walled mill that supplied flour to the soldiers of Fort Union. Pioneer rancher Vicente Romero's mill also supplied power to the area until 1950; at what is now called the Salman Ranch, you can pick raspberries early to mid-fall, or buy fresh berries, raspberry jam and vinegar, and dried flowers and herbs at the original La Cueva Ranch Store (open 9–5). Brilliantly colored wildflower gardens, and homemade tamales, burgers, and raspberry sundaes served at the café (11–4) draw families out for weekend excursions. The historic district's San Rafael Church, dating from the 1870s, is also worth a look. Call ahead for raspberry-picking hours. ⊠*NM 518 at NM 442, 10 mi south of Mora, 20 mi north of Las Vegas* ☎*575/387–2900* ⊙*Closed Mon.*

Southeastern New Mexico

WITH WHITE SANDS NATIONAL MONUMENT & TEXAS'S GUADALUPE MOUNTAINS

WORD OF MOUTH

"We made a loop to White Sands National Park (amazing), Alamogordo (space museum), Ruidoso, Roswell (great fun), and then Carlsbad Caverns (also amazing). Besides Carlsbad Caverns, you could make day trips to see most of these or visit on your drive in. To be honest, besides visiting the casino and shopping downtown, we didn't do much in Ruidoso but sit in our cabin and relax."

—seashell

"If you do decide to go to Carlsbad, I would highly recommend the Wild Cave Tour. Sign up for this now! Hall of the White Giants is the best one. Spider Cave would be my second choice."

—spirobulldog

Updated by
Georgia de
Katona

AWASH WITH GEOLOGICAL CONTRAST, THE landscapes of southeastern New Mexico shift before your eyes as you drive from one area to the next. Parched red earth sparsely dotted with scrub oak turns into miles of white gypsum dunes at White Sands National Monument. Making the 19-mi drive to Cloudcroft (8,600 feet) from Alamogordo will double your altitude, and take you into the cool mountain air of the heavily forested Lincoln National Forest. Curious, large-eared mule deer wander amid the juniper and pines, as well as among sand dunes near the Pecos River farther east. The seemingly monotonous Chihuahuan desert holds the underground wonderland of Carlsbad Caverns, the hulking El Capitan peak, and, in Guadalupe Mountains National Park, pure, bubbling streams, pine-laden basins, and prickly cactus. Sure, the terms "vast" and "desolate" are regularly applied to this area, but they're misleading, and only true until you look a bit closer at the amazing region you've wandered into.

Southeastern New Mexico retains a delicious feeling of wildness. The nearest interstate is generally as far as 200 mi away, and with no lights from strip malls or urban sprawl, the stargazing here is a treat for the expert and novice alike. Cloudcroft has one of the largest solar observatories in the world, the National Solar Observatory, because of the clarity of the skies and the absence of typical light pollution— Alamogordo, which lies at the base of the mountains, uses special lights to minimize glare. Of course, the area's seeming proximity to the heavens is what's made it the subject of an ongoing debate among UFO believers for almost 60 years: what was it, exactly, that fell from the sky over Roswell that night in July of 1947?

ORIENTATION & PLANNING

GETTING ORIENTED

The wildly rugged Guadalupe and Sacramento mountain ranges cut through the south-central portion of the state, dividing the Pecos River valley to the east from the Mesilla River valley to the west. The major highway south through southeastern New Mexico is U.S. 285, accessible from Interstate 40 at the Clines Corner exit, 59 mi east of Albuquerque. If you're destined for Roswell or Carlsbad from southwestern New Mexico, the best route is U.S. 70 east from Las Cruces or U.S. 62/180 east from El Paso, Texas. To get to Roswell and other points in southeastern New Mexico, drive east from Albuquerque on Interstate 40 for about 60 mi, exit on U.S. 285 heading south, and continue 140 mi to Roswell. From Roswell take U.S. 285 to Carlsbad, about 75 mi away (320 mi from Albuquerque). From El Paso, Texas, take U.S. 62/180 east and north 154 mi to Carlsbad Caverns (187 mi to Carlsbad).

The Southeast Corner. It's a lot more like Texas than other areas of New Mexico, and you'll notice lots of Texas drawls coming from the locals. Stark expanses of land are broken by the dramatic Guadalupe

TOP REASONS TO GO

■ **White Sands National Monument.** Journey to Mars....The otherworldly landscape of White Sands is an amazing place any time of day; the white gypsum sands glisten and remain surprisingly cooler than you'd think.

■ **Carlsbad Caverns.** Journey to the center of the earth....Nothing can prepare you for the visually stunning, massive scale of these incredible natural wonders. The comfortable subground temperatures are a delightful respite from the heat above.

■ **Roswell.** Journey beyond....Even if you aren't an alien enthusiast, visiting Roswell is a fun detour—especially with kids. You'll learn why rumors and stories persist and see every variety of alien souvenir—even plastic lawn aliens (à la those beloved pink flamingos).

■ **Cloudcroft and Ruidoso.** Journey to the clouds....Once you've gone down, head up—way, way up—where cool alpine breezes greet you. The towns remind you of their Old West history while offering all sorts of delightful respite from the blistering heat of the lowlands.

Mountains, and once you've visited Carlsbad Caverns you'll realize why so many passed by them without knowing what amazing things lay below.

East-Central Outposts. Cattle are the name of the game in the grassy plains of this region. You'll see huge open areas in between the small towns and amazing wildflowers if you're lucky enough to drive through after good rains. Tucumcari and Santa Rosa offer amazing displays of vintage neon along the famed Route 66.

Heading to High Country. After visiting the visually stunning and smoldering heat of White Sands, you'll be delightfully surprised by how fast the scenery and the temperature change as soon as you head into the mountains toward Cloudcroft or Ruidoso. The Wild West outpost of Lincoln is but one of the many fun historic towns to visit in the area.

SOUTHEASTERN NEW MEXICO PLANNER

WHEN TO GO

Winters tend to be gentle in the desert regions, but between May and early September blistering heat is not uncommon. Even the mountainous areas can be uncomfortably warm during a hot spell. Plan summer outdoor excursions for early morning or late afternoon. Spring is cooler, but it's often accompanied by blustery, dust-laden winds. One of the best times to visit is between September and early November, when skies are clear blue and the weather is usually balmy. The mountains typically get plenty of snow in the winter months, though the roads are well-maintained and navigable, and the snow wonderfully powdery and dry.

GETTING HERE AND AROUND

BY AIR Albuquerque International Sunport is 380 mi north of Carlsbad and 295 mi north of Roswell. El Paso International Airport in Texas is the main gateway to southern New Mexico. The major airlines with scheduled service to the airport are America West, American, Continental, Delta, Frontier, and Southwest. The municipal airports in Carlsbad and Roswell have daily shuttle-flight service on Mesa Airlines. Roswell is southeastern New Mexico's major flight hub, offering the most daily flights and scheduling options.

BY BUS Texas, New Mexico & Oklahoma Coaches, which is affiliated with Greyhound Lines, provides bus service to Carlsbad, White's City, and other destinations in southern New Mexico. Silver Stage Lines offers van service to Carlsbad Caverns National Park and Carlsbad by special charter.

BY CAR The quality of the roadways in southeastern New Mexico varies widely, particularly in remote rural areas. Drive with caution on the region's narrow highways, which particularly in mountainous areas have no shoulders. On minor roadways, even if paved, be alert for curves, dips, and steep drop-offs. You can rent a car at El Paso International Airport and Albuquerque International Sunport. Auto dealerships in some southeastern New Mexico cities rent cars. Your best bet for finding car rentals in smaller communities, such as Roswell and Carlsbad, is at municipal airports. Both Avis and Hertz rent cars at the Roswell airport, while Hertz has a site at Carlsbad's airport. Enterprise in downtown Ruidoso will deliver rental cars to the Sierra Blanca Airport upon request.

VISITOR **Alamogordo Chamber of Commerce** (⊠ *1301 N. White Sands Blvd.* ☎ *575/437–*
INFORMATION *6120 or 888/843–3441* ⊕ *www.alamogordo.com*). **Capitan Chamber of Commerce** (⌂ *Box 441 88316* ☎ *575/354–2273 www.villageofcapitan.com*). **Carlsbad Chamber of Commerce** (⊠ *302 S. Canal St. 88220* ☎ *575/887–6516* ⊕ *www. carlsbadchamber.com*). **Carrizozo Chamber of Commerce** (⌂ *Box 567 88301* ☎ *575/648–2732 www.townofcarrizozo.org*). **Cloudcroft Chamber of Commerce** (⌂ *Box 1290 88317* ☎ *866/874–4447* ⊕ *www.cloudcroft.net*). **Lincoln State Monument** (⊠ *U.S. 380, 88338* ⌂ *Box 36 88338* ☎ *575/653–4372*). **Portales Chamber of Commerce** (⊠ *100 S. Ave. A 88130* ☎ *575/356–8541 or 800/635– 8036* ⊕ *www.portales.com*). **Roswell Chamber of Commerce** (⊠ *131 W. 2nd St. 88202* ☎ *575/623–5695 or 877/849–7679* ⊕ *www.roswellnm.org*). **Ruidoso Valley Chamber & Visitor Center** (⊠ *720 Sudderth Dr. 88345* ☎ *575/257–7395* ⊕ *www.ruidoso.net*). **Santa Rosa Visitor Information Center** (⊠ *486 Historic Rte. 66 88435* ☎ *575/472–3763* ⊕ *www.santarosanm.org*). **Tucumcari/Quay County Chamber of Commerce** (⊠ *404 W. Rte. 66 88401* ☎ *575/461–1694* ⊕ *www.tucumcarinm.com*).

ESSENTIALS **Airline Contacts Mesa Airlines** (☎ *800/637–2247* ⊕ *www.mesa-air.com*).

Airports Albuquerque International Sunport (⊠ *2200 Sunport Blvd. SE, Albuquerque* ☎ *505/842–4366*). **El Paso International Airport** (⊠ *6701 Convair Dr., El Paso, TX* ☎ *915/772–4271*). **Sierra Blanca Regional Airport** (⊠ *1 Airport Rd., Ruidoso* ☎ *575/336–8111*).

Bus Contacts **Gray Line of Albuquerque** (✉ *300 2nd St. SW, Albuquerque* ☎ *866/242–4998*). **Silver Stage Lines** (☎ *800/522–0162*). **Texas, New Mexico & Oklahoma Coaches** (☎ *575/887–1108 in Carlsbad, 800/231–2222 all other destinations*).

ABOUT THE RESTAURANTS

Leave the fancy duds at home—you're unlikely to find a formal dining room to strut into. Casual dress reigns supreme in this part of the world. Although much of southeastern New Mexico is cowboy country, where thick steaks and barbecue make the meal, good Mexican food can be found, too.

ABOUT THE HOTELS

You'll find generally reliable chain motels to choose from if that's what suits you, but you can also choose from a luxury resort, numerous quaint cabins, and several charming and beautiful bed-and-breakfasts in the Sacramento Mountains. These private facilities serve some of the tastiest food in the region and can offer amenities like therapeutic massage, horseback riding, and guided fishing and hiking tours.

WHAT IT COSTS					
	¢	$	$$	$$$	$$$$
Restaurants	under $10	$10–$15	$16–$22	$23–$30	over $30
Hotels	under $70	$70–$120	$121–$175	$176–$250	over $250

Restaurant prices are per person for a main course at dinner. Hotel prices are for two people in a standard double room in high season, excluding 10%–12% tax.

PLANNING YOUR TIME

You can explore a cross section of the southeast's attractions in three days by moving quickly. If you start your trip from El Paso, Texas, swing through Guadalupe Mountains and Carlsbad Caverns national parks first. If you're dropping down from Albuquerque, reverse the itinerary and make cities such as Ruidoso and Roswell your first stops before traveling on to the national parks. *See also Great Itineraries, below.*

THE SOUTHEAST CORNER

Some folks refer to the southeast as "Little Texas," and indeed you'll find the easy smiles and small-town graciousness of the neighbor state in great abundance. The biggest attraction—Carlsbad Caverns National Park—is just above the Texas state line. Cattle and sheep still roam miles of arid pastures, much the way they have for well over a century. During the past two decades a steady migration of newer residents—many of them retirees leaving crowded metropolitan areas for wide-open spaces and clean air—has added significantly to the population and to the availability of such staples as espresso.

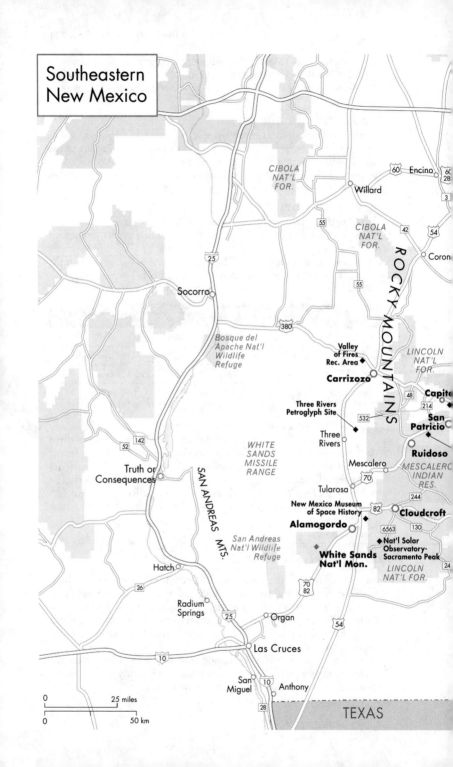

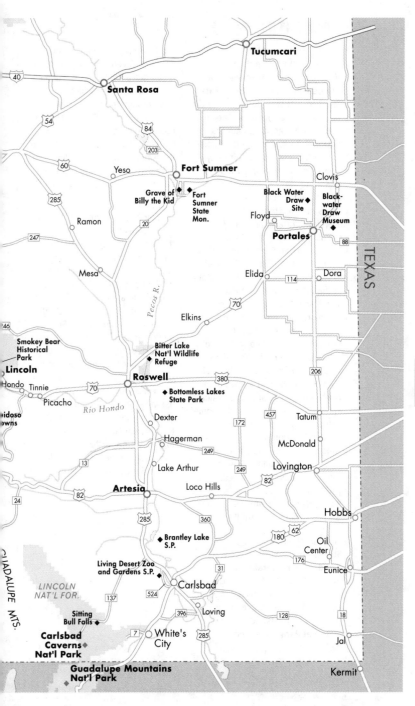

GREAT ITINERARIES

IF YOU HAVE 3 DAYS

It's best to start from the gateway of El Paso, Texas, and make **Guadalupe Mountains National Park** your first rest stop. Just north of the mountains, over the New Mexico state line, is **Carlsbad Caverns National Park**. Take the Big Room Tour in the late morning or early afternoon, and in warmer months, be sure to catch the spectacular evening bat exodus out of the cave's mouth. Afterward you can overnight in **Carlsbad**. On the morning of Day 2, stop by Living Desert Zoo and Gardens State Park before heading north to **Roswell** to learn about alleged alien visitors at the International UFO Museum and Research Center and view the impressive collections of the Roswell Museum and Art Center, including the Goddard rocketry display and paintings by Southwestern artists. Push on to overnight in **Lincoln**. You awaken in a town of 70, where the ghosts of past gunslingers loom large. Make time for some outdoor activities in the mountains surrounding **Ruidoso**. A ski resort is open in winter and horse racing takes place at Ruidoso Downs in summer. Arrange your schedule so you have at least an hour for **White Sands National Monument**, which is open in summer until 9.

IF YOU HAVE 5 DAYS

Spend most of your first day at **Guadalupe Mountains National Park** in Texas. At McKittrick Canyon are three trails of varying lengths. On your first evening, view the bat flight at **Carlsbad Caverns National Park** and spend the night there.

On the morning of Day 2, return to Carlsbad Caverns to take the Natural Entrance Route into the depths of the cavern, after which you can loop through the interior, and then take the Big Room Tour. That afternoon visit Living Desert Zoo and Gardens State Park in **Carlsbad**. In the evening consider strolling some of the scenic walkways along the Pecos River at the Lake Carlsbad Recreation Area.

On Day 3 drive north on U.S. 285 to **Roswell**, where you can stop at the Roswell Museum and Art Center and International UFO Museum and Research Center. Continue to **Lincoln** on U.S. 70/380 west and take in a bit of the Wild West before settling down for the night at one of the B&Bs there. Spend Day 4 perusing the museums and galleries of **Ruidoso** and Ruidoso Downs. Spend the night at Inn of the Mountain Gods, or at one of the many nice inns in Ruidoso. On Day 5, swing through **Cloudcroft** before examining the space ware at the New Mexico Museum of Space History in **Alamogordo**. Close your day and finish up the last roll of film at **White Sands National Monument**.

GUADALUPE MOUNTAINS NATIONAL PARK

8

Guadalupe Mountains National Park

Guadalupe Mountains National Park is a study in extremes: it has mountaintop forests but also rocky canyons, arid deserts, and a gurgling stream that winds through verdant woods. The park is home to the Texas madrone tree, found commonly only here and in Big Bend National Park. Guadalupe Mountains National Park also has the distinction of hosting the loftiest spot in Texas: 8,749-foot Guadalupe Peak. The mountain dominates the view from every approach, but it's just one member of a rugged range carved by wind, water, and time.

WELCOME TO GUADALUPE MOUNTAINS

El Capitan

NEW MEXICO
TEXAS

Cutoff Mountain
6,933 ft

TOP REASONS TO GO

★ **Tower over Texas:** The park is home to 8,749-foot Guadalupe Peak, the highest point in the state.

★ **Fall for fiery foliage:** Though surrounded by arid desert and rocky soil, the park has miles of beautiful foliage in McKittrick Canyon. In late October you can watch it burst into flaming colors.

★ **Hike unhindered:** The main activity at the park is hiking its rugged, remote, and often challenging trails: 80 mi worth will keep you captivated and spry—and far away from civilization.

★ **Eat with elk, loll with lions:** Despite the surrounding arid region, a variety of wildlife—including shaggy brown elk, sneaky mountain lions, and shy black bears—traipses the mountains, woods, and desert here.

★ **Catch a (ghost) stagecoach:** In the late 1830s a stagecoach line ran from St. Louis and San Francisco with a stop at what's now Guadalupe Mountains National Park. The stages are long gone, but ruins of an old station still remain in the park, along with old ranch houses.

1 Guadalupe Peak. This crude, rocky pinnacle tops 8,700 feet and towers over the rest of the park's peaks. Those who brave the seven hour–plus round-trip to the summit are rewarded with breathtaking views of New Mexico and southwestern Texas.

2 McKittrick Canyon. In late October and early November, the lush green foliage along McKittrick Canyon's trout-filled desert stream bursts into russet, amber, and gold hues. An easy, handicapped-accessible ramble takes visitors through this geological wonder.

3 El Capitan. Not to be confused with equally impressive El Capitan in Yosemite National Park, this 3,000-foot cliff dominates the view at the southern end of the Guadalupe Range. It has visitors talking and hikers walking: a 6- to 11-mi-plus trail winds around the base of this massive limestone formation.

4 Manzanita Spring. The area around this idyllic stream and picnic spot has a little bit of everything: a spring feeds lush grasses and trees, giving life to hundreds of wildflowers. Birds hang out here to enjoy the tasty seeds and insects that the water, shade, and vegetation provide. Plus, it's only a 0.2-mi, paved ramble from here to the Frijole Ranch Museum.

5 Frijole Ranch Museum. This easily accessible historic ranch site houses the stone ruins of the oldest structure in the park. The recently restored ranch-house museum injects a bit of man-made history into the natural surroundings. Five nearby springs are just a refreshing stroll away.

Texas Madrone

TEXAS

8

137

Dog Canyon

Pratt Cabin

BROKEOFF MOUNTAINS

OFF RIDGE

Lost Peak
7,830 ft

McKittrick Canyon 2

GUADALUPE MOUNTAINS

◆ **Grotto**

FRIJOLE RIDGE

62 180

Bush Mountain
8,631 ft

Bartlett Peak
8,508 ft

5 **Frijole Ranch Museum**

Shumard Peak
8,615 ft

Hunter Peak
8,368 ft

4

Guadalupe Peak 1
(highest point in Texas)
8,749 ft

Pine Springs ◆
Stay Station Ruins

Williams Ranch ◆

El Capitan 3
8,085 ft

Williams Ranch Rd.

Visitor Center

GETTING ORIENTED

The park is off U.S. 62/180, 110 mi east of El Paso, Texas; 40 mi southwest of Carlsbad Caverns National Park; and 55 mi southwest of Carlsbad, New Mexico. White's City, New Mexico, is 35 mi northeast of the park on U.S. 62/180.

0   2 mi
0   2 km

62 180

Quail Mountain
4,962 ft

KEY	
📛	Ranger Station
△	Campground
🛆	Picnic Area
🍴	Restaurant
🏨	Lodge
🥾	Trailhead
🚻	Restrooms
�ºᐟ	Scenic Viewpoint
⋯	Walking/Hiking Trails
⋯⋯	Bicycle Path

GUADALUPE MOUNTAINS NATIONAL PARK PLANNER

When to Go

Trails here are rarely crowded, except in fall, when foliage changes colors in McKittrick Canyon, and during spring break in March. Still, this is a very remote area, and you probably won't find too much congestion at any time. Hikers are more apt to explore back-country trails in spring and fall, when it's cooler but not too cold. Snow, not uncommon in the winter months, can linger in the higher elevations.

Getting There & Around

Since about half of the Guadalupe Mountains is a designated wilderness, few roadways penetrate the park. Most sites are accessible off U.S. 62/180. Dog Canyon Campground on the north end of the park can be reached via Route 137, which traverses the woodlands of Lincoln National Forest.

AVG. HIGH/LOW TEMPS

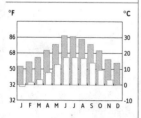

Flora & Fauna

Despite the constant wind and the arid conditions, more than a thousand species of plants populate the mountains, chasms, and salt dunes that make up the park's different geologic zones. Some grow many feet in a single night; others bloom so infrequently they're called "century plants." Some of the most spectacular sights, however, are seasonal. In fall, McKittrick Canyon's oaks, bigtooth maples, and velvet ashes go Technicolor above the little stream that traverses it. Barren-looking cacti burst into yellow, red, and purple bloom in spring, and wildflowers can carpet the park for thousands of acres after unusually heavy rains.

Hundreds of animal species haunt the diverse environments of the Guadalupes. At last count there were nearly 300 different bird species, 90 types of butterflies, and 16 species of bats alone. The park's furry residents include coyotes, black bears, and badgers. You may also spot elk, which were reintroduced here in the late 1920s after nearly becoming wiped out here.

Plenty of reptiles and insects make their homes here too: coachwhip snakes, diamondback rattlers, and lovelorn tarantulas (the only time you'll spy them is in the fall, when they search for mates), to name a few. Texas's famous horned lizards—affectionately called "horny toads"—can also be seen waddling across the soil in search of ants and other insects. Rangers caution parents not to let little ones run too far ahead on the trails. ■TIP→ **Be mindful that rattlesnakes are common in the park. They aren't aggressive, but be sure to give a wide berth to any snakes your hear or spot.**

8

MORE THAN 86,000 ACRES OF mountains, chasms, canyons, woods, and deserts house an incredible diversity of wildlife, including hallmark Southwestern species like roadrunners and long-limbed jackrabbits, which run so fast they appear to float on their enormous, black-tipped ears.

SCENIC DRIVE

Williams Ranch Road. You'll take in panoramic views and get an up-close look at limestone cliffs on this 7¼-mi, one-way drive over what was once the Butterfield Overland Mail Stage Line. The closest highway, U.S. 180, parallels the old trail. The rough route—you'll need a high-clearance, four-wheel-drive vehicle or a mountain bike—is enjoyable. To drive it, get a gate key at the Pine Springs visitor center and drive west on U.S. 62/180 for 8¼ mi until you see a brown metal gate on the north side with a National Park Service sign. Drive through two locked gates (be sure to lock them behind you), and follow the road to an old, lonely ranch house. James "Dolph" Williams operated this spread with his partner, an Indian named Geronimo (no relation to the historical figure). The road closes at night, though, so don't tarry too long.

WHAT TO SEE

HISTORIC SITES

★ **Frijole Ranch Museum.** You'll find displays and photographs depicting ranch life and early park history inside this old ranch-house museum. Hiking trails are adjacent to the shady, tree-lined grounds. Some of the trails, which are easy to travel and great for kids, lead to the **Manzanita Spring.** ⊠*Access road 1 mi northeast of Headquarters Visitor Center* ☎*915/828–3251* ☒*Free* ☉*Call for hours.*

★ **Pinery Butterfield Stage Station Ruins.** In the mid-1800s passengers en route from St. Louis or San Francisco would stop for rest and refreshment this structure, one of the stops along the old Butterfield Overland Mail stagecoach route. A paved ¾-mi round-trip trail leads here from the Headquarters Visitor Center, or you can drive directly here. ⊠½ *mi east of Headquarters Visitor Center.*

SCENIC STOP

Fodor'sChoice **McKittrick Canyon.** A desert creek flows through this canyon, which is
★ lined with walnut, maple, and other trees that explode into brilliant colors each fall. Call the visitor center to find out the progress of the colorful fall foliage; the spectacular changing of the leaves can often take until November, depending on the weather. You're likely to spot mule deer heading for the water here. ⊠*4 mi off U.S. 62/180, about 7 mi northeast of Headquarters Visitor Center* ☉*Highway gate open Nov.–Apr., daily 8–4:30; May–Sept., daily 8–6.*

VISITOR CENTERS

Headquarters Visitor Center. Exhibits and a slide show here give you a quick introduction to the park, half of which is a wilderness area. Some nicely crafted exhibits depict typical wildlife and plant scenes.

⊠*U.S. 62/180, 55 mi southwest of Carlsbad, 110 mi east of El Paso* ☏*915/828–3251* ☉*June–Aug., daily 8–6; Sept.–May, daily 8–4:30.*

McKittrick Contact Station. Poster-size illustrations in a shaded, outdoor patio area tell the geological story of the Guadalupe Mountains, believed to have been carved from an ancient sea. You can also hear the recorded memoirs of oilman Wallace Pratt, who donated his ranch and surrounding area to the federal government for preservation. ⊠*4 mi off U.S. 62/180, 7 mi northeast of Headquarters Visitor Center* ☏*915/828–3251 (Headquarters Visitor Center)* ☉*June–Aug., daily 8–6; Sept.–May, daily 8–4:30.*

SPORTS & THE OUTDOORS

BIRD-WATCHING

More than 300 species of birds have been spotted in the park, including the ladder-backed woodpecker, Scott's oriole, Say's phoebe, and white-throated swift. Many non-native birds—such as fleeting hummingbirds and larger but less graceful turkey vultures—stop at Guadalupe during spring and fall migrations. **Manzanita Springs,** located near the Frijole Ranch Museum, is an excellent birding spot. As with hiking, there aren't any local guides, but rangers at the Dog Canyon and Pine Springs stations can help you spot some native species. Books on birding are available at the Pine Springs station; visitors might find the Natural History Association's birding checklist for Guadalupe Mountains National Park especially helpful. It will be easy to spot the larger birds of prey circling overhead, such as keen-beaked golden eagles and swift, red-tailed hawks. Be on the lookout for owls in the **Bowl** area, and watch for swift-footed roadrunners in the desert areas (they're quick, but not as speedy as their cartoon counterpart).

HIKING

No matter which trail you select, be sure to pack wisely—the park doesn't sell anything. This includes the recommended gallon of water per day per person, as well as sunscreen and hats. (Bring a five, too—that's the additional cost to use the trails, payable at the visitor centers.) The area has a triple-whammy as far as sun ailments are concerned: it's very open, very sunny, and has a high altitude (which makes sunburns more likely). Slather up. And be sure to leave Fido at home—few of the park's trails allow pets. The staff at the **Dog Canyon ranger station** (☏*575/981–2418*) can help you plan your hike. The bookstore at the **Pine Springs ranger station** also sells hiking guides. These and other guides can also be found at ⊕*www.ccgma.org.*

EASY The **Indian Meadows Nature Trail** in Dog Canyon is a very easy, mostly level ½-mi hike that crosses an arroyo into meadowlands. It's a good way to spend about 45 minutes savoring the countryside.

The easiest McKittrick trail is the 1-mi **McKittrick Nature Loop.** Signs along the way explain the geological and biological history of the area. The trail is handicapped accessible and great for little ones. Plus, you can see the canyon's signature foliage in the late fall.

Fodor's Choice

MODERATE **Bush Mountain,** a moderate 4.5-mi round-trip, rewards you with a panoramic view of West Dog Canyon. It will take about half a day to complete. ⌧*Rte. 137, 60 mi southwest of U.S. 285.*

The moderate **Devil's Hall Trail** runs through about 4 mi of Chihuahua Desert habitat, thick with spiked agave plants, prickly pear cacti, and giant boulders, and Devil's Hall, a narrow canyon about 10 feet wide and 100 feet deep. This moderate hike, which begins at the Pine Springs trailhead, will take about a day if you travel at a leisurely pace.

★ The **El Capitan/Salt Basin Overlook Trails** form a popular loop through the low desert. El Capitan skirts the base of El Capitan peak for about 3.5 mi, leading to a junction with Salt Basin Overlook. The 4.5-mi Salt Basin Overlook trail begins at the Pine Springs trailhead and has views of the stark, white salt flat below and loops back onto the El Capitan Trail. Though moderate, the 11.3-mi round-trip is not recommended during the intense heat of summer, since there is absolutely no shade. ⌧*Behind Headquarters Visitor Center at Pine Springs campground.*

The **Frijole/Foothills Trail,** which branches off the Frijole Ranch trailhead, leads to the Pine Springs campground behind Headquarters Visitor Center. The moderate, 5.5-mi round-trip route through desert vistas takes about five hours.

The 6.75-mi round-trip to the **Grotto Picnic Area** starts at the McKittrick Contact Station. It affords views of a flowing stream and surface rock that resembles formations in an underground cave, with jagged overhangs. Plan on about five hours for a leisurely walk.

You can view stream and canyon woodland areas along the **Pratt Lodge Trail,** a 4.5-mi round-trip excursion that leads to the now vacant Pratt Lodge. Plan on at least two hours if you walk at a fast pace, but give yourself another hour or two if you want to take your time. ⌧*4 mi off U.S. 62/180, about 7 mi northeast of Headquarters Visitor Center.*

☾ The **Smith Spring Trail** also departs from the Frijole Ranch trailhead. The trail, a round-trip walk of 2.2 mi, takes you through a shady oasis where you're likely to spot mule deer alongside a spring and a small waterfall. Allow 1½ hours to complete the walk. This is a good hike for older kids, whose legs won't tire as easily. ⌧*Access road 1 mi northeast of Headquarters Visitor Center.*

DIFFICULT Cutting through forests of pine and Douglas fir, **The Bowl** is considered
Fodor'sChoice one of the most gorgeous trails in the park. The strenuous 9-mi round-
★ trip—which can take up to 10 hours, depending on your pace—begins at the Pine Springs trailhead. This is where rangers go when they want to enjoy themselves. Don't forget to bring lots of water and drink it!

The 8.5-mi **Guadalupe Peak Trail** is a strenuous workout over a steep grade, but it offers some great views of exposed cliff faces. The hike begins at the Pine Springs trailhead and can take up to eight hours to complete.

The somewhat strenuous **Lost Peak Trail** in Dog Canyon is 6.5-mi round-trip, which will take about six hours to complete if your pace is slower;

it leads from Dog Canyon into a coniferous forest.

If you're in shape and have a serious geological bent, you may want to hike the **Permian Ridge Geology Trail.** The 8.5-mi round-trip climb heads through open, expansive desert country to a forested ridge with Douglas fir and ponderosa pines. Panoramic views of McKittrick Canyon and the surrounding mountain ranges will allow you to see the many rock layers that have been built up over the millennia. Begin at the McKittrick Contact Station, and set aside at least eight hours for this trek.

> **OUTFITTERS**
>
> The staff at **Dog Canyon Ranger Station** can help you plan your hikes. ⊠ *Box 400, Pine Canyon Rd., Salt Flat* ☎ *915/825–3251.*
>
> Visit **Headquarters Visitor Center** for hiking advice. ⌂ *HC 60, Box 400, Salt Flat, 79847* ☎ *915/828–3251.*

MOUNTAIN BIKING

If you've got a mountain bike cruise to the **Williams Ranch Trail.** Skittering down it will only take about an hour and a half one way and will lead you to the **Williams Ranch House,** which sits alone at the base of a 3,000-foot cliff. ■ TIP➜ Before you set out, check out the gate key at the **Headquarters Visitor Center.** Then head west on Highway 62/180. Drive 8¼ mi to the brown metal gate with National Park signs; be sure to lock the gate behind you once you're through. Proceed for another ¾ mi to another gate; lock this one as well once you're through it. Follow the worn dirt road—which runs past arid scenery and cacti that bloom in the spring months—to the Ranch House, and enjoy a great view of El Capitan. Be sure to leave before sundown, and don't forget to return the key to the visitor center.

WHAT'S NEARBY

Tiny White's City, New Mexico, 35 mi to the northeast off U.S. 62/180, is more of a crossroads than a town, and it's offerings are meager. The town of **Carlsbad, New Mexico,** 55 mi northeast of the park, has more amenities. **Artesia,** a sweet little town 91 mi north from the park, has several very nice lodging and dining options—worth the extra drive time. *For more information about both towns, including dining, lodging, and attractions, see town listings below.*

WHERE TO EAT

The park has no snack bars or restaurants, but several picnic areas are available. Wood and charcoal fires are not allowed anywhere in the park. If you want to cook a hot meal, bring a camp stove and your own supplies. Ranger stations don't serve meals or sell picnic items, though nearby White's City offers some basics—sodas, snacks, and the like—but dining here is mediocre at best. It's worth your time to push on to Carlsbad or a bit farther to Artesia (⇨ *below*) for quality dining.

Dog Canyon Campground. Thirteen campsites have picnic tables, which you can use during the day for free. This is a lovely shaded area where you're very likely to see mule deer. Drinking water and restrooms are available at the site. This area is about a 2½-hour hike from the Headquarters Visitor Center (you can also drive there). ✉ *Off Rte. 137, 65 mi southwest of Carlsbad.*

Frijole Ranch Museum. This area is much cooler than nearby Pine Springs Campground. Two picnic tables are set up under tall trees; restrooms are available at the ranch-house museum. ✉ *Access road 1 mi northeast of Headquarters Visitor Center.*

Pine Springs Campground. Shade varies depending on the time of day, and it can be hard to find a cool spot in hot summer. You will find drinking water and restrooms here, though. ✉ *Behind Headquarters Visitor Center.*

WHERE TO STAY

There are no hotels within the park. If you can drive to Artesia, there are a couple very nice lodging options available (⇨ *Where to Stay in Carlsbad Caverns National Park, below*). Carlsbad has one good, consistent hotel. Avoid White's City unless you're exhausted and can't drive another mile.

The park has two developed campgrounds that charge fees, and a number of designated primitive, backcountry sites where you can camp for free (check with the visitor center about using primitive sites). Wood and charcoal fires are prohibited throughout the park, but you can use your camp stove. The same rules apply for backcountry sites; however, no restrooms are provided. Visitors may dig their own privies, but toilet paper and other paper waste should be packed out.

¢ ⚠ **Dog Canyon Campground.** This campground is remote and a little
★ tricky to find, but well worth the effort. Located on the north side of Guadalupe National Park, it can be accessed by turning west on County Road 408 off U.S. 62/180, about 9 mi south of Carlsbad. Drive 23 mi on this county road; then turn south on Highway 137. Travel 43 mi through Lincoln National Forest until the road dead-ends just at the park boundary, at the New Mexico–Texas state line. The very well-maintained camping area is located in a coniferous forest, with hiking trails nearby. ✉ *Guadalupe Mountains National Park, off Rte. 137, 65 mi southwest of Carlsbad* ☎ *575/981–2418* 🛏 *4 RV sites, 9 tent sites* ♿ *Flush toilets, drinking water, picnic tables, public telephone, ranger station* ▤ *AE, D, MC, V.*

¢ ⚠ **Pine Springs Campground.** You'll be snuggled amid piñon and juniper trees at the base of a tall mountain peak at this site behind the Guadalupe Mountains National Park Visitor Center. Wood and charcoal fires are prohibited, although camp stoves are allowed. Shade here can be a bit sparse in the intense summer heat. Advance reservations are accepted for group sites only. ✉ *Guadalupe Mountains National Park, off U.S. 62/180* ☎ *915/828–3251* 🛏 *20 tent sites, 18 RV sites, 1 wheel-*

chair-accessible site, 2 group sites △ Flush toilets, drinking water, picnic tables, public telephone, ranger station ⊟AE, D, MC, V.

GUADALUPE MOUNTAINS ESSENTIALS

For more general information on visiting national parks, go to ⊕fodors.com/parks.

ACCESSIBILITY
The wheelchair-accessible Headquarters Visitor Center has a wheelchair available for use. The ¾-mi round-trip Pinery Trail from the visitor center to Butterfield Stage Ruins is wheelchair accessible, as is McKittrick Contact Station.

ADMISSION FEES
An admission fee of $8 per camping site ($5 per day-use person) is collected at the visitor center.

ADMISSION HOURS
The park is open 24 hours daily, year-round; some sites, like McKittrick Canyon, are day-use only.

AUTOMOBILE SERVICE STATION
Contacts **White's City 24-Hour Shell** (⊠ *17 Carlsbad Caverns Hwy., White's City* ☎ *575/785–2291).*

EMERGENCIES
There are no fire boxes in this largely wilderness park, but cell phones with far-reaching service can pick up signals at key points along trails. Rangers have emergency medical technician training and are also law-enforcement officers. To reach them, call 911 or contact Headquarters Visitor Center or Dog Canyon Ranger Station.

PERMITS
For overnight backpacking trips, you must get a free permit from either Headquarters Visitor Center or Dog Canyon Ranger Station.

VISITOR INFORMATION
Contacts **Headquarters Visitor Center** (✑ *HC 60, Box 400, Salt Flat, 79847* ☎ *915/828–3251* ⊕ *www.nps.gov/gumo).*

Carlsbad Caverns National Park

On the surface, Carlsbad Caverns National Park is deceptively normal—but all bets are off once visitors set foot in the elevator, which plunges 75 stories underground. The country beneath the surface is part silky darkness, part subterranean hallucination. The snaky, illuminated walkway seems less like a trail and more like a foray across the river Styx and into the Underworld. Within more than 14 football fields of subterranean space are hundreds of formations that alternately resemble cakes, soda straws, ocean waves, and the large, leering face of a mountain troll.

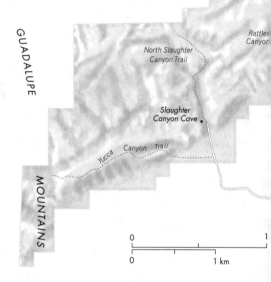

WELCOME TO CARLSBAD CAVERNS

TOP REASONS TO GO

★ **300,000 hungry bats:** Every night and every day, bats wing to and from the caverns in a swirling, visible tornado.

★ **Take a guided tour through the underworld:** Plummet 75 stories underground, and step into enormous caves hung with stalactites and bristling with stalagmites.

★ **Living Desert Zoo and Gardens:** More preserve than zoo, this 1,500-acre park houses scores of rare species, including endangered Mexican wolves and Bolson tortoises, and now boasts a new black bear exhibit.

★ **Birding at Rattlesnake Springs:** Nine-tenths of the park's 330 bird species, including roadrunners, golden eagles, and acrobatic cave swallows, visit this green desert oasis.

★ **Pecos River:** The Pecos River, a Southwest landmark, flows through the nearby town of Carlsbad. The river is always soothing, but gets festive for holiday floaters when riverside homeowners lavishly decorate their homes.

1 **Bat Flight.** Cowboy Jim White discovered the caverns after noticing that a swirling smokestack of bats appeared there each morning and evening. White is long gone, but the 300,000-member bat colony is still here, snatching up 3 tons of bugs a night. Watch them leave at dusk from the amphitheater located near the park visitor center.

2 **Carlsbad Caverns Big Room Tour.** Travel 75 stories below the surface to visit the Big Room, where you can traipse beneath a 255-foot-tall ceiling and take in immense and eerie cave formations. Situated directly beneath the park visitor center, the room can be accessed via quick-moving elevator or the natural cave entrance.

GUADALUPE

MOUNTAINS

Rattles Canyon

North Slaughter Canyon Trail

Slaughter Canyon Cave

Yucca   Canyon   Trail

0   1
0   1 km

TO
GUADALUPE MOUNT
NATIONAL PARK
& EL PASO, TEXAS

NEW MEXICO
TEXAS

3 Living Desert Zoo and Gardens. Endangered river cooters, Bolson tortoises, and Mexican wolves all roam in the Living Desert Zoo and Gardens. You can also skip alongside roadrunners and slim wild turkeys in the park's aviary, or visit a small group of cougars. The Living Desert is located within the town of Carlsbad, New Mexico, 23 mi to the north of the park.

4 The Pecos River. In the town of Carlsbad, a river runs through it—the Pecos River, that is. The river, a landmark of the Southwest, skims through town and makes for excellent boating, waterskiing, and fishing in some places. In the winter, residents gussy up dozens of riverside homes for the holiday season.

NEW MEXICO

GETTING ORIENTED

To get at the essence of Carlsbad Caverns National Park, you have to delve below the surface—literally. Most of the park's key sights are underground in a massive network of caves (there are 113 in all, although not all are open to visitors; a variety of tours leave from the visitor center). The park also has a handful of trails above ground, where you can experience the Chihuahua Desert and some magnificent geological formations.

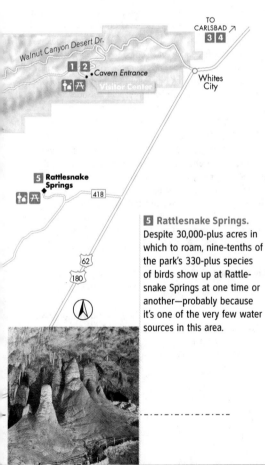

TO CARLSBAD ↗
3 4

Walnut Canyon Desert Dr.

1 2 •Cavern Entrance
Visitor Center

Whites City

5 **Rattlesnake Springs**

418

62
180

5 Rattlesnake Springs. Despite 30,000-plus acres in which to roam, nine-tenths of the park's 330-plus species of birds show up at Rattlesnake Springs at one time or another—probably because it's one of the very few water sources in this area.

KEY
🏠 *Ranger Station*
🔺 *Campground*
🌲 *Picnic Area*
🍴 *Restaurant*
🏨 *Lodge*
🥾 *Trailhead*
🚻 *Restrooms*
⟫ *Scenic Viewpoint*
...... *Walking/Hiking Trails*
...... *Bicycle Path*

CARLSBAD CAVERNS NATIONAL PARK PLANNER

When to Go

While the desert above may alternately bake or freeze, the caverns remain in the mid-50s; the fantastic formations don't change with the seasons either. If you're coming to see the Mexican free-tailed bat, however, come between spring and late fall.

Getting There & Around

Carlsbad Caverns is 27 mi southwest of Carlsbad, New Mexico, and 35 mi north of Guadalupe Mountains National Park via U.S. 62/180. The nearest full-service airport is in El Paso, 154 mi away. The 9.5-mi Walnut Canyon Desert Drive loop is one way. It's a curvy, gravel road and is not recommended for motor homes or trailers. Be alert for wildlife such as mule deer crossing roadways, especially in early morning and at night.

AVG. HIGH/LOW TEMPS

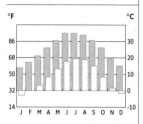

Flora & Fauna

Without a doubt, the park's most prominent and popular residents are Mexican free-tailed bats. These bats have bodies that barely span a woman's hand, yet sport wings that would cover a workingman's boot. Female bats give birth to a single pup each year, which usually weighs more than a quarter of what an adult bat does. Their tiny noses and big ears enable them to search for the many tons of bugs they consume over their lifetime. Numbering nearly a third of a million, these tiny creatures are the park's mascot.

Famous fanged flyers aside, there is much more wildlife to recommend in the park. One of New Mexico's best birding areas is at Rattlesnake Springs. Summer and fall migrations give you the best chance of spotting the most varieties of the more than 330 species of birds. Lucky visitors may spot a golden eagle, a rare visitor, or get the thrill of glimpsing a brilliant, gray-and-crimson vermilion flycatcher.

Snakes generally appear in summer. ■TIP→ **If you're out walking, be wary of different rattlesnake species, such as banded-rock and diamondbacks. If you see one, don't panic. Rangers say they are more scared of us than we are of them. Just don't make any sudden moves, and slowly walk away or back around the vipers.**

This area is also remarkable because of its location in the Chihuahua Desert, which sprouts unique plant life. There are thick stands of raspy-leaved yuccas, as well as the agave (mescal) plants that were once a food source for early Apache tribes. The leaves of this leggy plant are still roasted in sand pits by Apache elders during traditional celebrations.

In spring, thick stands of yucca plants unfold yellow flowers on their tall stalks. Blossoming cacti and desert wildflowers are one of the natural wonders of Walnut Canyon. You'll see bright red blossoms adorning ocotillo plants, and sunny yellow blooms sprouting from prickly pear cactus.

WHAT TO SEE

SCENIC STOPS

The Big Room. With a floor space equal in size to about 14 football fields, this underground focal point of Carlsbad Caverns clues visitors in to just how large the caverns really are. Its caverns are close enough to the trail to cause voices to echo, but the chamber itself is so vast voices don't echo far; the White House could fit in just one corner of the Big Room, and wouldn't come close to grazing the 255-foot ceiling. The 1-mi loop walk on a mostly level, paved trail is self-guided. An audio guide is also available from park rangers for a few dollars. ⊠ *At the visitor center* ⊠ *$6; free for kids under 15* ⊗ *Memorial Day–Labor Day, daily 8–5 (last entry into the Natural Entrance is at 3:30; last entry into the elevator is at 5); Labor Day–Memorial Day, daily 8:30–3:30 (last entry into the Natural Entrance at 2; last entry into the elevator at 3:30).*

*Fodor's*Choice ★

Natural Entrance. A self-guided, paved trail leads from the natural cave entrance. The route is winding and sometimes slick from water seepage aboveground. A steep descent of about 750 feet takes you about a mile through the main corridor and past features such as the Bat Cave and the Boneyard. (Despite its eerie name, the formations here don't look much like femurs and fibulas; they're more like spongy bone insides.) Iceberg Rock is a 200,000-ton boulder that dropped from the cave ceiling some millennia ago. After about a mile, you'll link up underground with the 1-mi Big Room trail and return to the surface via elevator. ⊠ *At the visitor center* ⊠ *$6* ⊗ *Memorial Day–Labor Day, daily 8:30–3:30; Labor Day–Memorial Day, daily 9–2.*

Rattlesnake Springs. Enormous cottonwood trees shade the picnic and recreation area at this cool oasis near Black River. The rare desert wetland harbors butterflies, mammals, and reptiles, as well as 90% of the park's 330 bird species. Don't let its name scare you; there may be rattlesnakes here, but not more than at any other similar site in the Southwest. Overnight camping and parking are not allowed. Take U.S. 62/180 5½ mi south of White's City and turn west onto Highway 418 for 2½ mi. ⊠ *Hwy. 418.*

VISITOR CENTER

A 75-seat theater offers an engrossing film about the different types of caves, as well as an orientation video that explains cave etiquette. Some of the rules include staying on paths so you don't get lost; keeping objects and trash in your pockets and not on the ground; and not touching the formations. Besides laying down the ground rules, visitor center exhibits offer a primer on bats, geology, wildlife, and the early tribes and nomads that once lived in and passed through the Carlsbad Caverns area. Friendly rangers staff an information desk, where tickets and maps are sold. Two gift shops also are on the premises. ⊠ *7 mi west of park entrance at White's City, off U.S. 62/180* ☎ *505/785–2232* ⊗ *Labor Day–Memorial Day, daily 8–5; Memorial Day–late Aug., daily 8–7.*

SPORTS & THE OUTDOORS

BIRD-WATCHING

From warty-headed turkey vultures to svelte golden eagles, about 330 species of birds have been identified in Carlsbad Caverns National Park. Ask for a checklist at the visitor center and then start looking for greater roadrunners, red-winged blackbirds, white-throated swifts, northern flickers, and pygmy nuthatches.

Rattlesnake Springs. Offering one of the best bird habitats in New Mexico, this is a natural wetland with old-growth cottonwoods. Because southern New Mexico is in the northernmost region of the Chihuahua Desert, you're likely to see birds that can't be found anywhere else in the United States outside extreme southern Texas and Arizona. If you see a flash of crimson, you might have spotted a vermilion flycatcher. Wild turkeys also flap around this oasis. ⊠ *Hwy. 418, 2½ mi west of U.S. 62/180, 5½ mi south of White's City.*

Fodor's Choice ★

HIKING

Deep, dark, and mysterious, the Carlsbad Caverns are such a park focal point that the 30,000-plus acres of wilderness above them have gone largely undeveloped. This is great news for people who pull on their hiking boots when they're looking for solitude. What you'll find are rudimentary trails that crisscross the dry, textured terrain and lead up to elevations of 6,000 feet or more. These routes often take a half day or more to travel; at least one, **Guadalupe Ridge Trail,** is long enough that it calls for an overnight stay. Walkers who just want a little dusty taste of desert flowers and wildlife should try the **Desert Nature Walk.**

Finding the older, less well-maintained trails can be difficult. Pick up a topographical map at the visitor center bookstore, and be sure to pack a lot of water. There's none out in the desert, and you'll need to drink at least a gallon per person per day. The high elevation coupled with potent sunshine can deliver a nasty sunburn, so be sure to pack SPF 30 (or higher) sunblock and a hat, even in winter. You can't bring a pet or a gun, but you do have to bring a backcountry permit if you're camping. They're free at the visitor center.

EASY   **Desert Nature Walk.** While waiting for the night bat-flight program, try taking the ½-mi self-guided hike. The tagged and identified flowers and plants make this a good place to get acquainted with much of the local desert flora. The paved trail is wheelchair accessible and an easy jaunt for even the littlest ones. The payoff is great for everyone, too: a big, vivid view of the desert basin. ⊠ *Off the cavern entrance trail, 200 yards east of the visitor center.*

Rattlesnake Canyon Overlook Trail. A ¼-mi stroll off Walnut Canyon Desert Drive offers a nice overlook of the greenery of Rattlesnake Canyon. ⊠ *Mile marker 9 on Walnut Canyon Desert Dr.*

MODERATE   **Juniper Ridge Trail.** Climb up in elevation as you head north on this nearly 3-mi trail, which leads to the northern edge of the park and then turns toward Crooked Canyon. While not the most notable trail, it's challenging enough to keep things interesting. Allow yourself half a

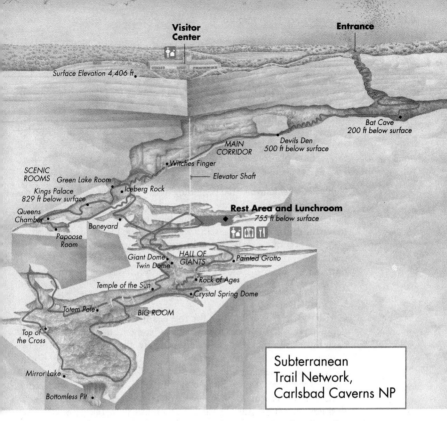

Visitor Center

Entrance

Surface Elevation 4,406 ft.

Bat Cave
200 ft below surface

MAIN CORRIDOR

Devils Den
500 ft below surface

Witches Finger

Elevator Shaft

SCENIC ROOMS

Green Lake Room

Iceberg Rock

Kings Palace
829 ft below surface

Rest Area and Lunchroom
755 ft below surface

Queens Chamber

Boneyard

Papoose Room

Giant Dome
Twin Dome

HALL OF GIANTS

Painted Grotto

Temple of the Sun

Rock of Ages

Crystal Spring Dome

Totem Pole

BIG ROOM

Top of the Cross

Mirror Lake

Bottomless Pit

Subterranean Trail Network, Carlsbad Caverns NP

day, and be sure to bring lots of water, especially when the temperature is high. ⊠ *Trailhead at 8.8 mi marker of Desert Loop Dr.*

Old Guano Road Trail. Meandering a little more than 3.5 mi one way on mostly flat terrain, the trail dips sharply toward White's City campground, where the trail ends. Give yourself about half a day to complete the walk. Depending on the temperature, this walk can be taxing. Drink lots of water. ⊠ *The trailhead is at the Bat Flight Amphitheater, near the Natural Cave Entrance and visitor center.*

Rattlesnake Canyon Trail. Rock cairns loom over this trail, which descends from 4,570 to 3,900 feet as it winds into the canyon. Allow half a day to trek down into the canyon and make the somewhat strenuous climb out; the total trip is about 6 mi. ⊠ *Mile marker 9 on Walnut Canyon Desert Dr.*

Fodor's Choice ★ **Yucca Canyon Trail.** Sweeping views of the Guadalupe Mountains and El Capitan give allure to this trail. Drive past Rattlesnake Springs and stop at the park boundary before reaching the Slaughter Canyon Cave parking lot. Turn west along the boundary fence line to the trailhead. The 6-mi round-trip begins at the mouth of Yucca Canyon, and climbs up to the top of the escarpment. Here you'll find the panoramic view. Most people turn around at this point; the hearty can continue along a poorly maintained route that follows the top of the ridge. The first part of the hike takes half a day. If you continue on, the hike takes a full day. ⊠ *Hwy. 418, 10 mi west of U.S. 62/180.*

DIFFICULT **Guadalupe Ridge Trail.** This long, winding ramble follows an old road all the way to the west edge of the park. Because of its length (about 12 mi), an overnight stay in the backcountry is suggested. The hike may be long, but for serious hikers the up-close-and-personal views into Rattlesnake and Slaughter canyons are more than worth it—not to mention the serenity of being miles and miles away from civilization. ⊠ *Follow Desert Loop Dr. 4.8 mi to the trailhead.*

North Slaughter Canyon Trail. Beginning at the Slaughter Canyon parking lot, the trail traverses a heavily vegetated canyon bottom into a remote part of the park. As you begin hiking, look off to the east (to your right) to see the dun-colored ridges and wrinkles of the Elephant Back formation, the first of many dramatic limestone formations visible from the trail. The route travels 5.5 mi one way, the last 3 mi steeply climbing onto a limestone ridge escarpment. Allow a full day for the round-trip. ⊠ *Hwy. 418, 10 mi west of U.S. 62/180.*

SPELUNKING

Carlsbad Caverns is famous for the beauty and breadth of its inky depths, as well as for the accessibility of some of its largest caves. All cave tours are ranger led, so safety is rarely an issue in the caves, no matter how remote. There are no other tour guides in the area, nor is there an equipment retailer other than the Wal-Mart located in Carlsbad, 23 mi away. Depending on the difficulty of your cave selection (Spider Cave is the hardest to navigate), you'll need at most knee pads, flashlight batteries, sturdy pants, hiking boots with ankle support, and some water.

Hall of the White Giant. Plan to squirm through some tight passages for long distances to access a very remote chamber, where you'll see towering, glistening white formations that explain the name of this feature. This strenuous, ranger-led tour lasts about four hours. Steep drop-offs might elate you—or make you queasy. Wear sturdy hiking shoes, and pick up four AA batteries for your flashlight before you come. Visitors must be at least 12 years old. ⊠ *At the visitor center* ☎ *877/444–6777* ⊡ *$20* ⚠ *Reservations essential* ⊙ *Tour Sat. at 1.*

King's Palace. Throughout King's Palace, you'll see leggy "soda straws" large enough for a giant to sip and multi-tiered curtains of stone—sometimes by the light of just a few flashlights. The mile-long walk is on a paved trail, but there's one very steep hill. This ranger-guided tour lasts about 1½ hours and gives you the chance to experience a blackout, when all lights are extinguished. While advance reservations are highly recommended, this is the one tour you might be able to sign up for on the spot; it's also the only tour that will take you to the Queen's Chamber. Children under 4 aren't allowed on this tour. ⊠ *At the visitor center* ☎ *877/444–6777* ⊡ *$8* ⊙ *Tours Labor Day–Memorial Day, daily 10 and 2; Memorial Day–Labor Day, daily 10, 11, 2, and 3.*

Left Hand Tunnel. Lantern light illuminates the easy walk on this detour in the main Carlsbad Cavern, which leads to Permian Age fossils—indicating that these caves were hollowed from the Permian Reef that still underlies the Guadalupe Mountain range above. The guided tour over a packed, dirt trail lasts about two hours. It's a moderate trek that older kids can easily negotiate, but children under 6 aren't allowed. ⊠ *At the visitor center* ☎ *877/444–6777* ⛏ *$8* ⊙ *Tour daily at 9.*

Lower Cave. Fifty-foot vertical ladders and a dirt path will take you into undeveloped portions of Carlsbad Caverns. It takes about half a day to negotiate this moderately strenuous side trip led by a knowledgeable ranger. Children younger than 12 are not allowed on this tour. ⊠ *At the visitor center* ☎ *877/444–6777* ⛏ *$20* ⚲ *Reservations essential* ⊙ *Tour weekdays at 1.*

★ **Slaughter Canyon Cave.** Discovered in the 1930s by a local goatherd, this cave is one of the most popular secondary sites in the park, about 23 mi southwest of the main Carlsbad Caverns and visitor center. Both the hike to the cave mouth and the tour will take about half a day, but it's worth it to view the deep cavern darkness as it's punctuated only by flashlights and, sometimes, headlamps. From the Slaughter Canyon parking area, give yourself 45 minutes to make the steep ½-mi climb up a trail leading to the mouth of the cave. Arrange to be there a quarter of an hour earlier than the appointed time. You'll find that the cave consists primarily of a single corridor, 1,140 feet long, with numerous side passages.

You can take some worthwhile pictures of this cave. Wear hiking shoes with ankle support, and carry plenty of water. You're also expected to bring your own two-D-cell flashlight. Children under age 6 are not permitted. It's a great adventure if you're in shape and love caving. ⊠ *End of Hwy. 418, 10 mi west of U.S. 62/180* ☎ *877/444–6777* ⛏ *$15* ⚲ *Reservations essential* ⊙ *Tours Memorial Day–Labor Day, daily 10 and 1; post–Labor Day–Dec., weekends at 10; Jan.–Memorial Day, weekends 10 and 1.*

Spider Cave. Visitors may not expect to have an adventure in a cavern system as developed and well stocked as Carlsbad Caverns, but serious cavers and energetic types have the chance to clamber up tight tunnels, stoop under overhangs, and climb up steep, rocky pitches. This back-country cave is listed as "wild," a clue that you might need a similar nature to attempt a visit. Plan to wear your warm, but least-favorite clothes, as they'll probably get streaked with grime. You'll also need soft knee pads, 4 AA batteries, leather gloves, and water. The gloves and pads are to protect you on long, craggy clambers and the batteries are for your flashlight. It will take you half a day to complete this ranger-led tour noted for its adventure. Visitors must be at least 12 years old and absolutely not claustrophobic. ⊠ *Meet at visitor center* ☎ *877/444–6777* ⛏ *$20* ⚲ *Reservations essential* ⊙ *Tour Sun. at 1.*

OUTFITTERS & EXPEDITIONS   Spelunkers who wish to explore both developed and wild caves are in luck; park rangers lead visitors on six different tours, including the **The Hall of the White Giant** and **Spider Cave,** known for its tight twists and grimy climbs. Reservations are required at least a day in advance. If you're making reservations 21 days or more before your visit, you can send a check; 20 days or less, and you must pay by credit card over the phone or online. ☎877/444–6777 ⊕*www.nps.gov/cave/planyourvisit/ feesandreservations.htm.*

Those who want to go it alone outside the more established caverns can get permits and information about 10 backcountry caves from the **Cave Resources Office** (☎575/785–2232). Heed rangers' advice for these remote, undeveloped, nearly unexplored caves.

EDUCATIONAL OFFERINGS

RANGER PROGRAMS

Ⓒ **Evening Bat Flight Program.** In the amphitheater at the Natural Cave
Fodor's Choice Entrance (off a short trail from main parking lot) a ranger discusses
★ the park's batty residents before the creatures begin their sundown exodus. The bats aren't on any predictable schedule, so times are a little iffy. ⊠*Natural Cave Entrance, at the visitor center* ☒*Free* ☉*Mid-May–mid-Oct., nightly at sundown.*

NEARBY TOWNS

On the Pecos River, with 2¾ mi of beaches and picturesque riverside pathways, **Carlsbad, New Mexico,** seems suspended between the past and the present. It's part university town, part Old West, with a robust Mexican kick. The Territorial town square, a block from the river, encircles a Pueblo-style country courthouse designed by New Mexican architect John Gaw Meem. Artesia is a quaint historical town with more dining and lodging options than Carlsbad in terms of quality. If you can make the drive after exploring, it is well worth it.

NEARBY ATTRACTIONS

Brantley Lake State Park. In addition to 42,000-acre Brantley Lake, this park 12 mi north of Carlsbad offers primitive camping areas, nature trails, a visitor center, more than 51 fully equipped campsites, and fine fishing for largemouth bass, bluegill, crappie, and walleye pike (though authorities recommend practicing catch-and-release due to the high levels of contaminants in fish caught here). You can boat here, too. ⊠*County Rd. 30 (Capitan Reef Rd.), 5 mi off U.S. 285, Carlsbad* ☎*575/457–2384* ⊕*www.emnrd.state.nm.us* ☒*$5 per vehicle* ☉*Open daily year-round.*

Carlsbad Museum and Arts Center. Here you'll find Pueblo pottery, American Indian artifacts, and early cowboy and ranch memorabilia along with exhibitions of contemporary art. The real treasure, though, is the McAdoo Collection, with works by painters of the Taos Society of Artists. ⊠*418 W. Fox St., Carlsbad* ☎*575/887–0276* ☒*Free* ☉*Mon.–Sat. 10–5.*

☾ **Living Desert Zoo and Gardens State Park.** The park contains impressive
★ plants and animals native to the Chihuahua Desert. The Desert Arbore-
tum has hundreds of exotic cacti and succulents, and the Living Desert
Zoo—more a reserve than a traditional zoo—is home to mountain
lions, deer, elk, wolves, bison, and endangered Mexican wolves, which
are more petite than their snarly kin. Nocturnal exhibits and dioramas let you in on the area's nighttime wildlife, too. Though there are
shaded rest areas, restrooms, and water fountains, in hot weather it's
best to visit during the early morning or early evening, when it's cooler.
✉ *1504 Miehls Dr., off U.S. 285* ☎ *575/887–5516* 💲 *$5* ☾ *Late May–
early Sept., daily 8–8; early Sept.–late May, daily 9–5; last admission
1½ hrs before closing.*

AREA ACTIVITIES

SPORTS & THE OUTDOORS

BOATING & FISHING

The **Lake Carlsbad Recreation Area** offers boat ramps, boating, and fishing; there are no admission fees. ✉ *Along Riverside and Park drives
in Carlsbad* ☎ *575/885–6262* ☾ *Open daily; swimming area open
Memorial Day weekend through Labor Day.*

ARTS & ENTERTAINMENT

The **Fiesta Drive-In Theater** (✉ *401 W. Fiesta, Carlsbad* ☎ *575/885–4126*
⊕ *www.fiestadrivein.com*) offers three current movie selections. The
theater is open Friday through Monday, and shows start at 8 PM. It's a
fun bit of Americana, and affordable at only $10 a carload.

WHERE TO EAT

INSIDE THE PARK

Choice isn't an issue inside Carlsbad Caverns National Park because
there are just three dining options—the surface-level café, the underground restaurant, and the bring-it-in-yourself option. Luckily, everything is reasonably priced (especially for national park eateries).

¢ ✗ **Carlsbad Caverns Restaurant.** This comfy, diner-style restaurant has
AMERICAN the essentials—hamburgers, sandwiches, and hot roast beef. ✉ *Visitor
center, 7 mi west of U.S. 62/180 at the end of the main park road*
☎ *575/785–2281* 💳 *AE, D, MC, V* ☾ *Closes at 6:30 Memorial Day
weekend–Labor Day, then at 5 after Labor Day.*

¢ ✗ **Underground Lunchroom.** Grab a treat, soft drink, or club sandwich for
AMERICAN a quick break. Service is quick, even when there's a crowd. ✉ *Visitor
center, 7 mi west of U.S. 62/180 at the end of the main park road*
☎ *575/785–2281* 💳 *AE, D, MC, V* ☾ *No dinner. Closes at 5 Memorial
Day weekend–Labor Day, then at 3:30 after Labor Day.*

PICNIC AREAS

There are only a couple of places to picnic in the park. The best by far
is at **Rattlesnake Springs.** There are about a dozen picnic tables and grills

here, and drinking water and chemical toilets are available. ⊠*Hwy. 418, 2½ mi west of U.S. 62/180.*

There are also a few picnic tables in the shade by the **visitor center.**

OUTSIDE THE PARK

CARLSBAD

¢ ✕**Blue House Bakery & Cafe.** Morning glories greet you at the front
AMERICAN fence, the pretty blue Queen Anne–style house beckons, and the aromas
★ coming from within are irresistible. Fabulous coffee and baked goods, and high quality, fresh ingredients in the food make the Blue House a delight. Check the board out front to see what the lunch selection is (there's only one per day), but the turkey-and-avocado sandwiches, Southwest chicken salad, and chicken gumbo are just a few of the tasty goods you might find at this great little spot. ⊠*609 N. Canyon Rd., Carlsbad* ☎*575/628–0555* ▭*No credit cards* ☉*No dinner. No lunch Mon. and Sat.*

¢ ✕**Pecos River Cafe.** If you find yourself in Carlsbad in need of a hearty
CAFÉ breakfast or lunch, this is the place to go. Omelets are fluffy and big, but these folks do great huevos rancheros with hash browns and yummy pinto beans—and their rich, mild red chili is delightful. The lunch menu includes great, fresh salads, basic Mexican dishes, and amazing grilled sandwiches—like the Pecos River Special of turkey, bacon, green chili, and avocado on wheat-berry bread. They've made quite a name for themselves with their homemade pies and delicious cinnamon rolls. Locals love this place and you'll understand why. ⊠*409 S. Canal St., Carlsbad ,* ☎*575/887–8882* ▭*AE, D, MC, V* ☉*No dinner. Closed weekends.*

$ ✕**Red Chimney.** If you hanker for sweet-and-tangy barbecue, this homey,
BARBECUE log cabin–style spot is the place for you. Sauce from an old family
★ recipe is slathered on chicken, pork, beef, turkey, and ham here; fried catfish and other home-style dishes are also served. If wall-mounted animal heads make you squeamish, though, you might want to dine elsewhere. ⊠*817 N. Canal St., Carlsbad* ☎*575/885–8744* ▭*AE, MC, V* ☉*Closed weekends and holidays.*

ARTESIA

¢ ✕**La Fonda.** For decades, residents of Carlsbad and Roswell have driven
MEXICAN to this Mexican restaurant to dine on celebrated specialties like the
Fodor's Choice palate-pleasing Guadalajara (beef, cheese, and guacamole on a corn
★ tortilla), or the combination plates—try the chiles rellenos alongside cheese enchiladas, tacos with sides of *refritos* (refried pinto beans), and rice, and top it all off with a sopaipilla (puffy fried bread) and honey. Aside from tasty Mexican food, it has a gorgeous interior with a trickling fountain and greenery, and wonderfully friendly service. Artesia is about 50 mi north of the park and it's worth the drive. ⊠*206 W. Main St., Artesia* ☎*575/746–9377* ▭*AE, D, MC, V.*

$ ✕**The Wellhead Restaurant & Brewpub.** After a long day of exploring, this
AMERICAN is the place to come for tasty food and tasty beer brewed right on the
☺ premises. The super-friendly staff love to talk about beer and the great
★ old building they're in. Pub favorites like burgers and fried catfish are no disappointment, they've got a couple of interesting and tasty pastas

(the BLT is bacon, leeks, and tomato on noodles). They serve a fine selection of steaks as well. The green chili can be added to anything and it's *tasty, and their red chili comes from the famed Shed restaurant in Santa Fe.* Their house root beer and cream sodas are a surefire bet for kids and adults alike; and be sure to save room for dessert. ✉*332 W. Main St., Artesia* ☎*575/746–0640* ⊕*www.thewellhead.com* ▭*D, MC, V* ⊘*Closed Sun.*

WHERE TO STAY

The only overnight option within the arid, rugged park is to make your own campsite in the backcountry, at least half a mile from any trail. Backcountry camping is by permit only (no campfires allowed) in the park; free permits can be obtained at the visitor center, where you can also pick up a map of areas closed to camping. You'll need to hike to campsites. There are no vehicle or RV camping areas in the park. Commercial sites can be found in White's City and Carlsbad.

In Carlsbad there is one good hotel among a number of choices. With the one exception, the hotels are aging and not particularly well maintained, and staff attention to customer service markedly less than in other nearby areas. Artesia offers a more options and isn't too far from the park. There are a couple of very nice, and reasonably priced, B&Bs.

ARTESIA

$ ★ **Adobe Rose.** What started out as the art studio for the College of Artesia in the '60s has been reimagined and re-created to be an amazingly relaxing and comfortable B&B. Thick adobe walls keep the spacious rooms cool, and the lush grounds have verandas to relax on throughout the heat of the day. Custom-made lodgepole pine furniture and some antiques help make this feel like you've landed in your own private hacienda. **Pros:** Private entrances make coming and going easy. **Cons:** Decorations tend to the cutesy; no hot tub or pool on the property. ✉*1614 N. 13th St.* ☎*888/909–7673 or 575/748–3082* ⊕*www. adoberosenm.com* ⇲*4 rooms* ♿*In-room: refrigerator, Wi-Fi. In-hotel: laundry facilities* ▭*D, MC, V* ⦿*CP.*

$ Fodor'sChoice ★ **The Heritage Inn.** You'll find this lovely inn in a 1905 building in the heart of Artesia's historic business district. The high-ceilinged rooms are beautifully furnished with colonial-style furniture, and the inn manages to be stately and elegant without being the least bit stuffy. The friendly staff can arrange tours for you, and will happily answer questions about the area. La Fonda Restaurant and the Wellhead Brewpub are across the street—both yummy places to eat—and there's a great old movie theatre a couple blocks away. Guests have privileges at the Artesia Racquet and Health Club. **Pros:** This is the best lodging option in the southeastern part of the state. **Cons:** There is a petroleum processing plant on the edge of downtown, somewhat spoiling the scenery in an otherwise neat little town. ✉*209 W. Main St.* ☎*866/207–0222 or 575/748–2552* ⊕*www.artesiaheritageinn.com* ⇲*11 rooms* ♿*In-room: Wi-Fi* ▭*D, MC, V* ⦿*CP.*

CARLSBAD

$$ ⌨**Holiday Inn Express.** Built in 2007, this hotel represents the best of what Carlsbad has to offer—by far. Rooms are clean and spacious, with contemporary wood furniture, including a desk and two phone lines in case you need dial-up Internet rather than the available Wi-Fi. The Continental breakfast is more like a full breakfast, and the public spaces are elegant, with cozy couches and nice stone detailing. **Pros:** You'd be hard-pressed to find a better hotel in Carlsbad than this one. **Cons:** Staff isn't always as professional as one would hope for at this price. ⊠*2210 W. Pierce* ☎*575/234–1252 or 877/863–4780* ⊕*www. ichotelsgroup.com* ⇕*80 rooms* ⋋*In-room: Wi-Fi, refrigerator, no-smoking rooms. In-hotel: gym, pool* ⊟*AE, D, DC, MC, V* ⍟*CP.*

CAMPING & RV PARKS

$$ ⚠**Brantley Lake State Park.** Thirteen miles north of Carlsbad, the campground in this state park is shaded with Afghan pines, Mexican elder trees, and desert plants. Some camping and picnic sites have views of the 3,000-acre lake and dam—an inviting haven in this upper Chihuahuan Desert region. Swimming is allowed (although there's no lifeguard), along with boating and fishing for largemouth bass, bluegill, crappie, and walleye pike. Release what you catch, though; there's DDT in them there gills (at least in some of them). ⊠*U.S. 285, Box 2288, Carlsbad* ☎*575/457–2384, 877/664–7787 reservations* ⇕*51 RV sites, unlimited primitive sites* ⋋*Flush toilets, full hookups, partial hookups, dump station, drinking water, showers, fire grates, grills, picnic tables, electricity, public telephone, play area, ranger station, swimming (lake)* ⊟*No credit cards.*

$$ ⚠**Carlsbad RV Park & Campgrounds.** This full-service campground inside the city limits has level gravel sites and an indoor swimming pool. Camping cabins with heating and air-conditioning are available, as are phone hookups and a meeting room. Reservations are recommended in summer. A professional RV service center where repairs can be made is next door. ⊠*4301 National Parks Hwy., Carlsbad* ☎*575/885–6333 or 888/878–7275* ⊕*www.carlsbadrvpark.com* ⇕*96 RV sites, 41 tent sites* ⋋*Flush toilets, full hookups, partial hookups, dump station, drinking water, guest laundry, showers, grills, picnic tables, electricity, public telephone, general store, play area, swimming (pool)* ⊟*MC, V.*

CARLSBAD CAVERNS ESSENTIALS

For more general information on visiting national parks, go to ⊕*fodors. com/parks.*

ADMISSION FEES

No fee is charged for parking or to enter the aboveground portion of the park. It costs $6 to descend into Carlsbad Cavern either by elevator or through the Natural Entrance. Costs for special tours range from $7 to $20 plus general admission.

ADMISSION HOURS

The park is open year-round, except Christmas Day. From Memorial Day weekend through Labor Day, tours are conducted from 8:30 to 5; the last entry into the cave via the Natural Entrance is at 3:30, and the last entry into the cave via the elevator is at 5. From Labor Day until Memorial Day weekend tours are conducted from 8:30 to 3:30; the last entry into the cave via the Natural Entrance is at 2, and the last entry into the cave via the elevator is at 3:30. Carlsbad Caverns is in the Mountain Time Zone.

AUTOMOBILE SERVICE STATIONS

Contacts **White's City 24-Hour Texaco** (⊠ *17 Carlsbad Caverns Hwy., White's City* ☎ *575/785–2291*).

EMERGENCIES

In the event of a medical emergency, dial 911, contact a park ranger, or report to the visitor center. To contact park police dial 575/785–2232, locate a park ranger, or report to the visitor center. Carlsbad Caverns has trained emergency medical technicians on duty and a first-aid room. White's City has emergency medical technicians available to respond to medical emergencies. A full-service hospital is in nearby Carlsbad.

PERMITS

All hikers are advised to stop at the visitor center information desk for current information about trails; those planning overnight hikes must obtain a free backcountry permit. Trails are poorly defined, but can be followed with a topographic map. Dogs are not allowed in the park, but a kennel is available at the park visitor center.

8

PUBLIC TELEPHONES

Public telephones are at the visitor center—handy, because cell phones only work about 10% of the time.

VISITOR INFORMATION

Contacts **Carlsbad Caverns National Park** (⊠ *3225 National Parks Hwy., Carlsbad, NM* ☎ *575/785–2232, 877/444–6777 reservations for special cave tours, 877/444–6777 cancellations* ⊕ *www.nps.gov/cave*).

LINCOLN NATIONAL FOREST

Access via NM 137, turn southwest off U.S. 285 12 mi northwest of Carlsbad; U.S. 82 west from Artesia; U.S. 70 west from Roswell; U.S. 82 east from Alamogordo; U.S. 70 east from Tularosa; and U.S. 380 east from Carrizozo. Numerous other gravel or dirt roads lead into the forest.

Covering 1.1 million acres of Eddy, Otero, Chaves, and Lincoln counties, this magnificent forest encompasses two distinct regions: the arid lower elevations near Carlsbad, and the towering pines and mountain peaks of the Ruidoso area. The piñon and juniper of the southernmost region stretch through the Guadalupe Mountains to connect with the Carlsbad Caverns and Guadalupe Mountains national parks. The forest land has many caves, some of which can be accessed with a free permit available at the Guadalupe Ranger District.

Call or visit the **Guadalupe Ranger District** (⊠ *Federal Bldg., Room 159, 114 S. Halagueno St., Carlsbad* ☎ *505/885–4181*) for permit information. These caves are not developed, so be prepared for primitive conditions. The only private development you can find other than scattered ranches is at **Queen** (49 mi southwest of Carlsbad, on NM 137). This site consists of a small mobile-home community, restaurant, store, gas station, and church camp. This forested area is hugely popular with hunters lured by ample populations of mule deer.

Fodor'sChoice You almost have to see **Sitting Bull Falls** to believe that a cascading, 150-
★ foot-tall waterfall flowing into beautiful, crystal-clear pools exists in southeastern New Mexico. It's no mirage—and you can even swim in the waters of this oasis. A 1-mi hike from the parking lot over a paved trail takes you to a desert riparian area lush with ferns, watercress, and cottonwoods. At the parking lot, the forest service provides rock ramadas for picnics. There are viewing decks and restrooms, and 16-mi of hiking trails lace the area. The park is open for day use only. If you want to camp overnight, drive southwest on NM 137 until you reach the New Mexico–Texas state line and Dog Canyon Campground in Guadalupe Mountains National Park. During extreme drought conditions, call first to make sure the area hasn't been closed. ⊠ *From Carlsbad take U.S. 285 north about 12 mi, then turn west on NM 137 for 27 mi* ☎ *575/885–4181* ☒ *$5 per vehicle, free Wed.* ☉ *Apr.–Sept., daily 8:30–6; Oct.–Mar., daily 8:30–5.*

The northernmost portion of the Lincoln forest, surrounding the resort community of Ruidoso, is a more traditional sanctuary, with snowy mountain peaks, lakes, and gurgling mountain streams. Developers have capitalized on this beauty, so the forest is interspersed with cabins, resorts, church camps, condos, and ski runs. Still, there are miles of pristine wilderness, many of which can be accessed by hiking trails.

More than 25 camping areas are scattered throughout Lincoln National Forest. Although fishing lakes and streams are available on private, municipal, or tribal lands, there's very little opportunity for the sport on these public forest lands. To obtain more information about hiking, camping, hunting, and other recreation, contact the forest service's main headquarters in Alamogordo. ☎ *575/434–7200.*

ARTESIA

36 mi north of Carlsbad on U.S. 285, 40 mi south of Roswell on U.S. 285, 110 mi west of Alamogordo on U.S. 82.

Artesia got its name from artesian wells that were dug here in the late 1800s to tap the abundant water supply just below the ground's surface. The region's subterranean bounty includes more than water, however; oil and gas were discovered here in the 1920s, and today there are more than 20,000 oil and 4,000 natural-gas wells in the area. Pumping jacks cover the dunes and fields to the east. The Navajo Oil Refinery, alongside U.S. 285, is a major employer for this city of about 12,000.

A Federal Law Enforcement Training Center took over the abandoned campus of a private liberal arts college here in 1989, and thousands of law-enforcement employees from agencies such as the U.S. Bureau of Land Management and U.S. Customs Service now train at its driving and shooting ranges. Other than grabbing a meal, there isn't a great deal to do here. On football-season Fridays you can't miss the array of orange banners and bulldog emblems touting the local high school team, the Bulldogs, in this highly sports-conscious town.

Artesia is a quick 36-mi drive north of Carlsbad. The two inns listed in the Carlsbad Caverns National Park section (⇨*above*), as well as the restaurants, are arguably good reasons to make the drive. They stand out as gems in a little town that doesn't generally draw much tourism and a region that is short on gems.

EN ROUTE For a closer look at the farms and dairies of the Pecos Valley, veer northeast off the main highway (U.S. 285) just north of Artesia and take Alt. U.S. 285. This 40-mi route meanders through quaint farming villages of Lake Arthur, Dexter, and Hagerman and will rejoin the main highway at Roswell.

To view one of the valley's little-known but fascinating attractions, turn east onto Hatchery Road in Dexter. One mile down you'll find the **Dexter National Fish Hatchery & Technology Center** (⊠*7116 Hatchery Rd., Dexter* ☎*575/734–5910*), a facility with the noble mission of studying, propagating, and possibly salvaging endangered species of warm-water fish like the pike minnow (once known as the Colorado squawfish, and once common to the Colorado River). You can view live exhibits and read all about the center's activities at a small visitor center on-site. A guide will accommodate tour groups if requests are made in advance.

ROSWELL

40 mi north of Artesia on U.S. 285; 205 mi southeast of Albuquerque, south on I–25 and east on U.S. 380; 78 mi southwest of Fort Sumner, via NM 20 and U.S. 285.

The true character of Roswell has been largely obscured over the last few decades by the brouhaha over UFOs. Rather than a hotbed of extraterrestrial activity, Roswell is in reality a simple, conservative city with an economy based on manufacturing, agriculture, oil, and gas. The population of around 50,000 grew out of a farming community founded in the fertile Pecos Valley about a century ago; artesian wells still provide the water used to irrigate crops like alfalfa, hay, and cotton. Residents may sigh over the fact that visitors only come here in search of spaceships—but they've also learned to have fun with it, and to cash in on the tourist trade.

Depending on your point of view, the **International UFO Museum and Research Center** will either seem like a display of only-in-America kitsch or a real opportunity to examine UFO documentation and other phenomena involving extraterrestrials. This homespun nonprofit facility is surprisingly low-tech—some of the displays look like they've seen previous duty on B-movie sets (the museum is, coincidentally, inside an old movie house). The blowups of newspaper stories about the 1947 Roswell crash, its fallout, and 1950s UFO mania make interesting reading, and you can view the videotaped recollections of residents who say they saw the crash firsthand. Dummies used in movies about the Roswell incident are also on exhibit. The gift shop sells all manner of souvenirs depicting wide-eyed extraterrestrials, along with books and videos. Though some of the exhibits are whimsical, the portion of the museum devoted to research accumulates serious written collections and investigations of reported UFOs. The museum organizes the UFO Festival over the first weekend of July each year. Lectures about UFOs and aliens, science fiction writers' workshops, and films are offered. Vendors and musicians set up in the parking lot and the atmosphere is festive. Five-day passes are $20, otherwise day visits are included with museum entrance. ⊠ *114 N. Main St.* ☎ *575/625–9495 or 800/822–3545* ⊕ *www.roswellufomuseum.com* ⊠ *$5* ☉ *Daily 9–5.*

Fodor's Choice
★

The impressive **Roswell Museum and Art Center** often gets overlooked in favor of alien hoopla, but it contains a good collection of Southwestern artists, including works by Georgia O'Keeffe, Henriette Wyeth, Peter Hurd, and the recently deceased El Paso native Luis Jiménez. The extensive Rogers Aston Collection has displays of Plains Indian artifacts and Spanish armor. Robert H. Goddard's collection exhibits the inventions and journals of the rocketry genius, who conducted some of his early experiments near Roswell. The **Robert H. Goddard Planetarium**, which is part of the museum, is open only occasionally, generally on holiday weekends and for celestial events—call ahead for the schedule. ⊠ *100 W. 11th St.* ☎ *575/624–6744* ⊕ *www.roswell museum.org* ⊠ *Free* ☉ *Mon.–Sat. 9–5, Sun. 1–5.*

NEED A BREAK?

Not Of This World (⊠ *209 N. Main St.* ☎ 575/627–0077 ☉ *No dinner*) is, despite its name, not an alien-themed coffee shop. Good coffees, pastries and muffins, and a nice selection of sandwiches are served with good cheer by the friendly staff. Free Wi-Fi, a public computer, and comfy seating make this a good spot to revive, or relax.

☾
★

The lakes at **Bottomless Lakes State Park** were created when an ancient sea that covered the area 240 million years ago evaporated, leaving behind salt and gypsum deposits. Those deposits then slowly dissolved with accumulations of rain, and ceilings collapsed into sinkholes. Scuba divers, boaters, and swimmers now take advantage of the crystal-clear, spring-fed water. The main Lea Lake facility has a bathhouse with modern showers and restrooms, and paddleboats and paddleboards can be rented from late May to early September. A visitor center has exhibits of park history, geology, and geography; during the peak season, interpretive lectures are given in the evenings. ⊠ *Off U.S. 380, 12 mi east of Roswell, turn south on NM 409 and continue 3 mi* ☎ *575/624–6058*

UFO Over Roswell

Of all the sightings of Unidentified Flying Objects in the world, it's the one that took place more than 50 years ago outside Roswell, New Mexico, that remains most credible in people's minds. Rumors of alien bodies and silenced witnesses are the real-life happenings that inspired fantastical entertainment like the TV series *The X-Files* and *Roswell.* The most likely reason so many people refuse to dismiss the Roswell Incident is the undisputed fact that in July 1947 *something* fell from the sky.

On July 8, 1947, officers at Roswell Army Airfield announced to the *Roswell Daily Record* that the military had retrieved wreckage of a UFO nearby. The next day Army Air Force officials retracted the story, saying it was in fact a weather balloon that had crashed. Over the years, theories of a cover-up and suspicions that the military had also recovered alien bodies linked the town of Roswell with aliens as strongly as Loch Ness is with its monster. Backing up the alien-bodies theory is the testimony of people like mortician Glen Dennis, who today works with Roswell's International UFO Museum and Research Center. He maintains that a nurse at the military hospital passed him sketches of aliens and that the military called him in 1947 to ask odd questions about embalming bodies.

In the 1990s a flood of information, including books like *UFO Crash at Roswell* and accounts from eyewitnesses who claim they were silenced, rekindled the conspiracy theories. The air force responded in 1994 with a report revealing that fragments mistaken for a flying saucer came not from a weather balloon but from an air force balloon used in the top-secret Project Mogul. The true nature of the balloon had to be concealed in 1947 because its purpose was to monitor evidence of Soviet nuclear tests. As this new explanation didn't address the alien-bodies issue, the air force issued a 231-page report, "The Roswell Report, Case Closed," in 1997. This document explains that from 1954 to 1959, life-size dummies were used in parachute drop experiments. That this time frame postdates the 1947 Roswell Incident is immaterial to the air force, which claims people have simply confused dates in their memories.

The holes in every story, whether from the military or eyewitnesses, have allowed the Roswell UFO legend to mushroom extravagantly. It now incorporates tales of captured aliens (alive and dead) that further feed our imaginations, thanks in part to the capitalizing media. You can see depictions of slender, doe-eyed aliens, known as the "Grays," all over storefronts and souvenir shops in Roswell. These spooky, diminutive creatures might even be called the New Mexico version of leprechauns, with only the rare treasure seeker truly hoping to encounter one.

8

🚗 *$5 per vehicle* ⏱ *Daily 6 AM–9 PM (day use); visitor center late May–early Sept., daily 9–6; early Sept.–late May, daily 8–5.*

From the viewing platforms along the 8½-mi self-guided tour at the **Bitter Lake National Wildlife Refuge,** you can watch for snow geese, sandhill cranes, and other exotic birds, along with more familiar species. ✉ *4065 Bitter Lakes Rd.; from Roswell, head north on U.S. 285, then turn east on Pine Lodge Rd. for 7 mi* ☎ *575/622–6755* 🚗 *Free* ⏱ *Daily dawn–dusk.*

WHERE TO EAT

$$ ✕ **Cattle Baron.** Grilled meats, seafood, and spicy sauces are the order of
STEAK the day at this restaurant, which is part of a regional chain, including
🌙 prime rib and chicken baked with jalapeño-flavored gravy. The dark-wood furnishings here are offset by big windows and a skylight. There are ample fresh veggie selections at the salad bar. ✉ *1113 N. Main St.* ☎ *575/622–2465* 🍴 *AE, D, DC, MC, V.*

$ ✕ **El Toro Bravo.** Next to the International UFO Museum and Research
MEXICAN Center, this Mexican restaurant achieves a Latin flair with matador
★ paintings, piñatas, and wrought-iron wall lamps. Owner Artie Acevas uses family recipes in the preparation of ethnic favorites such as fajitas, enchiladas, tacos, and burritos. Cold beer and wine help cool the delicious fire of the spicy dishes. ✉ *102 S. Main St.* ☎ *575/622–9280* 🍴 *AE, D, MC, V.*

$ ✕ **Pasta Café Italian Bistro.** A longtime local favorite, the Buonaiuto fam-
ITALIAN ily serves traditional Italian food in a beautiful wood-accented din-
Fodor's Choice ing room with lots of windows. A large selection of pastas is offered,
★ including rigatoni alla vodka topped with tender chicken breast slices, and deliciously spicy penne al'Arrabbiata. The large menu offers gourmet pizzas, savory chicken, veal and seafood dishes, and the house specialties, like the slow-roasted prime rib, are delectable. ✉ *109 W. 12th St.* ☎ *575/624–1111* 🍴 *AE, DC, MC, V.*

WHERE TO STAY

$$ 🏨 **Hampton Inn & Suites.** This newer hotel stands out even among the
🌙 reliable Hampton Inn chain properties. High ceilings, cozy comforters, and very good beds are bonuses in large, elegant, contemporary rooms. **Pros:** Friendly, professional staff; exceptionally clean rooms. **Cons:** 4 mi from downtown. ✉ *3607 N. Main St.* ☎ *575/623–5151* ⊕ *www.roswellsuites.hamptoninn.com* ⤴ *70 rooms* 🛏 *In-room: Wi-Fi, refrigerator. In-hotel: pool, gym, laundry facilities, laundry service* 🍴 *AE, D, DC, MC, V CP.*

$ 🏨 **Ramada Limited.** Large, contemporary rooms and convenient access to U.S. 70 are draws to this hotel on the outskirts of Roswell. The decor is Southwestern style throughout, and amenities include an outdoor heated pool and a parking lot big enough to accommodate large RVs and trucks. The Continental breakfast spread is impressive and substantial. **Pros:** The staff here is particularly accommodating and rooms are very clean. **Cons:** Not within walking distance of the downtown sights or restaurants. ✉ *2803 W. 2nd St.* ☎ *575/623–9440* 📠 *575/622–9708* ⤴ *58 rooms* 🛏 *In-room: Wi-Fi, refrigerator. In-hotel: pool, some pets allowed, laundry facilities* 🍴 *AE, MC, V* ⏱ *CP.*

CAMPING

△ **Bottomless Lakes State Park.** Lea Lake, 90 feet deep, is the only lake of the group where swimming is allowed. In summer, you can rent paddleboards and paddleboats for a small fee. The lakes stand in stark contrast to the hot, unshaded surroundings, although the campgrounds do have sheltered picnic tables. Rainbow trout are stocked in Devil's Inkwell during the winter months. ⊠ *Off U.S. 380, 12 mi east of Roswell, turn south on NM 409 and continue 3 mi* ☎ *877/664–7787* ⚒ *Flush toilets, pit toilets, full hookups, partial hookups (electric and water), dump station, drinking water, showers, grills, picnic tables, electricity, public telephone, play area, ranger station, swimming (lake)* ⇋ *32 RV sites, 27 tent sites* ▤ *No credit cards.*

EAST-CENTRAL OUTPOSTS

Vast herds of pronghorn (commonly, but erroneously, called antelope) graze alongside roadways in this wide-open area, known as the Eastern Plains of New Mexico. When rains have been generous to this usually parched region, green grass and wildflowers adorn the rolling hills; ordinarily, however, the grasslands struggle to survive the burning heat of the New Mexico summer and take on a golden-brown hue. The many miles of uninhabited prairie create a convenient cattle range, helping the many ranchers in this area continue a century-old tradition.

People in these agricultural and oil communities are busy making a living, so you won't find many touristy stops or shops along the highways. The purity of the rural life seen here is part of its charm, though. A note of caution: pay attention to winter snow storm warnings. You don't want to get caught in the blinding, blizzardlike conditions that can create huge drifts of snow.

PORTALES

From Roswell, take U.S. 285 north 5 mi and U.S. 70 east 92 mi. Or, if you want a nice drive through sand dunes and rural farmland, from Artesia, take U.S. 82 east 65 mi to Lovington and SR 206 north to Portales 109 mi.

Along with neighboring Clovis, this farming and ranching community bills itself as the world's top producer of Valencia peanuts, a specialty crop ideally suited to red, sandy soil. In October, Portales hosts a peanut festival where nuts are sold in raw form or cooked up in candies and other delicacies. Portales also is home to Eastern New Mexico University, a four-year college.

☾ The nation's largest **windmill collection** is found on Portales's Kilgore Street (you can't miss it). Resident Bill Dalley has collected the 85 windmills in his own backyard. Since he's the past president of the International Windmillers' Trade Fair Association, meetings of the group are sometimes conducted here.

☾ In the early 1930s, archaeologists in eastern New Mexico unearthed
★ remnants of prehistoric animals like mammoths, camels, and saber-
tooth tigers. More important, this was the first site in the contiguous
United States that provided conclusive evidence that humans lived here
at least 11,300 years ago. The culture and artifacts associated with these
earliest inhabitants take their name from the nearby city of Clovis. The
Black Water Draw Museum contains photographs of early excavations,
along with artifacts from Clovis, Folsom, and later Native American
civilizations. The museum looks a little lonely on the side of U.S. 70, 8
mi northeast of Portales, but its interior is cheerful, with informative,
well-presented exhibits and a "touch and feel" table for children.

★ The **Black Water Draw Archaeological Site** remains active and is open at
regular hours to visitors in summer and on weekends in spring and fall.
Self-guided tours on developed trails are well worth the effort for the
privilege of viewing work in progress at a major archaeological site.
Stay strictly on the trails, which offer options of ¾-mi or ½-mi round-
trips with about 20 different interpretive stops with signs describing
vegetation and geology (the wildflowers following spring rains can be
spectacular). On hot days, wear a hat, use sunscreen, and carry water
for these excursions. An exhibit building offers a fascinating look at
ongoing excavations of prehistoric animal bones, and an ancient, hand-
dug well can be viewed near the exhibit building. ⊠ *West side of NM
467, 5 mi north of Portales, turn at Mile Marker 5* ☎*575/356–5235*
☜*Site and museum $3* ⊙*Museum late May–early Sept., Mon.–Sat.
10–5, Sun. noon–5; museum early Sept.–late May, Tues.–Sat. 10–5,
Sun. noon–5. Site June–Aug. and Nov.–Mar., daily 9–5; Sept., Oct.,
Apr., and May, weekends 9–5.*

WHERE TO EAT & STAY

$ ✕**Cattle Baron.** This Portales steak house in the heart of cattle country
STEAK was the founding establishment for the popular chain that now extends
★ into Roswell, Ruidoso, and Las Cruces. Prime rib is the specialty, and
the trademark salad bar doesn't disappoint with its fresh greens, crisp
veggies, and homemade soups. The interior is decorated with plenty
of wooden accents and skylights. ⊠*1600 S. Ave. D* ☎*575/356–5587*
⊟*AE, D, DC, MC, V.*

$ ✕**Mark's Restaurant & Catering.** Tasty breakfast omelets, steaks, and
AMERICAN sandwiches attract the hungry college crowd from nearby Eastern New
Mexico University. Try the house specialty, a chicken-fried steak dinner.
This diner-style hangout has a fun atmosphere. The tables are inlaid
with tile, the chairs are covered with brightly colored vinyl, and there
are a few exotic parrot decorations. Their house-made salsa is tasty!
⊠*1126 W. 1st St., across from airplane display next to Eastern New
Mexico University* ☎*575/359–0857* ⊟*D, MC, V.*

$ ☷**Holiday Inn Express.** Locals send their guests to this updated facil-
☾ ity for the clean, comfortable rooms and down-home friendly staff. A
★ major 2006 renovation added appealing dark-wood furnishings and
comfortable chairs to the rooms, in addition to great beds. Good-size
bathrooms with large showers and adjustable showerhead height are
added amenities. **Pros:** A standout among other hotel options in town.

Cons: One mi from downtown Portales, no restaurants within walking distance. ⊠*1901 W. 2nd St.* ☎*575/356–4723* ➥*65 rooms* ⌂*In-room: Wi-Fi, refrigerator. In-hotel: laundry facilities, laundry service, pool* ▭*AE, D, DC, MC, V.*

CAMPING

⚠**Oasis State Park.** Sand dunes, huge cottonwood and elm trees, and the refreshing air from the 3-acre lake make this state park seem like an oasis. Especially pleasurable activities here include hiking, bird-watching (especially in winter), fishing, and camping. Horseback riding is allowed, although swimming and boating are not. Six miles north of Portales via U.S. 70 and NM 467. ⊠*Off NM 467, 6 mi north of Portales* ☎*505/356–5331, 877/665–7787 reservations* ⌂*Flush toilets, pit toilets, partial hookups (electric and water), dump station, drinking water, showers, grills, picnic tables, electricity, play area, ranger station* ➥*13 RV sites, 10 tent sites* ▭*No credit cards.*

FORT SUMNER

70 mi northwest of Black Water Draw Museum, north on U.S. 70 and west on U.S. 60/84; 85 mi northeast of Roswell, north on U.S. 285 and northeast on NM 20; 159 mi southeast of Albuquerque, east on I–40 and south on U.S. 84.

Besides its historic significance as one of the area's earliest military outposts and the place where Billy the Kid was killed, the town of Fort Sumner is known for its air park, where NASA launches balloons used in scientific research. Nearby Sumner Lake provides irrigation for area farms and ranches, as well as boating and fishing opportunities. In June the De Baca County Chamber of Commerce hosts the annual Old Fort Days here, with living-history demonstrations and mock shoot-outs.

Artifacts and photographs at **Fort Sumner State Monument** illustrate the history of the fort, which was established in 1862 on the east bank of the Pecos River. From 1863 to 1868 it was the headquarters for a disastrous attempt to force the Navajo people and some Apache bands—after their defeat on various battlefields in the Southwest—to farm the inhospitable land. Natural disasters destroyed crops, wood was scarce, and even the water from the Pecos proved unhealthy. Those who survived the harsh treatment and wretched conditions (3,000 didn't) were returned to reservations elsewhere in 1868. The post was then sold and converted into a large ranch. This is the same ranch where, in 1881, Sheriff Pat Garrett gunned down Billy the Kid. The Kid is now buried in a nearby cemetery, where his headstone is secured in a barred cage (this was erected after the headstone was stolen three times and later recovered). ⊠*Billy the Kid Rd.; from town of Fort Sumner, head east on U.S. 60/84 and south on Billy the Kid Rd., parts of which are signed NM 212* ☎*575/355–2573* ☞*$5* ⊘*Wed.–Mon. 8:30–5.*

The small **Old Fort Sumner Museum,** next to Fort Sumner, has displays about Billy the Kid and ranch life. ⊠*Billy the Kid Rd.* ☎*575/355–2942* ☞*$3.50* ⊘*Daily 8:30–5.*

☾ The **Billy the Kid Museum** houses 20,000 square feet of exhibits about
★ the young scofflaw, as well as antique wagon trains, guns, household
goods, and other artifacts of the frontier era. There's an interesting
film about the Kid and the Lincoln County wars he was involved in.
The museum is closed the first two weeks of January. ⊠ *1435 E. Sum-*
ner Ave., U.S. 60/84 ☎ *575/355–2380* ⊕ *www.billythekidmuseumfort*
sumner.com ⊡ *$5* ⊙ *Mid-May–Sept., daily 8:30–5; Oct.–Dec. and*
mid-Jan.–mid-May, Mon.–Sat. 8:30–5.

At **Sumner Lake State Park** you can boat, fish, camp, picnic, hike, sightsee,
swim, and water-ski. ⊠ *10 mi north of Fort Sumner on U.S. 84, then*
west on NM 203 for 6 mi ☎ *575/355–2541* ⊡ *Day use $5 per vehicle.*

CAMPING

⚠ **Sumner Lake State Park.** The choices at this popular recreational site
range from primitive, shoreline camping with no facilities to developed or partially developed sites. Shading in this desert location varies.
⊠ *10 mi north of Fort Sumner on U.S. 84, then west on NM 203 for*
6 mi ☎ *575/355–2541, 877/665–7787 reservations* ♿ *Flush toilets, pit*
toilets, partial hookups (electric and water), dump station, drinking
water, showers, fire grates, grills, picnic tables, electricity, play area,
ranger station, swimming (lake) ⇥ *40 developed sites, 18 sites with*
partial hookup, 50 primitive sites ⊟ *No credit cards.*

EN ROUTE

To continue touring southeastern New Mexico, the easiest route (132
mi) is to backtrack to Roswell via Highway 20 to U.S. 285 and head
west on U.S. 70/380 toward Lincoln County. Look for the pronghorns
grazing alongside roadways in the flat eastern plains, which is an ideal
habitat for these delicate creatures. Sometimes after a summer rain has
made grasses and flowers bloom you'll find more than 100 pronghorn
grazing along a short stretch of road.

A more adventurous route (178 mi) to Lincoln County would be a
loop west from Fort Sumner on U.S. 60. At the town of Vaughn head
south on U.S. 54 and travel through the southernmost region of Cibola
National Forest to the fringes of the Lincoln National Forest. These
areas are mountainous but semiarid, as evidenced by sparse hillsides
dotted with brush and junipers. On this route you pass through **Corona,**
near where the Roswell UFO is said to have crashed. No signs designate
the site. At Carrizozo head east on U.S. 380. You pass the towns of
Capitan and Lincoln before you reach U.S. 70. Cut back west on U.S.
70 to get to San Patricio.

SANTA ROSA

32 mi north of Fort Sumner on U.S. 84, at I–40; 117 mi east of Albu-
querque on I–40.

A charming little town loaded with history, Santa Rosa also has the
only body of water in the state—the Blue Hole—where divers can
obtain deep water certification. That spot, along with the Pecos River
and other natural bodies of water, were created by ancient sinkholes

in the bedrock that drew early peoples and animals as far back as the time of woolly mammoths.

Spanish explorer Francisco Vázquez de Coronado is said to have settled the quaint village of **Puerto de Luna**, 10 mi south of Santa Rosa on NM 91, back in 1541, and the area has been a crossroads of settlers, travelers, and the railroad ever since. The bypassing of Santa Rosa, when Route 66 was replaced by Interstate 40, has clearly impacted the town, although it maintains more vitality and economic activity than many of the towns along the route in this part of the state. There is a real pride among Santa Rosa's residents, and traditions of the town's deep Hispanic roots are still apparent.

About 8,000 diving permits are issued per year for folks who strap on tanks and plunge into the 80-foot-deep artesian spring–fed pool at the **Blue Hole** (⊠ *Blue Hole Rd.; turn south off Rte. 66 onto Lake Dr.; turn left onto Blue Hole Rd. just past Park Lake* ☎ *575/472–3763*). The Blue Hole is open for public swimming during daylight hours (no fee). Cliff diving is great fun here, as is snorkeling and coming face to face with the many koi and goldfish who've been deposited here over the years.

Stella Salazar runs the dive shop (☎ *575/472–3370*) adjacent to the Blue Hole; hours are generally restricted to the weekends, although the pool is open seven days a week. Tanks, air, weight belts, and a few other basics are available there. Weekly dive permits are $8.

The folks from **Sandia Snorkel** (☎ *505/247–8632*) in Albuquerque are out at the Hole every second weekend. The shop staff is full of helpful information about diving certification and the conditions of the pool (which remains a constant 62°F year-round).

Santa Rosa Lake State Park is 7 mi north of town and offers fishing, camping, and access to waterskiing and other water sports. The man-made lake was created to keep the flooding of the Pecos River under control, and it's become a resting spot for many different birds, including a number of gorgeous cormorants.

WHERE TO EAT

$ ✕ **The Comet II Drive-In & Restaurant.** Expect authentic, spicy, and satisfy-
MEXICAN ing New Mexican food here, such as the enchiladas and famed PDL
★ (Puerto de Luna) chili, made from the chiles grown in the village of the same name 10 mi south of town. Burgers, steaks, and seafood dishes are also available for the faint of heart. Cozy booths and walls covered with pictures of local history make this quasi-Mexican café a fun and casual place to go. ⊠ *217 Parker Ave., at Rte. 66* ☎ *575/472–3663* ▭ *AE, D, DC, MC, V* ⊘ *Closed Mon.*

$ ✕ **Lake City Diner.** In a charming old bank building on the corner of
AMERICAN Route 66 and 4th Street, this bright, clean restaurant serves some of
★ the best food in the region on *either* side of the Pecos. Fairly traditional dishes are notable because the ingredients are so fresh; you'll find rib-eye steak, chicken Milanesa, and a mouthwatering green-chili chicken enchilada casserole. Mixed green salads are a delight in an area where

"greens" often means iceberg lettuce. Desserts, such as the Mexican chocolate pie (with cinnamon), are a must. ⊠*101 4th St. (at Rte. 66)* ☎*575/472–5253* ⊟*AE, MC, V* ⊘*No lunch. Closed Sun.*

$ ✕**Western BBQ Restaurant.** At the Santa Rosa Campground on the east
AMERICAN   side of town, this spot serves fine baby back ribs, brisket, steaks, seafood, and a delectable peach cobbler—they'll even deliver right to your campsite. Side dishes like homemade coleslaw, potato salad, or corn on the cob come with the dinners. It's open only for dinner (5–8). ⊠*2136 Historic Rte. 66* ☎*575/472–3126* ⊟ *AE, D, MC, V.*

WHERE TO STAY

$ ⊡ **La Quinta Inn.** Perched on a high point in Santa Rosa, this motel offers
★   the nicest stay in town, and the wonderful views of the surrounding Pecos River Valley are a treat. The indoor pool is very clean, and relaxing in the outdoor spa, nestled amongst boulders, is a nice way to finish a day spent in the car. Rooms are spacious and immaculate, with contemporary furnishings in soft Southwestern colors. The staff is helpful and friendly. **Pros:** The free breakfast, though classified as Continental, is large and has lots of choices; the view. **Cons:** Not within walking distance of the Blue Hole or the historic downtown. ⊠*1701 Will Rogers Dr./Historic Rte. 66,* ☎*575/472–4800* 🖷*575/472–8809* ⋑*60 rooms* ♨*In-room: refrigerator, Wi-Fi. In-hotel: pool, laundry facilities, some pets allowed* ⊟*AE, D, DC, MC, V* ⓄⅠCP.*

CAMPING

⚠ **Santa Rosa Lake State Park.** For travelers wanting to do some fishing, this reservoir and campground is a quick and easy drive just north of Santa Rosa. Aside from fishing, waterskiing and boating are permitted, and there are numerous hiking trails. Weather in spring and fall is almost ideal at about 70°F, although summer tends to be at least 90°F. Beautiful, glossy black cormorants can be spotted on the shores and provide a real treat for bird-watchers. Reservations are allowed but are not generally necessary, even in spring. ⊠*7 mi north of Santa Rosa via NM 91, Box 384, Santa Rosa,* ☎*575/472–3110, 877/664–7787 reservations* ⊕*www.emnrd.state.nm.us/PRD/santarosa.htm* ♨*Showers, picnic tables, electricity (some)* ⋑*76 developed sites* ⊟*AE, D, DC, MC, V.*

TUCUMCARI

59 mi east of Santa Rosa on I–40.

Tucumcari is a tumble-down little town with intriguing early- to mid-20th-century architecture. Neat little houses on quiet, tree-shaded streets can keep you peeking around corners and down new streets for quite awhile. Along Route 66—the main, and only, route through town—you'll find low-slung motels in various stages of use and disuse, restaurants, markets, gas stations, curios stores, and, of course, *neon.* As hard as this town tries to develop itself economically, it's those neon signs and the still-living, old-time businesses that keep it alive.

The biggest attraction beyond the miles of neon and the Blue Swallow Motel is the **Mesalands Community College Dinosaur Museum,** where marvelous full-size bronze dinosaur skeletons are on display. This area was a hotbed of Triassic activity, when dinosaurs emerged in their development, and there are species here—like the Struthiomimus—that you won't find anywhere else in the world. The skeletons are cast in the local foundry, and they *are* touchable. The latest addition, a Parosaurolophus from the Farmington, New Mexico, area even "breathes" through re-created respiratory tubes—talk about realistic! ⊠*222 E. Laughlin, follow signs off Rte. 66* ☏*575/461–3466* ⊠*$6; children 5–11 $3.50* ☉*Mar.–Labor Day, Tues.–Sat. 10–6; Labor Day–Feb., noon–5.*

WHERE TO EAT & STAY

$ ✕**Del's.** The huge, fiberglass bull perched on the sign makes this land-
AMERICAN   mark easy to find. Del's has been serving Route 66 travelers since 1956 with American and Mexican food. Eggs, pancakes, and bacon fill the breakfast menu, and hand-cut steaks keep customers returning. This is the most reliable food in town, and it's rib-sticking good. Windows all around make for great nighttime neon viewing. ⊠*1202 E. Tucumcari Blvd./Rte. 66* ☏*575/461–1740* ▭*D, MC, V* ☉*Closed Sun.*

$ ✕**Rubee's Diner.** From breakfast to dinner, what you'll get at Rubee's
AMERICAN   is a square meal. Huevos rancheros in the morning come with fresh green lettuce, tomatoes, and some of the tastiest panfried potatoes around. Eggs are cooked exactly the way you ask. The red chili is rich—loaded with beef—and not spicy. Burritos, burgers, and a basic BLT are also available. They close at 7 PM weekdays, and at 4 PM on Saturday. ⊠*605 W. Tucumcari Blvd./Rte. 66* ☏*575/461–1463* ▭*No credit cards* ☉*Closed Sun.*

¢   **Blue Swallow Motel.** Here it is: the retro motor court of your dreams.
Fodor'sChoice   Built in 1939, the glowing neon, the tidy grounds, the spotlessly clean
★   rooms furnished with vintage and antique furniture, and the abundant charm of Bill and Terri, the proprietors, all come together in one neat, feel-good package. The Blue Swallow is a landmark and a genuine pleasure for an overnight. The rooms are not the super-size, super-modern ones you get at the chains down the road, but that just isn't what this place is all about. Arrive before sunset if you can and take a seat at a table on the front lawn; the views of the Western sky exploding with color are not to be missed. There is a feeling of camaraderie among the guests here—many of whom are diligently following Route 66 in its entirety—that lends a real sweetness to an already unique experience. **Pros:** One of the best-preserved hotels on all of Route 66. **Cons:** No pool or hot tub; Tucumcari is pretty run-down. ⊠*815 E. Rte. 66* ☏*575/461–9849 or 866/461–9489* ⊕*www.blueswallowmotel.com* ⤷*11 rooms* ⌕*In-hotel: Wi-Fi* ▭*AE, D, MC, V.*

8

HEADING TO HIGH COUNTRY

From the hub city of Roswell, U.S. 70 shoots out of the flatlands west toward mountain peaks. The route's slow climb in elevation is apparent beginning near San Patricio. Here, in an area known as the Hondo

Valley, the shrubs and scattered forest dotting the otherwise naked hillsides provided inspiration for many of the late artist Peter Hurd's stunning landscapes.

Onward and upward, the pines thicken and grow taller. The Rio Ruidoso (Spanish for "river of noisy water") dances alongside the highway as the air grows cooler and fragrant. It's easy to imagine this majestic land as it was when outlaws, Native Americans, merchants, ranchers, and lawmen battled each other for control of the frontier; you can contemplate the stillness by taking a solitary horseback ride or hike on a wilderness trail, or by lake fishing on reservation land controlled by the Mescalero Apaches. Near the town of Ruidoso, there are more modern diversions, like skiing, shopping, horse racing, and casino gambling.

LINCOLN

★ *12 mi east of Capitan on U.S. 380; 47 mi west of Roswell on U.S. 70/380 to Hondo, then 10 mi northwest on U.S. 380 to Lincoln.*

It may not be as well known as Tombstone, Arizona, or Deadwood, South Dakota, but Lincoln ranks right up there with the toughest of the tough old towns of the Old West. Mellowing with age, the notorious one-street town has become a National Historic Landmark and a state monument. Its well-preserved museums and historic houses at one time were managed by the state and Ruidoso's Hubbard Museum of the American West, but there's ongoing discussion about placing all the attractions under state management. As of this writing, nothing definitive has happened, and a single ticket ($5) still grants entry to all attractions, whether they're private or state-owned (you can purchase the ticket at Historic Lincoln Center, Tunstall Store Museum, or Lincoln County Courthouse Museum).

The violent, gang-style Lincoln County War consumed this region between 1878 and 1881, as two factions, the Tunstall-McSween and the Murphy-Dolan groups, clashed over lucrative government contracts to provide food for the U.S. Army at Fort Stanton and area Native American reservations. The local conflict made national news, and President Hayes ordered Lew Wallace, governor of New Mexico, to settle the conflict. One of the more infamous figures to emerge from the bloodshed was a short, slight, sallow young man with buckteeth, startling blue eyes, and curly reddish-brown hair called Billy the Kid.

He is said to have killed 21 men (probably an exaggeration), including Lincoln County's sheriff William Brady—for whose murder he was convicted in 1881 and sentenced to hang. Billy managed to elude the gallows, however; on April 28, 1881, though manacled and shackled, he made a daring escape from the old Lincoln County Courthouse, gunning down two men and receiving cheers from townspeople who supported his group, the Tunstall-McSweens. Three months later a posse led by Sheriff Pat Garrett tracked down Billy at a home in Fort Sumner, surprised him in the dark, and finished him off with two clean shots. One of the West's most notorious gunmen, and ultimately one of its best-known folk legends, was dead at age 21.

The **Historic Lincoln Center,** on the eastern end of town, serves as an information center for the Lincoln State Monument which encompasses the buildings listed below. There's a 12-minute video about Lincoln and exhibits devoted to Billy the Kid, the Lincoln County War, cowboys, Apaches, and Buffalo Soldiers, African-American cavalry troops who earned a sterling reputation as fierce protectors of Western frontiers. The center's guides and attendants dress in period costumes and lead a walking tour through town on the hour, vividly describing each building's role as a setting in the Lincoln County War. ⊠ *Main St./U.S. 380; far eastern end of Lincoln, on south side of road* ☎ *575/653–4025* 💰 *$5 pass grants access to all historic buildings* ☯ *Daily 8:30–4:30.*

Lincoln was first settled by Spanish settlers in the 1840s. The short, round **Torreon** fortress served as protection from Apache raids in those days; it came in handy during the Lincoln County War, too.

José Montaño ran a saloon and boardinghouse within his **Montaño Store** for more than 30 years after the Civil War. Governor Lew Wallace stayed here when trying to arrange a meeting with Billy the Kid. Today, displayed writings in both English and Spanish describe the history of the site. ⊠ *Main St./U.S. 380; on east end of town, south side of road* ☎ *No phone* 💰 *$5 pass grants access to all historic buildings* ☯ *Daily 9–4:30.*

Dr. Wood's House was once occupied by a country doctor specializing in treatments for chest ailments. The doctor's house is filled with pre-1920s furnishings along with books, instruments, and pharmaceutical supplies from his era. ⊠ *Main St./U.S. 380; on north side of highway, midway between Historic Lincoln Center and Tunstall Store Museum* ☎ *No phone* 💰 *$5 pass grants access to all historic buildings* ☯ *Daily 9–4:30.*

Nothing has changed much at the **Tunstall Store Museum** since the days of the Old West. When the state of New Mexico purchased the store in 1957, boxes of stock dating from the late 19th and early 20th centuries were discovered here, still unused. The clothes, hardware, butter churns, kerosene lamps, and other items are displayed in the store's original cases. ⊠ *Main St./U.S. 380; located about midway through town on north side of road* ☎ *575/653–4049* 💰 *$5 pass grants access to all historic buildings* ☯ *Daily 9–4:30.*

The **Lincoln County Courthouse Museum** is the building from which Billy the Kid made his famous escape. You can walk in the room where Billy was imprisoned and view a hole in the wall that just might have been caused by the gun he fired during his escape. Display cases contain historical documents, including one of Billy's handwritten, eloquent letters to Governor Lew Wallace, defending his reputation. The Lincoln State Monument office is here. ⊠ *Main St./U.S. 380; on far west side of town, south side of highway* ☎ *575/653–4372* 💰 *$5 pass grants access to all historic buildings* ☯ *Daily 8:30–4:30.*

8

When church services, weddings, funerals, and other regularly scheduled functions are not taking place here, Lincoln's historic **Iglesia de San Juan Bautista,** originally built in 1887, can be viewed free. The tiny church was built and restored entirely from local materials. Roof beams and other wood elements including *latillas* (small branches laid on top of larger, rounded wood beams known as vigas) were dragged by oxcart from the nearby Capitan Mountains. ⊠*Main St./U.S. 380; on south side of highway between Montaño Store and Lincoln County Courthouse Museum* ☎*575/257–7067* ✑*Free* ☉*Daily 8:30–4:30.*

WHERE TO STAY

$ ★ 🖾**Ellis Store Country Inn.** In 1850 this B&B was a modest two-room adobe in a territory where settlers and Mescaleros clashed; during the Lincoln County War, Billy the Kid was known to frequent the place. These days, rooms in the main house are decorated with antiques. Behind the main house is the Mill House, which has four guest rooms and a large common room and is ideal for families. Casa Nueva has two suites with reproduction antiques and a country-French feeling. Owner Jinny Vigil, who won *New Mexico* magazine's chef-of-the-year award in 2003, cooks six-course gourmet meals in the evening, which are served in a wood-paneled dining room. The breakfasts could stir even the most avid sleeper, and the lush, well-manicured garden is becoming increasingly popular for June weddings. Reservations for dinner are a must, and the public can have breakfast here, too, but only if you make reservations. **Pros:** Beautiful inn; excellent food. **Cons:** Management doesn't take kindly to guests who arrive with children without having informed them ahead of time; if you have kids, tell them in advance! ⊠*U.S. 380, Mile Marker 98* ⊡*Box 15, 88338* ☎*575/653–4609 or 800/653–6460* ⊕*www.ellisstore.com* ⤙*8 rooms (4 share 2 baths)* ♤*In-room: no a/c, no phone, no TV. In-hotel: restaurant, no-smoking rooms* ⊟*AE, D, DC, MC, V* ⦿*BP.*

$ ☾ Fodor'sChoice ★ 🖾**Wortley Hotel.** It's easy to imagine this hotel as it was during the days of the Lincoln County War. Rebuilt after a fire in 1935, the original inn was where Deputy U.S. Marshal Bob Ollinger ate his last meal at noontime on April 28, 1881. After hearing gunfire from the courthouse down the street, he ran outside—only to meet up with one of Billy the Kid's bullets during the outlaw's famous escape. These days, there isn't nearly so much action here, but there's plenty of charm—and you can soak it in while sitting in a rocker on the wooden porch or throwing a game of horseshoes. A major renovation has brought this property back to life, and the antique furnishings in the rooms are a nice touch. Guests are treated to a full breakfast, and can order dinner from the lunch menu—there aren't any dinner restaurants in town. In the **Wortley Dining Room** (¢), open Thursday through Sunday, 8 AM–3 PM, you'll find delicious basics cooked up with good cheer. Victor, the chef, cooks everything from amazing breakfasts—basics like eggs and bacon or Mexican classics like huevos rancheros or *migas*—to lunches of superfresh Cobb salads, enchiladas, grilled chicken, and tasty burgers. There is talk of serving dinners in the near future—call to confirm. **Pros:** Friendly, easygoing owners; good food; a great rest. **Cons:** Somewhat irregular hours based on occupancy; call ahead. ⊠*U.S. 380*

☎ 575/653–4300 ⊕ *www.wortleyhotel.com* ⌂5 rooms ⌂In-room: no a/c, no phone, no TV. In-hotel: restaurant ▭D, MC, V; restaurant, no credit cards ⊗Closed early Dec.–mid-Mar.

OFF THE BEATEN PATH

$$ ✕**Tinnie Silver Dollar.** Just 2 mi east of the NM 70 turnoff to Ruidoso
★ is the little town of Tinnie and this real find of a restaurant. The food at the Silver Dollar is more than worth the drive (it's owned by the well-run local Cattle Baron chain), and if you're in need of a place to stay, they have two well-appointed guest suites available. Aside from enjoying a really fine meal of traditional favorites like filet mignon, rack of lamb, lobster tail, or chicken piccata, you can relax knowing that you're supporting a business with a mission: the Silver Dollar's profits go to support the Second Chance Boys' Ranch, an on-site program geared to helping neglected boys between the ages of 10 and 16 regain self-esteem and learn the skills they need to make good life choices. Their Sunday champagne brunch ($) is a favorite that draws folks from miles around. Ask about the haunted mirror and the building's ghost. ⊠NM 70 ☎575/653–4425 ⊕*www.tinniesilverdollar.com* ⊗Dinner only, except for Sunday brunch ▭AE, D, MC, V.

SAN PATRICIO

14 mi south of Lincoln, 45 mi west of Roswell on U.S. 70/380.

Ranchers, farmers, artists, and others who appreciate the pastoral pleasures of the Hondo Valley live in San Patricio and the nearby villages of Tinnie and Hondo. The Rio Ruidoso flows into the Rio Hondo here, providing a watery boon to farmers and wildlife alike. During the harvest, fresh cider and produce are sold at roadside stands.

The late artist Peter Hurd lived in the Hondo Valley on the Sentinel Ranch, which is still owned by his son, Michael Hurd, whose paint-
★ ings are also displayed in the gallery. The **Hurd–La Rinconada Gallery** displays Peter's landscapes and portraits. The artist is famous for Western scenes but gained some notice when a portrait he painted of Lyndon B. Johnson displeased the president, who refused to hang it in the White House. Also on display are the works of Hurd's late wife, Henriette Wyeth (Andrew Wyeth's sister). Michael is an amiable host who has established an international reputation with a series of paintings he calls "The Road West," his vision of the lonely desert scenery surrounding his home. Michael's sister Carole Hurd Rogers and her husband, Peter Rogers, also an artist, live near the ranch as well. Paintings by Jamie Wyeth, father Andrew Wyeth, and grandfather N.C. Wyeth round out the impressive collection at the gallery. Signed reproductions and some original paintings are for sale. ⊠U.S. 70, Mile Marker 281 ☎575/653–4331 or 800/658–6912 ⊕*www.wyethartists.com* ⊗Mon.–Sat. 9–5.

WHERE TO STAY

$$$ ▦**Hurd Ranch Guest Homes.** Modern and Western furnishings and
★ paintings, sculpture, and Native American artifacts decorate the adobe casitas on the Sentinel Ranch. Peter Hurd made them avail-

able to friends and to customers who needed accommodations while he painted their portraits. The rooms have washing machines and dryers, fully equipped kitchens, and fireplaces. The newest one is named after actress Helen Hayes, who was a family friend and frequent visitor. Facilities also are available for weddings and conferences. **Pros:** Beautifully furnished casitas; rural, rustic and peaceful. **Cons:** No refunds on reservations made within 30 days of stay; nothing but nature around for miles. ⊠ *Off U.S. 70, turn south toward San Patricio at Mile Marker 281, 20 mi east of Ruidoso* ⌂ *Box 100, 88348* ☎ *575/653–4331 or 800/658–6912* 🖷 *575/653–4218* ⊕ *www. wyethartists.com* ➟ *5 casitas, 1 suite* ⚲ *In-room: kitchen, refrigerator. In-hotel: laundry facilities* ⊟ *AE, D, MC, V.*

RUIDOSO

20 mi west of San Patricio on U.S. 70

A sophisticated year-round resort town on the eastern slopes of the pine-covered Sacramento Mountains, Ruidoso retains a certain rustic charm. Shops, antiques stores, bars, and restaurants line its main street, and in winter, skiers flock to nearby Ski Apache. In summer, Ruidoso is a paradise for outdoors lovers seeking respite from the blazing heat of lower elevations.

Worth noting is that the general quality of lodging and dining options in town is very good. Service is delightfully friendly and laid-back, and you can eat everything from Greek food to Mexican food to good ol' American barbecue and walk away with *una panza llena y un corazon contento* (a full stomach and a happy heart).

Ruidoso Downs is so close to Ruidoso you won't realize it's a separate township, but its Ruidoso Downs Racetrack and museums are the area's huge draws. The summer horse-racing season keeps the 9,800 or so permanent residents entertained after the snow and ski bunnies disappear.

Ruidoso Downs Racetrack & Casino, the self-proclaimed Home of the World's Richest Quarter Horse Race, has a fabulous mountain vista as the setting for cheering the ponies. On Labor Day the track is the site of the All-American Quarter Horse Futurity, with a total purse of as much as $2.5 million. Twenty percent of revenues from the **Billy the Kid Casino,** with some 300 slot machines, boosts purses for the races. Casino gambling allowed at horse racing tracks is credited with reviving the sport in New Mexico by attracting quality horses and competition. The casino is decorated with murals suggesting nearby historic Lincoln, where Billy the Kid once hung out. The facility offers year-round, full-card simulcasting from the nation's largest tracks. ⊠ *U.S. 70W, Ruidoso Downs* ☎ *575/378–4431* ⊕ *www.ruidownsracing.com/* 🖾 *Racetrack open seating is free, reserved seating $5 and up; Turf Club $10, higher on special weekends* ☉ *Racing late May–early Sept., Thurs.–Sun. and Mon. holidays, post time 1 PM. Casino Sat.–Thurs. 11–11, Fri. noon–midnight.*

NEED A BREAK? **Sacred Grounds Coffee** (✉ *2929 Sudderth* ☎ *575/257–2273*) is a locally owned place with great organic coffee, an amazing variety of homemade pastries, muffins, and cookies, and yummy sandwiches and quiches for lunch (try the green chili chicken!). The space is open and full of natural light, but the patio out front is a great spot to enjoy the mountain air. Enjoy free Wi-Fi while you rejuvenate.

About a half-mile east of the racetrack you can pay further respects to horses at the **Hubbard Museum of the American West.** The museum houses the **Anne C. Stradling Collection** of more than 10,000 artworks and objects related to the horse—paintings, drawings, and bronzes by master artists; saddles from Mexico, China, and the Pony Express; carriages and wagons; a horse-drawn grain thresher; and clothing worn by Native Americans and cowboys. The **Racehorse Hall of Fame** celebrates accomplished horses and jockeys and screens rare and contemporary video footage. Activities at the children's interactive center include pony rides, horse demonstrations, and puzzles. In front of the museum is a dramatic bronze sculpture by Dave McGary of eight galloping horses—*Free Spirits at Noisy Water.* Aside from being beautiful, the monument represents a minor feat of engineering, since of the eight horses only nine hooves actually touch the ground. A new children's exhibit (indoors) offers kids the chance to climb and touch an adobe home, a tipi, and wagon, as well as lots of other hands-on activities. ✉ *U.S. 70 W, Ruidoso Downs* ☎ *575/378–4142* 🎫 *$6* ⏰ *Daily 9–5.*

The **Mescalero Apache Indian Reservation,** bordering Ruidoso to the west, is inhabited by more than 4,500 Mescalero Apaches, most of whom work for the tribal government or for the tribe-owned Inn of the Mountain Gods. One of the state's most elegant resorts, **Inn of the Mountain Gods** has become a major destination for visitors from all over the country. Also on the reservation are a general store, a trading post, and a museum where a 12-minute video about life on the reservation is screened. Regular talks are also given on the history and culture of the Mescalero Apaches. There are campsites here (with hookups at Silver and Eagle lakes only) and picnic areas. The July 4th weekend dances, which include a rodeo, powwow, and the lovely dances of young women going through puberty rites, are open to the public. *Tribal Office* ✉ *106 Central Mescalero Ave., off U.S. 70, Mescalero* ☎ *575/671–4494* 🎫 *Free* ⏰ *Reservation and tribal museum weekdays 8–4:30.*

WHERE TO EAT

✗ **Café Rio.** Eclectic international is the easiest way to describe this bright, fun restaurant. There simply isn't any other place in Ruidoso to find jambalaya, spanakopita, a delicious array of Greek soups (though the Portuguese kale soup is a real find, too), or hand-tossed, thin-crust pizzas that have made fans all over the West ($25 for the fabulous, large "Kitchen Sink" pizza). They close at 7:50 PM, so your dinner here should be on the early side. ✉ *2547 Sudderth Dr.* ☎ *575/257–7746* 💳 *No credit cards* ⏰ *Closed before Thanksgiving (for about 2–3 wks most years; call and check) and after Easter (for 1 wk).*

ECLECTIC

$ ✕ **Lincoln County Grill.** The locals come here for quick service and good
AMERICAN   inexpensive food. Step up to the counter to order hearty Texas chili,
★   old-fashioned hamburgers, or the local favorite green-chili chicken-
fried steak. At breakfast you can grab eggs served with fluffy, homemade "Lincoln County" biscuits. New Mexican food, like huevos
rancheros, and enchiladas, are also on the menu. Vinyl-covered tables
are decorated with old coffee-, tea-, and tobacco-tin images. This is a
great stop for families in a hurry and on a budget. ☒ *2717 Sudderth
Dr.* ☎ *575/257–7669* ☐ *AE, MC, V.*

$$$ ✕ **Morsels.** Farm-to-table devotee Kristian Markland runs this gem of
ECLECTIC   a restaurant—and eating in Ruidoso is much more exciting as a result.
☾   A far cry from the ubiquitous offerings of steak and Mexican food,
the kitchen in this little storefront restaurant puts out lunches ($) of,
say, corn-cob-smoked Scottish salmon with delicately spiced house-
made crème fraîche and a watermelon salad. For dinner you might
start with a Georgia peach and Rogue Creamery smoky blue quesa-
dilla, then move on to wild Mexican shrimp with Yukon gold mashed
potatoes, organic cumin-scented carrots and sugar snap peas, or pan-
roasted soft-shell crabs with roasted sweet corn, jicama, watermelon,
and organic greens. Desserts, like a dreamy, creamy buttermilk panna
cotta, or the sea salt–, sugar-, and black pepper–dusted *churros* served
with coffee chocolate mousse. ☒ *2919 Sudderth* ☎ *575/630–0113*
☐ *MC, V* ☉ *Closed Mon. No lunch Sun.*

WHERE TO STAY

$$ ⌂ **Black Bear Lodge.** Tucked into the secluded tall pines of the Upper
Fodor'sChoice   Canyon, each of this adults-only inn's four spacious rooms has its own
★   Jacuzzi, wood-panel ceiling, and fireplace. Owner Carol Olson, who
re-created the property from a 1930s-era restaurant, has created a great
room that has all the coziness of a family room. Privacy is empha-
sized above communal gatherings here, and you're on your own for
breakfast (although breakfast items, as well as homemade cookies and
other snacks, are stocked in the common-area refrigerator). The front
porch is a wonderful place to sit and watch dozens of hummingbirds
frolic during the spring and summer. **Pros:** Restful and romantic. **Cons:**
No children allowed (which can be a pro for some). ☒ *428 Main Rd.*
☎ *575/257–1459* ☐ *575/630–8310* ⊕ *www.blackbearruidoso.com*
⌕ *4 rooms* ☖ *In-room: no phone, Wi-Fi, DVD. In-hotel: parking
(free), Wi-Fi* ☐ *AE, D, MC, V* ⦿ *CP.*

$$$ ⌂ **Inn of the Mountain Gods.** There is nothing run-of-the-mill about this
Fodor'sChoice   beautifully designed hotel and resort. The luxurious rooms and com-
★   mon areas are decorated with contemporary Southwestern flourishes
and nods to the inn's Mescalero Apache ownership. Stunning bronze
crown dancer sculptures are found at the entrance to the resort, which
includes a 38,000-square-foot casino with 1,000 slot machines. The
views here are stunning; many windows overlook a serene lake and
(in winter) the nearby snow-crusted mountain peak of Sierra Blanca.
Big-game hunts, a championship golf course, guided fishing trips, wed-
ding facilities, excellent food; it's all here. This resort is more Aspen
in feel than southeastern New Mexico—with all the graciousness and
none of the pretense. **Pros:** Luxury and a great staff. **Cons:** If you don't

like the casino scene, even at the high end, this is probably not the place for you. ✉287 Carrizo Canyon Rd., Box 269 ☎800/545–9011 or 575/464–7777 ⊕www.innofthemountaingods.com ⌖273 rooms ♿In-hotel: 2 restaurants, bars, golf course, pool, bicycles, no-smoking rooms, Wi-Fi ▭AE, D, DC, MC, V.

$$ 🔲**The Lodge at Sierra Blanca.** This luxury resort is next door to a top-
★ rated New Mexico golf course (The Links at Sierra Blanca) and to the Ruidoso Convention Center. A dramatic rock fireplace looms majestically over the lobby; the huge indoor pool, enclosed within a two-story atrium, is Ruidoso's largest. A complimentary full breakfast (with eggs made to order) is served in a dining area that has views onto the 9th hole and surrounding mountains. Most rooms have extensive views of meadows, pine trees, or the golf course; soft yellow interiors with wood furnishings complete the feel of cozy luxury. King rooms have private balconies, fireplaces, in-room whirlpool tubs, and sitting rooms with kitchenettes. Discounts on green fees to hotel guests. ✉107 Sierra Blanca Dr. ☎575/258–5500 or 866/211–7727 🖷575/258–2419 ⊕www.ruidosohawthorn.com ⌖117 rooms ♿In-room: kitchen (some), refrigerator, Wi-Fi. In-hotel: bar, golf course, tennis courts, pool, gym, laundry facilities, parking (free), some pets allowed, Wi-Fi ▭AE, D, DC, MC, V ⦿BP.

$ 🔲**Ruidoso Lodge Cabins.** In the heart of Ruidoso's gorgeous, tree-filled
♺ Upper Canyon, owners Judy and Kurt Wilkie oversee a placid retreat
★ of renovated 1920s, knotty-pine abodes. The immaculate one- and two-bedroom cabins are adorned with Western and Southwestern decor. Some have whirlpool tubs, and all have fireplaces and decks with gas grills offering serene views. Porches with Adirondack chairs are great for barbecues and gatherings. The cabins are fully equipped with kitchen utensils and dishes. You can trout fish here, right along the Rio Ruidoso, but you must arrange for your own gear. Hiking trails lead off the property through the pine forest. These folks also own the romantic, adults only **Riverside Cottages** across the river (☎575/257–2548 or 800/497–7402). **Pros:** Great for families. **Cons:** Complaints surface occasionally about impatient service. ✉300 Main St. ⊹Take Sudderth Dr. north from U.S. 70 through downtown Ruidoso; continue west through Upper Canyon, where Sudderth turns into Main St. ☎575/257–2510 or 800/950–2510 ⊕www.ruidosolodge.com ⌖10 cabins ♿In-room: no phone, kitchen, refrigerator, DVD, Wi-Fi. In-hotel: no pets ▭D, MC, V.

$$ 🔲**Shadow Mountain Lodge.** Designed for couples, this lodge in the Upper
★ Canyon has king suites with fireplaces and furnished kitchens in the lodge, and cabins with queen beds, two-person whirlpools, and two-sided fireplaces opening into the living room and bedroom. The front veranda views tall pines and the lush, landscaped gardens. Separate cabins all have wood paneling and ample privacy. The staff here is gracious and attentive but not intrusive. The owners have other properties for families and larger groups—ask Debbie if you've got a family or a big group to house. **Pros:** Lodge is within easy walking distance of downtown restaurants and shops. **Cons:** Children are not allowed; rooms and cabins are two-person occupancy only. ✉107 Main Rd.

8

📠 575/257–4886 or 800/441–4331 📠 575/257–2000 ⊕ www.shadowmountainlodge.com ➪ 19 suites, 4 cabins ☜ In-room: kitchen, refrigerator, Wi-Fi. In-hotel: laundry facilities ☰ AE, D, MC, V.

NIGHTLIFE & THE ARTS

A 514-seat venue hosting top-tier performances from jazz musicians to international ballet dancers can be found in the **Spencer Theater for the Performing Arts** (✉ NM 220, north of NM 48 📠 575/336–4800, 888/818–7872, 575/336–0055 box office, 800/905–3315 ticket orders ⊕ www.spencertheater.com). The white, templelike building looms majestically amid mountain vistas just north of Ruidoso and is one of the state's cultural icons. Tickets run $20–$55, and free tours are given Tuesday and Thursday beginning at 10. Local children sometimes act in special free summer performances; outdoor summer music concerts are also offered.

SPORTS & THE OUTDOORS

Run by the Mescalero Apaches on 12,003-foot Sierra Blanca, **Ski Apache** (✉ Ski Run Rd. [NM 532] 📠 575/336–4356, 575/257–9001 snow report ⊕ www.skiapache.com) has powder skiing for all skill levels on 55 trails and 750 acres. One of Ski Apache's distinctions is its high mountain elevation surrounded by desert. This unique climate can produce heavy snowfall (averaging more than 15 feet each winter) followed by days of pleasant, sunny weather. With the largest lift capacity in New Mexico, this huge resort can transport more than 16,500 people hourly. Ski Apache also has the state's only gondola. The season typically runs from Thanksgiving through Easter, and the snowmaking system is able to cover a third of the trails. Lift operations are open daily from 8:45 to 4; the ski area charges adults $40 for full-day lift tickets and $28 for children 12 and under. Slightly higher fees apply for certain dates, including the week between December 26 and January 1, and special weekends in January and February. Snowboarding is allowed on all trails. Families should check out the Kiddie Korral Program for children ages four to six. Although there are no overnight accommodations at the resort, day lodges have two cafeterias, three snack bars, and outdoor grills. From Ruidoso take NM 48 6 mi, and turn west on NM 532 for 12 mi.

CAPITAN

22 mi north of Ruidoso on NM 48, 12 mi west of Lincoln on U.S. 380.

Capitan is famous as the birthplace and final home of Smokey Bear, the nation's symbol of wildfire prevention. The original bear concept was created in 1944, and the poster bear is still seen in public service announcements issued by the Ad Council. After a devastating 1950 forest fire in the Capitan Mountains, a bear cub was found badly burned and clinging to a tree. Named Smokey after the poster bear, he lived in the National Zoo in Washington until his death in 1976, when he was returned home for burial.

⟳ Displays at the **Smokey Bear Historical Park** visitor center explain forest-fire prevention and fire ecology. A theater with informational films is offered at the 3-acre park, which also contains a picnic area. Capitan's original train depot is adjacent to the museum and gift shop. The site hosts special events for youngsters, such as an Easter egg hunt, Halloween night, and Smokey's Christmas at the Park. ✉ *118 Smokey Bear Blvd., off NM 380* ☎ *575/354–2748* 🏷 *$2* ⊘ *Daily 9–5.*

WHERE TO EAT

$

CONTEMPORARY

★

✕ **Greenhouse Café.** Within this historic building that was once a hotel, you can sample creative dishes such as orange-coconut chicken, or Pacific dumplings, and savor organic salad greens grown right next door in a hydroponic (without soil) greenhouse. A tiny back porch patio is available for outdoor dining. Try the bread pudding even if you don't think you're a fan; you may develop a new favorite dessert. You may have to stand in line for a hugely popular Sunday brunch, served 9–11; dinner only, otherwise. Reservations are suggested. ✉ *103 Lincoln Ave.* ☎ *575/354–6025* 🖃 *MC, V* ⊘ *Closed Mon. and Tues.*

CARRIZOZO

37 mi northwest of Capitan on U.S. 380, 58 mi north of Alamogordo on U.S. 54.

Back when railroad crews began using this site as a supply center, the community that rose up was named after *carrizo*, the reedlike grass growing in the area. The extra "-zo" appeared when the carrizo grew so thick a ranch foreman added it to the town's name for emphasis. The ranching community incorporated in 1907 and in 1912 became the county seat of Lincoln County. About 1,000 residents live in this charming, isolated town at the junction of U.S. 54 and U.S. 380.

Near Carrizozo is the stark **Valley of Fires Recreation Area** operated by the Bureau of Land Management. According to Native American legend a volcanic eruption about 1,000 years ago created a valley of fire here. When the lava cooled, a dark, jagged landscape remained. A ¾-mi trail penetrates the lava-flow area, which looks like a *Star Trek* backdrop and covers 44 mi (it's 5-mi wide in some places). Crevices and bowls trapping precious water nurture ocotillo and blooming cactus, creating natural landscaping along the well-maintained trail. The visitor center has a gift shop with souvenirs and books. Caving is allowed; get permits at the visitor center. ✉ *U.S. 380, 4 mi west of Carrizozo* ☎ *575/648–2241* 🏷 *$3 per individual, $5 per carload* ⊘ *Information center daily 8–4.*

WHERE TO EAT & STAY

¢

AMERICAN

✕ **Outpost Bar & Grill.** Rural restaurants in southern New Mexico have a long-standing rivalry over who makes the best green-chili hamburgers in the region. Many fans will tell you that the winner is right here—and many will tell you this is the best one found *anywhere*. Besides cooking awesome burgers, this bar and grill has a wacky hunting-lodge decor full of animal heads, snakeskins, and painted cow skulls. The massive

8

antique wooden bar is the centerpiece of the establishment. ⊠ *U.S. 54 S* ☎ *575/648–9994* ⊟ *No credit cards.*

¢   🖵 **Sands RV Park & Motel.** The nicely maintained, modern rooms here have extras including refrigerators and microwaves, Wi-Fi, and cable TV. An RV park ($12) with extra-wide spaces, some shade trees, and full hookups and showers is also on the premises. **Pros:** This is a good place to stop if you don't want to continue on to Ruidoso. **Cons:** Beds are on the soft side. ⊠ *U.S. 54 S* ⌂ *Box 873, Carrizozo 88301* ☎☎ *575/648–2989* 🛏 *12 rooms, 16 RV sites* ♿ *In-room: refrigerator, Wi-Fi. In-hotel: laundry facilities, some pets allowed, Wi-Fi* ⊟ *AE, D, MC, V.*

CAMPING

⚠ **Valley of Fires Recreation Area.** This small campground sits atop an island of sandstone surrounded by lava. Continuous improvements, such as paving and updated facilities, are being made. ⊠ *U.S. 380, 4 mi west of Carrizozo* ☎ *575/648–2241* ♿ *Flush toilets, pit toilets, partial hookups (electric and water), dump station, drinking water, showers, fire grates, grills, picnic tables, electricity, public telephone, ranger station* 🛏 *20 RV sites with partial hookups, 5 tent sites.*

▐ EN
ROUTE
☾
★

Twenty-eight miles south of Carrizozo, take CR B-30 east off U.S. 54 and in 5 mi you come to **Three Rivers Petroglyph Site,** one of the Southwest's most comprehensive and fascinating examples of prehistoric rock art. The 21,000 sunbursts, lizards, birds, handprints, plants, masks, and other symbols are thought to represent the nature-worshipping religion of the Jornada Mogollon people, who lived in this region between AD 900 and 1400. Symbols were pinpointed and identified through the extensive work of two members of the Archaeological Society of New Mexico's Rock Art Recording Field School. Fragrant desert creosote and mesquite can be found here, along with cacti that blossom brilliantly in early summer. A rugged trail snakes for 1 mi, and from its top you can see the Tularosa Basin to the west and the Sacramento Mountains to the east. A short trail leads to a partially excavated prehistoric village. You can camp at the site, and there are 10 covered shelters with picnic tables, barbecue grills, restrooms, and water. Two RV sites with electricity and water are available for $10 per night. ⊠ *CR B-30 east off U.S. 54* ☎ *575/525–4300* 🏷 *$2 per vehicle.*

ALAMOGORDO

58 mi south of Carrizozo on U.S. 54, 46 mi southwest of Ruidoso; 68 mi northeast of Las Cruces on U.S. 70.

Defense-related activities are vital to the town of Alamogordo and to Otero County, which covers much of the Tularosa Basin desert. Look up and you might see the dark, bat-shaped outline of a Stealth fighter swooping overhead—Holloman Air Force Base is home to these high-tech fighter planes. Many residents work at White Sands Missile Range, where the nation's first atomic bomb exploded at Trinity Site on July 12, 1945. If you find U.S. 70 closed temporarily, it's due to test launches (locals have grown accustomed to this). South of Alamogordo huge military exercises involving both U.S. and foreign troops are conducted at the Fort Bliss Military Reservation along Route 54. It's not all that surprising that flying objects can be mistaken for Unidentified Flying Objects in this state.

☾ The multistory structure that houses the **New Mexico Museum of Space**
★ **History** gleams metallic gold when the sun hits it at certain angles. Its centerpiece is the **International Space Hall of Fame,** into which astronauts and other space-exploration celebrities are routinely inducted. A simulated red Mars landscape is among the indoor exhibits. Outside, the **Stapp Air and Space Park** displays a rocket sled from the 1950s and other space-related artifacts. The scenic **Astronaut Memorial Garden** has a view of White Sands National Monument. The **Clyde W. Tombaugh IMAX Dome Theater and Planetarium** screens films and presents planetarium and laser light shows. Weeklong annual space-shuttle camps for children take place from the first week in June through the first week in August. ⊠*At top of NM 2001, from U.S. 70 take Indian Wells Rd. to Scenic Dr.; from U.S. 54 take Florida Ave. to Scenic Dr.* ☏*505/437–2840 or 877/333–6589* ☒*Museum $6, IMAX tickets $6 ($6.50 for evening shows)* ☉*International Space Hall of Fame daily 9–5. Tombaugh IMAX Dome Theater and Planetarium shows Sun.–Thurs. on the hour 11–5, Fri. and Sat. on the hour 11–6.*

☾ If there's a train buff in your family, the **Toy Train Depot** in Alamogor-
★ do's Alameda Park is a must-see. Here, a narrow-gauge train rumbles along a 2½-mi track, and a depot, built in 1898, displays elaborate toy train layouts in five rooms. There are live steam engines on display, and you can hear real whistles and rumbles from nearby heavy freight trains (the attraction is only 50 yards from the Union Pacific main line). One room in the depot is an incredible re-creation of the railroad system between Alamogordo, Cloudcroft, and Ruidoso. ⊠*1991 N. White Sands Blvd., Alameda Park* ☏*575/437–2855 or 888/207–3564* ☒*Train $4, displays $4, combo ticket $6* ☉*Wed.–Sun. noon–4:30.*

Tasty nuts are the crop at **Eagle Ranch Pistachio Groves and Heart of the Desert Vineyards,** where you can buy pistachios baked into cranberry biscotti, pistachio-filled chocolate candies, and the nuts themselves, as well as the wines being produced in the proprietary winery. Linger in the coffee shop or art gallery. George and Marianne Schweers own the family farm here, which has been growing pistachios—an unusual crop for New Mexico—since 1972. The ranch has 12,000 pistachio trees and is the largest such grove in the state; a vineyard was planted in 2003 and is now producing wines—their signature wine is a crisp pistachio rosé, a zinfandel–chenin blanc blend with a hint of pistachio essence. They offer free wine tastings everyday, but not until noon on Sunday. If you have an RV and would like to camp overnight, ask for permission at the store to camp at the picnic area—there's no charge for self-contained vehicles. ⊠*7288 NM 54/70, 4 mi north of White Sands Mall* ☏*800/432–0999* ⊕*www.eagleranchpistachios.com* ☒*Mon.–Sat. 8–6, Sun. 9–6. Free farm tours late May–early Sept., weekdays at 10 and 1:30; early Sept.–late May, weekdays at 1:30.*

8

White Sands National Monument encompasses 145,344 acres of the largest deposit of gypsum sand in the world, where shifting sand dunes reach 60 feet high. The monument, one of the few landforms recognizable from space, has displays in its **visitor center** that describe how the dunes were (and are continually) formed from gypsum crystals originating at a dry lake bed called Lake Lucero, where winds and erosion break down the crystals into fine particles of sand. A 17-minute introductory video at the visitor center is very helpful if you intend to hike among the dunes. There are also a gift shop, snack bar, and bookstore.

Fodor'sChoice ★

A 16-mi round-trip car ride takes you into this eerie wonderland of gleaming white sand. You can climb to the top of the dunes for a photograph, then tumble or surf down on a sled sold at the visitor center. As you wade barefoot in the gypsum crystals you notice the sand is not hot, and there's even moisture to be felt a few inches below the surface. Gypsum is one of the most common minerals on earth and is finer than the silica sand on beaches. A walk on the 1-mi **Big Dune Trail** will give you a good overview of the site; other options are the 4¾-mi **Alkali Flat Trail** and the 600-yard **Boardwalk**. The **Nature Center in the Dunes** museum has exhibits and other information that includes interpretive displays with depictions of animals and plant life common to the dunes, along with illustrations of how the dunes shift through time. The center usually is open during regular hours, but is staffed by volunteers (so it sometimes closes unexpectedly). Call first to make sure it's open. The picnic area has shaded tables and grills. Backpackers' campsites are available by permit, obtainable at the visitor center, but there aren't any facilities. Once a month from May to September, White Sands celebrates the full moon by remaining open until 11, allowing you to experience the dunes by lunar light. Call for information and reservations for monthly auto caravans on Saturday to **Lake Lucero,** the source of the gypsum sand deposit. Rangers lead tours daily at sunset, starting at the visitor center. Each September there are two special events, a star party, where you can bring high-powered telescopes and gaze at the displays in the heavens, and a balloon fiesta, where about 50 balloons show up to float placidly over the gorgeous dunes. Call for specific dates for both events. ⊠ *Off U.S. 70, 15 mi southwest of Alamogordo, Holloman AFB* ☎ *575/479–6124* ⊕ *www.nps.gov/whsa* ☎ *$3* ☉ *Late May–early Sept., daily 7 AM–9 PM; visitor center 8–7. Early Sept.–late May, daily 7–sunset; visitor center 8–6.*

OFF THE
BEATEN
PATH

White Sands Missile Range Museum & Missile Park. Here you can see outdoor displays of more than 50 rockets and missiles along with indoor exhibits honoring historic contributions of scientists including rocketry genius and inventor Wernher von Braun. The museum also contains accounts of early Native American inhabitants who occupied the surrounding Tularosa Basin. A newer display is an exhibit building with a cutout of the interior of the V-2 missile. ⊠ *White Sands Missile Range, turn east off U.S. 70, 45 mi southwest of Alamogordo or 25 mi northeast of Las Cruces; take access road 5 mi to gate and stop for visitor's pass; you must have current driver's license and insurance to enter, as well as photo identification for all passengers* ☎ *575/678–8824*

⊕*www.wsmr-history.org* ⊠*Free* ⊗*Museum weekdays 8–4, weekends 10–3; Missile Park daily dawn–dusk.*

WHERE TO EAT & STAY

$$
AMERICAN
Fodor'sChoice
★

✕**Memories.** A delicious find in little Alamogordo! Inside a lovely, gray, two-story Victorian this restaurant operates an incredible kitchen, turning out soups, salads, and sandwiches for lunch (¢). Try the famous baked-potato soup—which is as wonderful as it sounds—and updated Continental favorites for dinner. You can order steak (hand cut), prime rib, and a very nice assortment of seafood, but the swordfish is outstanding—it's marinated in teriyaki sauce, then grilled and finished with ginger butter. Your choice of sides with dinner includes sweet-potato fries or homemade potato salad, and all come with soup or salad to start. Memories received the "best desserts" vote in a town survey, and once you taste the Italian cream cake or the coconut-cream pie you'll understand why. ⊠ *1223 New York Ave.* ☏*575/437–0077* ⊟*AE, D, MC, V* ⊗*Closed Sun.*

¢
AMERICAN
★

✕**Waffle and Pancake Shoppe.** This bustling restaurant is on the short list of locals and visitors in the know for tasty, and big, breakfasts and lunches. Aside from fluffy waffles and pancakes (which can come loaded with all sorts of toppings), they serve very good Mexican breakfasts and lunches—the chili verde plate for breakfast is great, as are the chicken enchiladas for lunch. Standard American fare, like eggs and bacon, and sandwiches round out the menu. A friendly greeting will almost certainly ring out the minute you walk through the door, making you feel like a long-lost friend. ⊠ *950 S. White Sands Blvd.* ☏*575/437–0433* ⊟*D, MC, V* ⊗*No dinner.*

$

⛉**Holiday Inn Express.** Alamogordo has a number of hotels, not many of them worth mentioning. This Holiday Inn, built in 2006, is the exception. A friendly, professional staff, immaculate grounds and hotel, and spacious, comfortable rooms more than make up for the lack of choices in town. Beds are triple sheeted with plush linens and comforters, and dark-wood furniture and cool, calming beige walls make for a pleasurable stay. This chain is known for its amenities and this property doesn't disappoint. Continental breakfasts are generous, to say the least. ⊠*100 Kerry Ave.* ☏*575/434–9773* ⬔*80 rooms* ⧖*In-room: refrigerator, Wi-Fi. In-hotel: laundry facilities, gym, pool* ⊟*AE, D, DC, MC, V* ⧇*CP.*

CAMPING

⟳
★

⛺**Alamogordo Roadrunner Campground.** Motel-style amenities, such as a lounge and a recreation room, are available at this facility. There are also inviting patches of green lawn and trees where you can pitch your tent. The staff here is friendly and it's one of the more fun campgrounds–RV parks you'll find. Two 12-foot by 12-foot log cabins each have a double bed and set of bunk beds. ⊠*412 24th St., 1 block east of U.S. 70/54* ☏*575/437–3003 or 877/437–3003* ⊕*www.roadrunnercampground.com* ⧖*Laundry facilities, flush toilets, full hookups, showers, grills, picnic tables, general store, play area, swimming (pool), Wi-Fi (limited range)* ⬔*67 RV sites, 10 tent sites, 2 cabins* ⊟*MC, V.*

8

CLOUDCROFT

19 mi east of Alamogordo on U.S. 82.

Cloudcroft was established in 1898 when the El Paso–Northeastern Railroad crew laid out the route for the Cloud Climbing Railroad. The natural beauty and business possibilities for creating a getaway from the blistering summer heat in the valley below were obvious and plans were quickly made for a mountaintop resort. You can still see the Mexican Canyon trestle from this era as you drive NM 82 to the west of town. This incredibly steep, twisty, and scenic drive links Cloudcroft to the desert basin below and gains 4,700 feet in elevation during its 30-mi stretch.

One way this sweet little mountain town promotes itself these days is with the slogan "9,000 feet above stress level," and from its perch high above the Tularosa desert valley the town lives up to the claim. Flowers and ponderosa and other greenery give the air an incredible mountain fragrance, and the boardwalks lining the main street, Burro Avenue, lend the town an Old West atmosphere that comes across as more charming than contrived. Despite a significant influx of retirees and big-city expats over the past few years, the town has held onto its country friendliness. People you don't know will stop and chat with you. Get used to it and enjoy; this kind of sweetness seems all too rare these days.

There are two festivals that bookend the warm season here, and a number of others in between. Mayfest happens over Memorial Day and Aspencade is held the first weekend of October. The July Jamboree, and a Labor Day weekend fiesta are two more events held, along with street dances and the melodramas that most of the residents seem to participate in. Festivals typically include arts-and-crafts booths and all sorts of perfectly delectable munchies.

Cloudcroft has the southernmost ski area in the United States, although it's a very small operation and only open during years when snow is abundant (it brings about 89 inches a year on average). It's a nice place for beginner skiers to get their snow legs. Contact the Chamber of Commerce for season info and ticket prices.

☾   The **National Solar Observatory–Sacramento Peak,** 20 mi south of Cloud-

Fodor's Choice   croft on the Sunspot Highway at an elevation of 9,200 feet, is desig-

★   nated for observations of the sun. The observatory, established in 1947, has four telescopes, including a 329-foot Vacuum Tower that resembles a pyramid. One observation point has a majestic view of White Sands and the Tularosa Basin. During the day you can inspect the telescopes on a self-guided tour and watch live, filtered television views of the sun. Interactive displays at the visitor center allow you to, among other activities, make infrared fingerprints. The community of Sunspot, home of the observatory, is an actual working community of scientists—not a tourist attraction—so you should stay within areas designated for visitors. ☒*3010 Coronal Loop, Sunspot Hwy., Sunspot* ☏*575/434–7000*

⊕*www.nso.edu* ✉*Visitor center $3, self-guided tours free* ☉*Visitor center daily 9–5.*

The headquarters of the **Lincoln National Forest Sacramento Ranger District** (✉*61 Curlew St., off U.S. 82* ☎*575/682–2551*) has maps showing area hiking trails. The office is open weekdays 7:30–4:30.

EN ROUTE

Two miles south of Cloudcroft on NM 24, take Forest Road 64 (paved) to **Nelson Canyon Vista Trail** for a well-marked walking trail with absolutely breathtaking views of White Sands. This walk among the shade of tall trees is made all the more sweet if you've recently spent time down in the blazing summer heat of the Tularosa desert.

WHERE TO EAT

¢
MEXICAN
★

✕**Gallo's Red Rooster Café.** With its brightly colored interior and *papel picado* banners hanging from the ceiling, you might think you've wandered into Mexico. Basic American food (burgers, hot dogs, grilled-cheese sandwiches) and a nice assortment of Mexican favorites are served. Try the *chile colorado*, chopped pork loin simmered to amazing tenderness in a smooth, rich, spicy, red chili. Start your day with huevos rancheros, or stop in just to snack on tasty fresh salsas, guacamole, and chips. ✉*306 Burro Ave.* ☎*575/682–2448* ▭ *D, MC, V* ☉ *Closed Tues. No dinner.*

¢
ECLECTIC
★

✕**Gnarly Charlie's Beer Brats & Burgers.** Savory bratwurst as well as some of the tastiest, juiciest burgers around are the draw here—and the super-friendly staff doesn't hurt either. Noteworthy is the enormous Mongrel Burger, a 1-pound cheeseburger topped with grilled onions and jalapeños. The ice-cream and fudge shop on premises is worth a stop if you're in need of rich and creamy coldness or super-rich chocolate truffles. ✉*Pine Stump Mall, 300 Burro Ave.* ☎*575/682–2127* ▭*No credit cards.*

$
AMERICAN

✕**Western Bar & Cafe.** Locals jokingly refer to the regular morning gatherings here as "the old men's club," where all the latest happenings in Cloudcroft are discussed at great length, and sometimes with great passion. Come in as you are (this place is casual personified) and get ready for great big helpings of local favorites such as chicken-fried steak. Don't ask for pepper-encrusted ahi here: this is basic, rib-sticking Western food served in a simple, no-frills room where the wood tables and chairs and paneled walls may remind you of your grandparents' living room. The bar next door is great if you require more than water and sodas, and it serves a number of good microbrews, like the amusingly named "Arrogant Bastard Ale." ✉*304 Burro Ave.* ☎*575/682–2445, 575/682–9910 bar* ▭*No credit cards.*

WHERE TO STAY

$

▦**Cloudcroft Hotel and Mall.** If you'd like to be in the thick of things, or just want to park your car and spend your time strolling around town, this is the hotel for you. You're within walking distance of dining and nightlife, shopping, and outdoor activities. The nine spacious rooms have ceiling fans (fine for the cooler temperatures at this altitude) and claw-foot tubs. Two suites overlook Burro Avenue and have balconies. Gallo's, a restaurant in the attached shopping arcade, offers room ser-

8

vice to guests. **Pros:** Very friendly staff, immaculate accommodations. **Cons:** Hotel is right downtown, there aren't any grounds or gardens. ✉ *306 Burro Ave.* ☎ *575/682–3414* ⊕ *www.cloudcrofthotel.com* ⟁ *In-room: kitchen (some)* ▤ *AE, D, MC, V* ⏀ *CP.*

$$ ▦ **The Lodge.** The imposing Bavarian-style architecture of the Lodge, ★ with its tower and dramatic details, has drawn all sorts of notable characters over the years, including Judy Garland, Clark Gable, and even the Mexican revolutionary Pancho Villa. The bar was owned by Al Capone. The outside looks like an Alpine lodge, but the interior, with its dark-wood furnishings and plush carpeted stairways, seems to have come right from a Gothic novel. Rooms are furnished with period antiques, comforters, and ceiling fans. **Rebecca's Restaurant** (**$$$**) serves Continental cuisine in a beautiful room that is full of sunlight during the day and romantically lighted with candles at night. Rebecca is the ghost of a chambermaid apparently murdered by her lumberjack lover in the 1930s in the hotel—and she's reputedly quite playful. **Pros:** Generally service is wonderful; the rooms lovely; it is a gorgeous, historic property. **Cons:** Wide variance in service and cleanliness; it's worth asking specifically not to be placed in the Pavillion, which is subpar and very different from the main lodge. ✉ *1 Corona Pl. Box 497,* ☎ *575/682–2566 or 800/395–6343* ⎙ *575/682–2715* ⊕ *www.thelodgeresort.com* ⟲ *47 rooms* ⟁ *In-room: Wi-Fi. In-hotel: restaurant, bar, golf course, pool, gym, spa, some pets allowed* ▤ *AE, D, DC, MC, V.*

$ ▦ **RavenWind Bed & Breakfast.** Morning dew on sparkling grass and the ★ fragrant scent of a juniper forest greet visitors awakening in sublime isolation at RavenWind (22 mi southeast of Cloudcroft). The 75-acre ranch owned by transplanted upstate New Yorkers Russ and Elaine Wright was built in 2000 specifically to create a refuge where people can rest and renew themselves—or hike, mountain bike, and explore to your heart's content. You have your choice of a separate, secluded two-bedroom house (where children are welcome) or rooms in the main lodge, which has wooden porches and native rock walls. RavenWind is popular with horse owners, who can transport and then board their animals in stables ($20 daily per horse). For some real pampering, or to work out the kinks from the busy life you left behind, talk to Russ—he's a licensed therapeutic massage therapist. RavenWind was chosen by *New Mexico Magazine* (June 2007) as *the* lodging of choice in Cloudcroft. **Pros:** Gorgeous mountain meadow setting; wonderful breakfasts. **Cons:** No kids allowed in main lodge; two-night minimum stay required. ✉ *1234 Hwy. 24, Weed* ☎ *575/687–3073* ⎙ *575/687–2039* ⊕ *www.ravenwindranch. com* ⟲ *2 rooms, 1 2-bedroom house* ⟁ *In-room: kitchen (some), refrigerator (some), Wi-Fi. In-hotel: spa, bicycles, laundry facilities, no-smoking rooms* ▤ *No credit cards* ⏀ *MAP.*

For cabin rental information, call the Cloudcroft Chamber of Commerce, or try **Cabins at Cloudcroft** (☎ *575/682–2396 or 800/248–7967* ⊕ *www.cloudcroftnm.com*). Rates are $75–$170 for one- to four-bedroom cabins.

CAMPING

⚠ **Deer Spring RV Park.** You can savor the forested surroundings and shade in this sanctuary far removed from any major community. The grassy site has full hookups and pull-through parking. ✉ *2089 Rio Penasco Rd., off NM 130, about 18 mi east of Cloudcroft, Mayhill* ☎ *575/687–3464* ⊕ *www.deerspringrvpark.com* ⇆ *60 RV sites* ⚙ *Laundry facilities, showers, recreation room, Wi-Fi* ▭ *No credit cards* ⊘ *Closed Nov.–Mar.*

8

Southwestern New Mexico

INCLUDING EL PASO, TEXAS & CIUDAD JUÁREZ, MEXICO

WORD OF MOUTH

"I love the drive from Albuquerque to Las Cruces—all those mountains in the desert! Reminds me of an old Zane Grey novel Riders of the Purple Sage. The desert scenery is ever-changing. In Las Cruces itself, especially off of Highway 70, there are these great views of the Organ Mountains."

—easytraveler

Updated by
Georgia de
Katona

CALLING SOUTHWESTERN NEW MEXICO A borderland may seem a bit obvious, but it is one in the broadest possible sense. The proximity of Mexico is inescapable as you travel through the region, but so is the delightful blend of the people whose cultures have met and mingled in this area since long before there was a border. Southwestern New Mexico is a trove of diversity, from the scenery, to the people and their cultures, to the food.

Historically, the lack of an international border didn't mean the area was without intense struggles. For centuries this region has been populated by peoples of various nations struggling to control and keep it. The Apaches and the Spaniards chased and harassed each other for three centuries, until the westward push of Americans threatened the existence of both of those cultures. By the mid-1800s the Apaches had been mostly subdued and moved onto reservations, the territory was appropriated by the United States, and the struggles shifted to those between lawmen and outlaws. It wasn't called the Wild West for nothing.

El Paso (The Pass) is so named because of its positioning in the natural pathway of the Spanish march northward through the area more than 400 years ago. Cabeza de Vaca led the first Spanish expedition into the area in 1593. Five years later Juan de Oñate brought 500 Spanish colonists from Mexico across the Rio Grande into what is now New Mexico. Trade between the northern Spanish colonial outposts and old Mexico followed El Camino Real (The Royal Road, named in honor of the Spanish monarchy for whom the colonies were established), a route that essentially ran parallel to the Rio Grande. The 100-mi stretch of the Camino Real from Las Cruces to San Marcial became known as Jornada del Muerto (Journey of Death, or Dead Man's Walk, depending on whom you're asking for translation) because it veered away from the Rio Grande (the only water source) and straight into Apache territory.

El Paso, Texas, is the region's largest city and most convenient gateway, but the hub of southern New Mexico is Las Cruces (The Crosses, so named because of the number of people buried in the area due to hardship and Apache attacks). With a population of about 75,000 (and growing quickly), Las Cruces is bordered to the east by the jagged and beautiful Organ Mountains. Sunset often colors the jagged peaks a brilliant magenta, called "Las Cruces purple," and they are depicted endlessly by local painters and photographers. Nearby, Old Mesilla once served as the Confederate territorial capital of New Mexico and Arizona.

The incredible, irrigated lushness in the fertile Mesilla Valley would surprise the hard-pressed Spanish settlers who passed through the area 400 years ago. Miles of green fields and orchards track the path of the Rio Grande from north of El Paso to north of Las Cruces, with water from the huge Elephant Butte reservoir irrigating some of the country's most prolific pecan and chile pepper farms. New Mexico's largest body of water, Elephant Butte Lake, is a mecca for water sports and fishing.

TOP REASONS TO GO

■ **Take a soak.** Immersing yourself in hot mineral water is an absolute delight, and between the healing waters in Truth or Consequences and the delightful springs near the Gila Cliff Dwellings you'll have ample opportunity to soak while exploring this region.

■ **Art walk.** Silver City's historical district is the locus for the town's friendly arts community and some very good, and accessible, galleries. Head to the Yankie Street arts district and have a leisurely breakfast or cup of coffee before wandering around.

■ **The Gila Wilderness.** If you can spare two full days to explore the cliff dwellings and the Catwalk, it will be time well spent. In an otherwise dry region, the lushness of the Gila will amaze you.

■ **Old mining towns.** Take some time to wander around Hillsboro, Mogollon, or Winston and Chloride. The remaining buildings, from well-preserved and open for business, to crumbling piles of adobe, are reminders that the area was once full of bustling towns.

Nearby, you can soak in natural hot springs and enjoy laid-back, small-town New Mexico in Truth or Consequences. The Bosque del Apache National Wildlife Refuge is a resting place for millions of migrating birds each year. Whether you're a bird enthusiast or not, it is quite a treat to witness the sky fill up with enormous varieties of birds taking off or landing in the marshy area.

Outdoors enthusiasts from all over head to the Gila National Forest (pronounced "heela") and Gila Wilderness areas for access to fantastic camping and hiking and natural hot springs. Old mining towns remind you of the thousands who came here on their quest for silver, copper, and other minerals once found abundantly in the ore-rich hills, Several small museums display the region's minerals, along with fine pottery created by early indigenous inhabitants. This rugged, mountainous area, with its breathtaking vistas and seemingly endless span of trees, was home at different times to two Western legends: Geronimo and Billy the Kid. The hub of the area is Silver City, one of the great small towns of the West. Here you'll find a burgeoning art scene, numerous community festivals, and friendly locals.

ORIENTATION & PLANNING

GETTING ORIENTED

Whether you're coming up from El Paso or down from Albuquerque, Interstate 25 and Interstate 10 make it easy to hit the highlights of southwestern New Mexico. Although hilly, the area's roads aren't mountainous until you get onto NM 152 between Interstate 25 and Silver City or up into the Gila National Forest, making most travel fairly quick. In the northern part of this region, many off-the-beaten-path treasures await via NM 60 heading west from Socorro.

Borderland. Southern New Mexico seemingly blends right into Texas and Mexico. The people and the pace of life reflect the influence of Mexico, as does the food, but equally as compelling is the landscape that provides the backdrop for all the cultural intermingling. Dramatic, sharply cut mountains and vast open spaces are unmistakably, almost archetypally, Western.

Gila National Forest area. In the central part of this region, about 10 mi north of Silver City, lies a vast wilderness—diverse and immense. You'll want to allow lots of time to explore the area. From the famed Gila Cliff Dwellings, to abandoned mining towns, to lush canyons replete with waterfalls, plan to devote a fair amount of time here; you won't regret a moment of it.

Heading west on U.S. 60. Farther north, out of the town of Socorro and on into Arizona, route 60 will take you through numerous villages. Enjoy fabulous pie in Pie Town; gape at expansive mountains, and marvel at the giant antennae at the Very Large Array. Touring this immutable area often feels like a trip through the Old West.

SOUTHWESTERN NEW MEXICO PLANNER

WHEN TO GO
Mild and sunny winters are this region's major draw. From May to September, though, it's just plain hot. Really hot. And dry. The mountain areas provide a respite and are generally 10 degrees cooler during the day. Unless you're used to dry, intense heat, plan summer outdoor excursions for early morning or late afternoon. Wear sunscreen, sunglasses, and a hat in the midday sun, and don't just carry plenty of water—drink it. Temperatures drop in the evenings, so keep a light jacket or sweater on hand. Spring is cooler, but it can bring strong, dusty winds. The weather between mid-September and early November tends to be delightful and balmy, and the sunsets and moonrises at this time are fantastic.

GETTING HERE & AROUND
BY AIR El Paso International Airport is the main gateway to southern New Mexico. The major airlines with scheduled service to the airport are America West, American, Continental, Delta, Frontier, and Southwest. Albuquerque International Sunport is 210 mi north of Las Cruces. *See Air Travel in New Mexico Essentials for national airline phone numbers.*

BY BUS Texas, New Mexico & Oklahoma Coaches provides bus service throughout southwestern New Mexico (though not Silver City). Silver Stage Lines provides shuttle service to Las Cruces and Silver City from El Paso International Airport. Las Cruces Shuttle Service makes regular runs daily between El Paso International Airport and Las Cruces, Deming, and Silver City. Roadrunner City Bus operates public buses in Las Cruces.

BY CAR   Two major interstates travel through southwestern New Mexico, Interstate 10 from west to east and Interstate 25 from north to south. U.S. 70 connects Las Cruces to Alamogordo and the southeast. From Albuquerque, the drive is about two hours to Truth or Consequences, three hours to Las Cruces. Silver City can be accessed from minor highways leading off Interstate 10 and Interstate 25. From Las Cruces, Interstate 10 leads south to El Paso.

The quality of the region's roadways varies widely, particularly in remote rural areas. Drive with caution on the narrow highways, which particularly in mountainous areas have no shoulders. On minor roadways, even if paved, be alert for curves, dips, and steep drop-offs. If you veer too far into unexplored territory with primitive, unpaved roads, make sure you have a vehicle with high clearance and four-wheel drive, such as an SUV.

You can rent a car from one of the national agencies at either Albuquerque International Airport or El Paso International Airport. Auto dealerships in some communities rent cars. Hertz has an office at the Las Cruces Hilton.

BY TRAIN   Amtrak serves El Paso and Deming, New Mexico, on the *Sunset Limited,* which operates between Los Angeles, New Orleans, and Florida.

TOUR INFORMATION   El Paso–Juárez Trolley Co. has daily guided tours into Juárez, Mexico, for a $12.50 fee. Call for schedules and rates for special tours to the old Spanish missions of El Paso, Texas. Around and About Tours specializes in El Paso, Texas; Ciudad Juárez, Mexico; and tours of several days or a week into southern New Mexico. Volunteers from El Paso Mission Trail Association lead groups of at least 10 people on visits to the old Spanish missions of the El Paso area. A donation of at least $2.50 per person is requested.

ESSENTIALS   **Air Contacts Albuquerque International Sunport** (✉ *2200 Sunport Blvd. SE, Albuquerque* ☎ *505/244–7700*). **El Paso International Airport** (✉ *6701 Convair Dr., El Paso TX* ☎ *915/780–4749*).

Bus Contacts Las Cruces Shuttle Service (☎ *575/525–1784* ⊕ *www.las crucesshuttle.com*). **Roadrunner City Bus** (☎ *575/525–2500*). **Silver Stage Lines** (☎ *800/522–0162*). **Texas, New Mexico & Oklahoma Coaches** (☎ *575/524–8518 in Las Cruces, 800/231–2222 for all other destinations* ⊕ *www.tnmo.com*).

Tour Contacts Around and About Tours (✉ *6716 Mesa Grande Ave., El Paso, TX* ☎ *915/833–2650*). **El Paso–Juárez Trolley Co.** (✉ *1 Civic Center Plaza, El Paso, TX* ☎ *915/544–0062*). **El Paso Mission Trail Association** (✉ *1 Civic Center Plaza, El Paso, TX* ☎ *915/851–9997* ⊕ *www.themissiontrail.net*).

Train Contacts Amtrak (✉ *Union Station, 700 San Francisco St., El Paso, TX* ☎ *915/545–2247 or 800/872–7245* ⊕ *www.amtrak.com*).

VISITOR INFORMATION

Information El Paso Convention & Tourism Department (✉ *1 Civic Center Plaza* ☎ *915/534–0601 or 800/351–6024* ⊕ *www.visitelpaso.com*). **Las Cruces Convention & Visitors Bureau** (✉ *211 Water St.* ☎ *575/541–2444* ⊕ *www.lascrucescvb. org*). **Mesilla Visitor's Center** (✉ *2340 Avenida de Mesilla* ☎ *575/524–3262 Ext.*

117 ⊕ www.oldmesilla.org). **Silver City Grant County Chamber of Commerce** (✉ 201 N. Hudson St. ☎ 575/538–3785 or 800/548–9378 ⊕ www.silvercity.org). **Truth or Consequences/Sierra County Chamber of Commerce** (✉ 400 W. 4th St. ☎ 575/894–3536 ⊕ www.truthorconsequencesnm.net).

ABOUT THE RESTAURANTS

The cost of a meal in this area is extremely reasonable, although the food options are limited compared to what you'll find farther north. There are a couple of outstanding restaurants in Truth or Consequences and Silver City. Mexican food is an almost sure bet in this area, especially if you're a fan of the locally grown green chiles (for some reason the red tends to be less compelling down here than up north). You won't get far before you realize that barbecue joints and steak houses are almost as numerous as the Mexican restaurants. Las Cruces has several tasty ethnic-food restaurants in the university district; again, generally at very reasonable prices.

ABOUT THE HOTELS

Whether they're historic lodgings or chain hotels, you'll find many of the accommodations in this part of the state incorporate Spanish influences in their architecture. Haciendas, mission-style buildings with tile roofs, and courtyards with fountains and gardens are everywhere here—evidence of the style first introduced by Spanish colonists more than four centuries ago.

WHAT IT COSTS					
	¢	$	$$	$$$	$$$$
Restaurants	under $10	$10–$15	$16–$22	$23–$30	over $30
Hotels	under $70	$70–$120	$121–$175	$176–$250	over $250

Restaurant prices are per person for a main course at dinner. Hotel prices are for two people in a standard double room in high season, excluding 10%–12% tax.

PLANNING YOUR TIME

Most routes in this area are on freeways or quick-moving highways, except for 152 east of Silver City and the 15 going to the Gila Cliff Dwellings. These roads are mountainous and winding and worth driving at a leisurely pace. Allow yourself plenty of time to get from town to town and to explore once you get there. There are old mining towns to visit, tasty chili to be tried, and lovely shaded forest trails to wander. If you normally stay in chain hotels, try a night or two in a cozy, rural B&B. Don't hesitate to stop in at a little café that beckons or to ask locals what they enjoy doing. El Paso, Texas, is listed here because its proximity and size make it a natural gateway.

IF YOU HAVE 3 DAYS

Spend the first day exploring the old Spanish missions of **El Paso.** In the late afternoon head up NM 28 to **Old Mesilla,** where you can easily find a delicious Mexican-style dinner and have a walk around the historic plaza and its surrounding streets. On Day 2, head out through Deming and go north on NM 180, stopping for an hour or so to explore

City of Rocks State Park and then going on to **Silver City**. Spend the afternoon exploring the walkable downtown area and its many shops and diverse arts and crafts galleries. If your third day involves driving, you should consider spending the second night in one of the B&Bs closer to the cliff dwellings, such as The Wilderness Lodge. The roads in the Gila are windy and slow and take longer than a map can tell you. On Day 3, enjoy the scenic drive through the Gila and a visit to the cliff dwellings.

IF YOU HAVE 7 DAYS
Enjoy the extra time to explore the areas above. Spend Day 1 exploring **El Paso** and Juárez. The morning of Day 2 can be spent in **Old Mesilla**, with an afternoon trip up to White Sands to enjoy the shifting shadows of the late afternoon and the gorgeous colors on the sands and surrounding mountains as the sun sets. Spend the night back in **Las Cruces**. Drive to **Silver City** on Day 3 and spend the afternoon wandering around town. Spend all of Day 4 in the **Gila National Forest**, visiting the cliff dwellings, canyons, and old mining towns. Spend the night in one of the lovely mountain B&Bs or inns. On Day 5, head west from Silver City on the very scenic NM 180. If you spend the night in Glenwood you can explore Mogollon and the unbelievably lush Whitewater Canyon. On Day 6, head north toward Datil and then east toward Magdalena, past the **Very Large Array**. Plan on spending the night in **Truth or Consequences** to take a good, long soak in the hot springs there. If you're a birder, make a point of visiting the **Bosque del Apache National Wildlife Refuge** before heading to Truth or Consequences. On Day 7, enjoy a morning soak and a stroll around T or C before heading down Interstate 25 to El Paso, stopping in Hatch for lunch and some green chiles to take home if time allows.

EXPLORING SOUTHWESTERN NEW MEXICO

9

The Rio Grande flows through the fertile Mesilla Valley, known for its plump green chile peppers and acres of thick, shaded pecan groves. Try leaving Interstate 10 and following the green agriculture fields along NM 28, which begins just north of El Paso and ends at Old Mesilla. The shops and restaurants in Old Mesilla's historic plaza make for an easy, leisurely afternoon of wandering. The adobe buildings are virtually unchanged from the way they appeared a century ago. From Las Cruces, take NM 185 north through the farm valley on the route that leads to Hatch, where you might want to stop for lunch and dinner to sample some of the famed chile. During the fall harvest this whole valley takes on the rich scent of roasting chiles. The annual Chile Fest happens on Labor Day weekend every year.

You could easily spend several days (or weeks) exploring the old, but still lively, mining town of Silver City and the vast Gila National Forest, which surrounds it. New Mexico's largest lake, Elephant Butte, begins at the hot springs haven of Truth or Consequences and tracks north for miles alongside Interstate 25. The Bosque del Apache Wildlife Refuge near Socorro provides a haven for countless species of birds.

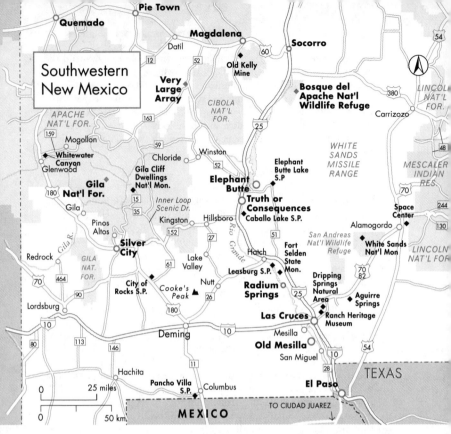

Heading west at Socorro on U.S. 60 to explore tiny rural villages such as Magdalena and Datil will show you more of New Mexico's charm. On the Plains of San Augustin, look for the awesome array of giant, gleaming, white radio antennae that are part of the National Radio Astronomy Observatory.

BORDERLAND

Lines drawn on a map do little to divide the inhabitants of two countries and three states (New Mexico, Texas, and the Mexican state of Chihuahua) who share a history dating back some 400 years. In the small border villages of Columbus and Las Palomas, Mexico, families live and do business on both sides of the international boundary line. Las Cruces, New Mexico, and El Paso, Texas, are both growing so quickly that they seem to be near the point of merging via housing developments. Anthony is the little town between the two, with a sweet, small-town feel and a dynamic community-minded sensibility. The borderland area also draws transplants from the eastern and western United States, who come to take advantage of the mild weather and placid way of life.

You might be surprised to find U.S. Border Patrol checkpoints on all major highways leading away from the El Paso area to destinations such as Carlsbad, Deming, Truth or Consequences, and Alamogordo. Uniformed officers will simply ask your citizenship, though trained dogs sometimes circle vehicles in searches for illegal drugs. The stops are routine, and law-abiding citizens should encounter no difficulty.

EL PASO

267 mi south of Albuquerque, I–25 to I–10.

Fabled El Paso, just barely in Texas and in fact on Mountain Time (rather than Central), was at one time part of the New Mexico Territory. It is still an important crossing point for those entering from or departing for Mexico. One glance at a map will show why this city along the Rio Grande has become the transportation and business hub for southern New Mexico and West Texas, as well as a destination for outdoors adventurers and history buffs. Most residents speak English and at least some Spanish, and the mix of American Indian, Spanish, and American cultures is evident in the city's art and music, architecture, and cuisine.

El Paso lies between the southern end of the Rockies and the northern terminus of Mexico's Sierra Madre, making it a major stopping point on the southern route west during the California gold rush. In 1850 the downtown area was sparsely settled, with a dirt trail leading to the Rio Grande. Eight years later there was an established roadway populated with adobe homes and businesses, and not long after that San Jacinto Plaza became the official town square. The arrival of the railroad in 1888 sealed El Paso's fate as a vital city of the west.

Many of El Paso's downtown gems, such as the historically protected Plaza Hotel (one of Conrad Hilton's first hotels), unfortunately today stand empty. Hotels during the 1950s were often full, sometimes with Hollywood stars and the wealthy heading for a cheap and easy divorce in Ciudad Juárez (often called just Juárez), across the river. Adding to the town's bravado back then were live alligators in the plaza pond. (A sculpture of writhing alligators has replaced the real reptiles, which ended their residency in the 1960s.)

Sixteenth-century Spanish explorer Don Juan de Oñate dubbed the entire Rio Grande Valley Paso del Rio del Norte ("the pass through the river of the north")—from which El Paso derives its name. Oñate was so grateful that the expedition of about 500 ragged colonists had reached the Rio Grande that he ordered his people to don their best clothes for a feast of thanksgiving on April 30, 1598—a celebration that preceded the arrival of the pilgrims in Massachusetts by nearly a quarter century.

WHAT TO SEE

Chamizal National Memorial. In 1964 nearly a century of dispute between Texas and Mexico, caused by the shifting banks of the Rio Grande, came to an end. Both the United States and Mexico founded memorials within their borders to commemorate this event. Texas created a 55-acre park, on formerly Mexican land, with a visitor center, three galleries, drama festivals, and long walking paths. Across the border, easily accessed by the Bridge of the Americas, is the Mexican counterpart, the 800-acre Parque Chamizal. ⊠ *800 S. San Marcial* ☎ *915/532–7232* ⊕ *www. nps.gov/cham* ☲ *Free* ⊙ *Daily 5 AM–10 PM.*

El Paso Desert Botanical Gardens. Located in Keystone Heritage Park, these gardens juxtapose the exotic—an Asian-style koi pond and little waterfall—with native cacti and other succulents set against the backdrop of the northern Chihuahua Desert. There's even a natural wetlands area. ⊠ *4200 Doniphan Rd.* ☎ *915/584–0563* ⊕ *www. elpasobotanicalgardens.org* ☲ *$2* ⊙ *Sept.–May, weekends noon–3; June–Aug., weekends 8–11 AM.*

El Paso Museum of Art. The museum features a striking array of Spanish and native art, from Picasso and Goya to Southwest artists Tom Lea and Henrietta Wyeth. ⊠ *1 Arts Festival Plaza* ☎ *915/532–1707* ⊕ *www.elpasoartmuseum.com* ☲ *Free* ⊙ *Tues., Wed., Fri., and Sat. 9–5, Thurs. 9–9, Sun. noon–5.*

★ **Franklin Mountains State Park.** Within the park's 37 square mi are hiking, mountain-biking, and horseback-riding trails, all offering amazing views of the city below. Plans are in the works for 100 mi more of trails. Rock climbing is permitted. This is a good place to get up close and personal with native species like foxes and kestrels and bluebirds, as well as plants found nowhere else in Texas, like the stout barrel cactus. Limited camping is available for tents; there are five RV sites. Tours are offered on the first and third weekends of the month; call ahead to reserve a space. ⊠ *1331 McKelligon Canyon Rd.* ☎ *915/566–6441* ☲ *$4, additional for camping* ⊙ *Daily 8–5.*

Hueco Tanks Historic Site. This park, named after natural, water-holding stone basins called *huecos,* is internationally renowned for its rock climbing and is a big draw for lovers of the pictographs left by the Apache, Kiowa, and Jornada Mogollon tribes who dwelt here. Due to past vandalism of the petroglyphs, rangers now accompany visitors to the sensitive areas of the park, and reservations for tours (such as the pictograph tour, as well as birding and bouldering tours) are required. Rock climbing without a guide is an option, and so is camping, since park staff are located throughout the park and keep an eye on visitors' activities. From downtown El Paso, take U.S. 62/180 32 mi northeast, turn north on Ranch Road 2775; follow signs. ■TIP➔ **Call two days before your trip, as the number of visitors allowed is limited. Reservations are required to get in the park, unless visitors are among the first 10 at the door when the park opens at 8 AM.** ⊠ *6900 Hueco Tanks Rd.,*

No. 1 ☎915/857–1135 or 800/792–1112, option 3 ☞$4 per person, per day; camping $12–$16 ☉Oct.–Apr., daily 8–6; May–Sept., Mon.–Thurs. 8–6, Fri.–Sun. 7–7. Tours times for the more protected areas vary ⚓Reservations required.

Magoffin Home State Historical Park. This 19-room Territorial-style adobe home near downtown El Paso was erected in 1875 by early El Paso pioneer Joseph Magoffin, and occupied by the Magoffin family for 110 years. The city of El Paso grew out of Magoffinsville, a town started by this prominent and powerful family that vastly influenced the area by encouraging trade, organizing area merchants, establishing perhaps the first alfalfa crop in the region, and later leasing buildings for the incipient Fort Bliss. ⊠1120 Magoffin St., follow signs off I–10; westbound traffic takes Cotton St. exit; eastbound traffic takes Downtown exit to Kansas St. ☎915/533–5147 ☞$3 ☉Tues.–Sun. 9–5.

FodorsChoice **Mission Ysleta.** Around 1681, Spanish refugees from the Pueblo Revolt
★ in and around Santa Fe established this ysleta (small island) mission. Like other old missions in the area, Ysleta is still an active church. Guided tours of the mission are available from downtown El Paso via Sun Metro Buses and the El Paso–Juárez Trolley Co. Nearby, the Tigua Indian Reservation sells Tigua pottery, jewelry, and art. ⊠Old Pueblo Rd. at Zaragosa and Alameda, take Zaragosa exit off I–10, east of El Paso ☎915/859–9848 ☞Free ☉Mon.–Sat. 9–5; Sun. openings vary with church schedule.

★ **Presidio Chapel San Elizario.** This 1789 Spanish fortress provided settlers protection from raiding Comanches and Apaches. It was near this site that the expedition of Spanish explorer Don Juan de Oñate stopped to conduct a thanksgiving celebration in 1598. It's located in the San Elizario Historical District, 17 mi southeast of downtown El Paso. Tours are conducted on-site by friendly volunteers but feature only the museum, and not the church. The **El Paso Mission Trail Association** (☎915/534–0677) offers more extensive tours. ■TIP➔ **Call ahead if you're planning to visit the church. The father might be able to leave it open a bit later than 11.** ⊠1556 San Elizario Rd., San Elizario ☎915/851–1682 ☞Free ☉Visitor center and museum Tues.–Sat. 10–2, Sun. 10–noon; church weekdays 10–11.

San Elizario County Jail. Thought to have been built as a private residence in the early 1800s, this adobe building at some point became El Paso County's first courthouse and jail, and, according to Pat Garrett's book Authentic Life of Billy the Kid, was the only jail the Kid broke into, which he did in order to free his friend Melquiades Segura. ⊠On Main Street (100 yards west of the chapel), San Elizario ☎915/851–1682 San Elizario Genealogy and Historical Society ☞Free guided tours of jail and plaza beginning at the Los Portales building ☉Tues.–Sun. 10–2, and after hrs by special arrangement.

☾ **Wyler Aerial Tramway.** Touted as the only public tram in Texas, this
★ tramway totes visitors up 5,632-foot Ranger Peak, which provides a striking view of three states, two nations, and 7,000 square mi. ⊠1700

McKinley Ave. ☎*915/566–6622* ✍*$7* ⊘*Sun., Mon., and Thurs. noon–6, Fri. and Sat. noon–8.*

SPORTS & THE OUTDOORS

El Paso has a landscape rife with hiking trails through desert flatlands and up mountain peaks, while southeastern New Mexico, not far away, offers isolated streams and rivers—the Gila River, for example, is a popular waterway for whitewater rafting.

There's a flood of fishing and boating opportunities just outside El Paso and just inside New Mexico, including Bonito Lake (Ruidoso, NM) and Caballo Lake (Truth or Consequences, NM), where skiers ski, boaters boat, and swimmers

> ### OVER RAMPARTS THEY WATCHED
>
> The Franklin Mountains that frame El Paso, bending it into its familiar horseshoe shape, are iconic at sunset, when the sky blushes then bursts into bloody color behind them. Sometimes called the northern ramparts of El Paso Del Norte, the mountains are similar to a range located nearby in Mexico but separated by the river valley. More than 24,000 acres of the arid, bald mountains—which fold, lava-like, into the landscape—are protected within Franklin Mountains State Park.

swim. There are fishing areas along the Pecos and Gila rivers. Within El Paso, anglers cast their lines into the lake at Ascarate Park. Catfish bite in Plain View and Hideaway lakes, private water bodies in El Paso County that charge a pittance to fish.

FISHING

Ascarate Park (⊠*6900 Delta Ave.* ☎*915/772–5605* ✍*$1 per vehicle Fri.–Sun. Free otherwise* ⊘*Daily 6 AM–11 PM*) has almost 70 picnic shelters with grills, two children's playgrounds, and a golf course, and offers activities such as boating and fishing on a 48-acre lake.

ARTS & ENTERTAINMENT

El Paso Opera. A dress-up, professional opera, this company presents classic operas by Verdi, Puccini, and other masters, and welcomes guests ages 7 and up. ⊠*Abraham Chavez Theatre, 1 Civic Center Plaza* ☎*915/581–5534* ⊕*www.epopera.org.*

Speaking Rock Entertainment Center. You never know what's playing, but a good guess is mariachi music. A bar and restaurant are on-site, and smoking is allowed. ⊠*Tigua Indian Reservation, 122 Old Pueblo Rd.* ☎*915/860–7777.*

WHERE TO EAT

The juiciest part of El Paso's culture could be the mélange of American Indian, Spanish, Mexican, and Texan cultures that meet on a plate.

$$$$ ✕**Café Central.** The old saw "evolve or perish" has served this restau-
ECLECTIC rant well. In 1918 Café Central opened in Juárez and served alco-
★ hol (and tasty food) to the Prohibition-weary masses from the United States. Once Prohibition ended, the café moved north across the border, changed hands, and became part of the local scene. Today, bold decoration, an airy courtyard, and innovative Southwestern–Asian food combine to make this urbane eatery a popular destination for the city's

hip crowds. The menu changes seasonally, according to the availability of ingredients. Although you can enjoy a gourmet experience for about fifteen bucks by ordering a soup and a salad, it's worth the splurge to explore other menu options. Lunch is a bit less expensive than dinner, yet equally tantalizing. ⊠*Texas Tower, 109 N. Oregon St.* ☎*915/545–2233* ⚷*Reservations required* ⊟*AE, D, DC, MC, V* ☾*Closed Sun.*

DID YOU KNOW?

Did you know that El Pasoans claim the cocktail classic known as the margarita was invented in a Juárez bar called Tommy's Place? Stories about the origin of the famous cocktail abound, but nobody really knows for sure if this one is a myth or a reality.

$$$
STEAK
☾
Fodor'sChoice
★

✕**Cattleman's Steakhouse.** Twenty miles east of El Paso, this is pretty much in the middle of nowhere, but it's worth the trip, as much for the quirky theme rooms as for the terrific steaks. Consistently voted a local favorite, the succulent steaks are so tender they almost melt in your mouth. The mesquite-smoked barbecue and seafood on the menu are as tempting as the steaks—note that strict vegetarians won't find a happy meal here. A children's zoo, playground, lake walk, hayrides (on Sunday), and a movie set are among the numerous nonculinary diversions. It opens at 12:30 PM on weekends. ⊠*Exit 49 off I–10 (follow signs), Fabens* ☎*915/544–3200* ⚷*Reservations not accepted* ⊟*AE, D, MC, V* ☾*No lunch weekdays.*

$
MEXICAN

✕**Leo's.** The Mexican food at Leo's four El Paso locations is repeatedly voted a favorite by locals. Enchiladas, tacos, combination plates, and fluffy sopapillas are served in helpings that will leave you stuffed—that is, if you can elbow your way through the crowds and get a table. ⊠*5103 Montana St.* ☎*915/566–4972* ✉*5315 Hondo Pass* ☎*915/757–9025* ✉*315 Mills Ave.* ☎*915/544–1001* ✉*7520 Remcon Circle* ☎*915/833–1189* ⊟*AE, D, MC, V.*

$$$
ECLECTIC
★

✕**The Magic Pan.** They've got the magic stick—or, the magic touch at least. The chefs at the Magic Pan dish up fusion cuisine, like Tex-Italian blend mesquite chicken penne. However, they also serve classy Asian standbys such as sesame-crusted ahi tuna and distinctly domestic selections like Angus rib eye. A strong Southwestern current underlies many of the dishes. Dine outside and take in the desert breeze. ⊠*5034 Doniphan, inside Placita Santa Fe* ☎*915/581–2121* ⊕*www.magicpanrestaurant.com* ⚷*Reservations essential* ⊟*AE, D, MC, V* ☾*Closed Mon. No dinner Sun. and Tues.*

WHERE TO STAY

$
★

🛏**El Paso Marriott.** This clean, spacious hotel is a free shuttle trip away from the airport and near plenty of restaurants. Though not fancy, it's a great place to stay for a couple of nights, and offers an in-hotel bar and restaurant. **Pros:** Free airport shuttle and free newspaper in the morning. **Cons:** You have to pay to use the Internet. ⊠*1600 Airway Blvd.* ☎*915/779–3300* ⊕*www.marriott.com* ⇨*296 rooms* ⚷*In-room: Internet. In-hotel: restaurant, bar, pool, no-smoking rooms* ⊟*AE, D, DC, MC, V.*

$$
Fodor'sChoice
★

🛏**Holiday Inn Sunland Park.** This Holiday Inn, on a hill with 6½ acres near Sunland Park Racetrack, has outdoor courtyards; the Southwestern-style rooms have ironing boards, hair dryers, and coffeemakers.

9

Breakfast buffets are served in the Sierra Grille Restaurant, and a Sunday brunch is available from 11 to 2. The service from the staff is attentive and noteworthy. **Pros:** There's a nice, well-maintained gym, and room service. **Cons:** Some rooms are on the small side. ☒*900 Sunland Park Dr.* ☎*915/833–2900 or 800/658–2744* ⊕*www.holidayinn.com* ⤶*178 rooms* ♿*In-room: Internet. In-hotel: restaurant, bar, pool, no-smoking rooms* ▭*AE, D, DC, MC, V.*

CIUDAD JUÁREZ, MEXICO

Across the Rio Grande from El Paso.

If what you want is a quick and easy Mexican experience, Juárez is worth a day's excursion. There are any number of goods to buy, and tastes to taste, but it's a border town at the very end of it, with all the good and bad that title entails. Walking across the border is easy enough, but taking the trolley makes it all so much easier. At the end of a hot day of exploring, eating, and drinking margaritas, hopping on the trolley to take you back across the border is a welcome respite. Avoid driving in Juárez if you can, as it tends to be stressful, and parking your car isn't always safe. ⚠ **The more than a decade-long string of serial murders of women (hundreds since 1993) has caused a great deal of legitimate concern. Travelers of all genders should be mindful of this and women should not travel alone at all. Also note that at the time of this writing, drug violence is wreaking havoc with safety and tourism here. Please exercise great caution, and check travel warnings on the Department of State Web site about visiting Mexico (⊕www.state.gov).**

GETTING THERE

Due to the stricter border-crossing rules, lines of cars now clog entrance checkpoints. Crossing on foot is substantially quicker, especially since there are three bridges that allow pedestrian traffic—the Sante Fe Bridge in downtown El Paso, the Zaragosa Bridge in far east El Paso, and The Bridge of the Americas, which is located close to museums, shopping, and a visitor center. The Bridge of the Americas doesn't charge a toll, but does have the longest lines because of the free pass. The other pedestrian bridges only charge a pittance, though, due to a favorable exchange rate. There are parking lots near the Santa Fe Bridge, but it's easier to bypass driving altogether by taking a taxi to the bridges.

If you don't want to walk to Juárez, catch a ride with the **El Paso–Juárez Trolley Co.** (☒*1 Civic Center Plaza, El Paso* ☎*915/544–0061*). Its Border Jumper trolley leaves hourly from 10 AM to 5 PM. For a $12.50 ticket you have a day's worth of transportation along the route weaving through Juárez's shopping areas and restaurants. Juárez is a sprawling city, and not necessarily a pretty one. The trolley stops keep you moving toward the areas most worth visiting. ■**TIP➜ No matter which route you take, stow your passport in a safe place.**

SHOPPING

West Texans, New Mexicans, and visitors cross the border in Juárez for beautiful handicrafts as well as dental procedures, eyeglasses, and even cheap prescription drugs. A warning, however: buying prescription drugs is not a good idea, as regulations are much more lax in Mexico, and possession of some controlled medications will land the bearer in jail on the U.S. side.

It's entertaining to browse the outdoor stalls here with their attendant tchotchkes. Outdoor stalls and indoor markets feature wares as diverse as velvet paintings, leather saddles, turquoise jewelry, and cheap, poorly painted wood carvings—along with better-made handicrafts. The Sante Fe Bridge may be the best port of entry; it's near copious shopping opportunities, including the Mexican government–owned, bustling and touristy Mercado Juárez near Avenida Juárez. The market offers a diverse selection of handicrafts and other items as well as several outdoor cafés.

There are hundreds of shops here, but the ones catering to tourists are clear. If your Spanish is good, venturing into side streets off the trolley route can yield all sorts of treasures. Be smart about what you purchase; if it seems too good to be true, it probably is. If you're not familiar with Mexico, stick to the tourist-oriented shops and you'll have a fun day of Mexican-flavored adventure. Many stores in Juárez are closed on Sunday.

FodorśChoice
★
Avenida de Juárez features artisan-oriented shops where you can find handwoven shawls or hand-embroidered *huipiles,* the traditional blouses worn by indigenous Mexican women. There are also duty-free stores here.

FodorśChoice
★
One avenue in town, **Avenida Lincoln,** provides the pathway to a well-rounded afternoon. Nicer shops line its length, which eventually gives way to a shopping district featuring the bustling and modern Plaza de las Americas Mall and Museo de Instituto Nacional de Bellas Artes (Museum of Fine Art). Though there are bridal shops throughout the major shopping areas in Juárez, they cluster densely in the **"Bridal district"** (⌧ *Av. Lerdo, near the main drag*). It isn't a well-defined district, per se, just a concentration of fancy-dress stores. One of the safest and most touristy sectors of Ciudad Juárez, **City Market Juarez** (⌧ *Av. 16 de Septiembre*) is just a stroll from where the Sante Fe Bridge spills foot travelers. It's on September 16 Street, named after Mexican Independence Day. At the **Mercado** (⌧ *Av. 16 de Septiembre*) merchants sell wares in a labyrinth of booths carrying piñatas (papier-mâché animals stuffed with candy, or left empty for you to stuff), wooden figurines, belts, and jewelry. *Please* try your hand at bartering with the vendors! They really, really do expect you to haggle about the price, and you'll look like a rube if you don't.

WHERE TO EAT

Food is everywhere in Juárez—in carts alongside the road, in storefront kitchen stalls open to the air, and in fine restaurants with all the trappings of civility. A lot of the food here is very, very good and genuinely authentic. Americans should keep in mind that food safety and sanitation are not regulated and enforced as aggressively as in the States. And yes, it's true about the water: don't drink it unless bottled.

Larger restaurants dish up bottled water, so hydration needn't be a problem. Just make sure that food is peeled, cooked, or packaged to minimize chances of stomach problems.

$ ✗**Ajuua!** Built in the style of a *pueblito* (small pueblo), this restaurant
MEXICAN is a popular stopover for passengers aboard the El Paso–Juárez Trolley
★ Co.'s Border Jumper. The traditional Mexican dishes are reliably good, as are the margaritas. On weekend evenings, expect mariachi bands and colorfully costumed dancers. It's customary to tip the mariachi's leader a dollar or two. (You'll need to dial 011 plus 52 for the country code if calling from El Paso.) ✉*162 N. Efren Ornelas, Av. Lincoln and Av. 16 de Septiembre* ☎*52–656/616–6935* ▭*AE, MC, V.*

$$ ✗**Barrigas.** There are Barrigas sites throughout the sister cities, and all of
MEXICAN them serve traditional Mexican food and live music. The chicken mole (a rich sauce made with chocolate) is wonderful, and so is the *ribojo*, or rib-eye steak. ✉*4850 Av. Triunfo de la República* ☎*915/611–4840* ▭*AE, MC, V.*

OLD MESILLA

★ *2 mi south of Las Cruces on NM 28.*

Historians disagree about the origins of Mesilla (called both Mesilla and Old Mesilla), which in Spanish means "little table." Some say the town occupies the exact spot that Don Juan de Oñate declared "the first pueblo of this kingdom." Don't confuse Mesilla with Mesilla Park, another little village nearby.

Many of the sturdy adobe structures abundant in this community date back as far as 150 years and are still in use today. The thick walls of the adobes in this area not only helped keep the interiors cool and comfortable during hot days, but also helped defend against attacks by Apache, who were none too excited about the influx of people into their territory.

Mesilla was established by a group of lifetime Mexican residents when the territory of New Mexico was acquired by the United States in 1848. Wishing to remain Mexican, they left Las Cruces, moved a few miles west across the new border of the Rio Grande, and established their village in Mexican territory. All this effort was for naught, because the Rio Grande not only changed its path in 1865 putting both Las Cruces and Mesilla east of the river, but the whole area had already been annexed by the United States in 1854. Mesilla had established itself well and was the largest station between El Paso and Los Angeles on the Butterfield Stage Line, and for a time served as the Confederate territorial capital, an area that covered Arizona and western New Mexico. In 1881 the Santa Fe Railroad extended its line into Las Cruces, bypassing Mesilla and establishing Las Cruces as the area's major hub of commerce and transportation.

Mesilla has seen celebrations, weddings, bloody political battles, and the milestone trial of Billy the Kid. A Mesilla jury convicted the Kid for the murder of Matthew Brady, the sheriff of Lincoln County. The Kid was transferred to the Lincoln County Courthouse to be hanged for the crime but briefly staved off the inevitable by escaping.

Today touristy shops, galleries, and restaurants line the cobbled streets of Old Mesilla. With a Mexican-style plaza and gazebo where many weddings and fiestas take place, the village retains the charm of bygone days. It is well worth parking your car and strolling around the village and the surrounding neighborhoods, where many of the adobe homes are lovingly maintained.

On the north side of the Plaza is the **San Albino Church** (⊠ *Old Mesilla Plaza*), an impressive brick-and-stained-glass building originally established in 1851.

OFF THE BEATEN PATH

Stahmann Farms. Pecan trees cover about 4,000 acres here, at the world's largest family-owned pecan orchard. You can take a shaded drive through the trees and drop by the farm's store to sample yummy pecan products, or take a tour of the farms (2:30 in winter, 10 AM in summer). They also have a store on the Plaza in Old Mesilla. ⊠ *NM 28, 8 mi south of Old Mesilla, San Miguel* ☎ *575/526–8974 or 800/654–6887* ☉ *Store Mon.–Sat. 9–6, Sun. 11–5.*

WHERE TO EAT

¢
MEXICAN
Fodor's Choice
★

✕ **Chope's Bar & Cafe.** Pronounced *chope es*, it looks like a run-of-the-mill adobe building from the outside, but inside you'll find happy locals eating fiery Southwestern-style food in the restaurant and drinking ice-cold beer and tasty margaritas in the bar. It's well worth the 15-mi drive south from Old Mesilla for the food and the local flavor. This is the real deal—and it's a blast. No credit cards are accepted in the bar. ⊠ *NM 28, La Mesa* ☎ *575/233–9976 bar, 575/233–3420 restaurant* ⊟ *MC, V.*

$$$$
CONTINENTAL
Fodor's Choice
★

✕ **Double Eagle.** Chandeliers, century-old wall tapestries, and gold-leaf ceilings set the scene at this elegant restaurant inside an 1848 mansion on Old Mesilla's plaza. Some say ghosts, including one of a young man who incurred his mother's wrath by falling in love with a servant girl, haunt the property. Continental cuisine, steaks, and flambé dishes are served, formally, in the main restaurant. The restaurant has its own aging room for it's renowned steaks, and you can sample all sorts of delicious alcoholic infusions from the bar (the chile vodka makes a fantastic Bloody Mary). **Pepper's,** the adjoining Southwestern-style café, has more casual fare including chiles rellenos served with colorful tortilla chips ($). The Double Eagle Sunday champagne brunch is excellent and a good deal ($$; reservations are recommended). ⊠ *2355 Calle de Guadalupe* ☎ *575/523–6700* ⊟ *AE, D, DC, MC, V.*

$
MEXICAN
★

✕ **La Posta.** Once a way station for the Butterfield Overland Mail and Wells Fargo stagecoaches, this restaurant in an old adobe structure has hosted many celebrities through the years, including Bob Hope and Mexican revolutionary Pancho Villa. Some of the Mexican recipes here date back more than a century; among the best menu choices are *tostadas compuestos* (red or green chili, meat, and pinto beans in

9

tortilla shells), and enchiladas with red or green chili. Exotic birds and tropical fish inhabit the lushly planted atrium. ⊠*2410 Calle de San Albino* ☎*575/524–3524* ▤*AE, D, DC, MC, V*

$$ ✕**Lorenzo's.** Walk into this restaurant and it's easy to imagine you're in

ITALIAN Sicily: a hand-painted mural of the Mesilla Valley decorates a wall, light floods in through windows. The warm, colorful decor, friendly service, and really good food make Lorenzo's a favorite among locals. Old Sicilian recipes are used to create the pastas, sauces, pizzas, sandwiches, and salads. An outdoor courtyard offers a relaxing spot for a leisurely lunch or dinner. ⊠*1750 Calle de Mercado, Suite 4, near Mercado shopping center* ☎*575/525–3170* ▤*AE, D, MC, V.*

THE ARTS

The Fountain Theater (⊠*2469 C. de Guadalupe, ½ block off plaza* ☎*575/524–8287* ⊕*www.fountaintheatre.org*), built in 1905 by the prominent Fountain family, is the oldest continuously operating theater in New Mexico and is still owned by the family. Vaudeville acts once graced the stage; today, independent films, amateur theater, and some chamber music are featured.

SHOPPING

High-quality Native American jewelry and crafts are sold at surprisingly good prices in the adobe shops of **Old Mesilla Plaza** if you have the patience to weed through multitudes of cheesy ceramic Indian dolls with feathered headdresses (not what the locals wore) and other various and sundry tourist tchotchkes. The **Farmers Market** offers homegrown produce such as watermelons and green chiles (in season), as well as handcrafted souvenirs and jewelry, noon–4 Sunday and 11–4 Thursday year-round. In mid-afternoon on Sunday from September to early November, you can enjoy live mariachi music here, too. Nearby there are a growing number of interesting contemporary art galleries, kitchen shops, and restaurants. **El Platero** (⊠*2350 C. de Principal* ☎*575/523–5561*) offers jewelry, touristy souvenirs, Southwestern gift items, and postcards. This is also a great place to grab an ice cream or a piece of fudge to eat on the outside benches.

An interior-design firm and art gallery, **Charles Inc.** (⊠*1885 W. Boutz St., at Av. de Mesilla* ☎*575/523–1888 Mon.–Fri. 9–5*) has an extensive collection of fine art, such as bronze and marble pieces by master stone carver Jesús Mata.

Las Cosas (⊠*1740 Calle de Mercado, Suite A* ☎*575/541–9735* ⊕*www. lascosascooking.com* ⊗*Mon.–Sat. 10–6, Sun. noon–5*), like its sister shop in Santa Fe, is a cook's nirvana, offering the latest and greatest in cookware, kitchen gadgets, and even cooking classes. The staff is helpful and very knowledgeable.

Preston Contemporary Art Center (⊠*1755 Avenida de Mercado* ☎*575/523– 8713* ⊕*www.prestoncontemporaryart.com* ⊗*Wed. and Thurs. 1–5, Fri. 1–7, Sat. 9–2, Sun. 2–4*) opened in 2008 to the delight of the arts community. Showcasing different facets of the contemporary-arts world, such as photography, sculpture, painting, and ceramics, the four annual exhibits feature works from local, national, and international artists.

LAS CRUCES

45 mi north of El Paso on I–10.

The Mesilla Valley has been populated for centuries. The Spanish passed through the region first in 1598 and continued to use the route to reach the northern territories around Santa Fe. Though the Spanish could not maintain settlements in the region at all during the 1700s, by the early 1800s people were able to move in and create hamlets that grew to become Doña Ana and, eventually, Las Cruces.

In 1848 the Treaty of Guadalupe Hidalgo ended the Mexican-American war, but rendered uncertain the sovereignty of Las Cruces. The Mesilla Valley ended up split between two nations, with the town of Mesilla on the west of the Rio Grande belonging to Mexico and Las Cruces, on the eastern banks of the river, belonging to the United States. The Gadsden Purchase in 1853 made the whole area U.S. territory and Las Cruces began its ascent as the area's power center. The railroad, irrigation, agriculture, and local ranching drove the city's growth. Much of the new city was built in the Territorial and Victorian styles popular at the time. The College of Las Cruces was founded in 1880 and eventually became New Mexico State University.

Mention Las Cruces to someone today and their reply is likely to be about its status as one of the fastest-growing cities in the United States—second fastest in New Mexico, behind Albuquerque. With growth spurred by retirees looking for sun and mild winters, the defense and commercial business at White Sands Missile Range, the increasing strength of New Mexico State University, and its proximity to the business on the border with Mexico, this city of about 75,000 people *is* growing. Las Cruces is following the lead of many U.S. cities by pushing a major revitalization of its historic downtown. The district and its surrounding residential neighborhoods date back more than a century, and a casual walk around will show all sorts of renovation—from simple painting and planting to the restabilization of entire buildings. Despite the revitalization, greater Las Cruces tends to be a bit sterile as its historical district is surrounded by ever-expanding rings of strip malls and cookie-cutter subdivisions.

Many artists (painters, sculptors, actors, writers, metalsmiths) make their homes here not just because the surrounding area offers a perpetually inspiring palette, but also because the arts community is supportive and the town an affordable alternative to chic and expensive Santa Fe. Museums, a performing arts center, a renovated movie theater, and new shops and some cafés are draws. A farmers' market on the weekends makes for a fun way to spend a Saturday morning.

The Hispanic population in Las Cruces is comprised of descendents from the Spanish settlers as well as many Mexican immigrants; both influences add unique cultural elements to the community as well as some seriously spicy food. The emphasis on family is strong here, and kids are welcome just about everywhere.

Although Mesilla is listed separately, it's so close to Las Cruces that you can comfortably go back and forth to eat, shop, or enjoy a night out.

The **Branigan Cultural Center** is the hub of the revitalized downtown and operates as a locus for educational activities, arts conferences, and traveling crafts exhibits. It also serves as the central contact point for other city-operated museums in the neighborhood. The **Museum of Fine Art And Culture,** open weekdays 10–4, Saturday 9–2, next door to the Cultural Center, features works of regional artists with an eclectic mix of styles, and an emphasis on the Southwest. Admission is free. The **New Mexico Railroad and Transportation Museum,** open Thursday through Saturday 10–4, is in the old Santa Fe Railroad Depot several blocks west of the Cultural Center at 351 N. Mesilla St. ⊠ *Cultural Center, 501 N. Main St.* ☎ *575/541–2155* ⊠ *Free* ☉ *Weekdays 10–4, Sat. 9–1.*

The handsomely designed **New Mexico Farm and Ranch Heritage Museum** documents 3,000 years of agriculture in New Mexico and the Southwest. Visit a re-creation of a 1,200-year-old Mogollon farmhouse, based on styles built by some of the first non-nomadic people to live in what is now New Mexico. Longhorn cattle, churro sheep, and dairy cows are among the heritage breeds—descendants of animals the Spanish brought from Mexico—raised at the museum. At milking times (11 and 3), you can learn about the history of dairy farming in New Mexico, or take a look in the "beef barn" where six different breeds of beef cattle are housed. A span of the historic Green Bridge, which used to span the Hondo River, has been reassembled over the arroyo on the grounds. Chuck-wagon cooking demonstrations are offered during special events. ⊠ *4100 Dripping Springs Rd.* ✛ *from Las Cruces head east on University Ave., which becomes Dripping Springs Rd.; ranch is 1½ mi east of I–25* ☎ *575/522–4100* ⊕ *www.nmfarmandranch museum.org* ⊠ *$5* ☉ *Mon.–Sat. 9–5, Sun. noon–5.*

WHERE TO EAT

¢ ✕ **Caliche's.** Instead of heading for one of the big fast-food joints, order
AMERICAN from the window at one of these local stands, and then enjoy specialty hot dogs, or mesquite-smoked turkey sandwiches on croissants in your car or on the outside benches. All kinds of delectable sundaes and sodas are made here, too, using delicious homemade, custard-style ice cream. ⊠ *590 S. Valley Dr.* ☎ *575/647–5066* ⊠ *131 N. Roadrunner Pkwy.* ☎ *575/521–1161* ▤ *MC, V.*

$ ✕ **Farley's Pub.** For a family evening out with no worries about the kids
AMERICAN being loud or throwing their peanut shells on the floor, Farley's is the
☉ place. Choose from a huge menu of typical but tasty pub fare; peel 'n' eat shrimp, burgers and sandwiches, salads, wood-fired pizzas, all sorts of appetizers, and truly decadent desserts. Video games and pool tables make for a fun evening. ⊠ *3499 Foothills Rd. (at Nacho Dr.)* ☎ *575/522–0466* ▤ *D, MC, V.*

$ ✕ **International Delights.** A popular place to sample specialty coffees and
MIDDLE teas, this downtown café pipes rhythmic Middle Eastern music among
EASTERN its tables and comfortable outdoor patio. Order hummus, falafel, or
★ lamb couscous here for amazingly reasonable prices (the chicken-and-lamb combo, at $14.95, is the most expensive item on the menu).

Sacred Ground

Symbols of Catholicism seem to be a hallmark of New Mexico, and visitors seek out adobe churches to photograph, and colorful religious icons and minishrines to buy as souvenirs. More intimate and poignant expressions of New Mexicans' deep religiosity are found in homemade shrines and centuries-old churches of healing.

Alongside the state's roadways are small memorials of flowers and crosses known in Spanish as *descansos,* or resting places, for those who have died in automobile and motorcycle accidents. The monuments, erected by family or friends to honor the memory of the dead, often on narrow, curving roads and steep embankments, serve as reminders to the living not to take safe passage for granted. Some of the descansos are elaborated decorated for various events and holidays throughout the year. Some historians say the custom of highway shrines was introduced to the Western hemisphere four centuries ago by the first Spanish explorers, who experienced so many losses of life that their trails were strewn with crosses marking the fallen. Las Cruces, New Mexico, is thought to have obtained its name, "The Crosses," after one such site where Spanish explorers were slaughtered in a Native American ambush.

In modern times, those of Hispanic descent and others practicing the Southwest's shrine tradition have seen their custom thwarted elsewhere in the country. State highway departments in more densely populated regions order the roadside shrines to be removed because of the problems they present for road maintenance crews. But in New Mexico, road department officials go out of their way to honor the shrines held so sacred by the loved ones who maintain them. If the shrines need to be temporarily moved for maintenance, crews work with families to make sure the monuments are returned to their original spots.

Crosses in general are a revered symbol in this state, where they often can be seen high atop a barren hill where religious treks are made. The crosses are placed either by a community or, as in Lincoln, by a single, devout individual. New Mexico also is known for a variety of spontaneous shrines, created by those who report experiencing miracles or religious visions. One woman in Lake Arthur, near Artesia in southeastern New Mexico, saw the image of Christ in a tortilla she was cooking. She built her own shrine surrounding the tortilla, complete with flickering candles, and the faithful and curious can make pilgrimages to it.

In an awesome display of religious faith during Holy Week, thousands of people journey miles by foot to reach Chimayó in northern New Mexico. They seek the blessing and healing of the holy soil found in the town's Santuario (sanctuary) church. The ground's sacredness dates from 1810, when a man discovered a crucifix glowing in the dirt. Though several attempts were made to relocate the cross, legend says the crucifix always reappeared where it was first found. Today the cross hangs above the altar, and the holy dirt can be taken from a sacred *pozito* (a small hole) in the floorboards of an adjoining room. Those seeking healing or giving thanks leave small photographs or tokens of their faith within an anteroom.

9

Imported olives, pastas, rice, and other items can be purchased in the attached grocery shop. ⊠ *1245 El Paseo Rd.* ☎ *575/647–5956* ⊟ *AE, D, MC, V.*

$ ✕ **Lemongrass.** Super-fresh ingredients and a truly outstanding pad thai
THAI   make this airy restaurant worth your time. The food isn't traditional
★   Thai, with nary a trace of fish sauce or chile paste to be found, but the Americanized flavors are clean and crisp and the wonderful freshness of ingredients can't be overstated. ⊠ *2540 El Paseo Rd., Hadley Center* ☎ *575/523–8778* ⊟ *AE, D, MC, V.*

$ ✕ **Lorenzo's.** Convenient to New Mexico State University, the largest of
ITALIAN   Lorenzo's three Las Cruces locations re-creates the relaxed feel of an
★   Italian country inn with ample greenery, a fountain, and large murals depicting Italian scenes. Grilled fish and chicken are served along with Sicilian sandwiches, pizzas, pastas, and salads. The smaller outlet on North Alameda Street is open only for lunch weekdays. ⊠ *University Plaza, 1753 E. University Ave.* ☎ *575/521–3505* ⊠ *3961 E. Lohman* ☎ *575/522–7755* ⊠ *741 N. Alameda St.* ☎ *575/524–2850* ⊟ *AE, D, MC, V.*

$ ✕ **My Brother's Place.** *Tostadas compuestos* (a concoction of red or green
MEXICAN   chili, meat, pinto beans, and cheese in a crispy tortilla cup) and other
★   Southwestern dishes are served with flair at this exceptional Mexican restaurant, where you can order pitchers of beer or margaritas to soothe the fire. Try an empanada (a Mexican turnover) or crème caramel flan for dessert. The upstairs lounge is a pleasant watering hole decorated with brightly colored chairs and piñatas. Several varieties of Mexican beer are served here, including Negra Modelo and Tecate. ⊠ *334 S. Main St.* ☎ *505/523–7681* ⊟ *AE, D, DC, MC, V.*

$ ✕ **Si Señor Restaurant.** Regularly voted a favorite by locals, this immacu-
MEXICAN   late restaurant has spacious rooms with Southwestern paintings. Mex-
★   ican entrées emphasize three distinct chile-sauce types—Las Cruces green (mild and flavorful), Deming red (medium hot), and a variety known as Hatch green "smoke," which may set your hair on fire, but you'll love it if you enjoy spice. The cooks here use family recipes and locally grown green chile peppers. Friendly service and laughter abound here. It's no wonder the locals love it. ⊠ *1551 E. Amador* ☎ *575/527–0817* ⊟ *AE, D, MC, V.*

WHERE TO STAY

$ 🛏 **Hotel Encanto.** What looks like a multistory chain hotel from the
Fodor's Choice   outside feels surprisingly like a gracious hacienda inside. Rooms are
★   furnished in a Spanish colonial motif, are generous in size, and have separate sitting rooms. The pool, an oasis with huge, shady palm trees, is delightful during the many hot months. **Café Espana** ($) serves good Spanish and Mexican food and the bar, Azul, is a hip spot sometimes offering entertainment at night. **Pros:** Excellent accommodations for the price; close to attractions; friendly, professional staff. **Cons:** Room service can be slow; no laundry facilities. ⊠ *705 S. Telshor Blvd.* ☎ *575/522–4300 or 866/383–0443* ⊕ *http://hhandr.com/las_main. php* ⇋ *203 rooms, 7 suites* ☼ *In-room: Wi-Fi, refrigerator. In-hotel: pool, gym, parking (free), bar, restaurant, some pets allowed* ⊟ *AE, D, DC, MC, V.*

$ ★ ⊞ **Lundeen Inn of the Arts.** This art-filled B&B has been the favored lodging in town for years. Architect Gerald Lundeen seamlessly joined two 1895 adobe houses to create the property; Linda, his wife, runs the impressionist gallery on the premises. Guest rooms pay homage to Western artists like Georgia O'Keeffe and Frederic Remington, and are furnished with a mix of antiques and newer handcrafted pieces. The beautiful old-world–style great room has 18-foot ceilings covered in pressed tin, dark floors, and Jacobean furniture—and towering windows looking out over the large garden. In the evenings you can carry a glass of wine upstairs into the newly added bell tower and gaze at the stars. **Pros:** The inn is loaded with character and convenient to everything. **Cons:** Bathrooms tend to be rather small; service can be spotty. ⊠*618 S. Alameda Blvd.* ☎*575/526–3326* ⊕*www.innofthearts.com* ⮐*16 rooms, 4 suites* ♻*In-room: Wi-Fi, kitchen. In-hotel: no-smoking rooms, some pets allowed* ☰*AE, D, DC, MC, V* ⓘ*BP.*

CAMPING

★ ⚠ **Aguirre Springs.** This beautiful high-elevation spot is tucked alongside the towering spires of the Organ Mountains, giving you an expansive view of the Tularosa Basin. During drought conditions, fires may be restricted or prohibited. If you're fortunate enough to be here when the moon is full, make sure you catch the moonrise—you're not likely to forget it. ⊠*Off U.S. 70, from Las Cruces take U.S. 70 northeast 12 mi; head south at road marked Aguirre Springs an additional 5 mi* ☎*575/525–4300* ♻*Pit toilets, fire grates, fire pits, grills, picnic tables* ⮐*55 sites, 2 group sites (by reservation)* ⚰*Reservations not accepted* ☰*No credit cards.*

OFF THE BEATEN PATH

La Viña Winery. Head 20 mi south of Las Cruces on NM 28 and you'll find the pride of proprietors Denise and Ken Stark, and the oldest winery in New Mexico. La Viña also hosts the popular Winefest (in October) and the Jazz & Blues Fest (in April). A wide variety of wines is produced here—from a crisp viognier, to pinot noir, to white zinfandel. Tasting room, daily tours, closed Wednesday. ⊠*4201 S. NM 28, La Union* ☎*575/882–7632* ⊕*www.lavinawinery.com.*

NIGHTLIFE & THE ARTS

Head over to **El Patio**, in the plaza in Old Mesilla, for some of the area's best live music. Established in 1934, this unassuming little adobe cantina is in the old office building of the Butterfield Stage Co. The cantina is open seven days a week, live music happens Wednesday–Saturday. ⊠*2171 Calle de Parian* ☎*575/526–9943.*

New Mexico State University (⊠*Corbett Center, University Park* ☎*575/646–4411 information center, 575/646–1420 special events office*) presents lectures, concerts, and other special events. Nightly live entertainment is featured at the **Hilton Las Cruces** (⊠*705 S. Telshor Blvd.* ☎*575/522–4300*) lounge. The locally based **Tierra del Encanto Ballet Folklorico** performs folk dances of Mexico at the annual weekend **International Mariachi Festival** (☎*575/525–1735* ⊕*www.lascrucesmariachi.org*) in November.

SPORTS & THE OUTDOORS

An 18-hole course that hosts men's and women's NCAA champion-ships, **New Mexico State University Golf Course** has a full-service bar and grill in addition to the pro shop, driving range, and practice green. Greens fees for an 18-hole game are $37 weekdays to ride, $25 to walk, slightly less for a 9-hole game. ✉ *3000 Herb Wimberley Dr.* ☎ *575/646–3219.*

At **Aguirre Springs,** beneath the towering spires of the Organ Moun-tains, hiking trails lead into the upper regions of the ponderosa pines, including **Pine Tree Trail** (4-mi loop) and **Baylor Pass National Rec-reation Trail** (6 mi one way). During drought conditions fires may be restricted or prohibited. ✉ *Off U.S. 70, from Las Cruces take U.S. 70 northeast 12 mi; head south at road marked Aguirre Springs an addi-tional 5 mi* ☎ *575/525–4300* 🔲 *$3* ⊘ *Apr.–Oct., daily 8–8; Nov.– Mar., daily 8–6.*

At the **Dripping Springs Natural Area** is an abandoned mountain resort built in the 1870s and converted decades later into a sanatorium for tuberculosis patients. You can tour the now-empty facility, or take a 1-mi round-trip hike on a trail following a scenic canyon (it even has a stream when it's been raining) amid mesquite and wildflowers. You might spot a few rock climbers testing their mettle on sheer rock walls jutting above you. When you reach **Hermit's Peak**—a hill where Agos-tini Justiniani, an Italian nobleman, lived in solitude and treated the sick during the 19th century—you can step inside the cave where he once lived, and wonder about the stories of his miraculous healing powers. This is the same hermit who lived in a cave northwest of Las Vegas, New Mexico, on what is also known as Hermit's Peak. Justini-ani was found murdered at the site in 1869. This site is for day use only. ✉ *Dripping Springs Rd., from Las Cruces head east on University Ave. 10 mi* ☎ *575/522–1219* 🔲 *$3 per vehicle* ⊘ *Daily 8 AM–dusk.*

SHOPPING

If you're in town on a Wednesday or Saturday, don't miss the excel-lent **outdoor market** on North Main Street, where approximately 200 vendors sell produce, handcrafted items, and baked goods. Mingle with the locals and enjoy the scene between 8 and 12:30. The **Picacho Street Antique District** (✉ *Between N. Valley Dr. and N. 3rd St.*) is a fun area to explore and look for treasures at, often, very reasonable prices. The upscale **Glenn Cutter Gallery** (✉ *2640 El Paseo Rd.* ☎ *575/524–4300*) carries paintings from regional artists like Fred Chilton, as well as fine jewelry. The small complex surrounding Glenn Cutter Gallery is developing into an arts zone with interesting contemporary work by local artists; be sure to walk around and see who's moved in and what they're showing. The only artist co-op in the Las Cruces area, the **Mesilla Valley Fine Arts Gallery** (✉ *2470A Calle de Guadalupe, southeast corner of Old Mesilla plaza* ☎ *575/522–2933*) has a broad range of art by 30 juried artists.

RADIUM SPRINGS

13 mi north of Las Cruces on I–25.

Fort Selden was established in 1865 to protect Mesilla Valley settlers and travelers. The flat-roofed adobe buildings at **Fort Selden State Monument** are arranged around a drill field. Several units of "Buffalo Soldiers" were stationed here. These were the acclaimed African American cavalry troops noted for their bravery and crucial role in helping protect frontier settlers from Native American attacks and desperadoes. Native Americans thought the soldiers' hair resembled that of a buffalo and gave the regiments their name. Knowing the respect the Apaches held for the animals, the soldiers did not take offense. Buffalo Soldiers were also stationed at Fort Bayard, near Silver City, and Fort Stanton, in Lincoln County, to shield miners and travelers from attacks by Apaches.

In the early 1880s Capt. Arthur MacArthur was appointed post commander of Fort Selden. His young son spent several years on the post and grew up to become World War II hero General Douglas MacArthur. A permanent exhibit called "Fort Selden: An Adobe Post on the Rio Grande" depicts the roles of officers, enlisted men, and women on the American frontier during the Indian Wars. Camping facilities can be found at Leasburg State Park. ⊠*Off I–25 Radium Springs Exit 19, 13 mi north of Las Cruces* ☎*575/526–8911* ⊕*www.nmmonuments. org* 🎫*$3* 🕙 *Wed.–Mon. 8:30–5.*

Built in 1908, Leasburg Dam retains irrigation water for Mesilla Valley farmland and recreational water for the **Leasburg State Park.** Kayakers and anglers enjoy boating and fishing here, and on hot days the cool water draws dozens of swimmers. ⊠*NM 157 west of I–25* 🎫*Day use $5 per vehicle* 🕙*Daily 7 AM–sunset.*

CAMPING

🏕 **Leasburg State Park Campground.** A favorite campground for locals, this nicely developed camping area also draws plenty of out-of-state visitors. Reservations are essential during peak times (weekends, holidays, and summer). ⊠*NM 157 west of I–25* ☎*575/524–4068, 877/664–7787 reservations* ♿*Flush toilets, partial hookups (electric and water), dump station, drinking water, showers, fire grates, fire pits, grills, picnic tables, electricity, public telephone, play area, ranger station, swimming (river)* 🛏*18 RV sites, 6 developed tent sites, 3 primitive sites* 🚫*No credit cards.*

DEMING

60 mi west of Las Cruces on I–10.

In the late 1800s Deming was considered such a wild, out-of-control place that Arizona outlaws were sent here (with one-way stage tickets) as punishment. A stop on the Butterfield Stage Trail, Deming received an economic boost when the Atchison, Topeka & Santa Fe Railway met up with the Southern Pacific line here in 1881. Far from the Wild

West town it once was, farming and small industry are now the main sources of income for the town's roughly 15,000 residents. The historic buildings in the downtown area are nicely preserved and mostly still in use.

OFF THE
BEATEN
PATH

⚠ **Pancho Villa State Park.** Early on the morning of March 9, 1916, Francisco "Pancho" Villa, the famed revolutionary from Mexico, crossed into New Mexico to attack the town of Columbus and nearby Camp Furlong, a U.S. military outpost. This was the first time since the War of 1812 that the United States had experienced an armed invasion. A general who later would be commander of Allied forces in World War I—General John Joseph "Black Jack" Pershing—led 10,000 troops into Mexico for a grueling but futile search for Villa that lasted almost a year. This park on the site of Camp Furlong has exhibits depicting the raid, along with a 20-minute documentary film. ⊠ *NM 11, 35 mi south of Deming, in Columbus* ☎ *575/531–2711* ☑ *$5 per vehicle* ☉ *Visitor center daily 8–5.*

☪ **Shakespeare Ghost Town.** If you're heading west, this is a fun stop. In the heart of a working ranch 50 mi west of Deming, portions of this settlement have been preserved as they were in the town's heyday as a gold and silver mining town in the late 1800s. Founded in 1856, the ghost town has been designated a National Historic Site, and original structures such as homes, saloons, and stables still stand. Living-history reenactments are staged four times a year—usually the fourth weekend of April, June, August, and October. You'll find no snack shops or other tourist amenities in Shakespeare, as owner Janaloo Hill (who grew up on the ranch, and died in May 2005) vowed not to compromise the authenticity of this genuine piece of the Old West. ⊠ *2½ mi southwest of Lordsburg, south of I–10 at Exit 22, Box 253, Lordsburg, NM* ☎ *575/542–9034* ⊕ *www.shakespeareghostown.com* ☑ *$5* ☉ *Tours: Mar.–Dec., call for tour times and dates.*

WHERE TO EAT & STAY

¢ ✕ **Si Señor Restaurant.** Tasty, spicy Mexican food and standard American dishes are served at this family-owned restaurant (a sister property to the Si Señor in Las Cruces). Try the chicken stuffed sopaipillas with green chile—they're not on the menu but are some of the best in the state. The dining experience here isn't fancy, but the food is good and the prices are reasonable. No alcohol is served. ⊠ *200 E. Pine St.* ☎ *575/546–3938* ▭ *AE, D, MC, V.*

MEXICAN

★

¢ 🕎 **Holiday Inn Deming.** This property offers the most luxurious lodgings in at least a 60-mi radius. It's also very accessible from the interstate (I–10). The spacious rooms have contemporary, Southwestern-style decor, and include irons and ironing boards. The on-site **Lazy Lizard Grill** ($) starts off the day with an all-you-can-eat buffet breakfast for $6.50. **Pros:** Friendly staff, easy jumping-off point for several areas. **Cons:** Right by the freeway; chain hotel character. ⊠ *Off I–10 Exit 85 east* ☎ *575/546–2661* ⇆ *116 rooms* ♨ *In-room: refrigerator, Wi-Fi. In-hotel: restaurant, bar, pool, gym, laundry facilities, laundry service, some pets allowed* ▭ *AE, D, DC, MC, V.*

CAMPING

⚲ **Pancho Villa State Park Campground.** This campground on the Mexican border is a comfortable place to stop for the night. You may feel you're in the middle of nowhere, but a general store and a service station are right next door, and showers are a dream for hot, sweaty desert travelers. Wandering around the little town of Columbus, and even across the border to eat at the Pink House in Palomas is a fun way to spend a few hours (you'll need your passports). ✉ *NM 11, 35 mi south of Deming* ☎ *575/531–2711* ♿ *Flush toilets, partial hookups (electric and water), dump station, drinking water, showers, fire grates, fire pits, grills, picnic tables, electricity, public telephone, play area, ranger station* ⤳ *61 RV sites, 5 primitive sites.*

GILA NATIONAL FOREST AREA

The cliff dwellings, ghost towns, and sprawling ranches scattered among hundreds of miles of desert, forest, and jagged canyons in the Gila (pronounced "heela") are the legacy of the hearty souls who have inhabited this remote area over the centuries. The early cliff dwellers mysteriously disappeared sometime after the year 1000, leaving behind the ruins and relics of a culture replaced half a millennium later by Spanish explorers, roving bands of Apaches, and occasional trappers. In the 1800s Apache leaders including Cochise, Geronimo, and Victorio waged war against the encroaching Mexican and American settlers, and for a time the sheer ruggedness of the mountains provided refuge for them. Any hope for the Apaches retaining freedom in the area vanished when prospectors discovered the area was rich with minerals in the late 1800s. The mining boom began and the area was flooded with settlers. Scenic drives lead to several ghost towns from this era, including the old gold-mining settlement of Mogollon. ■ TIP➔**It can't be stressed enough that the drive to the cliff dwellings is winding and slow and one of the most scenic you'll find. If you can spare the time, spend the night at one of the mountain inns close to the dwellings to maximize your time in the park.**

9

SILVER CITY

53 mi northwest of Deming; 115 mi northwest of Las Cruces, west on I–10 and northwest on U.S. 180.

Silver City began as a tough and lawless mining camp in 1870, and struggled for a long time to become a more respectable—and permanent—settlement. Henry McCarty spent part of his boyhood here, perhaps learning some of the ruthlessness that led to his later infamy under his nickname—Billy the Kid. Other mining towns in the area sparked briefly and then died, but Silver City eventually flourished and became the area's most populated city. Today, even though it has 12,000 residents, Silver City retains a sense of remote wildness—largely due to the nearby Gila National Forest and vast Gila Wilderness.

Since the area's copper ore is now close to depleted and the huge mine nearby all but officially closed, the town's traditional population of miners is being replaced by artists, outdoors enthusiasts, and retirees looking for a slightly more bohemian community than, say, Las Cruces. Thanks to efforts of preservationists, though, Silver City's origins are evident in the many distinctive houses and storefronts of the downtown area, making it ideal for exploring by foot (buy a self-guided walking tour map and guide at the Silver City Museum shop—several are offered). The characterless strip-style development of the surrounding town belies the charm of the compact, walkable historic downtown. By all means, park your car to do your exploring.

A stroll through the historic downtown district will take you by many of the town's three dozen or so art galleries, several tasty cafés, and antiques stores. Silver City has become fairly well-known for being artsy, and artists may well make up the bulk of new residents. Silver City's arts scene couldn't be more different from the one in Santa Fe. High dollar isn't king here, and art galleries tend to feel more like friendly gathering places than the dead-serious spaces found so often farther north. A local artist said "Silver City is where art is for *the* people, not *some* people."

Festivals and community events abound in this town, and almost every month sees some sort of community event in, or close to, Silver City. In early May the **Celebration of Spring** happens downtown in the Big Ditch Park, with crafts booths, activities, and lots of frolicking in the balmy weather. This fiesta marks the opening of the city's farmers' market at Bullard and 6th Street, where locally grown produce and locally produced crafts are available. The **Silver City Blues Festival** also happens in May, in Gough Park (downtown), and locals treat it as sort of a large-scale block party where young and old dance on the grass under beautiful, starry skies. September brings the **Taste of Silver City** event where, for the price of a ticket, you can walk around downtown sampling food and treats from many participating establishments. The calendar of events and activities at ⊕*www.silvercity.org* gives comprehensive information, or you can call the Silver City Main Street Project (☎*575/534–1700*) for downtown events.

In the historic district, the **Silver City Grant County Chamber of Commerce** (✉*201 N. Hudson St.* ☎*575/538–3785* ⊕*www.silvercity.org*) has an information center. The Web site is up-to-date and offers an excellent calendar of events for planning your trip, in addition to all sorts of information about the city and region. If you're traveling north on NM 90, the highway turns into Hudson Street. If you're traveling on U.S. 180, it turns into Silver Heights Boulevard within the city limits and intersects Hudson Street.

WHAT TO SEE

The Ailman House, built in 1881, serves as headquarters for the **Silver City Museum,** whose main gallery mural of the mining and ranching community circa 1882 provides a good overview of the area's colorful history. Displays include pottery and other relics from the area's ancient (and now extinct) Mimbres and Mogollon cultures. From the museum's tower you can catch a glimpse of Silver City's three historic districts. Self-guided walking tours, with maps, are sold in the museum's store, which carries Southwestern gifts and books. Free guided walking tours of the neighboring historic district are offered on Memorial Day and Labor Day. The museum also has a local-history research library. ✉ *312 W. Broadway www.silvercitymuseum.org* ☎ *575/538–5921* ✉ *$3 Suggested donation* ⊙ *Tues.–Fri. 9–4:30, weekends 10–4.*

NEED A BREAK?

Alotta Gelato. Made on-site, the gelato here is creamy and delicious. Flavors change regularly; espresso, chocolate hazelnut, and a very unordinary vanilla are regulars, as are sorbettos like raspberry and mango. It's open late if you need a nighttime snack. ✉ *619 N. Bullard St.* ☎ *575/534–4995.*

The **Western New Mexico University Museum** contains the world's largest permanent display of distinctive Mimbres pottery (which has influenced modern ceramic artists around the world), as well as basketry and other artifacts. Exhibits also include the intricately decorated Casas Grandes pottery from northern Mexico. The museum's fourth floor displays photos and other memorabilia of the university. From the photo archives on the fourth floor you get a 360-degree view of Silver City. ✉ *1000 W. College Ave., on campus, west end of 10th St.* ☎ *575/538–6386* ✉ *Free* ⊙ *Weekdays 9–4:30, weekends 10–4.*

OFF THE BEATEN PATH

City of Rocks State Park. One look at the spires here and you'll figure out how the area came by its name. The unusual rock formations were spewed from an ancient volcano and have been eroded over the centuries by wind and rain into the marvelous shapes there today—some more than 40 feet tall. You've got to walk through the city to fully appreciate the place—and it's a great, easy adventure to have with kids (make sure you wear tennis shoes or hiking shoes). The park has a visitor center, and a large developed campground ($10–$14) with 10 RV sites with water and electric hookups, 42 camping sites, picnic tables, grills, flush toilets, and showers. This is a great spot to camp, with sites nestled amongst the huge rocks. ✉ *Take NM 180 northwest from Deming for 24 mi; then turn northeast onto NM 61 for 4 mi, Faywood* ☎ *575/536–2800* ✉ *Day use $5 per vehicle* ⊙ *Visitor center daily 10–4.*

WHERE TO EAT

$$
ECLECTIC
Fodor's Choice
★

✕ **1zero6.** Chef and proprietor Jake Politte creates dishes to rival any big-city restaurant. His menu changes constantly, based on what's available and what he feels like cooking. Asia and the Pacific Rim are clearly passions, and Jake manages to mix flavors of Interior Mexico with Malaysian ones like they were long-lost cousins. He uses only fresh, hand-selected ingredients, makes all of his own sauces (no bottled pastes here), and his attention to detail is clear from your first bite. Giant prawns in a rich but delicate red curry on a bed of fresh spinach next to perfectly savory rice, or Khmer Krom spiced roasted pork with mild lemongrass, curried rice noodles, and fresh wok-fried vegetables are only two of the creations to emerge from his kitchen. The menu usually consists of two appetizers, three entrées, and one perfectly paired dessert. The dining room has a half-dozen tables and a big canvas theater sign from Jakarta on one wall. It's an airy, comfortable room where the food is the star—and how. ✉ *106 N. Texas St.* ☎ *575/313–4418* ▭ *MC, V* ⊘ *Closed Mon.–Thurs. No lunch.*

¢ **✕ Café at the Kumquat.** This little café inside the international grocery
CAFÉ   called the Curious Kumquat is a delightful find. Salads and sandwiches
★   are fresh and tasty and anything but run-of-the-mill, and the Attack of the Killer Tomato Basil Bisque is fantastic. Outdoor seating under big, shady trees in the summer is great, or grab lunch to go before heading into the Gila. ✉ *111 E. College Ave., at N. Bullard St.* ☎ *575/534–0337* ▭ *AE, D, MC, V.*

$ **✕ Diane's Restaurant.** Fresh flowers grace the wooden tables and light
SOUTHWESTERN   streams through the large windows at this cheerful bakery and eat-
★   ery. Chef-owner Diane Barrett's creative menu includes blackened pork loin with apple-bourbon demi-glace, and a terrific rack of lamb. The sandwiches are all made with wonderfully tasty house-baked bread; if you're in the mood for something sweet, don't miss the knockout cinnamon rolls. Imported beer and specialty wines are available. ✉ *510 N. Bullard St.* ☎ *575/538–8722* ▭ *AE, D, MC, V* ⊘ *Closed Mon.*

$ **✕ Jalisco's.** The Mesa family serves up hunger-busting traditional Mexi-
MEXICAN   can food here, all based on old family recipes. Enchiladas and chiles rel-
lenos (ask for the green chile on the rellenos—strangely, they charge $2 extra for it, but it's worth it) satisfy big appetites in the cheerful dining rooms decorated with art from local artists and packed with families. ✉ *103 S. Bullard St.* ☎ *575/388–2060* ▭ *MC, V* ⊘ *Closed Sun.*

$ **✕ Vicki's Eatery.** Owned by the same friendly folks who own Yankie
CONTEMPORARY   Creek Coffee House across the street, this colorful nook serves break-
★   fast, lunch, and dinner to happy locals who stream through the doors all day long. Their eggs Florentine, with spinach and hollandaise sauce on an English muffin, is wonderful for breakfast. Hearty deli sandwiches like pastrami Reubens, or grilled roast beef with havarti and green chile on a pita for lunch, or their fresh, satisfying Greek sampler for dinner, are prepared fresh, and they make a nice alternative to the ubiquitous Mexican food. It can feel a bit crowded indoors—the eating area is charming but very small—try for a table on the outdoor patio in summer. ✉ *107 W. Yankie St.* ☎ *575/388–5430* ▭ *AE, D, MC, V.*

¢ **✕ Yankie Creek Coffee House.** Locals discuss the state of the world and
CAFÉ   the latest Silver City gossip in this friendly, laid-back living-room-like space. Coffees, including lovely Cubanos, juices, homemade pastries and cakes (most from its kitchen at Vicki's across the street) are served. If you like carrot cake, ask about Greg's—it's mouthwateringly yummy. ✉ *112 W. Yankie St.* ☎ *575/534–9025* ▭ *D, MC, V.*

LOCAL WINE

The Twisted Vine (✉ *108 E. Broadway* ☎ *575/388–2828* ⊘ *Closed Sun.*) is a thriving wine bar, which is a rare find in a town this size. What adds a nice twist to this establishment is that every wine served is produced in the region—and there are some surprisingly good ones. The art-filled space in the heart of the historic downtown welcomes guests from far and wide, and owner Jim Kolb seems to know every single one.

WHERE TO STAY

$$ ▪ Bear Mountain Lodge. Owned and operated by the Nature Conser-
Fodor'sChoice vancy, this serene, isolated haven offers luxury accommodations for
★ bird-watchers and nature lovers. You have direct access to 178 acres
of Gila National Forest land, where you can spot bird species such as
the Gila woodpecker, vermilion flycatcher, and red-faced warbler. Four
second-story rooms in the main lodge have views of mountains and for-
est land. Two downstairs lodge rooms have outdoor access to a covered
porch. Four guest rooms are available in Myra's Retreat, a separate
building named for the former owner, and a great space for a larger
family or group. A one-room guesthouse known as the Wren's Nest
has an exposed wood ceiling and its own kitchen. Hardwood floors
and locally (and sustainably) handcrafted furniture add to the rustic
elegance. A naturalist is available to answer questions and conduct
regular activities for guests. Box lunches and dinner are available for
additional charge and by arrangement. **Pros:** Quiet, distinctive haven.
Cons: Don't be put off by the mobile homes on Alabama as you head
toward the lodge property. ⊠ *Cottage San Rd., 3 mi off Alabama St.,
3 mi north of Silver City, take U.S. 180 west and turn north onto Ala-
bama* ☎ *575/538–2538 or 877/620–2327* ⊕ *www.bearmountainlodge.
com* ⇆ *11 rooms, 1 house* ⚐ *In-room: no a/c, no TV, Wi-Fi. In-hotel:
no kids under 10, no-smoking rooms, Internet* ⊟ *AE, MC, V* ⏀ *BP.*

$ ▪ Econo Lodge Silver City. This lodge on a mesa overlooking Silver City
has comfortable rooms with work tables and contemporary decor. It
is quiet and clean. You'll find extra touches here ordinarily associated
with higher-end lodges, such as microwaves, refrigerators, a hot tub,
and a gym. **Pros:** Breakfast spread is ample and a great value with the
room costs. **Cons:** Service is all over the map, generally good, but can
be indifferent. ⊠ *1120 NM 180 E* ☎ *575/534–1111, 800/553–2666
central reservations* 🖶 *575/534–2222* ⊕ *www.econolodgesilvercity.
com* ⇆ *62 rooms* ⚐ *In-room: refrigerator, Internet. In-hotel: pool,
gym, laundry facilities, some pets allowed, Wi-Fi* ⊟ *AE, D, DC, MC,
V* ⏀ *CP.*

$ ▪ Inn on Broadway. Located on a quiet street in downtown Silver
City, this popular B&B occupies a beautifully renovated home built
in 1883. Well-appointed rooms are light and spacious, and a fabulous
front porch makes for an enjoyable stay. One room has a whirlpool
bath, another room has a lovely marble fireplace. ⊠ *411 Broadway*
☎ *575/388–5485 or 566/207–7075* ⊕ *www.innonbroadway.com* ⇆ *4*
⚐ *In-room: Wi-Fi, DVD* ⊟ *AE, MC, V* ⏀ *BP.*

¢ ▪ Palace Hotel. Originally this grand two-story building was used as
a bank, but it was reinvented as a hotel in 1900. News accounts at
the time touted the Palace as a first-class lodging with the intimacy
of a small European hotel. The New Mexico Historical Preservation
Office helped to restore and reopen the hotel in 1990, which helped
keep much of the historical detail intact. Some rooms have Western-
style furnishings, others have neo-Victorian decor such as ruffled pillow
coverings and bed skirts. The upstairs garden room is a peaceful spot
for playing board games or reading. Ongoing renovations, including
all the bathrooms in 2008, make this a great deal. **Pros:** The hotel is

9

right downtown and it's steeped in history. **Cons:** No a/c, which is okay most of the time at this elevation, but it can get downright hot. ✉*106 W. Broadway* ☎*575/388–1811* ⊕*www.zianet.com/palacehotel* ⤸*12 rooms, 7 suites* ♿*In-room: no a/c, Wi-Fi* ⊟*AE, D, DC, MC, V.*

SHOPPING

Shops, galleries, cafés, parks, and all sorts of building renovation make walking Silver City's downtown district a super way to explore this great little town. Yankie Street has a compact little arts district and a couple of restaurants that make it easy to while away the hours.

Fodor's Choice ★ A standout in any town, **Blue Dome Gallery** (✉*307 N. Texas St.* ☎*575/534–8671*) is a real find for contemporary-art collectors with an eye for fine crafts. Linda and John, the owners, make a point of knowing each of the artists they represent, and they have a real knack for spotting up-and-coming artists. Pottery is clearly a passion here, though sculpture, painting, jewelry, glass, even furniture, are well represented and compelling. It's closed Tuesday.

Seedboat Gallery (✉*214 W. Yankie St.* ☎*575/534–1136* ⊕*www.seed-boatgallery.com*) is housed in a wonderfully renovated old building that was once a feed and seed store, and before that a Chinese apothecary, this gallery shows fine arts, folk art, sculpture and jewelry—all with an evident aesthetic cohesion. The proprietors, Nan and Marcia, are keen on hosting community events in the courtyard—ask them what's on the schedule.

Vendors at the **Silver City Trading Co.'s Antique Mall** (✉*205 W. Broadway* ☎*505/388–8989*) stock antiques, collectibles, and various and sundry treasures and trinkets. There are some real finds here, for a lot less than you'll see in many areas. Take some time to look in the nooks and crannies.

GILA NATIONAL FOREST

8 mi northeast of Silver City via NM 15 to Pinos Altos range and Gila Cliff Dwellings portion of Gila National Forest; 60 mi northwest of Silver City via U.S. 180 to western portions of forest. From I–25 eastern edge of forest can be accessed via NM 152: 62 mi north of Las Cruces take NM 152 west toward Hillsboro; 91 mi north of Las Cruces take NM 52 west through Winston and Chloride.

The Gila, as it's called, covers 3.3 million acres—that's 65 mi by 100 mi—and was the first land in the nation to be set aside as "wilderness" by the U.S. Forest Service back in 1924. The area is vast and continues to feel like a great, relatively undiscovered treasure. You are unlikely to come across any crowds, even in peak summer months. Whether you're backpacking or doing day hikes, you have 1,500 mi of incredibly diverse trails to explore. Open camping is permitted throughout the forest, although there are 18 developed campgrounds (all with toilets and seven with potable water). The Gila is an outdoors-lover's paradise: with seemingly endless trails to explore on mountain bikes, white-water rafting (the season usually starts in April), and fishing in rivers, lakes (three of them), and streams. Thirty percent of the forest is closed to vehicular traffic entirely, but the rest is open for touring. ■ TIP→ Remember: the roads in the Gila are winding and it will take you longer than the mileage alone would suggest to get to your destination. Allow extra time for travel.

The **Inner Loop Scenic Drive** snakes through 75 mi of some of the most gorgeous and scenic forest in the wilderness. The roads are paved but the sharp, narrow, and steep turns make it inadvisable for large RVs. From Silver City, take NM 15 north to Gila Cliff Dwellings National Monument. From the monument backtrack on NM 15 to NM 35 heading southeast to NM 152, which leads west back to Silver City.

WHAT TO SEE

☾ The **Gila Cliff Dwellings National Monument** showcases a series of flat-roof, stone-and-mud adobe dwellings built into the shallow caves of sheer sandstone cliffs by the Mogollon (*mow-go-yone*) people some 700 years ago. The visitor center has a small museum with books and other materials about the wilderness and the Mogollon. A fairly steep trail leads to the dwellings (1 mi); there are interesting pictographs to be seen on the wheelchair-accessible Trail to the Past. ⊠ *Off NM 15, 44 mi north of Silver City* ☎ *575/536–9461 or 575/536–9344* 🎟 *$3* ☉ *Monument late May–early Sept., daily 8–6; early Sept.–late May, daily 9–4. Visitor center late May–early Sept., daily 8–5; early Sept.– late May, daily 8–4:30.*

Fodor'sChoice
★

U.S. 180 leads west about 50 mi from Silver City to Glenwood and the **Whitewater Canyon.** The **Catwalk** (⊠ *Catwalk Rd., NM 174; turn east 5 mi off U.S. 180*) is a 250-foot-long metal walkway drilled into the sides of massive rock cliffs of the breathtaking Whitewater Canyon— which is only 20 feet wide in places. This is one of the most verdant, beautiful canyons in the state, with the creek and tumbling waterfalls surrounded by gorgeous rocks and shade trees. The Catwalk was built in 1935 as an access route so water lines could be extended 3 mi into the canyon. A number of famous outlaws, including Butch Cassidy and the Wild Bunch, have used the canyon as a hideout because of its remote, and almost inaccessible, location. You need to be in reasonably good physical condition to scramble up some steep stairways, but the 2.2-mi round-trip trail is well maintained and worth the effort. Bring your bathing suit so you can enjoy standing under the waterfalls and splashing in the creek. Admission is $3. Several miles north of the Catwalk on U.S. 180 is the **Glenwood State Trout Hatchery** (⊠ *U.S. 180* ☎ *575/539–2461*). There are picnic tables and a fishing pond with Rocky Mountain bighorn sheep grazing nearby. East of the Glenwood State Trout Hatchery, on NM 159, is **Mogollon.** The gold-mining town, established in the 1880s, was a ghost town for many years but has been revived in the last few decades by a dozen or so residents who live there year-round. A small museum, an art gallery and a gift shop, and a café operate on the weekends. Book a stay at the Silver Creek Inn and you can spend the weekend exploring this interesting relic of the American West, as well as the breathtaking, and huge, Gila National Forest bordering it.

9

**EN
ROUTE**

A a great place to stop on NM 12 just northwest of the Gila National Forest is **Carmen's** (⊠*NM 12 at NM 435* ☎*575/533–6990* ⊟*MC, V*) —not just because of the spicy enchiladas and good New Mexican dishes, but because once you leave the hamlet of Reserve, New Mexico (population about 300), you won't find another place to eat for about 70 mi. It's sometimes closed on major holidays.

As you drop down into **Pinos Altos** 7 mi north of Silver City on NM 15, check out the **Log Cabin Museum** (⊠*33 Main St., off NM 15* ☎*575/388–1882* ✐*$1*), where you'll find the structure originally built in 1865 by the pioneer George Shafer (the property is still in his family). Dusty artifacts tell the story of more than a century of occupation. On the eastern edge of the Gila National Forest, NM 52 leads west from Interstate 25 to **Winston** and **Chloride,** two fascinating mining towns about 35 mi northwest of Truth or Consequences. Prospectors searching for silver in the nearby ore-rich mountains founded the towns in the late 1800s; abandoned saloons and false-front buildings, and pioneer relics still remain. Though the communities are designated ghost towns, the moniker is belied by the 50 or so residents currently living in each place, and Chloride has several businesses in operation. The **Pioneer Store Museum** (☎*575/743–2736* ⊕*www.pioneerstore museum.com*) is an amazing time-capsule-like building in Chloride. The owners have painstakingly restored the building using the complete stock of original goods and records—the store had been boarded up in its entirety in 1923. It's a treasure trove of Western boomtown history. The proprietors are great, and the Web site is a resource for current information.

WHERE TO EAT & STAY

$$
STEAK
Fodor's Choice
★

✕**Buckhorn Saloon and Opera House.** Come here to see 1860s Western decor and stay for the food—including some of the best steak and seafood in the region, with hamburgers topping the list. The bar is a friendly place to gather for a drink, and has live folk-flavored music Wednesday through Saturday; the dining rooms are cozy and the walls replete with photos from the last 140 years of the area's history. The property also includes the Opera House, where melodramas are performed (on Friday and Saturday at 8). Service isn't refined, but it's generally good, and the portions are huge. ⊠*32 Main St., Pinos Altos* ✛*7 mi north of Silver City on NM 15* ☎*575/538–9911, 575/388–3848 opera house* ⊟*MC, V* ⊘*Closed Sun. No lunch.*

$$
♻
★

🏠**Bear Creek Motel & Cabins.** Gold panning, hiking, and fishing are among the popular activities at this mountain getaway, one of the better accommodations in the Silver City area. A ponderosa pine forest surrounds the well-kept A-frame cabins, half of which have kitchens, cookware, and fireplaces. **Pros:** Close to town but feels remote. **Cons:** A bit far from Silver City (7 mi north). ⊠*NM 15, 7 mi north of Silver City* ✐*Box 53082, Pinos Altos 88053* ☎*888/388–4515* 🖷*575/538– 5583* ⊕*www.bearcreekcabins.com* ⇱*12 cabins* ⚴*In-room: no a/ c, kitchen (some), refrigerator (some), Internet. In-hotel: some pets allowed* ⊟*AE, D, DC, MC, V.*

$$ 🏠 **The Casitas de Gila.** On the western edge of the Gila are five private
Fodor'sChoice casitas ("little houses" in Spanish) overlooking Bear Creek, nestled
★ on 90 acres in gorgeous Gila country. The night skies are brilliant,
with countless stars twinkling, and the swath of the Milky Way glow-
ing brightly. Each casita has its own spotting telescope or high-pow-
ered binoculars. Watching the stars from the shared hot tub is not
to be missed. Guests have access to the organic herb garden (in sea-
son), which is super for those wanting to use the casitas' well-equipped
kitchens and barbecue grills. Southwestern-style furnishings, Mexican
rugs, and generously appointed baths make for a perfect getaway.
The hosts offer star parties and tips on hiking in the area. There's an
art gallery on-site. **Pros:** Peace and quiet, mountain vistas, the bright-
est stars you've ever seen, and a hot tub (shared). **Cons:** Be prepared
for a remote getaway—the town of Gila doesn't offer much. ⊠*50
Casita Flats Rd., off Hooker Loop ◌Box 325, Gila 88038–0325
☎575/535–4455 🖷575/535–4456 ⊕www.casitasdegila.com ⇩4 1-
bedroom casitas, 1 2-bedroom casita ⬧In-room: kitchen, refrigerator,
no TV, Wi-Fi ⊟AE, DC, MC, V ⊺◌CP.*

$$$$ 🏠 **Silver Creek Inn.** Just getting to this property in the ghost town of
Fodor'sChoice Mogollon in the western region of the Gila is something of a thrill; the
★ scenic and twisty mountain road that leads here has some heart-stop-
ping, steep drop-offs along the way. Once you've arrived, settle into
a room at one of the original, two-story adobe structures of this old
mining town, which is now all but abandoned (population about 15).
The 1885 Inn building has been refurbished beautifully. Each of the
four rooms has a private bath, and all (*delicious*) meals are included
in the room rate. Proprietors Kathy and Stan make some outstanding
pies—she's the famed pie-maker for the Pie-O-Neer café in Pie Town,
and the pie recipes at the inn are hers. Head here if you're looking for a
relaxing getaway in an out-of-the-ordinary locale. The inn is for adults
21 and over only. Reservations are required. **Pros:** A fantastic place to
explore a ghost town and the western Gila Wilderness; inclusive meal
plan makes the room rates a value. **Cons:** Bookings are for Friday
and Saturday; two-night minimum—open only on weekends. ⊠*Take
NM 180 toward Glenwood; about 4 mi north of Glenwood, turn east
onto NM 159 and travel about 9 mi of steep roadway to Mogollon,
☎866/276–4882 ⊕www.silvercreekinn.com ⇩4 rooms ⬧In-room:
no a/c, no phone, no TV ⊟AE, D, MC, V ⊺◌MAP.*

$ 🏠**Whitewater Motel & Rock Shop.** If driving back to Silver City or con-
tinuing on towards Socorro after exploring the vast Gila seems daunt-
ing, by all means stop and stay at this cozy haven of rustic Americana.
The motel opened for business in 1948 and the original, hand-carved
white-oak furniture is still in every room. Rooms are simple, comfort-
able and immaculate. Recent renovation has put a nice polish on this
place, and there's a long balcony off the back of all the rooms that
looks out to the huge grassy yard and Whitewater Creek. Relaxing at
the tables on the grass and listening to the creek rush by is a real treat.
The proprietor, Marianna, is also the postmistress (the post office is in
the parking lot)—so if she doesn't pick up the phone, leave a message
and be assured she'll call you back. There is one large family room that

9

sleeps 5 for $65 a night. Marianna is happy to tell you where to eat. ⊠*Hwy. 78, on the west side of the street* ☎*575/539–2581* ⌁*6 rooms* ⌂*In-room: no smoking* ⊟*AE, D, MC, V.*

$

Fodor'sChoice

★

🖵**The Wilderness Lodge.** This rustic retreat is a super place to stay if you want plenty of time to explore the Gila Cliff Dwellings. An added bonus is the relaxing hot-springs pools to come home to at the end of the day. The lodge is in a 100-year-old former schoolhouse and is surrounded by the Gila National Forest. The covered front porch is a great place to sit and enjoy coffee with the birds and trees. The stars at night are brilliant. **Pros:** Surrounded by mountains and rivers, this is a true getaway ideal for relaxing and unwinding after exploring. **Cons:** No restaurants or shops nearby; shared bathrooms. ⊠*Jackass Lane* ✛ *Hwy. 15 from Silver City to Gila Hot Springs, turn right on Access Rd., then turn left on Jackass Lane* ☎*575/536–9749* ⊕*www.gilahot. com* ⌁*7 rooms* ⌂*In-room: no a/c* ⊟*MC, V* ⦿*|BP.*

LAKE VALLEY NATIONAL BACK COUNTRY BYWAY

★ *From Silver City: head east on U.S. 180/NM 152 to junction with NM 27. From Hatch: head west on NM 26 and north on NM 27.*

The 48-mi Lake Valley National Back Country Byway provides an exciting link to the Wild West. This remote drive (there are no gas stations)—which encompasses the stretch of NM 27 between Nutt and Hillsboro (31 mi) and then NM 152 east from Hillsboro to Truth or Consequences (17 mi)—follows part of the route taken by the Kingston Lake Valley Stage Line, which operated when this region was terrorized by Apache leaders like Geronimo and outlaw bands led by the likes of Butch Cassidy. A Lake Valley–area landmark, west of NM 27, is Cooke's Peak, where the first wagon road through the Southwest to California was opened in 1846.

Not much is going on these days in the old silver mining town of **Lake Valley**—the last residents departed in the mid-1990s—but it once was home to 4,000 people. The mine produced 2.5 million ounces of pure silver and gave up one nugget weighing several hundred pounds. Visit the schoolhouse (which later served as a saloon), walk around the chapel, the railroad depot, and some of the few remaining old homes. At the junction of NM 152 and NM 27 is another mining-era boomtown, **Hillsboro,** where gold was discovered as well as silver (about $6 million worth of the two ores was extracted). The town, slowly coming back to life with the artists and retirees who've moved in, has a small museum, some shops, restaurants, and galleries. The Hillsboro Apple Festival draws visitors from all over the state on Labor Day weekend. Street vendors sell apples and apple pies, chiles, antiques, and arts and crafts.

Caballo Lake State Park provides a winter nesting grounds for golden and bald eagles, often sighted gliding aloft as they search for prey. Fishing and water sports are popular at the lake, and hiking trails lead through the desert areas where yucca, century plants, and numerous varieties of cacti are abundant. A great time to visit is late March or early April, when prickly pears and other succulents are in bloom. ⊠*Take state* *park exit off I–25, about 58 mi north of Las Cruces and 16 mi south of Truth or Consequences ☎575/743–3942 ✑$5 per vehicle �)Visitor center daily 7:30–4:30, later in summer.*

WHERE TO STAY

$

Fodor'sChoice

★

☷Black Range Lodge Bed & Breakfast. It's not quite enough to describe this lodge as "historic." Although true, and yes, this getaway has sturdy log-beam ceilings, massive stone walls, an interesting history, and an informal, rustic atmosphere that makes it nice for families—the charm here owes a lot to the care and tending, and presence, of the gently charismatic proprietors. The "town" of Kingston—a bustling boom-town around the turn of the century, population now about 30—and the surrounding area are fun to explore and fantastic by mountain bike. Guests have access to Percha Creek and miles of hiking trails. The rooms on the north side of the inn have views of the mountains, and the south rooms look into the amazing greenhouse. One-bedroom suites have cozy, vine-wrapped balconies in addition to sitting areas. Breakfasts are healthy and hearty, and the kitchen is open for you to cook in if you bring your own food. There is a five-bedroom house and a beautiful straw-bale luxury guesthouse available as well. **Pros:** Great for a group retreat or family reunion. **Cons:** No restaurants for miles. ⊠*119 Main St./NM 152, 88042 ⌂Star Rte. 2, Box 119, Kingston 88042 ☎575/895–5652 or 800/676–5622 ⊕www.blackrange lodge.com ✒3 rooms, 5 suites, 2 guesthouses, 1 studio ⌂In-room: no a/c, kitchen (some), refrigerator (some), Wi-Fi. In-hotel: no-smoking rooms, some pets allowed ⊟ MC, V ⦵BP.*

EN
ROUTE

The Percha Bank Gallery and Museum (⊠*119-B Main St., Kingston* ☎*575/895–5010* ✑*Donation* �)*Weekends 10–4*) is right next door to the Black Range Lodge and it's well worth a visit. The building itself is beautifully preserved and the original vault and teller windows are still in place. Art from local artists, including the luminous contemporary paintings of director Bonita Barlow, are on display. Photos of the town during its heyday in the late 1880s are fascinating.

9

CAMPING

⚠️**Caballo Lake State Park.** Three camping areas offer views of the lake, which is within walking distance of each site. Cottonwoods and other trees shade two sites; the other has desert landscaping. The tent sites ($8) are lakeside. You can stock up on goods at a grocery store, bait shop, and gasoline station 3 mi from the park. Developed sites for RVs cost $10–$14 ($18 with sewer). ⊠*Take state park exit off I–25, about 58 mi north of Las Cruces and 16 mi south of Truth or Consequences,* ☎*575/743–3942* ✑*575/743–0031* ✒*136 sites* ⌂*Flush toilets, full hookups, partial hookups, dump station, drinking water, showers, fire grates, fire pits, grills, picnic tables, electricity, public telephone, play area, ranger station, swimming (lake)* ⊟*No credit cards.*

EN
ROUTE

El Camino Real International Heritage Center. The beautiful, contemporary Heritage Center opened in 2005, after many years and much effort by New Mexicans to create a monument to El Camino Real. The 400-year history, and to some extent, the prehistory, of the Royal Road is the focus of the captivating exhibits here, more than the political and military struggles that happened along it. It was a vital trade route that linked ancient peoples from North America to Mesoamericans, and later linked the Spanish explorers to Mexico, Spain, Europe, Asia, and finally the United States of America. The exchange of cultural ideas, beliefs, and customs that occurred because of the extensive trade and travel along the route is amazing to consider—particularly while gazing at the stark environment it runs through. Today, this international trade route lives on in the form of the parallel-running Interstate 25. There are picnic tables here but no café or food is available. ✉ *30 mi south of Socorro, Exit 115, east to NM 1 frontage road, south 1½ mi, east onto CR 1598, 2.7 mi to center* 📬 *Box 175, Socorro, NM 87801* ☎ *575/854–3600* ⊕ *www.elcaminoreal.org* 💲 *$5* ⊙ *Wed.– Mon. 8:30–5.*

TRUTH OR CONSEQUENCES

72 mi north of Las Cruces on I–25, 140 mi south of Albuquerque on I–25.

Yes, Truth or Consequences really did get its name from the game show of the same name. The show's producer, Ralph Edwards, suggested that a town adopt the name to honor the production's 10th anniversary in 1950. The community, which had been known as Hot Springs, accepted the challenge, earning national publicity for the stunt. A portion of the community rebelled, though, withdrawing from T or C (as the town is frequently called) and incorporating as Williamsburg. T or C's name is a favorite point of contention for some of the old-school residents.

Centuries ago the area's earliest inhabitants came here for relaxation and the waters' healing properties—hot water being a universally enjoyed healing method. In the 1930s bathhouses tapping into the soothing mineral waters were established near the downtown district. This area, with street after street of neat old buildings, some covered in art deco tiling, struggles economically despite the draw of the springs—with many shops out of business or boarded up. Despite this, there is a casual, friendly vibe among the people here that leaves you rooting for the little town. There is much hope among locals that the developing Spaceport will bring needed revenue and business to the area.

T or C bills itself as the "most affordable spa town in America" and about a half-dozen spas operate at prices that are quite reasonable compared to those in other parts of the Southwest. Facilities, even in the most affordable establishments, are very clean and many offer therapeutic treatments like massage, Reiki, and reflexology. There is a small group of resorts and restaurants especially notable for the style and quality they bring to a town where amenities tend toward the modest, to say the least. Their proprietors' dedication to raising the standard and visibility of the town is commendable and their establishments make T or C a more interesting, and tasty, destination.

All of the lodgings listed offer soaks and treatments to the public, with the exception of the Pelican Spa, whether or not you are staying at the establishment. If possible, call ahead to check availability. River Bend Hot Springs offers private and shared hot pools right next to the Rio Grande, making for a scenic *and* relaxing soak.

T or C is in Sierra County, and the Sierra County Recreation and Tourism Advisory Board keeps an excellent Web site up-to-date with events and happenings in the region at ⊕ *www.sierracountynewmexico.info.*

WHAT TO SEE

At the **Geronimo Springs Museum** you can visit an authentic, well-maintained miner's log cabin from the early 20th century that was transported from the nearby Gila National Forest, or view the giant skull of a woolly mammoth. The real treat, however, is the outstanding collection of early Mimbres, Tularosa, Alma, and Hohokam pottery from the region. The farm and ranch section has tools used by early settlers. ⊠ *211 Main St.* ☎ *575/894–6600* ✉ *$5* ⊙ *Mon.–Sat. 9–5, Sun. 11–4.*

Hay-Yo-Kay Hot Springs has seven naturally flowing pools, including one that, at 10 feet by 20 feet, is the largest in the hot-springs district. The standard price for the hot baths is $6 per person for a half-hour soak indoors, $11 for a half hour in an outdoor pool. Massage, Reiki, and reflexology therapists are on call for varying fees. Packages are available; for instance a soak and a 50-minute massage cost $65. The property also includes three two-bedroom condominiums (ideal for housing small group retreats) with kitchens, refrigerators, microwaves, cable TV, in-room VCRs, and barbecues (standard rates of $125 nightly). Those staying on the property have unlimited free access to the pools. Closed Monday and Tuesday. ⊠ *300 Austin Ave.* ☎ *575/894–2228* ▭ *AE, D, DC, MC, V.*

WHERE TO EAT

$$

ITALIAN

Fodor's Choice

★

✕ **Bella Luca.** Run with love and care by the talented chef Byron Harrel and his wife Jessica, the Bella's kitchen hums, the dining room buzzes—and the food amazes. Over and over again, delicious Italian dishes emerge that please the most particular urban guest. Succulent calamari, a Caesar salad the emperor would love, wood-fired pizzas, and an Alfredo sauce that would make any Nonna weep are merely the basics on the menu. Get into the chef's specialties, like the sea scallop risotto, and you'll know you're in an extraordinary restaurant. The carefully chosen wine list has interesting options and prices are reasonable. The desserts are delicious, but the tiramisu should not be missed. Local and organic ingredients are used whenever possible. It's worth mentioning that the renovation of this old building, where they discovered a gorgeous pressed-copper ceiling hidden under dropped acoustic tiles, has created an airy, sophisticated room quite unlike any other in town. Just go. ⊠ *303 Jones St.* ☎ *575/894–9866* ▭ *AE, D, DC, MC, V* ⊙ *Closed Tues.*

¢

CAFÉ

✕ **Little Sprout Market & Juice Bar.** This little deli-style café in the co-op serves delicious breakfasts and lunches with organic, local ingredients.

The Eggs Pacifentine, with eggs, lox, spinach, red onion, and goat cheese on a bagel, at $5.50, is a delicious bargain. Salads and tasty sandwiches, like the Girl Cheese (with Havarti and tomatoes on your choice of bread) make for ideal light lunches. ⊠ *400 N. Broadway* ☎*505/894–4114* ▤*MC, V.*

$$ ✕**Los Arcos Restaurant and Bar.** Steaks and seafood are the draws at
STEAK this old-school, white stuccoed establishment with Spanish-style arches
★ across the front. Steaks are aged in-house and they are succulent. The lobster, despite the landlocked locale, is as mouthwatering and tender as can be. The Southwestern decor comes complete with a cactus garden. Homemade soups, desserts, and freshly baked bread add to the aromas and the cheery ambience. ⊠*1400 N. Date St.* ☎*575/894–6200* ▤*AE, D, MC, V* ⊙*No lunch.*

WHERE TO STAY

$ ▦**Blackstone Hotsprings Lodging & Baths.** It is amazing what can be done
Fodor'sChoice with a 1930s courtyard apartment building—and this hotel is a perfect
★ example. The courtyard has been transformed into a shaded, flowering oasis. Each unfussy yet luxurious room (themed after classic TV series or stars) has its own private soaking tub for unlimited indulgence in the healing waters, and a Continental kitchen (no stove). The lush wet room ($25 per hour), with plants, waterfalls, a shower, and hot pool, transports you somewhere far away from this desert locale. Two huge private tubs are available for $5 per half hour. Coffee lovers take note: the in-house coffee is a custom blend and it's fantastic. The owners, Rob and Ralph, and their staff are helpful and offer all sorts of tips on places to visit and eat. This is a real getaway spot. ⊠*410 Austin,* ☎*575/894–0894* ⊕*www.blackstonehotsprings.com* ➿*7 rooms* ⌂*In-hotel: Wi-Fi* ▤*AE, D, DC, MC, V.*

¢   ▦**Charles Motel & Spa.** The inexpensive rooms at the Charles are a favorite among artists and healers who espouse all sorts of interesting and unorthodox approaches to health. Various alternative therapies are practiced. Costs depend on the treatment and its length, but $5 will buy you an hour-long soak in one of the nine indoor soaking tubs fed from natural hot springs ($4 for a half hour). For $8 (and a reservation) you can soak in one of two outdoor Jacuzzis up on the roof. The huge (400 square foot) guest rooms, many of which have kitchenettes, have so much extra space you can easily imagine settling in for months rather than days; in fact, excellent weekly rates are offered. There is a nice gift shop on the premises with locally made pottery and other goods. **Pros:** Property is clean and you can't beat the price. **Cons:** Furnishings are aging, mattresses a bit soft. ⊠*601 Broadway* ☎*800/317–4518* or *575/894–7154* ⊕*www.charlesspa.com* ➿*20 rooms* ⌂*In-room: kitchen (some), refrigerator (some). In-hotel: spa, some pets allowed* ▤*AE, D, MC, V.*

¢   ▦**Pelican Spa.** Color is the name of the game at this great little hotel-
★ spa oriented around a rock courtyard and tucked behind a coyote fence right downtown. Soaking tubs in private, serene spaces are reserved for guests only. Rooms are vibrantly colored and furnished with a mixture of contemporary and retro furniture; many have separate sitting areas and kitchens. Not all rooms are located on-site, but all are within minutes

of the main building. The Aqua Room ($80) has an in-room soaking tub. ⊠*306 S. Pershing* ☎*575/894–0055* ⊕*www.pelican-spa.com* ⮒*8 rooms* ⌂*In-room: Wi-Fi. In-hotel: some pets allowed* ▭*D, MC, V.*

¢   ⚲**Riverbend Hot Springs.** All the tubs at the bathhouse and spa are
★   located right on the Rio Grande with sweeping views of Turtleback Mountain. It's a bohemian place with a good variety of rooms, many with separate bedrooms and kitchens or kitchenettes. Don't let the fact that a number of the rooms are located in vibrantly painted, single-wide mobile homes deter you. It may appear funky from the outside but mattresses are firm, and the rooms are extremely clean and in good condition. There are a casita and several larger suites that are ideal for families or multi-person groups. Private tubs at $15 an hour are a treat and a bargain. Massage treatments available by appointment. ⊠*100 Austin St.* ☎*575/894–7625* ⊕*www.riverbendhotsprings.com* ⮒*10 rooms, 1 casita* ⌂*In-room: kitchen (some), Wi-Fi (some). In-hotel: Wi-Fi, some pets allowed* ▭*D, MC, V.*

$$ ⚲**Sierra Grande Lodge & Spa.** This elegant property led the way for
Fodor'sChoice   the small but impressive upward trend in lodging in T or C. In a 1937
★   building downtown, this inn feels like a secluded retreat because of the massive walls and boulders surrounding its mission-style architecture. The airy rooms have hardwood floors, four-poster beds, and serene prints on the walls. Bathrooms are well-appointed with extra-large showers. Guests can soak in an outdoor or indoor kiva-style hot tub swirling with steamy water from natural, underground hot springs; massages, facials, and other holistic body therapies are available by appointment in the spa. Breakfasts are delicious and are made with mostly local ingredients. The lodge is within easy walking distance of several restaurants. **Pros:** This lodge is pure elegance and the staff is wonderful. **Cons:** Rooms are on the small side. ⊠*501 McAdoo St.* ☎*575/894–6976* 🖷*575/894–6999* ⊕*www.sierragrandelodge.com* ⮒*16 rooms, 1 suite* ⌂*In-hotel: Wi-Fi, no-smoking rooms* ▭*AE, D, MC, V* ⧦*CP.*

SHOPPING

Paintings and sculpture by contemporary local artists such as Delmas Howe can be found at the **Rio Bravo Gallery Fine Art Inc.** (⊠*110 E. Broadway Ave.* ☎*505/894–0572* ⊙ *Wed.–Sat. 10–5, Sun. noon–5*). **Redbone** (⊠*410 Broadway* ☎*575/894–9403* ⊙ *Wed.–Sat. 11–3*) is a fun and funky collection of antiques and used objects, from Mexican pottery, to cowboy boots, to midcentury furniture, to conga drums.

ELEPHANT BUTTE

5 mi east of Truth or Consequences on NM 51.

★   More than a million people each year visit **Elephant Butte Lake State Park,** whose 36,500-acre lake is New Mexico's largest. A world-class competition lake for bass fishing, it also offers catfish, pike, and crappie fishing year-round. Boaters come here in droves, and when the wind picks up so do the windsurfers. Special events include an April balloon festival and July drag-boat racing. The lake, known as Elephant Butte

Space Tourism

It may seem hard to imagine as you gaze into the infinite blue of New Mexico's sky near White Sands Missile Range and Alamogordo, but some day, and perhaps sooner than later, those wispy contrails you see lingering from rocket engines may be the residue of vehicles carrying tourists into Earth's orbit—and beyond.

In October 2005 the missile range hosted the first of a series of annual events known as the X-Prize Cup Exhibition aimed at enabling private industry to become involved in economical space travel. Funded through a private foundation, the exhibition bestows annual awards of $10 million to the winner of each competition, from among competing (nongovernment backed) teams of experts worldwide. The mission of the X Prize Foundation is to spur innovation in space and related technologies, and to create low-cost space vehicles

capable of (eventually) carrying civilian passengers into space.

Competing space vehicles must have the ability to lift three people up and beyond Earth's gravity to a height of 62½ mi. The feat then must be repeated with the same vehicle within two weeks, to demonstrate reliability and economic feasibility associated with quick turnaround.

With an eye on the potential of both the X-Prize competition and space tourism that could result from development of a successful vehicle, New Mexico has obtained a permit for a commercial spaceport license for a remote, unpopulated area near the western edge of the missile range. State tourism officials expect the X-Prize competition itself to become a major attraction luring thousands of visitors annually to watch launches of competing space vehicles as they reach for the sky.

Reservoir, was created in 1916 by **Elephant Butte Dam,** a concrete structure 306 feet high and 1,674 feet long. The stretch of the Rio Grande below the dam is stocked with trout during colder months; these fish attract anglers as well as many species of waterfowl, including raptors. The lake level is dependent on the water conditions in the state, which fluctuate wildly, and it's worth noting that there are no trees around this lake—making the hot months a challenging time to camp. It's best to check the conditions before you plan a vacation around the lake.

The state park straddles Elephant Butte Lake and the Rio Grande east of Interstate 25 for about 50 mi (from south of Fort Craig to just north of Truth or Consequences). To take a **scenic drive** from Truth or Consequences, head east on NM 51, turn north at NM 179 for about 2 mi, head southeast on NM 195, and take a loop drive of about 5 mi to Elephant Butte Dam. At the end of the dam turn north for overlooks of the lake and a view of the rocky elephant-shape island formation that inspired the name of the reservoir. To visit the **Dam Site Recreation Area** turn west on NM 177, where you'll find a terraced picnic area with striking views and tall shade trees. A private concessionaire operates a restaurant, lounge, marina, and cabins. ⊠ *3 mi north of Truth or Consequences* ☎ *505/744–5421* ✉ *$5 per vehicle.*

WHERE TO EAT & STAY

¢ ✕**Hodges Corner Restaurant.** Owner Ray Hodges believes in hearty food
AMERICAN and lots of it—so if you're in the mood for a heaping plate of thick barbecued pork ribs, cube steak, or deep-fried fish, this is the place for you.
Late in the day, the ultracasual dining area is usually filled with hungry
anglers who've stopped to relax and chow down after a day of fishing.
Come in earlier in the day to buy a bucket of home-fried chicken to take
with you to the lake. ✉915 NM 195 ☎575/744–5626 ▤D, MC, V.

$ ▦**Dam Site Resort.** The lodgings at this resort are a fun step back in
time. The lodge was built in 1911 for the dam's administration and engineering offices. The "cabins" are quaint, neo-pueblo, stucco structures
built by the Civilian Conservation Corps in the 1940s. The resort has
been established as an official historic district, and the restoration of the
buildings is top-notch. The lodge operates as a B&B and is furnished
with many period antiques. The spacious covered porch overlooks the
marina. The cabins ($60) are an experience in retro-chic, and all have
views of the lake, and kitchenettes (you must furnish utensils, plates,
etc.). The bar-restaurant ($), open weekends only, serves steaks, seafood,
and sandwiches—and some excellent margaritas. On Saturday nights
between about Easter and Labor Day, dance bands play blues or rock
on the outdoor patio, which also has a bar. Booking is done through the
Dam Site Marina office. **Pros:** Beautiful, historic property with great lake
views. **Cons:** Staffing is minimal (though down-home friendly). ✉*77B
Engle Star Rte.* ✛*5 mi east of 3rd St. light in Truth or Consequences*
☎*575/894–2041* ⊕*www.thedamsite.com* ⇥*8 rooms, 16 cabins* ⚏*In-
room: no a/c (some), no phone, kitchen (some), no TV. In-hotel: restaurant, bar, water sports, some pets allowed* ▤*AE, D, MC, V.*

$$ ▦**Elephant Butte Inn.** The mesa-top property feels like a resort and has
panoramic views of the lake. Get a lake-view room if you can and enjoy
the huge, lush lawn that seems to disappear into the water. Rooms have
either two queen-size beds or one king-size bed, and all have irons, hair
dryers, and coffeemakers. **The Ivory Tusk Tavern & Restaurant** ($$)
serves standard fare including hamburgers, and steak and seafood plat-
ters. A spa and full salon are on the premises for massage treatments and
beautification. **Pros:** Peaceful property with nice views. **Cons:** At this writing Mountain View rooms are being renovated. ✉*401 NM 195, Box E*
☎*575/744–5431* ⇥*45 rooms* ⚏*In-room: refrigerator (some) Wi-Fi. In-
hotel: restaurant, bar, pool, spa, some pets allowed* ▤*AE, D, MC, V.*

CAMPING

⚠**Dam Site Recreation Area.** At night, campfires flicker along the beaches
of the many sandy coves of Elephant Butte Lake. There are developed
and primitive campsites, many of them delightfully secluded. Sites
without hookups are first come, first served; sites with hookups can
be reserved. There's a restaurant on-site. ✉*3 mi north of Truth or
Consequences* ☎*877/664–7787 for reservations, 505/744–5923 for
information* ⊕*www.nmparks.com* ⚏*Flush toilets, pit toilets, partial
hookups (electric and water), dump station, drinking water, showers,
fire grates, fire pits, grills, picnic tables, electricity, public telephone,
play area, ranger station, swimming (lake)* ⇥*127 developed sites, several hundred primitive or partially developed tent sites.*

SPORTS & THE OUTDOORS

The **Dam Site Recreation Area Marina** (⊠ *77B Engle Star Rte., 5 mi east of 3rd St. traffic light in Truth or Consequences* ☎ *575/894–2041*) rents runabouts, ski boats, and pontoon boats late May–early September. The vessels cost between $20 and $45 hourly ($110 and $220 daily). A $250 deposit is required for use of any boat.

EN ROUTE

Heading north on Interstate 25 there are two interesting places to stop. The first one is **Fort Craig National Historic Site.** Fort Craig was established after the New Mexico Territory became part of the United States to prevent raids by the Apache and Navajo peoples and to secure the trade routes within the region. The growth of Socorro and what is now Truth or Consequences can be traced to the protection the fort provided between 1854 and the mid-1880s, when it was decommissioned. Battles west of the Mississippi River during the American Civil War were relatively rare, but in 1862 the Confederate army crossed the Rio Grande and headed to Valverde, north of Fort Craig, with the goal of cutting off the fort from the Union military headquarters in Santa Fe. Confederate forces first were sent into retreat but later won a few battles and made the Union forces withdraw. The Rebels later occupied Santa Fe for a few months. Today, signs describe the various buildings and solitary life at the outpost, where only a couple of masonry walls and numerous foundations remain. Historic markers are very informative, however, and a well-maintained gravel trail winds among the ruins. The roads to Fort Craig, which is about 40 mi south and east of Socorro, can become hard to pass during rainy weather. During the closest weekend to significant dates of February 21 and 22, historical reenactors re-create the Civil War Battle of Valverde and even "capture" the nearby city of Socorro in a grand finale. ⊠ *Off I–25 San Marcial Exit 124, follow signs from exit for about 10 mi* ☎ *575/835–0412* ☜ *Free* ☉ *Daily dawn–dusk.*

Fodor's Choice
★

Hundreds of different types of birds, including snow geese, cranes, falcons, and eagles, can be spotted from viewing platforms and directly through your car window at the popular **Bosque del Apache National Wildlife Refuge.** Besides serving as a rest stop for migrating birds, the Bosque del Apache also shelters mule deer, turkeys, quail, and other wildlife. Photo opportunities abound on the 15-mi auto loop tour; you can also hike through arid shrub land or bike through the refuge or take a van tour. October and November are the months the cottonwoods show their colors. In winter months, the refuge echoes with the haunting cries of whooping cranes flocking for the evening. Snow geese are so thick on lakes at times that shores are white with feathers washed ashore. Whether you're a bird-watcher or not, it is well worth bringing binoculars or a spotting scope to get some idea of how many varieties of birds land here (377 species have been spotted since 1940). The Festival of the Cranes in mid-November draws thousands of people. ⊠ *1001 NM 1, off I–25 San Marcial Exit 124 for northbound traffic and Exit 139 for southbound traffic, San Antonio* ☎ *575/835–1828* ☜ *$3 per vehicle* ☉ *Refuge daily dawn–dusk; visitor center weekdays 7:30–4, weekends 8–4:30; tour road open Apr.–Sept.*

SOCORRO

72 mi north of Truth or Consequences; 77 mi southwest of Albuquerque, south on I–25 and west on U.S. 60.

The town of Socorro, population about 9,000, traces its roots back to the earliest Spanish expeditions into New Mexico when explorer Juan de Oñate established a permanent settlement along the Rio Grande in 1598. Native Americans provided corn for the expedition, inspiring Oñate to give the community a name that means succor, or help. The San Miguel Mission church was established in 1628, but Spanish settlement was virtually erased during the Pueblo Revolt of 1680 and did not reestablish itself until 1816. If not for this early and lengthy period of dormancy in the area, the city might have been the capital of New Mexico, with its prime location in a large, fertile valley, amid then-thriving pueblos, abundant water sources, and tremendous mineral wealth.

Socorro's business district now occupies historic buildings that surround its sleepy square, which has a park with a gazebo and a plaque commemorating the arrival of Juan de Oñate. The town's claim to fame is the highly regarded New Mexico Institute of Mining and Technology (New Mexico Tech) founded in 1893—though, unfortunately, the student population doesn't translate into town vibrancy or any sort of nightlife. The institution's original specialties were chemistry and metallurgy, but along with scientific research now there are programs in medicine, engineering, and business.

More than 2,500 minerals and fossils are on display at the **New Mexico Bureau of Geology and Mineral Resources Mineralogical Museum,** among them samples from the area's ore-rich mining districts of Magdalena, Hansonburg, Santa Rita, and Tyrone. Many rocks here, from glittering pyrite to the deep-blue azurite, have exotic colors like those of tropical fish. Special tours can be arranged. ⊠ *New Mexico Institute of Mining and Technology, 801 Leroy Pl., from I–25 Exit 150, follow signs to institute* ☎ *575/835–5420* 🖾 *Free* ☯ *Weekdays 8–5, weekends 10–3.*

Only a monument remains at **Trinity Site,** where the world's first atomic bomb exploded, on July 16, 1945. The resulting crater has been filled in, but the test site and monument are open for public viewing and self-guided tours two days of the year. The McDonald ranch house, where the first plutonium core for the bomb was assembled, can be toured on those days. **NOTE:** There are no vehicle services or gas at the site, and visitors must bring their own food and water. Picnic tables are available. Handicapped accessible. ⊠ *Off I–25, 10 mi south of Socorro* ✛ *Exit at San Antonio and go east on NM 380. Drive 12 mi east on U.S. 380 and turn south onto paved road, NM 525 (there is a large sign for Trinity Site), for 5 mi until route reaches Stallion Range Gate. Visitors (everyone over age 16 must present photo ID) will be met at and the gate and escorted 17 mi east to site* ☎ *575/678–1134* 🖾 *Free* ☯ *1st Sat. of Apr. and Oct., gate opens 8–2.*

9

WHERE TO EAT

¢   ✕ **La Pasadita.** Wander off the main drag into this place and you'll real-
MEXICAN   ize that it's a well-kept secret among locals. The New Mexican food
★   here is really good, and really inexpensive. Don't be put off by the
lack of charm on the outside; order at the counter, sit down at a table,
and wait for the friendly staff to bring you a plate of their wonderful
food. The burrito plate with red chile is big and mouthwatering, and
the combo plates are H-U-G-E. Don't miss what may be the very best
sopaipillas in all of New Mexico—light, flaky, and soooo good with
honey. ⊠ *230 Garfield St.* ⊹ *Turn onto Garfield from southwest corner of plaza, restaurant is a few blocks on left* ☎575/835–3696 ☐No
credit cards ⊘ *No dinner. Closed weekends.*

$ ✕ **Socorro Springs Brewing Co.** This microbrewery and restaurant is housed
AMERICAN   in a renovated adobe building off the plaza and is almost always full of
★   happy locals drinking good beer and eating excellent calzones, thin-crust
pizzas, homemade soups, and big, fresh salads. It's hard to go wrong
here, unless you're in a hurry. "Hurry" isn't on this menu, though the
service is friendly. Good breakfasts, too, but no beer served in the morning! ⊠ *1012 N. California St.* ☎575/838–0650 ☐D, MC, V.

¢   ✕ **Stevie's Grill.** Stevie, the self-proclaimed "native son" of Socorro, has
AMERICAN   turned a former cabinet shop into quite a little restaurant—a locals'
secret. He dishes up a simple menu of American and some New Mexican
dishes, with super enchiladas, chicken-fried steak, and out-of-this-world
burgers. Stevie has a special way of preparing those burgers that makes
them some of the juiciest, tastiest ever. Many of his recipes came from
his Puerto Rican grandmother's own cookbook. Decor is simple, with
some great photos on the walls of baseball stars of yesteryear and other
memorabilia. ⊠ *110 Willow St., behind McDonald's* ☎575/835–1567
⧄*Reservations not accepted* ☐MC, V ⊘*Closed Sun.*

WHERE TO STAY

$ ⊞ **Best Western Hotel & Suites.** A favorite of groups and small conven-
tions that otherwise might have limited options in a town this size,
this haven offers condensed versions of some of the luxuries of larger
resorts. You can expect the chain's usual quality and contemporary,
modern flourishes in standard rooms; a friendly staff rounds out an
easy stay. **Pros:** Within walking distance of several restaurants. **Cons:**
Right off the freeway; typical chain-hotel charm. ⊠ *1100 California
NE,* ☎575/838–0556 ➹*120 rooms* ⧄*In-room: refrigerator, Wi-Fi.
In-hotel: pool, gym, laundry facilities, some pets allowed* ☐AE, D,
DC, MC, V ⦿CP.

HEADING WEST ON U.S. 60

Maybe you're a traveler who prefers to stay off the beaten path, and
venture to places you've never even heard of. If you're in the mood
to take the slow road and encounter an authentic Western America
decades removed from today's franchise operations, head west on old
NM 60 out of Socorro and keep going—as far as the Arizona border if

you like. The speed limit is 55 mph, there's not a chain restaurant for 200 mi, and the scenery hasn't changed much for 50 years.

This long, often lonely highway opened in 1917 as the first numbered auto route to cross the United States. Called the Ocean to Ocean Highway, U.S. 60 ran from Norfolk, Virginia, to Los Angeles. Earlier in the 20th century it was a "hoof highway," the route of cattle drives from Springerville, Arizona, to Magdalena, New Mexico. Walk into any café along this dusty roadside and you're still likely to be greeted by a blue-eyed cowboy in spurs fresh from tending to ranch business.

People really ranch here, much the way they have for more than 100 years—prior to the era of homesteaders and ranchers, the Apaches ruled and weren't much inclined to allow ranching or settlements of any kind. Livestock production and timber are still the leading industries. U.S. 60 takes you through the heart of Catron County, New Mexico's largest county by area, and least populated by square mile. Notoriously politically incorrect and proud of it, this is a place where Confederate flags fly and animal trophies are considered high art.

After you've headed as far west as Quemado, you can make an interesting and scenic loop by continuing north on NM 36 to NM 117, which skirts the east side of El Malpais National Monument, eventually hooking up with Interstate 40 east of Grant. To get to Albuquerque take Interstate 40 east.

MAGDALENA

27 mi west of Socorro on U.S. 60.

Magdalena, population 300, enjoyed its heyday about a hundred years ago as a raucous town of miners and cowboys. It was once the biggest livestock shipping point west of Chicago. The Atchison, Topeka & Santa Fe Railway built a spur line from Socorro in 1885 to transport timber, wool, cattle, and ore. Lead, zinc, silver, copper, and gold all were mined in the area, but now there are more ghosts than miners.

The town took its name from Mary Magdalene, protector of miners, whose face is supposedly visible on the east slope of Magdalena Peak, a spot held sacred by the Native Americans of the area. To get a feel for the place, walk down to the Atchison, Topeka & Santa Fe Railway depot, now the town hall and library. Across the street is the Charles Ilfeld Warehouse, where the company's motto, "wholesalers of everything," is a reminder of the great trade empire of the late 19th century.

Although there are arts festivals in spring and fall, the biggest event of the year in Magdalena is the **Magdalena Old Timers Reunion** (☎575/854–2401), held for three days in early July. The festival, which draws about 5,000 and has the biggest parade in New Mexico after the State Fair's, began quietly 30 years ago. With the end of cattle drives and the shutdown of the rail spur in the early 1970s, cowboys began returning at the same time each year to greet each other and reminisce. Over the past three decades, the reunion has grown into an event-packed weekend including both kids' and adult rodeos, Western swing dances on Friday and Saturday nights, a fiddling contest, a barbecue dinner, and an authentic chuck-wagon cook-off. The parade takes place Saturday morning, and the crowned reunion queen must be at least 60 years old. Most events are held at the Magdalena Fairgrounds, and admission is free.

The ghost town of **Kelly** (⊠*Kelly Rd. off U.S. 60* ☎*No phone*), 4 mi south of town, is reputed to be haunted, and during the Old Timers Reunion a 7K race finishes here (it begins in the village). During its boom time 3,000 people lived in the town. You cannot go into the mine, but you can get a permit to walk around and collect rocks at Tony's Rock Shop in Magdalena at 9th and Kelly (☎*575/854–2401*).

WHERE TO EAT & STAY

$ ✕**Magdalena Cafe.** Hearty, delicious fare including roast beef, burgers,
AMERICAN   hot sandwiches, homemade pie, Mexican pineapple cake, and delicious milk shakes are served on red-and-white checkered tablecloths here. The place is usually busy with all sorts of characters, all of whom seem very happy to be here. Staff is a bit harried, but friendly. ⊠*109 Main St. (NM 60)* ☎*575/854–2696* ▭*No credit cards* ⊘*No dinner.*

¢   ☷**Western Motel & RV Park.** To inspire dreams of riding the range, rooms of knotty pine are set off with Western paintings and Native American artifacts, and some have Victorian-style flowered upholstery and matching art. Locally handmade quilts and Mexican textiles decorate the walls. The facility was a maternity hospital for the region in the 1920s. There are also 14 RV sites with full hookups ($30; weekly and monthly rates available). **Pros:** Wi-Fi and a hot tub are nice additions. **Cons:** Motel is along the main highway, though there isn't much traffic in these parts. ⊠*404 1st St., U.S. NM 60, town center* ☎*575/854– 2417* ☐*575/854–3217* ⤳*6 rooms, 14 RV sites* ⏃*In-room: refrigerator, Wi-Fi. In-hotel: some pets allowed* ▭*AE, D, DC, MC, V.*

SHOPPING

Histories of some of the notable buildings in Magdalena and a guide for a walking tour are available on ⊕*www.magdalena-nm.com.* It's fun to have the print-out of the walking tour while exploring the shops and cafés.

Blue Canyon Gallery (⊠*NM 60* ☎*575/854–2953 or 888/854–8337*) carries photographs, pottery, paintings, and artwork by area artists.

EN ROUTE

★   With its 27 glistening-white 80-foot radio-telescope antennae arranged in patterns, the **Very Large Array** is a startling sight when spotted along the Plains of San Augustin. The complex's dish-shaped "ears," each weighing 230 tons, are tuned in to the cosmos. The array is part of a series of facilities that compose the National Radio Astronomy Observatory. The antennas, which provided an impressive backdrop for the movie *Contact,* based on the Carl Sagan book, form the largest, most advanced radio telescope in the world. The telescope chronicles the birth and death of stars and galaxies from 10 to 12 billion light-years away. Hundreds of scientists from around the world travel to this windy, remote spot to research black holes, colliding galaxies, and exploding stars, as well as to chart the movements of planets. Visitors are permitted to stroll right up to the array on a self-guided walking tour that begins at the unstaffed visitor center. Staff members emphasize that their work does *not* involve a search for life on other planets. ⊠*Off U.S. 60, 23 mi west of Magdalena* ☎*575/835–7000* ⊠*Free* ⊗*Daily 8:30–dusk.*

PIE TOWN

21 mi west of Datil on U.S. 60.

During the 1930s and '40s, it was said that the best pie in New Mexico was served at a little café in Pie Town, a homesteading community west of the Continental Divide. Cowboys on cattle drives and tourists heading to California spread stories of the legendary pies. Thanks to the still-operational Pie-O-Neer Cafe, the tradition of great pie in this part of the world is alive and well.

Pie Town's reputation can be traced to 1922 when World War I veteran Clyde Norman came from Texas and filed a mining claim on the Hound Pup Lode. Gold mining didn't go as well as he'd hoped, but he began selling kerosene and gasoline, as well as doughnuts he'd brought from Magdalena in his Model T. Eventually he learned to bake pies with dried apples, which were an immediate success. Spanish-American War veteran Harmon L. Craig, who made a great sourdough, arrived in 1923 or '24, and the two went into partnership. The post office granted the place the name Pie Town in 1927.

Craig bought Norman out in 1932. He ran the mercantile end while his wife, Theodora Baugh, and her two daughters took over the pie baking. Nowadays aficionados can dig in at the annual Pie Festival, held on the second weekend in September, with pie-eating and pie-baking contests, horny-toad races, and hot-air balloon flights.

9

WHERE TO EAT

$ ✕**Pie-O-Neer Cafe.** "Life goes on and days go by. That's why you should CAFÉ stop for pie." Such is the motto of one of New Mexico's most leg-★ endary roadside stops. Owner Kathy Knapp serves meals, including excellent green-chile cheeseburgers, from midmorning through early evening, but pie is her stock in trade. She keeps these delicious varieties on hand: apple, cherry, peach, coconut cream, lemon meringue, and banana cream. Her best sellers are the apple and the more rarely made oatmeal-pecan. On some Sunday afternoons, local talent drops by for guitar strumming. Kathy is also one of the proprietors at the lovely Silver Creek Inn in Mogollon. ⊠*U.S. 60* ☎*575/772–2711* ⊟*AE, D, MC, V* ⊗ *Closed Mon.–Thurs. No dinner.*

QUEMADO

22 mi west of Pie Town on U.S. 60.

Quemado (pronounced kay-*ma*-dough) means "burnt" in Spanish, and the town is supposedly named for a legendary Apache chief who burned his hand in a campfire. The bustling village, which contains several motels and cafés, is busiest in fall, when it is a favorite base for deer hunters.

Quemado Lake, about 20 mi south of town on NM 32 and NM 103, is a man-made fishing and hiking area where it's not unusual to spot herds of elk.

OFF THE BEATEN PATH

Lightning Field. The sculptor Walter De Maria created *Lightning Field*, a work of land art composed of 400 stainless-steel poles of varying heights (the average is 20 feet, although they create a horizontal plane) arranged in a rectangular grid over 1 mi by ½ mi of flat, isolated terrain. Groups of up to six people are permitted to stay overnight from May through October—the only way you can experience the artwork—at a rustic on-site 1930s cabin. Fees range from $150 to $250 per person, depending on the month (children and students are $100), although those who can afford it are asked to pay up to $300 per person to help cover actual expenses of providing visitor meals and transportation. Dia Center for the Arts administers *Lightning Field*, shuttling visitors from Quemado to the sculpture, which is on private land to the northeast. Thunder-and-lightning storms are most common from July to mid-September; book way ahead for visits during this time. If you're lucky, you'll see flashes you'll never forget (though lightning isn't required for the sculpture to be stunning in effect). The Web site is updated regularly and is a good source of information. ✉ *Box 2993, Corrales 87048* ☎ *505/898–3335 Corrales office and reservations, 575/773–4560 Quemado shuttle* ⊕ *www.lightningfield. org* ☝ *Reservations essential* ⊗ *Closed Nov.–Apr.*

WHERE TO STAY

¢ ▦ **Largo Motel.** The rooms in this brand-new single-story stucco motel with a metal roof (built in 2008) are simple and comfortable and are just right to wash off the trail dust and get a good night's rest. The Largo has the best café in town ($), a busy little spot known for homemade corn tortillas and biscuits, gravy, and chicken-fried steak, and excellent red-and-green chile on Mexican food dishes. The Navajo tacos are famous. They serve "a real full plate," too. Above the spacious booths are mounted trophies (the owner is a hunting guide). **Pros:** Motel is clean and new; staff is friendly and easygoing. **Cons:** Nothing fancy here; just your basic roadside stop; no tubs in bathrooms, just showers. ✉ *U.S. NM 60 on west side of town* ☎ *575/773–4686* ⇨ *20 rooms* △ *In-room: Wi-Fi* ▤ *MC, V.*

CAMPING

⚠ **Quemado Lake Campgrounds.** Six campgrounds surround Quemado Lake, providing convenient access to hiking trails or lake fishing for stocked rainbow trout. ✉ *20 mi south of Pie Town on NM 32 and NM 103* ☎ *575/773–4678* △ *Pit toilets, partial hookups (electric and water), dump station, drinking water, fire grates, fire pits, grills, picnic tables* ⇨ *Unlimited primitive sites, 60 developed sites, 16 sites with partial hookups* ▤ *No credit cards.*

Travel Smart
New Mexico

WORD OF MOUTH

"There is a tourist information desk with a huge number of maps and brochures in the ABQ airport next to the baggage claim. I got a great map of the Turquoise Trail which noted every store/gallery, and a bunch of other brochures too."

—hikrchick

GETTING HERE & AROUND

A tour bus or car is the best way to take in the entire state. Public transportation options do exist in some metropolitan areas, but they are not very convenient for visitors. City buses and taxi service are available only in a few larger communities such as Albuquerque, Santa Fe, and Las Cruces. Don't expect to find easy transportation for rural excursions.

▌ BY AIR

To reach New Mexico by air, you have two primary options: if you're visiting central or northern New Mexico, it's best to fly into Albuquerque, and if you're headed to the southern part of the state, El Paso may make more sense. However, El Paso is smaller and served by far fewer flights, so depending on where you're flying from, it can still be easier to fly into Albuquerque than El Paso even when visiting the southern part of the state. Some visitors to Taos and northeastern New Mexico may also want to consider flying into Denver, which is an hour or two farther than Albuquerque but receives a high number of direct domestic and international flights. From Albuquerque airport, ground transportation is available throughout North-Central New Mexico, and commuter air service is available to Farmington, Clovis, Ruidoso, Silver City, and a few other communities around the state. El Paso has ground transportation to Las Cruces. Although Albuquerque and El Paso have small, clean, and user-friendly airports, they also have relatively few direct flights compared with larger cities around the country. With a few exceptions, travelers coming from the East Coast and to a certain extent the West Coast have to connect through other airports to fly into Albuquerque and, especially, El Paso.

The least expensive airfares to New Mexico are priced for round-trip travel and must usually be purchased in advance. Because the discount airline Southwest serves Albuquerque and El Paso, fares from these cities to airports served by Southwest are often 20% to 40% less than to other airports (whether or not you actually fly Southwest, as competing airlines often match Southwest's fares).

Flying time between Albuquerque and Los Angeles is 2 hours for direct flights (available only on Southwest Airlines and United Airlines) and 3½ to 4 when connecting through another airport; Chicago, 2 hours and 45 minutes; New York, 5½ to 6½ hours (there are no direct flights, so this factors in time for connections); Dallas, 1 hour and 45 minutes.

AIRPORTS

The major gateway to New Mexico is Albuquerque International Sunport (ABQ), which is 65 mi southwest of Santa Fe, 130 mi south of Taos, and 180 mi southeast of Farmington. Some travelers to Chama, Raton, and Taos prefer to fly into Denver (four to five hours' drive), which has far more direct flights to the rest of the country than Albuquerque—it's a scenic drive, too.

The gateway to southern New Mexico is El Paso International Airport (ELP), 50 mi southeast of Las Cruces, 160 mi southeast of Silver City, 135 mi southwest of Ruidoso, and 160 mi southwest of Carlsbad. The flight between El Paso and Albuquerque takes 50 minutes. The state's easternmost side can also be accessed via major airports in Texas, including Lubbock (170 mi east of Roswell) and Amarillo (105 mi northeast of Clovis).

▌TIP→ Long layovers don't have to be only about sitting around or shopping. These days they can be about burning off vacation calories. Check out ⊕www.airportgyms.com for lists of health clubs that are in or near many U.S. and Canadian airports.

Airport Information Albuquerque International Sunport (☎505/244–7700 ⊕ www.cabq.gov/airport). **Denver International Airport** (☎303/342–2000 ⊕ www.flydenver.com). **El Paso International Airport** (☎915/780–4749 ⊕ www.elpasointernationalairport.com).

MUNICIPAL AIRPORTS

Cavern City Air Terminal (CNM), Carlsbad (☎575/887–6858). **Clovis Municipal Airport (CVN), Carlsbad** (☎575/389–1056). **Four Corners Regional Airport (FMN), Farmington** (☎505/599–1285). **Grant County Airport (SVC), Silver City area** (☎575/388–4554). **Roswell Municipal Airport (ROW)** (☎505/624–6700). **Santa Fe Municipal Airport (SAF)** (☎505/955–2908). **Sierra Blanca Regional Airport (SRR), Ruidoso area** (☎575/336–8111).

FLIGHTS

Most major domestic airlines provide service to the state's main airport in Albuquerque; just over the border in Texas (near Las Cruces and Carlsbad), El Paso International Airport is served by American, Southwest, Delta, Continental, Frontier, New Mexico Airlines, Northwest, United, and US Airways. The state is also served by a few regional carriers. Great Lakes Airlines flies from Denver to Farmington and from Albuquerque to Silver City and Clovis (and then from Clovis on to Amarillo, Texas). Frontier Airlines flies daily from Denver to El Paso and Albuquerque. Skywest Airlines, a subsidiary of Delta, flies between Albuquerque and Salt Lake City.

Ask the local tourist board about hotel and local transportation packages that include tickets to major museum exhibits or other special events.

GROUND TRANSPORTATION

From the terminal at Albuquerque Airport, it's 5 to 20 minutes by car to get anywhere in town. Taxis, available at clearly marked stands, charge about $10 to $25 for most trips from the airport to around Albuquerque. Sun Tran Buses stop at the sunburst signs every 30 minutes; the fare is $1. Some hotels provide shuttle service to and from the airport. Airport Shuttle and Sunport Shuttle both cost less than $10 to most downtown locations.

Shuttle buses between the Albuquerque International Sunport and Santa Fe take about 1 hour and 20 minutes and cost about $20 to $25 each way. Shuttle service runs from Albuquerque to Taos and nearby ski areas; the ride takes 2¾ to 3 hours and costs $40–$50. In southern New Mexico there are daily trips between El Paso International Airport and Las Cruces (1 hour), Deming (2½ hours), and Silver City (3½ hours); the trip costs $43–$75 each way.

There's also Greyhound bus service between Albuquerque International Sunport and many New Mexico towns and cities; fares are considerably less than those charged by the shuttle services listed here.

TRANSFERS BETWEEN AIRPORTS

Around Albuquerque Airport Shuttle (☎505/765–1234). **Sun Tran Bus** (☎505/843–9200 ⊕ www.cabq.gov/transit). **Sunport Shuttle** (☎505/883–4966 or 866/505–4966 ⊕ www.sunportshuttle.com)

Between Albuquerque & Santa Fe Faust's Transportation (☎575/758–3410 or 888/830–3410 ⊕ www.newmexiconet.com/trans/faust/faust.html). **Sandia Shuttle Express** (☎505/474–5696 or 888/775–5696 ⊕ www.sandiashuttle.com).

Between Albuquerque & Taos Faust's Transportation (☎575/758–3410 or 888/830–3410 ⊕ www.newmexiconet.com/trans/faust/faust.html).

Between El Paso & Southern New Mexico Destinations Las Cruces Shuttle Service (☎505/525–1784 or 800/288–1784 ⊕ www.lascrucesshuttle.com).

▌BY BUS

Bus service on Texas, New Mexico & Oklahoma Coaches, affiliated with Greyhound Lines, is available to Alamogordo, Albuquerque, Carlsbad, Clovis, El Paso (TX), Farmington, Gallup, Grants, Las Cruces, Las Vegas, Raton, Roswell, Santa Fe, Taos, and several other towns and cities. Las Cruces Shuttle Service can get you from Silver City to Deming, Las Cruces, and El Paso.

Greyhound offers the **North America Discovery Pass**, which allows unlimited travel in the United States (and certain parts of Canada and Mexico) within any 7-, 15-, 30-, or 60-day period ($329–$750, depending on length of the pass). You can also buy similar passes covering different areas (America and Canada, the West Coast of North America, the East Coast of North America, Canada exclusively), and international travelers can purchase international versions of these same passes, which offer a greater variety of travel periods and cost considerably less. Greyhound also has senior-citizen, military, children's, and student discounts, which apply to individual fares and to the Discovery Pass.

Approximate standard sample one-way fares (based on 7-day advance purchase—prices can be 10% to 50% higher otherwise), times, and routes (note that times vary greatly depending on the number of stops) on major carriers: Albuquerque to Santa Fe, 70 minutes, $15; Albuquerque to Taos, 3 hours, $35; Albuquerque to Las Cruces, 4–5 hours, $30; Albuquerque to Ruidoso, 6½ hours, $45; Denver to Santa Fe, 9–10 hours, $50; Dallas to Las Cruces, 14–16 hours, $65; Oklahoma City to Albuquerque, 11–12 hours, $70; Tucson to Las Cruces, 5–7 hours, $60; and Phoenix to Albuquerque, 9–10 hours, $65.

BUS INFORMATION

Greyhound/Texas, New Mexico & Oklahoma Coaches (☎800/231-2222 ⊕ www.tnmo.com). **Las Cruces Shuttle Service** (☎505/525-1784 or 800/288-1784 ⊕ www.lascrucesshuttle.com).

▌BY CAR

A car is a basic necessity in New Mexico, as even the few cities are challenging to get around strictly using public transportation. Distances are considerable, but you can make excellent time on long stretches of interstate and other four-lane highways with speed limits of up to 75 mph. If you wander off major thoroughfares, slow down. Speed limits here generally are only 55 mph, and for good reason. Many such roadways have no shoulders; on many twisting and turning mountain roads speed limits dip to 25 mph. For the most part, the scenery you'll take in while driving makes the drive a form of sightseeing in itself.

Interstate 40 runs east–west across the middle of the state. Interstate 10 cuts across the southern part of the state from the Texas border at El Paso to the Arizona line, through Las Cruces, Deming, and Lordsburg.

Interstate 25 runs north from the state line at El Paso through Albuquerque and Santa Fe, then angles northeast to the Colorado line through Raton.

U.S. highways connect all major cities and towns in the state with a good network of paved roads—many of the state's U.S. highways, including large stretches of U.S. 285 and U.S. 550, have four lanes and high speed limits. You can make nearly as good time on these roads as you can on interstates. State roads are mostly paved two-lane thoroughfares, but some are well-graded gravel. Roads on Native American lands are designated by wooden, arrow-shaped signs and you'd best adhere to the speed limit; some roads on reservation or forest land aren't paved. Even in cities, quite a few surface streets are unpaved and often bumpy and narrow—Santa Fe, for instance, has a higher percentage of dirt roads than any other state capital in the nation.

Morning and evening rush-hour traffic is light in most of New Mexico, although it can get a bit heavy in Albuquerque. Keep in mind also that from most cities in New Mexico, there are only one or two main routes to Albuquerque, so if you encounter an accident or some other delay on a major thoroughfare into Albuquerque (or even Santa Fe), you can expect significant delays. It's a big reason to leave early and give yourself extra time when attempting to drive to Albuquerque to catch a plane.

Parking is plentiful and either free or inexpensive in most New Mexico towns, even Albuquerque and Santa Fe. During busy times, however, such as summer weekends, parking in Santa Fe, Taos, Ruidoso, and parts of Albuquerque can be tougher to find.

Here are some common distances and approximate travel times between Albuquerque and several popular destinations, assuming no lengthy stops and averaging the 65 to 75 mph speed limits: Santa Fe is 65 mi and about an hour; Taos is 135 mi and about 2½ hours; Farmington is 185 mi and 3 hours; Gallup is 140 mi and 2 hours; Amarillo is 290 mi and 4 hours; Denver is 450 mi and 6–7 hours; Oklahoma City is 550 mi and 8–9 hours; Moab is 290 mi and 6–7 hours; Flagstaff is 320 mi and 4½ hours; Phoenix is 465 mi and 6½ to 7½ hours; Silver City is 230 mi and 3½–4 hours; Las Cruces is 225 mi and 3½ hours; Ruidoso is 190 mi and 3 hours; Carlsbad is 280 mi and 4½–5 hours; El Paso is 270 mi and 4 hours; Dallas is 650 mi and 10–11 hours; and San Antonio is 730 mi and 11–12 hours.

GASOLINE

There's a lot of high, dry, lonesome country in New Mexico—it's possible to go 50 or 60 mi in some of the less-populated areas between gas stations. For a safe trip **keep your gas tank full.** Self-service gas stations are the norm in New Mexico, though in some of the less-populated regions you can find stations with full service. The cost of unleaded gas at self-service stations in New Mexico is close to the U.S. average, but it's usually 15¢ to 30¢ more per gallon in Santa Fe, Taos, and certain spots off the beaten path.

RENTAL CARS

All the major car-rental agencies are represented at Albuquerque's and El Paso's airports, and you can also find a limited number of car-rental agencies in other communities throughout the state.

Rates at Albuquerque's airport begin at around $25 a day and $150 a week for an economy car with air-conditioning, automatic transmission, and unlimited mileage; although you should expect to pay more during busier times. The same car in El Paso typically goes for about the same or even a bit less, again depending on the time of year.

If you want to explore the backcountry, consider renting an SUV, which will cost you about $40 to $60 per day and $200 to $400 per week, depending on the size of the SUV and the time of year. Dollar in Albuquerque has a fleet of smaller SUVs, still good on dirt roads and with much better mileage than larger ones, and they often run extremely reasonable deals, as low as $160 a week. You can save money by renting at a nonairport location, as you then are able to avoid the hefty (roughly) 10% in extra taxes charged at airports.

ROAD CONDITIONS

Arroyos (dry washes or gullies) are bridged on major roads, but lesser roads often dip down through them. These can be a hazard during the rainy season, late June–early September. Even if it looks shallow, **don't try to cross an arroyo filled with water**—it may have an axle-breaking hole in the middle. Wait a little while, and it will drain off almost as quickly as it filled. If you stall in a flooded arroyo, get out of the car and onto high ground if possible. In the backcountry, never drive (or walk) in a dry arroyo bed if the sky is dark anywhere upstream. A sudden thunderstorm 15 mi away could send a raging flash flood down a wash in a matter of minutes.

Unless they are well graded and graveled, **avoid unpaved roads in New Mexico when they are wet.** The soil contains a lot of caliche, or clay, which gets slick when mixed with water. During winter storms roads may be shut down entirely; call the State Highway Department for road conditions.

At certain times in fall or spring, New Mexico winds can be vicious for large vehicles like RVs. Driving conditions can be particularly treacherous in passages through foothills or mountains where wind gusts are concentrated.

New Mexico has a high incidence of drunk driving and uninsured motorists. Factor in the state's high speed limits, many winding and steep roads, and eye-popping scenery, and you can see how important it is to drive as alertly and defensively as possible. On the plus side, major traffic jams are a rarity even in cities—and recent improvements to the state's busiest intersection, the I–40/I–25 interchange in Albuquerque, has helped to reduce rush-hour backups there. Additionally, a major highway widening and improvement along U.S. 285/84, north of Santa Fe, has also greatly smoothed the flow and speed of traffic up toward Taos.

State Highway Department (☎800/432–4269 ⊕ www.nmshtd.state.nm.us).

ROADSIDE EMERGENCIES
In the event of a roadside emergency, call 911. Depending on the location, either the New Mexico State Police or the county sheriff's department will respond. Call the city or village police department if you encounter trouble within the limits of a municipality. Indian reservations have tribal police headquarters, and rangers assist travelers within U.S. Forest Service boundaries.

▍BY TRAIN

Amtrak's *Sunset Limited,* from Orlando, Florida, to Los Angeles, stops in El Paso, Texas; Deming; and Lordsburg on Tues-day, Thursday, and Saturday eastbound, and Monday, Thursday, and Saturday westbound.

Amtrak's *Southwest Chief,* from Chicago to Los Angeles via Kansas City, stops in Raton, Las Vegas, Lamy (near Santa Fe), Albuquerque, and Gallup daily.

In 2006 the City of Albuquerque launched the state's first-ever commuter train line, the *New Mexico Rail Runner Express.* Service runs from Santa Fe south through Bernalillo and into the city of Albuquerque, continuing south through Los Lunas to the suburb of Belén, covering a distance of about 100 mi.

Amtrak offers a **North America rail pass** that gives you unlimited travel within the United States and Canada within any 30-day period ($999 peak, $709 off-peak), and several kinds of **USA Rail passes** (for non-U.S. residents only) offering unlimited travel for 15 to 30 days. Amtrak also has senior-citizen, children's, disability, and student discounts, as well as occasional deals that allow a second or third accompanying passenger to travel for half price or even free. The **Amtrak Vacations** program customizes entire vacations, including hotels, car rentals, and tours.

Sample one-way fares on the *Sunset Limited* are $100 to $200 from Los Angeles to El Paso, and $85 to $165 from San Antonio, Texas, to Deming.

Sample one-way fares on the *Southwest Chief* are $120 from Chicago to Lamy; $50 to $70 Denver to Las Vegas; and $65 Albuquerque to Los Angeles.

The *New Mexico Rail Runner Express* was running only on weekdays as of this writing, but it's expected to add weekend service eventually. Tickets cost $1 to $4 one-way, depending on the distance traveled.

Contact Amtrak (☎800/872–7245 ⊕ www.amtrak.com). **New Mexico Rail Runner Express** (☎866/795–7245 ⊕ www.nmrailrunner.com).

ESSENTIALS

▮ ACCOMMODATIONS

With the exceptions of Santa Fe and Taos, two rather upscale tourist-driven destinations with some of the higher lodging rates in the Southwest, New Mexico has fairly low hotel prices. Albuquerque is loaded with chain hotels, and four or five new ones seem to open each year, further saturating the market and driving down prices. During busy times or certain festivals (the Balloon Fiesta in Albuquerque, some of the art markets and events in Taos and Santa Fe), it can be extremely difficult to find a hotel room, and prices can be steep. Check to make sure there's not a major event planned for the time you're headed to New Mexico, and book well ahead if so. New Mexico Central Reservations offers good deals at a number of properties throughout the state, but you'll find an even bigger selection (and often better deals) by checking the usual major travel sites, such as ⊕ *www.expedia.com*. You'll be charged a hotel tax, which varies among towns and counties, throughout New Mexico.

Most hotels and other lodgings require you to give your credit-card details before they will confirm your reservation. If you don't feel comfortable e-mailing this information, ask if you can fax it (some places even prefer faxes). However you book, get confirmation in writing and have a copy of it handy when you check in.

If you book through an online travel agent, discounter, or wholesaler, you might even want to confirm your reservation with the hotel before leaving home—just to be sure everything was processed correctly.

Be sure you understand the hotel's cancellation policy. Some places allow you to cancel without any kind of penalty—even if you prepaid to secure a discounted rate—if you cancel at least 24 hours in advance. Others require you to cancel a week in advance or penalize you the cost of one night. Small inns and B&Bs are most likely to require you to cancel far in advance. Most hotels allow children under a certain age to stay in their parents' room at no extra charge, but others charge for them as extra adults; find out the cutoff age for discounts.

▮TIP→ Assume that hotels operate on the European Plan (EP, no meals) unless we specify that they use the Breakfast Plan (BP, with full breakfast), Continental Plan (CP, Continental breakfast), Full American Plan (FAP, all meals), Modified American Plan (MAP, breakfast and dinner) or are all-inclusive (AI, all meals and most activities).

Reservations **New Mexico Central Reservations** (☎800/466-7829 ⊕ www.nmtravel.com).

APARTMENT & HOUSE RENTALS

Some parts of New Mexico are popular for short- and long-term vacation rentals, such as Santa Fe, Taos, and Ruidoso. See the book's individual regional chapters for rental listings in these locations.

BED & BREAKFASTS

B&Bs in New Mexico run the gamut from rooms in locals' homes to grandly restored adobe or Victorian homes. Rates in Santa Fe and Taos tend to be high; they're a little lower in Albuquerque and rival those of chain motels in the outlying areas. Good deals can be found in southern New Mexico as well.

See the book's individual chapters for names of local reservation agencies.

Reservation Services **Bed & Breakfast. com** (☎512/322-2710 or 800/462-2632 ⊕ www.bedandbreakfast.com) also sends out an online newsletter. **Bed & Breakfast Inns Online** (☎615/868-1946 or 800/215-7365 ⊕ www.bbonline.com). **BnB Finder.com** (☎212/432-7693 or 888/547-8226 ⊕ www.

bnbfinder.com). **New Mexico Bed and Breakfast Association** (☎800/661-6649 ⊕ www.nmbba.org).

HOME EXCHANGES

With a direct home exchange you stay in someone else's home while they stay in yours. Some outfits also deal with vacation homes, so you're not actually staying in someone's full-time residence, just their vacant weekend place.

Exchange Clubs **Home Exchange.com** (☎800/877-8723 ⊕ www.homeexchange.com); $59.95 for a 1-year online listing. **HomeLink International** (☎800/638-3841 ⊕ www.homelink.org); $80 yearly for Web-only membership; $125 includes Web access and 2 catalogs. **Intervac U.S.** (☎800/756-4663 ⊕ www.intervacus.com); $78.88 for Web-only membership; $126 includes Web access and a catalog.

HOSTELS

Hostels offer bare-bones lodging at low, low prices—often in shared dorm rooms with shared baths—to people of all ages, though the primary market is young travelers, especially students. Most hostels serve breakfast; dinner and/or shared cooking facilities may also be available. In some hostels you aren't allowed to be in your room during the day, and there may be a curfew at night. Nevertheless, hostels provide a sense of community, with public rooms where travelers often gather to share stories. Many hostels are affiliated with Hostelling International (HI), an umbrella group of hostel associations with some 4,500 member properties in more than 70 countries. Other hostels are completely independent and may be nothing more than a really cheap hotel.

Membership in any HI association, open to travelers of all ages, allows you to stay in HI-affiliated hostels at member rates. One-year membership is about $28 for adults; hostels charge about $10–$30 per night. Members have priority if the hostel is full; they're also eligible for discounts around the world, even on rail and bus travel in some countries.

Several New Mexico communities have hostels, including Albuquerque (there are two), Cloudcroft, Cuba, Oscuro (south of Carrizozo), Santa Fe, Taos, Truth or Consequences, and Tucumcari.

Information **Hostelling International—USA** (☎301/495-1240 ⊕ www.hiusa.org).

▌COMMUNICATIONS

INTERNET

In most of New Mexico Wi-Fi is available in-room or in-hotel. However, there are still a few smaller communities where you may encounter properties that have only dial-up Internet capacity. If it's important to you, check ahead. In the larger cities and primary tourist destinations in the region, you can find at least one or two coffeehouses or cafés with computer terminals that have Internet access as well as a library. Restaurants, coffeehouses, and bars with Wi-Fi are common throughout the state.

Contact **Cybercafes** (⊕ www.cybercafes.com) lists over 4,000 Internet cafés worldwide.

▌EATING OUT

New Mexico is justly famous for its distinctive cuisine, which utilizes ingredients and recipes common to Mexico, the Rockies, the Southwest, and the West's Native American communities. Most longtime residents like their chili sauces and salsas with some fire—in the Santa Fe, Albuquerque, and Las Cruces areas, chili is sometimes celebrated for its ability to set off smoke alarms. Most restaurants offer a choice of red or green chili with one type typically being milder than the other. If you want both kinds with your meal, when your server asks you if you'd like "red or green," reply "Christmas." If you're not used to spicy foods, you may find even the average chili served with chips to be quite a lot hotter than back home—so proceed with caution. Excellent barbecue and steaks also can be found throughout New Mexico, with other specialties being local game (especially elk) and trout. The restaurants we list are the cream of the crop in each price category.

MEALS & MEALTIMES

Statewide, many kitchens stop serving around 8 PM, so **don't arrive too late** if you're looking forward to a leisurely dinner.

Unless otherwise noted, the restaurants listed in this guide are open daily for lunch and dinner.

PAYING

Credit cards are widely accepted at restaurants in major towns and cities and even most smaller communities, but in the latter places, you may occasionally encounter smaller, independent restaurants that are cash only.

For guidelines on tipping see Tipping below.

RESERVATIONS & DRESS

Regardless of where you are, it's a good idea to make a reservation if you can. In some places (the top restaurants in Santa Fe, for example), it's expected. We only mention them specifically when reservations are essential (there's no other way you'll ever get a table) or when they are not accepted. For popular restaurants, book as far ahead as you can (often 30 days), and reconfirm as soon as you arrive. (Large parties should always call ahead to check the reservations policy.) We mention dress only when men are required to wear a jacket or a jacket and tie.

Online reservation services make it easy to book a table before you even leave home. OpenTable covers most states, including 20 major cities, and has limited listings in Canada, Mexico, the United Kingdom, and elsewhere. DinnerBroker has restaurants throughout the United States as well as a few in Canada.

Contacts **OpenTable** (⊕ www.opentable.com). **DinnerBroker** (⊕ www.dinnerbroker.com).

WINES, BEER & SPIRITS

Like many other states, New Mexico has some fine microbreweries, with the most prominent producer, Sierra Blanca Brewing Co., found in the unlikely and highly remote location of Carrizozo, in south-central New Mexico—Sierra Blanca's excellent beers are served throughout the state. New Mexico also has a growing number of wineries, some of them producing first-rate vintages. Franciscan monks first planted their vines here before moving more successfully to northern California, and the state's winemaking industry has really taken off since the late '90s. The New Mexico Wine Growers Association provides extensive information on the many fine wineries around the state as well as details on several prominent wine festivals.

▌ EMERGENCIES

In an emergency dial 911.

ALBUQUERQUE

Hospitals **Presbyterian Hospital** (✉ 1100 Central Ave. SE, Downtown ☎ 505/841–1234). **University Hospital** (✉ 2211 Lomas Blvd. NE, University of New Mexico ☎ 505/272–2111).

SANTA FE

St. Vincent Hospital (✉ 455 St. Michael's Dr. ☎ 505/983–3361).

TAOS

Holy Cross Hospital (✉ 1397 Weimer Rd. ☎ 505/758–8883 ⊕ www.taoshospital.org).

NORTHWEST NEW MEXICO

Rehoboth McKinley Christian Health Care Services (✉ 1901 Red Rock Dr., Gallup ☎ 505/863–7141). **San Juan Regional Health Center** (✉ 801 W. Maple St., Farmington ☎ 505/325–5011).

NORTHEAST NEW MEXICO

Alta Vista Regional Hospital (✉ 104 Legion., Las Vegas ☎ 575/426–3500).

SOUTHEAST NEW MEXICO
Carlsbad Medical Center (⊠2430 W. Pierce, Carlsbad ☎575/887–4100). **Dr. Dan Trigg Memorial Hospital** (⊠301 E. Miel de Luna, Tucumcari ☎575/461–7000). **Eastern New Mexico Medical Center** (⊠405 W. Country Club Rd., Roswell ☎575/622–8170). **Guadalupe County Hospital** (⊠535 Lake Dr., Santa Rosa ☎575/472–3417).

SOUTHWESTERN NEW MEXICO
Hospitals **Gila Regional Medical Center** (⊠1313 E. 32nd St., Silver City ☎575/538–4000). **Memorial Medical Center** (⊠2450 S. Telshor Blvd., Las Cruces ☎575/522–8641). **Socorro General Hospital** (⊠1202 NM 60 W, Socorro ☎575/835–1140).

▊ HOURS OF OPERATION

Although hours differ little in New Mexico from other parts of the United States, some businesses do keep shorter hours here than in more densely populated parts of the country. In particular, outside of the larger towns in New Mexico, it can be hard to find shops and restaurants open past 8 or 9 in the evening. Within the state, businesses tend to keep later hours in Albuquerque, Las Cruces, and Santa Fe than in rural areas.

Most major museums and attractions are open daily or six days a week (with Monday or Tuesday being the most likely day of closing). Hours are often shorter on Saturday and especially Sunday, and a handful of museums in larger cities stay open late one or two nights a week, usually Tuesday, Thursday, or Friday. New Mexico's less populous areas also have quite a few smaller museums—historical societies, small art galleries, highly specialized collections—that open only a few days a week, and sometimes only by appointment during slow times. It's always a good idea to call ahead if you're planning to go out of your way to visit a smaller museum.

Banks are usually open weekdays from 9 to 3 or a bit later and some Saturday mornings, the post office from 8 to 5 or 6 weekdays and often on Saturday mornings. Shops in urban and touristy areas, particularly in indoor and strip malls, typically open at 9 or 10 daily and stay open until anywhere from 6 PM to 10 PM on weekdays and Saturday, and until 5 or 6 on Sunday. Hours vary greatly, so call ahead when in doubt.

On major highways and in densely populated areas you can usually find at least one or two supermarkets, drugstores, and gas stations open 24 hours, and in Albuquerque, you can find a smattering of all-night fast-food restaurants, diners, and coffeehouses. Bars and discos stay open until 1 or 2 AM.

▊ MONEY

In New Mexico, Santa Fe is by far the priciest city: meals, gasoline, and motel rates are all significantly higher in the state's capital. Overall travel costs in Santa Fe, including dining and lodging, typically run 30% to 50% higher than in any other New Mexico city. Taos, too, can be a little expensive because it's such a popular tourist destination, but you have more choices for economizing there than in Santa Fe. Lodging and dining throughout much of the rest of the state are a genuine bargain. Depending on the establishment, $8 can buy you a savory Mexican dinner in Farmington, Old Mesilla, or Silver City. As the state's largest metropolitan area, Albuquerque has a full range of price choices.

CREDIT CARDS

Throughout this guide, the following abbreviations are used: **AE,** American Express; **D,** Discover; **DC,** Diners Club; **MC,** MasterCard; and **V,** Visa.

It's a good idea to inform your credit-card company before you travel, especially if you're going abroad and don't travel internationally very often. Otherwise, the credit-card company might put a hold on your card owing to unusual activity—not a good thing halfway through your trip. Record all your credit-card numbers—as well as the phone numbers to call if your cards are lost or stolen—in a safe place, so you're prepared should something go wrong. Both MasterCard and Visa have general numbers you can call (collect if you're abroad) if your card is lost, but you're better off calling the number of your issuing bank, since MasterCard and Visa usually just transfer you to your bank; your bank's number is usually printed on your card.

Reporting Lost Cards American Express (☎800/992–3404 in U.S., 336/393–1111 collect from abroad ⊕ www.americanexpress.com). **Diners Club** (☎800/234–6377 in U.S., 303/799–1504 collect from abroad ⊕ www.dinersclub.com). **Discover** (☎800/347–2683 in U.S., 801/902–3100 collect from abroad ⊕ www.discovercard.com). **MasterCard** (☎800/622–7747 in U.S., 636/722–7111 collect from abroad ⊕ www.mastercard.com). **Visa** (☎800/847–2911 in U.S., 410/581–9994 collect from abroad ⊕ www.visa.com).

▌PACKING

Typical of the Southwest, temperatures can vary considerably from sunup to sundown. Generally, you should **pack for warm days and chilly nights** from spring through fall, but this is a huge state with a tremendous range of elevations, so the most important thing is to check local weather conditions before you leave home and pack accordingly. In April for instance, you may need to pack for nighttime lows in the 20s and daytime highs in the 60s in Taos, but daytime highs in the 80s and nighttime lows in the 50s in Las Cruces. Any time of year pack at least a few warm outfits and a jacket; in winter pack very warm clothes—coats, parkas, and whatever else your body's thermostat and your ultimate destination dictate. Sweaters and jackets are also needed in summer at higher elevations, because though days are warm, nights can dip well below 50°F.

And **bring comfortable shoes**; you're likely to be doing a lot of walking.

New Mexico is one of the most informal and laid-back areas of the country, which for many is part of its appeal. Probably no more than three or four restaurants in the entire state enforce a dress code, even for dinner, though men are likely to feel more comfortable wearing a jacket in the major hotel dining rooms, and anyone wearing tennis shoes may feel out of place.

The Western look has, of course, never lost its hold on the West, though Western-style clothes now get mixed with tweed jackets, for example, for a more conservative, sophisticated image. You can wear your boots and big belt buckles in even the best places in Santa Fe, Taos, or Albuquerque, but if you come strolling through the lobby of the Eldorado Hotel looking like Hopalong Cassidy, you'll get some funny looks.

Bring skin moisturizer; even people who rarely need this elsewhere in the country can suffer from dry and itchy skin in New Mexico. And **bring sunglasses** to protect your eyes from the glare of lakes or ski slopes. High altitude can cause headaches and dizziness, so check with your doctor about medication to alleviate symptoms. Sunscreen is a necessity. When planning even a short day trip, especially if there's hiking or exercise involved, always pack a bottle or two of water—it's very easy to become dehydrated in New Mexico.

▌RESOURCES

ONLINE TRAVEL TOOLS
Check out the New Mexico Home page (⊕ *www.state.nm.us*) for information on state government, and for links to state agencies on doing business, working, learning, living, and visiting in the Land of Enchantment. A terrific general resource for just about every kind of recreational activity is ⊕ *www.gorp.com*; just click on the New Mexico link under "Destinations," and you'll be flooded with links

to myriad topics, from wildlife refuges to ski trips to backpacking advice. Also excellent for information on the state's recreation pursuits is the New Mexico Outdoor Sports Guide (⊕*www.nmosg. com*). Check the site of the New Mexico Film Office (⊕ *www.nmfilm.com*) for a list of movies shot in New Mexico as well as links to downloadable clips of upcoming made–in–New Mexico movies. A wide range of reviews and links to dining, culture, and services in Albuquerque and Santa Fe is available at ⊕ *www.city search.com* and ⊕ *www.yelp.com*, and ⊕ *www.999dine.com* is a site that sells steeply discounted meal certificates to dozens of top restaurants in Albuquerque, Santa Fe, and Taos. Visit ⊕ *www.farmers marketsnm.org* for information on the dozens of great farmers' markets around the state, and see ⊕ *www.nmwine.com* for tours and details related to the region's burgeoning wine-making industry.

ALL ABOUT NEW MEXICO

Safety Transportation Security Administration (TSA ⊕ www.tsa.gov).

Time Zones Timeanddate.com (⊕ www.timeanddate.com/worldclock) can help you figure out the correct time anywhere.

Weather Accuweather.com (⊕ www.accuweather.com) is an independent weather-forecasting service with good coverage of hurricanes.

Other Resources Weather.com (⊕ www.weather.com) is the Web site for the Weather Channel. **CIA World Factbook** (⊕ www.odci.gov/cia/publications/factbook/index.html) has profiles of every country in the world. It's a good source if you need some quick facts and figures.

VISITOR INFORMATION

The New Mexico Department of Tourism can provide general information on the state, but you'll find more specific and useful information by consulting the local chambers of commerce, tourism offices, and convention and visitors bureaus in individual communities

throughout the state (⇨ *See individual chapter Essentials*).

Contacts New Mexico Department of Tourism (☎505/827–7400 or 800/733–6396 ⊕ www.newmexico.org). **Indian Pueblo Cultural Center** (☎505/843–7270 or 866/855–7902 ⊕ www.indianpueblo.org). **USDA Forest Service, Southwestern Region** (☎505/842–3292, 877/864–6985 for fire restrictions and closures ⊕ www.fs.fed.us/r3).

PASSPORTS & VISAS

PASSPORTS

We're always surprised at how few Americans have passports—only 25% at this writing. This number is expected to grow in coming years, when it becomes impossible to reenter the United States from trips to neighboring Canada or Mexico without one. Remember this: a passport verifies both your identity and nationality—a great reason to have one.

U.S. passports are valid for 10 years. You must apply in person if you're getting a passport for the first time; if your previous passport was lost, stolen, or damaged; or if your previous passport has expired and was issued more than 15 years ago or when you were under 16. All children under 18 must appear in person to apply for or renew a passport. Both parents must accompany any child under 14 (or send a notarized statement with their permission) and provide proof of their relationship to the child.

There are 13 regional passport offices, as well as 7,000 passport acceptance facilities in post offices, public libraries, and other governmental offices. If you're renewing a passport, you can do so by mail. Forms are available at passport acceptance facilities and online.

The cost to apply for a new passport is $97 for adults, $82 for children under 16; renewals are $67. Allow six weeks for processing, both for first-time passports and renewals. For an expediting fee of $60 you can reduce this time to about two weeks. If your trip is less than two weeks away, you can get a passport even more rapidly by going to a passport office with the necessary documentation. Private expediters can get things done in as little as 48 hours, but charge hefty fees for their services.

■TIP→ Before your trip, make two copies of your passport's data page (one for someone at home and another for you to carry separately). Or scan the page and e-mail it to someone at home and/or yourself.

U.S. Passport Information U.S. Department of State (☎877/487–2778 ⊕ http://travel.state.gov/passport).

U.S. Passport & Visa Expediters A. Briggs Passport & Visa Expediters (☎800/806–0581 or 202/464–3000 ⊕ www.abriggs.com). American Passport Express (☎800/455–5166 or 603/559–9888 ⊕ www.americanpassport.com). Passport Express (☎800/362–8196 or 401/272–4612 ⊕ www.passportexpress.com). Travel Document Systems (☎800/874–5100 or 202/638–3800 ⊕ www.traveldocs.com). Travel the World Visas (☎866/886–8472 or 301/495–7700 ⊕ www.world-visa.com).

▌ TAXES

The standard state gross receipts tax rate is 5%, but municipalities and counties enact additional charges at varying rates. Even with additional charges, you will encounter no sales tax higher than 7%.

▌ TIME

New Mexico and a small portion of west Texas (including El Paso) observe mountain standard time, switching over with most of the rest of the country to daylight saving time in the spring through fall. In New Mexico, you'll be two hours behind New York and one hour ahead of Arizona (except during daylight saving time, which Arizona does not observe) and California.

▌ TIPPING

The customary tipping rate for taxi drivers is 15%–20%, with a minimum of $2; bellhops are usually given $2 per bag in luxury hotels, $1 per bag elsewhere. Hotel maids should be tipped $2 per day of your stay. A doorman who hails or helps you into a cab can be tipped $1–$2. You should also tip your hotel concierge for services rendered; the size of the tip depends on the difficulty of your request, as well as the quality of the concierge's work. For an ordinary dinner reservation or tour arrangements, $3–$5 should do; if the concierge scores seats at a popular restaurant or show or performs unusual services (getting your laptop repaired, finding a good pet-sitter, etc.), $10 or more is appropriate.

Waiters should be tipped 15%–20%, though at higher-end restaurants, a solid 20% is more the norm. Many restaurants add a gratuity to the bill for parties of six or more. Ask what the percentage is if the menu or bill doesn't state it. Tip $1 per drink you order at the bar, though if at an upscale establishment, those $15 martinis might warrant a $2 tip.

INDEX

NOTES

NOTES

ABOUT OUR WRITERS

Splitting her time between New Mexico and New York these days, Lynne Arany enjoys the best of two places remarkable for their distinct charms and extreme diversity. Author of the Little Museums guide to all 50 states, contributor to the *New York Times*, and a freelance travel writer and editor, she's covered areas from Glasgow, Budapest, and London to the southwestern United States and Mexico. Well-practiced in the art of uncovering the less-known gems wherever she is, she finds the serendipity of the search most appealing.

Former Fodor's staff editor Andrew Collins lives in Portland Oregon, but resided in New Mexico for many years and still visits often (usually stuffing his carry-on bag with fresh green chiles). A long-time contributor to this guide, he's also the author of Fodor's *Gay Guide to the USA* and has written or contributed to dozens of other guidebooks. He's the expert "guide" on gay travel for About.com, and he writes for a variety of publications (including *Travel + Leisure, New Mexico Journey, Sunset, Out Traveler,* and *New Mexico Magazine*).

Barbara Floria, who updated the Taos, Side Trips and Northeastern New Mexico chapters, has been to 46 states and 27 countries since becoming a travel writer and photographer in the 1970s. She lives in Glenwood Springs, Colorado, and has been visiting the Taos area for 30 years. She loves New Mexico's expansive high desert and never tires of roasted green chiles.

Georgia de Katona, who updated the Santa Fe, Side Trips, Southeast and Southwestern New Mexico chapters, is a freelance writer and Kundalini yoga instructor. A born-and-bred Westerner, she has spent her life exploring the nooks and crannies of the West by foot, car, bicycle, and motorcyle. Exploring Latin America has occupied much of her travel for the past few years, but it's the beauty of the high desert and the quirky individuality of Western people that always makes coming home to Santa Fe a pleasure.